Media and Entertainment Law

SANDI TOWERS-ROMERO

DELMAR
CENGAGE Learning™

Australia • Brazil • Japan • Korea • Mexico • Singapore • Spain • United Kingdom • United States

DELMAR
CENGAGE Learning

Media and Entertainment Law
Sandi Towers-Romero

Vice President, Career and Professional
    Editorial: Dave Garza

Director of Learning Solutions: Sandy Clark

Acquisitions Editor: Shelley Esposito

Managing Editor: Larry Main

Product Manager: Melissa Riveglia

Editorial Assistant: Lyss Zaza

Vice President, Career and Professional
    Marketing: Jennifer McAvey

Marketing Director: Debbie Yarnell

Marketing Coordinator: Jonathan Sheehan

Production Director: Wendy Troeger

Production Manager: Mark Bernard

Production Assistant: Matthew McGuire

Art Director: Joy Kocsis

Technology Project Manager: Tom Smith

Production Technology Analyst: Thomas
    Stover

For product information and technology assistance, contact us at
Professional & Career Group Customer Support, 1-800-648-7450

For permission to use material from this text or product, submit all
requests online at **cengage.com/permissions**.
Further permissions questions can be e-mailed to
permissionrequest@cengage.com.

Library of Congress Control Number: 2007940815

ISBN-13: 978-1-4180-3912-7

ISBN-10: 1-4180-3912-8

Delmar Cengage Learning
5 Maxwell Drive
Clifton Park, NY 12065-2919
USA

Cengage Learning is a leading provider of customized learning solutions with office locations around the globe, including Singapore, the United Kingdom, Australia, Mexico, Brazil, and Japan. Locate your local office at: **international.cengage.com/region**

Cengage Learning products are represented in Canada by Nelson Education, Ltd.

For your lifelong learning solutions, visit **delmar.cengage.com**

Visit our corporate website at **cengage.com**.

NOTICE TO THE READER
Publisher does not warrant or guarantee any of the products described herein or perform any independent analysis in connection with any of the product information contained herein. Publisher does not assume, and expressly disclaims, any obligation to obtain and include information other than that provided to it by the manufacturer. The reader is expressly warned to consider and adopt all safety precautions that might be indicated by the activities described herein and to avoid all potential hazards. By following the instructions contained herein, the reader willingly assumes all risks in connection with such instructions. The reader is notified that this text is an educational tool, not a practice book. Since the law in constant change, no rule or statement of law in this book should be relied upon for any service to any client. The reader should always refer to standard legal sources for the current rule or law. If legal advice or other expert assistance is required, the services of the appropriate professional should be sought. The publisher makes no representations or warranties of any kind, including but not limited to, the warranties of fitness for particular purpose or merchantability, nor are any such representations implied with respect to the material set forth herein, and the publisher takes no responsibility with respect to such material. The publisher shall not be liable for any special, consequential, or exemplary damages resulting, in whole or part, from the readers' use of, or reliance upon, this material.

Printed in Canada
1 2 3 4 5 6 7 12 11 10 09 08

Contents

Dedication

I am dedicating this book to all my friends, family, colleagues, and students who came to my need when I needed it most. Their acts of kindness will never be forgotten, and are deeply appreciated.

Sandi

Preface

MEDIA AND ENTERTAINMENT LAW

One of the most influential aspects of modern life is the role that the media and the entertainment industries play. Whether one is reading a newspaper, watching a television show, listening to the radio, or surfing the Internet, the media and the entertainment industries are involved. There is not a day that passes when one is not confronted with news and legal issues associated with these businesses.

Whether one is a lawyer, a law student, a paralegal or communications student, or a member of the public, it is important to know and understand the basics of media and entertainment law.

WHY AND HOW *MEDIA AND ENTERTAINMENT LAW* WAS CONCEIVED

Media and Entertainment Law has been purposely designed and written to engage the reader with up-to-date legal issues. Landmark cases are pulled from the main text to emphasize the importance of these litigations, and relevant quotes from U.S. Supreme Court Justices are highlighted to facilitate a better understanding of the thinking of the Court. Historical background of subjects has been emphasized so that the reader can obtain a better grasp of societal issues at the time of the ruling. International media and entertainment law issues are discussed at length. A full glossary is provided which includes definitions of legal terminology, bills and legislation introduced in Congress, and media and entertainment Laws and Acts.

Throughout the book, media and entertainment law ethics issues are discussed, and a chapter devoted to ethics has been added with suggestions presented on how to make better ethical choices, how to guide ethical considerations, and how to correct ethical issues that are not in alignment with corporate or business guidelines.

In Part 2 of the text, the reader will find title 17 of the United States Code, including all amendments enacted through the end of the second session of the 109th Congress, in 2006. Title 17 includes the Copyright Act of 1976 and all subsequent amendments to copyright law; the Semiconductor Chip Protection Act (SCPA) of 1984, as amended; and the Vessel Hull Design Protection Act (VHDPA), as amended. The Copyright Office is responsible for registering claims under all three.

Also in Part 2 is the Digital Millennium Copyright Act (DMCA), Pub. L. No.105-304, 112 Stat. 2860, 2905, and subsequent amendments to the SCPA and the VHDPA Significant copyright legislation enacted since June 2003 is included—the Copyright Royalty and Distribution Reform Act of 2004, the Satellite Home Viewer Extension and Reauthorization Act of 2004, and the Family Entertainment and Copyright Act of 2005 (including the Artists' Rights and Theft Prevention Act of 2005, the Family Movie Act of 2005, and the Preservation of Orphan Works Act).

CHAPTER ORGANIZATION

The text is divided into 11 easy-to-read chapters, and each contains the following:

- Chapter Outline
- Learning Objectives
- Text of the Chapter
- Summary
- Questions for Discussion
- Cases for Review
- Key Terms (emphasized in the text)
- End Notes

These chapter features are to promote further insight into the fields.

Chapters are arranged in a thoughtful and logical order, to take the student, practitioner, or interested reader from the beginnings of freedom of speech, press, and expression into cutting-edge current events that highlight areas such as copyrights, advertising, pornography, censorship of the media, cable and satellite television, digital and satellite radio, and the Internet.

SUPPLEMENTAL TEACHING MATERIALS

An Instructor's Manual is provided both in print and online at <http://www.paralegal.delmar.cengage.com>. Written by the author of the text, the Instructor's Manual contains:

- Chapter Outlines
- Teaching Suggestions

- Class Discussion Ideas
- Answers to the Text Questions
- Chapter Summaries
- Lesson Plans
- Test Bank and Answers
- PowerPoint Presentations

Student CD-ROM
For additional materials, please go to the
CD in this book.

Student CD-ROM

The new accompanying CD-ROM provides additional material to help students master the important concepts in the course. This CD-ROM includes a study guide, discussions of the Case for Review assignments, and a complete entertainment contract.

Online Companion™
For additional resources, please go to
http://www.paralegal.delmar.cengage.com

Online Companion™

The Online Companion™ provides students with additional support materials in the form of

- Updates to the Text
- New Case Law
- Recent Law Review Articles
- Web Site Links
- Quizzes for Review

The Online Companion™ can be found at <http://www.paralegal.delmar.cengage.com> in the Online Companion™ section of the Web Site.

Web page

Come visit our Web site at <http://www.paralegal.delmar.cengage.com> where you will find valuable information such as hot links and and sample materials to download, as well as other Delmar Cengage Learning products.

Please note that the Internet resources are of a time-sensitive nature and URL addresses may often change or be deleted.

ABOUT THE AUTHOR

Sandi Towers-Romero has been part of the entertainment and media business for over 30 years. Her first experiences with the fields were as a professional entertainer and booking agent for stage acts at resorts in Pennsylvania and New York.

During her studies at Arizona State University, she was a consumer advocate, reporting on such issues as price fixing in grocery stores and insurance fraud. While at law school, she wrote for the law school paper, *The Dictim*, and was hired as a reporter for the *News Times* syndicate of papers. After receiving her Juris Doctor degree, this journalism background followed her to the Orange County California Legal Aid Society, where she was the editor of a nationally recognized legal paper, *Speaking of Legal Aid.* She also taught classes at the University of California, Irvine, on how the media affects the legal rights of senior citizens.

When she moved to Hawaii, she became the assistant to the president of the television station KBFD. Beginning in 1994, she and her husband began publishing three Hawaii-based magazines—*Big Island of Hawaii Magazine, Big Island Business Magazine,* and *Maui Business Magazine.* She also developed, wrote, and was featured in her own television program, *Big Island Business News.*

In 1996, the U.S. Small Business Administration (SBA) awarded her the Media Advocate of the Year Award for the County of Hawaii, and in 1998 the SBA awarded her the Women in Business of the Year Award for the County of Hawaii.

Back in her home state of Florida, in 2001, her book on the history of the Seminole Indians, *Those of Distant Campfires,* was published. In 2007, her book *The Essentials of Florida Real Estate Law* was published.

She presently is Program Advisor for Professional and Technical studies at Edison College, where she also taught law. Sandi also has taught at South Florida Community College, and Florida Southern College's DeSoto/Charlotte Campus. She is listed in *Who's Who Among America's Teachers*.

ACKNOWLEDGMENTS

Valuable contributions were made to the text by the team at Delmar Cengage Learning and the reviewers that evaluated the book.

Michael Botein
New York Law School
New York, N.Y.

Mary Conwell
Edison College
Fort Myers, FL

Ramona DeSalvo
Southeastern Career College
Nashville, TN

Bob Diotalevi
Florida Gulf Coast University
Fort Myers, FL

Patricia Greer
Berkeley College
West Paterson, N.J.

Nicholas Johnson
University of Iowa
Iowa City, IA

Wendy Vonnegut
Methodist College
Fayetteville, N.C.

Table of Cases

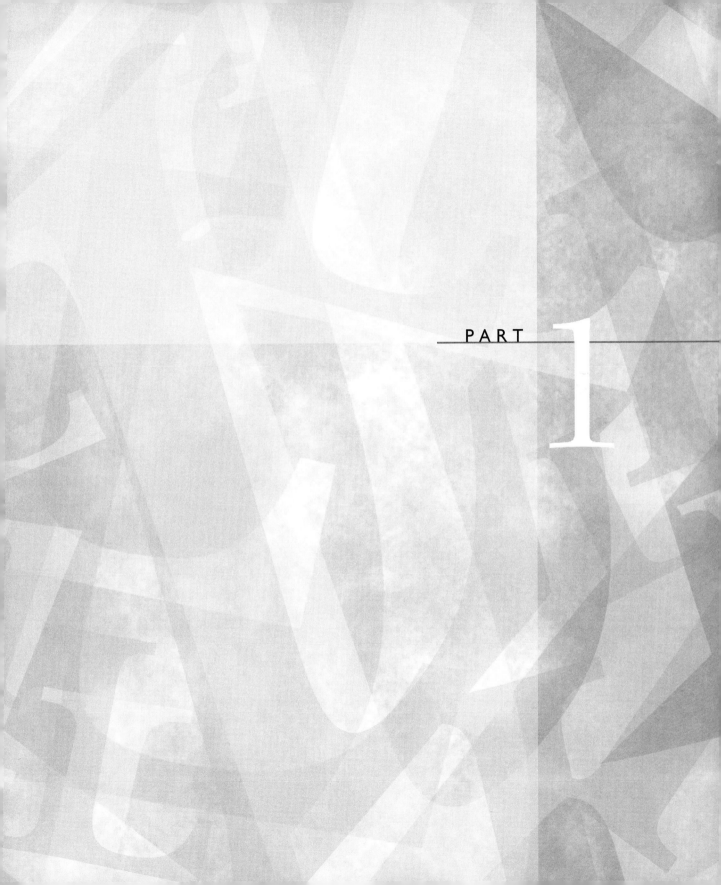

PART 1

The Road Leading to the First Amendment

■ **OBJECTIVES**_____

After completing this chapter, you will be able to:

- Understand how the governments of Europe and the Colonies attempted to control the media with libel laws, prior restraints, and monetary bonds.

- Understand how the First Amendment came into being, giving the rights of free speech and freedom of expression.

- Understand how the government, since the inception of the First Amendment up to World War II, tried to control freedom of expression with injunctions, and alien and espionage acts.

HISTORICAL BACKGROUND LEADING TO THE FIRST AMENDMENT

First Amendment-United States Constitution—Freedom of Religion, Press, Expression

Congress shall make no law respecting an establishment of religion, or prohibiting the free exercise thereof; or abridging the freedom of speech, or of the press; or the right of the people peaceably to assemble, and to petition the Government for a redress of grievances.[1]

These 45 words, and the rights they represent, are routinely taken for granted by citizens of the United States. The concept of freedom of speech and freedom of the press are well-known doctrines. These freedoms that we take for granted are only enjoyed by a few dozen democracies in the world. Less than one-half of the world's population has any freedom of expression. In most of the world, it is commonplace for governments to censor speech and the media. In some countries, even if there is no direct censorship, a journalist who advocates reform may just disappear. Yet, the First Amendment right of freedom of expression is not absolute.

A recent example of the hindrance on constitutional freedoms, are the laws passed since September 11, 2001. The threat of terrorism has placed new restrictions on civil liberties. The **USA Patriot Act** has created a new crime of domestic terrorism, broadened the federal government's ability to monitor the Internet and telephonic communications, and allowed the attorney general to detain any foreigner considered a national security threat.

Under revisions to the Patriot Act, implemented under House of Representatives (HR) bill 3199 (2005), an FBI (Federal Bureau of Investigation) agent, with a valid order, can compel a telecommunications company to disclose the name, address, and service usage of a particular subscriber. The Act's revision allows the creation of a uniformed division of the Secret Service. This police force has arrest authority at any events where the president or other dignitaries are meeting. HR 3199 makes it a crime for anyone to "willfully and knowingly . . . enter or remain in any posted, cordoned off, or otherwise restricted area of a building or grounds where the President or other person protected by the Secret Service is or will be temporarily visiting." Criminal penalties were added for the interference with maritime vessels or ports, money laundering, and false entry.

Further evidence in regard to curtailment of civil liberties occurred on September 9, 2005, when a unanimous decision by the federal appeals court of the 4th Circuit ruled that Jose Padilla could be held indefinitely without trial (*Padilla v. Hanft*). Mr. Padilla, an American citizen, was accused of planning to set off "dirty bombs." He was arrested in the United States and had been held for three and a half years without benefit of any judicial proceedings. The provision of the law under which he had been held is the Authorization for Use of Military Force. Congress enacted this act after the 9/11 attacks. This law allows the president to detain suspected terrorists indefinitely, in order to prevent any future acts of terrorism against the United States.

■ **USA PATRIOT ACT**

The USA Patriot Act was implemented after September 11, 2001, to combat terrorism.

The Padilla detention, without trial, finally ended when he was criminally charged in a terrorism conspiracy and support case in November 2005. At that time, the Justice Department requested that Padilla be removed from military control so that he could be tried on criminal charges in Florida. Padilla was found guilty of all charges against him on August 16, 2007, by a federal jury, which found that he conspired to kill people in an overseas jihad and to fund and support overseas terrorism. He was scheduled to be sentenced on December 5, 2007, but his sentencing was postponed to January 2008, due to the death of a family member of the judge who will sentence him. The expansion of governmental authority since 9/11 has been under serious criticism by many in the United States, as it is considered to be a denial of basic constitutional rights. Yet, it can be argued, if this is truly a time of "war," then the U.S. government, as all governments, can take extraordinary measures to protect its country and citizens.

In June 2006, the U.S. Supreme Court held in a 5–3 vote that President Bush exceeded his authority by setting up a trial system that denied terrorist suspects, held at Guantánamo Bay, Cuba, access to evidence against them or the right to attend all court hearings in their case. The Supreme Court held that this was a violation of the U.S. Military Code of Justice and the Geneva Convention on treatment of prisoners of war.[2]

EARLY RESTRICTIONS ON FREEDOM OF EXPRESSION

To fully understand how the United States developed the rights to **freedom of expression**, we must take a trip back to the 1500s. The whole issue of **freedom of the press** was nonexistent before the European invention of the printing press. At first, all books and publications were painstakingly handwritten by scribes and calligraphers. This meant that, except for the Bible (the most published work at the time), there were only a few copies of any one publication in circulation at any one time. Thus, if a monarch felt threatened by a book or publication, all she had to do was order the destruction of the few copies in existence. With the introduction of the printing press, there could be hundreds or thousands of copies of a publication produced in a short time, which was potentially a big problem for an all-powerful monarch.

Pope Alexander VI issued a notice in 1501 requiring printers to submit copies of works to church authorities before publication. He was trying to prevent heresy. Printing presses allowed easy communication with many people. Thus, the spread of "heresy" could run rampant. If printers did not comply with the pope's edict, they were subject to fines or excommunication from the Church.

In England in 1534, the appearance of publications that were unauthorized by the monarch (Henry VIII) led to a royal proclamation requiring publishers obtain a prepublication license. Henry limited the keeping of a printing press and required

FREEDOM OF EXPRESSION
Allows an individual to speak freely without censorship.

FREEDOM OF THE PRESS
The guarantee by a government of free public press.

the inspection of any publications by a licenser. British monarchs knew that the printing press was an extreme threat to their power. Whoever controlled the presses potentially could control the populace.

In an attempt to control what was being printed, the British imposed **seditious libel laws**. Interestingly enough, it did not make any difference if the information was true or not. The British also imposed **prior restraints**. Under prior restraints printers had to get approval before printing anything. Another way to gain control of publishing was to insist that a printer acquire **monetary bonds**. If the Crown felt that the information was unacceptable, but the item was printed anyway, the bond would be forfeited.

There were protests against such laws. John Locke, a political philosopher of the 17th century, stated in his *social contract theory* that the only legitimate civil government is instituted with the explicit consent of the individuals governed. Locke felt that all "men" were endowed with the natural rights of life, liberty, and ownership of property. According to Locke, government only has authority if it preserves these natural rights. Part of the right of liberty was freedom of expression.[3]

In 1644, John Milton, in his work *Areopagitica*, criticized licensing laws and asked the British parliament to punish publishers for offensive publications *after* their appearance, if necessary. He felt true ideas would prevail over false ones automatically.[4] Although he was much more open-minded about freedom of expression than most of his contemporaries, he would not go so far as to advocate the free publication of ideas that he considered dangerously subversive. Milton's objections to prior restraints were pivotal in press freedom. Yet, despite Locke's and Milton's objections to restraints on the press, it still took until 1695 for licensing and censorship laws to be repealed in England.

Complicating freedom of expression, truth was not a defense to defamation. The legal doctrine at that time was, "The greater the truth, the greater the libel." It took until the mid-1800s for truth to become a defense to defamation in England.

The problem for the English government was that the seeds of democracy were being planted all over Europe, as well as in a new and politically volatile land called the American Colonies. These seeds of democracy were being spread by use of the printing press and the dissemination of masses of printed material.

The Colonies Strike Back

In 1690, the first newspaper appeared in the Colonies Boston—*Publick Occurrences*. From that time until the actual ratification of the first 10 amendments to the U.S. Constitution in 1791, the newspapers of the Colonies were of utmost importance in shaping the population's opinions. This was an age without other forms of communication across any distance.

■ **SEDITIOUS LIBEL LAWS**

Sedition is when the government or its officers is criticized. The Sedition Act of 1798 made it a federal crime to publish contemptible writings against the government.

■ **PRIOR RESTRAINTS**

A form of censorship by the government where it prevents or stops the publication of certain material.

■ **MONETARY BONDS**

A form of insurance that would protect the government from the publishing of information against it.

During colonial times, newspapers were very careful not to offend the authorities. Colonial rulers felt it was their right to censor any dissenting views from a newspaper. Benjamin Franklin's older brother James was jailed in 1722 for not obtaining prior government approval when he published the *New England Courant*.

There also was the notorious **Tax Stamp Act**. These taxes, an attempt to raise revenue, were nonetheless considered censorship by the colonial newspaper publishers, and most did not buy them. Interesting enough, the British did little to enforce these laws.

The most famous case of government censorship in the Colonies was the seditious libel trial of John Peter Zenger.

■ **TAX STAMP ACT**

The act required all legal documents, permits, commercial contracts, newspapers, wills, pamphlets, and playing cards in the American Colonies to carry a tax stamp.

CASE STUDY **New York v. John Peter Zenger**

17 Howell's State Trials 675 (1735)

Facts:	In the early 1730s, *The New York Weekly Journal*, America's first independent political paper, was a voice for opposition to the unpopular royal governor— William Cosby. Zenger's paper had published articles critical of Cosby, and was sued by the governor, "for printing and publishing several seditious libels . . . as having in them many things tending to raise factions and tumults among the people of this Province, inflaming their minds with contempt of His Majesty's Government, and greatly disturbing the peace thereof." [Bench warrant for the arrest of John Peter Zenger, November 2, 1734.] Although the article's charges against the governor were exaggerated, they had a basis in fact. James Alexander had authored the articles, and Zenger printed them, knowing the printer would suffer the consequences of the governor's displeasure and hostility. This was the first time an American newspaper had openly criticized a government official.
Issue:	Was this seditious libel during colonial times?
Decision:	No.
Reason:	Andrew Hamilton (no relation to Alexander) represented Zenger. Hamilton ignored the orders of the judge not to address the jury and appealed to them stating published statements were not libelous if true. [Remember, at this time, truth was not a defense to libel.] Hamilton told the jury the case before them was of utmost importance, a case that would affect every free man living in the Colonies. His argument was that the common law of the Colonies was not the common law of England. Even if Zenger's conduct would be seditious libel in England, the citizens of the Colonies enjoyed greater freedom, and the right to directly criticize their leaders, if the accusations were true. The jury returned a not-guilty verdict.

■ **LEGAL PRECEDENT**

This is a court decision that gives an example or authority, to other courts, on how to decide subsequent cases involving similar or identical facts.

The Zenger trial did not create a binding **legal precedent**, and more printers were arrested and tried for seditious libel even after his acquittal. This decision did, however, set the stage for a change in defamation law (truth is an absolute defense), and it laid the foundation for freedom of the press, as we know it today.

Despite all of the attempts by the colonial government to control the press, papers, and pamphlets produced at the time, the government seemingly was unconcerned about sanctions. Printers published what they wished and suffered little retaliation.

THE FIRST AMENDMENT

■ **U.S. CONSTITUTION**

The supreme law of the United States.

■ **ARTICLES OF CONFEDERATION**

The first governing document, or constitution, of the United States.

Before the writing of the **U.S. Constitution**, the **Articles of Confederation** was adopted in 1781. It was the first attempt at creating a new government for the new nation of the United States. The Articles of Confederation contained no guarantees of any freedoms, and it did not give the new federal government sufficient power, thus allowing the new 13 states to do as they pleased. The Articles of Confederation was doomed to failure.

In the summer of 1787, it was decided there needed to be a new form of a government created in place of the defective Articles of Confederation. Twelve of the 13 states sent 55 delegates to Philadelphia to create something new, a U.S. Constitution. The constitutional delegates shared a common background in history, political philosophy, and science. Some wanted to merely revise the Articles of Confederation. Most knew that a new form of government was needed, a government that gave significant power to the central government and granted states rights in certain areas.

■ **BILL OF RIGHTS**

These are the first 10 amendments to the Constitution of the United States. Included in them are the freedoms of speech and freedom of the press.

Despite all of the thought and work put into this new Constitution, it had no provision for a **Bill of Rights**. Some delegates argued there was no need for such an addition. Roger Sherman, of Connecticut, said that the states' constitutions were a sufficient guarantee of rights for the people, and Congress could be trusted to protect their rights. The American populace feared this new Constitution. Although ratified by a sufficient number of states by 1788, Americans were concerned that this all-powerful federal government would not protect their civil rights. Some states would not ratify the Constitution until they were assured that a Bill of Rights would be added at a later date.

During the debate for the addition of a Bill of Rights, the *Freeman's Journal,* a Philadelphia publication, discussed the need for the liberty of the press. The *Freeman's Journal* wrote,

> "As long as the liberty of the press continues unviolated, and the people have the right of expressing and publishing their sentiments upon every public measure, it is next to impossible to enslave a free nation. Men of aspiring and tyrannical disposition, sensible of this truth, have ever been inimical to the press, and have considered the shackling of it, as the first step towards the accomplishment of their hateful domination, and the entire

suppression of all liberty of public discussion, as necessary to its support . . . . The reason assigned for the omission of a bill of rights, securing the liberty of the press, and other invaluable personal rights, is an insult on the understanding of the people."

Although the populace knew there was a need to protect its civil rights, passage of the Bill of Rights was difficult. From the time that these amendments went to the states for approval, it took two years for three-quarters of the states to ratify them and thus become part of the Constitution. Finally, on December 15, 1791, the state of Virginia ratified the Constitution, giving the sufficient number of states required for adoption.

Congress and First Amendment Restraints

America finally had its Bill of Rights, yet within seven years of the passage of these amendments Congress passed **Alien and Sedition Acts**. These were laws passed that intended to suppress seditious newspapers, and extended the time required for aliens to live in the United States to gain the right to become naturalized citizens.[5]

During the late 1790s, newspapers attacked the U.S. government. The government had declared the United States to be neutral in the war between England and the new Republic of France. The U.S. citizens supported the populace of France in its revolution against King Louis the XVI and Queen Marie Antoinette. U.S. citizens also remembered they may not have won the Revolutionary War if the French had not fought alongside them. The belief by U.S. citizens was that the United States should get involved in this conflict, and newspapers reflected this sentiment. In response, Congress passed the Alien and Sedition Acts to quell this dissention.

Rather than stopping dissent, these laws only fanned the flames. Although these Acts were never heard before a full Supreme Court, three of the Court's justices had heard cases involving these laws, while on the circuit, and they all had sustained their provisions. The Alien and Sedition Acts of 1798 expired by limitation on March 3, 1801, but they would only be the beginning of a string of attempts by the federal government to control freedom of expression in the United States.

Civil War–Era Restraints

The 18th-century view of enlightenment and natural rights of American citizens was over with the death of Thomas Jefferson in 1826. After the slave rebellions of Denmark Vessey in 1822 and Nat Turner in 1831, in South Carolina and Virginia, many Southern states passed laws forbidding distribution of **abolitionist literature**. This literature encouraged the freeing of the slaves and ending the importation of slaves. In Virginia, a law was passed stating that anyone who ". . . by speaking or writing maintains that owners have no right of property in slaves . . ." could be sentenced to a year in prison.

■ **ALIEN AND SEDITION ACTS**

These were laws passed that intended to suppress seditious newspapers, and extending the time required for aliens to live in the United States to gain the right to become naturalized citizens.

■ **ABOLITIONIST LITERATURE**

Literature encouraging the freeing of the slaves and ending the importation of slaves.

Tensions between slave owners and publishers increased as the issue of slavery became more intense. Elijah Lovejoy, editor of the Alton, Illinois, *Observer*, was shot to death by a pro-Southern mob in 1837, as he defended a printing press. Pro-slavery mobs had previously destroyed three other presses that he had used.[6] Lovejoy was a fervent abolitionist and was hated by Southern slaveholders. The press that Lovejoy died defending was carried to a window and thrown out onto the riverbank. It was broken into pieces, and ultimately these pieces were scattered into the Mississippi River. When the **Civil War** broke out, criticism of Abraham Lincoln and the war itself was rampant, although censorship was sporadic.

■ **CIVIL WAR**

The War Between the States.

EARLY 20TH-CENTURY CONTROLS ON FREEDOM OF EXPRESSION

With the coming of the early 20th century, there were new issues that renewed the attempt to control freedom of expression. With the publication of the premiere issue of *The Woman Rebel* in 1914, free speech issues again came to the forefront. Margaret Sanger, a nurse, was appalled at the lack of information available regarding reproductive health and birth control. In response, she published a militantly feminist newspaper advocating the right to practice birth control. Her publication was banned, and she was indicted for violating postal obscenity laws. Undaunted, she went into exile and later returned to open birth control clinics. Her advocacy of reproductive rights ultimately became what we know now as Planned Parenthood.

■ **INJUNCTIONS**

Judicial orders restraining or compelling some form of action. To obtain an injunction, one must show that there is potentially irreparable damage if the injunction order is not granted.

During the early 20th century, the nascent labor unions faced great scrutiny, and the union movement created great turmoil in the United States. Employers did not want to allow unionization of their employees, yet many employees desperately sought the protections that the unions offered. In response to attempts to unionize, police banned trade union meetings. Courts would issue **injunctions** against strikes or employee protests. There were symbolic flags in the early 20th century—black for anarchism, red for communism. In some states, displaying either of these would result in arrest.

■ **ESPIONAGE ACT OF 1917**

This is a federal law that made it a crime for a person to convey information with intent to interfere with the operation or success of the armed forces of the United States.

Adding to the tensions between the federal government and U.S. citizens was the entrance of the United States into World War I. Many Americans felt that the United States should not be involved in a war "a half a world away," and there were tremendous protests against entering that conflict. As a result, the government invoked significant suppression of free speech. People were sent to jail for merely opposing the war, lost their jobs, or were harassed for their dissent to the war.

On June 15, 1917, the government struck back against war protestors with the passage of the **Espionage Act of 1917**.[7] In 1918, an amendment was added to the Espionage Act—the **Sedition Act**.

■ **SEDITION ACT**

The Sedition Act made it illegal to speak out against the government.

This act and its amendment, unlike the Alien and Sedition Acts of 1798, were vigorously enforced. Under the Alien and Sedition Acts of 1798, there were only 15 prosecutions. Under the Espionage Act and sedition laws of 1917 and 1918, there were approximately 2,000 arrests and some 1,000 convictions. Penalty for violation of these laws was a fine of up to $10,000, or a jail term of up to 20 years. In response to the passage of the Espionage Act, the Civil Liberties Bureau, a forerunner of the **American Civil Liberties Union (ACLU)** was organized. Both organizations were formed to protect the constitutional rights of Americans.

Modern First Amendment law was born in a series of World War I–era prosecutions for violation of the Espionage Act of 1917 and the Sedition Act of 1918. Although all of the defendants lost in their arguments before the U.S. Supreme Court, their challenges to the Espionage Act and sedition laws would eventually lead to greater freedom of expression.

One of the cases prosecuted under these laws was that of *Schenck v. U.S.*

■ **AMERICAN CIVIL LIBERTIES UNION (ACLU)**

The ACLU is a national organization advocating individual rights, by litigating, legislating, and educating the public on a broad array of issues affecting individual freedoms.

CASE STUDY **Schenck v. United States**

249 U.S. 47 (1919)

Facts:	This case involved a three-count indictment. The first charge was a conspiracy to violate the Espionage Act of 1917. The defendants were charged with willfully conspiring to print and circulate information that would obstruct the recruiting and enlistment of men who had been called and accepted for military service. The defendants were found guilty on all counts. The defendants alleged that the First Amendment forbids Congress to make any law abridging the freedom of speech, or of the press.
	Schenck was the general secretary of the Socialist Party, and was in charge of the Socialist headquarters where the circulars were sent. Fifteen thousand leaflets were mailed to men who had passed exemption boards and had been accepted for military service. Schenck had personally attended to the printing.
	The circulars recited the Thirteenth Amendment, and equated the Conscription Act for World War I to involuntary servitude [slavery]. It stated that men should not be going on a ruthless venture for the profit of big business, and that Americans should oppose the Conscription Act.
Issue:	Was the distribution of the circulars a violation of the Espionage Act? Did it create a clear and present danger?
Decision:	Yes.
Reason:	The opinion by Justice Holmes stated that in ordinary times what the defendants said in the circular would have been within their constitutional rights. "But the character of every act depends upon the circumstances in which it is done. The question in every case is whether the words used are used in such circumstances and are of a nature as to create a clear and present danger that they will bring about the substantive evils that Congress has a right to prevent."

The conclusion to be drawn from this case is that the First Amendment is not the final word. Congress can pass laws antithetical to free speech if that speech presents a **clear and present danger** to an important national interest. Justice Holmes made his famous statement in this case, "The most stringent protection of free speech would not protect a man in falsely shouting fire in a theatre and causing a panic."

In *Debs v. U.S.*, 249 U.S. 211 (1919), a speech, "Socialism is the Answer," given by Eugene Debs in 1918 was at issue. Mr. Debs spoke before 1,200 people in Ohio. He was prosecuted for remarks that implied people were better than "common fodder or slaves." Debs's speech was quite mild, as compared to speeches made against the Vietnam War in the 1970s; nonetheless, the Supreme Court, using the definition of *clear and present danger*, voted to uphold Debs's 10-year sentence.

In 1919, the Supreme Court ruled on another case involving the Espionage Act —*Abrams v. U.S.* In this case, five individuals had published antiwar publications. The Court upheld their lower court convictions.

■ CLEAR AND PRESENT DANGER

If there is a clear and present danger it requires a governmental limitation on Constitutional First Amendment freedoms of speech to avoid damage to the government.

CASE STUDY Abrams v. U.S.

250 U.S. 616 (1919)

Facts:	The defendants in this case were convicted of violating the Espionage Act based on their printing of two leaflets and subsequently throwing them out of windows. One of the leaflets denounced sending troops to Russia. The other leaflet denounced World War I and the U.S. attempt to stop the Russian Revolution. This second leaflet was printed in Yiddish. The five individuals were convicted of inciting resistance to the war and for urging the curtailment of wartime material production. They were sentenced to 20 years.
Issue:	Does the Espionage Act and its amendment violate the free speech clause of the First Amendment?
Decision:	No.
Reason:	The Espionage Act and its amendments do not violate free speech and are constitutional. The majority opinion, expressed by Justice John Clarke, stated that the leaflets were to aid the enemy. They were a call for revolution. This was a clear and present danger to the national interest.
	Justice Louis Brandeis joined by Justice Holmes dissented.
	Holmes's dissent said, ". . . Congress certainly cannot forbid all effort to change the mind of the country . . . nobody can suppose that . . . a silly leaflet by an unknown man, would present any immediate danger . . . . I wholly disagree with the argument of the Government that the First Amendment left the common law as to seditious libel in force. History seems to me against the notion. I had conceived that the United States through many years had shown its repentance for the Sedition Act of 1798, by repaying fines that it

(continues)

CASE STUDY   Abrams v. U.S. *(continued)*

imposed." The necessary intent to create a clear and present danger of an *immediate evil* was not met, and according to Justice Holmes and Justice Brandeis, that is the only thing that would warrant Congress in setting limits on the expression of opinion.

Not only was the federal government concerned about political unrest, so were the states. In response, many enacted their own laws against radicalism. These laws mainly concerned themselves with the fear that nonconforming groups would attempt to change the politics and even the government of the United States. One of the cases that addressed one of these laws was *Gitlow v. New York*.

Gitlow v. New York, 268 U.S. 652 (1925), involved the publication of the *Left Wing Manifesto*, a paper urging general strikes, which was critical of moderates who would seek changes only through the ballot box. Gitlow and three others also distributed a paper called *The Revolutionary Age*. Gitlow and his companions were convicted of violating state criminal anarchy laws. Gitlow argued that the New York law violated his freedom of expression as guaranteed by the First Amendment.

He asserted that the First Amendment requires states to safeguard the civil liberties granted under the Bill of Rights. Even though the U.S. Supreme Court upheld Gitlow's conviction on the anarchy charge, of great importance, the Court agreed with Gitlow's position that states as well as the federal government are bound to comply with the commands of the First Amendment. The Court held the term *liberty* in the **Fourteenth Amendment's due process clause** encompasses the freedoms of the First Amendment, and, as such, states are bound to grant such freedoms to their citizens. Before this amendment, and the cases defining it, citizens would only be entitled to due process in federal cases. Never again would the Supreme Court question the applicability, to the states, of the free speech protections of the Bill of Rights.

Justices Holmes and Brandeis again dissented as to the majority opinion upholding the anarchy conviction. They argued that the First Amendment protects the abstract advocacy of the type appearing in the *Manifesto*, and that the government must show that speech presents a *real and immediate danger* in order to be punishable.

The only judicial decision of this era that could be called a First Amendment victory was *Masses Publishing Co. v. Patten*, 244 F. 535, 536, 541 (S.D.N.Y. 1917), rev'd, 246 F. 24 (2d Cir. 1917). In this case, Judge Learned Hand ruled a postmaster's refusal to allow the mailing of a revolutionary journal violated the defendant's First Amendment rights. Judge Hand proposed another test to decide if the words used in the literature were truly *"triggers to action,"* or merely *"keys to persuasion,"* and only the former would create legal liability.

■ **FOURTEENTH AMENDMENT'S DUE PROCESS CLAUSE**

"No state shall make or enforce any law, which shall abridge the privileges or immunities of citizens of the United States, nor shall any state deprive any person of life, liberty or property without due process of law . . . ."

SIDEBAR

Before *Gitlow*, only individuals in federal cases were afforded the rights under the first 10 amendments to the Constitution. In 1833, in the Supreme Court case of *Barron v. Baltimore*, 7 Pet. 243, the Supreme Court ruled the Bill of Rights did *not* apply to the states. In this case, Chief Justice Marshall stated that the U.S. Constitution was established for the federal government, *not* for the government of the states. Actually, in 1789 when the Bill of Rights was under debate, the U.S. Senate had rejected a resolution extending the civil rights afforded by the Bill of Rights to state actions.

After the Civil War, and the passage of the Fourteenth Amendment in 1868, the issues of the rights of the individual in state cases arouse. The Fourteenth Amendment states, "No state shall make or enforce any law, which shall abridge the privileges or immunities of citizens of the United States, nor shall any state deprive any person of life, liberty or property without due process of law; nor deny to any person within its jurisdiction the equal protection of the laws." The Supreme Court in the *Gitlow* decision inferred the term liberty means the right to freedom of expression, found in the First Amendment, must apply to the states. Today, most state constitutions contain clauses that are similar to the Fourteenth Amendment.

In 1927, the U.S. Supreme Court upheld another state political conviction in *Whitney v. California*, 274 U.S. 357. This case addressed the Criminal Syndicalism Act of California. The facts: Charlotte Anita Whitney was a member of the Communist Labor Party and, according to California law, she was in violation of the Act because of her party affiliation. This Act prohibited advocating, teaching, or aiding the commission of a crime, including, ". . . terrorism as a means of accomplishing a change in industrial ownership . . . or effecting any political change."

The Supreme Court sustained the lower court's decision, stating that the Act did not violate her rights under due process or equal protection. Justice Sanford, writing for the majority of the Court, ruled that the state has the power to punish those who abuse their rights to speech, ". . . by utterances inimical to the public welfare, tending to incite crime, disturb the public peace, or endanger the foundations of organized government and threaten its overthrow."

Justice Brandeis, with Justice Holmes, concurred with the decision because of technical reasons, but he wrote a powerful appeal for freedom. Justice Brandeis stated that free speech should only be abridged in times of emergency.

> ". . . There must be reasonable ground to believe that the evil to be prevented is a serious one . . . Those who won our independence by revolution were not cowards. They did not fear political change. They did not exalt order at the cost of liberty. . . . No danger flowing from speech can be deemed clear and present unless the incidence of the evil apprehended is so *imminent* [emphasis added] that it may befall before there is opportunity for full discussion . . . ."

It appears that U.S. laws and the courts were extremely oppressive as to freedom of expression at this time. However, one must look to the circumstances surrounding these decisions. World War I was the first time that the United States had fought on foreign soil; thus, this was a new and frightening experience. Also, the United States was not the only country involved in the war that decided to reign in its press. All of the combatant countries during "The Great War" had some sort of censorship of the press. Only neutral countries such as Spain allowed the press to freely report on the war and the flu pandemic that killed millions of civilians and soldiers worldwide.

Further contributing to the great concern and trepidation in the U.S. government was the communist revolution occurring in Russia. As noted in many of the cases discussed in this chapter, the doctrines of communism and socialism were considered by some Americans to be a viable option to capitalism. On the domestic front, there was the beginning of the women's movement and the start of labor unions. The question on the minds of many in power was, "Would anything stay the same?" It surely must have appeared that the entire fabric of society was unraveling.

It also should be remembered that although the Supreme Court often is put on a "legal pedestal"; that is, the justices are thought to be disconnected to what is happening around them—they are not. Since 1803, the date of the landmark case of *Marbury v. Madison*, 1 Cranch 137, the case that gave the Supreme Court the power to interpret the constitutionality of the law, the majority rulings of the Court have *not* been made in a vacuum. Quite the contrary, most rulings have reflected the views of the society at that time.

Government Restraints 1940–1960

The Depression began in October 1929. With the collapse of the stock market and the resulting implosion of the U.S. economy, many people felt that capitalism had failed. With the 1917 Russian Revolution, communism seemed a way out of the abject poverty of the Depression, and some Americans felt that this "new" form of government was the answer. In response to this renewed communist threat to the U.S. government, Congress passed the **Smith Act** in 1940 (named after its sponsor, Congressman Howard Smith, of Virginia).[8]

The Smith Act made it a criminal offense to advocate the violent overthrow of the federal or state government, or for anyone to organize any association that teaches or encourages such overthrow, or for anyone to belong to or affiliate with such an association that would advocate such overthrow. The law did not require actual acts of violence, or the ability to overthrow the government. Unlike the Espionage Act of 1917, this bill applied to other than wartime, giving it almost an unlimited effective period. Interestingly enough, the Smith Act was hardly used before and during World War II. Its application truly took hold with the advent of the **Cold War**. After World War II, the Cold War was based on the ideological struggle between communism and democracy.

■ **SMITH ACT**

This act made it a criminal offense to advocate the violent overthrow of the federal or state government, or for anyone to organize any association that teaches or encourages such overthrow, or for anyone to belong to or affiliate with such an association that would advocate such overthrow.

■ **COLD WAR**

A Cold War is a state of political hostility between two countries, stopping just short of full scale conflict.

A few Socialist Workers Party sympathizers were convicted under the Smith Act in 1943, but the first real test of the constitutionality of the Act was after World War II in *Dennis v. U.S.*, 341 U.S. 494 (1951). In this case, the U.S. Supreme Court considered the Smith Act convictions of 12 Communist Party leaders. These individuals violated the Act's advocacy and organizing sections. Eugene Dennis et al. were tried on charges of willfully and knowingly conspiring to overthrow the U.S. government.

The opinion of Chief Justice Fred Vinson and three other justices applied a revised test for clear and present danger. This plurality opinion found the evil prevented by the Act was serious enough to allow suppression of freedom of expression. ". . . If, then, this interest may be protected, the literal problem which is presented is what has been meant by the use of the phrase clear and present danger of the utterances bringing about the evil within the power of Congress to punish.

Obviously, the words cannot mean that before the government may act, it must wait until the putsch is about to be executed, the plans have been laid and the signal is awaited. If Government is aware that a group aiming at its overthrow is attempting to indoctrinate its members and to commit them to a course whereby they will strike when the leaders feel the circumstances permit, action by the Government is required . . . ."

Although the group had in no way acted to overthrow the government; the chief justice did not consider this and was convinced that the group was ready to make the attempt.

Justice Frankfurter concurred using a balancing test, ". . . there is ample justification for a legislative judgment that the conspiracy now before us is a substantial threat to national order and security. If the Smith Act is justified at all, it is justified precisely because it may serve to prohibit the type of conspiracy for which these defendants were convicted . . . ."

Justice Black dissented, stating that the Smith Act is an invalid prior restraint, and the convictions should be reversed because there was no clear and present danger shown. Justice Douglas applied the Holmes–Brandeis definition of clear and present danger, and concluded that the petitioners were not in any pivotal position to be a real and immediate danger to the government: ". . . No matter how it is worded, this is a virulent form of prior censorship of speech and press, which I believe the First Amendment forbids . . . ."

After the *Dennis* case, the U.S. Department of Justice felt empowered and began trying more individuals under the Smith Act. Over 120 people were prosecuted for conspiracy to overthrow the government or for belonging to organizations deemed to advocate the overthrow of the government.

In 1953, the Supreme Court took on a new direction, under new leadership. The *Yates v. U.S.*, 354 U.S. 298 (1957) decision was an example of a more liberal attitude of the Court, under the new Chief Justice Earl Warren. In this case, the convictions of several lower-echelon Communist Party leaders were set aside, some were **acquitted**, and some cases were **remanded** for a retrial.

■ **ACQUITTED**

The finding of insufficient evidence to prove guilt.

■ **REMANDED**

To remand is to return a case to a lower court for further proceedings.

In *Yates*, Justice John Marshall Harlan wrote the majority opinion, stating that the trial judge, in the case, had given faulty jury instructions. He said that the judge in the lower court had instructed the jury that all advocacy or teaching of government overthrow was punishable, whether it was meant to incite action or not, as long as there was *intent* to produce that purpose. Justice Harlan concluded the statute prohibited *"advocacy of action,"* not merely *"advocacy in the realm of ideas."* Justice Harlan stated, ". . . We are thus faced with the question whether the Smith Act prohibits advocacy and teaching of forcible overthrow as an abstract principle, divorced from any effort to instigate action to that end, so long as such advocacy or teaching is engaged in with evil intent. We hold that it does not . . . ." The Court found insufficient evidence to prove that the Communist Party was advocating the required action. The Court stated that the government had to prove such advocacy in each individual instance, not paint the entire Communist Party as a catalyst to action.

After *Yates*, the **burden of proof** was put on the government to prove advocacy of action in every case. This made it extremely difficult to prosecute communists, and as such there were fewer cases.

In *Noto v. U.S.*, 367 U.S. 290 (1961), the Supreme Court reversed a conviction under the membership clause of the Smith Act. The court held that there was not enough evidence to prove that the Communist Party had engaged in unlawful activity. The Court stated that the mere abstract teaching of a need to resort to force and violence is not the same as preparing a group to conduct such action. There must be a sufficiently strong and pervasive connection to a present or future call to violence, not just ambiguous theoretical material as to the teachings of the Communist Party to infer that the entire party advocates violence. Justice Harlan, giving the opinion of the Court, stated, ". . . There is a danger that one in sympathy with the legitimate aims of such an organization, but not specifically intending to accomplish them by resort to violence, might be punished for his adherence to lawful and constitutionally protected purposes, because of other and unprotected purposes which he does not necessarily share . . . ."

The last time the Supreme Court would hear a sedition appeal was in *Brandenburg v. Ohio*. In this case, it overturned the conviction of a Ku Klux Klan leader.

The *Brandenburg* case reversed the 1927 case of *Whitney v. California*. In *Whitney*, the Supreme Court upheld the California Syndicalism Act, a law that punished utterances *tending to incite*. Remember, in *Whitney*, Justice Brandeis's *concurring* opinion had argued for the need to show the potential for "imminent danger" for him to consider the California law constitutional. In *Brandenburg*, the Court adopted, as the constitutional litmus test for state criminal syndicalism statutes, Justice Brandeis's requirement of imminent lawless action.

Although the federal government has tried, in recent years, to prosecute neo-Nazis and other right-wing groups for sedition, juries have acquitted these defendants under the *Brandenburg* doctrine.

In the next chapter, we will look at some of the more recent attempts by the states to pass laws limiting expressions, such as that of Brandenburg, and the more recent role that the federal government has played in efforts to restrain freedom of expression.

■ **BURDEN OF PROOF**

The obligation on a party, to establish the facts at issue in a case, to the required degree of certainty in order to prove its case.

SIDEBAR

During the Cold War, the tension between free nations and communist nations was palpable. During the early 1950s, "McCarthyism" hit its peak. Senator Joseph McCarthy, of Wisconsin, accused many prominent people in the United States of being a communist sympathizer. He would proceed against those accused, in Senate hearings. It did not seem to matter if there was proof against the alleged sympathizer or not. Although Senator McCarthy finally fell into disrepute as a result of his zealousness, still he affected the lives of many with his accusations.

CASE STUDY Brandenburg v. Ohio

395 U.S. 444 (1969)

Facts:

This case involves another criminal syndicalism act—that in Ohio. The Ohio law stated that it was illegal to advocate any ". . . crime, sabotage, violence, or unlawful methods of terrorism as a means of accomplishing industrial or political reform." Furthermore, one could not assemble ". . . with any society, group, or assemblage of persons formed to teach or advocate the doctrines of criminal syndicalism."

A Ku Klux Klan (KKK) leader, Clarence Brandenburg, was convicted of violating this law. He had given an inflammatory speech at a KKK convention. This speech was filmed and was later shown on nationwide television. The speech included derogatory remarks toward black and Jewish people. He also spoke of the need for revenge. The Supreme Court, in deciding this case, had to consider if this was a "call to action" under *Yates*, or merely a teaching of some abstract doctrine. Brandenburg argued that his conduct was protected under the First Amendment.

Issue:

Was Brandenburg's conduct protected under the First Amendment? Did the criminal syndicalism act of Ohio violate Brandenburg's rights under the First and Fourteenth Amendments?

Decision:

The answer is yes to both queries. Brandenburg's conviction was reversed.

Reason:

In this case, the Supreme Court went beyond *Yates*, and stated that the First Amendment protects speech even if it calls for action. In *Brandenburg*, the Court stated that the constitutional guarantees of free speech do not allow state regulation unless the speech is ". . . directed to inciting or producing *imminent lawless action* [emphasis added], and is likely to incite or produce such action." The Supreme Court ruled that the Ohio act made unlawful the advocacy and teaching of doctrines, without considering if such advocacy or teaching would incite action. Thus, the Ohio law is too broad and violates the constitutional right of freedom of expression.

SUMMARY

The history leading to a free press has been and continues to be a constant struggle among the media, the government, and the courts. The media seeks a robust right to freedom of expression, whereas the government and the courts have many times sought to curtail this freedom.

With the advent of the U.S. Constitution and the first 10 amendments—the Bill of Rights, assuring rights such as freedom of the press and assembly—laws such as the Alien and Sedition Acts of 1798 were passed in an attempt to control political dissent and freedom of expression. Even with the passage of the Fourteenth Amendment, in 1868, it took another 57 years for the U.S. Supreme Court to agree that these rights should apply to state court proceedings.

World War I saw the passage of the Espionage and Sedition Acts. The Supreme Court has held the Espionage Act does not violate freedom of expression.

The Smith Act, passed in 1940, was another attempt to control dissent. Under this Act, all one had to do to violate the law was to advocate the overthrow of the government. In the *Brandenburg* case, the Supreme Court reversed its former rulings when it held that the constitutional guarantees of free speech do not allow regulation unless it is directed at producing "imminent lawless action"; mere advocacy was not enough.

▉ DISCUSSION QUESTIONS_____

1. Compare and contrast the limitations on the freedom of the press during colonial times versus today; during World War I versus today; and during the Cold War versus today.

2. Does the Constitution alone assure sufficient civil liberties without the Bill of Rights? Argue for and against the ability of Congress to protect the rights of the American people.

3. Compare and contrast the passage of the Alien and Sedition Acts of 1798 with the passage of the USA Patriot Act in 2001.

4. Discuss why the Fourteenth Amendment should *not* apply to the states.

5. Discuss what standard should be put in place to control freedom of expression in peacetime versus wartime.

6. Was the Smith Act too broad in its restrictions? Discuss how much of a chilling effect such an act would have on freedom of expression.

7. How much freedom should the courts and the government allow when speech involves hatred toward another? Argue against the right to express any hateful speech.

■ CASE FOR REVIEW

Compare and contrast *Whitney v. California* and *Brandenburg v. Ohio*. Were the differences between the California and Ohio laws sufficient for a totally different Supreme Court verdict? Did the change in the Supreme Court to a more liberal one under *Brandenburg* make the difference? Was the difference in decision based on Whitney being a member of the Communist Labor Party and Brandenburg making a hate speech?

■ KEY TERMS

abolitionist literature

acquitted

Alien and Sedition Acts

American Civil Liberties Union (ACLU)

Articles of Confederation

Bill of Rights

burden of proof

Civil War

clear and present danger

Cold War

Espionage Act of 1917

Fourteenth Amendment's due process clause

freedom of expression

freedom of the press

injunctions

legal precedent

monetary bonds

prior restraints

remanded

Sedition Act

seditious libel laws

Smith Act

Tax Stamp Act

U.S. Constitution

USA Patriot Act

■ ENDNOTES

[1] *The First Amendment to the U.S. Constitution.*

[2] *Hamdan v. Rumsfeld*, 126 S.Ct. 2749 (2006).

[3] Locke, John. 1690. *Two Treatises of Civil Government.*

[4] Milton, John. 1644. *Areopagitica.*

[5] *An Act Respecting Alien Enemies.* July 6, 1798. *An Act for the Punishment of Certain Crimes Against the United States.* July 14, 1798.

[6] *Alton Observer.* Alton, Illinois. November 7, 1837.

[7] June 15, 1917, U.S.C. Ch. 30, title I, Sec. 1, 6, 40 Stat. 217, 219.

[8] *Alien Registration Act of 1940. US Statutes at Large.* 76th Congress, 3rd Session 670–676. Also known as the Smith Act.

 Online Companion™
For additional resources, please go to
http://www.paralegal.delmar.cengage.com

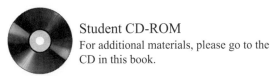 Student CD-ROM
For additional materials, please go to the CD in this book.

The Constitution and Its Interpretation as to Prior Restraint and Obscenity

▪ CHAPTER OUTLINE

▪ OBJECTIVES

After completing this chapter, you will be able to:

- Give examples of prior restraint—when the government attempts to control the publishing of information before the media disseminates it to the public.

- Determine what can and cannot be expressed in school publications—such as issues of pregnancy, divorce, and political dissention.

- Define obscenity based on the *Miller v. California* decision.

GOVERNMENT AND ITS ATTEMPT TO CONTROL WHAT IS EXPRESSED

Justice Brandeis in 1927 stated, "Those who won our independence believed liberty to be the secret of happiness and courage to be the secret of liberty. They believed that freedom to think as you will and to speak as you think are means indispensable to the discovery and spread of political truth."[1]

When the Founding Fathers wrote the Constitution, it was clear that they did not want to go back to the days of English rule and the requirements for licensing prior to publication—a form of prior restraint on freedom of expression. Yet U.S. courts have held that there can be injunctions issued against the publishing of information that is so controversial that almost everyone would agree it should not be published. There have been injunctions issued against the media to prevent it from printing confidential information or evidence that may jeopardize a defendant from having a fair trial. The courts have held that schools may limit student freedom of expression if it is considered vulgar or lewd, or if the speech is inconsistent with the shared values of a civilized society. The courts have, in many cases, held that expression that is deemed **obscene** is not entitled to First Amendment guarantees. Yet the Supreme Court has stated that any injunction or any attempt to limit freedom of expression should be looked at carefully, since all such limits on speech could be unconstitutional.

The following pages will examine the balancing act of the courts in determining what should and should not be censored, the courts taking into consideration the constitutional issues involved, and the tenor of society at the time.

▨ **OBSCENE**

For something to be obscene means it is offensively indecent.

CASE STUDY **Near v. Minnesota ex rel. Olson**

283 U.S. 697 (1931)

Facts:
Chapter 285 of the Session Laws of Minnesota provides for the abatement, as a public nuisance, of any malicious, scandalous, and defamatory newspaper, magazine, or other periodical. Anyone that is in the business of regularly publishing or circulating a newspaper, magazine, or other periodical that is obscene, lewd, and lascivious, or that is malicious, scandalous, and defamatory is guilty of a nuisance, and all persons guilty of such nuisance may be enjoined from such publication.

This action was brought to enjoin the publication of what was described as a malicious, scandalous, and defamatory periodical known as *The Saturday Press*. This periodical published by the defendants, in the city of Minneapolis. Nine editions of the periodical in question were published on successive dates. They were devoted to charges against public officers—that they were implicated to be working with gangsters.

(continues)

CASE STUDY   **Near v. Minnesota ex rel. Olson** *(continued)*

Issue: Does the Minnesota statute violate the First Amendment right of freedom of the press?

Decision: Yes.

Reason: Chief Justice Hughes felt the question that needs to be addressed is whether a statute authorizing such proceedings, in restraint of publication, is consistent with the conception of the liberty of the press. "In determining the extent of the constitutional protection, it has been generally, if not universally, considered that it is the chief purpose of the guaranty to prevent previous restraints upon publication. ... Charges of reprehensible conduct, and in particular of official malfeasance, unquestionably create a public scandal, but the theory of the constitutional guaranty is that even a more serious public evil would be caused by authority to prevent publication."

In *Near*, the Court made it clear that after publication punishment was preferable to **prior restraint**. In this way, the state is less likely to suppress free speech, and yet the individuals professing injury can pursue their claims in court after the information has been disseminated.

Forty years after *Near*, the *New York Times v. U.S.* case again addressed the issue of prior restraint. This case is also referred to as the Pentagon Papers case.

It is interesting to note, in the Pentagon Papers case, that Justice Brennan did not consider the Vietnam War to be in the same league as previous wars that prompted prior restraints on the press.

■ **PRIOR RESTRAINT**

This is the requirement to get prepublication approval. It is censorship that forbids the publishing of objectionable material.

CASE STUDY   **New York Times v. United States**

403 U.S. 713 (1971)

Facts: In these cases, the government sought to enjoin newspapers—the *New York Times* and the *Washington Post*—from publishing contents of a classified study on the *History of U. S. Decision-Making Process on Viet Nam Policy*. By the time of this case, in 1971, the United States had officially been in conflict with North Vietnam for six years. The Nixon administration faced widespread antiwar sentiment from American citizens. In 1967, then Secretary of Defense Robert McNamara commissioned a top-secret study on the role of the United States in Indochina. "Daniel Ellsberg, a former Defense Department economist who had grown disillusioned with the war, copied major portions of the study and then turned them over to the press. On June 13, 1971, the *New York Times* began publishing the papers, and the Nixon administration immediately sought to stop further publication."[2]

(continues)

CASE STUDY New York Times v. United States *(continued)*

Issue: Is the prevention of publishing this classified study a prior restraint that violates the First Amendment?

Decision: Yes. The Court stated, "Government failed to meet its burden of showing justification for imposition of such restraint."

Reason: The Court held any system of prior restraint bears a heavy presumption against its constitutionality. Mr. Justice Black with whom Mr. Justice Douglas joined, concurring, stated, ". . . that every moment's continuance of the injunctions against these newspapers amounts to a flagrant, indefensible, and continuing violation of the First Amendment . . . . Now, for the first time in the 182 years since the founding of the Republic, the federal courts are asked to hold that the First Amendment does not mean what it says, but rather means that the Government can halt the publication of current news of vital importance to the people of this country.

In seeking injunctions against these newspapers and in its presentation to the Court, the Executive Branch seems to have forgotten the essential purpose and history of the First Amendment." Justices Black and Douglas further stated, "The word 'security' is a broad, vague generality whose contours should not be invoked to abrogate the fundamental law embodied in the First Amendment. The guarding of military and diplomatic secrets at the expense of informed representative government provides no real security for our Republic."

Justice Brennan further added, concurring in the Court's decision, "Our cases, it is true, have indicated that there is a single, extremely narrow class of cases in which the First Amendment's ban on prior judicial restraint may be overridden. Our cases have thus far indicated that such cases may arise only when the Nation 'is at war,' *Schenck v. United States*, 249 U.S. 47, 52, 39 S. Ct. 247, 249, 63 L.Ed. 470 (1919) ... Even if the present world situation were assumed to be tantamount to a time of war, or if the power of presently available armaments would justify even in peacetime the suppression of information that would set in motion a nuclear holocaust, in neither of these actions has the Government presented or even alleged that publication of items from or based upon the material at issue would cause the happening of an event of that nature."

In *Smith v. Daily Mail Publishing Co.*, 443 U.S. 97 (1979), newspapers owned by Daily Mail Publishing published articles containing the name of a juvenile arrested for allegedly killing another youth. The publishers had learned the name from monitoring police band radio and asking eyewitnesses what had happened. The *Daily Mail* was indicted for violating a West Virginia statute that makes it a crime for a newspaper to publish an alleged juvenile offender's name without the written approval of the juvenile court. Was this a violation of freedom of the press? The

Supreme Court held that the State couldn't punish the truthful publication of an alleged juvenile offender's name, as long as the name is lawfully obtained, and still be consistent with the guarantees of the First and Fourteenth Amendments. The alleged state interest of protecting the anonymity of a juvenile offender, to further rehabilitation of the juvenile, could not be used to suppress freedom of the press.

A similar but different issue was addressed in *Bartnicki v. Vopper*, 532 U.S. 514 (2001). In this case, the Supreme Court extended First Amendment rights in speech that disclosed information from an illegally intercepted wire communication. The communication was collective-bargaining negotiations between a union representing teachers at a Pennsylvania high school and the local school board. An unidentified person intercepted and recorded a cell phone conversation between the union negotiator and the union president. After the parties accepted a nonbinding arbitration proposal, favorable to the teachers, Vopper, a radio talk show commentator, played a tape of the intercepted conversation. The Court accepted that the publishers of the information played no part in the illegal interception of the information, that their access to the information was obtained lawfully, and, "... a stranger's illegal conduct does not suffice to remove the First Amendment shield from speech about a matter of public concern. .... Privacy of communication is an important interest. However, in this suit, privacy concerns give way when balanced against the interest in publishing matters of public importance."

Other attempts to impose prior restraint on the media have ranged from taxing newspaper paper, printing ink, and even the number of copies a newspaper sells.[3] In *Leathers v. Medlock*, 499 U.S. 439 (1991), the restraint on the media had a slight twist. Arkansas had imposed a tax on cable television but not on the print media. Cable companies sued based on violation of their First Amendment rights. The Supreme Court ruled this tax was merely a generally applicable sales tax that was not indicative that Arkansas was attempting to target the content of cable television. Thus, this was not a violation of First Amendment rights.

The key—as with taxation of the media and its potential violation of the First Amendment—is whether it is normal taxation of a business, which all businesses must pay, or a special tax on the press that could censor content. If the Court finds that taxation is merely a ruse to impose prior restraint, it will be scrutinized and usually held to be unconstitutional.

SCHOOLS AND THE FIRST AMENDMENT

Until the 1960s, the concept of freedom of expression in a school setting was of little importance. Young people were viewed as second-class individuals; their parents and teachers controlled everything in their lives. Until the era of the late 1960s and early 1970s, very little controversy occurred on school campuses. Most students were just glad to be there. With the coming of the Baby Boomers' vehement protests against the **Vietnam War**, conditions on school campuses changed. These protests were vocal, visual, and visceral in nature.

■ **VIETNAM WAR**
The Vietnam War occurred from 1965 to April 30, 1975. This war was fought between the Democratic Republic of Vietnam—North Vietnam and the Republic of Vietnam—South Vietnam. The United States supported South Vietnam.

The 1969 case of *Tinker v. Des Moines* addressed the issue of whether the wearing of black armbands in protest to the war in Vietnam was protected speech or not.

The eloquent words of Justice Fortas met with much opposition after the *Tinker* case, both in state court decisions, and ultimately in the 1986 case of *Bethel School District v. Fraser*, and a 1988 case—*Hazelwood School District v. Kuhlmeier*. The 1980s,

---

CASE STUDY **Tinker v. Des Moines School District**

393 U.S. 503 (1969)

Facts:
In December 1965, a group of adults and students in Des Moines, determined to protest against the Vietnam War, decided to wear black armbands during the holiday season. John F. Tinker, 15 years old, and Christopher Eckhardt, 16 years old, attended high schools in Des Moines, Iowa. Mary Beth Tinker, John's sister, was a 13-year-old student in junior high school.

The principals of the schools met on December 14, 1965, and adopted the following policy: "that any student wearing an armband to school would be asked to remove it, and if he refused he would be suspended until he returned without the armband." The teenagers were aware of the regulation that the school authorities adopted. When they peacefully wore their armbands to school, they were suspended.

Issue:
Was this prohibition as to the wearing of the armbands a violation of the teenagers First Amendment rights?

Decision:
Yes.

Reason:
Justice Fortas delivered the opinion of the Court, stating, "First Amendment rights, applied in light of the special characteristics of the school environment, are available to teachers and students. It can hardly be argued that either students or teachers shed their constitutional rights to freedom of speech or expression at the schoolhouse gate." The Court held the school officials wanted to punish the students for a passive expression of opinion, there was no disorder or disturbance by the teenagers. There was no interference with the work of the school, or the right of other students to be left alone. School authorities argued this restraint on the wearing of black armbands was reasonable because it was based upon their fear of a disturbance.

The Court stated, "But, in our system, undifferentiated fear or apprehension of disturbance is not enough to overcome the right to freedom of expression. Any departure from absolute regimentation may cause trouble. Any variation from the majority's opinion may inspire fear. Any word spoken, in class, in the lunchroom, or on the campus, that deviates from the views of another person may start an argument or cause a disturbance. But our Constitution says we must take this risk." The Constitution does not allow officials of the state to restrain this form of expression—the wearing of the armbands.

unlike the 1960s, were not as kind to First Amendment rights. It was a more conservative time, with a more conservative political and judicial view, and a more conservative view of society and the school system.

In *Bethel School District Number 403 v. Fraser*, 478 U.S. 675 (1986), the issue revolved around a nominating campaign speech given by 17-year-old Matthew Fraser. The speech was given to a group of 600 teenagers, most of them around 14 years old. The speech contained sexual innuendoes, a sexual metaphor comparing the candidate's abilities to a specific sexual organ. Before Fraser gave the speech, he discussed it with several teachers, and two had said that it was inappropriate and should not be given.

As a result of Fraser giving the speech, he was told the school considered his speech a violation of the school's "disruptive conduct rule." This rule prohibited any conduct that substantially interferes with the educational process, and included the use of profane language or gestures, or the use of obscenities. Fraser, an honors student, was suspended for three days and his name was taken off the list of potential graduation speakers.

Chief Justice Burger delivered the opinion of the Court.

> "The process of educating our youth for citizenship in public schools is not confined to books, the curriculum, and the civics class; schools must teach by example the shared values of a civilized social order. Consciously or otherwise, teachers—and indeed the older students—demonstrate the appropriate form of civil discourse and political expression by their conduct and deportment in and out of class. Inescapably, like parents, they are role models. The schools, as instruments of the state, may determine that the essential lessons of civil, mature conduct cannot be conveyed in a school that tolerates lewd, indecent, or offensive speech and conduct such as that indulged in by this confused boy."

Chief Justice Burger held that the school district acted within its authority to sanction Fraser. "Unlike the sanctions imposed on the students wearing armbands in *Tinker*, the penalties imposed in this case were unrelated to any political viewpoint." School officials can determine not to allow a vulgar and lewd speech. To allow such a speech "would undermine the school's basic educational mission."

In *Hazelwood,* the Court determined the student's right to freedom of expression must be balanced with the interests of the school in maintaining order and a good learning environment.

The *Hazelwood* decision left undecided if the same ruling would be applicable in a college or university setting. In a footnote, the Court stated, "We need not now decide whether the same degree of deference is appropriate with respect to school-sponsored expressive activities at the college and university level." In view of this ambiguousness, federal appeals courts usually find the *Hazelwood* case inapplicable to college and university campuses (*contra* the Seventh Circuit *Hosty* decision, to be discussed later in this chapter).

CASE STUDY   **Hazelwood School District v. Kuhlmeier**

484 U.S. 260 (1988)

Facts: Former high school students that were staff members of the school's newspaper, the *Spectrum*, alleged that their First Amendment rights were violated when two pages of an issue were deleted from the paper. The articles deleted were those that discussed student pregnancies and the impact on the students, and an article discussing the effect of divorce on students. The paper was written and edited by a journalism class that was part of the school's curriculum. Before publishing, the teacher in charge of the paper would have to submit page proofs to the school's principal. The principal objected to the pregnancy article, because the students depicted, although not named, could be identified from the information in the article. Also, the reference to sexual activity and birth control were not appropriate for the younger students. There was an objection to the divorce article, because the original proofs contained the names of the parties (although the teacher deleted the names in the final draft). The principal also felt that the parties should have been given the opportunity to respond or give consent to the printing of the articles. The principal decided that there was insufficient time to change the articles before the publication date, and pulled the two pages of text, even though there were other noncontroversial articles on the two pages pulled.

Issue: Was the pulling of the two pages of the *Spectrum* a violation of freedom of expression?

Decision: No.

Reason: "The question whether the First Amendment requires a school to tolerate particular student speech—the question that we addressed in *Tinker*—is different from the question whether the First Amendment requires a school affirmatively to promote particular student speech. The former question addresses educators' ability to silence a student's personal expression that happens to occur on the school premises. The latter question concerns educators' authority over school-sponsored publications, theatrical productions, and other expressive activities that students, parents, and members of the public might reasonably perceive to bear the imprimatur of the school." The Court held the school is entitled to exercise greater control over activities that appear to have approval from the school, than activities that are merely an individual's expression. Readers or listeners should not be exposed to material that may be inappropriate for their age.

Justice Brennan, joined by Justice Marshall, and Justice Blackmun dissented: "In my view the principal broke more than just a promise. He violated the First Amendment's prohibitions against censorship of any student expression that neither disrupts class work nor invades the rights of others, and against any censorship that is not narrowly tailored to serve its purpose."

In *Kincaid v. Gibson*, 236 F. 3d 342 (6th Cir. 2001), an avant-garde yearbook was at issue. Kincaid and Coffer were registered students at Kentucky State University, a public, state-funded university. Gibson was KSU's Vice President for Student Affairs. KSU funded production and distribution of the *Thorobred*, the student yearbook.

Coffer, editor of the yearbook, took over the entire task of producing the yearbook after the others involved lost interest. She decided to gear the yearbook more toward the 1990s by covering the book with purple foil and giving the publication a theme—"destination unknown." When the yearbook came back from the printers, Gibson objected to the purple cover (KSU's colors are green and gold), its theme, and the inclusion of current events basically unrelated to KSU. Gibson consulted the KSU president and other university officials, and it was decided to confiscate the yearbooks and to withhold them from circulation.

Kincaid and Coffer sued Gibson; the president of the university, and other members of the KSU Board of Regents, alleging the university violated their First and Fourteenth Amendment rights when they confiscated the yearbooks. Was this a violation of their constitutional rights?

The Sixth Circuit held, "The university environment is the quintessential 'marketplace of ideas,' which merits full, or indeed heightened, First Amendment protection." University students are young adults, and thus are not immature. "The university's confiscation of this journal of expression was arbitrary and unreasonable. As such, it violated Kincaid's and Coffer's First Amendment rights." Thus, the college journalists were *not* subject to the same constraints as the high school students in *Hazelwood*.

The *Kincaid* case may be good law in the Sixth Circuit, but the 2005 case of *Hosty v. Carter*, 412 F.3d 731 (7th Cir. 2005), cert. denied U.S. 05-377 (February 21, 2006), leaves First Amendment freedoms on college and university campuses nonexistent in the Seventh Circuit.

The *Hosty* case revolved around the issue of the dean of student affairs, Patricia Carter, at Governors State University in University Park, Illinois, asking for prepublication review of the campus newspaper *The Innovator*.

Margaret Hosty, Jeni Porche, and Steven Barba sued in federal court contending Carter, the state-run school, and other university officials violated their constitutional rights, and the demand for prepublication review is a prior restraint on the freedom of expression. Is prepublication review of a university paper a violation of constitutional rights and a prior restraint?

The Seventh Circuit held that the analysis the Supreme Court used in *Hazelwood* was applicable to public colleges and university levels, not just elementary and high school publications. Circuit Judge Frank Easterbrook, writing for the majority, held that the university had the right to reasonably regulate *The Innovator's* content because it was published under the auspices of the university, and *Hazelwood* applies to *subsidized* student newspapers at colleges as well as to elementary and secondary schools.

In response to the Seventh Circuit's decision, Margaret L. Hosty, Jeni S. Porche, and Steven P. Barba filed a Petition for a Writ of Certiorari before the U.S. Supreme Court on September 15, 2005. In February 2006, the Court decided *not* to hear this case and thus let the lower court's decision stand.[4] Thus, *Hosty* is good law in the Seventh Circuit—Illinois, Indiana, and Wisconsin—and could have significant ramifications for student expression on college and university campuses throughout the nation.

California, in response to the decision by the U.S. Supreme Court not to hear the *Hosty* case, introduced, on February 24, 2006, Assembly Bill 2581 (The *Hosty* Bill). This bill was passed in the California Assembly on May 11, 2006, and passed the California Senate on August 10, 2006. It has been signed into law by the governor. This makes California the first state to grant college journalists the same free-speech protection enjoyed by professionals. The bill, authored by assemblymen Leland Yee, D-San Francisco and Joe Nation, D-Martin prohibits the censorship of student newspapers at a California college, university, or community college by specifically prohibiting UC (Universities of California), CSU (California State Universities), or community college officials from exercising prior restraint of *student speech or the student press*.[5] Under the bill, college and university campus administrators could still discipline students for publishing hate speech, and campus newspapers would still be liable for any libel printed.

What about private universities and colleges? Do First Amendment rights extend to those institutions? Usually, no. The only time that First Amendment rights attach is if the *administration* of the school allows freedom of expression.

There has been one major U.S. Supreme Court case on the issue—*Rendell-Baker v. Kohn,* 457 U.S. 830 (1982). In this case, the Court held that a nonprofit private high school, 90 percent funded by the government, did not give rise to constitutional rights. Rendell-Baker had been discharged from the school when she supported a student petition that sought greater responsibilities for the student–staff council. Rendell-Baker advised the board of directors she had been discharged without due process because she had exercised her First Amendment rights. She demanded to be reinstated or have a hearing into the matter. The school adopted a new policy and appointed a grievance committee to consider her claim.

The Supreme Court held,

> "The core issue presented in this case is not whether petitioners were discharged because of their speech or without adequate procedural protections, but whether the school's action in discharging them can fairly be seen as state action. If the action of the respondent school is not state action, our inquiry ends . . . . Here the school's fiscal relationship with the state is not different from that of many contractors performing services for the Government."

The school is not acting as a governmental entity or under state action, and thus constitutional rights do not attach.

The Banning of Books in Schools and Libraries

The banning of books, thus the banning of ideas, is not a new concept. The Greek philosopher Plato, in 360 b.c., said that the ideal Republic would be where fables and legends would be supervised. Those fables and legends that were not deemed satisfactory should not be disseminated to the public.

As was discussed in Chapter 1, political and religious leaders tried to control the dissemination of information, once the printing press came into use. Throughout history, books that went against societal norms have been banned or burned. Even today, there are attempts to ban books from libraries and schools. The individuals that attempt to do this usually do not consider their work censorship; rather, they feel that they occupy the moral high ground, preventing others from free access to books that are, in their view, profane, vulgar, too sexually explicit, depict homosexuality, depict witchcraft or the occult, or use racist or sexist language.

Books that have been banned include:

- Shakespeare's *Hamlet*, *Macbeth*, and *King Lear* for adult language and sexual and violence references.

- Shakespeare's *Twelfth Night* for its description of an alternative lifestyle—a young woman disguises herself as a boy.

- *Grimm's Fairy Tales* for the possible use of alcohol when the heroine brings food and wine to her grandmother.

- Mark Twain's *Tom Sawyer* and *Huckleberry Finn* for racist language. In fact, *Huckleberry Finn* has been the most banned book, ever.

- Voltaire's *Candide*, banned for obscenity.

- And, of course, the most recent controversy over J. K. Rowling's *Harry Potter* series for witchcraft and the occult.

In 1982, the most important case, to date, regarding the First Amendment and school libraries was decided. *Board of Education v. Pico* held that the First Amendment rights of students were impacted with the removal of books from a school library, and, as such, that schools officials have a limited right of book removal.

The *Pico* case did not give a decisive ruling as to what could be banned and why. What is educationally suitable? How could the Board limit acquisition of books without violating the First Amendment?

There have been few cases since *Pico*; one of them is *Virgil v. School Board of Columbia County (Florida)*, 862 F.2d 1517 (11th Cir. 1989). This case held that the school board could remove books from the *curriculum* if they are deemed to be vulgar or sexually explicit.

The facts in the *Virgil* case were that a public high school stopped using a textbook for humanities after receiving a complaint from a parent. The parent believed that the English translation of *Lysistrata*, a work of the Greek dramatist Aristophanes, and *The Miller's Tale* by the English poet Geoffrey Chaucer, were too vulgar. In response to the removal of these books from the curriculum, several other parents sued based on violation of the First Amendment. Can school officials remove the books from the curriculum based on the opinion that the books are vulgar and sexually explicit?

The court said the school officials could do so. Schools may remove books from the curriculum if there is a legitimate educational reason for doing so. (Educationally suitable as in *Pico*?) If a book is considered vulgar or too sexually explicit, there is a legitimate educational reason.

CASE STUDY   **Board of Education v. Pico**

457 U.S. 853 (1982)

Facts:	Members of the school board from Island Trees School District obtained a list of books considered objectionable by Parents of New York United, a conservative parents' organization. The Board found that the high school had nine titles on this list and that the junior high had one title listed. The school board, ". . . gave an 'unofficial direction' that the listed books be removed from the library shelves and delivered to the Board's offices, so that Board members could read them. When this directive was carried out, it became publicized, and the Board issued a press release justifying its action. It characterized the removed books as 'anti-American, anti-Christian, anti-Sem[i]tic, and just plain filthy', and concluded that '[i]t is our duty, our moral obligation, to protect the children in our schools from this moral danger as surely as from physical and medical dangers'."

The books removed were *The Fixer* by Bernard Malamud; *Slaughterhouse Five* by Kurt Vonnegut, Jr.; *The Naked Ape* by Desmond Morris; *Down These Mean Streets* by Piri Thomas; *Best Short Stories of Negro Writers* edited by Langston Hughes; *Go Ask Alice* by Anonymous; *Laughing Boy* by Oliver LaFarge; *Black Boy* by Richard Wright; *A Hero Ain't Nothin' But a Sandwich* by Alice Childress; *Soul on Ice* by Eldridge Cleaver; and *A Reader for Writers* edited by Jerome Archer.

The Board decided to appoint a review committee to decide what to do with these titles, but when the committee came back with its report, the Board ignored the directive and withdrew the books from the shelves. The Board gave no reasons for their rejection of the committee's recommendations. Steven Pico, a 17-year-old high school student, and several other students sued for denial of their First Amendment rights.

Issue:	Was the withdrawal of the books from the libraries a denial of First Amendment rights?
Decision:	Yes.

(continues)

CASE STUDY **Board of Education v. Pico** *(continued)*

Reason: Justice Brennan announced the judgment of the Court and delivered the following opinion, ". . . just as access to ideas makes it possible for citizens generally to exercise their rights of free speech and press in a meaningful manner, such access prepares students for active and effective participation in the pluralistic, often contentious society in which they will soon be adult members." The Court rejected the Board's claim of absolute discretion to remove books from the library shelves, yet stated, ". . . we do not deny that local school boards have a substantial legitimate role to play in the determination of school library content. [Yet] Our Constitution does not permit the official suppression of ideas." If the Board removed books from the school libraries only to deny the students access to ideas with which they disagree, and this was the decisive factor in the Board's decision, then this would be in violation of the Constitution. ". . . If it were demonstrated that the removal decision was based solely upon the 'educational suitability' of the books in question, then their removal would be 'perfectly permissible'." Thus, the Court limited the applicability of First Amendment rights to the removal of books from shelves, and did not extend constitutional rights to the acquisition of books or use of books in the school's curriculum. The Court recognized the school board's possession of ". . . broad discretion in the management of school affairs."

Judge R. Lanier Anderson did comment on the issue, saying, ". . . we seriously question how young persons just below the age of majority can be harmed by these masterpieces of Western literature. However, having concluded that there is no constitutional violation, our role is not to second guess the wisdom of the Board's action."

Now the question is, what is vulgar, sexually explicit, to the point, obscene? The next section of this chapter will address the attempts by society, and the courts, to determine this very difficult, even transcendent, concept.

OBSCENITY, WHAT IS IT?

For something to be obscene means it is offensively **indecent**. Interestingly enough, obscenity is not given constitutional protections, yet if something is merely indecent, the Court has held that it is protected speech, even if the indecency is punishable by a regulating agency such as the **Federal Communications Commission (FCC)**. Furthermore, if something is indecent, it is not necessarily obscene, yet if it is obscene it *is* indecent. Confused? So are the courts. Currently, there is a growing debate as to what can and cannot be shown on television, on the Internet, and in other forms of mass media. The Janet Jackson incident of Super Bowl 2004 was deemed indecent, and there were substantial fines handed out by the FCC, but was the bearing of a breast obscene? The courts have been struggling with

■ INDECENT

Something that is indecent offends decency.

■ FEDERAL COMMUNICATIONS COMMISSION (FCC)

The FCC regulates interstate and international communications, for example, radio and television that comes over the airwaves, and telecommunications.

how to legally define obscenity. Justice Stewart coined the most famous quote as to what obscenity is in the case *Jacobellis v. Ohio*, 378 U.S. 184, 197 (1964)—"I know it when I see it"—if it were only that simple.

To put obscenity into perspective, the question could be asked, why try to control speech that, for the most part, is performed and seen by consenting adults? Should society control what someone can and cannot see? Some societies are more accepting of sexually oriented materials, yet other cultures are very intolerant of anything that even suggests indecency.

Prosecutions for obscene speech in the United States began in the 1800s. The most comprehensive federal statute adopted to control obscenity became law in 1873 —The **Comstock Act**. This act made any "obscene" books, pamphlets, pictures, or other literature incapable of being mailed. The act criminalized the publication, distribution, or possession of information about any medications or devices concerning unlawful abortion or contraception.

Anthony Comstock, the innovator of this law, was truly a reflection of Victorian values of the times. Comstock, and other social conservatives of the time, worried that the women's suffrage movement (the right to give women the vote), "free love," and spiritualism would undermine morality in America.

The early 20th century saw the Comstock Act challenged. Margaret Sanger, a nurse, had published candid discussions about contraception, venereal disease, and sex education. She was indicted for violating the Comstock Act, but the charges were later dismissed. Ms. Sanger would continuously do battle with the censors throughout her life, but her work initiated a new way of viewing life and sexuality.

During the 1920s, in the United States, there was a sexual revolution going on. Women no longer had to cover themselves from neck to foot; hems were raised and clothes actually showed legs; and horribly constraining corsets were discarded. It truly was a new age.

The problem with the Comstock Act was that Congress never defined what was obscene. Ironically, the Comstock Act is federal law to this day. In 1971, Congress eliminated the referral to contraception in the act, and even after *Roe v. Wade*, 410 U.S. 113, was decided in 1973, it is still a crime to disseminate information about abortion. Although the law has not been enforced, it has been expanded to ban publication of abortion-related information on the Internet.

Along with the Comstock Act, an English case, *Regina v. Hicklin*, L.R. 3 Q.B. 360 (1868), defined obscenity in the United States until the 1950s. Obscenity, under *Hicklin*, was based on whether a passage, considered out of context and judged on its apparent influence on the most susceptible of readers, such as children or weak-minded adults, would corrupt such a reader. *Hicklin* made anything a child could find objectionable, obscene for all. Courts under the *Hicklin* test found an entire book obscene even if only one passage was deemed obscene.

In continuation of the corruption of the weak-minded theme, in *Mutual Film Corporation v. Industrial Commission of Ohio*, 236 U.S. 230 (1915), the Supreme Court considered an Ohio statute that required a board of censors to approve or disapprove this new technology called motion pictures (the Court referred to a film as

■ **COMSTOCK ACT**

The Comstock Act, a U.S. federal law, made it illegal to send any "obscene, lewd, and/or lascivious" materials through the mail, including contraceptive devices and information. The act also banned the distribution of information on abortion.

a series of positive prints shown in rapid succession to fool the eye into seeing motion). The Ohio statute gave the censors the power to decide if a film conformed to a moral, educational, or amusing and harmless character. If the film did not so conform, it would not receive the required censor board stamp.

Justice McKenna delivered the opinion of the Court. From that decision, it is clear that the Justices and society were enthralled by motion pictures but afraid of their potential hold over their audiences. Justice McKenna stated that although the motion picture could be used for moral, educational, and amusing purposes, still they could be used for evil.

> "Their power of amusement, and, it may be, education, the audiences they assemble, not of women alone nor of men alone, but together, not of adults only, but of children, make them the more insidious in corruption by a pretense of worthy purpose or if they should degenerate from worthy purpose. Indeed, we may go beyond that possibility. They take their attraction from the general interest, eager and wholesome it may be, in their subjects, but a prurient interest may be excited and appealed to. Besides, there are some things which should not have pictorial representation in public places and to all audiences."

(Sound like *Hicklin*?)

The Court held that freedom of speech does not apply to spectacles and circuses (obviously it was difficult for the Court to categorize this new form of entertainment). Thus, the Court upheld the state constitution's censorship review board. In fact, this form of censorship continued on a national level through the 1960s. Finally, instead of censors, the rating system that we have today came into being—G, PG, PG-13, R, and NC-17. Now it is up to parents and theaters to decide what age group will see what, and in what film.

In 1933, there was finally the demise of the *Hicklin* test, on the federal level. In *One Book Entitled "Ulysses" v. U.S.*, 72 F.2d 705 (2d Cir. 1933), Judge John Woolsey found *Ulysses* to be not obscene. He did not apply the *Hicklin* test; instead, he said that the material to be obscene must be *judged by its effect on the average person*, not those most susceptible, and *the work must be looked at as an entire unit* not just individual passages that could be interpreted out of context. Finally, adults could read something without worrying if it would corrupt a child.

In 1957, the Supreme Court took *Ulysses* a step further and began to apply an entirely different standard as to the definition of obscenity, in *Roth v. United States*.

Remember the *Mutual Film* decision, which allowed censors to approve or disapprove a motion picture? Finally in 1965, the case *Freedman v. Maryland*, 380 U.S. 51, held the use of censorship was not constitutional, because the Maryland law was too likely to suppress protected expression.

CASE STUDY Roth v. United States

354 U.S. 476 (1957)

Facts:	This case represented two lower court cases. One involved Roth, a New York businessman whose business was the publication and sale of books, photographs, and magazines. He used circulars and advertising to solicit sales. He was convicted of mailing obscene circulars and advertising, and an obscene book, in violation of federal obscenity statute.
	Alberts had a mail-order business in Los Angeles. He was convicted of lewdly keeping for sale obscene and indecent books. He was also convicted of writing, composing, and publishing an obscene advertisement of them. This was a violation of California Penal Code.
Issue:	Is obscenity a form of protected speech under federal law in the *Roth* case, or under the Due Process clause of the Fourteenth Amendment as to the California Penal Code in the *Alberts* case?
Decision:	No, ". . . it is apparent that the unconditional phrasing of the First Amendment was not intended to protect every utterance." Thus, the First Amendment will not protect obscene materials in the federal law, and the Fourteenth Amendment would not incorporate protection for obscenity under the Due Process clause, as to the California law.
Reason:	Justice Brennan delivered the opinion of the Court. The Court stated, ". . . sex and obscenity are not synonymous. Obscene material is material that deals with sex in a manner appealing to prurient interest. The portrayal of sex, e.g., in art, literature and scientific works, is not itself sufficient reason to deny material the constitutional protection of freedom of speech and press."
	Justice Brennan alluded to the fact, the early standard of obscenity was the *Hicklin* test—the material could be judged by an isolated excerpt upon susceptible group of people, but later decisions have substituted the test, ". . . whether to the **average person** applying **contemporary community standards**, the dominant theme of the material taken as a whole appeals to **prurient interest.**" The Court held that this more recent judicial standard provided sufficient safeguards and warning as to what is obscene, to protect the rights of due process and constitutional infirmities.

■ **AVERAGE PERSON**

An average person is one with an average and normal attitude toward, and interest in, sex.

■ **CONTEMPORARY COMMUNITY STANDARDS**

Contemporary community standards are set by what is accepted in the community as a whole —by society at large, or people in general.

■ **PRURIENT INTEREST**

An appeal to "prurient" interest is an appeal to a morbid, degrading and unhealthy interest in sex, as distinguished from a mere interest in sex.

Mr. Freedman was convicted of publicly exhibiting a film that was not submitted to the board of censors. Justice Brennan held the procedure involved in the Maryland censorship statute did not provide adequate safeguards against the possible inhibition of protected expression. If the censor disapproved the film, then the exhibitor was required to institute judicial proceedings to persuade the court the film was protected expression. Once the board had decided against the film, there could be no exhibition until the conclusion of judicial review, no matter how long that took. Finally, the statute had no provisions there would be prompt judicial review.

Justice Brennan suggested,

> "One possible scheme would be to allow the exhibitor or distributor to submit his film early enough to ensure an orderly final disposition of the case before the scheduled exhibition date—far enough in advance so that the exhibitor could safely advertise the opening on a normal basis. Failing such a scheme or sufficiently early submission under such a scheme, the statute would have to require adjudication considerably more prompt than has been the case under the Maryland statute."

Justice Douglas and Justice Black concurred in the reversal of the conviction of Freedman, but for different reasons. They stated that movies are entitled to the same protection as any other forms of expression. "If censors are banned from the publishing business, from the pulpit, from the public platform—as they are—they should be banned from the theatre."

Justice Douglas and Justice Black were constitutional absolutists—First Amendment rights should extend to all forms of expression, even obscenity. The problem for the Court was that because these two Justices consistently voted to overturn obscenity convictions, the Court never had the majority vote it needed to express a clear consensus on the law. The Court would hand down rulings with **plurality** decisions. Therefore, obscenity law is an unsettled venue.

In 1966, the Supreme Court further defined what obscenity was and was not. In *Memoirs v. Massachusetts*, 383 U.S. 413, the Court found the state courts of Massachusetts had erroneously found the book *Memoirs of a Woman of Pleasure (Fanny Hill)* obscene. *Memoirs* is a work completed in 1750 by John Cleland. It is a firsthand account of a high-class prostitute of London. Since its publication, it had been attracting the attention of censors; by 1966, it was widely translated and distributed. It was even found in the Library of Congress.

In a plurality decision (again Justices Douglas and Black maintaining there should be no censorship of expression) Justice Brennan gave the Court's decision. The Court held, this work was not obscene based on a three part test—first it applied the ruling in *Roth*—". . . whether to the average person, applying contemporary community standards, the dominant theme of the material taken as a whole appeals to prurient interest," but then the Court added two more parts to the obscenity test —the work had to be **patently offensive**, and it had to be **utterly without redeeming social value**. Thus, the Court was saying if a work had *any* redeeming social value of any kind whatsoever, it could not be considered obscene.

> "All possible uses of the book must therefore be considered, and the mere risk that the book might be exploited by panderers because it so pervasively treats sexual matters cannot alter the fact—given the view of the Massachusetts court attributing to *Memoirs* a modicum of literary and historical value—that the book will have redeeming social importance in the hands of those who publish or distribute it on the basis of that value."

PLURALITY

If a court cannot come to a majority opinion, two or more judges will publish concurring opinions. The other judges will then decide which concurring opinion they will join. The concurring opinion with the most number of judges creates a plurality opinion and, thus, a decision for the case.

PATENTLY OFFENSIVE

Whether material so exceeds the generally accepted limits of candor as to be clearly offensive.

UTTERLY WITHOUT REDEEMING SOCIAL VALUE

Material that has not even a modicum of redeeming social value.

■ TIME, PLACE, AND MANNER RESTRICTIONS

Limits that government can impose on the occasion, location, and type of individual expression in some circumstances.

After the *Memoirs* case, the Supreme Court backed away from trying to further substantiate the *content* aspect of obscenity; instead, **time, place, and manner restrictions** were used to distinguish if a work was to be held obscene or not—who, when, where, and how the material would be read or viewed would be the determining factors.

In *Ginzburg v. U.S.*, 383 U.S. 463 (1966), the Court dealt with a new consideration as to obscenity—the circumstances of production, sale, and publicity of circulars advertising potentially obscene material as being the offense, not the fact the materials themselves were necessarily obscene. Ralph Ginzburg was convicted in federal district court in Pennsylvania for sending three obscene publications through the mail—promotional material meant to titillate the receiver into buying what he was selling. An example of one of the advertisements sent out stated, "Documentary Books, Inc. unconditionally guarantees full refund of the price of *The Housewife's Handbook on Selective Promiscuity* if the book fails to reach you because of U.S. Post Office censorship interference." This basically was implying that the "*Handbook*" was "too hot to handle"!

Justice Brennan gave the opinion of the Court. The Court held, the deliberate representation of the publications in question as erotically arousing, made the reader accept them as prurient. The reader is seeking titillation, not intellectual content. "Where the purveyor's sole emphasis is on the sexually provocative aspects of his publications, that fact may be decisive in the determination of obscenity." Certainly in a prosecution that, as here, does not necessarily imply suppression of the materials involved as being obscene, the fact that they originate or are used as a subject of pandering is relevant to the application of the *Roth* test. Mr. Ginzburg was sentenced to five years in prison for his mailings.

SIDEBAR

TIME, PLACE, AND MANNER

Time, place, and manner are methods that the courts use in determining the degree speech can be restricted. If the restriction is content-based (what is being expressed), the government must show that the restriction serves a compelling state interest. If the restriction comes from a content-neutral (not based on the content of the expression) basis, all the government must show is the law serves an important objective, other than the suppression of free speech. The government will have to show the law is narrowly tailored, and there are ample means of alternative communication.

Justice Black dissented stating, "I believe the Federal Government is without any power whatever under the Constitution to put any type of burden on speech and expression of ideas of any kind (as distinguished from conduct), I agree with . . . the dissent of my Brother Douglas in this case, and I would reverse Ginzburg's conviction on this ground alone."

What if an individual already has possession of potentially obscene materials at home? In *Stanley v. Georgia*, 394 U.S. 557 (1969), police had a warrant to search Stanley's home for evidence of alleged bookmaking activities. While they were searching, the officers found three reels of 8 mm film. The officers reviewed the films, concluded they were obscene, and seized them. Stanley was tried and convicted under a Georgia law prohibiting the possession of obscene materials. Stanley argued the statute, because it punishes private possession of obscene material, violates his First Amendment rights, as applied to the states by the Fourteenth Amendment. The Supreme Court agreed. "Whatever may be the justifications for other statutes regulating obscenity, we do not think they reach into the privacy of one's own home. If the First Amendment means anything, it means that a State has no business telling a man, sitting alone in his own house, what books he may read or what films he may watch." Mere possession cannot be regulated. The production and distribution of obscene materials can.

In 1973, the Court finally adopted the obscenity standard still in effect today in *Miller v. California*.

Thus, under the *Miller* test, many materials dealing with sex, including pornography, do not qualify as being legally obscene; to be obscene, they must be of patently offensive, hard-core sexual conduct. Does nudity constitute obscenity? Not according to the *Jenkins v. Georgia* case.

In *Jenkins v. Georgia* 418 U.S. 153 (1974), a Georgia theater owner was convicted under a Georgia obscenity law when he showed the picture *Carnal Knowledge*. This film, starring Jack Nicholson and Ann Margret, explored sexuality in a social context. It is the story of two college roommates and lifelong friends preoccupied with their sex lives.

Justice Rehnquist gave the opinion of the Court. The Court stated that nothing in the movie falls into the purview of the patently offensive standard of *Miller*. Although the subject matter of the movie is of sexual conduct, there are no ultimate sex acts, nor exhibition of private parts. There is some nudity, ". . . but nudity alone is not enough to make material legally obscene under the *Miller* standards." Thus, the movie *does* merit constitutional protection.

Justice Douglas concurred in the decision, stating that there should be no ban on obscenity.

CASE STUDY Miller v. California

413 U.S. 15 (1973)

Facts: Miller conducted a mass mailing campaign to advertise the sale of illustrated books, alluded to as "adult" material. He was convicted of violating California Penal Code—"by knowingly distributing obscene matter." The conviction was based on his mailing five unsolicited advertising brochures addressed to a restaurant in Newport Beach, California (Orange County). The brochures consisted mainly of pictures and drawings explicitly depicting sexual activities with genitalia prominently displayed. The parties receiving them did not request the advertisements; the manager of the restaurant and his mother opened the envelope. They immediately complained to the police.

Issue: Is the sale and distribution of obscene materials, through the mails, protected under the Constitution?

Decision: No.

Reason: Chief Justice Burger delivered the opinion of the Court; Justices White, Blackmun, Powell, and Rehnquist joined. Justice Douglas dissented, and Justice Brennan filed a dissent with which Justice Stewart and Justice Marshall joined.

Chief Justice Burger held that the Court must define the standards that must be used to identify obscene material, so that a state may regulate it without infringing on First Amendment rights as applied to the states through the Fourteenth Amendment.

He stated obscene material is not protected under the First Amendment. The First and Fourteenth Amendments are not absolutes. The Court held, for a state law banning obscenity to withstand constitutional muster, ". . . The basic guidelines for the trier of fact must be: (a) whether 'the average person, applying contemporary community standards' would find that the work, taken as a whole, appeals to the prurient interest . . . quoting *Roth v. United States* . . . (b) whether the work depicts or describes, in a patently offensive way, sexual conduct specifically defined by the applicable state law; and (c) whether the work, taken as a whole, lacks serious literary, artistic, political, or scientific value. If a state law that regulates obscene material is thus limited, as written or construed, the First Amendment values applicable to the States through the Fourteenth Amendment are adequately protected . . . . We do not adopt as a constitutional standard the 'utterly without redeeming social value' test of *Memoirs v. Massachusetts*, . . . that concept has never commanded the adherence of more than three Justices at one time."

(continues)

CASE STUDY **Miller v. California** *(continued)*

Chief Justice Burger further stated, ". . . no one will be subject to prosecution for the sale or exposure of obscene materials unless these materials depict or describe patently offensive 'hard core' sexual conduct specifically defined by the regulating state law, as written or construed. We are satisfied that these specific prerequisites will provide fair notice to a dealer in such materials that his public and commercial activities may bring prosecution."

Addressing the issue of how to define "contemporary community standards"—nationally or locally—the Chief Justice noted, ". . . It would be unrealistic to require that the answer be based on some abstract formulation. The adversary system, with lay jurors as the usual ultimate fact finders in criminal prosecutions, has historically permitted triers of fact to draw on the standards of their community, guided always by limiting instructions on the law. To require a State to structure obscenity proceedings around evidence of a national 'community standard' would be an exercise in futility." It is not realistic for the standards of Mississippi or Maine to be applied to the standards of Las Vegas or New York City. Thus, the majority decision left these issues to be decided locally.

Justice Douglas dissented, stating, ". . . Obscenity cases usually generate tremendous emotional outbursts. They have no business being in the courts. If a constitutional amendment authorized censorship, the censor would probably be an administrative agency. Then criminal prosecutions could follow as, if, and when publishers defied the censor and sold their literature. Under that regime a publisher would know when he was on dangerous ground. Under the present regime—whether the old standards or the new ones are used—the criminal law becomes a trap. A brand new test would put a publisher behind bars under a new law improvised by the courts after the publication. That was done in *Ginzburg* and has all the evils of an ex post facto law."

Justice Brennan, with whom Justice Stewart and Justice Marshall joined, dissented. The consensus of these dissenting Justices was the California statute is overly broad, and invalid on its face.

Justices Brennan, Stewart, and Marshall concurred, stating that if the material is not distributed to juveniles or nonconsenting adults, the First and Fourteenth Amendments prohibit the state and federal governments from suppressing sexually oriented material on the basis of their alleged obscenity. Georgia's statute is constitutionally overbroad and facially invalid.

The issue of obscenity and its distribution was revisited in the case *United States v. Extreme Associates*, 352 F. Supp. 2d 578 (WD Pa. 2005). In this Federal District Court case, Judge Lancaster threw out a ten-count criminal indictment charging a California video distributor—Extreme Associates, and the husband-and-wife team that owns the business, with violation of federal obscenity laws—18 U.S.C. sections 1461 and 1465. These laws criminalize the commercial distribution of obscene materials, either through the mails or in interstate commerce. Extreme Associates boasts of having "the hardest of hard core porn," and declares, "See why the U.S. Government is after us!"

Extreme Associates argued that the antiobscenity laws violated their customers' privacy rights under the Fifth Amendment's doctrine of substantive due process; *Stanley v. Georgia* (cited earlier), allowing the mere possession of obscene material; and *Lawrence v. Texas* 539 U.S. 558 (2003), a case that struck down the criminal prohibition of homosexual sodomy in Texas. (The *Lawrence* case holding based on the violation of Fourteenth Amendment rights of adults to engage in private intimate conduct.) The District Court Judge agreed with Extreme's arguments and held the federal antiobscenity laws are unconstitutional.

In response to the Federal District Court's dismissal of the case, in February 2005 the Department of Justice appealed this ruling. That appeal was filed with the Third Circuit Court of Appeals in April of 2005 (Case No: 05-1555), argued in October 2005, and decided in December 2005. The appeals court reversed the lower court and reinstated the charges against the parties. The appeals court ruling, the lower court had erred in setting aside the federal obscenity statutes because the U.S. Supreme Court has repeatedly upheld federal statutes regulating the *distribution* of obscenity, both on First Amendment and substantive due process attacks.

In April 2006, Extreme Associates filed a petition to the U.S. Supreme Court for a Writ of Certiorari. In May 2006, the Supreme Court refused to issue the Writ, thus Extreme Associates will have to return to U.S. District Court to stand trial on trafficking obscenity. Pretrial motions in this case are scheduled to continue through June 1, 2007.

The *Extreme Associates* case highlights the contradictions found in United States obscenity laws. Under *Stanley*, the right to possession of obscene material is constitutionally protected, yet the distribution of such material is a crime under 18 U.S.C. sections 1461 and 1465.

Indecent Speech and the Courts

Remember the issue of obscenity versus indecency was raised earlier in this chapter? The Supreme Court, in 1978, ruled the FCC could limit the transmission of *indecent* speech when minors are likely to be part of the listening audience—from 6 AM to 10 PM (obscene speech is never allowed on the airwaves). In *FCC v. Pacifica Foundation*, 438 U.S. 726 (1978), the Court concerned itself with the issuance of a declaratory order by the FCC, that Pacifica could be subject to administrative sanctions for the playing of George Carlin's "Filthy Words" monologue in the mid-afternoon. The station had issued a warning prior to the broadcast that sensitive listeners may be offended.

The issue in *Pacifica* is, does the First Amendment deny the government any power to restrict broadcast of what is considered indecent language in any circumstance? According to the Court, "In this case it is undisputed that the content of Pacifica's broadcast was 'vulgar', 'offensive', and 'shocking'. Because content of that character is not entitled to absolute constitutional protection under all circumstances, we must consider its context in order to determine whether the Commission's action was constitutionally permissible." The Court held the broadcast was available to children, even those too young to read. The warning by the radio station, before playing the monologue, was not sufficient, because it was not a guarantee it would protect minors from this broadcast. The audience, time of day, and method of transmitting the message must be taken into consideration whether to impose sanctions. ". . . [N]uisance may be merely a right thing in the wrong place, - like a pig in the parlor instead of the barnyard . . . . We simply hold that when the Commission finds that a pig has entered the parlor, the exercise of its regulatory power does not depend on proof that the pig is obscene."

In 1989, the Supreme Court in *Sable Communications of California, Inc. v. FCC*, 492 U.S. 115, took on the topic of indecency and obscenity again. In *Sable*, the Court looked at the 1988 amendment to the **Communications Act of 1934**.[6] This amendment to the Communications Act deals with a ban on indecent and obscene interstate commercial phone messages—dial-a-porn.

In the *Sable* case, Sable Communications, a dial-a-porn business, brought suit in Federal District Court seeking injunctive relief against enforcement of the 1988 amendment to the Communications Act. This amendment gave a blanket prohibition on indecent as well as obscene interstate telephone messages. Sable sought to enjoin the FCC and the Justice Department from initiating any criminal, civil, or administrative action under this act. Sable also alleged the amendment is unconstitutional under the First and Fourteenth Amendments, since it included indecency and obscenity regulations. The District Court judge upheld the ban on obscenity but granted the injunction against the Act as to indecent messages. Thus, the District Court held obscenity was not protected under the Constitution, but *indecent* communications were.

When this case went to the Supreme Court, the Court upheld the lower court's ruling. "We agree with that judgment. In contrast to the prohibition on indecent communications, there is no constitutional barrier to the ban on obscene dial-a-porn recordings. We have repeatedly held that the protection of the First Amendment does not extend to obscene speech."

The Court further opined government may regulate constitutionally protected speech to promote a compelling interest, if it chooses the least restrictive means to do so, and there is a compelling interest to protect the physical and psychological well being of minors. Yet, this amendment to the Communications Act denies adults access to indecent telephone messages. The amendment far exceeds what is necessary to limit access to minors to such messages, thus the ban is not constitutional.

■ **COMMUNICATIONS ACT OF 1934**

The Communications Act of 1934 replaced the Federal Radio Commission with the Federal Communications Commission (FCC). The 1988 amendment to this act, dealt with dial-a-porn. Sections of the act were amended or repealed with the Telecommunications Act of 1996.

The Court differentiated the *Pacifica* case, from the *Sable* case, under time, place, and manner considerations. It is not protected speech if there are no controls as to access to minors of indecent expression on the ubiquitous radio, especially if the program is aired at a time when minors are likely to be listening, but it is protected speech if access to indecent expression reaches a limited audience, as in telephone messages. Obscene speech is never protected.

In April 2006, the four major television networks, and their 800 affiliated stations, sued in several federal courts, around the country, to overturn recent indecency rulings by the FCC. The networks and stations stating, the government "overstepped its authority" when it ruled an episode of CBS's *The Early Show*, several episodes of ABC's *NYPD Blue*, and two music awards shows on Fox, violated the agency's language decency standards. The broadcasters feel the rulings by the FCC are unconstitutional, and inconsistent with over 20 years of previous FCC decisions.

On June 4, 2007, a decision was reached in the U.S. Court of Appeals for the Second District as to one of the cases—*Fox v. FCC*; dockets number 06-1760-ag (L), 06-2750-ag (CON), 06-5358-ag (CON). The court found the new FCC policy sanctioning "fleeting expletives" is arbitrary and capricious for failing to state a reasoned basis for such a change.

The case before the court stemmed from Fox's broadcast of the Billboard Music Awards in 2002 and 2003. Receiving an award in 2002, Cher cursed. The following year, in presenting an award, Nicole Richie cursed twice. The FCC had argued the curse words, used by both women, are invariably indecent because they always connote a sexual or excretory function. The court rejected that reasoning, stating, "This defies any commonsense understanding of these words, which, as the general public well knows, are often used in everyday conversation, without any 'sexual or excretory' meaning."

Although the Court of Appeals did not outlaw the imposing of fines for indecency, the court returned the case to the FCC to find a more reasonable analysis for their implementation of fines. FCC Chairman Kevin Martin said this ruling, ". . . makes it difficult to go forward on a lot of the cases that are in front of us."

The FCC is especially concerned as to the disposition of the *Fox* case, since in June 2006, Congress passed legislation—the **Broadcast Decency Enforcement Act**. This act allows the Federal Communications Commission to increase the fine for airing indecent material on broadcast channels by 10 times—from $32,500 to $325,000 per incident. This bill does not apply to cable or satellite broadcasts, because the FCC does not regulate them.

The Internet has posed even more perplexing problems for the Supreme Court. Can protections of minors from unsuitable Internet messages withstand constitutional scrutiny? In *Reno v. ACLU* 521 U.S. 844 (1997), several litigants challenged the constitutionality of two provisions of the **Communications Decency Act**. The CDA was passed to protect minors from unsuitable expression on the Internet. The act under, "Title 47 U.S.C.A. §223(a)(1)(B)(ii) (Supp. 1997), criminalizes the 'knowing' transmission of 'obscene or indecent' messages to any recipient under 18 years of age.

■ BROADCAST DECENCY ENFORCEMENT ACT

The Broadcast Decency Enforcement Act was passed by Congress, and became Public Law 109-235 on 6/15/2006. This act was passed to increase the penalties for violations by television and radio broadcasters of the prohibitions against transmission of obscene, indecent, and profane material, and for other purposes.

■ COMMUNICATIONS DECENCY ACT

The 1996 federal legislation which attempted to ban the transmission of obscene or indecent material across the Internet.

Section 223(d) prohibits the 'knowin[g]' sending or displaying to a person under 18 of any message 'that, in context, depicts or describes, in terms patently offensive as measured by contemporary community standards, sexual or excretory activities or organs.' Affirmative defenses are provided for those who take 'good faith, . . . effective . . . actions' to restrict access by minors to the prohibited communications, §223(e)(5) (A), and those who restrict such access by requiring certain designated forms of age proof, such as a verified credit card or an adult identification number, §223(e)(5)(B)."

A three-judge District Court panel entered a preliminary injunction against enforcement of the challenged provisions—the government is enjoined from enforcing §223(a)(1)(B)'s prohibitions insofar as they relate to "indecent" communications. The court expressly preserved the government's right to investigate and prosecute obscenity or child pornography activities. The injunction against enforcement of §223(d) is unqualified since that section contains no separate reference to obscenity or child pornography. In response, the government appealed to the Supreme Court, under the CDA's special review provisions. The government argued it was an error to hold that the CDA violated the First Amendment for **over breadth**, and the Fifth Amendment because it is vague.

The Supreme Court ruled against the government. The Court found that the CDA does not allow parents to consent to their children's use of restricted materials; the act is not limited to commercial transactions; it does not define "indecent"; there is no requirement that the material be "patently offensive," or lacking in any socially redeeming value; the CDA does not limit the prohibitions to any particular time, place, or manner because it is a **content-based** blanket restriction on speech; the act does not allow for an evaluation by an agency familiar with the uniqueness of the Internet; the CDA is punitive; and the act applies to a medium that receives full First Amendment protection (unlike radio). The most stringent review of the act's provisions must be applied. "The CDA lacks the precision that the First Amendment requires when a statute regulates the content of speech." (The Court refused to address the Fifth Amendment issues.)

In 1998, Congress passed the **Child Online Protection Act (COPA)** in an attempt to protect minors from accessing sexually explicit material online. This Act was in response to *Reno v. ACLU* (*supra*). In response to COPA, the ACLU and online publishers sought an injunction to prevent enforcement of this act. They argued that it violated the First Amendment's Free Speech clause. The Federal District Court granted the injunction, and the Supreme Court ruled on the issue of the constitutionality of COPA in *Ashcroft v. American Civil Liberties Union*, Docket Number: 03-218, 542 U.S. 656 (2004).

Justice Kennedy delivered the opinion of the Court, stating, "Content-based prohibitions, enforced by severe criminal penalties, have the constant potential to be a repressive force in the lives and thoughts of a free people. To guard against that threat, the Constitution demands that content-based restrictions on speech be presumed invalid." For this regulation to be constitutionally valid, the Court should ask if the questioned regulation is the least restrictive means available to achieve the desired results. He continued, the granting of the injunction by the Federal District

■ **OVER BREADTH**

When a law proscribes constitutionally *unprotected* speech, but it also potentially proscribes constitutionally *protected* speech.

■ **CONTENT-BASED**

Content based regulation of speech means restrictions are placed on specific speech depending on what is says.

■ **CHILD ONLINE PROTECTION ACT (COPA)**

A law passed with the declared purpose of protecting minors from harmful sexual material on the Internet.

Court was not improper because there are other more plausible, less restrictive means of accomplishing COPA's goals. "The primary alternative considered by the District Court was blocking and filtering software. Blocking and filtering software is an alternative that is less restrictive than COPA, and, in addition, likely more effective as a means of restricting children's access to materials harmful to them . . . a filter can prevent minors from seeing all pornography, not just pornography posted to the Web from America." The Court estimated 40 percent of Web content harmful to minors comes from overseas, something that COPA does not address.

The Court let the injunction stand until final decision on the merits of the case. The Court held that to do otherwise would potentially lead to extraordinary harm and create a potential for a serious chill on protected speech. Because online publishers would likely self-censor, than run the risk of trial.

In March 2007, in a suit filed by the ACLU against the enforcement of COPA in U.S. District Court, Eastern District of Pennsylvania, Judge Reed permanently barred the enforcement of the Act, stating it was overly broad, and could potentially, ". . . chill a substantial amount of constitutionally protected speech for adults." Judge Reed stated current filtering systems are more effective than ever in blocking minors from accessing sexually explicit materials.[7]

The U.S. Justice Department is considering what the government's next step should be in response to this decision. Their option would be to appeal to the 3rd Circuit Court of Appeals.

Child Pornography

Child pornography is a form of expression that receives no First Amendment protections. The Court has consistently held there is a **compelling state interest** in protecting minors from exploitation. Yet, the Court has held child pornography statutes that are overbroad, and thus may inhibit or restrict free expression, other than actual child pornography—such as virtual child pornography, may be held to violate constitutional protections. In *Ferber*, the Court found the state law in question did pass constitutional scrutiny, since its intent was to protect minors, and the law was carefully written.

In *New York v. Ferber*, 458 U.S. 747 (1982), a New York criminal child pornography law was challenged. The law stated a person is guilty of this crime if they employ, authorize, or induce a child, less than sixteen, to engage in a sexual performance. The law is also violated if a parent, legal guardian, or custodian of the child in question consents to the participation of the child in the said sexual performance.

This case arose when Paul Ferber, the owner of a bookstore specializing in sexually oriented products, sold two films to an undercover police officer. The films depicted young boys masturbating. The U.S. Supreme Court dealt with one

■ COMPELLING STATE INTEREST

Compelling state interest is when the speech restriction by the government is justifiable based on a superior governmental interest, and as such, an individual's rights must cede to such interest.

issue—could the New York legislature pass a law that criminalizes the dissemination of child sexual activity, whether that activity is deemed obscene or not, and still have the law be constitutional?

Justice White, delivering the Supreme Court's opinion, stated, "The prevention of sexual exploitation and abuse of children constitutes a government objective of surpassing importance. The legislative findings accompanying passage of the New York laws reflect this concern." The recording of such acts by a child can potentially haunt the child for the rest of his life. The Court found the New York law to be carefully drawn to protect children, and thus did not violate the First and Fourteenth Amendments.

Yet, the Court in *Ferber* did express that there are limits for a statute to pass constitutional muster. The state law must adequately define any legislation, written or construed, prohibiting the conduct. The harm to be combated must be limited to works that visually depict sexual conduct by minors below a specified age, and the sexual conduct proscribed must be limited and described. If the law is not so written, it could be considered overbroad and, thus, a potential interference with constitutionally protected speech.

In a 1990 case, the Supreme Court reviewed an Ohio state law that made the mere possession of child pornography a crime. In *Osborne v. Ohio*, 495 U.S. 103, the Court considered if an Ohio statute violated the First Amendment. The statute prohibited the possession or viewing of any material or performance that shows a minor, not the person's child or ward, in any state of nudity, unless it is for artistic, scientific, or other *proper* purpose. Clyde Osborne's home was searched under a valid search warrant, and, during the search, four pictures of four nude male adolescents, posed in sexually explicit positions, were found.

The Court held the Ohio law was constitutional—it could proscribe the possession of child pornography. The Court distinguished this case from the *Stanley* case (*supra*), holding the *Osborne* case is different because it involves child pornography not mere obscenity, ". . . the interests underlying child pornography prohibitions far exceed the interests justifying the Georgia law at issue in *Stanley*."

As discussed earlier, not all child pornography statutes withstand constitutional scrutiny. In 2002, the Court struck down two provisions of the 1996 **Child Pornography Prevention Act (CPPA)**. In *Ashcroft v. Free Speech Coalition*, Docket Number: 00-795, 535 U.S. 234 (2002), the Court held, the CPPA was overbroad thus unconstitutional. The CPPA prohibits, ". . . 'any visual depiction, including any photograph, film, video, picture, or computer or computer-generated image or picture 'that' is, or appears to be, of a minor engaging in sexually explicit conduct', §2256(8)(B), and any sexually explicit image that is 'advertised, promoted, presented, described, or distributed in such a manner that conveys the impression 'it depicts' a minor engaging in sexually explicit conduct', §2256(8)(D). Thus, §2256(8) (B) bans a range of sexually explicit images, sometimes called 'virtual child pornography'." Virtual child pornography appears to depict minors, but it is produced by means other than using real children, such as the use of youthful-looking adults, or computer-imaging technology.

■ **CHILD PORNOGRAPHY PREVENTION ACT (CPPA)**

The Child Pornography Prevention Act extended the existing federal criminal laws against child pornography to the new computer media. As part of the overhaul, the definition of "child pornography" was extended to include "morphed" or computer generated images.

The Free Speech Coalition, an adult entertainment trade association, challenged these provisions as violations of First Amendment freedoms. They alleged that the CPPA provisions as to "appears to be" and "conveys the impression" were overbroad and vague.

The Supreme Court opinion, delivered by Justice Kennedy, held that the CPPA is inconsistent with *Miller* (*supra*). Materials under the CPPA need not have to appeal to prurient interests; the CPPA proscribes any depiction of sexually explicit activity, no matter how presented. There are no standards as to obscenity under the CPPA. *Miller* requires the government to prove the work taken as a whole, appeals to the prurient interest, is patently offensive in light of community standards, and lacks any serious literary, artistic, political, or scientific value.

The CPPA, unlike the issues in *Ferber* (*supra*), prohibits speech that records no crime and creates no victims by the material's production. Virtual pornography is not "intrinsically related" to the sexual exploitation of children.

The Court rejected the government's argument that CPPA is necessary to control pedophilia. This argument, the Court held, "runs afoul of the principle that speech within the rights of adults to hear may not be silenced completely in an attempt to shield children from it. . . . That the evil in question depends upon the actor's unlawful conduct, defined as criminal quite apart from any link to the speech in question, establishes that the speech ban is not narrowly drawn." Thus, the Court found these provisions of the CPPA abridge the freedom to engage in a substantial amount of lawful speech.

This chapter has examined the legal application of First Amendment rights to various forms of expression from banned books, to obscenity, and even child pornography. The next chapter will build on this background, and examine how journalists can gather the information they need for their careers.

SUMMARY

The Supreme Court has consistently held that prior restraints on free expression are less acceptable than punishment for the questioned material after its publication.

Time, place, and manner are methods of determining the degree of speech that can be restricted.

First Amendment rights are not vitiated in a school setting. Yet, under *Hosty*, college and university subsidized publications are subject to censorship. School officials have a limited right of book removal from libraries, but can regulate the acquisition of books, or use of books in the school's curriculum.

Obscenity is not given constitutional protections, yet indecent speech is, although it can be regulated. The Court has ruled obscenity cannot be sent through the mail or in interstate commerce. It has also held obscenity that already is within your home, for private viewing, is constitutionally protected—*contra* child pornography. The Court has held that child pornography statutes that are overbroad, and thus may inhibit free expression, or restrict other than actual child pornography (virtual child pornography) may be held to violate constitutional protections.

DISCUSSION QUESTIONS

1. Argue why or why not the press should be restricted in what they report. What if the report jeopardizes national security? Who is to say what is and what is not national security?

2. Discuss whether a juvenile's name should be withheld from publication at all times.

3. How can the media prove a tax on content is a prior restraint, and not just a legitimate revenue source for the governmental interest imposing it?

4. Is California helping or hurting college newspapers with the passage of AB2581? Discuss both sides of the issue.

5. Define obscenity.

CASE FOR REVIEW

A 1959 case, *Smith v. California*, 361 U.S. 147, would address the issue if the seller of books, or other material could be held criminally liable for obscenity if they did not know the content of the material was obscene. Mr. Smith owned a bookstore in Los Angeles; he was convicted under a Los Angeles City ordinance that makes it unlawful, ". . . for any person to have in his possession any obscene or indecent writing. [or] book . . . [i]n any place of business where . . . books . . . are sold or kept for sale." The ordinance included no element of knowledge of the contents of the book—thus the ordinance imposed strict or absolute criminal liability for the mere possession of such a book. Discuss whether this Los Angeles ordinance violates the rights of freedom of speech and the press.

KEY TERMS

average person	Comstock Act	patently offensive
Broadcast Decency Enforcement Act	contemporary community	plurality
Child Online Protection Act	standards	prior restraint
(COPA)	content-based	prurient interest
Child Pornography Prevention Act	Federal Communications	time, place, and manner restrictions
(CPPA)	Commission (FCC)	utterly without redeeming social
Communications Act of 1934	indecent	value
Communications Decency Act	obscene	Vietnam War
compelling state interest	over breadth	

▮ ENDNOTES

1 *Whitney v. California*, 274 U.S. 357 (1927).

2 http://usinfo.state.gov.

3 *Grosjean v. American Press Co.*, 297 U.S. 233 (1936), tax on circulation numbers, *Minneapolis Star v. Minnesota Commission of Revenue*, 460 U.S. 575 (1983), tax on paper and ink

4 *Hosty v. Carter*, Cert. denied U.S. 05-377 (February 21, 2006).

5 http://www.leginfo.ca.gov.

6 http://www.fcc.gov.

7 Docket number 2:98-CV-05591-LR.

 Online Companion™
For additional resources, please go to
http://www.paralegal.delmar.cengage.com

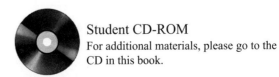 Student CD-ROM
For additional materials, please go to the
CD in this book.

3

Freedom of the Press versus a Fair Trial

▪ CHAPTER OUTLINE

▪ OBJECTIVES

After completing this chapter, you will be able to:

- Know why the courts' view media coverage of a case as potential prejudicial trial publicity.

- Know what "gag orders" are, and how they are invoked on the media.

- Know what the judiciary's view is regarding closed or open access to courtrooms by the media.

- Compare how having cameras in the courtroom versus not having cameras in a courtroom can affect the impartiality of a trial.

- Know how the courts handled media access in high-profile cases such as those of O .J. Simpson, Kobe Bryant, and Michael Jackson.

THE PRESS VERSUS A FAIR TRIAL

■ **PUBLIC TRIAL**

Proceedings
presumptively open to the
public.

■ **IMPARTIAL JURY**

An impartial jury is one
without bias, prejudice, or
other preconceptions as
to the case before it. The
juror should have no
opinion about or vested
interest in a case at the
start of the trial and
should base his verdict
only on competent legal
evidence presented during
the trial.

"In all criminal prosecutions, the accused shall enjoy the right to a speedy and **public trial** by an **impartial jury** of the State and district wherein the crime shall have been committed, which district shall have been previously ascertained by law, and to be informed of the nature and cause of the accusation; to be confronted with the witnesses against him; to have compulsory process for obtaining witnesses in his favor, and to have the Assistance of Counsel for his defence [*sic*]." This is the Sixth Amendment of the U.S. Constitution.

What exactly does this amendment mean? Does a *public* trial mean that every journalist in the country can attend, coming in with stage lights and cameras, and report on every aspect of the trial? If this is done, is it possible to give the defendant a fair trial? Or is this just a media circus? The courts have been struggling with this issue for years. With the advent of 24/7 news and media coverage, the Internet, blogs, and a plethora of talk and informational shows, it has been a struggle for courts to adhere to the concept of a public trial. Many times, the courts place restraints on such an open door policy; sometimes the public's right to know must give way to a defendant's right to a fair trial.

In 1884, then Massachusetts Supreme Court Justice Oliver Wendell Holmes in *Cowley v. Pulsifer*, 137 Mass. 392, expressed his opinion that members of the public enjoy a right of openness in *civil* judicial proceedings.

> "It is desirable that the trial of causes should take place under the public eye…not because the controversies of one citizen with another are of public concern, but because it is of the highest moment that those who administer justice should always act under the sense of public responsibility, and that every citizen should be able to satisfy himself with his own eyes as to the mode in which a public duty is performed."

In 1966, the U.S. Supreme Court handed down a landmark decision regarding prejudicial media publicity. In *Sheppard v. Maxwell*, the Court reversed Sheppard's conviction for murder and granted him a new trial based on the fact that he had not received a fair trial as a result of all the media publicity before and during his trial.

CASE STUDY   ⚖   **Sheppard v. Maxwell**

384 U.S. 333 (1966)

Facts: Dr. Samuel Sheppard was convicted of second-degree murder for the bludgeoning death of his wife. The murder occurred at their lakeshore home near Cleveland, Ohio. Dr. Sheppard consistently maintained he was asleep downstairs when his wife was killed. He stated that the screams of his wife, in the upstairs bedroom, awakened him, and he immediately ran upstairs to investigate. While running up the stairs, he stated that he was struck in the

(continues)

CASE STUDY Sheppard v. Maxwell *(continued)*

back of the head and knocked unconscious by the intruder. When he awoke from the blow, he followed the intruder outside to the shore of the lake and confronted him. He further stated that while he fought the intruder, he again lost consciousness.

From the outset of the case, the focus of suspicion was on Dr. Sheppard. The local media leapt on this and demanded the conviction of Dr. Sheppard. His account of the evening in question was very vague and confusing. Sheppard always maintained that he was innocent of the crime. Dr. Sheppard alleged that the trial judge did nothing to protect him from the intense and prejudicial publicity that accompanied his trial.

Issue: Did the massive, pervasive, and prejudicial publicity in the Sheppard trial prevent him from receiving a fair trial under the Due Process Clause of the Fourteenth Amendment?

Decision: Yes.

Reason: The Court held, "Though freedom of discussion should be given the widest range compatible with the fair and orderly administration of justice, it must not be allowed to divert a trial from its purpose of adjudicating controversies according to legal procedures based on evidence received only in open court." Both criminal and civil matters must be adjudicated in, "the calmness and solemnity of the courtroom according to legal procedures." The Court held that the pervasive media attention to this trial inflamed the minds' of the jurors against Dr. Sheppard, thus denying him a fair trial. The Court reversed the Sheppard conviction and he was granted a new trial. At the new trial, he was acquitted.

In the *Sheppard* holding, the Supreme Court made some suggestions on how the case should have been handled by the lower court:

1. He should have been granted a change in **venue** to a locale away from the publicity.
2. The jury should have been **sequestered**.
3. The lower court judge should have warned the jurors to disregard the media coverage.
4. The lower court judge should have imposed a **gag order** to control out of court statements, especially those from the prosecution and the defense.
5. The judge should have adopted rules to avoid the carnival-like atmosphere within the courtroom.
6. If there is likelihood that prejudicial news, before trial, will prevent a fair trial, the judge should **continue** the case until the threat abates.

▪ VENUE
The place of a trial.

▪ SEQUESTERED
To sequester a jury is to remove or set it apart from the public.

▪ GAG ORDER
A tool to prevent the media from publishing unwanted information on a particular topic.

▪ CONTINUE
To continue a case is to postpone the trial date to a later time.

It appears that the actual killer in the Sheppard case was a handyman, Richard Eberling, who had done work around the Sheppards' house. Dr. Sheppard spent 10 years in jail, based on the accusations against him; he died four years after his acquittal. If this case sounds familiar, it is the case on which the television program and motion picture *The Fugitive* were based.

Media Access to Miscellaneous Court Procedures

Regarding media access to videotapes, audios, and other documents that are introduced into evidence, lower courts have not agreed on what the media can view or hear. Usually the courts will not allow access to information that has not been made public, or allow the media to attend **depositions**. Only a few courts have held that depositions and other discovery proceedings are open to the press.

State statutes also limit information as to minors and sexual assault victims, although the Supreme Court has held that if the information is lawfully obtained, the media cannot be punished for publishing it, demonstrated for example, in the *Smith v. Daily Mail Publishing Co.* case discussed earlier.

Since September 11, 2001, a recent issue concerning the judiciary is whether **Immigration and Naturalization Service (INS)** administrative hearings are open to the press. INS regulations require these hearings to be open, but after September 11, as a result of security reasons, these hearings are now closed. INS records are also sealed. The appellate courts disagree on whether these new rules violate the First Amendment. The 6th U.S. Circuit Court of Appeals held in August 2002 that the new rules were unconstitutional, yet the 3rd Circuit upheld these secrecy rules in October 2002—the 3rd Circuit yielding to the executive branch of government's national security interests.

The media can only wait to see if the Supreme Court will consider the constitutionality of the new INS rules. So far, post-9/11 court rulings have not been favorable for the doctrine of openness. The Supreme Court denied certiorari in the 2004 INS case of *M.K.B. v. Warden* (cert. denied No. 03-6747),[1] the Court did not cite any precedent, and the government's brief in the case was kept under seal.

GAG ORDERS

The *Sheppard* decision, as discussed earlier, gave the judiciary the legitimate means of containing an out-of-control press, attorneys, and anyone involved in a court case. The Supreme Court criticized the lower court in the *Sheppard* case for not restricting the media's remarks. Yet the Court did not state what was required to impose such a restriction on expression. As a result, lower courts do not have a uniform test to apply when they need to quiet prejudicial publicity. Some jurisdictions use a *reasonable likelihood* of prejudice test, some use a *substantial likelihood* test of prejudice, and others use a *serious and imminent threat* of prejudice test.

■ DEPOSITIONS

A deposition is a form of discovery during which a person is questioned while under oath.

■ IMMIGRATION AND NATURALIZATION SERVICE (INS)

The INS, now called the U.S. Citizenship and Immigration Services, enforces the laws that apply to the entry of non-U.S. citizens—foreign nationals—into the United States.

In 1968, in an attempt to define when and how a restrictive gag order should be imposed, the American Bar Association (ABA) adopted the recommendations of its Committee on Fair Trial and Free Press. Justice Reardon of the Supreme Court of Massachusetts headed this committee, leading to the name of the report—the **Reardon Report**.

The standards in the Reardon Report were directed toward prosecutors, judges, jurors, defense attorneys, witnesses, law enforcement, and others involved in the trial. The report allowed use of the accused's name, age, and family status, the charge against the accused, and a description of the arrest. The report banned disclosure of potentially prejudicial information, for example, the suspect's record of actual priors, any confessions or admission contents, lie detector results, or refusals to submit to a polygraph test. Furthermore, the Reardon Report barred identifying witnesses, revealing their testimony, or delving into the credibility, or lack thereof, of a witness. Yet, Justice Reardon did state that these standards would not prohibit police or prosecutors from making public statements on the facts of the arrest, or the crime. In September 1968, the Reardon Report was made a federal standard by the U.S. Judicial Conference.

The ABA also suggested that if the parties to the case do not adhere to the prohibition as to dissemination of prejudicial information, judges should invoke their **contempt powers**.

In *Butterworth v. Smith*, 494 U.S. 624 (1990), the Supreme Court ruled that a Florida court could *not* prohibit a **grand jury** witness (a reporter for a Charlotte County newspaper) from discussing his testimony after the grand jury investigation was terminated. Florida's interests in preserving the confidentiality of its grand jury proceedings must be balanced against First Amendment rights, and Florida's interests do not warrant a permanent ban on disclosure by a witness of his *own* testimony once a grand jury has been discharged.

A 10th Circuit Court of Appeals case, *Hoffman-Pugh v. Keenan*, No. 01-1385 (2003), held that *Butterworth* did not prevent Colorado from forbidding a grand jury witness from disclosing information that he *gained through grand jury participation*. This case involved Linda Hoffman-Pugh, the housekeeper for John and Patsy Ramsey. The Ramseys, before the murder of their daughter JonBenet Ramsey, had employed Hoffman-Pugh. Because of her association with the Ramsey household, she was involved in the grand jury investigation of the crime.

Based on her experiences with the Ramseys, Ms. Hoffman-Pugh sought to publish a book. Colorado law requires a grand jury witness to take an oath that he will not disclose his testimony until an indictment or report is issued. The only exceptions are to discuss testimony with his attorney or with the prosecutor. The law also states that a grand jury witness cannot divulge his testimony even after the term of the grand jury has ended, if the investigation of the crime continues. The Federal District Court granted Ms. Hoffman-Pugh a judgment declaring she could not be prosecuted for revealing the information in question. The District Court holding the Colorado secrecy rule violates the First and Fourteenth Amendments.

■ **REARDON REPORT**

A study that advocated restrictions on the release and publication of information about people accused of crimes.

■ **CONTEMPT POWERS**

Contempt powers allow the highest remedy of a judge to impose sanctions on an individual for acts that excessively disrupt the normal process of a court hearing.

■ **GRAND JURY**

A grand jury reviews the evidence presented by the prosecutor and determines whether there is probable cause to return an indictment against the accused. An indictment is a formal accusation of a criminal offense.

The state appeals court and the 10th Circuit Court of Appeals reversed this decision, saying that the Colorado law did not violate Hoffman-Pugh's constitutional rights. They stated that *Butterworth* did not apply. Florida's law was found unconstitutional because it prohibited grand jury witnesses from discussing their *own* information after the grand jury investigation was complete. Colorado law forbade the divulging of *information gained* during the grand jury participation, and this prohibition is only in force as long as an investigation into the case continues.

Not only are grand juries' participants of interest in the implementation of gag orders, restrictive orders are imposed on **petit jurors** as well. Gag orders on petit jurors usually occur after the trial. This allows state trial judges to impose restraints on news interviews with jurors as to how they deliberated; restraints on questions as to how the juror voted; and restraints on repeated requests by the media for information after the juror has stated he does not wish to discuss the matter.

In *Gentile v. State Bar of Nevada*, 501 U.S. 1030 (1991), the Supreme Court held that lawyers participating in a pending case may be prohibited from making statements that may be prejudicial to the case. The Court stated, "... the 'substantial likelihood of material prejudice' test applied by Nevada and most other States satisfies the First Amendment." The state may demand some adherence by attorneys in the regulation of their speech and conduct. Their comments, out of court, pose a threat to a pending proceeding's fairness, since attorneys, in the case, have special access to information through discovery and client communication, and their statements are likely to be received as especially authoritative. It is permissible to subordinate the attorney's First Amendment rights to the party's interest in obtaining a fair trial.

Before the issuance of a gag order, a judge must conduct a hearing to consider the nature of the pretrial coverage and if other less restrictive measures can prevent prejudicial pretrial publicity. In *Nebraska Press Association v. Stuart*, the Supreme Court finally announced a test the judiciary must follow before the issuance of a gag order.

■ **PETIT JUROR**

A petit juror is one that sits on a trial jury.

CASE STUDY — Nebraska Press Association v. Judge Stuart, et al

427 U.S. 539 (1976)

Facts: In October 1975, local police found six members of the Henry Kellie family murdered in their home in Sutherland, Nebraska, a town of some 850 people. The suspect, Simants, was an unemployed handyman who had an IQ of 75.

Simants's brother-in-law lived next door to the Kellies, and Simants borrowed a rifle from him. Simants then walked over to the Kellies' house, and shot and killed the Kellie family. Simants turned himself in the next day and confessed to the murders. There was controversy whether or not Simants had sufficient mental capability to make a confession.

The crime attracted widespread news coverage. The county attorney and Simants' attorney requested the County Court to, "... enter a restrictive order relating to 'matters that may or may not be publicly reported or disclosed to

(continues)

CASE STUDY **Nebraska Press Association v. Judge Stuart, et al**
(continued)

the public', because of the 'mass coverage by news media' and the 'reasonable likelihood of prejudicial news that would make it difficult, if not impossible, in the impaneling of an impartial jury and tend to prevent a fair trial'. The County Court heard oral arguments but took no evidence; no attorney for members of the press appeared at this stage. The County Court granted the prosecutor's motion for a restrictive order."

The District Judge modified the County Court's order and entered its own restrictive order. "The judge found 'because of the nature of the crimes charged in the complaint that there is a clear and present danger that pre-trial publicity could impinge upon the defendant's right to a fair trial'."

The Nebraska Supreme Court modified the District Court's order to accommodate the defendant's right to a fair trial and the media's interest in reporting pretrial events. "The order as modified prohibited reporting of only three matters: (a) the existence and nature of any confessions or admissions made by the defendant to law enforcement officers, (b) any confessions or admissions made to any third parties, except members of the press, and (c) other facts 'strongly implicative' of the accused."

Issue: Does this restrictive order violate constitutional rights?

Decision: Yes.

Reason: Chief Justice Burger wrote the opinion of the Court: "... prior restraints on speech and publication are the most serious and the least tolerable infringement on First Amendment rights." The Court stated in the *Sheppard* case that there were other alternatives to prior restraints: (1) a change of venue to a locale less exposed to intense publicity; (2) postponement of the trial to allow public attention to subside; (3) the screening of jurors to eliminate those with set opinions as to guilt or innocence; (4) clear instructions to jurors on their sworn duty to decide the case only on the evidence presented in court; and (5) possible sequestration of jurors. A gag order is a last resort after all other alternatives are considered.

The Court held that before prior restraints can be directed against the media:

- There must be intense and pervasive publicity.
- No other alternative measures can be used to mitigate the effects of pretrial publicity.
- The gag order will actually prevent the prejudicial material from reaching the jurors.

The Court stated that it was not clear that the imposition of a prior restraint would have protected Simants's right to a fair trial.

Many states, joint commissions of bar associations, and the media have issued *voluntary* guidelines for *ethical* behavior of the press and legal professions as to potential prejudicial pretrial publicity. The emphasis in these guidelines is the attempt to balance the rights of the press and the rights of the accused. The principles include:

- The public is entitled to information, as long as that information does not interfere with a fair trial.

- The responsibility for assuring a fair trial is for the most part on the judge, as he has the power to use all means to see justice is done. (Sound like *Sheppard*?) The media is also responsible to see that their information is accurate and objective.

- The editor of the publication should keep in mind that an accused is innocent until proven guilty; readers, listeners, and viewers are potentially in the jury pool of the case and should do no unnecessary harm to a person's reputation.

- Attorneys should not exploit their access to information, and the prosecution should make available information to which the public is entitled.

- All parties to a case should ensure a free flow of information, but not to the extent that it may jeopardize a fair trial.

Remember, these are only ethical guidelines, not legal imperatives.

CLOSED THEN OPEN COURTROOMS

In *Gannett Co. v. DePasquale*, 443 U.S. 368 (1979), Wayne Clapp had disappeared on a fishing trip. The two male companions that accompanied him on this trip were the last people that saw him alive. The boat Clapp was fishing in with his two friends was found with multiple bullet holes in it. It was clear that foul play was involved. An intensive search was launched to look for his body and for his two male companions that had disappeared after the trip.

Gannett Company, Inc. published two newspapers. Each paper carried stories about Clapp's disappearance, giving the few details known about the case, and mentioning the names of the suspects in the crime—the missing friends, and the name of one of the suspects' wives. As more facts came in regarding the crime, the newspapers published information as they received it.

The two male suspects in the case were finally apprehended and charged with murder, robbery, and grand larceny, and one of the suspects' wives was charged with grand larceny. The defendants and their attorneys asked the court to exclude the public from the pre-trial hearing dealing with the admissibility of evidence. The defense attorneys argued that "… the unabated buildup of adverse publicity had jeopardized the ability of the defendants to receive a fair trial." The District Attorney did not oppose the motion, nor did a reporter for Gannett, who was present in the courtroom at the time of the closure motion.

The next day, the reporter wrote a letter to the trial judge, asserting a "right to cover this hearing," and requested, "we ... be given access to the transcript." The judge responded the same day, stating that the suppression hearing was concluded and that any decision as to the immediate release of the transcript had been reserved. Gannett moved the court to set aside its motion. The issue in this case is, do the press and public have a constitutional right, under the Sixth Amendment, to attend these pretrial proceedings?

The Court held, "The Constitution nowhere mentions any right of access to a criminal trial on the part of the public; its guarantee, like the others enumerated, is personal to the accused." Members of the public have no right to attend criminal trials under the Sixth and Fourteenth Amendments. There is no history to demonstrate the Framers of the Sixth Amendment intended to create a constitutional right to strangers to attend a pre-trial proceeding. Judges, the Court noted, have an affirmative duty to mitigate the effects of prejudicial pretrial publicity. Closure of pretrial proceedings is an effective way to accomplish this. Also, because the suppression of the transcript in question was only temporary, the First Amendment was not violated.

In reaction to the *Gannett* decision, many pretrial courtrooms began to be closed to the public. It appears that the *Gannett* decision was what the judiciary was waiting for.

In 1980, there was a case that clarified and distinguished the *Gannett* decision— *Richmond Newspapers, Inc. v. Virginia.*

CASE STUDY   **Richmond Newspapers, Inc. v. Virginia**

448 U.S. 555 (1980)

Facts: On the beginning of a fourth trial on a murder charge (the defendant's conviction after the first trial was reversed on appeal based on a technicality, and two subsequent retrials resulted in mistrials), the Virginia trial court granted the defense counsel's motion to close the fourth trial to the public. There was no objection to this by the prosecutor or the two reporters from the newspaper that were in attendance during the motion hearing. The defense counsel stated that he did not "... want any information being shuffled back and forth when we have a recess as to ... who testified to what." Later the same day, the newspaper and reporters challenged the judge's action, contending that constitutional considerations mandated that before closure of the courtroom, the court should look to see if alternative means could be used to protect the defendant's right to a fair trial. The trial judge denied that motion, stating he was inclined to order closure—the press and public were excluded.

(continues)

CASE STUDY   **Richmond Newspapers, Inc. v. Virginia** *(continued)*

Issue: Does the closure of the court to the press and public violate the First or Sixth Amendments?

Decision: Yes. The Supreme Court held that the right to attend criminal trials was "implicit in the guarantees of the First Amendment."

Reason: Chief Justice Burger gave the decision of the Court. The Court began consideration of the case by noting this precise issue had never been presented to the Court for decision. Gannett, supra, dealt with pretrial motions, not trials themselves. The Court held that the First Amendment calls for the right to receive information and ideas. In the context of trials, guarantees of speech and press standing alone prohibit government from summarily closing courtroom doors that had been open to the public at the time the First Amendment was adopted.

"Moreover, the right of assembly is also relevant, having been regarded not only as an independent right but also as a catalyst to augment the free exercise of the other First Amendment rights with which it was deliberately linked by the draftsmen. A trial courtroom is a public place where the people generally—and representatives of the media—have a right to be present, and where their presence historically has been thought to enhance the integrity and quality of what takes place. Even though the Constitution contains no provision which by its terms guarantees to the public the right to attend criminal trials, various fundamental rights, not expressly guaranteed, have been recognized as indispensable to the enjoyment of enumerated rights. The right to attend criminal trials is implicit in the guarantees of the First Amendment."

The result of the *Richmond* case was to limit the discretion of the judge to close trials to the public. The Court did not totally ban the closure of trials; trials could be closed under extraordinary circumstances. Chief Justice Burger did not set forth any guidelines for closures, but, the Court held in *Richmond*, "... the trial judge made no findings to support closure: no inquiry was made as to whether alternative solutions would have met the need to ensure fairness." One thing that the *Richmond* decision did do was to curtail the trend for judges to decide for automatic closure.

In 1984, the U.S. Supreme Court took the *Richmond* ruling one step further, and applied it to jury selection. In *Press-Enterprise Co. v. Superior Court of California*, 464 U.S. 501, Albert Brown Jr. was tried and convicted of the rape and murder of a teenage girl, and sentenced to death. Before the **voir dire** examination of prospective jurors, Press-Enterprise Co., moved to have the voir dire be open to the press and public. Press-Enterprise contended the public had an absolute right to attend the trial, asserting that the trial commenced with voir dire. The state opposed

■ **VOIR DIRE**

The questioning of prospective jurors by a judge and attorneys in court. It is used to determine if any juror cannot deal with the trial issues fairly.

this motion on the grounds that if the press were present, juror responses would lack the candor needed to ensure a fair trial. Does the public have a constitutional right to attend jury selection? The Court said yes.

The Court held that in the beginning of the sixteenth century jurors were selected in public, "This open process gave assurance to those not attending trials that others were able to observe the proceedings and enhanced public confidence." The Court held the presumption of openness may only be overcome "… by an overriding interest based on findings that closure is essential to preserve higher values and is narrowly tailored to serve that interest."

The Supreme Court, in a second *Press-Enterprise Co. v. Superior Court*, 478 U.S. 1 (1986) case, applied the same analysis it did in the first *Press-Enterprise* case. This time the Court dealt with public access to **preliminary hearings**.

In this case, California filed a complaint against a nurse, charging him with murdering 12 patients by administering massive doses of the drug lidocaine. The magistrate granted the defendant's motion to exclude the public from the preliminary hearing under a California statute that states that such proceedings are to be open unless "… exclusion of the public is necessary in order to protect the defendant's right to a fair and impartial trial." The Press-Enterprise sought to have the transcript of these proceedings released. Although the transcripts were finally released to the public, the issue of the case was whether these proceedings—preliminary hearings—should, as a matter of constitutional guarantees, be open to the public.

The Court held "… public access to such preliminary hearings is essential to the proper functioning of the criminal justice system. This proper functioning is not made any less essential by the fact that a preliminary hearing cannot result in a conviction and the adjudication is before a magistrate without a jury. The absence of a jury makes the importance of public access even more significant."

It was further held that a qualified First Amendment right of access attaches to preliminary hearings. The proceedings cannot be closed unless specific, on the record findings are made that show "… closure is essential to preserve higher values and is narrowly tailored to serve that interest." (This is the same language as that used in the first *Press-Enterprise* case.)

The Court has not yet extended the constitutional right of the public to attend civil trials; nonetheless, lower courts following the *Richmond* case have had little difficulty in granting public access to such trials.

CAMERAS IN THE COURTROOM

As has been discussed, courts have ruled that allowing the public into various stages of a trial is, for the most part, a constitutionally protected right. However, courts refuse to extend First Amendment rights to the bringing of cameras into a trial. Cameras are not allowed in Federal District Court criminal or civil trials. Yet, in November 2005 the House of Representatives voted to give Federal Courts of

> ■ **PRELIMINARY HEARING**
>
> A hearing to determine if there is sufficient evidence to charge and try a person for a felony (a serious crime punishable by a term in the state prison).

Appeal judges the power to decide to allow, or not to allow, the televising of court hearings. So far only the San Francisco–based 9th Circuit permits print and television cameras during hearings.

The U.S. Supreme Court is adamant about barring cameras. Case in point: the requests by the media to televise the arguments of the *Bush v. Gore* (cert. granted 00-949) case. (This was the case to decide if Florida should continue to recount ballots in the 2000 presidential election.)

In July 2006, the new Chief Justice Roberts stated, at a meeting of federal judges and attorneys, that the Supreme Court is not interested in televising its hearings. He emphasized, "All of the justices view themselves as trustees of an extremely valuable institution … we're going to be very careful before we do anything that will have an adverse impact on that." The Supreme Court does release audiotapes of its hearings.

All 50 state courts allow some photo or television coverage of some court proceedings, yet only 41 states allow any coverage of criminal trials. Some states require the consent of the defendant or the trial participants before cameras are allowed into the courtroom, whereas others allow the trial judge to decide if the admission of cameras is appropriate. Still others only allow coverage in appellate proceedings. Many states limit the coverage of sexual-abuse cases or coverage of trials in which minors are involved.

The consensus by the courts is that television and photo coverage distracts the participants in the trial and potentially diminishes the dignity and solemnity of a courtroom. Of course, broadcasters argue that cameras in the courtroom are not disruptive, and the courts and public benefit with the televising of court proceedings.

In 1965, the U.S. Supreme Court held in *Estes v. Texas*, 381 U.S. 532 that live television coverage was distracting to the trial participants, and likely to impair the testimony of witnesses. (Television equipment in the mid-1960s was extremely bulky and intrusive.)

The facts of the case: Billie Sol Estes, a Texas grain dealer, had swindled several investors. The case garnered national media attention. The original jury panel, Mr. Estes, counsel, and the trial judge were all subject to wide coverage by the media; the publicity was not favorable to the trial. Four of the jurors selected had seen or heard all or part of the media broadcasts concerning the upcoming trial. Under Texas court rules, televising two days of preliminary hearings was allowed.

Before the trial, the defendant had moved to exclude photography and broadcasting of the proceedings. The trial court denied his motion but granted a continuance for a month, and a booth was erected in the back of the courtroom for the media and their cameras.

After Estes was convicted, he appealed, arguing that he had been denied a fair trial as a result of the television coverage. The U.S. Supreme Court agreed. The Court held that the televising of the trial over Estes' objections violated his due process rights for a fair trial under the Fourteenth Amendment.

The Court held, "There are numerous respects in which televising court proceedings may alone, and in combination almost certainly will, cause unfairness, such as: (1) improperly influencing jurors by emphasizing the notoriety of the trial and affecting their impartial judgment, distracting their attention, facilitating (in States which do not sequester jurors) their viewing of selected parts of the proceedings, and improperly influencing potential jurors and thus jeopardizing the fairness of new trials; (2) impairing the testimony of witnesses, as by causing some to be frightened and others to overstate their testimony, and generally influencing the testimony of witnesses, thus frustrating invocation of the 'rule' against witnesses; (3) distracting judges generally and exercising an adverse psychological effect particularly upon those who are elected; and (4) imposing pressures upon the defendant and intruding into the confidential attorney-client relationship." The desire of the media to televise a trial must give way to the rights of the criminal defendant. The Court did add that if and when technology made cameras less obtrusive, perhaps they could be allowed into certain trial proceedings.

In 1981, the Supreme Court again looked at the issue of cameras in the courtroom in *Chandler v. Florida*.

CASE STUDY **Chandler v. Florida**

449 U.S. 560 (1981)

Facts:	Two Miami police officers were charged with burglarizing a restaurant. Their trial attracted a considerable amount of media attention. The officers objected to the televising of part of the trial, stating this denied them of their constitutional rights. They were found guilty of the charges.
	Under Florida rule, Canon 3A(7) of the Florida Code of Judicial Conduct, the media is allowed to televise and photograph judicial proceedings, subject to the control of the presiding judge, and subject to the guidelines placed on judges to protect the fundamental right of a fair trial for the accused.
Issue:	Does the Florida rule that allows radio, television, and still photographs of the trial violate the accused's right of a fair trial under the Sixth and Fourteenth Amendments?
Decision:	No. The Supreme Court found no violation of the Constitution under Florida's law.
Reason:	Chief Justice Burger delivered the opinion of the Court and held, "*Estes v. Texas* did not announce a constitutional rule that all photographic, radio, and television coverage of criminal trials is inherently a denial of due process. It does not stand as an absolute ban on state experimentation with an evolving technology, which, in terms of modes of mass communication, was in its relative infancy in 1964 when Estes was decided, and is, even now, in a state of continuing change."

(continues)

CASE STUDY Chandler v. Florida *(continued)*

The Supreme Court gave the background of how the Florida rule came into being and why it did not violate the Constitution. In 1937, the American Bar Association's House of Delegates adopted Judicial Canon 35 declaring all photographic and broadcast [at that time radio] coverage of courtroom proceedings should be prohibited. In 1952, the House of Delegates amended Canon 35 to proscribe television coverage as well. This was reaffirmed in 1972 when the Code of Judicial Conduct replaced the Canons of Judicial Ethics The Canon's proscription was reaffirmed in 1972 when the Code of Judicial Conduct replaced the Canons of Judicial Ethics and Canon 3A (7) superseded Canon 35. A majority of states including Florida adopted the ABA provision—Canon 3A (7) as its own law.

In 1978, the ABA Committee on Fair Trial-Free Press proposed revised standards, allowing courtroom coverage by the electronic media under local rule and under the control of the trial judge. Coverage would only be allowed if the coverage was unobtrusive and did not affect the trial. The ABA's Standing Committee on Standards for Criminal Justice endorsed this revision as did the Committee on Criminal Justice and the Media, but the House of Delegates rejected it in 1979.

In 1978, the Conference of State Chief Justices approved a resolution to allow the highest court in each state to put forth standards and guidelines regulating radio, television, and other photographic coverage of judicial proceedings.

From July 1977 to July 1978, Florida established a pilot program in which the electronic media were permitted to cover all judicial proceedings, without reference to the consent of the participants, but subject to detailed standards of conduct. Florida concluded after this pilot program, "... that on balance there [was] more to be gained than lost by permitting electronic media coverage of judicial proceedings subject to standards for such coverage. ... The Florida court was of the view that because of the significant effect of the courts on the day-to-day lives of the citizenry, it was essential that the people have confidence in the process. It felt that broadcast coverage of trials would contribute to wider public acceptance and understanding of decisions."

The U.S. Supreme Court found Florida's policy was implemented with strict guidelines. The Florida rule was intended to protect the accused's right to a fair trial. The Florida rule promulgated, "Subject at all times to the authority of the presiding judge to (i) control the conduct of proceedings before the court, (ii) ensure decorum and prevent distractions, and (iii) ensure the fair administration of justice in the pending cause, electronic media and still photography coverage of public judicial proceedings in the appellate and trial courts of this state shall be allowed in accordance with standards of conduct and technology promulgated by the Supreme Court of Florida."

RECENT CASES OF FREEDOM OF THE PRESS VERSUS FAIR TRIAL

In the wake of worldwide, 24/7 news coverage, and fierce competition for audiences, the media has been anxious to gain camera access to courtroom proceedings. Of special interest to the media are high-profile celebrity cases such as those of Scott Peterson, O. J. Simpson, Kobe Bryant, and Michael Jackson.

The 1995 trial of O. J. Simpson for the murders of his ex-wife Nicole Brown Simpson and Ronald Goldman was the stuff of any good mystery movie. It enthralled the American public for months. The topic of conversation around water coolers, during the proceedings, inevitably turned to, "Do you think he did it?" The televised courtroom testimony lasted for 133 days. Millions of people around the world watched as Mr. Simpson tried on the infamous too-tight glove, viewed the colorful testimony of Kato Kaelin, and observed O. J.'s famous "dream team" of attorneys in action. On October 3, 1995, when the jury's verdict of "Not Guilty" was handed down, the largest number of television viewers ever watched intently.

The live television coverage of the Simpson trial forced Judge Lance Ito to change regular courtroom proceedings. Testimony that television viewers saw jurors were not allowed to hear, for fear that the evidence would be too inflammatory. Judge Ito had the jury sequestered, but he allowed conjugal visits. The problem with televising the Simpson trial was that the media coverage was so intense that judges throughout the country questioned the wisdom of admitting the media into the courtroom.

In the Scott Peterson trial, a case that convicted Peterson of killing his wife Laci and the couple's unborn son in December 2002, the judge barred cameras from the courtroom. Both the prosecution and defense argued against the use of cameras. Judge Delucchi agreed. His concerns included the privacy of the trial participants, the affect on jury selection, and the media interfering with the ability to maintain order and fairness in such a publicized trial.

Attorneys for print and broadcast media argued it was in the public's best interest for cameras to be allowed in the courtroom. Defense attorney Mark Geragos disagreed, saying that the introduction of cameras would make the trial "a bigger zoo than it already is."

Other trials in which cameras were not allowed were the Michael Jackson child molestation trial; the Susan Smith trial (the woman who confessed to drowning her two sons in a lake); and the retrial of the Menendez brothers, who had been convicted of the shotgun slayings of their parents.

In the Kobe Bryant rape case, Judge Ruckriegle restricted how the news media could cover the trial, fearing that too much exposure could threaten the fairness of the court proceeding. There were no cameras allowed during witness testimony or jury selection. There were no photos allowed of jurors, or audio coverage, or closeup photographs of conferences at the bench, or of attorney-client discussions, or discussions between the attorneys in the case.

Judge Ruckriegle was concerned about witness intimidation, and physical threats made against the alleged victim, prosecutors, and others involved in the trial. If the witnesses were in a state of anxiety, the judge felt that it would reduce the court's ability to maintain a fair trial. He did allow still photography during opening statements and closing arguments, as well as video and audio coverage during closing arguments. Attorneys for various news organizations asked the entire trial to be open to cameras, yet defense and prosecution agreed with the restrictions placed on the media by the judge.

This balancing act between the rights of those on trial and the rights of the media to report on these newsworthy events will continue as long as the United States is a country that values constitutional rights. Yet cameras in the courtroom are not the only issues involved in the conflict between the courts, the law, and the media. The next chapters will discuss how the law and the courts may impinge on the media and its attempt to gather the news.

SUMMARY

For years, the courts have been struggling with the balance of the public's right to know what transpires in a court case, the rights of the media to cover judicial proceedings, and the rights of the accused on trial.

Lower courts have disagreed regarding what access the media should have to court information. The U.S. Supreme Court never defined what standard a lower court should use to lessen prejudicial media coverage of a trial. Before the imposition of a gag order, the Supreme Court would rather see the imposition of a means of assuring a fair trial, such as those listed in the *Sheppard* case.

The closure of courtrooms during various stages of a trial is left to the discretion of the judge. The Supreme Court has not given specific guidelines as to when a judicial proceeding should be open or closed, but there must be a balance of rights between free press and a fair trial.

The consensus by the courts is that television and photo coverage in court proceedings distracts the trial participants and possibly creates an unfair trial. The U.S. Supreme Court has upheld state rules allowing cameras in the courtroom as long as they are implemented with strict guidelines, so the accused's right to a fair trial is guaranteed.

▊ DISCUSSION QUESTIONS_____

1. How can the courts balance the public's right to know and the rights of the defendant to a fair and impartial trial?

2. Just because potentially prejudicial evidence may infiltrate the minds of jurors, is this enough to grant the defendant an entirely new trial?

3. Argue for media attendance at depositions.

4. Discuss the advantages of opening Immigration and Naturalization Service (INS) hearings to the public.

5. Discuss the pros and cons of allowing grand jury witnesses to make public comments on their testimony while the case is still under investigation.

6. Argue that gag orders are never appropriate.

7. Discuss the advantages of opening all trials to television cameras.

▊ CASE FOR REVIEW_____

Compare and contrast the Peterson, Bryant, and Simpson trials with regard to cameras in the courtroom. Discuss the pros and cons of live television coverage in the Simpson trial.

▊ KEY TERMS_____

contempt powers	Immigration and Naturalization	public trial
continue	Service (INS)	Reardon Report
depositions	impartial jury	sequestered
gag order	petit juror	venue
grand jury	preliminary hearing	voir dire

▊ ENDNOTES_____

[1] http://www.usdoj.gov

Online Companion™
For additional resources, please go to
http://www.paralegal.delmar.cengage.com

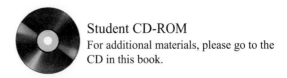

Student CD-ROM
For additional materials, please go to the
CD in this book.

Defamation—Libel and Slander: What It Is and How to Defend Against It

■ CHAPTER OUTLINE

■ OBJECTIVES_____

After completing this chapter, you will be able to:

- Know how there is a blurring of the line between libel and slander in today's mass media environment.
- Know the difference between public officials, public figures, and a private person, and what the consequences are of their classification in regard to defamation.
- Understand what the elements of libel are, and how the media can use them to their advantage.
- Know what constitutes a SLAPP lawsuit, and how to defend against them.
- Determine when an anti-SLAPP lawsuit is appropriate, and the mechanics of such a lawsuit.
- Know the defenses available if sued for libel, and how to invoke them.
- Be aware of the potential damage judgment, against you and your media company, if you are found liable for libel.
- Know if retractions help? Know how, when, and where to do them.
- Be able to define criminal libel, and know how to defend against it.
- Know how to avoid emotional distress causes of action.

DEFAMATION: WHAT IS LIBEL? WHAT IS SLANDER?

Under the First Amendment's guarantee of freedom of expression, the media should be allowed to report on anything it deems proper. If the media were constrained from doing so, this would have a severe chilling effect on the reporting of information. However, many times the right to free speech and the right of a free press are at odds with each other when it comes to the laws of **defamation**.

Let us take two hypothetical situations. A reporter, with the consent of her editor, decides to do a story on a local political official that brings up controversial subjects, but nonetheless contains factual and true statements. This report leads to the defeat of the political leader in the next election. Is this defamation? No. Although the report caused damage to the politician, the story was only exposing the facts of what was actually happening. The second hypothetical involves the same reporter and the same politician, but this time the reporter decides to stray from the facts and knowingly and with actual malice adds some untruthful hyperbole. This story causes the politician to lose the election, impugns the politician's reputation falsely, and causes a breakup of the politician's marriage. Is this defamation? Probably yes. If the politician sues the reporter and the publication for which the reporter works, and the politician wins, the publication could face a

■ **DEFAMATION**

The publication of false statements that causes a person to suffer damages.

judgment in the millions of dollars. Although the press is in existence to report on issues that concern the public, the press cannot subject individuals to falsehoods that damage their reputations and their lives.

So what are defamation, **slander**, and **libel**? Defamation is the publication of false statements that causes a person to suffer damages. Slander is the making of defamatory statements via the spoken word. Libel is making defamatory statements in printed form, or via the spoken word if it is disseminated to a large audience, such as through television broadcasts. That is why when a television station is sued for defamation it will be under the **tort** of libel, even though the communication is via the spoken word. The rationale behind this is that if the audience of the spoken word is large, there is much more likelihood of greater damage to one's reputation. Thus, for all intents and purposes, because we now live in the electronic age, almost all defamation suits are suits for libel.

The history of libel and slander cases in the United States dates back to a case discussed in a former chapter—*New York v. John Peter Zenger.* In that case, John Peter Zenger was imprisoned (under criminal libel) for printing political attacks against the then colonial governor of New York, but his attorney convinced the jury that truth is a complete defense to libel. Zenger also established that libel cases are mainly civil proceedings, not criminal; juries should hear such cases; and the jury should decide how much compensation should be given to the person libeled. (There are very few criminal libel cases today—most are tort actions—although they do still exist. There will be a discussion of criminal libel at the end of this chapter.)

In *Chaplinsky v. State of New Hampshire*, 315 U.S. 568 (1941), the Supreme Court put libel and fighting words into the same genre—both categories of expression received no constitutional protections.

> "There are certain well-defined and narrowly limited classes of speech, the prevention and punishment of which has never been thought to raise any Constitutional problem. These include the lewd and obscene, the profane, the *libelous*, and the insulting or 'fighting words'—those which by their very utterance inflict injury or tend to incite an immediate breach of the peace."

Until the mid-1960s, it appeared the law-favored defamation plaintiffs. Under the common law, a defamation defendant could be liable even if expressing an opinion about the plaintiff. The U.S. Supreme Court left libel law to the states, and many state laws shifted the burden of proof, as to the truth of the statement, to the defendant, since the law presumed the statement to be false. The media was left with defamation being **strict liability**—the defendant was held liable regardless of fault. Thus the prospect of being the defendant in a defamation action could definitely put a chill on media reporting.

SLANDER

The making of defamatory statements via the spoken word.

LIBEL

The making of defamatory statements in printed form, or via the spoken word if it is disseminated to a large audience.

TORT

The breach of a legal duty that proximately causes injury or harm to another. This is a civil wrong, not a criminal, or a contractual wrong.

STRICT LIABILITY

The imposition of liability regardless of fault.

Public Officials, Public Figures, and Actual Malice

In 1964, the United States Supreme Court decided to hear a defamation case—*New York Times Co. v. Sullivan.* It would be a case that would revolutionize the law of libel in the United States. Finally, there would be a national libel law in place, a law that did take into consideration the guarantees of the First Amendment. In this case, the Court held that **public officials** could *not* be successful in their tort libel suits unless they proved a reporter or editor was shown to publish the false statement with *actual malice.* Gone were the days of defamation and strict liability.

This case was critical at the time it was heard. During the 1960s, state libel suits were so onerous, they threatened to extinguish media coverage of the civil rights movement. The *New York Times v. Sullivan* case, by eliminating strict liability of the media in defamation suits, allowed the media to report on one of the most important issues of the 20th century.

The Chief Justice of the Supreme Court at the time, Earl Warren, considered the promotion of racial equality to be one of his greatest contributions in his Supreme Court career. (Chief Justice Warren wrote for a unanimous court in banning segregation in the nation's schools in the landmark ruling in *Brown v. Board of Education*, 347 U.S. 483 [1954].) With the decision in the *Sullivan* case, in a backdoor fashion, he and the Court brethren furthered that cause by removing the strait jacket from the media on reporting civil rights issues.

■ **PUBLIC OFFICIALS**

A public official is a person in public office.

CASE STUDY **New York Times Co. v. Sullivan**

376 U.S. 254 (1964)

Facts: This case revolves around a full-page ad placed in the *New York Times.* The ad detailed abuses endured by black students at the hands of the police, especially abuses in Montgomery, Alabama. Some of the ad was correct, but two paragraphs contained factual errors. Although the ad did not mention anyone specifically by name, L. B. Sullivan, the Montgomery city commissioner, who was in charge of the police, contended the ad tarnished his reputation. The third and sixth paragraphs were the basis of Mr. Sullivan's libel suit.

The third paragraph read as follows: "In Montgomery, Alabama, after students sang 'My Country, 'Tis of Thee' on the State Capitol steps, their leaders were expelled from school, and truckloads of police armed with shotguns and tear-gas ringed the Alabama State College Campus. When the entire student body protested to state authorities by refusing to re-register, their dining hall was padlocked in an attempt to starve them into submission."

(continues)

CASE STUDY **New York Times Co. v. Sullivan** *(continued)*

The sixth paragraph stated: "Again and again the Southern violators have answered Dr. King's peaceful protests with intimidation and violence. They have bombed his home almost killing his wife and child. They have assaulted his person. They have arrested him seven times—for 'speeding', 'loitering' and similar 'offenses'. And now they have charged him with 'perjury'—a felony under which they could imprison him for ten years . . ."

What actually happened was that nine students were expelled from school for demanding service at a lunch counter in the Montgomery County Courthouse, not for singing "My County 'Tis of Thee" on the Capitol steps. The police never padlocked the dining hall entrance, nor did they "ring" the college campus. Also, Dr. King was only arrested four times, not seven.

Mr. Sullivan sued the *New York Times* and four black clergymen who were listed as officers of the Committee to Defend Martin Luther King Jr. and endorsers of the ad. Mr. Sullivan demanded a retraction from the *Times;* the paper refused issue one.

Under Alabama law, the trial judge instructed the jury that these statements against Sullivan were "libelous per se," thus not privileged. The judge instructed the jury that falsity of the statements and malice in the publication were presumed. Under the state law, Sullivan did not have to prove he had been harmed, only that the statements published were "of and concerning" Sullivan. The jury awarded Sullivan $500,000. The Alabama appellate court affirmed. The *Times* appealed to the U.S. Supreme Court.

Issue: Is the Alabama law constitutionally deficient for failure to provide the safeguards for freedom of speech and freedom of the press required by the First and Fourteenth Amendments?

Decision: Yes, the Alabama law is constitutionally deficient.

Reason: Justice Brennan delivered the opinion of the Court. "The constitutional guarantees require, we think, a federal rule that prohibits a public official from recovering damages for a defamatory falsehood relating to his official conduct unless he proves that the statement was made with 'actual malice'— that is, with knowledge that it was false or with reckless disregard of whether it was false or not."

The Court held that even though the *Times* published the advertisement without checking its accuracy against news stories in the *Times'* own files, still the mere possession of the files does not establish that the *Times* "knew" the ad was false. To prove the state of mind for actual malice, the *knowledge of the falsity* would have to be brought to the attention of those in the *Times* that had the responsibility of publishing the ad.

After *Times v. Sullivan*, the Court began to define how to apply that decision. In the 1966 *Rosenblatt v. Baer*, 383 U.S. 75 case, the Supreme Court looked to the essence of defamation—the right to protect one's good name and reputation. The facts of the case were Rosenblatt, a newspaper columnist, had accused the former supervisor of a county recreation area of financial mismanagement of public funds. Rosenblatt asked the questions in his column, "What happened to all the money last year? And every other year?" There was no direct mention of the supervisor's name. Yet the supervisor sued; he offered extrinsic proof the column imputed mismanagement during his tenure. At the trial court level, the jury was permitted to find that *negligent* misstatement of fact would defeat Rosenblatt's privilege of free expression. The jury awarded the supervisor damages and the State Supreme Court affirmed, finding no bar in *New York Times Co. v. Sullivan*.

The question is, then, who is a public official to which the *Times v. Sullivan* decision applies? The U.S. Supreme Court held in *Times v. Sullivan* that it did not determine "… how far down into the lower ranks of government the 'public official' designation extends," or the specific categories of persons included in this designation. Nor did the Court feel precise lines had to be drawn for the purposes of the *Rosenblatt* case. The Court held in *Rosenblatt*,

> "Criticism of government is at the very center of the constitutionally protected area of free discussion. Criticism of those responsible for government operations must be free, lest criticism of government itself be penalized. It is clear, therefore, that the 'public official' designation applies at the very least to those among the hierarchy of government employees who have, or appear to the public to have, *substantial responsibility* [emphasis added] for or control over the conduct of governmental affairs."

There are important social values that underlie the law of defamation. Society has a strong interest in preventing and giving redress to attacks on one's reputation. Yet, there is a tension between this interest and the values propounded in the First and Fourteenth Amendments. If interests in public discussion are strong, the Constitution limits the protections of defamation law. In *Rosenblatt*, the Court extended the "public official" designation to even minor public employees: even a supervisor of a county recreation area would have to show actual malice to win a libel suit.

■ **PUBLIC FIGURES**

A public figure is someone that is newsworthy and in the public eye.

Over the years, the U.S. Supreme Court has extended the term "public official" to those not in public office but who are newsworthy and in the public eye—**public figures**. A public figure today includes celebrities, well-known writers, athletes, and others that are in the public spotlight.

In 1967, the Court in two consolidated cases—*Curtis Publishing Co. v. Butts*, 388 U.S. 130, and *Associated Press v. Walker*, 389 U.S. 28, further defined the term public figure by extending the term to a former athletic director at the University of Georgia, and a former general that had been in command of the federal troops involved in the desegregation of schools in Little Rock, Arkansas, during the 1950s.

The *Curtis* case revolved around an article the *Saturday Evening Post* had run—"The Story of a College Football Fix." The story stated that Wally Butts, the athletic director at the University of Georgia, gave coach "Bear" Bryant of the University of Alabama information about the upcoming game between the two schools. The article was based on a conversation between the two coaches that was overheard. The problem with this article was the *Saturday Evening Post* did not check the accuracy of the information, despite the fact the *Post* had plenty of time to do so. The *Post* also assigned the article to a non-football-savvy journalist, and did not have a football expert check the story for accuracy.

The *Walker* case arose from the distribution of a news dispatch relating an eyewitness account of events at the University of Mississippi, on September 30, 1962. On that night, there were massive riots as a result of federal efforts to enforce the enrollment of James Meredith, a black man, as a student at the university. This dispatch said that Walker, present on campus at the time, had taken command of the crowd, and personally led them against federal marshals sent to enforce the court's decree. The dispatch also said Walker encouraged rioters to use violence. Although Walker was a private citizen at the time, he had formerly commanded federal troops during the school segregation confrontation in Little Rock, Arkansas, in 1957.

The cases went to the U.S. Supreme Court and the Court affirmed Butts's libel judgment against the *Post*, but the court unanimously overruled Walker's judgment against the Associated Press.

The Court noted, "… the public interest in the circulation of the materials here involved, and the publisher's interest in circulating them, is not less than that involved in *New York Times*. And both Butts and Walker commanded a substantial amount of independent public interest at the time of the publications; both, in our opinion, would have been labeled 'public figures' under ordinary tort rules." Thus, both Butts and Walker would have to show reckless disregard of the truth or actual malice to prevail at a libel trial. With these decisions in mind, why did Butts's libel judgment stand, yet Walker's judgment did not? The answer lies in the meaning of reckless disregard of the truth.

The difference between the two cases is that the *Saturday Evening Post* article was published without any specific time limit, in fact, the *Post* had plenty of time to investigate if the article was true or not. By contrast, the Associated Press article was written and dispatched under tremendous time pressure. There was almost no time to examine the eyewitness's statements for their veracity. The AP had to get the story out, and they were relying on the fact the journalist involved had an excellent reputation for accurate reporting. Thus, the *Post* was publishing with reckless disregard for the truth, whereas the AP was not.

This trend by the U.S. Supreme Court, to be tough on libel plaintiffs (especially public official and public figure plaintiffs), and more forgiving of the media continued through many other cases. In *Rosenbloom v. Metromedia*, 403 U.S. 29 (1971), it appeared the Court would actually do away with the threat of libel suits against the media. The plurality opinion—three justices deciding the case—stated if an issue were of *public interest* even if a private citizen was involved, the plaintiff would have to show actual malice to recover under libel.

The facts of this case were that a Metromedia radio station broadcast news stories of Rosenbloom's arrest for possession of obscene literature, and the police seizure of supposedly obscene books and stories from his business. Rosenbloom, a magazine dealer, was never convicted of the charges, and the lower court granted an injunction ordering the police not to harass him. The radio station stories did not mention Rosenbloom's name, but did use the terms "smut literature racket" and "girlie-book peddlers." Rosenbloom sued Metromedia. The jury returned a verdict for Rosenbloom, and awarded $25,000 in general damages, and $725,000 in punitive damages. The judge reduced the punitive damages award to $250,000.

The Court of Appeals reversed the lower court's judgments, emphasizing the fact the broadcasts concerned matters of public interest, and involved "hot news" prepared under deadline pressure. The Court of Appeals concluded that the fact that Rosenbloom was not a public figure could not be of decisive importance if we are to recognize the important guarantees of the First Amendment's right of free expression. Rosenbloom alleged he was not a public figure and thus he did *not* have to prove actual malice in a libel suit.

The U.S. Supreme Court agreed with the appellate court. The Court stated,

> "Although the limitations upon civil libel actions, first held in *New York Times* to be required by the First Amendment, were applied in that case in the context of defamatory falsehoods about the official conduct of a public official, later decisions have disclosed the artificiality, in terms of the public's interest, of a simple distinction between 'public' and 'private' individuals or institutions."

If a matter is of public or general interest, the matter does not lose the status of public interest merely because a private individual is involved. The public's primary interest is in the event itself, and the conduct of the participant in the event. It does not matter as to, "the participant's prior anonymity or notoriety."

The *Rosenbloom* decision did not stay the law of the land for long. In 1974, the U.S. Supreme Court further clarified the parameters of when actual malice would be required for proof of libel in *Gertz v. Robert Welch, Inc.*, 418 U.S. 323.

Elmer Gertz, an attorney, was hired to sue police officer Richard Nuccio. The police officer was tried and convicted of the crime of murder in the second degree. Robert Welch, Inc. published a magazine called *American Opinion*, a monthly venue for the views of the John Birch Society. In the early 1960s, the magazine began to warn of a national conspiracy to discredit local law enforcement agencies and create a national police force that would support a communist dictatorship. (It was during the early 1960s that some of the U.S. populace coined the name "pig" for those in law enforcement. It also was a time of unrest by a growing counterculture, as well as the beginnings of the "Cold War.") The John Birch Society and *American Opinion* commissioned an article on the murder trial of Officer Nuccio. In March 1969,

Robert Welch, Inc. published an article called "Frame-up: Richard Nuccio and the War on Police." The article proposed that the testimony against Officer Nuccio, at his homicide trial, was false, and that his prosecution was merely a plot of the communist campaign against the police. The article labeled Gertz a "Leninist" and a "communist-fronter" because he chose to represent clients who would sue a law enforcement officer. The article also stated that Gertz had been an officer of the National Lawyers Guild, described as a Communist organization that, "… probably did more than any other outfit to plan the Communist attack on the Chicago police during the 1968 Democratic Convention." (The 1968 Democratic Convention had significant demonstrations against authority, whether it was the government or the police. There were especially vocal and physical demonstrations against the escalating war in Vietnam.)

It was implied in the article that Gertz had a criminal record; this was false. True, he had been a member and officer of the National Lawyers Guild 15 years earlier, but there was no evidence this Guild had anything to do with the demonstrations at the 1968 Democratic Convention. Nor was there any basis he was a Leninist or communist-fronter.

The managing editor of *American Opinion* made no effort to substantiate or verify the charges against Gertz. In fact, he inserted a picture of Gertz with the caption "Elmer Gertz of Red Guild harasses Nuccio" into the article. Gertz lost his libel suit in the lower court because the court found the magazine had not violated the actual malice test for libel.

The issue that went before the U.S. Supreme Court was whether the publisher of defamatory falsehoods, about an individual who is neither a public official nor a public figure, may assert a constitutional privilege against liability for those statements.

The Court, in reversing the lower court's decision, held that Gertz's rights were violated. "The First Amendment requires that we protect some falsehood in order to protect speech that matters. The need to avoid self-censorship by the news media is, however, not the only societal value at issue. If it were, this Court would have embraced long ago the view that publishers and broadcasters enjoy an unconditional and indefeasible immunity from liability for defamation."

Justice Powell, writing for the Court, argued the application of the need to show actual malice for Mr. Gertz to prevail was not appropriate in this case, since he was not a public official, nor a public figure. The Court held, "The first remedy of any victim of defamation is self-help—using available opportunities to contradict the lie or correct the error and thereby to minimize its adverse impact on reputation. Public officials and public figures usually enjoy significantly greater access to the channels of effective communication and hence have a more realistic opportunity to counteract false statements than private individuals normally enjoy. Private individuals are therefore more vulnerable to injury, and the state interest in protecting them is correspondingly greater." The Court also stated,

"… the States should retain substantial latitude in their efforts to enforce a legal remedy for defamatory falsehood injurious to the reputation of a private individual. The extension of the *New York Times* test proposed by the *Rosenbloom* plurality would abridge this legitimate state interest to a degree that we find unacceptable. And it would occasion the additional difficulty of forcing state and federal judges to decide on an ad hoc basis which publications address issues of 'general or public interest' and which do not."

Ordinary citizens should be afforded more protections from libelous statements than individuals in the public eye. The Court holding the states may decide "… the appropriate standard of liability for a publisher or broadcaster of defamatory falsehood injurious to a private individual."

Since *Gertz*, most states have adopted defamation laws that only require some degree of **negligence** on the part of the media for a private person to prevail in a libel suit. However, there are a few states that have decided to require both public and private individuals to prove actual malice if the case involves issues of public concern, or is of general interest to media readers, listeners, or viewers.

The *Gertz* ruling also affected damages awarded in a libel suit. The Court held that most private, libel plaintiffs would have to prove some *actual damages* before they could recover, and because there would be no showing of actual malice there would be no automatic presumption of actual or punitive damages.

From these cases, it is clear the most important legal consideration in a libel suit is the status of the plaintiff. If the plaintiff is a public official, public figure, or even a public figure in a limited way as in *Rosenbloom*—when a private individual became a public figure based on the story involved, then the plaintiff must show actual malice on the part of the media. Yet, if the person is merely a private individual, in most states the plaintiff will merely have to prove the media acted negligently, although the plaintiff will have to show some actual damages to prevail in the case. If a private individual wants punitive damages, she will have the more difficult burden of proving the media acted with actual malice.

Since *Gertz*, there have been many lower court cases attempting to determine who is a public and private individual. For the most part, decisions have created a general rule: if individuals are in the news, but they have not purposely put themselves in a newsworthy situation, they are merely private individuals. Yet, there are state courts that have handed down decisions that have put newsworthy individuals in the classification of public figures.

In a 1985 case, *Dun & Bradstreet v. Greenmoss Builders*, 472 U.S. 749, the U.S. Supreme Court looked to the award of damages in cases involving *purely private matters*. The Court held that states could decide if a libel plaintiff could recover

■ **NEGLIGENCE**

Negligence is a violation of a duty of due care—a reckless disregard for the truth. In media law, negligence may occur from sloppy journalism, not adequately checking a source based on a how a "reasonable man" would check on information in a story.

SIDEBAR

A media practitioner must be prudent to protect herself from potential libel suits. It behooves one to check on local libel cases to see how the local courts have decided the issue of who is or who is not a public or private individual.

presumed and punitive damages absent a showing of "actual malice." The Court held, "… courts for centuries have allowed juries to presume that some damage occurred from many defamatory utterances and publications."

The facts of the *Greenmoss* case are that Dun & Bradstreet, a credit-reporting agency that provides subscribers with financial and other information about businesses, sent a report to five subscribers indicating Greenmoss, a construction contractor, had filed for voluntary bankruptcy. This report was false and grossly misrepresented Greenmoss's assets and liabilities. Greenmoss discovered this information when he was discussing financing with his bank, and the bank stated they had received such report. Greenmoss immediately called Dun & Bradstreet and asked for a correction, and asked for the names of the firms that had received the false report. Dun & Bradstreet said they would look into the matter but would not reveal who received the reports.

Dun & Bradstreet determined that the report was false, and issued a corrective notice to the subscribers that had received the first report. The corrected report stated one of Greenmoss's employees had filed for bankruptcy, not the firm. Dun & Bradstreet still refused to divulge the names of the parties that had received the first report, and Greenmoss sued for defamation, seeking compensatory and punitive damages for injury to his reputation.

The Vermont trial court found that Dun & Bradstreet's error occurred when a 17-year-old high school student had inadvertently attributed the employee's bankruptcy to Greenmoss. Dun & Bradstreet said its practice is to check with the business prior to issuing a report, but it did not do so in this instance. The trial court jury ruled in favor of Greenmoss, awarding him $50,000 in compensatory (presumed) damages, and $300,000 in punitive damages. Dun & Bradstreet moved for a new trial, arguing *Gertz* ruled, "… the States may not permit recovery of presumed or punitive damages, at least when liability is not based on a showing of knowledge of falsity or reckless disregard for the truth." Dun and Bradstreet also argued that the judge's instructions in this case permitted the jury to award such damages on a lesser showing.

The Vermont Supreme Court held that Dun & Bradstreet is in the business of selling financial information to a limited number of subscribers who pay high fees for such a service. The Vermont Supreme Court concluded such firms are not the type of media worthy of First Amendment protection as contemplated by *New York Times v. Sullivan*, and thus an award of damages can be made by a lesser showing than actual malice.

The U.S. Supreme Court agreed with the Vermont Supreme Court's decision, with further discussion. The Court held that while such speech as is represented in *Greenmoss* is not totally unprotected by the First Amendment, its protections are less stringent. "In light of the reduced constitutional value of speech involving no matters of public concern, we hold that the state interest adequately supports awards of presumed and punitive damages—even absent a showing of 'actual malice'."

The Court then addressed the issue of whether the credit report was of "public concern." Whether something is

"… of public concern must be determined by [the expression's] content, form, and context … as revealed by the whole record. … These factors indicate that petitioner's credit report concerns no public issue. It was speech solely in the individual interest of the speaker and its specific business audience. … This particular interest warrants no special protection when—as in this case—the speech is wholly false and clearly damaging to the victim's business reputation. … Moreover, since the credit report was made available to only five subscribers, who, under the terms of the subscription agreement, could not disseminate it further, it cannot be said that the report involves any 'strong interest in the free flow of commercial information.' … There is simply no credible argument that this type of credit reporting requires special protection to ensure that 'debate on public issues [will] be uninhibited, robust, and wide-open'."

The Court concluded the permitting of presumed and punitive damages in defamation cases, without the showing of actual malice, does not violate the First Amendment, when the defamatory statements do not involve matters of public concern.

THE ELEMENTS OF A DEFAMATION SUIT

Up to this point, the status of the plaintiff in a libel suit has been the issue under consideration, but, even before the plaintiff can bring her case to court, she must satisfy the elements of the tort of defamation. The following list highlights these elements.

Identification

Before a potential libel plaintiff can even begin to start a suit, it must be established that the publication was concerning the plaintiff. In other words, the plaintiff must establish that she was the subject of the libel, or that someone reading or listening to the story understood it was the plaintiff being referred to. This sounds simple enough; either one is mentioned in the article, or not. It is not that easy.

If someone's name was mentioned, it would appear identification has been established. Right? Not necessarily. What if the name mentioned is John Smith? There are many John Smiths in the world. By mentioning just the name in this situation, and attaching the name to a potentially libelous statement, the journalist is potentially looking for problems. So what is the solution? If a true but potentially defamatory statement is published, the journalist must identify the subject of the story as completely as possible. Explaining that this is John Smith the attorney, living in Yourtown, U.S.A., can do this. Or, a story can explain who the person is by the use of negatives, for example, explaining the John Smith in the story is *not* the prominent physician of Los Angeles, California. Good journalism identifies the person with her full name, especially middle names or initials if possible, where she lives, and what she does for a living. To do less, exposes the journalist to liability. Not properly identifying the subject is a serious problem.

Even the *New York Times* had problems in *New York Times v. Sullivan*. In that case, even though the plaintiff in the case was not mentioned by name, the fact that the *New York Times* alleged there was police misconduct, and Sullivan oversaw the police department, allowed Sullivan to convince the court the article referred to him. The lesson from *Sullivan* is to not make vague descriptions of a subject of a story, hoping to avoid a libel suit. It can cost a publication many years of litigation and expensive legal fees.

Publication

Another element of defamation is the requirement that the statement has been disseminated to a third person. Yes, all it takes is one other person to read or hear the defamatory statement. Of course, if only one other person or even a few people heard the defamation, can the plaintiff actually prove she has suffered any damages? Usually, the publication issue is not hard to prove by the plaintiff, especially if the media are the ones disseminating the information.

Many in the media think that if they let another publication publish the information first, and then they just reiterate what was printed by the first publication, they are immune from suit. Think again. Unless the republisher can establish a defense to the suit, it is potentially liable for defamation. Thus, the original publication and the republication can be sued.

Defamatory Statement

This seems the easiest of the elements, but not so. The courts have divided defamatory statements into two categories.

Libel per se is where the words themselves would injure the person's reputation. Such statements would include:

1. The accusation of a heinous crime—murder, rape, and so on.
2. The accusation of immorality. (This original definition applied to accusing an unmarried woman of being unchaste.)
3. The accusation of a loathsome disease. (Today, this would be HIV or the like. Previously it could have included tuberculosis.)
4. The accusation of incompetence in one's professional life.
5. Any communication that would lead someone to avoid another person.

LIBEL PER SE
Libel per se is where the words themselves would injure the person's reputation.

■ **LIBEL PER QUOD**

Libel per quod is where more information is needed to determine if a statement is libelous.

■ **SPECIAL DAMAGES**

Special damages are those that are actually caused by the tort; they are out-of-pocket damages, for example, loss of wages, loss of money due on a contract, and medical bills.

■ **GENERAL DAMAGES**

General damages are subjective in determination, for example, pain and suffering, mental anguish, loss of reputation (especially in libel suits), and loss of anticipated business.

■ **PUNITIVE DAMAGES**

Punitive or exemplary damages are meant to punish or set a public example to others not to commit the tort.

■ **FAULT**

Fault is a neglect of care, an error, or a defect of judgment.

Libel per quod is where more information is needed to determine if a statement is libelous. For example, it is not usually libelous to state a politician has been seen in the company of someone regularly. Yet, that statement could become libelous if it is well known the person the politician was seen with has criminal connections, and is noted for manipulating politicians.

Damages

There are **special damages** available to a libel plaintiff if she can show she actually incurred out-of-pocket damages, and there are **general damages** available for embarrassment and loss of reputation. The plaintiff will have to prove her injury, and if she prevails, the court will decide how much money to award.

Gertz made **punitive damages** (punishing damages) available only if it can be proven the statements published were done so with actual malice, unless as in *Greenmoss*, it is a defamation matter of *purely private concern*; then a lesser standard than actual malice can be imposed by the states.

False Statements and Statements of Fact

For a plaintiff to succeed in a libel suit she must prove that whatever was said about her was false. *Truth is a complete defense to the tort of libel*. So, even if a statement hurts the plaintiff's reputation and holds her up to ridicule, if the comment is true the plaintiff will not win a libel suit. That is why in so many of the sensational tabloids, anything that is questionable usually will be labeled as some form of satire to protect the publication from a defamation suit.

To be actionable for libel, a statement must be one of fact. The reason for this is that facts can be proven to be true or false. It is much harder to show that opinions are true or false. The exception to this rule is expressions of opinions that *imply objective facts*. In this situation, the publisher of the "opinions" may be facing a libel suit, since they have taken the statements to an actionable level.

In *Milkovich v. Lorain Journal Co.*, 497 U.S. 1 (1990), the U.S. Supreme Court held that even though a mere opinion could not be the basis for a libel suit, if an opinion implies *false objective facts*, the statement may be actionable. Although the line between facts and opinions may be very narrow, it may have to go before a judge or jury to decide if the statement is constitutionally protected or not. *Milkovich* will be studied in more detail in the discussion of defenses to libel.

Fault

The last element of defamation is one of **fault**. In *New York Times v. Sullivan*, the standard of fault was *actual malice* on the part of the media.

A case that allows the media to appeal a holding of actual malice, thus giving more protection to the media, is the 1984 case of *Bose v. Consumers Union*, 466 U.S. 485. Bose, an audio receiving and speaker manufacturer, sued Consumers Union for product disparagement. The Consumers Union's article said Bose speakers caused the sound of musical instruments to wander "about the room." The engineer reporting on the speakers should have stated that the sound wandered "along the wall[s]."

The Federal District Court judge deemed the article factually wrong and written with actual malice. The Court of Appeals reversed, finding the District Court's ruling erroneous. The U.S. Supreme Court agreed to hear the case on the premise the media *needs the right to appeal the issue of actual malice* in order to protect vital First Amendment rights. The Court held that the constitutional values protected under the *New York Times* rule, as to actual malice, require judges to make sure they exercise a review to preserve constitutional liberties. If this were not done, it would deny the media the right to challenge libel judgments that may be awarded by trial judges or juries.

The Supreme Court agreed with the Court of Appeals, and ruled for Consumers Union, stating that there was not much difference between the statement—sounds that "wander about the room" and sounds that wander "along the wall[s]."

DEFENSES TO LIBEL

For a plaintiff to win a libel suit she must show that all of the elements of the tort of libel are met; it is said the plaintiff has the *burden of proof* in a libel case. When it comes to the defense of a libel case, the defendant must prove, under the rules of evidence, that an applicable defense will absolve her from liability. This may be more problematic than one imagines.

As a reporter, one may have garnered a story from various sources, all of them reliable, and had the facts checked many times for accuracy, yet, under the court's rules of evidence some or all of this evidence as to the correctness of the story may not be admissible because the rules of evidence do not usually allow what is termed **hearsay**—secondhand information. Hearsay occurs if a witness testifies about something she did not personally see or hear—someone else told her what occurred. The problem with hearsay is a constitutional one—the danger that someone accused of something cannot confront and cross-examine the witness that actually saw or heard the information. This is a big problem for a reporter, since most journalists rely on information from someone else for their story. (There are some 15 exceptions to the hearsay rule—for example, where such evidence is admissible even though it comes from a secondhand source. However, do not rely on the exceptions to get the evidence into court.)

Another issue for journalists in getting evidence into court to verify the correctness of their story is the aspect of keeping a source confidential. A journalist faces an ethical dilemma—do I keep a trusted and relied on source confidential, as promised, and thus lose the libel suit, or do I reveal my source, and lose my source, to potentially win the tort action?

■ **HEARSAY**

Hearsay is secondhand information that occurs if a witness testifies about something that she did not personally see or hear— that is, someone else told her what occurred.

Truth

The oldest and most concrete of all defamation defenses is **truth**. Some jurisdictions have even adopted the "**substantial-truth**" doctrine. In these jurisdictions, substantial truth protects the libel defendant as long as the "gist" of the information is true. Although before the media defendant asserts the defense of truth, since *Gertz*, the plaintiff will have to show the information is false.

This issue was revisited in *Philadelphia Newspapers v. Hepps*, 475 U.S. 767 (1986). In this case, Hepps is the principal stockholder of a corporation that franchises a chain of stores selling beer, soft drinks, and snacks. Philadelphia Newspapers published a series of articles whose general theme was that Hepps, the franchisor corporation, and its franchisees had links to organized crime, and used some of those links to influence the state's governmental processes. Hepps, the corporation, and the franchisees sued for defamation in a Pennsylvania State Court against the newspaper owner and the authors of the articles in question. The trial court instructed the jury, Hepps, the corporation, and the franchisees (the plaintiffs) had to prove falsity of the statements. The trial court jury ruled for the newspaper.

The Pennsylvania Supreme Court, favoring Hepps, concluded that placing the burden of showing the truth on the defendant (the newspaper) did not unconstitutionally inhibit free debate, and sent the case back for a new trial for the newspaper to prove the truth of the statements.

The U.S. Supreme Court reversed the State Supreme Court's decision, stating that the plaintiff must show falsity and fault prior to prevailing in a defamation suit, this based on *Gertz*.

Justice O'Connor, writing for the majority of the Court stated,

> "Here, as in *Gertz*, the plaintiff is a private figure and the newspaper articles are of public concern. In *Gertz*, as in *New York Times*, the common-law rule was superseded by a constitutional rule. We believe that the common law's rule on falsity—that the defendant must bear the burden of proving truth—must similarly fall here to a constitutional requirement that the plaintiff bear the burden of showing falsity, as well as fault, before recovering damages. ... We note that our decision adds only marginally to the burdens that the plaintiff must already bear as a result of our earlier decisions in the law of defamation. ... A jury is obviously more likely to accept a plaintiff's contention that the defendant was at fault in publishing the statements at issue if convinced that the relevant statements were false. As a practical matter, then, evidence offered by plaintiffs on the publisher's fault in adequately investigating the truth of the published statements will generally encompass evidence of the falsity of the matters asserted."

So it is quite clear, the U.S. Supreme Court has decided that if the case revolves around the media covering issues of *public concern*, the *plaintiff* will have to show the statements are false. But what if the case does not involve issues of public concern? The Supreme Court has left this to the states to decide who has the burden of proof as to truth or falsity.

SIDEBAR

A caveat: just because a story may be true and the libel suit is won, there are other possible actionable torts against the media, such as invasion of privacy, placing someone in a false light, intentional infliction of emotional distress, or public disclosure of private facts.

Absolute and Qualified Privilege

Certain communications are protected by an absolute privilege. For example, statements made in legislative or judicial proceedings are protected by an absolute privilege. The rationale behind protecting statements made within the context of legislative or judicial proceedings is that individuals should not be deterred from commenting freely, thereby contributing to a more complete and truthful exploration of a particular issue. There are certain occasions of qualified privilege when the media can report on deliberations of a public body or governmental records as long as this is not done with actual malice.

Absolute Privilege

Defamatory statements made during the course of a trial within a legislative or administrative proceeding, by the participants, are considered to have **absolute privilege**. Thus, what an attorney states *during a trial*, or what a state legislator says *during a lawmaking session* is privileged and not actionable for libel. The caveat here is when the attorney or legislator steps outside of the courthouse or the debate floor.

Article I, Section 6 of the U.S. Constitution, called the Speech and Debate Clause, grants members of Congress, engaged in debates on the floor of Congress, an absolute privilege to say what they wish and never be liable for libel. This privilege now extends to government officials; government proceedings; government documents; local, state, and national legislative branches of government; and to court proceedings. This means governmental officials, making comments while carrying out their official duties, are immune from libel suits. This privilege allows for a free flow of information during governmental, administrative, or judicial proceedings, without the potential "chill" of a libel suit.

But not all activities that appear to be part of an official's duties are so protected. In 1979, in *Hutchinson v. Proxmire,* 43 U.S. 111, the U.S. Supreme Court ruled that Senator William Proxmire was *not* afforded an absolute privilege of comment in regards to his development of the "Golden Fleece" award. Senator Proxmire had

■ **ABSOLUTE PRIVILEGE**

Absolute privilege is immunity from libel, given government officials, administrative proceedings, and judicial proceedings.

facetiously awarded Dr. Ronald Hutchinson, a behavioral scientist, such an award for his receipt of an almost half-million dollar government grant. Senator Proxmire felt this was nonsensical and a waste of taxpayer money. Proxmire stated so on the floor of the Senate, in staff conferences, and in a newsletter sent to his constituents. There were also press releases printed as to this "newsworthy" situation. Dr. Hutchinson claimed this award defamed him causing him to lose professional standing, and as a result suffer financial loss. He sued for libel.

The U.S. Supreme Court concluded Proxmire's comments in newsletters and press releases were not protected under Article I, Section 6 of the Constitution, since these items were not "essential to the deliberations of the Senate," nor were they part of Congress's "deliberative process." However, his speeches in Congress and discussions with his staff were so protected, because they were important to the workings of that legislative body.

An area where the media has an absolute privilege defense to defamation is under Section 315 of the Communications Act of 1934. Under this act, broadcasters are required to provide equal access to airtime for all opposing political candidates. The act does not allow the broadcaster to control any of the information given; the broadcaster has no way of preventing the politician of defaming her opponent, thus the broadcaster is not held potentially liable for defamation.

Qualified Privilege

■ **QUALIFIED PRIVILEGE**

A qualified privilege in defamation suits may be defeated especially by a showing of actual malice on the part of the media.

A **qualified privilege** allows the media to report on deliberations of a public body or governmental records without the fear of facing a defamation suit. There are a few problems with this defense: 1. Not all jurisdictions are the same as to immunity from suit. 2. Who and what are within the scope of this privilege? 3. What are the parameters under which this privilege applies? Would it apply to a governmental official privately negotiating a contract with a private business? It probably would not. Would the privilege apply if a reporter were covering a legislative hearing? It probably would.

The privilege is almost always applicable to formal official proceedings. The privilege gets more attenuated if the meeting is more informal and, thus, less official. Also, be careful as to the level of the individual making the comment. The lower the ranking of the person making the comment, the less likely the privilege will apply.

In judicial proceedings, usually the key to whether the privilege will apply will be whether the proceeding is usually open to the public, or if the records are official. If they are, it is more likely there will be qualified privilege attached to the reporting of the information. If the proceeding is held behind closed doors, or if the records are not official, the privilege will probably not apply.

Another potential pitfall area is a non-public record that somehow becomes public. If a reporter decides to report on this information, beware—the privilege will probably not apply. Even if a record is public, some jurisdictions will not extend the qualified privilege to the media if *actual malice* is found in the publication of the information. Be careful as to records that are public but are not yet ruled on by a judge. Some jurisdictions will not extend a privilege to the reporting on such information; they want the imprimatur of the judge before considering the information public.

If one is assigned to a police beat, or is *allowed* access to police information, reports as to an individual's arrest and booking are usually privileged. But when reporting this information be sure to always "couch" the report by stating the "alleged" criminal.

Make sure the person has actually been charged with the crime. If the person has only been "taken into custody for questioning" and it is reported as an arrest, be ready for a suit for libel. If the person is only being questioned, this is all that can be reported. Also, if one is privy to nonpublic police information, reporting on this information is usually *not* privileged. Reporting potentially false charges that may appear in a public record may raise ethical questions, but as to its legality, it is usually privileged, as long as the report is a fair and accurate reflection of the public record.

Fair Comment or Opinion Privilege

The **fair comment** privilege protects the media from a libel suit when they publish statements about a *public figure*—a person that voluntarily puts herself before the public. This privilege extends to expressions of *opinion*, if they are labeled as such. The query may be how does this differ from a qualified privilege? The fair comment privilege applies *outside* of official government proceedings or records, while the qualified privilege only applies to deliberations of a public body or governmental records. Be aware that not all jurisdictions embrace the fair comment privilege, although the U.S. Supreme Court has alluded to it in the *Gertz*, *Milkovich*, and *Hepps* cases.

In *Gertz (supra)*, the Court opined,

> "Under the First Amendment there is no such thing as a false idea. However pernicious an opinion may seem, we depend for its correction not on the conscience of judges and juries but on the competition of other ideas. But there is no constitutional value in *false statements of fact* [emphasis added]. Neither the intentional lie nor the careless error materially advances society's interest in 'uninhibited, robust, and wide-open' debate on public issues."

In *Milkovich*, cited earlier, the U.S. Supreme Court held that mere opinion could not be a basis for a libel suit, but if false objective facts were involved, the statement might be libelous. The line between opinion and fact would have to be decided by a **trier of fact** (a judge or jury) as to whether the case is actionable or not.

In *Milkovich*, a news column had accused a high school wrestling coach of perjury. The column stated Milkovich had lied under oath in reference to an altercation at a match involving his team and another high school's team.

FAIR COMMENT
Fair comments are statements of opinion made by the media in an honest belief in their truth, even though the statements are not in fact true.

TRIER OF FACT
The trier of fact is the authority at a trial, be it jury or judge, who decides what the truth is.

The Court held, "Since the latter half of the 16th century, the common law has afforded a cause of action for damage to a person's reputation by the publication of false and defamatory statements." Here the Court held that the connotation that Milkovich committed perjury is sufficiently *factual* to lend itself to being proved true or false, thus taking it out of the realm of mere opinion. It is not difficult to determine by objective evidence whether Milkovich lied or not in his testimony. Chief Justice Rehnquist stated,

> "First Amendment protection for defendants in defamation actions surely demonstrate the Court's recognition of the Amendment's vital guarantee of free and uninhibited discussion of public issues. But there is also another side to the equation; we have regularly acknowledged the 'important social values which underlie the law of defamation,' and recognize that '[s]ociety has a pervasive and strong interest in preventing and redressing attacks upon reputation'."

In *Hepps*, discussed and cited earlier, the United States Supreme Court ruled the plaintiff must show falsity and fault prior to prevailing in a defamation suit. As long as a statement cannot be proven true or false, a mere opinion cannot be actionable.

So what are the criteria to decide if a report is libelous fact or protected opinion?

1. Be careful if there is some specificity in the article—facts that can be proven are probably *not* opinion.

2. Courts will look at how the article is written and to whom it is disseminated. If the article is on the op/ed page and written by someone from the public, usually this will be mere opinion and protected, unless it can be proven to be a libelous statement of fact. Remember, if the information is of a public record or of a governmental proceeding it may be under *privilege*, as discussed earlier.

3. If the statement is of debate on public issues and is uninhibited, robust, and wide open, it is more likely to be protected by the First Amendment.

Other Libel Defenses

Some other defenses to libel include **neutral-reporting privilege**, **right of reply**, **consent**, **statute of limitations**, **libel-proof plaintiffs**, and **retraction**. These are less used defenses to libel than those discussed earlier, but they are still worthy of discussion.

Neutral-reporting privilege is invoked when the media attempts to cover all aspects of a controversy. The media feels if they are merely acting as a news bulletin board—airing all sides of the story—they should be protected from a libel suit. The media in these situations are only a means to disseminate the news. They are not espousing any view. The media may not even believe in the views expressed; they are

■ **NEUTRAL-REPORTING PRIVILEGE**

The neutral-reporting privilege extends to the media when they function as a "bulletin board," serving merely as a vehicle for the dissemination of newsworthy statements, without espousing or even necessarily believing the contradictory charges and countercharges made by participants in a public debate.

only stating what is occurring in the controversy, and covering a newsworthy event. Of course, under *New York Times v. Sullivan* this disbelief could lead to libel liability, because this could be interpreted as reckless disregard of the truth.

In *Edwards v. National Audubon Society*, 556 F. 2d 113 (2d Cir.1977), the *New York Times* attempted to cover a dispute between a group of scientists and the National Audubon Society. In this case, the Audubon Society accused several pro-DDT pesticide scientists as being "paid to lie." The *New York Times*' environmental reporter did not believe these charges, but nonetheless reported the charges, feeling they were newsworthy. In this case the federal appeals court reversed a libel judgment against the *Times*, recognizing a constitutional privilege of *neutral reporting*. This defense is not well recognized by other courts.

In March 2005, the U.S. Supreme Court declined to hear a case considering if journalists have a constitutional privilege to report defamatory remarks made by public figures, as long as the remarks are reported in a neutral fashion. This let stand a Pennsylvania Supreme Court ruling—*Norton v. Glenn*,[1] that stated no such privilege exists under U.S. or Pennsylvania Constitutions.

The article in question in *Norton* reported some members of a local borough council had accused other members of the council of being homosexuals. The reaction to these charges from the council members was to deny the charges, and they called the comments "bizarre." The jury for the trial court found the reporter, editor, and the newspaper not liable for defamation under the neutral reportage privilege. The Pennsylvania Supreme Court disagreed, stating no such privilege exists, and ordered a new trial to determine the journalists' liability under an "actual malice" standard.

More than a dozen news-media organizations argued such a ruling would put a chill on news reporting of charges and countercharges, but without comment the U.S. Supreme Court let the *Norton* ruling stand.

What does *Norton* mean to a journalist? It will have to be determined, if the jurisdiction being covered recognizes the neutral-reporting privilege or not. Be careful: the story may end up in a jurisdiction that does not apply the privilege. If so, the plaintiff may decide to sue in that jurisdiction rather than the one that recognizes neutral reporting.

Another defense to libel is *right of reply*. This defense is usually used where two publishers are printing libelous statements about each other and one finally sues. The defendant will answer, "I was only replying to what was stated in the article." Some state courts recognize this defense, and many do not. Sometimes a plaintiff will actually give *consent* to a libelous statement. If this happens, it is a valid defense to libel. Be careful as to the scope of the consent. If the scope is exceeded, the potential for liability has been reopened.

There is also the defense of the *statute of limitations* (the time limit to file a suit has passed). This defense is very straightforward; all the defendant to a suit has to show is that it is too late for the plaintiff to sue. Be aware, however, that each jurisdiction has its own time limit, and there may actually be something that has occurred that extends the time limit—the statute of limitations has been *tolled* for

RIGHT OF REPLY

The right of reply is when the media or an individual feels that when she has been misrepresented she should have the right to respond to the allegations.

CONSENT

Giving consent is giving permission to do something.

STATUTE OF LIMITATIONS

A statute of limitations limits the amount of time within which legal action may be taken.

LIBEL-PROOF PLAINTIFFS

A person is libel-proof if her character is so bad that anything else bad said about her still would not lead to an action for defamation.

RETRACTION

Retraction is a formal recanting of the libelous material.

some reason. For example, the plaintiff may not have known of the story before the expiration of time under the statute of limitations. Also, the plaintiff may go forum shopping for a jurisdiction that has a longer time period to sue. This actually happened in *Keeton v. Hustler* under long arm statutes.

There are some *libel-proof plaintiffs*—they really cannot sue for defamation, because their reputations are so bad. The theory is that someone with a lousy reputation cannot be harmed any further.

Retraction or correction is another possible defense. Each state has its own rules as to how and when a retraction must be published. Usually, the retraction must be published as prominently as the original story so as to give the retraction as much "play" as the potentially libelous piece, and the retraction must be published in a timely manner. If the retraction law is followed, in some states this will reduce the possibility of the plaintiff winning a libel suit; in other states it will merely prevent the plaintiff from recovering punitive damages.

In many states, a timely retraction will limit damages to special damages—provable out-of-pocket damages, which are hard to prove, and thus potentially fatal to a libel suit. Some state laws hold that a retraction only "mitigates" the damage done. A retraction may also be used to show a lack of actual malice on the part of the media.

There are two major problems with retractions. If the publisher feels that it is right, and it refusese to retract, this leaves the door to a potential suit wide open. Also, does a retraction truly protect the person potentially libeled? If the viewer of the story saw only the first story, and not the retraction, is the retraction of any value? Is it not human nature to believe the initial story and not the retraction?

There has been an attempt to make state retraction laws uniform. In 1994, the **Uniform Correction or Clarification of Defamation Act (UCCDA)** came into being. (As of this writing, only a few states have adopted this act.) The UCCDA encourages prompt corrections of potentially defamatory statements, and changes the damages a plaintiff could recover to actual economic loss, not presumed loss of reputation or punitive damages. The act applies to print, electronic, Internet media, business, and personal contexts. The law addresses the major reason plaintiffs sue the media—the restoration of their reputations.

The UCCDA works by requiring that anyone who believes a publisher of information has made a damaging statement contact the publisher to show the statement was false and demand a retraction. The publisher then must decide if a retraction should be made. If a correction is published, it must reach the same audience as the original publication to invoke UCCDA protection. If the retraction is done accordingly, the plaintiff could only sue for special damages—out-of-pocket damages. If the retraction is made during the lawsuit, the publisher will have to pay the plaintiff's attorney and court fees. If no retraction is made, or a court decides the correction is not sufficient, the libel case would continue as it would under current law. This act would not affect any other common law or constitutional laws that presently exist for libel actions.

■ UNIFORM CORRECTION OR CLARIFICATION OF DEFAMATION ACT (UCCDA)

This act is a proposal by the National Conference of Commissioners on Uniform State Laws (NCCUSL) to make the retraction laws more uniform among the states.

SLAPP SUITS

In recent years, journalistic and private citizen constitutional protections of freedom of expression have been threatened by what is called a **Strategic Lawsuits Against Public Participation (SLAPP) suit**. These suits are not specifically labeled SLAPPs—yet they involve various and sundry tort actions ranging from product disparagement to defamation, abuse of process, interference with contractual relations, and other common-law torts. Corporations or private citizens initiate SLAPP suits; these entities sue journalists or citizen advocates when they speak out against specific projects or corporate policies.

A typical example of a SLAPP suit is when Oprah Winfrey was sued by the cattle industry. Ironically, she was sued under Texas's "**veggie libel**" law. The judge ultimately dismissed the veggie libel cause of action and allowed the cattle industry to continue the suit under business defamation.

The case began when Ms. Winfrey interviewed an author on her talk show. The author was warning the beef industry not to feed ground-up dead cows to beef cattle, attributing this practice to the potential spread of "mad cow" disease. In response to this allegation, Ms. Winfrey stated, "It has stopped me cold from eating another hamburger." She was sued for this comment in *Engler v. Winfrey*, 201 F.3d 680 (5th Cir. 2000). Although Ms. Winfrey won the suit, will it make her think twice about making such a comment again?

SLAPP suits are not only in the United States but overseas as well. One of the more publicized cases in Europe was the "McLibel" case when McDonald's in the United Kingdom SLAPPed Helen Steel and David Morris with a lawsuit. The two, along with others, had distributed a leaflet accusing McDonald's of selling unhealthy food, being cruel to animals, and exploiting its workforce. They were found liable in 1994 of libeling McDonald's, but the European Court of Human Rights ruled they had not received a fair trial, because legal aid had not been afforded them as libel defendants. Thus, their right to freedom of expression under the European Convention on Human Rights had been violated. They were awarded £24,000 in damages plus costs.

Although almost all SLAPP litigation is dismissed, or **summary judgment** is entered for the defendant, and most case law is in favor of the defendant in a SLAPP suit, potential litigation is definitely still a chill on freedom of expression.

Anti-SLAPP Laws

As a response to this proliferation of SLAPP suits, many states have enacted anti-SLAPP laws. California has the most extensive of these laws. In 1993, the **Code of Civil Procedure section 425.16** took effect. This law allows a judge to decide if the SLAPP suit has any merit—any chance of winning. If the judge rules that the case has no chance of success, the SLAPP will be dismissed, and the SLAPP defendant will win costs and attorney's fees.

■ **STRATEGIC LAWSUITS AGAINST PUBLIC PARTICIPATION (SLAPP) SUIT**

SLAPP stands for Strategic Lawsuits Against Public Participation. They are suits usually filed by citizens or companies against journalists or citizen advocates when they speak out against specific projects or corporate policies.

■ **VEGGIE LIBEL**

Veggie libel is the false disparagement of a perishable food item.

■ **SUMMARY JUDGMENT**

A summary judgment is a decision based on the statements and evidence presented on the record without a trial. Summary judgment is used if there are no disputed facts in the case, and it is decided one party is entitled to judgment in its favor as a matter of law.

■ CODE OF CIVIL PROCEDURE SECTION 425.16

The California Code of Civil Procedure section 425.16—anti-SLAPP legislation, states, "A cause of action against a person arising from any act of that person in furtherance of the person's right of petition or free speech under the United States or California Constitution in connection with a public issue shall be subject to a special motion to strike, unless the court determines that the plaintiff has established that there is a probability that the plaintiff will prevail on the claim."

The statements covered under the California law include:

(1) Any written or oral statement or writing made before a legislative, executive, or judicial proceeding, or any other official proceeding authorized by law;

(2) Any written or oral statement or writing made in connection with an issue under consideration or review by a legislative, executive, or judicial body, or any other official proceeding authorized by law;

(3) Any written or oral statement or writing made in a place open to the public or a public forum in connection with an issue of public interest;

(4) Or any other conduct in furtherance of the exercise of the constitutional right of petition or the constitutional right of free speech in connection with a public issue or an issue of public interest."

Other states have anti-SLAPP laws that are generally similar to California's but may be more narrowly drawn. Some do not require the plaintiff to pay expenses if the suit is dismissed. State anti-SLAPP laws have caused the dismissal of thousands of lawsuits, and the courts have upheld the right of the media to use anti-SLAPP laws to get frivolous lawsuits dismissed against them, even if a private individual has filed the suit. In *Braun v. Chronicle Publishing Co.*, 52 Cal.App.4th 1036, 61 Cal.Rptr.2d 58 (1997), the court upheld the *San Francisco Chronicle's* right to report on a state investigation of alleged wrongdoing by a university medical center. The court held that "… the anti-SLAPP statute is designed to nip SLAPP litigation in the bud by striking offending causes of actions which 'chill the valid exercise of the constitutional rights of freedom of speech and petition . . .' (section 425.16, subd. (a))."

If there is no anti-SLAPP law in the state where the publication is being sued, the U.S. Supreme Court in *Anderson v. Liberty Lobby*, 477 U.S. 242 (1986), ruled that if a defamation suit is considered frivolous, and a reasonable jury could not conclude with "convincing clarity" that actual malice existed, under the *New York Times v. Sullivan* ruling the lawsuit should be dismissed on a motion for summary judgment.

In the *Anderson* case, Liberty Lobby, Inc., a "citizens' lobby," and its founder filed a libel action in Federal District Court against a magazine published by Jack Anderson. Liberty Lobby claimed one of the magazine's articles contained libelous statements. After discovery, Anderson moved for summary judgment, pursuant to Federal Rule of Civil Procedure 56. Asserting, since Liberty Lobby were, "public figures, they were required to prove their case under the *New York Times* standards, and that summary judgment was proper because actual malice was absent as a matter of law in view of an affidavit by the author of the articles in question that they had been thoroughly researched and that the facts were obtained from numerous sources." Opposing the motion, Liberty Lobby claimed an issue of actual malice was presented because the author had relied on patently unreliable sources in preparing the articles.

The Federal District Court ruled in favor of Anderson and granted summary judgment; the appellate court reversed, holding the lower court had erroneously applied the actual malice standard at the summary judgment phase of the trial. Anderson appealed to the U.S. Supreme Court. The Supreme Court ruling was, "In essence, the inquiry [as to the granting of a summary judgment] (emphasis added) is whether the evidence presents a sufficient disagreement to require submission to a jury or whether it is so one-sided that one party must prevail as a matter of law." If a libel plaintiff cannot show by clear and convincing proof that she could win the suit, the case should be dismissed.

MISCELLANEOUS LIBEL ISSUES

As has been discussed previously, in a defamation suit, the plaintiff must prove fault on the part of the defendant, in the case of the media, fault could be an issue of negligence or actual malice, depending on the plaintiff and/or the jurisdiction. To defeat the libel action, all the media has to do is prove there was no negligence or actual malice. The easiest way of accomplishing this would be to bring in the source of the information, have her testify as to the correctness of the information, case closed. That may not sound difficult to do, but what if a journalist has promised her source confidentiality?

Under the rules of discovery, if the party that is asked to comply does not, the court will merely conclude the evidence—the truthful and accurate source of the reported information—does *not* exist. If that happens, the court will have to conclude the story was published with reckless disregard of the truth—the media loses the libel suit. Thus, the journalist must choose between violating ethics and revealing a confidential source, or losing the suit.

This confidentiality issue is of great concern to **libel insurance** companies as well. In response the **National Association of Broadcasters (NAB)** offers libel insurance coverage to broadcasters—radio and television. This insurance does not require the broadcaster to reveal confidential sources, and the broadcaster is still covered. Although this insurance is expensive and requires surcharges if a broadcaster does business in states that are high risk for a libel suit, nonetheless it is comforting for broadcasters to know they are afforded some protection from suit. The insurance that the NAB provides even protects against punitive damages, where permitted by law. Other media trade associations have also arranged for libel insurance through private insurance companies.

The Long-Arm of the Law

Minimum contacts—in which forum the media can be sued—is another issue that must be considered in libel cases. In 1945, the U.S. Supreme Court ruled in *International Shoe v. Washington*, 326 U.S. 310, that anyone engaging in interstate

■ LIBEL INSURANCE

Insurance against claims arising from alleged defamation of character.

■ NATIONAL ASSOCIATION OF BROADCASTERS (NAB)

The National Association of Broadcasters (NAB) is a nonprofit, incorporated association of radio and television broadcast stations. NAB serves and represents the American broadcasting industry.

■ MINIMUM CONTACTS

Minimum contacts are that degree of contact with a forum state sufficient to maintain a suit there and not offend traditional notions of fair play and substantial justice.

commerce may be sued in any state where they have minimum contacts. The minimum contacts in this situation was the hiring of salesmen, and their selling of shoes in the state of Washington, despite the fact the home office of International Shoe was located in St. Louis, Missouri.

Calder v. Jones, 465 U.S. 783 and *Keeton v. Hustler*, 465 U.S. 770, both decided on the same day in 1984, held that journalists would have to defend themselves in other states courts based on the doctrine of minimum contacts. The U.S. Supreme Court held that this would not have a "chilling" effect on freedom of the press.

In the *Calder* case, actress Shirley Jones and her husband brought suit for libel in the California Superior Court against the *National Enquirer*; South, the writer of the story; and Calder, the editor of the *Enquirer*. The *Enquirer*, South, and Calder are all based in Florida. The *Enquirer* is a national publication with a large circulation in California. The *Enquirer*, South, and Calder were served with process by mail in Florida. The *Enquirer* and the distributing company answered the complaint, and made no objection to the jurisdictional issue, but South and Calder felt they should not be subject to California jurisdiction, and caused special appearances to be entered on their behalf. They moved to quash the service of process, for lack of personal jurisdiction on the part of the California court. The California Superior Court granted the motion to quash service of process on the grounds there were First Amendment concerns, and a possible "chilling effect" on freedom of the press. The court stated that this outweighed an assertion of jurisdiction otherwise proper under the Due Process Clause. The California Court of Appeals reversed, rejecting the suggestion that First Amendment considerations enter into the jurisdictional analysis.

The U.S. Supreme Court agreed with the Court of Appeals stating, "The Due Process Clause of the Fourteenth Amendment to the United States Constitution permits personal jurisdiction over a defendant in any State with which the defendant has 'certain minimum contacts … such that the maintenance of the suit does not offend 'traditional notions of fair play and substantial justice'." The Court held that "… intentional, and allegedly tortious, actions were expressly aimed at California." South wrote and Calder edited an article they knew would have a potentially devastating impact on Ms. Jones, and they knew the brunt of the injury would be felt in California, the state where Ms. Jones lives and works, and in which the *National Enquirer* has its largest circulation—600,000 readers. Under the circumstances, South and Calder must "reasonably anticipate being ha[u]led into court there" to answer for the truth of the statements made in their article.

In *Keeton v. Hustler,* Kathy Keeton sued *Hustler Magazine* and other defendants for libel in the U.S. District Court for the District of New Hampshire. She sued because of a derogatory cartoon published in *Hustler* in 1976. Kathy Keeton, then girlfriend of Penthouse publisher Bob Guccione, felt that she had been libeled in the cartoon. She originally had sued in Ohio, but her suit was dismissed since she missed the statute of limitations. Keeton was a resident of New York, and *Hustler* is an Ohio corporation and its principal place of business is in California. Keeton sued based on **diversity of citizenship**—the parties of a suit being from different states. She chose to sue in New Hampshire because that state offers a six-year statute of limitations for

■ DIVERSITY OF CITIZENSHIP

Diversity of citizenship occurs when the plaintiff and defendant are from different jurisdictions. This can lead to the case being heard in federal court.

libel, the longest in the United States. *Hustler* did sell magazines in New Hampshire —approximately 10,000–15,000 per month, and Keeton's only contact with New Hampshire was the circulation of a magazine she assisted in producing. The District Court dismissed the suit on the grounds the Due Process Clause did not allow for the application of the long arm statute of New Hampshire to apply to *Hustler*, and the First Circuit Court of Appeals affirmed this decision, finding Keeton's contacts too attenuated for an assertion of personal jurisdiction over *Hustler*. The Court of Appeals also addressed the issue of damages, stating that if Keeton were to prevail in New Hampshire, it would be unfair, because most of her injuries occurred outside that state.

The U.S. Supreme Court held that *Hustler's* regular circulation of magazines in New Hampshire was sufficient to allow personal jurisdiction over the magazine based on the magazine's content. The Court held,

> "… the Court of Appeals' analysis of New Hampshire's interest is an emphasis on the extremely limited contacts of the plaintiff with New Hampshire. But we have not to date required a plaintiff to have "minimum contacts" with the forum State before permitting that State to assert personal jurisdiction over a nonresident defendant. … Where, as in this case … *Hustler Magazine*, Inc., has continuously and deliberately exploited the New Hampshire market, it must reasonably anticipate being ha[u]led into court there in a libel action based on the contents of its magazine."

Hustler "… produces a national publication aimed at a nationwide audience. There is no unfairness in calling it to answer for the contents of that publication wherever a substantial number of copies are regularly sold and distributed." As to damages, the Court held that though most of the harm done to Keeton occurred outside New Hampshire, the same is true for any libel case brought in other than the plaintiff's state of domicile.

Although *Calder* was a blow for the media, *Keeton* was an atomic bomb. According to *Keeton*, anywhere the media has "a substantial number of copies" regularly sold is sufficient to allow jurisdiction, thus basically allowing the plaintiff to shop for the most favorable forum possible in a defamation suit.

What about online defamation and long-arm statutes? Until 2003, the plaintiff could only sue the defendant for defamation where the defamation was directed. In *Young v. New Haven Advocate*, 315 F.3d 256 (4th Cir. 2002), the U.S. Court of Appeals held that the warden of a Virginia prison could not sue Connecticut papers for their Web site articles, because the articles were directed at a Connecticut audience not a Virginia audience.

A year later, in a North Dakota case—*Wagner v. Mishkin*, ND 69 (2003)—the North Dakota Supreme Court upheld a $3 million libel verdict against a former University of North Dakota student accused of using an Internet site to spread defamatory statements about a UND professor. The court held that a North Dakota court could assert jurisdiction, because at the time of the defamatory statements the defendant lived in North Dakota, even though she now lives in Minnesota.

Fiction and Libel Suits

It would seem if a journalist wrote a piece of fiction, there could be no libel suit based on the fictional story written, because by definition fiction is not based on fact. Think again. If a writer comes too close to a real person in her depictions, and the real person claims this has caused defamation, beware of a potential suit. Even if the writer of the story puts in the caveat, "the story is purely fictional and does not depict a real person," this will not always protect one from a suit.

For a plaintiff to get such a suit into court, she will have to prove she is actually that fictional character. All that is needed to prove this is for the people that know the person allegedly defamed to understand that the character in the story depicts the plaintiff. The key here is the fictional character and the plaintiff must be very close in description.

In *Carter-Clark v. Random House, Inc.*, 793 NYS 2d 394, 2005 the court held that the plaintiff in this case did not show that she could be the same as a character in the book *Primary Colors*.

The plaintiff sued the publisher, Random House, and the author of *Primary Colors,* Joe Klein, for libel and negligence. She alleged that the librarian character depicted in the first chapter of the book was based on her. The court held that although a real person and real events inspired the book, it was still fiction, and thus must be analyzed as such. For a fictional character to be able to sue for libel it must be shown "… the description of the fictional character is so closely akin to her that a reader of the book, knowing the real person, would have no difficulty linking the two." In this case, any supposed similarities were superficial. The ruling focused on the difference between the plaintiff and the character in the book—they had different names, different jobs, and different physical characteristics. It was clear the book, as a work of fiction, did not depict the plaintiff. Thus, it was appropriate to dismiss the libel suit and the suit for negligence against the publisher, because as a work of fiction Random House had no duty to investigate the writing any further than it did.

What about taking a "poke" at a public official? Here the plaintiff will have to show a "reasonable reader" would interpret the satire as actual facts about the plaintiff. The key is to create as ludicrous a satire as possible, so that no reasonable person could interpret it as an actual fact.

In *New Times, Inc. v. Isaacks*, 146 S.W.3d 144 (Tex. 2004), the Texas Supreme Court held that there were enough exaggerations in a story to take it out of the realm of actual facts. In November 1999, 13-year-old Christopher Beamon, a seventh grader, was arrested and detained for five days in a juvenile detention facility after the Halloween story he wrote as a school assignment was deemed to contain violent threats. According to Beamon, his teacher assigned students the task of writing a scary story about being home alone in the dark and hearing scary noises. Beamon penned a story that described shooting a teacher and two classmates. He received a grade of 100, plus extra credit for reading it aloud in class. The school principal read the story and called juvenile authorities, which sent sheriff's deputies to remove

Beamon from school. Denton County Juvenile Court Judge Darlene Whitten ordered Christopher detained at the Denton County Juvenile Detention Facility for 10 days. She later approved an early release after five days, and Denton County District Attorney Bruce Isaacks declined to prosecute the case—it appeared all Christopher did was what the teacher assigned him to do.

The *Dallas Observer*, a self-described alternative paper, wrote a story lampooning the Denton County District Attorney Isaaks and the Denton County Juvenile Court Judge Whitten for the prosecution of a six-year-old girl for writing a book on cannibalism and disorderly conduct. In the satire, the author referred to a religious group called GOOF.

The Texas Supreme Court held that this was clearly a satire and could not reasonably interpreted as actual facts about Isaaks or Whitten. The "Stop the Madness" article does have a superficial degree of plausibility, but such is the nature of satire. The nature of a parody is to catch the reader off guard, after which the victim of the satire realizes the joke is on her because she has been caught unaware. This does not necessarily make the parody actionable for libel. Although a reader may first think that the parody is real news, this article in question is so preposterous it is unlikely a reasonable reader could construe it to be actual facts, especially because it could not be construed as an article depicting the Beamon incident.

Criminal Libel

Although all 50 states have civil libel laws, only 20 states have criminal libel statutes. What criminal libel means to journalists and publishers is that not only are they potentially monetarily liable for a civil defamation case, but, if they are found to have committed criminal libel, they can be jailed as well.

Criminal libel is an ancient doctrine dating back to Roman times. The U.S. basis for this action dates to the late 15th century and the notorious Star Chamber of England. (This is the court in which one was brought before a judge, but could not confront one's accuser or bring witnesses on one's behalf. If charged and brought before the Star Chamber, jail or death would almost be a certainty.) Criminal libel laws ban statements that tend to blacken the memory of one who is dead, or impeach the honesty, integrity, virtue, or reputation of someone living. The John Peter *Zenger* case (*supra*) was the first criminal libel case on American soil.

In 1964, shortly after the *New York Times v. Sullivan* civil libel case, the U.S. Supreme Court handed down an important *criminal* libel case—*Garrison v. Louisiana*, 379 U.S. 64. In *Garrison*, the Court upheld the need to prove actual malice with regard to false statements made against a public official or public figure, to uphold a criminal libel case.

This case revolved around a district attorney in Louisiana. The district attorney, during a dispute with certain state court judges of his parish, "accused them at a press conference of laziness and inefficiency and of hampering his efforts to enforce the vice laws." The U.S. Supreme Court stated that the reasonable-belief standard applied by the Louisiana trial judge is not the same as the reckless-disregard-of-truth standard held in the *New York Times* case. "The test which we laid down in *New York Times* is not keyed to ordinary care; defeasance of the privilege is conditioned, not on mere negligence, but on reckless disregard for the truth." Thus, *actual malice* would have to be shown before conviction on criminal libel.

Although criminal libel laws have not been used to a great extent, there is a case that came out of Kansas that must be discussed: *Kansas v. Carson*, No. 01-CR-301 (Kansas Dist. Ct. Wyandotte County July 17, 2002). The facts are that Carson, the publisher, and Powers, the editor, of *The New Observer,* were convicted of seven counts of criminal defamation, fined $700 each, and given one year of unsupervised probation. Their crime was criticizing the mayor in one of their stories. They had questioned whether Mayor Marinovich lived in the proper county. In fact she did; therefore, their statements were false.

Carson and Powers have appealed. Kansas criminal libel law requires the false statement be made with *reckless disregard of the truth* or with *actual malice*—the standard applied in the U.S. Supreme Court case of *Garrison*. If this case gets to the U.S. Supreme Court, it will be interesting to see how it will be voted on, considering that at the time of writing there is a new Chief Justice—John Roberts—and a new Associate Justice—Samuel Alito.

In August 2005, an Idaho man, L. D. Bryson, was arrested for criminal libel for putting out several yard signs on his parent's property. The signs put forth the question of whether a sex offender lived in the neighborhood. His neighbors found the signs offensive and felt he was accusing one of them of being a criminal. He spent one day in jail, and was told he could face a $300 fine and six months in jail for each sign. Since the arrest, Mr. Bryson has moved from Osborn to Kellogg, Idaho. He claims that the police will not allow him to return home until the dispute is resolved.

Mr. Bryson is now suing the northern Idaho town of Osborn, the police department, and its police chief. He is asking for $1 million for an alleged violation of his First Amendment rights, harassment, intimidation, emotional distress, and attorneys' fees.

Although criminal libel cases are rare in the United States, as seen in the prior cited cases, they are a remote possibility and should be kept under consideration. Again, the key is to avoid reckless disregard of the truth or actual malice in reporting potentially false statements against public officials or public figures.

Emotional Distress

Often associated with defamation lawsuits is another cause of action, called infliction of **emotional distress**. There are four elements that the plaintiff must prove to recover under this cause of action: 1. The media must act intentionally or recklessly (some jurisdictions allow recovery for negligent infliction of emotional distress); 2. The media's conduct must be extreme and outrageous; 3. The media's conduct must be the cause; and 4. The story must create severe emotional distress to

■ **EMOTIONAL DISTRESS**

For a plaintiff to recover for emotional distress she must prove that the media acted intentionally or recklessly (some jurisdictions allow recovery for negligent infliction of emotional distress), that the media's conduct was extreme and outrageous, and that the media's conduct was the cause of severe emotional distress.

the plaintiff. The law defines extreme and outrageous as to go beyond all possible bounds of decency, and to be regarded as atrocious and intolerable in a civilized community.

According to The Restatement (Second) of Torts section 46 cmt. d and h (1965), liability does not extend to mere insults, indignities, threats, annoyances, or petty oppressions. The court must determine whether an average member of the community upon learning of the facts alleged by plaintiff would exclaim "outrageous!"

In 1988, the U.S. Supreme Court ruled that public figures and public officials may not recover for intentional infliction of emotional distress unless they can show that the media acted with *actual malice*, thus applying the *New York Times v. Sullivan* libel rule to emotional distress.

In *Hustler Magazine v. Falwell*, 485 U.S. 46 (1988), the Court held that cartoonists and satirists must be protected from libel and emotional distress suits if commenting on matters of public concern. This case began when *Hustler* magazine ran an advertisement "parody" about Reverend Jerry Falwell. Reverend Falwell was a Fundamentalist minister and political leader. The ad portrayed him as having engaged in a drunken incestuous rendezvous with his mother in an outhouse. The ad stated, "Jerry Falwell talks about his first time." This parody was modeled after actual Campari ads that included interviews with various celebrities about their "first times." Although it was apparent by the end of each interview that this meant the first time they sampled Campari, the ads clearly played on the sexual double entendre of the general subject of "first times." In small print, at the bottom of the page, the ad contained the disclaimer, "ad parody—not to be taken seriously." The magazine's table of contents listed the ad as "Fiction; Ad and Personality Parody." Falwell sued for libel, invasion of privacy, and intentional infliction of emotional distress.

The U.S. Supreme Court, in a unanimous decision, held that public figures such as Falwell may not recover for emotional distress unless they show the publication contained a false statement of fact made with actual malice. The Court added that the First Amendment right to free speech must take precedence over a state's interest in protecting public figures from offensive speech, as long as that speech cannot be construed to relate to actual facts about the one portrayed. This was merely a parody, and the advertisement and magazine specifically stated that it was.

The next chapter will discuss invasion of privacy, another tort issue the media must consider when publishing a story. Libel and emotional distress, although very important, are only the beginning of potential liability for the media.

SUMMARY

Although the press is in existence to report on issues that concern the public, the press cannot subject individuals to falsehoods that damage their reputations and their lives—defamation.

The 1964 *New York Times Co. v. Sullivan* case had the U.S. Supreme Court rule that public officials could not be successful in their libel suits unless they proved a reporter or editor was shown to publish the false statement with *actual malice*. Over the years, the Court has extended the term "public official" to those not in public office, but yet newsworthy—"public figures." In most states, those deemed to be private figures only have to prove some negligence on the part of the media to win a libel suit.

SLAPP suits occur when corporations or private citizens sue journalists or citizen advocates for defamation and other torts when specific projects or corporate policies are denounced. As a response to the proliferation of SLAPP suits many states have enacted anti-SLAPP laws.

Criminal libel laws are usually used against journalists when their stories are politically explosive. These laws have the same constitutional requirement as civil libel for recovery—actual malice on the part of the publisher or reporter must be shown for a public official or public figure to win a criminal libel suit.

▍ DISCUSSION QUESTIONS

1. Argue why the First Amendment should protect the media against defamation suits.

2. What is the difference between slander and libel? Has this distinction changed with the coming of the electronic age?

3. How did the *Zenger* case affect the issue of libel?

4. How did the *New York Times v. Sullivan* case change the law of libel?

5. What is the difference between a public official and a public figure?

6. Discuss why a public interest story should be given more constitutional protections.

7. Argue why private individuals should have to show actual malice to win a defamation suit against the media.

▍ CASE FOR REVIEW

Compare the *Associated Press* case and the *Rosenbloom* case with regard to the courts *not* finding libel, as the media in both cases were under tight journalistic deadlines.

■ KEY TERMS

absolute privilege

Code of Civil Procedure section
   425.16

consent

defamation

diversity of citizenship

emotional distress

fair comment

fault

general damages

hearsay

libel

libel insurance

libel per quod

libel per se

libel-proof plaintiffs

minimum contacts

National Association of
   Broadcasters (NAB)

negligence

neutral-reporting privilege

public figures

public officials

punitive damages

qualified privilege

retraction

right of reply

slander

special damages

statute of limitations

Strategic Lawsuits Against Public
   Participation (SLAPP) suit

strict liability

substantial-truth

summary judgment

tort

trier of fact

truth

Uniform Correction or Clarification
   of Defamation Act (UCCDA)

veggie libel

■ ENDNOTES

[1] *Troy Publishing Co. v. Norton*, 125 S. Ct. 1700 (2005) and *Norton v. Glenn*, 860 A.2d 48 (Pa. 2004)

Online Companion™
For additional resources, please go to
http://www.paralegal.delmar.cengage.com

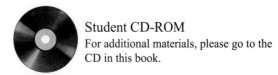

Student CD-ROM
For additional materials, please go to the
CD in this book.

Invasion of Privacy

▪ CHAPTER OUTLINE_____

▪ OBJECTIVES_____

After completing this chapter, you will be able to:

- Know what is meant when the media invades someone's privacy.

- Know when and how to gather news and information without intruding into another's privacy.

- Know when and if a photo or news story places an individual in a false light.

- Understand commercial appropriation and know how to avoid misappropriating a "celebrity's" name or likeness.

- Define and list the possible defenses to invasion of privacy.

INVASION OF PRIVACY

The Founding Fathers of the United States did not put anything about an individual's right to privacy in the text of the U.S. Constitution. It was not until 1965, when the U.S. Supreme Court ruled in *Griswold v. Connecticut*, 381 U.S. 479, that a right to privacy was implied in the Bill of Rights. The *Griswold* case held that there was privacy that allowed married couples to be counseled as to the use of contraceptives, thus striking down a Connecticut law that criminalized such advice. The Court stated, there were various guarantees within the Bill of Rights that create "penumbras," or zones, that establish a right to privacy. If taken together, the First, Third, Fourth, Fifth, and Ninth Amendments, create this constitutional right of privacy.

When the Constitution was written in the 18th century, America was a rural country without cameras, surveillance equipment, or the Internet. Although, by the 19th century, the right to privacy became an important issue. By the 1800s, the United States was in the throes of the Industrial Revolution and was becoming an urban nation. The newspapers in these teeming cities wanted to attract readers to their publications, so the more tawdry and sensational the story, the better. The population of the cities was mainly poor and the titillation of living vicariously through stories concerning the wealthy and those in the upper reaches of society would definitely sell papers. Also in the 1800s, there was this new invention—cameras. These new contraptions could actually catch people in less than flattering situations.

In 1890, Samuel Warren and Louis Brandeis in a *Harvard Law Review* article proposed the concept of a right to privacy. They stated, "... the right to be let alone; the right to liberty secures the exercise of extensive civil privileges; and the term 'property' has grown to comprise every form of possession—intangible, as well as tangible. ... Instantaneous photographs and newspaper enterprise have invaded the sacred precincts of private and domestic life." The two lawyers suggested there be a new legal right—one of privacy.

Today, all but a few states recognize the legal right to privacy, either by state statute or under case law. Most states try to perform the difficult balancing act of the public interest and freedom of the press versus the individual's right to privacy. Sometimes this balancing act is more difficult than not.

This legal right stems from the concept of protecting one's reasonable expectation to be left alone. It is an action that is personal to the individual, thus it is not available to corporate entities or labor unions, or any nonnatural person. It usually does not survive the individual whose privacy has been interfered with, unless it affects surviving relatives as in commercial appropriation cases, or as in the publication of autopsy photos.

Case in point: the blocking of autopsy photos of racecar driver Dale Earnhardt after his death in the 2001 Daytona 500 NASCAR race. His wife, Teresa Earnhardt, had successfully lobbied for legislation making it a felony for a medical examiner to make autopsy photos public. (Florida had not previously protected such photos.)

Under invasion of privacy, public figures have a limited right to claim their privacy has been violated, because it is held they have voluntarily exposed themselves to public scrutiny. Private individuals have more rights with regard to privacy, but beware: if they are part of a newsworthy event, their privacy rights may become more limited.

The law of privacy is not just one concept it is actually divided into four categories, depending on the wrong incurred by the individual: **intrusion**—when one intentionally intrudes on a person's solitude and into their private affairs; **publication of private facts**—publication of truthful information about the private life of a person that would be highly offensive; putting one in a **false light**—publishing information that is false or puts a person in a false light, this information is highly offensive, and it is published with malice (sound like defamation? It is similar but not the same); and **commercial appropriation**—the use of a person's name or likeness for commercial gain. Commercial appropriation is the use of a person's name or picture for another person's gain or commercial advantage.

Intrusion

Intrusion is usually claimed against the media when there is some sort of invasion of privacy during the newsgathering process. It could be how a reporter, photographer, or videographer gets the photo or the story. Telephoto lenses, hidden cameras, camouflaged microphones, and going through one's trash all could lead to intrusion charges. Intrusion is often associated with civil or criminal **trespass**, although a reporter does not have to trespass to intrude on an individual's privacy. Not all intrusions are trespass, not all trespass is intrusion. For example, physically going onto an individual's land without consent would be a trespass, yet a reporter does not have to physically step on to the land to intrude on one's privacy. The intrusion could be by use of a telephoto lens, or a high-powered listening device.

The tort of intrusion focuses specifically on how the information is gathered. The most important aspect of an intrusion case is, what is a "reasonable expectation of privacy"? If the media can show the plaintiff did not expect privacy in a specific situation the suit will fail. For example, if the plaintiff is in a public place and speaking loudly, is there an expectation of privacy? Probably not, because the entire world can

▪ INTRUSION

Intrusion is the unlawful entry upon or appropriation of the property of another.

▪ PUBLICATION OF PRIVATE FACTS

Publication of private facts is the public disclosure of embarrassing private information.

▪ FALSE LIGHT

False light is publicity that invades a person's privacy by disseminating a false statement that would be highly offensive to a reasonable person.

▪ COMMERCIAL APPROPRIATION

Commercial appropriation is the use of a person's name or picture for another person's gain or commercial advantage.

▪ TRESPASS

Trespass is an unauthorized entry upon land.

hear him. If the plaintiff is at home speaking on the phone quietly, but the media is eavesdropping on the conversation, has an expectation of privacy been breached? Probably yes, because the plaintiff expected the conversation to be private.

One of the major areas the media must be careful as to intrusion is when a journalist is taken on a "ride-along" with the police. In 1999 the U.S. Supreme Court in *Wilson v. Layne* held that the media and law enforcement officers risk suit if a journalist on a ride-along with the police enters a private home along with the officer. Although a search warrant gives the officer the right to enter the home, it is a violation of the Fourth Amendment for a journalist to enter the home without the occupant's permission.

CASE STUDY **Wilson v. Layne**

526 U.S. 603 (1999)

Facts: Charles Wilson, father of Dominic Wilson, challenged the constitutionality of an arrest procedure conducted by U.S. marshals and state officers seeking to arrest his son. The officers were in possession of arrest warrants, and entered the private dwelling of Charles Wilson. A journalist and photographer from the *Washington Post* entered the home with the officers. The officers' early morning entry into the home prompted a confrontation with the Wilsons and a sweep of the home revealed to the officers the son was not in the house. The reporters from the *Post* observed and photographed the incident, but were not involved in the execution of the warrant. Their newspaper never published the photographs they took of the incident. The officers departed when they realized they were in the wrong home. The Wilsons sued the officers based on violation of their Fourth Amendment rights.

Issue: Is the entrance of a home by a journalist on a ride-along a violation of the homeowner's Fourth Amendment rights as to unreasonable searches and seizures?

Decision: Yes, it is a violation of the Fourth Amendment.

Reason: Justice Rehnquist, writing for a unanimous Court on the Fourth Amendment issue, based the decision on the primacy of common law and Fourth Amendment respect for the privacy of the home. The Court held that the presence of the media, while officers are executing a warrant, was in no way related to the officers' duties. The presence of the media does not assist the officers with the execution of the warrant. However, the Court did state that if a third party could aid in the execution of a warrant, his presence inside the home would not constitute a Fourth Amendment violation—for example, if the third party could help identify property to be seized.

(continues)

> ### CASE STUDY Wilson v. Layne (continued)
>
> The Court held in the *Wilson* case, and because no prior rule existed as to permitting the media into a home during the execution of a warrant, the officers did not know this would be an unlawful act. Thus, the Court granted the officers qualified immunity.

> ### SIDEBAR
>
> Ignorance of the law is no excuse, but in the *Wilson* case because there was no law in place at the time with regard to allowing the media into a home along with officers executing a warrant, the officers could not know of a nonexistent law. Thus, they were not held accountable for their actions.

As a journalist, it can be legally hazardous to one's health to videotape or photograph anything that goes on during a ride-along. Even if the photos or video are not published, it still can be considered an intrusion. Officers, now aware of this legal liability, will not allow journalists onto private property while performing their duties, unless someone in authority gives **consent** to the presence of the media.

Another area of great concern for potential liability for intrusion is when the media places hidden cameras in private places, or when the media conducts surreptitious recordings.

In October 2005, California Governor Arnold Schwarzenegger signed a law toughening the 1998 **California Anti-Paparazzi Act**, Cal. Civ. Code sec. 1708.8. The original Act was passed in response to the death of Diana, Princess of Wales. Her death was attributed to the fact her car was fleeing aggressive paparazzi. The new act is to thwart the profit motive behind these paparazzi photos.

The revised Act creates greater penalties if a person *trespasses*, "... in order to physically invade the privacy of the plaintiff with the intent to capture any type of visual image, sound recording, or other physical impression of the plaintiff engaging in a personal or familial activity, and the physical invasion occurs in a manner that is offensive to a reasonable person." Liability attaches even if there is no trespass if one, "... attempts to capture, [through the use of a visual or auditory enhancing device] in a manner that is offensive to a reasonable person, any type of visual image, sound recording, or other physical impression of the plaintiff engaging in a personal or familial activity under circumstances in which the plaintiff had a reasonable expectation of privacy."

If the Act is violated, a victim may sue for treble damages (three times the amount of any general and special damages proximately caused by the Act's violation), and punitive damages. The stripping of paparazzi proceeds from the sale of the photos is also imposed as a penalty. The Act punishes anyone who "... directs,

■ **CONSENT**

Giving consent is giving permission to do something.

■ **CALIFORNIA ANTI-PAPARAZZI ACT**

The California Anti-Paparazzi Act imposed heightened penalties on people who physically invaded another's privacy "with the intent to capture any type of visual image, sound recording, or other physical impression of the plaintiff engaging in personal or familial activity and the physical invasion occurs in a manner that is offensive to a reasonable person."

solicits, actually induces, or actually causes" someone to violate the law, under section 1708.8(d), and under section 1708.8(i), the act applies even if no image or recording is ever taken or sold.

In the United States, 13 states have *criminal* laws that expressly prohibit the unauthorized placement or use of cameras in private places. They are Alabama, Arkansas, California, Delaware, Georgia, Hawaii, Kansas, Maine, Michigan, Minnesota, New Hampshire, South Dakota, and Utah.[1] These laws provide that any use of a device that photographs, observes, or eavesdrops on events in a *private place*—where one reasonably expects to be safe from unauthorized intrusion—is against the law.

Ten states—Alabama, Delaware, Georgia, Hawaii, Kansas, Maine, Michigan, Minnesota, South Dakota, and Utah—prohibit the *trespassing* on private property to conduct surveillance. In Maine, violation of privacy is a felony, and in Michigan unauthorized installation or use of a hidden camera is a felony.[2]

In all 50 states, if all of the parties to a conversation consent to the recording, filming, or broadcasting of that conversation, it is legal. It is always legal to tape or record an interview if the reporter's camera is in full view of the person interviewed, because consent is therefore presumed.

SIDEBAR

In June 2004, the European Court of Human Rights ruled, paparazzi photos in German magazines showing Princess Caroline of Monaco doing familial things, such as shopping and on vacation with her family, violated her right to be left alone.

Princess Caroline, daughter of Prince Rainier of Monaco and actress Grace Kelly, had been trying to prevent the European media from publishing pictures of her in what she considers private situations.

In a 1999 case, Germany's constitutional court ruled that the princess was a public figure and thus had to tolerate such photos. Princess Caroline argued, under Article 8 of the Human Rights Convention that these photos were a breach of her right to privacy ("Everyone has the right to respect for his private and family life, his home and his correspondence"). The German government disagreed, stating the public had a legitimate right to know how she behaved in public because she was a public figure.

In the 2004 case, the European Court of Human Rights drew a distinction between reporting facts about politicians and reporting information about someone without official duties. They said that the published photos of Princess Caroline made no contribution to a debate of general interest, and even those known to the public could expect protection of their privacy. The public has no legitimate interest in knowing where Princess Caroline is or how she behaves in her private life, even if she is not in a secluded place when the photo is taken.

If consent is needed, be sure to get it in writing, so that there is a physical record that can be referred to at a later time. When obtaining consent, do not be timid and get less consent than needed for the story. For example, if the conversation will be broadcast in full, do not ask for consent for a 30-second sound bite. If the full conversation is aired, the consent received has been exceeded. Exceeded consent is the same as no consent.

Thirty-eight states and the District of Columbia allow the recording of a conversation if the reporter is a party to the conversation. The reporter need not tell the other party that they are being recorded. Federal wiretap statutes allow similar recordings, in most situations. Under 18 U.S.C. 2511 (d),

> "It shall *not* be unlawful under this for a person *not acting under color of law* to intercept a wire, oral, or electronic communication where such person is a party to the communication or where one of the parties to the communication has given prior consent to such interception unless such communication is intercepted for the purpose of committing any criminal or tortious act in violation of the Constitution or laws of the United States or of any State."[3]

Most states have adopted the federal law as to surreptitious recording of a conversation. Twelve states have expanded the federal law's language and prohibit all surreptitious recording or videotaping without *all* the parties consent. Those states are California, Connecticut, Florida, Illinois, Maryland, Massachusetts, Michigan, Montana, Nevada, New Hampshire, Pennsylvania, and Washington.[4] Most state statutes allow the recording of conversations when the parties have a reasonable expectation of being recorded.

Usually, state statutes apply within their respective states. If there is a conflict between the states' law, usually federal law will prevail, although a reporter must be careful. The more stringent state may choose to enforce its law against the eavesdropping violator. It is not clear if federal law will prevail over state law in interstate conversations, and in *Krauss v. Globe International, Inc.*, No. 18008-92 (N.Y. Supreme Court Sept. 11, 1995) it was held that New York law would apply to an interstate phone conversation as long as the injury occurred in New York.

As discussed in an earlier chapter, *Bartnicki v. Vopper* (2001) held that the media could not be liable for damages for publishing information the media obtained from a source that had conducted an illegal wiretap. In this case, the Supreme Court extended constitutional rights in speech that disclosed information from an illegally intercepted wire communication. The communication was collective-bargaining

---

SIDEBAR

It is imperative when gathering news that one knows his state law and the law of the state one is calling *before* secretly recording a conversation. If one calls someone in a state that requires consent of all parties to a conversation, ignoring that state's law could land the reporter in court or in jail.

▥ U.S. NATIONAL SECURITY AGENCY (NSA)

The NSA coordinates, directs, and performs highly specialized activities to protect U.S. government information systems and produce foreign intelligence information.

▥ FOREIGN INTELLIGENCE SURVEILLANCE ACT (FISA)

FISA prescribes procedures for requesting judicial authorization for electronic surveillance and physical search of persons engaged in espionage or international terrorism against the United States on behalf of a foreign power.

▥ AUTHORIZATION FOR THE USE OF MILITARY FORCE

The Authorization for use of Military Force, Public Law 107-40, of September 18, 2001, states the President has authority, under the Constitution, to take action to deter and prevent acts of international terrorism against the United States.

negotiations between a union representing teachers at a Pennsylvania high school and the local school board. An unidentified person intercepted and recorded a cell phone conversation between the union negotiator and the union president. Vopper, a radio talk show commentator, and in no way party to the illegal wiretap, played a tape of the intercepted conversation. The Court stated privacy concerns give way to publishing matters of serious public importance. The *Bartnicki* Court did not rule on whether the media would be protected for publishing illegally recorded conversations under different circumstances.

As of this writing, there is controversy as to the **U.S. National Security Agency's (NSA)** monitoring of private telephone conversations and email content, called the "Terrorist Surveillance Program." This program uses the NSA to perform warrantless eavesdropping on U.S. citizens communicating overseas. The federal government alleges that only potential terrorists or enemies of the country are having their communications scrutinized.

In August 2006, a Detroit U.S. District Court judge declared, the warrantless wiretaps conducted since 2002, by the Bush administration, were unconstitutional. Judge Anna Taylor held, in this case brought by the American Civil Liberties Union (ACLU) against the government, these electronic dragnets violate the First and Fourth Amendments and the separation of powers mandated by the Constitution. She stated, "It was never the intent of the Framers to give the president such unfettered control, particularly where his actions blatantly disregard the parameters clearly enumerated in the Bill of Rights."[5]

She added these actions are a violation of the **Foreign Intelligence Surveillance Act (FISA)**. FISA was enacted to assure the Executive Branch would be able to conduct legitimate electronic surveillance for foreign intelligence, yet not violate the nation's commitment to the Fourth Amendment.[6] FISA also admonishes, "… no United States person may be considered … an agent of a foreign power solely upon the basis of activities protected by the First Amendment to the Constitution of the United States."[7]

The government argued it has such powers to conduct surveillance based on congressional authorization given post-9/11 under the **Authorization for the use of Military Force**. The government further alleged that this authorization allows the conducting of surveillance in violation of FISA and the Constitution.

Judge Taylor stated that it is clear that FISA was meant to supercede all other statutory law as to surveillance, and FISA has strict limitations on the duration and scope of use of electronic surveillance. "Even if the [congressional authorization] superseded all other statutory law, Defendants [the government] have violated the Constitutional rights of their citizens, including the First Amendment, Fourth Amendment, and the Separation of Powers doctrine."[8]

"Implicit in the term 'national defense' is the notion of defending those values and ideas which set this Nation apart. … It would indeed be ironic if, in the name of national defense, we would sanction the subversion of … those liberties … which makes the defense of the Nation worthwhile."[9]

The U.S. Department of Justice has appealed this ruling, and has stated that this program is imperative in the ongoing conflict with terrorists. The government complained that it could not prove these claims without revealing state secrets. Judge Taylor rejected this argument as "disingenuous and without merit."

This is only one of nearly three dozen lawsuits nationwide challenging the warrantless interception of communications.

Some government officials are perturbed at the media for having "leaked" information about this monitoring of telephone and email communications. Journalists, that exposed this governmental practice, are fearful of being charged with espionage under the 1917 Espionage Act, which makes it a crime to print, write, or comment on anything that would put the federal government in disrepute.

Publication of Private Facts

The key to liability under publication of private facts is that it is truthful information, but it concerns the private life of an individual, and the publication of such information would be *highly offensive*, and the information is *not of legitimate public concern*. Under defamation law, if a reporter could prove the statements were true, this was a defense to the tort. Truth is *not* a defense to publication of private facts. How the information is obtained and whether it is newsworthy will determine liability.

So what can a reporter safely report on?

Public Records

There is usually no liability for a reporter to use information from public records, such as a birth certificate, judicial proceeding, or police reports, even if the dissemination of this information is highly embarrassing.

In 1975, the U.S. Supreme Court ruled in *Cox Broadcasting v. Cohn*, 420 U.S. 469 that it is unconstitutional to hold the media liable for civil liability for invasion of privacy if they accurately publish information lawfully obtained from court records or other public documents. In the *Cox* case, Martin Cohn, the father of a 17-year-old girl that was raped and killed in Georgia, sued Cox Broadcasting for invasion of privacy. Cox Broadcasting had obtained the name of the victim through public records, and used the name of the victim, Cynthia Cohn, in its coverage of the trial. This violated a Georgia privacy statute, which prevented members of the media from publicizing the names or identities of rape victims.

The Georgia Supreme Court upheld the law against publishing the name of a rape victim, based on invasion of privacy. The U.S. Supreme Court did not agree, and reversed that decision. Justice White, writing for the Court, held that the Georgia statute violated the Constitution. The Court held the news media is an important resource for citizens to scrutinize government proceedings, such as adjudication of crimes. "Thus even the prevailing law of invasion of privacy generally recognizes that the interests in privacy fade when the information involved already appears on the public record." To restrict the media, as the law in Georgia did, "... would invite timidity and self-censorship and very likely lead to the suppression of many items that would otherwise be published and that should be made available to the public."

In 1989, *Florida Star v. B.J.F.*, 491 U.S. 524, the Court again overturned an invasion of privacy civil judgment against a news organization for publishing a rape victim's name. The *Florida Star* is a newspaper that publishes a "Police Reports" section containing brief articles describing local criminal incidents under police investigation. B. J. F. reported to the Sheriff's Department and told them she had been robbed and sexually assaulted. The Department prepared a report, which identified B. J. F. by her full name, and placed it in the Department's pressroom. The Department does not restrict access to the room or to the reports available there. A *Star* reporter-trainee, sent to the pressroom, copied the police report verbatim, including B. J. F.'s full name. B. J. F.'s name was included in a "Police Reports" story in the paper. This reporting of her name was in violation of the *Star's* internal policy, and Florida Stat. 794.03 makes it unlawful to "... print, publish, or broadcast . . . in any instrument of mass communication" the name of the victim of a sexual offense. B. J. F. filed suit in a Florida court alleging, *inter alia,* that the *Star* had negligently violated 794.03.

When the case reached the U.S. Supreme Court, it was held that if the press lawfully obtains truthful information about a public concern from a governmental source, the state cannot constitutionally punish publication of the information, *unless the state shows the need to further a substantial state interest in preventing the publication of the information.*

The U.S. Supreme Court in the *B.J.F.* case did state, however, "... our holding today is limited. We do not hold that truthful publication is automatically constitutionally protected, or that there is no zone of personal privacy within which the State may protect the individual from intrusion by the press, or even that a State may never punish publication of the name of a victim of a sexual offense." The key here is if the State can prove they are promoting a substantial state interest in preventing the publication of lawfully obtained and truthful information, the state's statute may pass constitutional muster.

SIDEBAR

A journalist must be very cautious in publishing information from semipublic sources such as a police officer's notes that are not incorporated into the police report. These notes may not be deemed public record and leave the reporter in jeopardy for an invasion of privacy suit.

Reporting on Juveniles

Another issue for the media is how to handle the publication of information concerning juveniles.

The case *Smith v. Daily Mail Publishing Co.*, 443 U.S. 97 (1979), was a test of a West Virginia statute that made it a *crime* to publish, without approval of the juvenile court, the name of any youth charged as a juvenile offender. Newspapers owned by Daily Mail Publishing published articles containing the name of a juvenile arrested for allegedly killing another youth. The publishers had learned the name from monitoring a police band radio, and asking eyewitnesses what had happened. Does this law violate constitutional freedoms granted in the First and Fourteenth Amendments? The Supreme Court held the state could not punish the *truthful* publication of an alleged juvenile offender's name, as long as the name is *lawfully* obtained. The state's alleged interest of protecting the anonymity of a juvenile offender could not be used to suppress freedom of the press. To make publication of such information a *crime* the state would have to show the restriction would advance a substantial state interest. No such interest was shown in this case.

Yet Chief Justice Burger writing for the Court did state that if the publication were false, or there was unlawful access by the press to a confidential judicial proceeding, or the publication led to privacy or prejudicial pretrial publicity, then the Court may hold *contra* to the *Smith* decision.

Smith protects the media from *criminal* prosecution for the publication of a juvenile's name in a juvenile judicial proceeding, if the juvenile's name is *lawfully* obtained. *Smith* does not provide a defense to possible invasion of privacy suits if information is not part of public record. Also, *Smith* did not create any special circumstances for the media to obtain names of rape or juvenile offenders; a state may still decide to keep that information private. What *Smith* did do was allow then the media to publish lawfully obtained information and publish it without fear of criminal sanctions.

Newsworthiness

An area that may produce publication of private facts lawsuits is in the area of whether a topic or individual is **newsworthy** or not. If the facts are correct and current, but nonetheless embarrassing, the issue that will determine whether there may be a successful tort action is its newsworthiness. If the facts are not considered newsworthy, it is more likely the media will lose in an invasion of privacy suit. Courts consider several factors as to the newsworthiness of information. They look to the social value of the facts published, how much the article intrudes into the supposedly private affairs of the individual, and if the person has assumed a position of public notoriety (celebrity).

Although most cases that revolve around the issue of newsworthiness are resolved in favor of the media, still to be involved in such a suit can definitely give one pause before publishing a story.

■ **NEWSWORTHY**
If something is newsworthy is has generated sufficient interest or importance to the public to warrant reporting in the media.

When reporting a story, a journalist must not only consider if the topic or person is newsworthy, but if all the facts of the story reported are pertinent. In *Garner v. Triangle Publications Inc.*, 97 F. Supp. 546 (S.D.N.Y. 1951), a woman sued when she was involved in an auto accident, and as part of the story, it was reported that she was living with a man who was not her spouse. This information had nothing to do with the auto accident, and the reporter was held liable.

Thus, it is important when reporting on a story to decide if the information can be considered newsworthy, and stick only to those facts that are pertinent to the story. It may be titillating to reveal the person in the story has an interesting past, but step back and consider if this is truly important to what is being covered. If it is not, although tempting, do not publish the information.

Celebrity

Another consideration in publishing a newsworthy story: is this person a sufficient enough celebrity to bring his actions into the realm of newsworthiness? The courts are not clear as to what defines celebrity. Should a reporter be able to make a person a celebrity by merely reporting on them, and thus have a defense to an invasion of privacy lawsuit?

Although, public officials and public figures, for the most part, remain "celebrities" for the sake of reporting, what about ordinary people? An ordinary person may have his "fifteen minutes of fame" and thus achieve celebrity status, but the passage of time can negate his remaining a celebrity. Thus, facts that may have been permissible to publish during his time as a "celebrity," may now lead to an invasion of privacy lawsuit. A reporter should also consider the community where the story will run. If the facts may be considered indecent or obscene, be ethical and avoid a potential lawsuit, omit them.

In March 2006, a new Web site was developed by Justin Blecher and Ian Van Ness—the "Gawker Stalker." This Web site tracks the movement of celebrities in New York City. How it works is, people spot a celebrity and report his whereabouts to the site, a pin is then put on the Web site map. Clicking on the individual pin shows a photo of the star along with details on when and where he was seen.

Celebrities have stated that this is an invasion of privacy, and is potentially dangerous to them. "Gawker Stalker" is claiming that because they are in public and are celebrities, there is no invasion of privacy, and there is a 15-minute lag time between the report of the celebrity citing and the posting of the location.

Placing an Individual in a False Light

False light, invasion of privacy, involves publicity about a person that is false, or places the person in a false light. The information published must be highly offensive to a reasonable person, and it must be published with the knowledge that it is false, or with reckless disregard as to its falsehood, or if the information would place the person in a false light. Although this tort is similar to defamation, it is not. The information does *not* have to be defamatory to be actionable.

An example of false light is when actress Jessica Alba demanded *Playboy* magazine pull all of its March 2006 issues from newsstands. *Playboy* used a picture of Ms. Alba, taken for the promotion of the movie "Into the Blue," on the cover of the March issue, without her permission. *Playboy* had asked Ms. Alba's publicist for a picture, but the publicist refused. *Playboy* was running an article on the 25 sexiest people, and Ms. Alba was one of them. Ms. Alba contended that the placement of her picture on the cover of *Playboy misleads* the public into thinking she will be seen in the issue nude or seminude and, as such, damaged her career and reputation.

Ultimately, Ms. Alba forgave *Playboy* magazine, after founder Hugh Hefner sent her a letter of apology and pledged to donate money to her favorite charity. Ms. Alba stated that her concerns were never about money, it was to set the record straight "about something that was done without my knowledge or consent."

False light includes adding false material to a story, arranging the story or photograph to give a false impression, and fictionalizing characters that really represent real people or refer to real people. (This also may be defamation. See Chapter 4 on defamation.)

When fictionalizing a story, be careful not to place anyone in a false light. Although the story may not have been a tort before turning it into fiction, once it is fictionalized, check to see if any of the story's characters could claim it is highly offensive. Be careful of stock pictures. They may seem inane, but it actually may put the people photographed in an objectionable situation. For example, a picture of a couple holding hands, used to illustrate true love, would probably not place them in a false light, but if the same picture is used as an illustration for a prostitute and their client, look for a false light and defamation lawsuit to be filed.[10]

Although the tort of false light is recognized in 30 of the 50 states, 11 states have decided not to recognize this as a cause of action in a lawsuit. The states that do not recognize this tort feel this is a duplication of the tort of defamation, and would have a "chilling effect" on the news media's free speech activities, because elements of the claim are vague and subjective. The states that have ruled as such are North Carolina, Texas, Massachusetts, Minnesota, Mississippi, Missouri, Ohio, Virginia, Washington, Wisconsin, and Colorado.[11]

In 1967, the U.S. Supreme Court ruled in *Time, Inc. v. Hill*, 385 U.S. 374, that the First Amendment bars recovery for "... false reports of matters of public interest in the absence of proof that the defendant published the report with knowledge of falsity or in reckless disregard of the truth." Thus, the Court applied the *New York Times v. Sullivan* rule to privacy issues.

The facts of the case were: James Hill, his wife, and five children had involuntarily become the subjects of a front-page news story, after being held hostage by three escaped convicts in their suburban Whitemarsh, Pennsylvania, home for 19 hours on September 11–12, 1952. The family was released unharmed. In an interview with reporters, after the convicts departed, Hill stressed that the convicts had treated the family courteously, had not molested them, and had not been at all violent. The convicts were thereafter apprehended in a widely publicized encounter with the police that resulted in the killing of two of the convicts. Shortly thereafter the family moved to Connecticut. The Hills discouraged all efforts to keep them in the public spotlight.

A *Life* magazine article and photo essay, in February 1955, discussed the ordeal of a family trapped by convicts, and this incident lead to a Broadway play and movie, —*The Desperate Hours*. The story in the play and movie depicted the experience of a family of four held hostage by three escaped convicts in the family's suburban home. But, unlike the Hills' experience, the family of the story did suffer violence at the hands of the convicts; the father and son are beaten, and the daughter is subjected to a verbal sexual insult.

Life's article about the play was the subject of the cause of action. The complaint by the Hills sought damages on allegations that the *Life* article was intended to, and did, give the impression that the play mirrored the Hill family's experience, which, to the knowledge of *Life*, " . . . was false and untrue." Time Inc.'s defense was that the article was "... a subject of legitimate news interest ... a subject of general interest and of value and concern to the public," at the time of publication; and it was "... published in good faith without any malice whatsoever . . . " There were pictures in the article depicting the son of the family being roughed up by one of the convicts, the daughter biting one of the convicts to have him drop the gun he was holding, and the father throwing the gun out the door, trying to save his family.

The Supreme Court did find applicable the standard of knowing or reckless falsehood, but not through blind application of *New York Times Co. v. Sullivan*. The Court stated this is neither a libel action by a private individual nor a statutory action by a public official. Therefore, although the First Amendment principles pronounced in *New York Times* guided the conclusion, the Court reached that conclusion only by applying these principles in this discrete context—the *Hill* case.

Since the *Hill* case, many state courts have followed the Supreme Court opinion and now apply the *New York Times v. Sullivan* standard in false light cases.

Cantrell v. Forest City Publishing Co., 419 U.S. 245 (1974), was an opportunity for the Supreme Court to abandon the *Hill* decision, but the Court did not address the *Hill* issue. The Court upheld an invasion of privacy judgment against the publication the *Plain Dealer*, for printing "calculated falsehoods" and "reckless untruth."

In December 1967, Margaret Cantrell's husband Melvin was killed along with 43 others when the Silver Bridge across the Ohio River at Point Pleasant, West Virginia, collapsed. *The Plain Dealer* assigned a reporter named Eszterhas, to cover the story of the disaster. He wrote a "news feature" story focusing on the funeral of Melvin Cantrell, and the impact of his death on the Cantrell family.

Eszterhas and photographer Conway went to the Cantrell residence, where Eszterhas talked with the children, and Conway took 50 pictures. Mrs. Cantrell was not at home at any time during the hour to hour and a half that the men were at the Cantrell residence. Eszterhas' story appeared as the lead feature in the August 4,

1968, edition of the *Plain Dealer* Sunday Magazine. The article stressed the family's abject poverty, the children's old, ill-fitting clothes, and the deteriorating condition of the house. All were detailed in both the text and accompanying photographs. Eszterhas used the Cantrell family to illustrate the impact of the bridge collapse on the lives of the people in the Point Pleasant area.

It has been conceded that the story contained a number of inaccuracies and false statements. Most conspicuously, although Mrs. Cantrell was not present at any time during the reporter's visit to her home, Eszterhas wrote, "Margaret Cantrell will talk neither about what happened nor about how they are doing. She wears the same mask of non-expression she wore at the funeral. She is a proud woman. Her world has changed. She says that after it happened, the people in town offered to help them out with money and they refused to take it." Other significant misrepresentations were contained in details of Eszterhas' descriptions of the poverty in which the Cantrells were living, and the dirty and dilapidated conditions of the Cantrell home.

The case went to the jury on a so-called false light theory of invasion of privacy. In essence, the theory of the case was that by publishing the false feature story about the Cantrells, and thereby making them the objects of pity and ridicule, this damaged Mrs. Cantrell and her son William by causing them to suffer outrage, mental distress, shame, and humiliation.

The Supreme Court held that the story was published with "calculated falsehoods" and the jury was justified in finding the Cantrells were placed in a false light through knowing or reckless untruth. The Court did not find that the photos were actionable because there was no misrepresentation in the pictures.

Commercial Appropriation

Commercial appropriation, sometimes referred to as misappropriation or right of publicity, is when a person's name, likeness, catch phrase ("Here's Johnny" for a toilet), tangible object associated with the celebrity (a race car), the sound of his voice, or depicting them as a futuristic robot is used for commercial purposes without their consent.[12] There is no need for the person's entire name to be used, or even for every detail of his face or body be mimicked. The tort occurs as long as the person reasonably could be identified. Unlike the other aspects of invasion of privacy, this tort involves economic rights of well-known people, not personal rights of individuals that want to be left alone. Thus, celebrities file most of these lawsuits, where their name or likeness has commercial value. The issue is not that their name or likeness is being used, the issue is they are not being *paid* for its use.

In *Cher v. Forum International Ltd.*, 692 F.2d 634 (9th Cir. 1982), cert. denied, 462 U.S. 1120 (1983), Cher, a well-known singer and actress, sued a tabloid magazine and freelance writer, Fred Robbins, based on a published article billed as an "exclusive" interview with her.

She had given Robbins an interview for a story to be published in *Us* magazine. *Us* declined to publish the article. Robbins eventually sold the interview to *Forum* and *Star* magazines. Based on the headlines, cover page promotions, and related advertising, Cher alleged breach of contract, unfair competition, misappropriation of name and likeness, misappropriation of her right of publicity, and violations of the Lanham Act (federal trademark law).

The Ninth Circuit held, among other things, that Cher was not damaged by the *Star*'s allegedly exaggerated "exclusivity" claims, and the First Amendment protected the magazines from Cher's right of publicity claims, so long as, the publications were not published with actual malice.

However, the Ninth Circuit went on to hold that *Forum* misappropriated Cher's right of publicity, by falsely indicating that she had revealed facts to *Forum* that she would not reveal to a rival magazine, "There are certain things that Cher won't tell *People* and would never tell *Us*. She tells *Forum* ..." and by falsely indicating that she endorsed the magazine. The Ninth Circuit affirmed an award of $100,000 in special damages, $69,000 in general damages, and $100,000 in punitive damages.

Commercial appropriation does not bar the media from using a photo or information in a news story, whether the person does or does not give permission. The First Amendment protects the media in this instance. The problem is, to define the line between a news story and a commercial venue. The question to ask is, does the story or photo seriously impair the person's ability to make a profit? If the answer is yes, there is probably commercial appropriation.

In *Zacchini v. Scripps-Howard Broadcasting Co.*, 433 U.S. 562 (1977), the U.S. Supreme Court ruled on the issue as to what is newsworthy and what is a violation of an entertainer's state law, right of publicity.

In this case, Hugo Zacchini sued Scripps-Howard Broadcasting for airing, on the nightly news, a performance of his entire human cannonball act without his permission. Zacchini alleged unlawful appropriation of his professional property. The Ohio Supreme Court ruled in favor of Scripps-Howard, finding they were constitutionally protected to air newscasts of public interest, as long as these newscasts did not intend to injure or commercially appropriate information for use that was not privileged.

The U.S. Supreme Court held, Scripps-Howard's constitutional privilege to broadcast news events did *not* extend to airing Zacchini's entire act without his permission. This was categorically different from airing a news story, since it imposed a substantial threat to the economic value of the performance. Justice Powell Jr., Justice Brennan Jr., and Justice Marshall dissented saying this was news and Scripps-Howard was constitutionally privileged to air the segment.

To avoid the tort of commercial appropriation in using photos or information, make sure that it cannot be inferred by the reader this is an ad or an endorsement. Of course, always take into consideration when using a photo and text, that the person is not being put into a false light, as discussed earlier. Even though there may not be a cause of action for misappropriation, there may be one for false light, or even defamation.

Although commercial appropriation cases are usually tried in federal court, because there is usually **diversity of citizenship**—the plaintiff and defendant are from different jurisdictions—federal courts apply state law, because there is no applicable federal law in this cause of action.

One area of commercial appropriation that is not settled law is whether the right to sue survives the individual. Is this a personal right, so that only the person affected can bring suit, or is this a property right, the right to sue survives their death? The cases conflict in this area. In an attempt to resolve the issue, California passed the **Celebrity Rights Act** in 1985. The California Act gives heirs of a deceased celebrity the right to profit from the commercial use of their departed celebrity relative for 70 years after his death. This Act does not transcend state borders, however, and only applies to residents of California.

Take note, there may not only be commercial appropriation at issue in suits involving a deceased celebrity, there may be copyright issues as well, and as will be discussed in the chapter on copyrights, these are always property rights that survive the celebrity's or artist's death. Copyrights are federal law, and thus are applicable to all 50 states and beyond, and as long as the copyright has not expired, infringement on that copyright is actionable.

DEFENSES TO INVASION OF PRIVACY

The best defense to this tort is consent. If the person consents there is no invasion of privacy. As discussed earlier, be sure that the consent covers all aspects of the scope of the story—not only does the consent need to cover the interview or photo, but also it must include the publication of the information. Consent exceeded is no consent. Always use written releases. They are formal contracts signed by the individual interviewed or photographed. If that person is under 18, or appears to be mentally incompetent, then a parent or guardian will need to sign for them because these individuals are incapable of giving consent. Be careful that consent has not been revoked.

■ DIVERSITY OF CITIZENSHIP

Diversity of citizenship is a case involving questions that must be answered according to state law, but the case may be heard in federal court if the parties on the two sides of the case are from different states.

■ CELEBRITY RIGHTS ACT

The Celebrity Rights Act grants statutory post-mortem rights which prohibit the unsanctioned use of the "name, voice, signature, photograph or likeness on or in products, merchandise, or goods" of any person for 70 years after a celebrity's death.

■ **PUBLIC INTEREST OR NEWSWORTHY**

Public interest refers to the information that affects the well-being of the general public.

■ **TRUTH**

Truth is the actual state of things.

If the information is of **public interest or newsworthy**, courts usually will rule for the defendant in a privacy case. Public officials and public figures, and individuals that become involved in newsworthy events, have less right to privacy than a truly private person. Just be sure that the reporting is accurate and does not contain information that is not pertinent to the story.

Time v. Hill, cited previously, does provide some protection for the media in a false light case, as long as the information is not published with malice. **Truth** is also a defense in false light cases, although truth will *not* protect a reporter in publication of private facts.

Information lawfully obtained from court records is a constitutional defense to invasion of privacy. Avoid use of information that has not made it to public record; this can lead to invasion of privacy causes of action.

The next chapter will discuss other issues that affect the media in gathering the news, such as confidential sources, contempt, and access to documents and governmental records.

SUMMARY

The law of privacy is not one concept it is actually divided into four categories, depending on the wrong incurred by the individual: intrusion—when one intentionally intrudes on a person's solitude and into his private affairs; publication of private facts— publication of truthful information about the private life of a person that would be highly offensive; putting one in a false light—publishing information that is false or puts a person in a false light, this information is highly offensive and it is published with malice; and commercial appropriation—the use of a person's name or likeness for commercial gain.

Not all states recognize all four forms of invasion of privacy; some states allow suits for some of them.

Commercial appropriation, also referred to as misappropriation or right of publicity, involves a property right. False light, publication of private facts, and intrusion are personal rights. Because commercial appropriation is a property right, the right to sue may survive the individual whose property rights have been violated. Thus, the heirs of the individual suffering the misappropriation can sue on his behalf.

Defenses to invasion of privacy include consent, newsworthiness, truth in false light cases (although truth is not a defense in publication of private facts), and the information reported on was lawfully obtained from public records.

■ DISCUSSION QUESTIONS_____

1. Argue why a celebrity should *not* be able to sue for invasion of privacy, unless the invasion is totally egregious.

2. Discuss why the media should be allowed to enter a crime scene.

3. Argue for the government—why it should be allowed to continue its warrantless eavesdropping of U.S. citizens.

4. Discuss the rationale in not reporting alleged juvenile offenders' names.

5. Argue that sexual assault victims should always have their names withheld from the media.

6. What are the potential ramifications for the media of the *Stanton v. Metro* case, cited in footnote 10.

■ CASE FOR REVIEW_____

In *Deteresa v. ABC*, 121 F.3d 460 (9th Cir.1997) the Ninth Circuit U.S. Court of Appeals interpreted California privacy law. The court allowed an ABC producer secretly to tape and air a conversation between the producer and a reluctant interviewee. Beverly Deteresa was a flight attendant on the flight that took O. J. Simpson to Chicago the night of the murders of his ex-wife Nicole Brown Simpson and Ron Goldman. ABC had gone to Ms. Deteresa's condominium and asked her to appear on an ABC program concerning the flight. She refused, but as she knew that some of the facts regarding that flight that were being reported were false, she did speak to the producer on her porch. The producer called Ms. Deteresa and informed her that the conversation on the porch had been videotaped from a public street, and again asked her to appear on the show. She declined, and asked her husband to call ABC and tell them not to air the taped conversation. ABC did decide to air a five-second spot of the conversation, as well as a summary of Ms. Deteresa's recollections of Mr. Simpson on the flight. The U.S. appellate court held that Ms. Deteresa had no expectation of privacy when talking to a television producer on her porch, because her porch was viewable from a nearby street. Ms. Deteresa knew she was talking to the media and the conversation was viewable; thus, she could not reasonably expect the conversation to be a confidential communication. Would the new California Anti-Paparazzi Act apply to the *Deteresa* case? Why or why not? Would this taping be offensive to a reasonable person? Could it be argued, when Ms. Deteresa asked her husband to call ABC and tell them not to air the tape of the porch conversation, the conversation became a confidential communication?

■ KEY TERMS_____

Authorization for the use of Military Force	diversity of citizenship	public interest or newsworthy
California Anti-Paparazzi Act	false light	publication of private facts
Celebrity Rights Act	Foreign Intelligence Surveillance Act (FISA)	trespass
commercial appropriation	intrusion	truth
consent	newsworthy	U.S. National Security Agency (NSA)

■ ENDNOTES

[1] Ala. Code sec. 13A-11-31, 13A-11-32; Ark. Code sec. 5-16-101; Cal. Penal Code sec. 632; Del. Code Ann. Tit. 11 sec. 1335, 1336; Ga. Code Ann. sec. 16-11-60 to 16-11-64; Hawaii Rev. Stat. sec. 711-1111; Kan. Stat. Ann sec. 21-4001; Me. Rev. Stat. Ann. tit 17-A sec. 511; Mich. Comp Laws Ann. sec. 750.539d; Minn. Stat. sec. 609.746; N.H. Rev. Stat. Ann. sec. 644:9; S.D. Codified Laws Ann. sec. 22-21-1; Utah Code Ann. sec. 76-9-401, 76-9-403,76-9-702.7.

[2] Ala. Code sec. 13A-11-31, 13A-11-32; Del. Code Ann. Tit. 11 sec. 1335, 1336; Ga. Code Ann. sec. 16-11-60 to 16-11-64; Hawaii Rev. Stat. sec. 711-1111; Kan. Stat. Ann sec. 21-4001; Me. Rev. Stat. Ann. tit 17-A sec. 511; Mich. Comp Laws Ann. sec. 750.539d; Minn. Stat. sec. 609.746; S.D. Codified Laws Ann. sec. 22-21-1; Utah Code Ann. sec. 76-9-402.

[3] 18 U.S.C. sec. 2510 *et seq.* (1999) (Wire and Electronic Communications Interception and Interception of Oral Communications).

[4] Cal. Penal Code sec. 631, 632; Conn. Gen. Stat. sec. 52-570d; Fla. Stat. Ann. sec. 934.03; Ill. Rev. Stat. ch. 720, para. 5/14-1 to 5/14-6; Md. Code Ann., Cts & Jud. Proc. Sec 10-402; Mass. Ann. Law ch. 272, sec. 99; Mich. Comp. Laws sec. 750-539c; Mont. Code Ann. sec. 45-8-213; Nev. Rev. Stat. Ann. sec. 200.620; N.H. Rev. Stat. Ann. sec. 570-A:2; 18 Pa. Cons. Stat. Ann. sec. 5703, 5704; Wash. Rev. Code sec. 9.73.030.

[5] *American Civil Liberties Union v. National Security Agency*, Case No. 06-CV-10204 (S.D.E.D. Mich. 2006).

[6] *United States v. Falvey*, 540 F.Supp. 1306 (E.D.N.Y 1982).

[7] 50 U.S.C. section 1805(a)(3)(A).

[8] *American Civil Liberties Union v. National Security Agency*, Case No. 06-CV-10204 (S.D.E.D. Mich. 2006).

[9] Justice Warren, *U.S. v. Robel*, 389 U.S. 258 (1967) as quoted *ibid.*

[10] *Stanton v. Metro Corp.*, 438 F.3d 119 (1st Cir. 2006) a case that illustrates the potential issue of defamation, depending on the context in which the photo is shown. Ms. Stanton's picture had been used in an article depicting promiscuous teens. Even though there was a disclaimer printed with the picture, the Court of Appeals held, this was not enough to deprive Ms. Stanton of the right to sue for defamation.

[11] *Renwick v. News and Observer*, 312 S.E. 2d 405 (1984); *Cain v. Hearst Corp.*, 878 S.W. 2d 577 (1994); *Denver Publishing Co. v. Bueno*, 54 P.3d 892 (2002).

[12] *Carson v. Here's Johnny*, 698 F.2d 831 (9th Cir. 1983); *Motschenbacher v. R.J. Reynolds Tobacco*, 498 F.2d 821 (9th Cir. 1973) *Midler v. Ford Motor Co.*, 849 F.2d 460 (9th Cir. 1988), cert. denied sub nom *Young Rubican, Inc. v. Midler*; *Waits v. Frito-Lay, Inc.*, 978 F.2d 1093 (9th Cir. 1992), cert. denied, 506 U.S. 1080 (1993); *White v. Samsung*, 971 F.2d 1395 (9th Cir. 1992), cert. denied, 113 S.Ct. 2443 (1993).

Online Companion™
For additional resources, please go to
http://www.paralegal.delmar.cengage.com

Student CD-ROM
For additional materials, please go to the
CD in this book.

6

The News, The Courts, and Contempt

■ CHAPTER OUTLINE_____

I. The Media and the Courts
  A. Shield Laws
  B. Contempt of Court
  C. Confidential Sources and Current Contempt Cases
  D. Newsroom Searches
  E. Foreign Intelligence Surveillance Act
  F. Press Access to the News
  G. Freedom of Information
II. Press Credentials

■ OBJECTIVES_____

After completing this chapter, you will be able to:

- Know the role of the courts and how they affect the gathering of information, especially as to what a journalist is required to disclose in a judicial proceeding.

- Know how shield laws can protect the media from the judiciary, either with an absolute or qualified immunity.

- Know what contempt of court is, and what to do if found in contempt.

- Know how the media should handle newsroom searches and what to do if searched.

- Know what access the press has to information, such as the Freedom of Information Act.

- Know what press credentials are, who issues them, and what they allow a journalist to do.

THE MEDIA AND THE COURTS

The First Amendment guarantees freedom of speech and the freedom of the press. Yet these rights extend mainly to the publishing of information, not protection in gathering that information.

In 1972, the U.S. Supreme Court held in the *Branzburg v. Hayes* case, the right of a free press "could be eviscerated." (This case was also heard with two other cases —*In re Pappas*, on certiorari to the Supreme Judicial Court of Massachusetts, argued February 23, 1972, and *United States v. Caldwell*, on certiorari to the United States Court of Appeals for the Ninth Circuit, argued February 22, 1972.) All three cases had a common theme—reporters refused to answer grand juries' questions about potential criminal activity they had allegedly witnessed.

CASE STUDY **Branzburg v. Hayes**

408 U.S. 665 (1972)

Facts: Branzburg wrote an article that appeared in the *Courier-Journal*, a Louisville newspaper. The story discussed his observation of two people using and synthesizing hashish from marijuana. The article stated that the reporter had promised not to reveal the identity of the two hashish makers. Branzburg was subpoenaed by the Jefferson County, Kentucky, grand jury; he appeared but refused to identify the individuals he had seen possessing marijuana, or the persons he had seen making hashish from marijuana. A state trial court judge ordered Branzburg to answer these questions and rejected his contention that the Kentucky reporters' privilege statute, Ky. Rev. Stat. 421.100 (1962), the First Amendment of the U.S. Constitution, or the Kentucky Constitution authorized his refusal to answer.

The *In re Pappas* case dealt with a television newsman-photographer, Pappas, reporting on civil disorders in New Bedford, Massachusetts. He intended to cover a Black Panther news conference at the group's boarded-up store headquarters. Pappas found the streets around the store barricaded, but he ultimately gained entrance to the area and recorded and photographed a prepared statement read by one of the Black Panther leaders. He then asked for and received permission to reenter the area later in the evening. At that time, he was allowed to enter and remain inside Panther headquarters. As a condition of entry, Pappas agreed not to disclose anything he saw or heard inside the store except an anticipated police raid, which Pappas, "on his own," was free to photograph and report as he wished. Pappas stayed inside the headquarters for about three hours, but there was no police raid; thus, he wrote no story and did not otherwise reveal what had occurred in the store while he was there. Two months later, Pappas was summoned and appeared before the Bristol County Grand Jury. He answered questions as to his name,

(continues)

CASE STUDY **Branzburg v. Hayes** *(continued)*

address, employment, and what he had seen and heard *outside* Panther headquarters, but he refused to answer any questions about what had taken place inside headquarters, claiming that the First Amendment afforded him a privilege to protect confidential informants and their information.

United States v. Caldwell arose from subpoenas issued by a federal grand jury in the Northern District of California against Earl Caldwell, a reporter for the *New York Times*. He had been assigned to cover the Black Panther Party and other black militant groups. A subpoena was served, ordering him to appear before the grand jury to testify, and to bring with him notes and tape recordings of interviews given to him for publication by officers and spokesmen of the Black Panther Party. These notes and recordings concerned the aims, purposes, and activities of that organization. Caldwell objected to the scope of this subpoena. A second subpoena, omitted the documentary requirement, and simply ordered Caldwell "... to appear ... to testify before the Grand Jury." Caldwell and his employer, the *New York Times*, moved to **quash the subpoenas** based on the ground of their unlimited breadth, and if Caldwell had to appear in secret, before the grand jury, it would destroy his working relationship with the Black Panther Party and, "... suppress vital First Amendment freedoms ... by driving a wedge of distrust and silence between the news media and the militants." Caldwell argued, "... so drastic an incursion upon First Amendment freedoms [should not be permitted] in the absence of a compelling governmental interest—not shown here."

Issue:

The sole issue before the Supreme Court was what is the obligation of reporters to respond to grand jury subpoenas to answer questions concerning investigations into the commission of a crime?

Decision:

The U.S. Supreme Court held that citizens generally are not constitutionally immune from grand jury subpoenas; and neither the First Amendment nor any other constitutional provision protects the average citizen from disclosing to a grand jury information that they have received in confidence. The reporters involved in these cases claim that they are exempt from such obligations because if they were forced to testify as to their sources, or disclose other confidences, their informants would be reluctant to furnish information in the future. Thus, this burden compelling testimony from reporters is constitutionally suspect. The Court did not agree with the reporters.

Reason:

The Court stated the requirement the reporters disclose confidential information to a grand jury does serve a "compelling" and "paramount" state interest, and does not violate constitutional rights. "The role of the grand jury as an important instrument of effective law enforcement necessarily includes an investigatory function with respect to determining whether a crime has been committed and who committed it. To this end it must call witnesses, in the manner best suited to perform its task."

(continues)

■ **QUASH THE SUBPOENAS**

To quash a subpoena means to attempt to nullify or void it.

> **CASE STUDY** **Branzburg v. Hayes** *(continued)*
>
> Justice White, writing for the Court, stated that because there was no governmental intervention in imposing prior restraints, and no directive to publish sources or disclose them indiscriminately, then the Constitution is not violated.
>
> The Court stated that if a conditional privilege were granted to these reporters not to testify before a grand jury, then there would have to be a judicial interpretation of every time a reporter refused to testify, a path that the Court refused to follow. "We are unwilling to embark the judiciary on a long and difficult journey to such an uncertain destination. The administration of a constitutional newsman's privilege would present practical and conceptual difficulties of a high order."
>
> Although the Court did state that "[A]t the federal level, Congress has freedom to determine whether a statutory newsman's privilege is necessary and desirable and to fashion standards and rules as narrow or broad as deemed necessary to deal with the evil discerned and, equally important, to refashion those rules as experience from time to time may dictate. There is also merit in leaving state legislatures free, within First Amendment limits, to fashion their own standards in light of the conditions and problems with respect to the relations between law enforcement officials and press in their own areas." (These also are known as **shield laws**.)

■ **SHIELD LAWS**

Shield laws vary significantly from state to state, but most provide that privileged information cannot be obtained unless the party seeking the information can allege that the information is highly material and relevant to the case at issue; a compelling need exists for the information, and the information cannot be obtained by other means.

These cited cases were ruled on during a volatile time in United States history. At the time of *Branzburg*—the 1960s and 1970s—the United States experienced tremendous civil unrest because of tensions between blacks and whites in this country. The Black Panther Party was especially looked at with suspicion. The then chief of the Federal Bureau of Investigation (FBI), J. Edgar Hoover, viewed the Black Panther Party as one of "... the greatest threats to the internal security of the United States." Also the use of drugs in the 1960s was running rampant, and law enforcement was anxious to stop this criminal behavior.

Shield Laws

Shield laws vary significantly from state to state, but most provide that privileged journalistic information cannot be obtained unless the party seeking the information can allege that the information is highly material and relevant to the case at issue; a compelling need exists for the information, and the information cannot be obtained by other means. Shield laws for the media range from an absolute privilege in some states to laws that only apply if the information is actually published or broadcast, as well as to qualified or limited privileges, which the courts in that state can decide to allow or disregard.

Thirty-one states and the District of Columbia have statutory shield laws in place for journalists as of this writing.[1] These laws vary from state to state. New Mexico had a statutory shield law in place until 1976. In that year, the New Mexico Supreme Court ruled that the statutory shield law was an unconstitutional legislative encroachment on judicial prerogative, and held only the courts could decide the privilege.[2] California has placed its shield law in the California State Constitution to help protect it from judicial decision. In some states, there are no statutory shield laws, yet state courts have recognized some qualified privilege.[3] Utah has no shield law, although Utah lies in the Federal 10th Circuit, which does recognize a qualified privilege in civil cases applying to confidential information. It is possible that Utah would look to federal law to help decide the question of a reporters' privilege, as other states in the 10th Circuit have done. As of this writing, there are no Utah cases as to privilege. Hawaii[4] has no shield law, and does not recognize a reporter privilege, and Wyoming has no shield law and has not had any cases dealing with privilege.

As it was noted in *Branzburg*, the Supreme Court alluded to the fact that Congress did have the right to look into a federal shield law. In May 2007, a bipartisan coalition of House and Senate lawmakers vowed to pass federal legislation in 2007 to shield journalists from being forced under subpoena to reveal their confidential sources. Rep. Mike Pence (R-Indiana) and Rep. Rick Boucher (D-Virginia) spearheaded this initiative. Rep. Pence stated, "As a conservative who believes in limited government, I know the only check on government power in real time is a free and independent press." (This Bill called H.R. 2102: Free Flow of Information Act of 2007 has been passed in the House on October 16, 2007. The bill now goes on to be voted on in the Senate.)

Under this bill, disclosure of sources can only be compelled when a judge deems it necessary "to prevent imminent and actual harm to national security" and "to prevent imminent death or significant bodily injury." Furthermore, the bill would allow a court to compel disclosure of sources that reveal valuable trade secrets or personal financial information in violation of federal law. The bill also would require a court to balance the public's right to know interest, against the public interest in the free gathering of the news.

The Justice Department has not taken a stand on this bill, although in 2005 they came out opposing a federal reporters' shield law, stating to the Senate Judiciary Committee there is no need for a federal law since the rules in subpoenaing reporters have worked well for 33 years (since *Branzburg*), and to create a shield law could slow the Justice Department's subpoena process in case of national security threats. The Justice Department stated they only seek information about reporters' confidential sources when it truly matters.

The business community fears the 2007 bill will protect people who illegally obtain or leak legitimate private information, and allow them to cover their tracks by giving it to a reporter and hiding behind the proposed federal shield law.

Why, just recently, is there a call for a national shield law? Could it be the result of recent cases of journalists being imprisoned for **contempt of court** for not revealing confidential sources?

■ **CONTEMPT OF COURT**

Any willful disobedience to, or disregard of, a court order or any misconduct in the presence of a court; action that interferes with a judge's ability to administer justice or that insults the dignity of the court the judge has the power to declare the defiant person (called the contemnor) in contempt of court.

Contempt of Court

Contempt of court is now becoming a major issue for journalists. It is a court ruling that deems an individual "holds contempt for the court," be it the judicial process, or its powers. Contempt of court may be found if a journalist disobeys a lawful order of the court, disrupts court proceedings, shows disrespect for the judge, or publishes information that criticizes the judicial process. The background of this concept began when judges were given the power to control the courtroom. Penalties for contempt may include fines or jail time.

There are two types of contempt of court—**criminal contempt** and **civil contempt**. Criminal contempt is used to punish a journalist, for example, if it is clear that the reporter will not disclose the information wanted. Because it is a criminal charge, the individual charged with contempt (if she is facing more than six months in jail) has the constitutional right to trial by jury, to examine and call witnesses, and to testify on her own behalf.[5]

Civil contempt is not a criminal charge. It is a show of force by the court. In civil contempt, the journalist determines the time she spends in jail. With civil contempt, it is said that the "contemnor has the key to the jail door in her pocket." This means that if one cooperates with the court, she can be released from custody immediately.

Under the U.S. jurisprudence system, civil and criminal contempt are divided into two types—**direct contempt** and **indirect contempt**. Direct contempt occurs in the courtroom; the presiding judge decides summarily the individual has held contempt for the court. For the media, this form of contempt usually occurs near the court, or there is a refusal to obey a court order—for example, a reporter who refuses to reveal a source of information, or a photographer who violates a court order by taking a picture that the court did not allow. Direct contempt can be criminal or civil in nature, if the judge feels that the decorum of the court or respect for the court has been violated the judge can pass contempt sanctions immediately.

Indirect contempt does *not* occur in the immediate presence of the court; it consists of publishing information that criticizes a judge or the justice system, or other disrespectful acts, away from the courtroom. Indirect contempt can be civil or criminal in nature. This form of contempt was a major problem for journalists until 1941 when the U.S. Supreme Court curtailed the use of this charge against the media.

In 1941, the U.S. Supreme Court ruled in *Bridges v. California*, 314 U.S. 252, and in a companion case *Times-Mirror Company et al. v. Superior Court of State of California, in and for Los Angeles County* (cited with *Bridges*) that the indirect contempt orders issued in both cases were unconstitutional. Both convictions rested on comments pertaining to pending litigation.

In *Bridges*, Longshoreman Union leader Harry Bridges had sent a telegram to the U.S. Secretary of Labor threatening a West Coast dock strike if a court ruling that was not favorable to him was enforced. In the *Times* case, several antilabor editorials that the judge disliked brought on the contempt charge. Both publications were statements of possible future events. The U.S. Supreme Court prohibited contempt

CRIMINAL CONTEMPT

Criminal contempt occurs when the contemnor actually interferes with the ability of the court to function properly.

CIVIL CONTEMPT

Civil contempt occurs when the contemnor willfully disobeys a court order.

DIRECT CONTEMPT

Direct contempt occurs under the court's own eye

INDIRECT CONTEMPT

Contempt is indirect when it occurs out of the presence of the court, thereby requiring the court to rely on the testimony of third parties citations for such publications unless it was shown that the publications had created a *clear and present danger* to the judicial process. They had to be threats to justice that are imminent or immediate to allow contempt citations to prevail.

Five years later, in *Pennekamp v. Florida*, 328 U.S. 331 (1946), the Court held that the *Miami Herald* could not be held in contempt of court for publishing articles critical of the trial courts in Dade County, Florida. The articles criticized the courts for being more in favor of the criminals than the victims of the crimes. The U.S. Supreme Court ruled such articles were not a clear and present danger to the administration of justice in Florida. The Court stating, free discussion of issues is critical to the proper administration of justice.

In 1947, *Craig v. Harney*, 331 U.S. 367, the *Corpus Christi Caller-Times* was highly critical of a judge in his handling of a civil suit against a well-liked citizen of the area. The Supreme Court struck down the contempt of court conviction against the paper. The Court held contempt powers should not be used against a newspaper for what they print. For contempt citations to be upheld, the articles "must constitute an imminent, not merely a likely, threat to the administration of justice."

Thus, these three cases all but eliminated the potential for indirect contempt by the media, therefore leaving direct contempt as the remaining journalistic threat.

SIDEBAR

In England, the law of contempt is partially set in case law, and partly in the *Contempt of Court Act of 1981*. There is criminal contempt for contempt "in the face of the court " disobedience of a court order, and breaches of undertakings to the court. It is also contempt of court in England to bring a tape recorder or camera into an English court without consent of the court.

It is not contempt for a journalist to refuse to disclose her sources unless the court has deemed the information is, "… necessary in the interests of justice or national security or for the prevention of disorder or crime." Penalties for contempt violation are imprisonment for up to one month and a fine of £1500.

Under the Contempt of Court Act, there is strict liability to publish anything that may create a real risk of impeding an active case. The media cannot publish material that is too sensational until the trial is over.

Civil contempt in England occurs if a journalist fails to honor a subpoena requiring court attendance. A bench warrant is issued and the journalist can be arrested and imprisoned. (If the journalist sends a truly apologetic letter explaining why she did not attend, this will usually avoid imprisonment, although the arrest will be made and then bail will be set.) Failure to comply with a court order can also land a journalist in jail. (This rarely happens; again, a letter of apology or payment of a fine suffices.)

Confidential Sources and Current Contempt Cases

The cases of *Miller v. United States* and *Cooper v. United States*, petitions for writs of certiorari, highlight how a court uses its contempt powers.

CASE STUDY **Miller v. United States and Cooper v. United States**

Nos. 04-1507 and 04-1508 (2005)

During the spring and summer of 2003 (after the United States had entered Iraq to overthrow its leader, Saddam Hussein), a controversy arose concerning a statement made by President George W. Bush during the State of the Union address, delivered on January 28, 2003. In that address, President Bush stated: "The British government has learned that Saddam Hussein recently sought significant quantities of uranium from Africa." The implication was that Iraq was potentially using the uranium to create weapons of mass destruction, thus making Iraq a viable threat to the United States.

The accuracy of this statement was called into question by a series of articles, including one by Joseph C. Wilson IV, a retired career State Department official. This article was published in the *New York Times* on July 6, 2003. In this article, Wilson asserted that he had taken a trip to Niger in 2002, at the request of the Central Intelligence Agency (CIA), to investigate a report stating that Iraq had sought or obtained uranium from Niger. On his return, he reported his conclusion to the CIA—it was "highly doubtful that any such transaction had ever taken place." Wilson stated, "Some of the intelligence related to Iraq's nuclear weapons program was twisted to exaggerate the Iraqi threat."

On July 14, 2003, syndicated columnist Robert Novak published a column in the *Chicago Sun-Times* stating, "two senior administration officials" told him that Wilson had been selected for the Niger trip at the suggestion of Wilson's wife, whom Novak described as a CIA "operative on weapons of mass destruction."

After Novak's column was published, it was reported that government officials had told other reporters that Wilson's wife worked at the CIA monitoring weapons of mass destruction, and that she was involved in having her husband sent to Africa. Matthew Cooper related this information in an article published by *Time.com* on July 17, 2003, and later put it into print. The article mentioned Wilson's wife name—Valerie Plame—and stated, based on the comments by some government officials, she was involved in her husband's trip to Niger. On September 28, 2003, the *Washington Post* reported that in July 2003, "... two top White House officials called at least six Washington journalists and disclosed the identity and occupation of Wilson's wife."

In the fall of 2003, special prosecutor Patrick Fitzgerald, assigned to this case, issued subpoenas to several reporters, including Judith Miller of the *New York Times* and Matthew

(continues)

CASE STUDY **Miller v. United States and Cooper v. United States** *(continued)*

Cooper of *Time* magazine. Mr. Fitzgerald was seeking information as to whom had leaked CIA operative Plame's name to the media. A grand jury investigation into this matter began in January 2004.

Between January and May 2004, the grand jury determined that it was necessary to obtain information from Matthew Cooper of Time, Inc. and Judith Miller of the *New York Times* in regards to this investigation. Special Counsel first sought voluntary cooperation from Cooper and Miller. Cooper provided limited testimony. Then Fitzgerald issued a second broader subpoena; Cooper refused to comply with this second subpoena. On October 13, 2004, after a hearing, the district court held Cooper and Time, Inc. in civil contempt of court based on their refusal to comply with the subpoenas.

On August 12 and August 20, 2004, grand jury subpoenas were issued to reporter Judith Miller and the *New York Times* seeking documents and testimony related to conversations between Miller and a specified government official occurring between on or about July 6, 2003, and on or about July 13, 2003, "... concerning Valerie Plame Wilson ... concerning Iraqi efforts to obtain uranium." (Miller had done interviews and research for an article about Plame but never actually wrote a story.) Miller refused to comply, and the *New York Times* stated that they had no documents relating to the subpoenas. The district court held her in civil contempt of court.

Miller and Cooper were ordered to serve time in jail, and Cooper was fined $1,000 per day. The sentences were suspended pending appeal.

Cooper, Time, Inc., and Miller brought a consolidated appeal to the United States Court of Appeals for the District of Columbia Circuit. On February 15, 2005, a panel of the court of appeals affirmed the orders of the district court.

The panel was unanimous in its rejection of petitioners' claimed First Amendment privilege in the grand jury context. In the opinion for the court, the panel thoroughly analyzed *Branzburg v. Hayes* (see earlier) and found no material distinction between the facts of *Branzburg* and this case before the court of appeals, and held that *Branzburg* foreclosed petitioners' claim of protection based on a reporter's privilege rooted in the First Amendment. (The Branzburg decision stating a requirement that reporters disclose confidential information to a grand jury *does* serve a "compelling" and "paramount" state interest and does not violate constitutional rights.)

Thus Cooper and Miller had to comply with the subpoenas, or face jail time.

In April 2005, the case was appealed to the full District of Columbia Circuit; they refused to hear the case. A stay of execution was granted to Cooper and Miller until the U.S. Supreme Court decided to hear or not to hear the case.

(continues)

CASE STUDY **Miller v. United States and Cooper v. United States** *(continued)*

On June 27, 2005, the U.S. Supreme Court refused to grant certiorari. On July 1, *Time* editor-in-chief Norman Pearlstein agreed to turn over the information sought by the subpoenas, and Cooper agreed to testify, thus he was spared jail time. Judith Miller refused to comply and was taken into custody on July 6. She was held in jail until September 29 and was released after reaching an agreement with the special prosecutor. She testified before the grand jury on September 30, after her source I. Lewis "Scooter" Libby (Vice President Cheney's chief of staff) released her from her promise of confidentiality. Judith Miller ultimately resigned from the *New York Times* after 28 years of reporting. Ms. Miller is now advocating for a federal shield law. She states that without such a protection a free press cannot exist.

In October 2005, I. Lewis Libby was indicted on charges of perjury, obstruction of justice, and lying to FBI investigators probing into the Plame case. As of April 6, 2006, in grand jury testimony, Mr. Libby testified that Vice President Cheney had authorized him to disclose the Plame information. Vice President Cheney stated that he and the president have the authority to declassify information and release such information as needed. On April 8, 2006, President George W. Bush was implicated in the leak of Ms. Plame's name. As of September 9, 2006, Deputy Secretary of State Richard L. Armitage informed his superiors and the Justice Department he had been Novak's primary source for the Plame name leak. Why Armitage talked to Novak remains unclear, although he is known for his penchant to gossip, as well as for his skepticism concerning the Iraq war. Even with this news, "Scooter" Libby still faced criminal charges on the matter.

On March 6, 2007, I. Lewis "Scooter" Libby was convicted of obstruction, perjury, and lying to the FBI. On June 14, 2007, United States District Judge for the District of Columbia Reggie Walton denied Libby's request that he remain free pending his appeal of his two-and-a-half-year sentence. President Bush commuted Libby's 30-month prison sentence, leaving the other parts of his sentence intact. In commuting Libby's prison term, Bush stated: "I am commuting the portion of Mr. Libby's sentence that required him to spend thirty months in prison. ... My decision to commute his prison sentence leaves in place a harsh punishment for Mr. Libby. The reputation he gained through his years of public service and professional work in the legal community is forever damaged." After Libby paid his monetary fine and penalty totaling $250,400, Judge Walton queried aspects of the presidential commutation, and lawyers filed their briefs supporting Libby's serving supervised release, resolving the issue and thus clearing the way for Libby to begin the rest of his sentence, the two years of supervised release and 400 hours of community service.

Another case involving confidential sources and contempt highlights the issue not only of possible jail time or fines but also of actually losing a libel case by default. The loss of the defamation suit was based on the fact that if the media did not reveal the source of the information, they could not adequately defend themselves in the tort action. This case raised a problem—a public figure plaintiff was allowed to win a libel suit against the media without having to prove that the information published was false, or that it was published with actual malice.

In *Ayash v. Dana-Faber Cancer Institute*, 46 Mass. App. Ct. 384, 392-393 (1999), the *Boston Globe* ran a series of articles in 1995 dealing with the accidental chemotherapy overdoses of two patients at the Dana-Farber Cancer Institute, one of the patients was a *Globe* health columnist, Betsy Lehman. As a result of the overdose, Ms. Lehman died. The articles in the *Globe* were based on information gained from confidential sources. *Globe* reporter Richard A. Knox identified Dr. Lois Ayash as the leader of the medical team overseeing the chemotherapy treatment, and identified Dr. Ayash as one of the physicians that countersigned the order for the treatment. The *Globe* articles contained information about internal investigations into the incident, and corrective actions taken by Dana-Farber. The *Globe* did later publish a correction as to the countersigning of the treatment order by Dr. Ayash, but maintained that all the other information was correct.

Dr. Ayash sued the *Globe* and Dana-Farber for libel and breach of confidentiality. Ayash subpoenaed Knox to gain the identity of the person that disclosed the information as to the internal actions of Dana-Farber. Ayash maintaining this information should have been kept confidential.

The Massachusetts Superior Court conducted a required "balancing test" to determine if disclosure of the identity of the source of information was required for Ayash's suit. The court held that Ayash's need for this information is "... tangible and substantial and outweighs the public interests in protecting the free flow of information."[6]

Knox and the *Globe* refused to reveal their confidential source, and the court found them in contempt. This ultimately led to a default judgment of $2.1 million in favor of Ayash. This amount based on evidence that the *Globe* articles impugned the plaintiff, and thus affected her career and caused her emotional and psychological anguish.

In February 2005, the Massachusetts Supreme Judicial Court upheld the lower court ruling. On October 3, 2005, the U.S. Supreme Court refused to hear an appeal by the *Globe*.[7] The Supreme Court justices had been urged by the Associated Press and more than a dozen media companies and journalist associations to review the case. The media stating, a review of this case was important for protecting news sources, a subject of special interest with the jailing of *New York Times* reporter Judith Miller for contempt (supra), and the ruling against the *Globe* is constitutionally problematic because it allows a public-figure plaintiff—Ayash, to recover damages for libel without having to prove the publication was false, or that the *Globe* acted with actual malice, this ruling *contra* to *New York Times v. Sullivan*.

The *Miller*, *Cooper*, and *Ayash* cases bring up the issue of what a reporter's obligation to a confidential source is. Did Judith Miller, Richard Knox, and the *Globe* go too far in protecting their confidential sources?

In light of such cases, many news organizations have reexamined their views on promises of unconditional confidentiality of a source. Some editors have decided to overrule such agreements to avoid potential contempt citations or legal difficulties for the publication. Journalists must become familiar with the policies of their own news organization as to how much they can promise in keeping a source confidential, and how far their organization will support them in case a subpoena is issued seeking the identity of the source.

What to Do if Subpoenaed

First of all do not panic, no one will show up at the door with an arrest warrant. All a subpoena is asking is for the journalist to appear at a deposition (discovery) or other court proceeding to answer specific questions, or to supply certain documents.

A subpoena cannot be ignored, to do so is contempt of court and could result in fines or jail time. When a subpoena is received, the following steps must be followed:

1. Consult an attorney. The legal counsel for the news organization must be notified immediately.

2. The attorney will determine if there is a shield law in place that will protect the journalist or the publication from court proceedings. If there is no shield law applicable for the jurisdiction, the attorney will look to see if there is common law (case law) or constitutional law that may act as a form of shield. (See earlier as to shield laws.)

3. The attorney and the editor of the news organization will then determine a strategy as to how to deal with the subpoena. Both will look to the information requested and the publication's policy as to subpoena compliance. If the material has been published, usually the materials will be turned over voluntarily. If the material consists of reporter's notes, interviews, or exposing confidential sources, most news organizations will not automatically comply with the subpoena. Do not attempt to destroy the information requested in the subpoena. This is only inviting more legal problems, and it is, potentially, obstruction of justice.

4. As a journalist, the subpoena policy of the publication worked for must be followed. If there is no policy, it is important one be established to avoid legal problems. If the publication's policies conflict with the journalist's policies as to revealing sources or turning over journalistic notes, the journalist should hire separate legal counsel as further protection.

Newsroom Searches

The media potentially face subpoenas for revelation of information, or documents obtained in the newsgathering process. However, as of 1978, the U.S. Supreme Court ruled warrants could be issued to search a reporter's home or a newsroom if there is possible evidence of a crime to be found. In *Zurcher v. Stanford Daily*, 436 U.S. 547 (1978), rehearing denied 439 U.S. 885, the Court upheld the searching of a college newspaper newsroom for evidence that would potentially identify demonstrators that injured several policemen.

The facts of the case are: in April 1971, nine police officers were injured when they sought to remove demonstrators from the administrative offices of Stanford University's Hospital. The officers could only identify two of the assailants, but they did notice someone taking pictures during the melee.

Two days later, the *Stanford Daily*, a student newspaper, published a special edition of the paper, in which pictures of the attack on the police were printed. The next day, the District Attorney's office secured a warrant to search the newsroom of the paper, allowing a search for negatives, film, and pictures depicting the demonstration at the Stanford Hospital. The warrant was based solely on the statements that there was probable cause to believe that there were photographs depicting the assault in the newsroom; the warrant was not based on any assertion that the paper or its staff had committed a crime.

Four officers searched the newsroom and did not find any other pictures than those already published. They left without taking anything.

The *Stanford Daily*, and some staff members, filed suit in U.S. District Court against the officers who had conducted the search, the chief of police, the assistant district attorney, the district attorney, and the judge who had issued the warrant.

The suit alleged the search had deprived the paper and its staff their rights under the First, Fourth, and Fourteenth Amendments. The District Court ruled that the Fourth and Fourteenth Amendments prohibit search warrants for third parties not suspected of involvement in a crime, unless it can be proven that the third party will ignore a subpoena or destroy needed documents.

The District Court also held that if the search involves a newspaper, the First Amendment places further limits on issuing a warrant. A warrant would only be appropriate if materials would be destroyed or removed, and a restraining order would be ineffective.

The Ninth Circuit Court of Appeals agreed with the District Court's findings, and the case was appealed to the U.S. Supreme Court.

Justice White, writing for the Court, disagreed with the lower courts and held the interest of the state is the same as to uncovering evidence relating to a crime whether the area to be searched belongs to a suspect or nonsuspect of the crime.

Thus, innocent third parties have no greater protection from searches than guilty parties, and the interests of law enforcement outweigh an individual's privacy. Newsrooms do not merit different or higher standards for issuance of search warrants. The Court found sufficient media protection under the First Amendment cases requiring courts to "apply the warrant requirements with particular exactitude," and newsroom searches do not constitute the threat of prior restraints.

The Court refused to reinterpret the Fourth Amendment as to imposing a constitutional barrier against warrants in the search of newspaper premises.

In reaction to this ruling, Congress passed the **Privacy Protection Act of 1980**. This act limits the circumstances under which law enforcement may obtain warrants for a journalist's "work product," or "documents." These items may be seized under a search warrant if "... there is probable cause to believe that the person possessing such materials has committed or is committing the criminal offense to which the materials relate," or if the information is needed to prevent death or serious injury to someone. Work products and documents may be searched for and seized if they are related to national defense or child pornography.

Documents may be seized, under a search warrant, if the advance notice, provided by a subpoena, would possibly result in destruction of the materials, or if the subpoena would be ignored, or all legal remedies have been exhausted to enforce the subpoena, and to further delay the obtaining of the materials would "threaten the interests of justice."[8]

Although the Privacy Protection Act applies to federal, state, and local searches, eight states have implemented their own search warrant acts. Some of these acts provide more protection for the media—the requirement search warrants are only directed to parties suspected of actually committing the crime.[9] (Hopefully, this excludes the journalist.)

■ PRIVACY PROTECTION ACT OF 1980

The Privacy Protection Act of 1980 protects journalists from being required to turn over to law enforcement any work product and documentary materials, including sources, before it is disseminated to the public.

SIDEBAR

If presented with a search warrant, call the news organization's attorney immediately. Try to have the attorney review the warrant before the search, if possible. If the search proceeds under the warrant, it should be videotaped. There is no requirement that the newsroom staff assist with the search, but they cannot impede it, either.

Consult with the organization's attorney as to whether to file suit or seek an administrative hearing as to the search. There may be sanctions available against the officials that violated the Privacy Protection Act, or a judge may do an emergency review of the warrant.

Foreign Intelligence Surveillance Act

Congress passed the Foreign Intelligence Surveillance Act (FISA) in 1978. This created a court that has powers to issue warrants that allow officials to secretly wiretap communication devises and perform searches. Proceedings under FISA are done without the person knowing they are under investigation.

With the passage of the USA Patriot Act, after the attacks on the World Trade Center in 2001, the powers of the FISA courts were expanded. Under the Patriot Act, an investigator only needs to show the issue concerns national security to obtain a FISA warrant. The media's concern with such warrants is that because the investigation is done in secret, there is no way for a journalist to know if her confidential sources are being compromised.

The Patriot Act allows government officials to obtain an order from the FISA court to take any documents from a business (including a newsroom) that may affect foreign intelligence. Thus, a news organization could likely be a potential subject to such an investigation, and again potentially compromising a journalist's confidential source.[10] This aspect of the Patriot Act allows for such searches despite the provisions of the Privacy Protection Act.

Press Access to the News

So what access does the press have in gathering news information? In 1974, in *Pell v. Procunier*, 417 U.S. 817, the United States Supreme Court held the press had no greater rights in access in gathering the news than the general public. In the *Pell* case, four California prison inmates and three professional journalists brought suit challenging the constitutionality of regulation 415.071 of the California Department of Corrections Manual, which provides that "... [p]ress and other media interviews with specific individual inmates will not be permitted." The provision was put in place following a violent prison episode that correction authorities attributed, at least in part to, the former policy of face-to-face prisoner-press interviews. These interviews had resulted in a few inmates gaining a disproportionate influence with other prisoners, and this practice potentially created, "... a *clear and present danger* [emphasis added] to prison security."

The Court held that the press could interview inmates randomly but could not freely interview certain prisoners. In the *Pell* case, the media plaintiffs contend that 415.071 constitutes governmental interference with their newsgathering activities, and that no substantial governmental interest can be shown to justify the denial of press access to specifically designated prison inmates.

> "More particularly, the media plaintiffs assert that, despite the substantial access to California prisons and their inmates accorded representatives of the press—access broader than is accorded members of the public generally—face-to-face interviews with specifically designated inmates is such an effective and superior method of newsgathering that its curtailment amounts to unconstitutional state interference with a free press."

The Court did not agree. The Court held that the Constitution does not impose on government the duty, "... to make available to journalists sources of information not available to members of the public generally."

In 1978, the Supreme Court again denied journalists access to a particular part of a prison where an inmate had committed suicide. Although journalists argued the conditions in the prison were of public concern, the Court held journalists have no constitutional right of access to prisons. Chief Justice Burger, writing for the court, stated that if journalists want to know about prison conditions, they could interview individuals that knew of the prison conditions, such as former inmates, and attorneys that visit the prison.[11]

At the end of August 2006, the California legislature passed SB 1521, sponsored by State Senator Romero (no known relation to the author). This bill, titled "Media Access to Prisons," would restore the ability of journalists to conduct prearranged face-to-face interviews with prison inmates. Governor Schwarzenegger vetoed two previous versions, expressing concerns that inmate interviews could "glamorize criminals," and, as of October 2006, he vetoed SB 1521.

Accident or Crime Scenes

A journalist must follow police protocols as to reasonable restrictions at accident or crime scenes. The media cannot interfere with emergency situations, nor can they affect any evidence of a crime.

The courts usually stand behind journalists that act reasonably to get information. Courts have held that as long as the press is not unreasonably interfering with police procedures, there is a First Amendment privilege for them to be at the scene and be left alone. Although the courts have not looked favorably at the media that blatantly ignores police instructions—either interfering with police activities, or putting themselves in harm's way. In a 1990 New Hampshire case, a federal district court held a news photographer had the right to be at a car accident scene.[12]

A reporter cannot conceal or destroy evidence of a crime, nor can she tamper with a witness, informant, or any other source of information, regardless if this information is later admissible or not in a court proceeding.[13] Nor should a reporter inadvertently become a weapons transport or become any other means of escape or avoidance of capture by the alleged criminal.[14]

Or should the reporter be the one who accidentally warns the alleged criminal of impending discovery or apprehension?[15] This actually happened in 1993, when a reporter asked for directions to a roadblock outside of the Branch Davidian compound near Waco, Texas. The reporter told compound lookouts that FBI agents were on the way. When the agents arrived at the scene, many lives were lost in an intense gunfight.[16]

Freedom of Information

Enacted in 1966, **The Freedom of Information Act (FOIA)**, 5 U.S.C. Section 552, is a federal law that establishes the public's and the media's right to obtain information from federal government agencies. Anyone can file a FOIA request,

■ **THE FREEDOM OF INFORMATION ACT (FOIA)**

The Freedom of Information Act (FOIA) is a federal law that establishes the public's and the media's right to obtain information from federal government agencies.

including U.S. citizens, foreign nationals, organizations, the media, and universities. After the Watergate scandal in 1974, the act was amended to make government more transparent, and in 1996 the FOIA was expanded to electronic information.

FOIA applies to all executive branch departments, agencies, and offices; federal regulatory agencies; federal corporations; Congress; and the federal courts. Records obtainable include photographs, printed documents, videos, electronic records, and e-mail, as long as the items were created or obtained by the federal agency and are, at the time that the record is requested, in the agency's possession and control.

Exempt from the FOIA is national security information; internal personnel rules and practices; confidential business information; inter- or intra-agency communication that is subject to any deliberative process; litigation and other privileges; if the information involves personal privacy issues; certain law enforcement records; financial institution information; geological information; and any information exempt under other laws.

Once an agency receives a formal request for information (each agency has its own forms to fill out), it is supposed to either supply the record or explain why the request is denied, within 20 business days.

In a 1999 federal appellate court case concerning the FOIA, the court stated, "Congress gave agencies 20 days, not years, to decide whether to comply with" FOIA requests. Although the FOIA poses difficulties for federal agencies, the judicial branch cannot repeal a law enacted by Congress by a "construction that vitiates any practical utility it [FOIA] may have." In this case, in which a plaintiff's FOIA request required the processing of voluminous materials but had been pending for more than six years, clearly the practicality of the FOIA is in question.[17]

FOIA requests are not free. In 1974, an amendment to FOIA required all agencies to publish lists of accessible records and their fees for making copies. Fees may be waived or reduced if the agency feels the release of the document would benefit the general public. In 1986, the FOIA was amended by Congress to reduce fees charged to news organizations and nonprofit educational or scientific agencies. Journalists and nonprofits usually do not have to pay for the time searching for the information, while businesses requesting such information do.

If the agency does not comply with providing the requested information, the journalist can sue, and if successful in the suit recover legal costs from the government, but if the journalist loses there will be a large legal bill to pay.

Of course, the major issue with the FOIA in recent years is the fact that the federal bureaucracy has tried to weaken the act. In 1982, Congress restricted access to information as to the Central Intelligence Agency. The **Intelligence Identities Protection Act** made it a crime to engage in activities that would identify and expose covert CIA agents. (See the Judith Miller case earlier in this chapter.)

In 1986, Congress authorized the FBI and other federal law enforcement agencies to reject FOIA requests without confirming or denying the existence of such information. Thus, there is no way to know if a FBI report exists or not, although, under the 1974 Privacy Act, individuals have a limited right to inspect their own files.[18]

■ **INTELLIGENCE IDENTITIES PROTECTION ACT**

The Intelligence Identities Protection Act is a U.S. federal law that makes it a federal crime to intentionally reveal the identity of an agent whom one knows to be in or recently in certain covert roles with a U.S. intelligence agency.

In December 2005, President Bush issued Executive Order 13,392 to establish new FOIA compliance and review policies for federal agencies. It, "... calls upon all agencies to improve their FOIA operations with both efficiency and customer service in mind. Pursuant to this first-of-its-kind FOIA executive order, the head of each federal agency now has designated a Chief FOIA Officer to oversee all ongoing agency implementation activities under it, as well as the agency's administration of the FOIA overall."[19]

There are also state public records laws, and all 50 states have them. Access is usually denied for personnel records, law enforcement investigation records, records of juvenile courts, and adoptions. Access to state public records has to be balanced with an individual's right to privacy. Most states have privacy statutes that limit access to personal information.

As with the FOIA, most states allow judicial review if access to a permissible record is denied, and some allow payment of attorney's fees if the requester of the information is successful in the suit.

Open Meeting Laws

Each state has its own open meeting laws. These laws usually apply to state and local governmental sessions. At these open meetings anyone can attend, as long as they do not create a disturbance. Not all meetings are open; for example, if the issue involves pending lawsuits, national security, or a personnel issue, the meeting may be closed to the public. It is up to the journalist to determine which meeting is available for coverage.

It took until 1976 for the federal government to enact an open-meeting law—the **Government in the Sunshine Act**. Under this law, it requires some 50 administrative agencies to allow access to public meetings. Closed sessions are still allowed for the same items exempted from the FOIA (see earlier), and there can be closed meetings if the issue is pending litigation or other judicial matters.[20]

A journalist may initiate litigation against the federal government if there is a violation of the Sunshine Act, and federal district courts can issue injunctions ordering the agency to comply with the law.

■ **GOVERNMENT IN THE SUNSHINE ACT**

The Government in the Sunshine Act was intended to create greater openness in government. The purpose of the act is to provide the public with information while protecting the rights of individuals and the ability of the government to carry out its responsibilities.

> **SIDEBAR**
>
> All over the world, freedom of information (FOI) is an extremely important issue for journalists and citizens alike. Some countries are doing well with the concept, but some are struggling with their FOI laws.
>
> A draft of a freedom of information bill was proposed formally in the Cayman Islands. The Cayman Island's journalists have stated that they hope their FOI bill will be similar to the U.S. or the U.K. laws.
>
> *(continues)*

SIDEBAR   *(continued)*

The Indian freedom of information law guarantees public inspection of information held by governmental agencies, but the fees charged are often prohibitive for many in India.

Germany has a Federal Freedom of Information Act, but the fees are high, and no information will be given unless payment is made in advance.

Mexico's Federal Institute for Access to Public Information is an attempt by Mexico to increase government transparency.

PRESS CREDENTIALS

The function of press credentials or press passes is to identify reporters and other members of the press at police and fire lines or barricades, and to allow the bearers to pass such lines. Press passes are normally provided on request of an officer or administrator of a particular medium on behalf of the firm's reporters. The local police department will usually issue a journalist's press pass; sometimes the event itself will issue the appropriate credentials.

Courts may limit media credentials in a specific case, but it cannot do so arbitrarily. Credentials cannot be refused because of the potential content of the journalist's work. In 1971, an Iowa case held that credentialing systems must use "narrow and specific standards which advance a compelling state interest."[21] In this case, the publication complained it had been denied press passes, even though the police department had issued such passes to the staffs of other media. The publication was given no criteria by the government on how to obtain press passes for its reporters, and as such was given no specific standard on how to comply to receive the proper credentials. The court held that this practice by the police department served to penalize or restrain the exercise of a First Amendment right.

In *Consumers Union of the U.S. v. Periodical Correspondents' Association*, 515 F.2d 1341 (DCC 1975), it was held; rules as to credentialing are fashioned so that *due process* is provided before denying press credentials. There must be opportunity for adequate impartial review if a publication is denied such credentials. Thus, Fifth and Fourteenth Amendment due process issues must be addressed if credentialing is denied.

In the next chapter, we will look further into the gathering of information—what can and cannot be acquired under copyright and trademark law.

SUMMARY

In *Branzburg*, it was held that there was no privilege of the media to refuse to disclose confidential information to a grand jury. The grand jury does serve a "compelling" and "paramount" state interest and it does not violate constitutional rights to require a reporter to reveal such information.

Shield laws vary significantly from state to state, but most provide that privileged information cannot be obtained unless the party seeking the information can allege that the information is highly material and relevant to the case at issue; a compelling need exists for the information; and the information cannot be obtained by other means. A federal shield law has been introduced in Congress; it has been passed by the House, and awaits a Senate vote.

Contempt of court—showing disrespect for the court—is becoming more of a problem for journalists. There is criminal and civil contempt, and these can be direct or indirect. Penalties for contempt can be fines and/or jail time.

Subpoenas are orders for an individual to appear in court to testify, or to produce documents the court asks for. Subpoenas cannot be ignored or the journalist potentially faces contempt charges. Subpoenas must be discussed with the news organization's editor and attorney to determine what strategy will be used in answering this order.

The U.S. Supreme Court in the *Zurcher* case held that the media have no special rights as to the issuing of warrants to search a newsroom, whether or not the media is an innocent third party. In 1980, the Privacy Protection Act attempted to limit the issuing of warrants for such searches. Eight states have enacted similar limitations on the issuance of such warrants.

The Foreign Intelligence Surveillance Act of 1978 (FISA) established a court that can secretly wiretap and perform searches, and the USA Patriot Act of 2001 expanded FISA's powers.

The *Pell* and *Houchins* cases held that the media has no greater right to gather the news than the public. The media cannot interfere with police activities, and should heed reasonable police requests.

The Freedom of Information Act (FOIA) is a federal law that establishes the public's and the media's right to obtain information from federal government agencies.

Press credentials are issued so that a journalist may pass police or fire barricades, or gain other access to better cover the story.

■ DISCUSSION QUESTIONS

1. Argue why a reporter should not be required to reveal their confidential sources.
2. Does requiring a reporter to give information gathered in confidence to the grand jury interfere with the gathering of the news?
3. Would a federal shield law help journalists? Why or why not?
4. Discuss both sides of a court's power to imprison a journalist for contempt of court.
5. Did Judith Miller deserve 85 days in jail for not revealing her source?
6. How did the award of $2.1 million in the *Ayash* suit affect the media?

7. Argue why the police should have the right to search a newsroom or a journalist's home without the need to show the news organization or the journalist committed a crime.

8. In recent years, the Freedom of Information Act has been called the Freedom From Information Act. Which is true? Why?

■ CASE FOR REVIEW

After the *Branzburg* case, in late 1972, the Second Circuit U.S. Court of Appeals ruled a journalist has a constitutional right not to reveal their sources under certain circumstances (*Baker v. F & F Investments*, 470 F.2d 778 (2d Cir. 1972) cert. denied, 411 U.S. 966 (1973). The *Baker* case involved an article exposing the practice of "blockbusting"—when real estate agents try to panic a neighborhood by disclosing that a black family was moving into the neighborhood. In the 1970s, this usually caused property values to plummet in the area, thus allowing real estate agents to make money when white homeowners sold their homes at a discount. Unlike *Branzburg*, *Baker* was a civil lawsuit between black homebuyers and the real estate firms attempting to panic the white homeowners. In *Baker*, the journalist's source for the information in the article was someone in the real estate business. The writer of the article feared harassment if they revealed their source. The appellate court ruled that this case was different than *Branzburg* because it was a civil suit, not a grand jury investigation, and thus the journalist could keep their source confidential under the protections afforded in the First Amendment. What is the difference between a criminal and civil trial as to keeping a source confidential?

■ KEY TERMS

civil contempt

contempt of court

criminal contempt

direct contempt

Government in the Sunshine Act

indirect contempt

Intelligence Identities Protection Act

Privacy Protection Act of 1980

quash the subpoenas

shield laws

The Freedom of Information Act (FOIA)

■ ENDNOTES

[1] Code of Alabama Sec. 12-21-142, Alaska Statutes Sec. 09.25.300, Arizona Revised Statutes Sec. 12-2237, Arkansas Code Sec. 16-85-510, California Code Sec. 1070, Colorado Revised Statutes 13-90-119, Delaware Code Sec. 4321, District of Columbia Code Sec. 16-4702, Florida Statutes Sec. 90.5015, Official Code of Georgia Annotated Sec. 24-9-30, Illinois Compiled Statutes Sec. 735 ILCS 5/8-901, Indiana Statutes Sec. 34-46-4-2, Kentucky Revised Statutes Sec. 421.100, Louisiana Revised Statutes Sec. 45:1452, Annotated Code of Maryland Sec. 9-112, Michigan Compiled Laws Service Sec. 767.5a, Minnesota Statutes 595.022, Montana Code Annotated 26-1-902, Nebraska Revised Statutes Sec. 20-146, Nevada Revised Statutes Sec. 49.275, New Jersey Statutes Sec. 2A:84A-21, New Mexico, New York Consolidated Law Sec. 79-h, North Carolina General Statutes Sec. 8-53.11, North Dakota Century Code Sec. 31-01-06.2, Ohio Revised Code Sec. 2739.04, Oklahoma Statutes Sec. 2506, Oregon Revised Statutes 44.520, Pennsylvania Consolidated Statutes Sec. 5942, General Laws of Rhode Island Sec. 9-19.1-2, South Carolina Code Sec. 19-11-100, and Tennessee Code Annotated 24-1-208.

[2] *Ammerman v. Hubbard Broadcasting*, 89 NM 307, 551 P.2d 1354 (1976).

[3] Connecticut, Idaho, Iowa, Kansas, Maine, Massachusetts, Mississippi, Missouri, New Hampshire, South Dakota, Texas, Vermont, Virginia, Washington, West Virginia, and Wisconsin.

[4] *Appeal of Goodfader*, 45 Haw. 317 (Haw. 1961).

[5] *Bloom v. Illinois*, 391 U.S. 194 (1968), *Baldwin v. New York*, 399 U.S. 117 (1970).

[6] *Ayash v. Dana-Farber Cancer Institute*, 13 Mass L. Rep. 1 (Mass. Super. 2001).

[7] *Globe Newspaper Co. v. Ayash*, (docket #: 04-1634) (2005).

[8] 42 U.S.C. section 2000aa.

[9] Cal. Penal Code section 1524 (g); Connecticut General Statutes sections 54-33i and j; Illinois Statutes Chapter 38 section 108-3; Nebraska Revised Statutes section 29-813 (2); New Jersey Statutes section 2A:84A-21.9; Oregon Revised Statutes section 44:520(2); Texas Code Criminal Procedure, article 18.01(e); Washington Revised Code section 10.79.015(3).

[10] 50 U.S.C. sections 1801-1811.

[11] *Houchins v. KQED*, 438 U.S. 1 (1978).

[12] *Connell v. Town of Hudson*, 733 F.Supp. 465 (D.N.H. 1990).

[13] Model Penal Code section 242.3 (c). The purpose of the Model Penal Code was to stimulate and assist legislatures in making a major effort to appraise the content of the criminal law.

[14] Model Penal Code section 242.3 (b).

[15] Model Penal Code section 242.3 (d).

[16] *Risenhoover v. England*, 936 F.Supp 392, 401 (W.D. Tex. 1995).

[17] *Fiduccia v. Department of Justice*, 185 F.3d 1035 (9th Cir. 1999).

[18] 5 U.S.C. 552a.

[19] http://www.usdoj.gov.

[20] 5 U.S.C. 552b.

[21] *Quad-City Community News Service v. Hon. John H. Jebens*, 334 F.Supp. 8 (Cal. 1971).

Online Companion™
For additional resources, please go to
http://www.paralegal.delmar.cengage.com

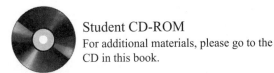

Student CD-ROM
For additional materials, please go to the
CD in this book.

CHAPTER 7

Copyrights and Marks

CHAPTER OUTLINE

■ OBJECTIVES_____

After completing this chapter, you will be able to:

- Know what can be copyrighted and when copyright protection comes into effect.

- Know when copyright infringement occurs, and how to avoid it.

- Know what a work for hire is, and who holds the copyright if it is a work for hire.

- Know what Fair Use means—what can be used of a copyrighted work, without infringing on the copyright.

- Define misappropriation and unfair competition with regard to use of copyrighted materials.

- Understand the Digital Millennium Copyright Act—what its parameters are as to copyrighted works.

- Know what a trademark and service mark is, how to get one, and how to defend them from going back into generic terms.

INTRODUCTION TO COPYRIGHTS

■ **COPYRIGHTS**

Copyrights are a group of exclusive rights granted by the federal government, which can be obtained for a variety of intellectual works from movies to literature.

Copyrights are a group of exclusive rights granted by the federal government. The Congress of the United States has the power "[T]o promote the progress of science and useful arts, by securing for limited times to authors and inventors the exclusive right to their respective writings and discoveries." This is known as the Intellectual Property Clause.[1]

The issuance of a copyright gives the owner of the copyright the right to reproduce the copyrighted work. It means only that the owner of the copyright can produce *derivative* works (those works that are based on the original copyrighted material). A copyright protects its owner based on the *form of expression of the work*. It does not cover the idea, facts, style, or technique of the work. For example, only J. K. Rowling can allow her series of *Harry Potter* books be made into movies, but the copyright on the books and movies does not protect Ms. Rowling from another author writing a totally different fantasy based on the lives of wizards, and ultimately putting that book into a movie medium.

Copyrights can be obtained for a variety of intellectual works—literary works, movies, dances and ballets, musical compositions and recordings, art pieces, software, photographs, and television broadcasts. In March 2006, Congress proposed fashion designs be made part of copyright law.[2]

Some forms of expression cannot be copyrighted. One of the most important exceptions to copyrights, for the media, are that the facts of the news cannot obtain a copyright. Only the description of the event can be protected. Although this is not good for the first journalist on the scene, because other journalists will be able to report on the same incident, with a different description, it is good news for the journalist arriving at the scene later, because they can report on the news albeit with a different depiction of the event. Thus, journalists are constantly rewriting each other's news stories.

When Does Copyright Protection Attach?

Copyright protection is automatic. Once the work is completed, and fixed in a **tangible medium of expression**, the creator of the work obtains a common law copyright whether or not they actually register the work with the federal government, although there are advantages to actual registration:

- Registration establishes a public record of the copyright claim.

- Before an infringement suit may be filed in court, registration is necessary for works of U.S. origin.

- If made before or within five years of publication, registration will establish prima facie evidence, in court, of the validity of the copyright and of the facts stated in the certificate.

- If registration is made within three months after publication of the work, or before an infringement of the work, statutory damages and attorney's fees will be available to the copyright owner in court actions. Otherwise, only an award of actual damages and profits is available to the copyright owner.

- Registration allows, the owner of the copyright, to record the registration with the U.S. Customs Service for protection against the importation of infringing copies.[3]

Most journalists will not have to concern themselves with copyright registration, because they will be working under the copyright of the news organization for which they work—a work for hire. If a journalist produces their own column or news item, then it will be in their best interest to register the item as their own work.

It is important to realize that it is important to discuss with one's employer when a news item will be considered part of a "work product," or a journalist's own property. If there is a conflict in opinion, it may be necessary to consult an attorney.

There is no longer any need to put the copyright symbol on a work to establish a copyright, although it is suggested that one does so.[4] The usual notice is: "Copyright © 2009 by [the name of the creator of the work, or other holder of the copyright such as a publishing house or news organization]." The reason that it remains important to put a copyright notice on a work is that if no copyright notice is included, a person using the work may be unaware that the work is copyrighted. The person may think that the work is in the **public domain**— it is available for anyone to use. Of course, once an individual is notified that there is a copyright on the material, they are no longer an innocent party to infringement. To prove copyright infringement, the holder of the copyright

TANGIBLE MEDIUM OF EXPRESSION

A tangible medium of expression means a work is embodied in a material object of some kind, such as the pages of a book, a canvas, magnetic tape, or a computer's hard disk.

PUBLIC DOMAIN

Works in the public domain are considered to be a part of the public's cultural heritage. They are open for anybody to make use of, for any purpose.

must show that the new work is substantially similar to the original work, that the copyright is still in force (there is an expiration date, to be discussed later), and that the person infringing on the work had violated the copyright.

Once a work has been copyrighted, anyone that copies it, uses it for a derivative work, displays the work to the public as their own, or performs the work without the copyright holder's permission is guilty of copyright infringement. The only exception to this would be what is called the **fair use** of the material (this concept will be discussed in detail later in the chapter).

■ **FAIR USE**

Fair use is when you can use material that is copyrighted, by someone else, without paying them royalties, or getting permission to use the work.

How to Register a Copyright

If one decides to register their work, rather than rely on a common-law copyright, there are three steps to registration:

1. A properly completed application form.
2. A nonrefundable filing fee for each application. It is best to consult //www. copyright.gov for the latest schedule of fees.
3. A deposit of the work being registered (take note—the work will not be returned).

The deposit requirements vary in particular situations:

- If the work was first published in the United States on or after January 1, 1978, two complete copies or phonorecords *of the best edition.*
- If the work was first published in the United States before January 1, 1978, two complete copies or phonorecords of the work *as first published.*
- If the work was first published outside the United States, one complete copy or phonorecord of the work *as first published.*[5]

The Early History of Copyright Laws

Before the European invention of the printing press, there was not much need for copyrights because scribes painstakingly handwrote all books. By the 15th century, there was the development of a more literate citizenry, and they wanted information. With the coming of the printing press, their needs were answered. The problem with this new invention was that books and other printed materials could be more easily reproduced, and thus the original author of the work potentially would lose revenue to literary thieves.

■ **STATUTE OF ANNE**

The Statute of Anne vested authors, rather than printers, with the monopoly on the reproduction of their works.

In 1710, the British instituted the **Statute of Anne**, an act to encourage learning. This statute gave authors, not publishers, exclusive right to their works, and ensured that publishers could not interfere with the buyers' rights to the work after the sale of the printed material. This statute limited the copyright to 14 years plus an additional renewal of 14 years if the author were still alive; after that time, the work would go into the public domain. The problem with this act was that it did not extend to all of British territory, and there was a debate as to how long the copyright should be valid.

In 1886, there was the first recognition of copyrights between sovereign nations —**The Berne Convention for the Protection of Literary and Artistic Works**. This Convention began the assigning of a copyright to a creative work, whether or not the work was registered. As soon as the work was "fixed" in a tangible medium, the copyright would apply; also, there was no need to attach a copyright notice to the work. Berne allowed foreign authors to be treated the same as a domestic author in any country that was a signatory to the Convention. Interestingly, the United States did not sign this document until 1989.

Part of the controversy over the United States signing of the Berne Convention was the concept of "**moral rights**." The concept of moral rights gives an author of literary, dramatic, musical, and artistic works the right to be identified as the author of the work, or the director of a film, for example, when copies are made for the public. Moral rights also give the author the right to object to derogatory treatment of the work, such as a distortion or mutilation of the work, colorization of a formerly monochrome movie, or if something is prejudicial to the honor or reputation of the author or director. In most of Europe, an author cannot assign their moral rights; they can only agree not to enforce them, which some do.

When the United States signed the Berne Convention, they stipulated that the "moral rights" provisions were already sufficiently addressed under U.S. laws such as trademark and libel.

■ **THE BERNE CONVENTION FOR THE PROTECTION OF LITERARY AND ARTISTIC WORKS**

The Berne Convention is an international agreement about copyrights, which was first adopted in Berne, Switzerland.

■ **MORAL RIGHTS**

Moral rights, under copyrights, refer to the ability of authors to control the eventual fate of their works.

U.S. COPYRIGHT LAW

The first United States copyright law was implemented in 1790—The Copyright Act. There have been many revisions of this Act leading ultimately to the **Copyright Act of 1976** (U.S. Code Title 17). This 1976 act became law on January 1, 1978, and, although modified in recent years, it is the basis for copyright law in the United States. The 1976 Act preempts the former copyright act of 1909, and all relevant common law and state copyright laws that may conflict with it.

One of the major differences between the 1976 Act and the 1909 law was that copyright protection now was granted as soon as the original work was *fixed in a tangible medium of expression*, unlike the 1909 law that required the work to be *published*. The 1909 law also required there be the *proper affixing of the copyright to the work*. If there was no proper notice of copyright on the work, under the 1909 law, the work became part of the public domain. (As was discussed earlier, because the United States signed the Berne Convention in 1989, there is no need to put any copyright notice on the work to give it copyright protection.)

■ **COPYRIGHT ACT OF 1976**

The 1976 Copyright Act preempts the former copyright act of 1909, and all relevant common law and state copyright laws that conflict with this Act.

The 1976 Act gave five exclusive rights to the copyright holder:

1. The right to copy the work.
2. The right to create derivative works.
3. The right to sell, lease, or rent copies to the public.
4. The right to perform the work publicly.
5. The right to display the work publicly.
6. The right to perform a sound recording by means of a digital audio (this was added in 1995).

The 1976 Copyright Act allows an unpublished author to register and copyright their work before "shopping" it around to a publisher before publication. This protects the author from the possibility that they will not be paid for their creative work if a publisher accidentally uses the author's ideas.

The term of copyright protection under the 1976 Act was extended as well. Prior copyright law set the duration of a copyright to 28 years, with the possibility of extending it for another 28 years. The 1976 Act, however, substantially increased the term of protection, and the **1998 Sonny Bono Copyright Term Extension Act (CTEA)**, extended copyright protection even more—the duration of the author's life plus 70 years, or 95 years for works made for hire. CTEA applied to existing as well as future copyrights. The practical result of this was to prevent a number of works, beginning with those published in 1923, from entering the public domain in 1998, and beyond.

Not everyone favored this extension of time for copyrights. In 2003, there was a challenge to the Bono Act, *Eldred v. Ashcroft*, 537 U.S. 186. This case dealt with the assertion that Congress was attempting to create perpetual copyrights.

In *Eldred*, individuals that relied for their products or services, based on the fact an item had become part of the public domain and thus could then be republished, argued that the copyright extension violated the "limited times" prescribed by the Copyright Clause, and the First Amendment's right to free speech. They claimed that Congress could not extend the copyright terms for works that had existing copyrights.

Supporting the new extension of time for copyrights included the U.S. Government (represented by the Attorney General), the **Motion Picture Association of America (MPAA)**, the **Recoding Industry Association of America (RIAA)**, **American Society of Composers, Authors, and Publishers (ASCAP)**, and **Broadcast Music Incorporated (BMI)** (ASCAP and BMI will be discussed in the next chapter). The entertainment industry, of course, was interested in keeping a product out of the public domain as long as possible.

The United States District Court for the District of Columbia and the District of Columbia Court of Appeals did not agree that the extension of time violated the Constitution of the United States, nor did the U.S. Supreme Court. Justice Ginsburg delivered the opinion of a 7–2 decision. The Court held that Congress did not transgress constitutional limits by extending existing and future copyrights. There is "...the unbroken congressional practice of treating future and existing copyrights in

---

■ 1998 SONNY BONO COPYRIGHT TERM EXTENSION ACT (CTEA)

The 1998 Sonny Bono Copyright Term Extension Act (CTEA), extended copyright protection to the duration of the author's life plus 70 years, or 95 years for works made for hire.

■ MOTION PICTURE ASSOCIATION OF AMERICA (MPAA)

The Motion Picture Association of America was formed to advance the business interests of the movie studios.

■ RECODING INDUSTRY ASSOCIATION OF AMERICA (RIAA)

The Recording Industry Association of America is a trade group that represents the U.S. recording industry.

parity." Justice Ginsburg also noted that the Founding Fathers did not intend for the First Amendment to limit copyrights, and copyrights are usually exempt for First Amendment scrutiny.

Another case that took the new copyright laws to task is *Kahle v. Gonzales* (previously named *Kahle v. Ashcroft)*. Plaintiffs in the *Kahle* case are Internet archivists that want to put books that are out of copyright, or "**orphan works**" (works that are still under copyright protection but no longer of economic interest to the copyright holder), on the Internet for all to read. They argue the difficulty and expense of obtaining permission to place these works on the Internet is overwhelming; and ownership of these "orphan works" is often difficult, and sometimes impossible, to ascertain.

They are contending that the current system, put in place by the recent changes to the copyright law—changing conditional copyrights to unconditional copyrights— is unconstitutional. The plaintiffs argue that by granting a copyright automatically once a creative work is fixed in a tangible medium, regardless of attaching copyright notice and regardless if the creator of the work wants a copyright or not, leads to indiscriminate copyright protection. It is argued that this change in the copyright law, has not benefited authors, and imposes burdens on free speech.

When there was conditional copyright, the great majority of works were not copyrighted, or were copyrighted only for the first 28 years, and then not renewed. Therefore, these works would automatically go into the public domain. Only works that the author or publisher felt required a copyright were so registered. The new laws create works that are still under copyright, but they are no longer economically viable, and thus are of no interest to the creator of the work, or the publisher, to keep them under copyright. Thus, they should be in the public domain.

On January 22, 2007, the United States Court of Appeals for the 9th Circuit, 487 F.3d 697 (9th Cir. 2007). released an opinion on the *Kahle* case, given by Senior Circuit Judge Farris.

The District Court's dismissal of plaintiffs' complaint was affirmed by the Court of Appeals. Judge Farris held the Supreme Court had already adjudicated the plaintiffs' allegations as to the change from a conditional copyright to an unconditional copyright system, and the copyright term extension. The Supreme Court holding both issues were not in violation of the Constitution, as per *Eldred v. Ashcroft*, cited previously.

Infringing on a Copyright

When a copyright is *registered*, it allows the holder several remedies in case of infringement. The holder can seek an injunction to stop the infringer from continuing their actions; all copies of the infringement may be impounded under court order; there can be statutory or actual damages awarded; and attorney's fees incurred, in defending the copyright, may be given the copyright holder (the plaintiff). Attorney's fees also can be given to the defendant in the copyright suit if they prevail.[6]

■ **AMERICAN SOCIETY OF COMPOSERS, AUTHORS, AND PUBLISHERS (ASCAP)**

The American Society of Composers, Authors and Publishers is a membership association of composers, songwriters, lyricists, and music publishers. Its function is to protect the rights of its members by licensing and paying royalties for the public performances of their copyrighted works.

■ **BROADCAST MUSIC INCORPORATED (BMI)**

Broadcast Music Incorporated is a performance rights organization that collects license fees on behalf of its composers, songwriters, and music publishers and distributes them as royalties to members whose works have been performed.

■ **ORPHAN WORKS**

Orphan works are copyrighted works whose owners may be impossible to identify and locate.

If the copyright was not registered, at the time of the infringement, the copyright must be registered before taking any legal action. Once the copyright is registered, the holder may then sue for actual damages. There can be an injunction sought against the infringer, or there can be the impounding of infringing copies, but if the copyright was not registered at the time of the infringement, or within three months of publication, the holder *cannot* recover statutory damages, nor can the holder seek attorney's fees. Thus, it does behoove the creator of a work to register the copyright when the work is created.

Title 17 USC 504 sets forth the statutory damages for copyright infringement. The court has the discretion to award an amount anywhere from $750 to $30,000 per work. If a plaintiff can show willful infringement, damages can go up to $150,000 per work. Innocent infringers may only be liable for $200 in damages per work.

Title 17 USC 412 only allows statutory damages if the work was registered with the Copyright Office before the infringement, or within three months of publication.

In 1998, the U.S. Supreme Court ruled there is a right to a jury trial in the determination of either statutory or actual damages—*Feltner v. Columbia Pictures Television*, 523 U.S. 340.

An example of potential copyright infringement came in September 2005, when the Authors' Guild filed a class action suit against the search engine Google.[7] In October 2005, several other major publishers filed their own suit against Google. Earlier that year, Google announced that it would be scanning millions of books, in their entirety, from the world's largest libraries (entitled Book Search), and make them available on the Internet. Some of these books are still under copyright. The suit filed claims that Google is guilty of copyright infringement. Google is saying only small excerpts of copyrighted works will be viewable, and as such falls within the exemption in copyright law—allowing small reproductions for the sake of research. (This will be discussed more in the section on fair use.)

In March 2007, Thomas Rubin, associate general counsel for copyright, trademark, and trade secrets at Microsoft, accused Google of violation of copyright law via its "Book Search" project. Rubin stated, "In my view, Google has chosen the wrong path for the longer term, because it systematically violates copyright and deprives authors and publishers of an important avenue for monetizing [sic] their works."

Microsoft is in the midst of its own book scanning called "Live Search Books." Microsoft claims that it is only scanning books that are out of copyright or in the public domain. Thomas Rubin states the company asks for permission from publishers for works currently under copyright.

Google's senior vice president for corporate development and chief legal officer stated,

> "The goal of search engines, and of products like Google Book Search and YouTube (YouTube was purchased by Google in 2006 for $1.6 billion dollars), is to help users find information from content producers of every size. ... We do this by complying with international copyright laws, and the result has been more exposure and in many cases more revenue for authors, publishers, and producers of content ..."

In another controversy against Google, in April 2007, Viacom, the U.S. media giant demanded all its content that was available on YouTube be removed from the site. This includes MTV, Nickelodeon, or Paramount Pictures productions. Viacom alleges that YouTube users had copied over 100,000 clips of its shows and movies, and that these shows and movies were put on the site without Viacom's permission.

Viacom's actions against Google and YouTube commenced three weeks after it introduced its own Web site to feature some of its own videos—"Acceptable TV."

Works for Hire

Most of the time, the articles created and the copyright associated with a journalist are not actually the journalist's; they are under the copyright of the news organization for which they work, under the Copyright Act's "**works made for hire**" provision. If a journalist is doing freelance work, and it is very important that particular work not be under the organization's copyright, the journalist should have a contract with the organization's editor or publisher, to ensure that this will be his or her own copyrighted work. If a journalist does not, and the work is considered a "work made for hire," the journalist will lose all rights to the piece.

In 1989, the U.S. Supreme Court ruled on this issue in *Community for Creative Non-Violence v. Reid*, 490 U.S. 730. In the *Reid* case, the Court examined what might or might not be a work for hire.

In the fall of 1985, the Community for Creative Non-Violence (CCNV), an organization dedicated to eliminating homelessness, entered into an oral contract to commission a sculpture from James Earl Reid, a Baltimore sculptor. The sculpture was to be displayed in Washington, D.C., and it was to be a modern "Nativity" scene, in which a homeless black couple and their child were huddled on top of a street steam grate. The sculpture, entitled "Third World America," was to be placed on a base so that there was steam coming from the base, and thus swirled around the huddled family. Reid worked on the sculpture at his studio in Baltimore, and CCNV members would visit regularly to check on the status of the work.

When the completed sculpture was delivered to Washington, CCNV paid Reid the final installment of the price, joined the sculpture to its base, and put it on display. CCNV and Reid filed for competing copyrights. The District Court ruled, CCNV had commissioned a "work made for hire" and thus deserved the copyright. The Court of Appeals reversed, holding that the sculpture was not made by an employee "under the terms of their employment" because Reid was an independent contractor. The Court of Appeals held that it was never agreed the sculpture would be a work for hire. The Court of Appeals did remand the case to the District Court for a determination of a possible joint ownership of the statute, thus, a possible joint copyright ownership.

The U.S. Supreme Court, in a unanimous decision, held that CCNV was not the employer of Reid. Reid was an independent contractor, because even though CCNV members would check on the specifications of the work (mainly to make sure it fit

WORKS MADE FOR HIRE

A work made for hire is a work prepared by an employee within the scope of his or her employment. In this case the employer, and not the employee, is considered the author of the work.

onto the planned base); still Reid had creative control over the project. Reid is a skilled artisan, he supplied his own tools, worked away from Washington, did not have daily supervision of CCNV, and CCNV paid him as one would pay an independent contractor. CCNV did not put Reid on their payroll, nor did they pay his Social Security taxes, nor provide employee benefits (all items looked at to determine if one is an employee or an independent contractor). The Court did make note, CCNV may be a "joint author" of the sculpture, thus entitled to co-ownership of the copyright, if the District Court, on remand, determines CCNV and Reid prepared the work, "... with the intention that their contributions be merged into inseparable or interdependent parts of a unitary whole."[8]

Publishers and Rights to a Work

So how can a publisher of a work protect themselves in copyright matters? There are several ways to buy the rights to a work.

- The most prevalent is when **all rights** are purchased. This means that the publisher has exclusive control and ownership over the work.
- **First serial rights** means that the publisher has the right to use the work *once* in a periodical, anywhere in the world, and then rights revert to the creator.
- **First North American rights** limit the publisher to publish *once*, but only in North America.
- Sometimes publishers will buy what are called **simultaneous rights**. In this case, rights are sold to multiple publishers, and all publishers must know all the other publishers that have purchased simultaneous rights have the right to print the material in other publications all at the same time.
- There are **one-time rights**; a publisher purchases the right to use the work one time, but there are no guarantees that it has not been previously published in another publication.

Fair Use

Federal courts have been using the common law form of fair use since the mid-1800s, but the 1976 Copyright Act, Section 107, codified this defense to copyright infringement. Fair use is a legal doctrine that recognizes scholarly quoting of brief passages, or use of a work for teaching purposes, would not dilute the economic returns of the copyright holder, and thus should be a defense to copyright infringement. What fair use allows is the use of a copyrighted work for criticism, teaching, scholarship, research, or the reporting of the news. There are four factors to be considered to determine if there is fair use of a work (of course it will up to a court to make a final determination of "fair use"):

1. The purpose and character of the use, including whether such use is of a commercial nature, or is for nonprofit educational purposes;

2. The nature of the copyrighted work—fictional or factual, the degree of creativity;

3. The amount and substantiality of the portion used in relation to the copyrighted work as a whole.

4. The affect of the use on the potential market of the copyrighted work.[9]

Harper & Row Publishers, Inc. v. Nation Enterprises, Inc., 471 U.S. 539 (1988), is a case dealing with the concept of unpublished information and the Fair Use Doctrine. In this case, the U.S. Supreme Court held that *The Nation* magazine was guilty of copyright infringement for publishing critical verbatim quotations from President Gerald Ford's memoirs concerning the pardon of former President Nixon, before the authorized publisher of a book could get the memoirs in print. *The Nation* magazine had cut substantially into the profits of the upcoming work. In response to this, and other cases concerning the use of quotations of important individuals from unpublished sources, in 1992 Congress added a sentence as to unpublished works and fair use—a work that is unpublished shall not, in and of itself, bar a finding of fair use if such finding is made on consideration of all the factors of the four-part test as to fair use.[10] (See earlier.)

The Doctrine of Fair Use has been adjudicated many times, especially since the advent of the photocopy machine. In *Basic Books, Inc. v. Kinko's Graphics Corp.*, 758 F.Supp. 1522 (S.D.N.Y. 1991), a federal court ruled that Kinko's had to pay royalties for all the course packages that they had produced for college classrooms. The court held these copyrighted materials were copied at such a large scale that it was not a fair use. The problem with Kinko's arguing for fair use was the copying was for commercial purposes—to make money, not strictly for educational purposes. The court looked to the percentage of the copying, as to the works themselves, and found 5 to 25 percent of the books were being copied—the court held this was excessive. The court decided that this would be direct competition to a student purchasing these books. Thus, even though most of the books were factual, a plus for the Fair Use Doctrine to apply, nonetheless, the court held this copying was not fair use.

Princeton University Press v. Michigan Document Services, Inc., 99 F.3d 1381 (6th Cir. 1996), reaffirmed the holding in the *Kinko's* case. A private copy shop created and sold course information under circumstances similar to the *Kinko's* case. The copy shop was also found to have acted outside the limits of fair use. Although there were five judges that did dissent, asserting such copying should be under fair use. The court did not address the issue that the production of these course packs would be fair use if a college or a nonprofit copy shop produced them.

Los Angeles Times v. Free Republic, 54 U.S.P.Q.2D 1453 (C.D. Cal. 2000), dealt with the issue of a bulletin board Web site allowing members to post full articles (copy them completely) from newspapers, so as to generate discussion.

Access to the site was available for free, but the purpose of the articles was to draw "hits" to the Web site. Although the site was for profit, at the time of the posting of the articles, it was seeking to become a nonprofit site. The court looked to the articles and found that they were copied directly from the newspapers, and the posting of these articles drew individuals away from the newspapers' commercial Web sites. It also was found that copying the articles completely was more extensive copying than that required to generate discussion. The court held that even though the articles were mainly factual, and there was a move by the site to become a nonprofit entity, both factors favoring a fair use ruling. The court decided that the Web site was only in existence to exploit the articles for their own commercial purposes, and thus infringed on the original copyright holders.

One area in which there is a glimmer of hope regarding the use of copyrighted materials for a commercial purpose and it being considered fair use is when it is considered by the courts to be used to inform individuals of the facts of a situation. In *Rosemont Enterprises, Inc. v. Random House, Inc.*, 366 F.2d 303 (2d Cir. 1966), cert. denied 385 U.S. 1009 (1967), a company—Rosemont, established by Howard Hughes—tried to prevent publication of a biography of Mr. Hughes.

Rosemont had learned that there was a biography being written about Howard Hughes. The biographer was relying on *Look* magazine articles for information about Mr. Hughes. The trial court held for Rosemont, but the federal appellate court reversed, stating that there could be no copyrighting of history, and the articles, although important to the book on Hughes, nonetheless amounted to only a small percentage of the book. The book's authors had done extensive research into Mr. Hughes' life. The court ruled that there is a legitimate public interest in the doings of such celebrities as Mr. Hughes; thus, Random House could publish its book without incurring liability for copyright infringement. Fair use was the "... privilege in others than the owner of a copyright to use the copyrighted material in a reasonable manner without his consent, notwithstanding the monopoly granted to the owner ...".

For fair use to apply, consider how important the copyrighted passage used is to the work. Even though a work may be 100,000 words, the most important part of the work may only consist of 2,000 words. If those are the words used, under the guise of fair use, it is likely that a court will find them a copyright infringement.

In 1999, *contra* to the *Random House* decision, a federal appellate court held that the estate of Dr. Martin Luther King Jr. could sue CBS for copyright infringement. This holding was based on the speech entering the *public domain*, not based on the Fair Use Doctrine.

CBS had used a significant amount of Dr. King's historic "I Have a Dream" speech of August 28, 1963, for a documentary on the 20th century. This work was entitled "The 20th Century with Mike Wallace." One segment was devoted to Martin Luther King Jr. The episode contained material filmed by CBS, including extensive footage of the speech—approximately 60 percent of the speech's total content. CBS did not seek the King estate's permission to use the speech, and refused to pay royalties to the King estate, even though the King estate had obtained a copyright on the speech on October 2, 1963—approximately a month after the speech—and the estate continued to maintain a copyright on the speech.

In the suit, the estate claimed copyright infringement, CBS claimed that the speech had been heard by such a large audience, and had been quoted so many times since the delivery of the speech, that no one should be able to prevent the media from using it for journalistic purposes.

The District Court held that the speech had entered the public domain and thus there was no copyright infringement. The federal appellate court disagreed. The federal court holding there are two tests if work enters the public domain:

1. if tangible copies of the work are distributed to the general public in such a manner as it allows the public to exercise dominion and control over the work, or

2. if the work is exhibited or displayed in such a manner as to permit unrestricted copying by the general public.

The federal court did not consider that the mere fact that many had seen and heard the speech, or the fact that the speech was newsworthy, put the speech in the criteria of entering the public domain.[11] Ultimately, CBS settled with the King estate.

In the *King* case, it is interesting that the rule of law applicable to copyrights in the 1960s was the Copyright Act of 1909. The 1909 Act did not grant automatic statutory protection before publication as is in place today under the Berne Convention. Completing all formalities required—registering the work with the Registrar of Copyrights and properly affixing the copyright notice—both had to be done to obtain a statutory copyright under the 1909 Act.

CBS argued that because the speech was first published and then later copyrighted (a little over a month after its airing), it entered the public domain. The King estate argued that the work was not published when the speech was given, and thus retained a common law copyright under the 1909 Act. The public performance of the speech was not the "general publication" required to put it into the public domain; instead, it was a "limited publication" that maintained a common-law copyright.

A major area of concern to journalists, and fair use, is the area of **video clip businesses**. These are businesses that make videotapes or record to DVD segments of a news or public affairs show that mentions a specific individual or business. There are also businesses that clip articles from newspapers, these businesses then sell these newspaper clips to the individual or business so mentioned in the news story.

In 1993, a federal court held that video clipping was not under the Fair Use Doctrine, nor were video clipping services protected under the First Amendment. Instead, they were actually infringing on a copyright.[12] Clipping services now pay a small license fee to use the newscasts.

What about one station using video from another station in covering a very newsworthy event? Is that fair use? In *Los Angeles News Service v. KCAL-TV Channel 9*, 108 F.3d 1119 (9th Cir.1997), the appellate court ruled it would take a

■ **VIDEO CLIP BUSINESSES**

Video clip businesses make videotapes or DVDs of segments of a news or public affairs show.

full trial to determine if KCAL's unauthorized use of a video, taken by Los Angeles News Service of the beating of Reginald Denny by black youths, after the first trial and acquittal of the officers that beat Rodney King, was or was not copyright infringement. KCAL had used 30 seconds from a four-minute copyrighted tape of the 1992 beating. KCAL alleged that because the riots were so newsworthy, they should be available for use under the Fair Use Doctrine. The appellate court held newsworthiness must be balanced against the potential economic damage that KCAL would impose in their unauthorized use of the tape. By KCAL using the heart of the tape, it affected the copyright owner's ability to market the video. The *KCAL* decision is a warning to journalists to gain permission before airing any video, even if it is extremely newsworthy.

Interestingly, the same federal court in 2002 held that the same Reginald Denny tape played on Court TV was under the Fair Use Doctrine. This *contra* decision was based on the fact that, Court TV used it to promote its coverage of the trial of the individuals that beat Denny, not news coverage that could be deemed competition with another news organization. Also, only a few seconds were used, not 30 as in the *KCAL* case.[13]

International Copyrights and Fair Use

Canada statute allows private copying for personal use called "fair dealing." The term of a copyright shall be "... the life of the author, the remainder of the calendar year in which the author dies, and a period of fifty years following the end of that calendar year."[14]

Australia allows copying of copyrighted materials for research or study, review and criticism, news coverage, or the giving of professional (legal) advice, under limited circumstances. Unlike fair use in the United States, fair dealing in Australia also must be "fair." The definition of fair will depend on all circumstances, for example, the nature of the work, the nature of the use of the work, and the possible economic affect on a copyrighted work. The term of a copyright in Australia is the life of the creator plus 70 years.[15]

Misappropriation of a Work

■ **MISAPPROPRIATION** OR **UNFAIR COMPETITION**

Misappropriation or unfair competition is a "taking," of a business value of another without consent.

A journalist must not only look to possible copyright infringement when using another's work, often called using another's "sweat of their brow," but the tort of **misappropriation** or **unfair competition** must be considered as well. Unlike copyright law, made a federal standard with the Copyright Act of 1976, Section 301, and thus preempting all state laws dealing with copyrights, misappropriation is a tort that is decided by state court decisions.

In *International News Service v. Associated Press*, 248 U.S. 215 (1918), the U.S. Supreme Court's decision went to the heart of the issue dealing with pirated use of another's work. In this case, the Associated Press (AP) gathered the news from all over the world and would supply it to their AP members for publication in their newspapers.

AP members were only to publish this information in their own newspapers; they were not to disseminate this information in any other way. The estimated cost to AP for this newsgathering was approximately $3.5 million per year. This amount would be divided up among the AP members, each paying their share.

International News Service (INS), the defendant in this case, is a corporation that gathers the news and sells it to its participating members. Estimated annual revenue to INS is some $2 million. Some of INS clients are also clients of the AP wire service. INS and AP are fierce competitors.

The case filed was to restrain the pirating by INS of "hot news" gathered by AP. AP claimed employees of its members' newspapers were being bribed by INS to furnish AP news to INS, before publication, thus violating the agreement between AP and its members. INS also was charged with copying the news from bulletin boards or early editions of AP newspapers and selling this news as it was published.

The issues presented to the Supreme Court in this case were: "(1) Whether there is any property in news; (2) Whether, if there be property in news collected for the purpose of being published, it survives the instant of its publication in the first newspaper to which it is communicated by the news-gatherer; and (3) Whether defendant's [INS] admitted course of conduct in appropriating for commercial use matter taken from bulletins or early editions of Associated Press publications constitutes unfair competition in trade."

INS argued that once AP members communicate the news to the general public via bulletin boards or by publishing the information in a newspaper, AP loses control of the use of this information, "... when it thus reaches the light of day it becomes the common possession of all to whom it is accessible; and that any purchaser of a newspaper has the right to communicate the intelligence which it contains to anybody and for any purpose, even for the purpose of selling it for profit to newspapers published for profit in competition with complainant's [AP] members."

The Court did not agree, and held that it was different for an individual to buy a paper and spread knowledge of its contents for free, as opposed to INS using that information for a commercial use. The Supreme Court held INS seeks to justify taking the information that AP had worked so hard to gather. Furthermore, INS sells this information as if they had gathered it. The Court held this amounts to an unauthorized interference with the AP, and INS is diverting, "... a material portion of the profit from those who have earned it to those who have not." The Court thus took the *INS* case out of the preemption of federal copyright law, and placed the issue into the area of misappropriation or unfair competition.

The National Basketball Association v. Motorola, Inc., 105 F.3d 841 (2d Cir. 1997), case dealt with the sale of statistical information about National Basketball Association (NBA) games on Motorola's handheld pager—"SportsTrax." SportsTrax's operation relies on a "data feed" supplied by reporters who watch the games on television or listen to them on the radio. This information in "real time" is then relayed to a host computer, and that information is sent out to local FM radio stations, which in turn emit the signal received by the SportsTrax device. In producing and marketing its basketball games, the NBA derives great commercial value from the sale of its broadcasting rights; thus, it has a great interest in preventing any competition. The NBA filed suit under *state law* alleging commercial misappropriation by Motorola.

The heart of the dispute concerns the extent to which a state law "hot-news" misappropriation claim based on *International News Service (INS) v. Associated Press* case, survives preemption by the federal Copyright Act of 1976, and whether the NBA's claim fits within the surviving *INS* misappropriation case.

The federal court held that the "hot news" exception under *INS* does survive preemption of the Copyright Act—thus, it is actionable in state court, as long as the case passes the "extra elements test." If other elements, in addition to the elements of copyright infringement, are needed to constitute a state created cause of action, then it takes it out of the scope of copyright law, and thus there is no federal preemption. The court announced the elements of a misappropriation claim which survives federal copyright preemption are,

> "... (i) a plaintiff generates or gathers information at a cost; (ii) the information is time sensitive; (iii) the defendant's use of the information constitutes free-riding on the plaintiff's efforts; (iv) the defendant is in direct competition with a product or service offered by the plaintiffs; *and* (v) the ability of other parties to free-ride on the effort of the plaintiff or others would so reduce the incentive to produce the product or service that its existence or quality would be substantially threatened."

The court held that the NBA did not prove these extra elements, and thus this was not "hot news"— copyright law preempted this misappropriation claim by the NBA. The court found no competition between the actual games and game statistics, nor was there "free-riding" because Motorola had its own reporters expend time and energy in gathering this information, and there was further effort made in disseminating this information to the pagers.

THE DIGITAL MILLENNIUM COPYRIGHT ACT

The advent of the Internet has created many copyright issues. On the Net, access to information, software piracy, and peer-to-peer file sharing produced much controversy between copyright holders and individuals potentially infringing on these intellectual rights. In response to these issues, on October 12, 1998, Congress passed the **Digital Millennium Copyright Act (DMCA)**, and President Clinton signed it into law on October 28 of the same year.

The Digital Millennium Copyright Act was supported by the software and entertainment industry but opposed by researchers, librarians, and scientists, because it puts restrictions on what and what cannot be legally done with digital works.

The DMCA was designed to assist in implementing the treaties that were signed in Geneva, Switzerland, at the **World Intellectual Property Organization (WIPO)** conference in December 1996. WIPO is an international organization

■ **DIGITAL MILLENNIUM COPYRIGHT ACT (DMCA)**

The Digital Millennium Copyright Act (DMCA) makes it a crime to use any measures that circumvent antipiracy measures built into software. The DMCA does offer limited protection to Internet Service Providers in merely distributing information over the Net.

■ **WORLD INTELLECTUAL PROPERTY ORGANIZATION (WIPO)**

WIPO administers the Madrid system for international registration of marks.

dedicated to promoting the use and protection of creative works. WIPO is one of 16 specialized agencies of the United Nations, and counts 183 nations as member states.[16]

The DMCA makes it a crime to circumvent any antipiracy measures built into software, for example, encryptions or serial numbers, and outlaws the manufacture, sale, or distribution of code-cracking devices used to unlawfully copy software. It *does* allow for the cracking of copyright protection to conduct encryption research, assess product operation, or test computer security systems.

It limits the liability for Internet Service Providers (ISPs) for copyright infringement for merely transmitting information over the Net, although ISPs are expected to remove material from a Web site that a copyright owner has notified the ISP of a "good faith belief" that there has been an infringement. This provision is one of the most controversial of the DMCA, because once a complaint comes into the ISP, the service provider must notify the Web site owner of the copyright complaint and shut down the site. There is no judicial proceeding before the shutting down of the site, and if the ISP does not shut down the "offending" site, the service provider can be held liable for any copyright infringement that occurs.

The Act also states that "... [n]othing in this section shall affect rights, remedies, limitations, or defenses to copyright infringement, including fair use ..." (See the discussion of fair use earlier.)

And the DMCA requires that "webcasters" pay licensing fees to record companies.

Despite the attempt by the DMCA to assist copyright holders, digital files are easily copied, and copyright holders such as software companies, music companies, and movie producers have become painfully aware of this problem. Producers of copyrighted material complain that online piracy cuts into their profits.

By the year 2000, the problem of peer-to-peer file sharing of "MP3s" (a music file compression technology) was escalating. The creation of MP3 files allow the exchange of files that otherwise would be too large or cumbersome to share. Enter into this a Web site that encouraged the exchange of MP3s—Napster. The major record companies did not take long to react to the sharing of these files and filed suit against Napster in an effort to protect their copyrights. In *A & M Records v. Napster*, 239 F.3d 1004 (9th Cir. 2001), it was found Napster facilitated the transmission of MP3 files between and among its users through a process called peer-to-peer file sharing. Napster allowed its users to search for and make MP3 music files, stored on other users' hard drives, and transfer these exact files from one computer to another. Napster provided technical support for the indexing and searching of MP3 files, in a central computer bank, and had a chat room for users to discuss music.

The court held in the *Napster* case that the record companies had sufficiently shown copyright ownership of most of the works Napster was facilitating the downloading of; thus, this was a violation of copyright law. Napster argued that its use of these files came under the Fair Use Doctrine, but the court did not agree with Napster. The works that Napster allowed for download were not transformed in any way. Napster was a commercial enterprise, these were creative works, Napster was allowing the copying of the entire work, and by Napster allowing this downloading, it could affect the market for such works. The court also did not agree with the contention of Napster that they were only offering "samples" of the works—an entire work is an entire work.

Napster further contended that they were an ISP and the Digital Millennium Copyright Act protected them from charges of copyright infringement. The court did not rule on this issue, instead stating that if Napster was an ISP, that would have to be decided at a later trial.

Ultimately, Napster had to prevent its users from exchanging songs the record industry identified as holding valid copyrights. Once so identified, Napster had to pull them from their download list. By 2002–2003, Napster was on a downward spiral, and the free version of Napster finally collapsed. The new Napster, charging monthly fees for its service and paying royalties to the record industry, now competed with other paid file sharing entities such Apple Computer's "I-Tunes" and even free file-sharing sites. These free sites eluded U.S. copyright issues for a while, because they did not have a central coordination point as did Napster—they only had file sharing between users' computers. Some survived because they were based overseas.

One of these free file-sharing sites that continued to survive was KaZaA. As with the creators of similar Web-based products, KaZaA's owners have been taken to court by music publishers to restrict their facilitating the sharing of works under copyright. In 2001, in a case in the Netherlands, KaZaA's owners were told to prevent their users from violating copyrights or face stiff fines. In response to this ruling, the holding company of KaZaA—Consumer Empowerment—chose not to comply with the court order, and sold KaZaA to Sharman Networks. Sharman is located in Australia and incorporated in Vanuatu.

In 2002, the Recording Industry Association of America (RIAA) and the Motion Picture Association of America (MPAA) sued Sharman Networks in California. This suit resulted in a judgment, concluding that the users of KaZaA engaged in copyright infringement, and required Sharman Networks modify their software to prevent such infringement.

■ AUSTRALIAN RECORD INDUSTRY ASSOCIATION (ARIA)

The Australian Record Industry Association is a trade group representing the Australian recording industry.

In February 2004, the **Australian Record Industry Association (ARIA)** sued KaZaA for copyright infringement. In February 2005, the homes of two Sharman Networks executives and the offices of Sharman Networks in Australia were raided under court order to gather evidence for trial. In September 2005, the Federal Court of Australia held that Sharman itself was *not* guilty of copyright infringement but was authorizing KaZaA users to share copyrighted songs *illegally*. The company was ordered to modify its software and pay millions of dollars to the record labels that had sued them.

In December 2005, the Federal Court of Australia ceased KaZaA downloads in Australia, because they had not made the necessary modifications in software. A warning to Australian users of KaZaA was put on the KaZaA Web site—that they were not to download files from the KaZaA site. In March 2006, the Full Federal Court of Australia handed down its decision concerning the trial judge's powers in relation to failure by Sharman Networks to comply with the Australian court's orders to modify their software to limit future copyright infringement. The Full Court held that the trial judge was entitled to make a finding of contempt against Sharman Networks and its associates in relation to their alleged failure to implement orders made by the trial judge.[17]

On July 27, 2006, KaZaA reached an agreement with the music industry over illicit file sharing. Sharman Networks to pay four music labels—Universal Music, Sony BMG, EMI, and Warner Music, over $100 million, and vowed to introduce filtering technology to block illegal file trading. Under the agreement, KaZaA networks will no longer be under scrutiny and will operate as a completely legal network. Nikki Hemming, CEO of Sharman Networks, stated that this "... marks the dawn of a new age of cooperation between P2P technology and content industries ..."

A landmark United States case that involved downloading of copyrighted movies and music was *MGM v. Grokster*, 125 S. Ct. 2764. This case, decided in June 2005, shocked the peer-to-peer file sharing community, and put them on notice that intentional copyright infringement on the Net would not be tolerated.

The *Grokster* case is often thought of as a reexamination of *Sony Corporation v. Universal City Studios*, 464 U.S. 417 (1984). The *Sony* case protected manufacturers of VCRs from contributory copyright infringement. The Supreme Court held in that case, VCR technology could not be barred if it was, "... capable of substantial noninfringing [copyright] uses."

When it came before the U.S. Supreme Court, Grokster had already won in its case before the U.S. District Court for the Central District of California. The District Court held that those who used the Grokster software to download copyrighted media files directly infringed on MGM's copyrights, but the court nonetheless granted summary judgment in favor of Grokster as to any liability arising from distribution of the then current versions of their software. "Distributing that software gave rise to no liability in the court's view, because its use did not provide the distributors with actual knowledge of specific acts of infringement." The Ninth Circuit Court of Appeals upheld the lower court's decision. The appeals court holding a commercial product capable of substantial noninfringing uses could not give rise to contributory liability for infringement; unless Grokster had actual knowledge of specific instances of infringement, and did not act on that knowledge. The appeals court held that because there was a decentralized architecture of their software, Grokster had no such knowledge.[18] (KaZaA was originally one of the defendants in this case but was dropped since the company is incorporated in Vanuatu. See *KaZaA* earlier.) In the Supreme Court case against Grokster, Intel, AT&T, Verizon, and Sun Microsystems filed amicus curiae (friends of the court) briefs in favor of file sharing; the RIAA and MPAA sided with MGM.

CASE STUDY MGM v. Grokster

125 S. Ct. 2764 (2005)

Facts:
Justice Souter delivered the opinion of the Court. Grokster, Ltd. and StreamCast Networks, Inc. distribute free software products that allow computer users to share electronic files through peer-to-peer networks. These network users communicate directly with each other, not via a central server. The recipients of Grokster and StreamCast software usually use it to share copyrighted music and video files without the authorization of the copyright holder. A group of movie studios and other copyright holders filed suit against Grokster and Streamcast for copyright infringement, alleging Grokster and Streamcast intentionally distributed their software to allow their users to infringe on copyrighted works, in violation of the Copyright Act of 1976.

Issue:
Is a distributor of a product that is capable of being lawful and unlawful, in its use, liable for copyright infringement by third parties using the product?

Decision:
Yes.

Reason:
The court held that the *Sony* case does not require the courts to ignore evidence of *intent* to infringe on copyright, if there is such evidence. The *Sony* case was not meant to foreclose rules of fault based liability based on common law. If the evidence shows the product's characteristics, or if there is knowledge the product may be put to infringing uses, liability will not be precluded. Here the court held that "... one who distributes a device with the object of promoting its use to infringe copyright, as shown by clear expression or other affirmative steps taken to foster infringement, is liable for the resulting acts of infringement by third parties. ... Grokster and StreamCast's efforts to supply services to former Napster users, deprived of a mechanism to copy and distribute what were overwhelmingly infringing files, indicate a principal, if not exclusive, intent on the part of each to bring about infringement."

Furthermore, Grokster and StreamCast make money by selling advertising space; thus, the more the software is used, the more the ads are seen, and the greater the ad revenue. This then makes this a commercial enterprise that turns on high-volume use, which the record shows is infringement.

(Shortly after this ruling, Grokster agreed to a permanent injunction barring direct or indirect infringement of copyrighted works, and stopped offering and supporting its original software.)

A consortium of the world's largest record labels sued LimeWire, another file-sharing program, for copyright infringement, on August 7, 2006. The record labels—Universal Music, Sony BMG, EMI, and Warner Music Group—seek $150,000 in damages for each song "willfully infringed" on by LimeWire. They allege that LimeWire has profited from unlawful music downloads, calling the "scope of infringement ... massive." The suit, filed in New York federal court, lists Lime Group, LLC, the company's chief executive Mark Gorton, and chief operating officer Greg Bildson as defendants.

LimeWire is fighting a RIAA shutdown with a countersuit of its own. LimeWire's contention is that the RIAA is an antitrust operation out to destroy any online music distribution service they did not own or control, or force such services to do business with them. The countersuit charges that the RIAA is carrying out antitrust violations, consumer fraud, and other misconduct.[19]

On December 4, 2007, U.S. District Judge Gerard E. Lynch dismissed the antitrust lawsuit filed by LimeWire against the major record labels. Judge Lynch stated LimeWire's claims "fail to allege an adverse affect on competition market-wide." Judge Lynch viewed the record companies' actions as "independent decision-making by each company to refrain from doing business" with LimeWire.

Judge Lynch also dismissed several claims brought by LimeWire against the record labels under state laws "**without prejudice**," which gives the New York-based LimeWire the option to pursue their claims in state court.

TRADEMARKS, SERVICE MARKS

Other ways that the creator of a work can protect their intellectual property rights is under **trademark** and **service mark** registration. The federal law of trademarks and service marks was established in the United States in 1946, under the **Lanham Act**. Unlike the Copyright Act, the Lanham Act is not exclusive to the federal government, states can and do establish their own trademark laws and methods of trademark registration. Many local businesses operating in one state do not register federally, but will register in the state in which they do business. In most jurisdictions, rights to having a trademark on a product can be established by actual use or by registering it with the trademark registration office. It is in the best interest of a product or business to register the trademark; otherwise, the extent of enforcement of the trademark against potential infringement can be jeopardized.

Trademark laws cover such items as distinctive and unique packaging, color combinations, building designs, slogans, symbols, product styles, and overall presentations.

A service mark is registered the same as a trademark. It is attached to a service business' advertisement or signage, for example, such as a carpet cleaning company's logo. There may be a copyright, a trademark, and a service mark, all held by one

WITHOUT PREJUDICE

Without prejudice is when a case is dismissed but the plaintiff is allowed to bring a new suit on the same claim.

TRADEMARK

A trademark is a form of intellectual property. It is a distinctive indication used by a business, organization, or other legal entity to uniquely identify and distinguish its products from other businesses, organizations, or other legal entities—a brand name.

SERVICE MARK

A service mark is any word, name, symbol, device, or any combination, used, or intended to be used, in commerce, to identify and distinguish the services of one provider from services provided by others, and to indicate the source of the services.

LANHAM ACT

The Lanham Act defines the scope of a trademark, the process by which a federal registration can be obtained from the Patent and Trademark Office for a trademark, and penalties for trademark infringement.

project. For example, a movie company releases a movie DVD. There will be a copyright on the contents of the movie, a service mark associated with the production company, and a trademark associated with the symbol or slogan of the movie studio.

Trademarks are identifiable with the letters "TM" if they have not yet been registered with the trademark office. Unregistered service marks will have an "SM" attached to the name. When marks have been registered, it is required that the mark holder attach to the mark "'Registered in U.S. Patent and Trademark Office' or 'Reg. U.S. Pat. & Tm. Off.' or the letter R enclosed within a circle, thus ®; and in any suit for infringement under this by such a registrant failing to give such notice of registration, no profits and no damages shall be recovered under the provisions of this unless the defendant had actual notice of the registration."[20]

Trademarks and service marks are considered intellectual property, and anyone knowingly infringing on a mark can be sued for injunctive relief and damages in either federal or state court, whichever is appropriate. Marks are usually good only *where* registered, although there are international mark laws that allow one registration that covers many jurisdictions. (See later for a discussion of international mark laws.)

A major concern for companies in the use of their mark is that it will be used in a generic way, for example, the term "aspirin," "linoleum," or "cornflakes." At one time, all these terms were registered marks, but because the owners of these marks let them be used in a generic way, they reentered the public domain, and now anyone can use the terms as part of their product description. This is where the media and owners of marks come into conflict. A company always must defend its mark from generic use. When the media insists on calling any cola product "Coca-Cola®," the trademark holder will send a letter to the journalist reminding them that not all colas can be labeled as a "Coke® or Coca-Cola®." The company is merely establishing the use of their mark, to the courts, so it does not revert to a generic form.

If a mark is used in an advertising venue, and the advertiser or publisher misuses the mark, such as not labeling it as a marked item, or potentially holding the item out as their own, be assured a suit will follow.[21]

Mark law not only prevents companies and products from using marks that may confuse the public, but even an entertainment group such as the Beach Boys can insist there is no other musical group using the term Beach Boys. For example, a group calling itself "Beach Boys Family and Friends" implied an endorsement by the original group's record company, when one was not given.[22]

Copyright versus Trademark

In 2003, the U.S. Supreme Court differentiated a copyright from a trademark. In *Dastar Corp. v. Twentieth Century Fox Film Corp.*, 539 U.S. 23, the Court held a new release of a video, based on a 1949 film series dealing with World War II, was not a violation of trademark as was alleged by Twentieth Century Fox Films. The Court held that Fox was improperly trying to use trademark law to prevent the release of the new video by Dastar. The Court found copyright law should be applied, and because the copyright had not been renewed, the film was now in the public domain and Dastar had the right to release the video.

Be advised that if a work has entered the public domain by nonrenewal of its copyright, the courts will not look favorably on bringing a mark suit in attempt to protect the intellectual property.

Trademark Law Revision Act

In 1988, Congress revised the original Lanham Act. These revisions affected advertisers in the media, because, under the new Act, it was made a federal right for a mark owner to sue a competitor for falsely disparaging their product or service. Treble damages were available to the wronged trademark holder.[23]

In 1995, Congress passed the **Federal Trademark Dilution Act**, which gave a federal right to a trademark holder to sue an infringer for "... lessening of the capacity of a famous mark to identify and distinguish goods or services, regardless of the presence or absence of competition between the parties or likelihood of confusion, mistake, or deception."[24]

However, there are limits on what is confusing and what is not. In Kentucky, a sex shop had named itself "Victor's Little Secrets," after one of its owners Victor Moseley. The major lingerie store Victoria's Secret® felt that this was a dilution of their trademark and sued. The U.S. Supreme Court held this was not trademark dilution. For Victoria's Secret® to win its case, they would have to show "... a lessening of the capacity of a famous mark to identify and distinguish goods or services"—actual dilution. It would be difficult for Victoria's Secrets® to show that a small sex shop in Kentucky could have such an effect on such a famous trademark.[25]

In reaction to the Victoria's Secret® case decision, U.S. Representative Lamar Smith (R-TX) proposed an amendment to the Federal Trademark Dilution Act (FTDA)—H.R. 683. This bill, approved by the House in April 2005, and the Senate in March 2006, amends provisions of the (FTDA), so that a famous mark holder will not have to prove "actual dilution" to pursue a claim of either blurring or tarnishing a trademark. Now the mark holder will only have to show a "likelihood of dilution." This bill became Public Law No: 109-312, on October 6, 2006.

Exclusions for mark dilution under section (3) E of this law are:

> "...(A) Fair use of a famous mark by another person in comparative commercial advertising or promotion to identify the competing goods or services of the owner of the famous mark.
>
> (B) Noncommercial use of a designation of source.
>
> (C) All forms of news reporting and news commentary."[26]

■ **FEDERAL TRADEMARK DILUTION ACT**

The Federal Trademark Dilution Act gives a federal right to a mark holder to sue an infringer if they lessen the ability of a mark to identify goods or services, or if the infringer creates confusion in the mind of the consumer.

International Trademarks

On November 2, 2003, the United States became a signatory to the **Madrid system for international registration of marks**. Under this system, one mark registration can cover up to the 78 members of the Madrid union under the Madrid Agreement and Protocol. The registration of a mark in one participating country will be protected in any or all member states of the system. The International Bureau of the World Intellectual Property Organization (WIPO), which maintains the International Register of marks, administers the Madrid system for the international registration of trademarks.

There is also the **Community Trade Mark (CTM)** system this applies to the European Union. Registration of a mark with the Office of Harmonization in the Internal Market gives effective protection throughout the European Union—all 27 member states indivisibly. It is not possible to limit the mark to any particular member state or states.

A country that has given many mark holders a problem is Mainland China. Although piracy is an issue in the People's Republic of China (PRC), they have signed the Madrid system, and they have their own trademark office. The Trademark Law and the Unfair Competition Law form the PRC's trademark system. In the PRC, there is no common-law protection for unregistered marks (unless they are "well known"). The courts and administrative bodies decide what is "well known." Some determinations that are considered are the amount of publicity of the mark in the PRC, and if consumers are aware of the mark.

Recently, the Beijing No. 2 Intermediate People's Court upheld trademark infringement for Louis Vuitton® handbags. The suit involved the selling of Vuitton® "knockoffs" for a substantially lower price than the real items. The Shanghai No. 2 Intermediate People's Court also upheld the trademark of Starbucks® against a local Chinese competitor that had essentially the same name as Starbucks® in Chinese. The court held Starbucks® was a "well-known" mark and as such deserved protection.

In the next chapters, the concept of intellectual property—copyrights and marks—will be discussed with regard to how they relate to entertainment law and in cyberspace.

SUMMARY

Copyrights are a group of exclusive rights granted by the federal government. They can be obtained for all types of intellectual works from literature to movies. Facts cannot be copyrighted, but how the facts are depicted can be.

Copyright protection is automatic. Once the work is completed and fixed in a *tangible medium of expression*, the creator of the work obtains a common-law copyright whether or not they actually register the work. There is no longer any need to attach a copyright symbol to establish the right, although it is suggested that one does so.

Once a work has been copyrighted, anyone that copies it, uses it for a derivative work, displays the work to the public as their own, or performs the work without the copyright holder's permission is guilty of copyright infringement. The only exception to this would be what is called the *fair use* of the material.

Fair use is a defense to charges of copyright infringement. Another defense argument is that the work has entered the public domain.

The 1976 Copyright Act preempts the former copyright act of 1909, and all relevant common law and state copyright laws that conflict with this law. The 1998 Sonny Bono Copyright Term Extension Act (CTEA) extended copyright protection to the duration of the author's life plus 70 years, or 95 years for works made for hire. The media must not only consider potential copyright infringement but also the tort of misappropriation must be kept in mind.

The Digital Millennium Copyright Act (DMCA) makes it a crime to use any measures that circumvent antipiracy measures built into software. The DMCA does offer limited protection to Internet Service Providers in merely distributing information over the Net.

Trademarks and service marks are other ways of protecting intellectual property. The Lanham Act defines how to register a mark with the Patent and Trademark Office, and puts forth penalties for infringement.

■ DISCUSSION QUESTIONS

1. Should there be automatic copyright recognition on fixing the work in a *tangible medium of expression*, or should registration be required? Why or why not?

2. Should the United States recognize the concept of *moral rights*, as does Europe? Do the laws as to libel and slander protect the creator of a work as much as the concept of moral rights?

3. Should the Copyright Act of 1976 do away with all other copyright laws? Why or why not? Should the states still be able to determine what should be protected under copyright?

4. The 1998 Sonny Bono Copyright Term Extension Act (CTEA) extended the term of copyright ownership, should a copyright protection be granted for such a long time?

5. Should the "I Have a Dream" speech given by Dr. Martin Luther King Jr. be considered part of the public domain? Why or why not?

6. If an event is newsworthy, should others in the media be able to use the information under the Fair Use Doctrine?

7. Should the courts have ruled against Napster, Grokster, and KaZaA? Why or why not?

8. Does Victor's Little Secrets likely dilute the famous mark Victoria's Secret®? Why or why not?

■ CASE FOR REVIEW

In *Playboy Enterprises v. Welles*, 162 F.3d 1169 (9th Circuit 1998) 279 F.3d 796 (9th Circuit 2002), Terri Welles was sued by Playboy® for trademark infringement when she used her title as 1981 *Playboy Magazine's* Playmate of the Year® on her Web site. The court held that "Playmate of the Year®," although a registered trademark, was not trademark infringement by Ms. Welles. She was merely using it to identify herself, and so this was fair use of the mark. Argue why this was mark infringement.

■ KEY TERMS

1998 Sonny Bono Copyright Term
   Extension Act (CTEA)
all rights
American Society of Composers,
   Authors, and Publishers (ASCAP)
Australian Record Industry
   Association (ARIA)
Broadcast Music Incorporated
   (BMI)
Community Trade Mark (CTM)
Copyright Act of 1976
Copyrights
Digital Millennium Copyright Act
   (DMCA)
fair use

Federal Trademark Dilution Act
First North American rights
First serial rights
Lanham Act
Madrid system for international
   registration of marks
misappropriation or unfair
   competition
moral rights
Motion Picture Association of
   America (MPAA)
one-time rights
orphan works
public domain
Recoding Industry Association of

America (RIAA)
service mark
simultaneous rights
Statute of Anne
tangible medium of expression
The Berne Convention for the
   Protection of Literary and Artistic
   Works
trademark
video clip businesses
without prejudice
works made for hire
World Intellectual Property
   Organization (WIPO)

■ ENDNOTES

1 U.S. Constitution Article I, section 8, Clause 8.

2 HR 5055 IH Mr. GOODLATTE (for himself, Mr. DELAHUNT, Mr. COBLE, and Mr. WEXLER) introduced the following bill; which was referred to the Committee on the Judiciary.

3 http://www.copyright.gov

4 Berne Convention Implementation Act of 1988, signed by the United States March 1, 1989.

5 Ibid.

6 *Fogerty v. Fantasy*, 510 U.S. 517 (1994).

[7] *Author's Guild v. Google*, Case number 05cv8136 (S.D.N.Y. 2005).

[8] 17 U.S.C. 101.

[9] Copyright Law of the United States of America and Related Laws Contained in Title 17 of the *United States Code.*

[10] Ibid.

[11] *Estate of Martin Luther King, Jr., Inc. v. CBS, Inc.*, 194 F.3d 1211 (11th Cir. 1999).

[12] *Georgia Television Company v. Television News Clips of Atlanta*, 983 F.2d 238 (11th Cir. 1993).

[13] *Los Angeles News Service v. CBS Broadcasting*, 305 F.3d 924 (9th Cir. 2002).

[14] Copyright Board of Canada.

[15] Australian Copyright Council.

[16] World Intellectual Property Organization

[17] *Universal Music v. Sharman*, FCAFC 41 (2006).

[18] 259 F. Supp. 2d 1029, 1033 (CD Cal. 2003), 380 F.3d 1154 (9th Cir. 2004).

[19] *RIAA v. Lime Wire*, Case number 06cv5936 (S.D.N.Y. 2006).

[20] U.S. Code Title 15, , SubIII, section 1111.

[21] U.S. Code Title 15, , SubIII, section 1114.

[22] *Brother Records Inc. v. Jardine*, 318 F.3d 900 (9th Cir. 2003).

[23] Lanham Act, Section III (15 U.S.C. section 1117(b).

[24] Lanham Act, Section 43 (15 U.S.C. 1125).

[25] *Moseley v. V Secret Catalogue, Inc.*, 537 U.S. 418 (2003).

[26] Public Law No: 109-312.

Online Companion™
For additional resources, please go to
http://www.paralegal.delmar.cengage.com

Student CD-ROM
For additional materials, please go to the
CD in this book.

Entertainment Law

■ **CHAPTER OUTLINE**

■ FEDERAL TRADE COMMISSION (FTC)

Congress created the FTC in 1914 to prevent "unfair methods of competition," and was designed to complement the antitrust laws.

■ FEDERAL COMMUNICATIONS COMMISSION (FCC)

The FCC regulates interstate and international communications, for example, radio and television that comes over the airwaves, and telecommunications.

■ SHERMAN ANTITRUST ACT

The Sherman Antitrust Act declared every contract, combination, or conspiracy in restraint of interstate and foreign trade to be illegal, based on Congress' right to control interstate commerce.

■ CLAYTON ACT

The Clayton Antitrust Act of 1914 was passed by the U.S. Congress as an amendment to clarify and supplement the Sherman Antitrust Act of 1890.

■ OBJECTIVES

After completing this chapter, you will be able to:

- Know how antitrust laws have affected entertainment law, especially in the area of mergers.
- Understand the role of the Federal Communications Commission, and how its regulations affect the entertainment industry.
- Understand governmental regulations concerning cable and satellite television.
- Have a background of the evolution of radio—from analog, to digital, and now to satellite.
- Understand the impact of movies on the media.
- Have a background of the recording industry, that is, contracts and how they are negotiated, and how artists are compensated.
- Discuss issues involved in publishing, such as copyrights, and how to get one's work published.

THOSE WHO CONTROL ENTERTAINMENT LAW

Major influences on entertainment law come from federal government regulations—the antitrust acts under the **Federal Trade Commission (FTC)**, and the regulations of the **Federal Communications Commission (FCC)**.

Antitrust laws are to prohibit restraint of trade—one company creating a monopoly, and thus not allowing other companies to compete. The U.S. government decreed that the creation of monopolies adversely affects consumers and the economy. There have been several antitrust laws starting in 1890 with the **Sherman Antitrust Act**. This act was passed as an attempt to break up the concentration of economic power in large corporations, and in combinations of business concerns. It is based on the constitutional power of Congress to regulate interstate commerce. It declared every contract, combination, or conspiracy in restraint of interstate and foreign trade to be illegal.

In 1914, the **Clayton Act** was adopted. This act expanded the federal government's antitrust enforcement powers under the Sherman Act. In 1950, the **Celler-Kefauver Act** strengthened the Clayton Act. The Celler-Kefauver Anti-merger Act amended Section 7 of the Clayton Act to close a legal loophole. The Clayton Act prohibited stock purchase mergers that resulted in reduced competition, but it did not prevent one business from buying another business' assets. The Celler-Kefauver Act prohibited this practice if competition would be reduced because of the acquisition of such assets.

In 1976, the **Hart-Scoss-Rodino Antitrust Improvement Act** facilitated federal regulators in scrutinizing mergers for potential antitrust violations. The 1970s saw severe scrutiny by the FTC into mergers. Since the 1980s, the FTC has looked less at the effect of the merger and more at the benefit or burden that the merger will have on the consumer.

Some major mergers that have occurred recently include: in 2006, two newspaper giants merged—McClatchy Company acquired Knight-Ridder in a deal valued at approximately $6.5 billion. General Electric, the parent of NBC, was allowed to merge with Vivendi Universal, creating not only a media merger but also an entertainment giant that consisted of theme parks, studios, and GE's other nonmedia and entertainment interests. Comcast in 2004 made a hostile takeover bid for Disney, but later withdrew the offer. In 2000, the largest media company in the world was created with the merger of Time Warner and AOL.

In 1999, Viacom bought CBS (these companies split apart in December 2005). Also in 1999, Clear Channel Communication acquired Jacor Communication. Walt Disney and Capital Cities/ABC merged in 1996. Also in 1996, Time Warner bought Turner Broadcasting. Viacom acquired Paramount and Blockbuster Entertainment in 1994; in 1991 Matsushita Electric bought MCA, and Time Inc. bought Warner Communications in 1990 (becoming Time Warner).

The other arm of the federal government that puts tight regulation on the entertainment industry is the Federal Communications Commission (FCC). The FCC was an offshoot of the **Communications Act of 1934**—the first federal act to control the airwaves. The FCC controls everything from decency on the airwaves, to deceptive advertising, to how powerful a radio or television broadcast transmission can be—the FCC allocates spectrum space (frequency) that a broadcaster may use. The FCC's function is to see that all spectrum space is fairly distributed.

The FCC also gets involved with license transfers. One of the largest has been the sale of almost all of Adelphia's cable systems and assets to Time Warner Inc. and Comcast Corporation in July 2006.

The Organization of the FCC

The FCC is composed of five commissioners that serve five-year terms; they are appointed by the president and approved by the Senate.

"Consumer and Governmental Affairs Bureau—educates and informs consumers about telecommunications goods and services and engages their input to help guide the work of the Commission. CGB coordinates telecommunications policy efforts with industry and with other governmental agencies—federal, tribal, state and local—in serving the public interest.

Enforcement Bureau—enforces the Communications Act, as well as the Commission's rules, orders and authorizations.

■ **CELLER-KEFAUVER ACT**

The Cellar-Kefauver Act reformed and strengthened the Clayton Antitrust Act of 1914. The Cellar-Kefauver Act was passed to close a loophole regarding certain asset acquisitions and acquisitions involving firms that were not direct competitors.

■ **HART-SCOSS-RODINO ANTITRUST IMPROVEMENT ACT**

The Hart-Scoss-Rodino Antitrust Improvement Act (1976) made it easier for regulators to investigate mergers for antitrust violations.

■ **COMMUNICATIONS ACT OF 1934**

The Communications Act of 1934 replaced the Federal Radio Commission with the Federal Communications Commission (FCC).

International Bureau—represents the Commission in satellite and international matters.

Media Bureau—regulates AM, FM radio and television broadcast stations, as well as cable television and satellite services.

Wireless Telecommunications—oversees cellular and PCS phones, pagers and two-way radios. This bureau also regulates the use of radio spectrum to fulfill the communications needs of businesses, local and state governments, public safety service providers, aircraft and ship operators, and individuals."[1]

The FCC makes the rules, judges the alleged rule violator, and then carries out the enforcement of the rules. The FCC must abide by the United States Constitution, and its decisions can be appealed to the U.S. Courts of Appeals and the U.S. Supreme Court, if the Supreme Court grants certiorari.

When the FCC considers making a new rule, and they need further information, they first publish a **Notice of Inquiry** or a **Notice of Proposed Rule Making** and wait for interested parties to respond. Both notices are published at the FCC Web site (http://www.fcc.gov)—and in the *Federal Register*.

After comments have been received, the five commissioners may decide to make the rule or hold hearings on the matter. If the commissioners vote to accept the new rule, it is entered into the *Code of Federal Regulations*, Title 47.

The FCC and Broadcasting Licenses

Of great concern to broadcasters is the FCC's total power to grant a new license, revoke a license, or refuse to renew a license. There are two different licensing procedures depending on whether the station is seeking a new license or renewing a license.

It is extremely costly and time-consuming to seek a new license. There are issues as to allocation of a frequency to the new station (if a frequency is available, the FCC holds an auction and it goes to the highest bidder), antenna issues, and whether the new station will interfere with a station already in existence. The application process delves into whether the station will serve the needs of the community, the background of its owners, the financial backing of the owners, and plans for programming. If an owner wins a frequency, they then obtain a construction permit for the station, and finally a broadcast license for an initial term of eight years.

Once a broadcast license is in place, a station must begin to prepare for renewal immediately. The 1934 Communications Act specifically states, a license is never a vested right that potentially remains with the licensee forever. A broadcaster must show on renewal that they have had a *substantial record of service*. "During the license renewal process, listeners of the stations whose licenses are up for renewal

---

■ **NOTICE OF INQUIRY**

A notice of inquiry is issued by the FCC when it is seeking information or ideas on a given topic.

■ **NOTICE OF PROPOSED RULE MAKING**

A notice of proposed rule making is issued by the FCC when it proposes a new body of regulations or changes to existing regulations. Before any changes to regulations can be made, interested parties are given a time period during which they can comment on the proposed changes.

may participate in the process either by filing a petition to deny or informal objection against a renewal or by filing positive comments about a broadcaster's service."[2] The length of license extension on renewal is eight years.[3]

If the FCC plans to revoke a license, as a result of noncompliance, it must give the owner notice so that the licensee can prepare for a challenge to the revocation. Burden of proof is on the FCC—they must prove why the license should be revoked.

In 2003, the FCC decided to allow corporations to own more TV stations in the same market; expand the percentage of TV households a media corporation could reach from 35 percent to 45 percent; and made it easier for a corporation to cross-own TV stations, newspapers, and radio stations in the same market.

In a Third Circuit Court case, *Prometheus Project v. FCC*, No. 03–3388 (3d Cir. Sept. 16, 2003), it was ruled that the FCC viewed cross-ownership of the media was "irrational assumptions and inconsistencies." The circuit court stayed and remanded several media ownership rules the FCC adopted in 2003. The U.S. Supreme Court refused to hear the case; thus, the FCC is now required to reconsider its broadcast ownership rights.

In June 2006, the FCC announced a 120-day public comment cycle on its broadcast ownership policies. In September 2006, the FCC announced the first public hearing on media ownership issues would be held in Los Angeles, California, on Tuesday, October 3, 2006. Chairman Kevin Martin said, "Public input is integral to this process. The Commission will hold public hearings in diverse locations around the country to fully involve the American people in its review of our media ownership rules."

On December 18, 2007, the Federal Communications Commission approved two new rules that are likely to reshape the nation's media landscape by setting new parameters for the size and scope of the largest news and cable companies. One rule will tighten the reins on the cable television industry—by stipulating that no one company can control more than 30 percent of the market.

The second rule, passed in a 3-to-2 party-line vote, eliminated the longstanding ban on "newspaper/broadcast cross-ownership." This rule gives owners of newspapers more leeway to buy radio and television stations in the largest cities. It is intended to help the newspaper industry. This rule recognizes that the conditions that gave rise to cross-ownership restrictions have changed, now that more news sources are available on the Internet and via cable television.

On December 19, 2007, two members of Congress from Washington State, Representatives Jay Inslee (D-Wash.) and Dave Reichert (R-Wash.) introduced the "Media Ownership Act of 2007" (H.R.4835). This is the House companion bill to Senate bill (S. 2332). The Senate bill was first introduced on November 18, 2007, and was sponsored by Senators Byron Dorgan (D-N.D.) and Trent Lott (R-Miss.). The Media Ownership Act would overturn the Federal Communications Commission's vote on December 18, 2007, as to further consolidation of the media, as well as set new standards for the FCC to be more responsive to public input. The act would prevent the FCC's hurried December 18th rule from becoming law, and it would require more time for public comment. It would also change the timeframe for proposed revisions to be published. The act would go into effect retroactively, on October 1, 2007.

The FCC and Broadcast Content Regulation

In addition to issuing a license for the right to broadcast, the FCC supervises all aspects of the licensee's business, especially programming content. Yet, one could argue, that can put a broadcaster at a disadvantage to a newspaper or magazine that does not have to comply with FCC regulations. In response, the FCC would say that they are granting a license to one particular individual and denying that privilege to others; as such, they have the right to monitor the licensee's programming content.

An area about which the FCC is especially concerned is political broadcasting. The Communications Act Section 315, the **Equal Time Rule**, has been in existence since 1934. This section requires broadcasters to provide equal access to the airwaves during an election to all legally qualified candidates. If a station gives a 30-minute interview to one candidate, it must provide the same amount of time to opposing candidates, although the Rule does not apply to news interviews, news documentaries, political debates, or political conventions. Thus, if a candidate is merely a subject of a news story, the other candidate does not have to be given equal time, but if a candidate is invited to speak on a particular show and discuss their political views, the other candidate must be given equal time. Section 315 does not require a broadcaster to give politicians free time for political advertising; it merely requires a broadcaster to treat each candidate equally.

In the 1990s, President Clinton sought to give free advertising time to major political candidates. The FCC responded by issuing a Notice of Inquiry, thus soliciting input from the public, but it did not take any other action.

The Equal Time Rule also requires radio, television stations, and cable systems, which originate their own programming, to treat legally qualified political candidates equally when it comes to selling or giving away air time. The station must sell a candidate the same amount of time, at the same part of a broadcast, and at the same price her opponent has purchased. If any candidate is given free airtime, then her opponent must be given free air time as well.

Under the Communications Act, a broadcaster must provide reasonable advertising access to candidates in federal elections—Congress and presidential[4]— although a broadcaster is not required to provide access to candidates for state or local offices. If time is sold to a nonfederal office seeker, her opponent must have equal advertising access.

Another area of political broadcasting and the FCC, involves a provision of the Communications Act Section 315(b). This provision requires broadcasters to charge candidates the lowest rate they charge their most favored commercial advertisers within 45 days of a primary election and 60 days of a general election. This provision applies to *all* candidates! Under the revision of the law in 1991, a broadcaster must

■ **EQUAL TIME RULE**

The equal-time rule specifies that radio and television stations must provide equal access to the airwaves to any opposing political candidates who requests it.

tell a candidate all rates and classes of rates available and allow a candidate to purchase the lowest rate. If a candidate's ads are taken off the air for some reason—for example, if they are preempted—a station must "make good" on the ad before the election. The FCC has declared that it has exclusive jurisdiction over the lowest unit rate, and the 9th Circuit U.S. Court of Appeals let that jurisdiction stand.[5]

International Control of Broadcasting

The FCC does not control international broadcasts. In Europe, members of the European Union have established a single EU market in television—"Television Without Frontiers [TWF] Directive." The TWF Directive enacted in 1989, and revised in 1997, assures access for viewers and listeners in all EU states to broadcasting signals from any other member state. TWF also seeks the harmonization of EU advertising standards.

The directive sets forth minimum standards for television programming, and, if those standards are met, this will allow broadcasts to freely circulate through the EU. The TWF concerns itself with protection of minors, advertising, rights of reply, and the promotion of television program production and distribution.

Any advertising that promotes discrimination based on race, sex, or nationality; is offensive to religious beliefs; or encourages behavior *contra* to health, safety, or environmental protection is prohibited or restricted under the directive. If any individual or organization feels a television program has damaged her, then she is given a right of reply to correct the issue.

The TWF requires EU member states to reserve a majority of their transmission time for "European Works"—to protect EU members from non-EU competition. Furthermore, 10 percent or more of transmission time or programming budget is to be reserved for European works created by producers that are independent of a broadcaster.

Also involved in the international broadcast arena is the International Telecommunications Union (ITU). The ITU was created to facilitate telecommunications between the world's countries. This includes the Internet, telephony, radio, television, and satellite matters. The ITU assures proper allocation of radio and television frequencies worldwide. Although each country can decide which channel to assign to a broadcaster; how much a country can use of the broadcasting frequency spectrum is determined on an international basis.

CABLE TELEVISION

With the beginning of television's popularity in the 1950s, there was a need for more reliable television service to rural communities. Although metropolitan areas could "pick up" the three major U.S. TV networks—ABC, CBS, and NBC—with either an outdoor antenna or "rabbit ears," the rural community was left with poor or no reception at all. In answer to this problem, "community antenna television"—CATV—was implemented. CATV allowed a community to set up a large antenna system with signal boosters so those that were connected to the CATV cable could receive TV reception. By the 1960s and 1970s, cable TV changed its focus from merely providing clear television reception to providing additional viewing channels.

These new cable channels were not under FCC regulation because they were not being transmitted over the airwaves; instead, they were coming over underground or aboveground wires. They did not need an FCC license to operate. Thus, cable TV developed with very little federal regulation. Finally, in 1966, the FCC decided to regulate cable TV. This FCC action came about mainly as a result of protests by broadcasters and program producers as to cable TV's importation of distant signals—not the closest station affiliate. Under the 1966 directive, a cable station had to carry the nearest station affiliate, not a more distant one, and the FCC put forth rules as to local governments granting franchises to cable systems. The FCC said that it was authorized to put forth such rules to protect the airwaves broadcasters. The U.S. Supreme Court agreed with the FCC in *U.S. v. Southwestern Cable Co.*, 392 U.S. 157 (1968). The Court held that the FCC had jurisdiction under the Communications Act because that act allowed the FCC "... regulatory power over all forms of electrical communication, whether by telephone, telegraph, cable, or radio."

In 1984, Congress affirmed the FCC's role in cable TV when it amended the Communications Act with the **Cable Communications Act**. This act was put into effect to establish a national policy concerning cable communications, establish procedures that encourage the growth of cable systems, assure cable systems are responsive to the needs of the local community, establish guidelines for the exercise of federal and local governments as to regulation of cable systems, assure a wide diversity of information and sources to the public, establish a policy for franchise renewal that protects cable operators from unfair renewal denials, and promote competition between cable systems and minimize unnecessary regulation.[6] This act gave the cable industry freedom to grow with minimal regulation.

In light of the minimal regulations put on the cable companies, they became the subjects of many complaints from consumers for poor service and high prices. In response to these complaints, in 1992, Congress instituted the **Cable Television Consumer Protection and Competition Act**.

Although this act did little for service and rates, it did require cable operators to carry noncable stations under **must carry**. Must carry means that all cable systems in a service area are required to carry a particular station, yet they are not required to carry duplicative broadcasts. (For example, if there are two independent stations in a

CABLE COMMUNICATIONS ACT

The purpose of the Cable Communications Act is to establish a national policy concerning cable communications and establish franchise procedures and standards which encourage the growth and development of cable systems and which assure that cable systems are responsive to the needs and interests of the local community.

CABLE TELEVISION CONSUMER PROTECTION AND COMPETITION ACT

The Cable Television Consumer Protection and Competition Act was passed to amend the Communication Act of 1934 to provide increased consumer protection and to promote increased competition in the cable television and related markets.

service area carrying the same programming, the local cable company need only carry one of the stations, not both of them.) The station carried, under must carry, does not get paid for its programming—usually these are less preferred stations that merely want to be carried on the cable system.

The must carry rule has been upheld in two U.S. Supreme Court cases, one in 1994 and one in 1997. In both cases, the Court held that the must carry rule was necessary to foster free local broadcast and competition. The Court held the impact on the cable systems was minimal, thus not a violation of cable's First Amendment rights.[7]

In October 1994, the FCC gave stations a choice of being carried under the must carry rules, or under a new regulation requiring cable companies to obtain **retransmission consent** before carrying a broadcast signal. The retransmission consent ruling gave *desirable* local stations increased power to negotiate the terms of carriage the cable company would provide, including channel preference and payment of royalty fees. (The three Copyright Royalty Judges, housed within the U.S. Copyright Office, determine these royalty rates.[8])

In June 2006, the FCC was scheduled to vote if cable companies *must carry* both analog and digital signals until the final total switch to digital broadcasting occurs on February 17, 2009. The FCC abandoned that vote when FCC Chair Kevin Martin concluded a consensus on the matter could not be reached. Martin favors holding the cable companies to the carrying of both signals.

SATELLITE TELEVISION

When satellite TV started in the 1980s, as competition to cable television, it was a horrible failure. All the firms that began their operations at that time decided not to continue. It took until the 1990s for these ventures to begin to gain subscribers. The leading satellite television companies, EchoStar and DirecTV, were given the opportunity to be competitive with cable in 1999 when Congress passed the **Satellite Home Viewer Improvement Act (SHVIA)**.

"The SHVIA amends both the 1988 copyright laws and the Communications Act of 1934. One of the key elements of the SHVIA is that it, for the first time, permits satellite carriers to transmit local television broadcast signals into local markets, also known as 'local-into-local.' This act also authorizes satellite carriers to provide distant or national broadcast programming to subscribers."[9]

Of course, royalties must be paid for station use. Before this act, a satellite system could only carry the major broadcasting networks in rural areas that were so far away from a broadcast station that these stations could not be received.

The FCC further helped satellite TV compete with cable when, in August 1996, it adopted a new rule that is intended to eliminate unnecessary restrictions on antenna placement. The FCC overruled local zoning regulations banning the dish

■ MUST CARRY

The must carry rule mandates that cable companies carry various local and public television stations within a cable provider's service area.

■ RETRANSMISSION CONSENT

Retransmission consent is an alternative to must carry. Under retransmission a local station can demand compensation from a cable company when the cable company carries their station signal.

■ SATELLITE HOME VIEWER IMPROVEMENT ACT (SHVIA)

The Satellite Home Viewer Improvement Act, for the first time, permitted satellite carriers to transmit local television broadcast signals into local markets, also known as "local-into-local." This act also authorizes satellite carriers to provide distant or national broadcast programming to subscribers.

antennas required for satellite reception, thus balancing the right to receive satellite service with those of issues of public concern. The rule does allow local governments and homeowners' associations to enforce restrictions for safety or historic preservation.

RADIO

Radio had its humble beginnings in 1896 when one of the inventors of the technology—Guglielmo Marconi—was awarded a British patent. In 1897, the first radio station was launched on the Isle of Wight in England. Another founder of radio was Nikola Tesla, who launched his transmissions in 1900. However, it took another two decades to begin regular radio broadcasts.

Radio is sent out on particular frequencies. AM stations broadcast from 0.300 megahertz to 3 megahertz, a rather low frequency. AM translates into amplitude modulation—the height of the waves being transmitted. FM stations broadcast with higher fidelity—they can send out more information on their frequencies. FM refers to frequency modulation—the number of waves being transmitted. One drawback that FM stations have is that their reception range is limited—usually 50 to 100 miles. FM radio broadcasts in the VHF (very high frequency) range of 30 megahertz to 300 megahertz power. This requires more radio frequency space than AM; fortunately, there are more frequencies available at these megahertz powers. Still, there are not enough commercial frequencies for all that wish to broadcast, and as discussed earlier, the FCC keeps tight rein on the licensing of broadcast stations, including radio.

A new development in radio is the introduction of digital audio broadcasting called **In-Band On-Channel (IBOC)**. This digital broadcasting began in the late 1980s. It was implemented to give higher fidelity than the FM or AM analog stations could provide. By 2005, the FCC had approved IBOC digital radio operation for AM and FM broadcast stations. AM broadcast stations are limited, at the time of this writing, to digital operation during daytime hours only.

So what is IBOC? This terminology refers to a method of transmitting a digital radio broadcast signal that is centered on the present AM or FM station's frequency, but the digital transmission occupies the sidebands above and below the carrier's frequency. Thus, the digital signal is transmitted in addition to the existing analog signal. The IBOC is a hybrid, because it is not fully analog nor is it fully digital. Only receivers that can pick up both forms of transmissions will allow the digital reception. The goal of IBOC is to provide near CD quality for FM stations, and for AM stations their quality will improve to FM analog reception.

For an AM or FM licensee to transmit digitally, it must notify the FCC within 10 days of commencing its IBOC transmission. Once notice is received, it will be entered into the FCC's database as a hybrid station. The station itself will need to advertise to its listeners the fact it is transmitting in digital format.[10]

■ **IN-BAND ON-CHANNEL (IBOC)**

In-Band On-Channel is a method of transmitting digital radio and analog radio broadcast signals simultaneously on the same frequency.

Satellite Radio

Satellite radio (SR), also called subscription radio, is digital radio that receives its signal from a communication satellite circling the earth. Anywhere that there is line of sight between the receiving antenna and the satellite, there is reception.

The reason that satellite radio is called subscription radio is because the technology behind it is extremely costly and, as such, there are commercial entities that sell this service for a monthly fee. In North America, the companies offering SR are XM Radio and Sirius. Both of these services require a proprietary receiver for each service. XM radio offers some 170 digital channels featuring music, news, sports, weather and traffic reports, and talk stations. XM boasts that it has over eight million listeners. Sirius offers some 130 channels of radio coverage and has implemented a few satellite TV stations geared to a young, back seat-of-the-car audience. Sirius boasts that it has over six million listeners.

One of the most controversial aspects of Sirius radio is its channel addition of "shock jock" Howard Stern, a talk-show host who is noted for his ribald humor. In April 2004, the FCC fined Clear Channel Communications, the station that had formerly aired the Howard Stern show, $495,000 for indecency. Acting on a listener complaint regarding an April 2003 broadcast in which Stern and his cohorts on the show discussed their sex lives, the FCC took action. In response, Clear Channel radio decided to drop Stern from their radio lineup. Stern took this opportunity to leave Clear Channel Communications in 2005, and he joined ranks with Sirius. The contract amount for Stern signing with the SR was $500 million over five years. Some Sirius money!

Satellite radio, at this time, is not subject to FCC regulation or scrutiny, and it appears the FCC has no intention of regulating this medium. The question is without the constant conflict with the FCC, will Howard Stern be as controversial? Sirius is hoping that he is. (Because Sirius picked up Stern, its stock price has increased almost 60 percent, and its subscriber base has increased by over a million subscribers. Perhaps Sirius' gamble has paid off.)

As of this writing, Sirius and XM are in the beginnings of a merger process, although this merger will not be an automatic one. In addition to getting shareholder approval, XM and Sirius also will have to get the endorsement of regulators, including the FCC.

Furthermore, the **National Association of Broadcasters (NAB)**, a trade group that represents local radio and TV stations, urged policy makers to reject the deal, calling it an "anticonsumer proposal." The NAB actually would be shocked if federal regulators allowed the merger, considering the government's history of opposing monopolies. The NAB stated, "It bears mentioning that regulators summarily rejected a similar monopoly merger of the nation's only two satellite television companies—DirecTV and DISH Network—just a few years back."

The Department of Justice (DOJ) also may have a say regarding the merger, and may require a price cap on the subscription price on the combined company, for example, there would be a very low, or even no, increase in subscription rates.

■ **NATIONAL ASSOCIATION OF BROADCASTERS (NAB)**

The NAB exists to advance the rights and interests of free, local radio and television broadcasters.

As more listeners are tuning into satellite radio and tuning out of terrestrial stations, land-based stations are beginning to see their earnings fall. In July 2006, CBS Radio told its employees that there is increased competition from satellite radio. CBS is seeing its stock value, and thus its corporate value, fall, as are other terrestrial stations. Is this the beginning of the end for "free" radio? Will listeners choose to pay $12.95 per month for a more controversial and commercial-free venue? Will the fierce competition for FCC granted frequency licenses slow? Only time will tell.

Satellite Radio and the World

Not only has the satellite radio phenomenon come to North America, but the rest of the world has satellite radio options as well. In Europe, Asia, and Africa, WorldSpace is the SR provider. Founded in 1990 to provide digital satellite radio to emerging underserved markets, WorldSpace is a subscription-based service using low-cost portable satellite radios. WorldSpace serves over 130 countries including India, China, all of Africa, the Middle East, and most of Western Europe. Broadcasts include news, sports, music, and educational programming.

Low Power Radio Transmission

With the advent of satellite radio, the continued fierce competition for terrestrial station frequencies, and the desire for alternative venues for individuals to express their views, the FCC has adopted a way for someone with even the most modest means to actually own a noncommercial radio station. In response to a growing communication area—"pirate" stations (those transmitting without FCC approval)—the FCC in 2000 created low power FM broadcast service (LPFM).

These stations are only authorized for noncommercial educational broadcasting. The maximum power at which they can operate is 100 watts with a service range of 3.5 miles (although some LPFMs actually can be heard up to 100 miles away). Antenna height cannot be taller than 100 feet above the average terrain. A LPFM station is not protected from interference from other FM stations. Nor are LPFM stations available to current broadcast licensees with interests in other media—broadcast or newspapers.

LPFM stations must protect authorized radio broadcast stations on the same channel or frequency, as well as broadcast stations in adjacent channel frequencies. This is accomplished through use of mileage separation requirements set forth in Title 47 CFR 73.807.[11]

Are LPFMs popular? Although over 250 LPFMs were initially licensed very few are still on the air. Those that have survived maintain they are filling a need in the field of alternative media.

MOVIES

Movies are one of the most prominent forms of entertainment in the world. The United States is the largest producer of movies, and as such the most influential in cinematography. Movies, because of their high profile, have garnered much legal controversy. There are issues of copyright infringement, either in the editing of the movie, the colorization of it, or in its production; there is the issue of unions and their affect on a production, and there are issues as to the rights of artists in the work.

The Screenplay

A movie begins with the writing of a screenplay. This either can be developed as an original piece for a particular work, or it can be an adaptation from a book or short story. The screenplay is different from a literature piece because screenplays only concern themselves with the action and dialogue of the characters, not their emotional state or other aspects that may be seen in the final product. That is left up to the director and actors.

In the early days of movies, most screenwriters were under contract to one studio, and thus screenplays were merely works for hire. Today, with so many independent studios, independent contractors produce most of the screenplays, although most writers that are established will write on assignment—when a production company or studio commissions them. In this way, they are assured of getting paid for what they write. Very famous writers usually only "spec" write—they are not under assignment from a particular production company or studio. They do this so that they can get a better price by creating competition among studios.

When writing a spec script, a writer hopes that their work will go under option. An option is a contractual agreement made by a producer, with a writer, whereby the producer gets the right to buy a screenplay from a writer by a certain date. The writer hopes that the option will turn into the purchase of the screenplay.

What the writer does not want to happen is to have a producer "shop" the screenplay around to studios without an option agreement. If the studios reject the screenplay, and there is no option agreement, the writer will not get paid for her work. The Writers' Guild of America (WGA), the major union involved in screenplay issues, mandates that a producer cannot "shop" it around to a third party unless an option contract is in place. If a producer shops a script without an option contract, she will have to pay a fine to the WGA. The WGA also mandates other contract terms for the protection of its members. Some contract issues that a writer must consider are how payment will be provided for an option, or how payment will be provided if the screenplay is turned into a movie; to whom and how the movie will be distributed; and who will hold the copyright on the finished product.

If an option is exercised, an agreed amount will be paid either as a lump sum or over several payments (called an exercise price). A writer also may get an agreed percentage of the actual film budget, or she may get a bonus based on the credit given to her in the film as screenplay writer or merely as a revision writer. If credited as the screenplay writer, she will receive more compensation than if her work had to go under extreme revisions. Net or gross profit percentages also can be negotiated. If net profits—revenue less expenses—are accepted as the form of payment on a film contract, the writer must realize she may actually get no payment on the film. A percentage of the "net" on a film could be nothing, since after expenses there may be no profits left. Many a writer, director, producer, or even an actor has sworn, "The next time I negotiate a contract percentage it will be based on gross profits, not net."

Producers or directors who are hired by a studio for multiple projects may sign what is called a cross-collateralization agreement. Cross collateralization is when the costs of the two projects are linked together, and the eventual percentage amount to be paid will be based on the total profits between the projects. Thus, the studio is protected if one project does not do well and the other is a success. This is also done in the recording industry, and in publishing.

Cross-collateralization is a potentially losing proposition for all except the studio, recording industry, or publisher. For example, a producer finishes one picture and it is a horrible failure. It loses over $4 million. The other project is a great success and net profits are $4 million. If the producer is paid based on net percentage, because of the cross-collateralization clause in their contract, then they will make nothing because there was no net profit.

A case that highlights a screenwriter versus powers in the movie industry is when, in July 2006, screenwriter Royce Mathew sued Walt Disney Co. and the other companies involved in the production of the initial *Pirates of the Caribbean* film—*The Curse of the Black Pearl*.[12] The suit alleges that in the 1980s, Mr. Mathew created and wrote drawings, screenplays, outlines, and other original materials for a supernatural pirate. He alleges Disney, Buena Vista Home Entertainment, and Jerry Bruckheimer stole his ideas. Mr. Mathew stated that he had pitched the story line to producers in Hollywood, and had documents from the U.S. Copyright Office to prove it. He even had a copyrighted drawing of a pirate ship called the Black Pearl. Mr. Mathew asked that all copies of the film be impounded, and he demanded an injunction against other infringing works and asked for unspecified damages. A Disney spokeswoman stated that the suit had no merit.

The first *Pirates* movie—*The Curse of the Black Pearl*—grossed some $655 million worldwide since its release in 2003. The sequel—*Dead Man's Chest* —grossed over $1 billion worldwide, and the third movie—*At World's End*—grossed $142 million in its first weekend.

Unions and the Creative Process

The movies and unions have been synonymous since the 1930s. The **Screen Actors Guild (SAG)** is a labor union that was established in 1933. It is affiliated with the American Federation of Labor-Congress of Industrial Organizations (AFL-CIO), via the Associated Actors and Artists of America. Its primary concerns are wages and

■ **SCREEN ACTORS GUILD (SAG)**

The Screen Actors Guild is an American labor union that represents film and television performers. The Guild seeks to negotiate and enforce collective bargaining agreements that establish equitable levels of compensation, benefits, and working conditions for its performers.

working conditions for performers. It accomplishes its mission via collective bargaining agreements, thus creating equitable levels of pay, benefits, and working conditions for its member performers.

To join SAG, a performer must qualify for at least one of the following:

1. Worked as a principal performer for one day on a SAG project produced by a company that has signed with SAG, and that hires SAG members.

2. If a performer is a background actor and completes three days of work as a SAG-covered background actor under a SAG contract. The three days can be on different projects.

3. Or, a performer may be a member of The American Federation of Television and Radio Artists (AFTRA), Actors Equity, American Guild of Musical Artists (AGMA), Alliance of Canadian Television and Radio Artists (ACTRA), or the American Guild of Variety Artists (AGVA) for at least one year, and also has been a principal performer while a member of any of the named unions during that time.

With the advent of many movies being made abroad because of much lower production costs, creative artists also will want to look into non-American unions. The British Columbia Council of Film Unions (BCCFU), established in 1996, was a result of an order of the Labour Relations Board of Canada. The BCCFU and its member unions have agreements with more than 80 percent of all film production in British Columbia. It is a resource for producers and filmmakers, and it provides provisions for all to work collaboratively so as to fulfill the artistic visions of creative artists, and promote a healthy film and television industry. The BCCFU wants filmmakers to come back to British Columbia again and again.

In the United Kingdom, the U.K. Film Council is a government-sponsored agency, the main aim of which is to stimulate a successful and vibrant U.K. film industry. It also promotes cinematography throughout all regions of the United Kingdom.

The Australian Film Commission promotes everything from protecting its indigenous peoples in the moviemaking process to the promotion of Australian films worldwide. Ausfilm represents the movie and television industry, promoting Australia as a destination for screen productions. At Ausfilm, a producer can find information about locations in Australia, studios, available technicians, and creative talent. She also will inform a production about governmental regulations and other legal and financial issues. Ausfilm represents a collaboration of Australia's film agencies such as Austrade, the Department of Communications, Information Technology and the Arts, and over 60 private sector companies.

Colorization

The issue of colorizing a movie, which originally was in a black-and-white format, includes how much power the creator of the copyrighted work should have, even if the copyright has been sold to another. Does colorization violate the *moral rights* of the original producer of the movie?

As discussed in Chapter 7, the Berne Convention and the doctrine of moral rights gives an artist complete control over the artistic content of her work. The belief is that the artist's creation is an extension of the artist and cannot be changed or tarnished by anyone else. No matter who holds the copyright, the artist retains these rights to the creative work. Although moral rights are recognized in other countries that have signed the Berne Convention, the United States, as a signatory, does not recognize such rights.

In the mid-1980s, Ted Turner's company purchased the entire MGM library of classic films, and their copyrights, and then colorized most of them. The U.S. Congress agreed with Mr. Turner's actions, and refused to honor the moral rights provision of the Berne Convention.

In 1988, Congress established the National Film Registry, a legacy of the colorization controversy. This registry is a list of films that are selected by the creative community and copyright holders. The copyright owner may colorize a film that is selected by the registry, but now it must be labeled with a disclaimer—that is, that the film has been altered from its original monochromatic format.

There have been arguments made that U.S. trademark law protects the moral rights of a copyright holder because a copyright holder can sue under the Lanham Act for not receiving proper credit for their creative work.[13] Yet, in *Dastar Corp. v. Twentieth Century Fox Film Corp.* (cited earlier), the Court did away with the protection of giving the original copyright owner credit for her work if the work is now in the public domain. In *Dastar*, the U.S. Supreme Court held trademark law could not be used to prevent the rerelease of a television series even if the origin of the series was not revealed. Once the work is in the public domain, the original copyright holder has no further rights in the work.

■ FAMILY ENTERTAINMENT AND COPYRIGHT ACT

The Family Entertainment and Copyright Act provides for the protection of intellectual property rights, and for other purposes.

Censorship of DVDs

In 2005, President Bush signed into law the **Family Entertainment and Copyright Act**. This act was a win and a loss for Hollywood and its movie studios. The win was that it became a federal crime for someone to "camcord" a movie while viewing it in a movie theater, or produce other bootlegged audio or video materials. The motion picture industry attributes 90 percent of the illicit DVD films are a result of camcording in movie theaters.

The loss for the movie industry was that the act made it legal for distributors to release movies that have had all the sex, violence, and questionable language edited out (although it did not take long for this issue to end up in federal court. See later in this chapter). Hollywood moviemakers argued that this was a violation of their copyrights every time that a "sanitized" version of a movie was distributed for profit.

Companies such as CleanFilms, Family Flix, CleanFlicks, and Play it Clean Video are among over 90 companies that produce such edited DVDs. CleanFlicks, Family Flix, and CleanFilms takes an original DVD and copies it on to their computer hard drives. They then edit it accordingly, and either sell or rent the new version to their customers.

Another company that censors DVDs without actually altering them is ClearPlay. ClearPlay uses downloadable filtering systems that skip past objectionable material without the physical alteration of the disc. The technology allows the viewer to control how much or little violence, sex, or other objectionable material they wish to see. ClearPlay allows its users to decide what material is suppressed. The company is not selling censored DVDs but is selling filtering templates. Filter selections include nudity, violence, homosexuality, profanity, sexual scenes, and so forth.

In July 2006, the issue of copyright infringement, via the physical alteration of a movie, and the selling or renting of this "sanitized" version, went to trial in *Clean Flicks v. Soderbergh*, 433 F.Supp.2d 1236 (D. Colo. 2006). In this case, the court struck down the altering of DVDs or VHS tapes for censorship purposes. The judge held that such alteration violates copyright laws, stating that this is an "illegitimate business."

The applicable law in this case is the Copyright Act, 17 U.S.C. sections 101–122. The movie studios hold the copyrights for the movies identified, and have the exclusive copyright rights under section 106 of the act. Although the movie studios do edit such films for use by airlines, network and syndicated television broadcasts, for conformation of ratings, run times, and other industry standards, the studios do not sell or rent such copies to the general public. The movie studios claimed that CleanFlicks et al. are infringing on their exclusive right to reproduce the copyrighted works, as well as on their exclusive right to distribution of copies of the movies.

CleanFlicks et al. claimed that they are only making "fair use" of the copyrighted material, and, under public policy, their edits are much appreciated by families viewing these altered DVDs. The court held "There is nothing transformative about the edited copies. Therefore, the first statutory factor in the fair use defense does not support the infringers." As to public policy "This Court is not free to determine the social value of copyrighted works. What is protected are the creator's rights to protect its creation in the form in which it was created."

The court ordered the infringing companies to hand over their inventories within five days to the studios for destruction of the altered movies, and issued a permanent injunction for the companies to immediately stop producing, creating, renting, and selling the altered movies. CleanFlicks plans to appeal this ruling. CleanFlicks did relaunch their site in 2007.

As for ClearPlay, this business was not affected by the *CleanFlicks* ruling because the company does not physically alter movies. As such, unless there is a stay of injunction issued as to the *CleanFlicks* case, ClearPlay will be the only product on the market offering the legal filtering of potentially objectionable material in movies.

In addition to the censorship of movie DVDs, there have been attempts by state governments to limit a minor's access to computer and videogames that are rated for mature audiences. Yet, six times in the last five years, courts have held that state laws that attempt to limit access to such games violates the First Amendment of the Constitution. The courts have held that such games are protected speech.[14]

THE RECORDING INDUSTRY

Before the time of radio, sheet music and even player piano rolls (devices that would allow a player piano to play the music by itself) were the main sources of revenue for the music industry. With the advent of radio and phonograph records, sheet music became less popular. When records could be mass-produced, phonographs became electric instead of hand-cranked, and the radio began playing more popular songs; the music industry began to grow. Now the industry is dominated by the record (CD) industry.

The **Recording Industry Association of America (RIAA)** is a trade group that represents its *record (CD) company* members. The members of the RIAA create and distribute some 90 percent of all legal sound recordings produced and sold in the United States. As was discussed in the last chapter, the RIAA has been involved in litigation connected with the downloading of copyrighted music, the *Napster* and *Grokster* cases (cited earlier), and the RIAA has been seriously criticized for its aggressive legal suits against individuals that have participated in music file sharing.

Yet many musical artists do not feel that the RIAA adequately represents their interests because the RIAA is established to work with its company members, and not with the music artist. In response to this need artists have formed their own association—the **Recording Artist's Coalition (RAC)**.

The RAC was formed to represent the interests of recording artists in legislative, corporation, and public policy areas. Areas such as Internet music policies, recording contracts, and other industry issues have been addressed by the RAC.

Internet Music Policies

In 1995, Congress passed the **Digital Performance Right in Sound Recordings Act**. This act allowed record companies the right to charge royalties when a digital audio broadcast is played on the Internet. Congress concluded that playing copyrighted music on the Internet could interfere with the sale of such works, and, as such, the copyright holder has the right to compensation.

■ RECORDING INDUSTRY ASSOCIATION OF AMERICA (RIAA)

The Recording Industry Association of America is a trade group that represents the U.S. recording industry.

■ RECORDING ARTIST'S COALITION (RAC)

The Recording Artist's Coalition is an American music industry organization that represents the recording artist, and attempts to defend her rights and interests.

■ DIGITAL PERFORMANCE RIGHT IN SOUND RECORDINGS ACT

The Digital Performance Right in Sound Recordings Act allows the record companies, who hold the rights in sound recordings, to collect a royalty on digital "performances" of the sound recording.

In 1998, with the enactment of the Digital Millennium Copyright Act, a royalty schedule was implemented for such digital audio broadcasts. These webcasting rates apply to *noninteractive formats* such as streaming audio. SoundExchange, originally part of the RIAA, and now its own separate entity, collects these royalties and distributes them—50 percent to the copyright holder, usually the record company, 45 percent to the main artist, and 5 percent to background artists. A panel of artists and record labels runs the SoundExchange, and each group has equal representation.

These royalty amounts are not small. In 2002, a rate of $0.0007 per song performance, per listener for an on-the-air radio station, and $0.0014 per performance, per listener for a nonbroadcast webcaster was set.[15] Nonbroadcast webcasters complained that this was more than they made from their digital broadcasts. In 2004, the Copyright Office established the same rate for both on-air and nonbroadcast stations—$0.0007 per song performance, per listener.

In response to the imposition of royalty amounts by the **Copyright Royalty Board**, in 2006, an administrative trial began. The copyright owners and SoundExchange presented evidence in May. The webcasters presented their direct case in June. In 2007, the United States Copyright Royalty Board made a decision; they passed a rate increase in the royalties payable by webcasters. The new rates for a commercial webcaster include a minimum fee of $500 per year per channel, with escalating fees for each song played.

Furthermore, the decision and rates are retroactive to January 1, 2006, and the applicable fee for the retroactive period is $0.0008 per performance, per listener. This per song fee increases approximately 30 percent per year, which by 2010 will be $0.0019 per song, per listener. It is estimated by many webcasters that these fees assessed would represent 100–200 percent or more of their revenue received during their Internet broadcasts.

■ **COPYRIGHT ROYALTY BOARD**

The three Copyright Royalty Judges, who make up the Copyright Royalty Board, determine the rates and terms for the copyright statutory licenses and make determinations on distribution of statutory license royalties collected by the copyright office.

SIDEBAR

On November 30, 2004, the Copyright Royalty and Distribution Reform Act of 2004 was signed into law. The act became effective on May 31, 2005. It amends the Copyright Act, title 17 of the United States Code with respect to the administration of the various statutory copyright licenses, phasing out the Copyright Arbitration Royalty Panel ("CARP") system and replacing the arbitrators with three permanent Copyright Royalty Judges (Board). This Board conducts proceedings to, "... make determinations and adjustments of reasonable terms and rates of royalty payments as provided in [Copyright Act] sections 112(e), 114, 115, 116, 118, 119 and 1004 ... and to make determinations concerning the adjustment of the copyright royalty rates under [Copyright Act] section 111, to authorize distributions under sections 111, 119, and 1007 of the Act, and [t]o determine the status of a digital audio recording device or a digital audio interface device under sections 1002 and 1003, as provided in section 1010." 17 U.S.C. 801(b).

■ AGGREGATE TUNING HOURS

Aggregate Tuning Hours are the cumulative hours of reception of a broadcast, per listener, for a given timeframe.

For noncommercial webcasters the fee will be $500 per channel for up to 159,140 ATH—**Aggregate Tuning Hours**—per month. (ATH is the total number of reception hours, of a broadcast, per listener, for any given time period.) Any transmissions above that number would require the noncommercial webcaster pay the commercial rate.

Not only are webcasters concerned about this action by the Copyright Royalty Board; performers also are worried; fearing that the rate increases will cripple or kill many webcasters and thus reduce the exposure that Internet broadcasting of their works has given them. Some webcasters are considering taking their stations to Canada, or to other countries that do not impose such fees.

In response to these new rate increases, on April 26, 2007, a bill was introduced in the House of Representatives—HR 2060, by Rep. Jay Inslee (D-WA) and Rep. Donald Manzullo (R-IL) and has been cosponsored by some 100 members of Congress to reverse the CRB's decision; a companion bill was introduced in the Senate on May 10, 2007, by U.S. Senators Ron Wyden (D-Ore.) and Sam Brownback (R-Kans.).

The new rates webcasting rates were scheduled to go into effect on July 15th, 2007. This has been appealed.

In November 2007, the U.S. Court of Appeals for the District of Columbia, released a briefing schedule for the appeal of webcasting royalty rates. This appeal will begin in February 2008, but is not likely to be resolved until sometime in 2009.

Briefs from the groups who filed the appeal—include the Digital Media Association, National Public Radio, and others are due on February 25, 2008. The Department of Justice, representing the Copyright Royalty Board, will then file its brief defending the existing rates by April 25, 2008; and SoundExchange will submit a brief defending the fairness of the rates it recommended to the Copyright Royalty Board by May 15, 2008.

The parties will then have until June 12, 2008 to reply to one another's briefs.

The argument is then likely to be heard by the court during the Fall of 2008. A decision would not likely come until very late in 2008 or, more likely, in 2009.

As to royalties, if a song is played on interactive media such as My.MP3.com, Pressplay, MusicNet, and so on, artists are left without the high mandatory royalties of streaming audio (discussed earlier) because the mandated royalties do not apply to interactive formats. With interactive venues, an artist must settle for whatever royalties she has agreed to in her contracts. Even before an artist sees these smaller interactive format royalties, the record company can deduct any outstanding balances they have with the artist—for example, advances or record production costs—so there may be no royalty left.

Artists get no royalties on webcasting, when a record label negotiates an equity deal with a webcaster. In such a deal, instead of payment of money to the record company, the company takes an equity interest in the webcaster. Because no money has changed hands, there are no royalties to pay the artist.

Music Licensing Societies

A particularly difficult issue regarding royalties in the use of copyrighted music is that of how a composer, lyricist, and music publisher gets a licensing fee from everyone performing a copyrighted song. **ASCAP—The American Society of Composers, Authors, and Publishers**, **BMI—Broadcast Music Incorporated**, and **SESAC—Society of European Stage Authors and Composers**, were created to solve this problem. These organizations keep track of whose music is being played. They then collect royalties from restaurants, nightclubs, radio and television stations, and other businesses that play copyrighted music. Churches, schools, and even nonprofits may have to pay licensing fees unless they are exempt under Section 110 of the Copyright Act.

The organizations sell a **blanket license**, which allows a music user to perform any of the groups' copyrighted works as much or as little as they wish. Licensees pay an annual fee—from $500 up. The license saves the music user from having to keep track of all the music used, and avoids the necessity of negotiating licenses with all the copyright holders. It also prevents the inadvertent copyright infringement on ASCAP's, SESAC's, and BMI's members.

There are also "per program" licenses. These authorize a broadcaster to use all the works under the groups' copyright, but the user will have to keep track of all music used. A complication to this form of license is that a music user must get rights for any music used in programs not covered under the "per program" license. The main advantage of the "per program" license is that it is less expensive than the blanket license. When fees have been collected under either license, BMI, SESAC, and ASCAP then distribute these amounts to the copyright holders they represent.

Recording Contracts

For record companies, standard recording contracts are a blessing, although many artists maintain such contracts range from unfair, to indentured servitude, to a restraint of trade. Record labels require an artist to sign an **exclusivity agreement**—the artist may not be able to enter other contracts while under contract with the record company. This is good for the label because it gives them control over the artist, yet limits what the artist can do.

Record companies will require the artist to agree to produce a minimum number of albums—usually six to eight. Of this number, there will be an initial number of albums the artist must produce in a specified period of time, and the record label must produce these or face a penalty for not producing them—called pay-or-play. Pay-or-play is good for the artist because she is guaranteed that either the album will be produced, or that she gets some money for her work. (The compensation will be whatever the record company agreed to pay the artist for the album, less the expected costs to produce the album.) After the initial albums are produced, it is up to the record label to decide whether to renew the artist's contract (option). This

ASCAP—THE AMERICAN SOCIETY OF COMPOSERS, AUTHORS, AND PUBLISHERS

The American Society of Composers, Authors and Publishers, is a membership association of composers, songwriters, lyricists and music publishers. Its function is to protect the rights of its members by licensing and paying royalties for the public performances of their copyrighted works.

BMI—BROADCAST MUSIC INCORPORATED

Broadcast Music Incorporated is a performance rights organization that collects license fees on behalf of its composers, songwriters, and music publishers and distributes them as royalties to members whose works have been performed.

■ SESAC—SOCIETY OF EUROPEAN STAGE AUTHORS AND COMPOSERS

SESAC, originally the Society of European Stage Authors & Composers, is the smallest of the three performance rights organizations in the U.S. Based in Nashville, Tennessee, SESAC deals with all aspects of the music business from creation, to licensing, and administration.

■ BLANKET LICENSE

A blanket license allows the music user to perform a performance rights organization's entire copyrighted song list as much or as little as they like.

■ EXCLUSIVITY AGREEMENT

An exclusivity agreement would prevent an artist from entering a similar recording agreement with another recording company.

means that, as long as the record company wants that artist's product, the artist is obligated to produce the originally agreed to number of albums. This may result in an artist working for that particular label for 10 or more years. Interestingly, only the record company can decide whether to extend a contract or not; the artist has no say in the matter.

> **SIDEBAR**
>
> It is in the artist's best interest to negotiate a contract that requires a record label to commit to the production of a high number of albums in the initial term, and then limit the number of times a label can renew a contract (option). Thus, the artist is given a certain number of produced albums, yet the artist will be tied to the label for the shortest period of time.

California attempted to address this issue of inordinately long record contracts when it passed Labor Code 2855. Under subsection (a), the termination of contracts between creative artists and entertainment companies after seven years is allowed. However, in 1987, after much lobbying by the record labels, and much to the chagrin of music artists, California added subsection (b), which states:

"(1) Any employee who is a party to a contract to render personal service in the production of phonorecords in which sounds are first fixed, as defined in Section 101 of Title 17 of the United States Code, may not invoke the provisions of subdivision (a) without first giving written notice to the employer in accordance with Section 1020 of the Code of Civil Procedure. ... In the event a party to such a contract is, or could contractually be, required to render personal service in the production of a specified quantity of the phonorecords and fails to render all of the required service prior to the date specified in the notice provided in paragraph (1), the party damaged by the failure shall have the right to recover damages for each phonorecord as to which that party has failed to render service ..."

In 2001, recording artist Courtney Love filed a counterclaim against UMG Recordings for violating California Labor Code Section 2855.[16] This counterclaim was the result of a complaint filed by UMG (Universal Music Group) Recordings against Love when she attempted to end her contractual relationship with the recording company. The counterclaim alleged major record companies force unconscionable, impossible-to-perform contracts on recording artists with the full knowledge that the artists have no choice except to sign them if they want access to the marketing campaigns that only a major label can provide. Standard recording agreements require artists to bear so many of their own production, packaging, and marketing costs that they virtually guarantee little or no financial return for almost every recording artist. By the time that all costs of the record production and any advances to the artist are repaid to the record label, there may be no royalties left to be paid to the artist.

In 2002, Ms. Love and UMG settled. Ms. Love is now free to record with whomever she pleases. The issue as to the validity of subsection (b), with regard to recording artists, was not fully resolved with this settlement; perhaps it will be in the future.

The recording industry, as does the film industry, has cross-collateralization of projects. Thus, even if an artist has a huge success with one album but two miserable failures, the costs of the failures will be taken out of the royalties of the successful work. An artist should attempt to negotiate the best possible scenario as to cross-collateralization in their recording contract.

PUBLISHING

The oldest area of entertainment law is the publishing of books. This form of entertainment has been around since humans began to put their thoughts down on paper. When an individual decides to publish, there are some initial considerations on how to go about this process. Formerly, an author had only three possible options—find a publisher that would publish what the writer has written, find a publisher that would hire the writer for a specific book, or pay a printer to print the work, that is, self-publish. Today, with the advent of the Internet and on-demand printing, a writer also can decide to e-publish—that is, put the book online, or have one's book published by an on-demand publisher, a much less expensive proposition than going to a print shop. No matter how a writer proceeds, there are specific legal issues that must be addressed.

The most important consideration is what type of contractual agreement will be entered into between the publisher and writer. Issues as to control of the material, copyright ownership, advances, and royalties all must be considered.

If a writer signs a contract with a publishing firm for a work that she has created, usually there is an agent representing the author. An agent receives a commission from the author, usually 15 to 20 percent of the royalties or fees that the author receives from the work. Agents are valuable to an author because they have contacts with publishers that an author may not have. They also will assist a writer in marketing her work to other media forms such as a screenplay.

A contract for such a book usually will allow the author to retain the copyright and other property rights in the work, because the publisher has had very little control over the writing of the book, and the publisher did not initiate the concept for the book. Remuneration from the publisher will usually consist of royalties from the sale of the work. A royalty is a set percentage amount, negotiated between author/agent and publisher. A publisher taking on such a work is gambling that the cost of compiling, marketing, and printing the first run of the book (usually 5,000 copies) will be made up in sales of the book.

If a publisher contacts an author to write a specific book, the publisher wants control over its writing and contents. In that case, an author will not have any rights in the work, except for the right to get paid. The publisher will hold the copyright and all other property rights in the work, because it is a work for hire. Remuneration in this case could be in the form of an advance, an amount paid to the author before publication, or even before the writing of the book. The advance is then paid back when the book sells; any royalties to the author are withheld until the advance is satisfied. The publisher is taking the chance the work will sell, and will pay off the advance and the cost of publishing and marketing the work.

An author writing a work for hire may only be paid in the form of royalties, and no advance is given. This usually happens if the author is not well known, or has not had prior publishing experience.

SIDEBAR

When Hillary Rodham Clinton was approached to write a book on her life, she was given an $8 million advance from her publisher, Scribner.

When an author negotiates a royalty, and agrees to a percentage, she needs to be very specific in how the royalty will be calculated. Will it apply to the gross amount of book sales, or will it apply to the net amount on the work's sale after the publisher has deducted all expenses? Also, an author should ask for the right to audit the financial sales records of the publisher to substantiate what has and has not been paid and or deducted from royalty amounts.

The publisher should be sure a delivery date for the manuscript is specified, the term "**time is of the essence**" should be put in the contract. This puts the author on notice that the publisher needs the chapter, first draft, or final manuscript by a specific date. If the author does not comply, she can be held for contractual breach.

A publishing contract will require an author to warrant that her work is original, or, if she uses another's work, that she will receive a release for its use. Contracts also require that the publisher and the author will not compete with each other—they will not produce a work that will interfere with the contracted book. All publishing contracts allow a publisher to reject a work, if it is deemed not publishable. If a manuscript is rejected, most contracts require the publisher to relinquish its rights in the project, and thus the author can take the work to another publisher.

If a writer cannot find a publisher that will take on her work, and she is convinced that her work is worth publishing, she can self-publish. There are three options available. The first is what is called a vanity publisher. In this situation, an author takes her manuscript to a company that specializes in the printing of books. The cost of printing the book will be based how much effort the printer must put into turning the manuscript into the book. Usually in vanity publications, 500 copies are printed, and, of course, the author will keep all rights in the book. The drawbacks to this, as compared to signing a contract with a publisher, are (1) the author is taking the financial chance the book will sell; (2) most major bookstores will not stock such a book, and (3) the author will have to market the book without the help of a publisher.

■ **TIME IS OF THE ESSENCE**

It is a contract term, and it is meant to specify that the time and dates mentioned in contract are very important to maintain and should not be ignored by any of the parties under any circumstances.

A less costly way of getting a book into print is to go to a print-on-demand publisher. The advantages of this form of publishing are that it will cost a fraction of what a vanity press would charge, the author will not have 500 copies of the book sitting around because copies are only printed when actually purchased, and the author usually will get a royalty on each copy sold. The disadvantages include (1) there is limited marketing of the book—the author is mainly responsible for selling the book; and (2) the author will have to be familiar with desktop publishing because much of the layout of the book will be in the author's hands (unless the author wishes to pay for the preparation of her manuscript).

E-publishing is another form of publishing and has emerged with the growth of the Internet. E-publishers can help with editorial services, as well as arrange for an ISBN (**international standard book number**) for the author. The cost for e-publishing is even less than publishing via print-on-demand. The e-publisher will require the author to supply a hardcopy of the work as well as a CD. Once this is supplied, the publisher will upload the content to the site, and then interested readers worldwide will pay a fee to access the online encrypted book. The author receives a royalty from the fees collected from readers.

The next chapter will discuss the role advertising plays in media law.

■ INTERNATIONAL STANDARD BOOK NUMBER

The ISBN (International Standard Book Number) is a 13-digit number that uniquely identifies books and book-like products published internationally.

SUMMARY

Congress created the FTC to prevent "unfair methods of competition"—prohibiting one company from creating a monopoly and thus not allowing other companies to compete. It was designed to complement the antitrust laws.

The FCC controls everything from decency on the airwaves, to deceptive advertising, to how powerful a radio or television broadcast transmission can be—the FCC allocates spectrum space (frequency) a broadcaster may use. The FCC has complete control over broadcast licenses.

Cable television, in its infancy, merely assured those in rural areas had over-the-air television access equal to urban dwellers. Cable has now grown into a major force in the transmission of over-the-air and purely cable channels. Satellite television, competition to the cable companies, needed federal regulations to help it succeed.

Radio had its humble beginnings in the late 19th century, evolving into a well-received medium in the early 1900s. Today, radio has gone digital and is being broadcast via satellite.

Movies have garnered much legal controversy because of their high profile. There are issues of copyright infringement; there is the issue of unions and their affect on a production, and there are issues as to the rights of artists in the work.

Record companies dominate the music industry, leaving music artists at a disadvantage as to contract negotiations and royalty payments. Many artists make most of their income from tours, not from the sale of records (CDs).

When publishing a manuscript, an author originally had limited options. Today, with the growth of the Internet and on-demand printing, a writer can also decide to e-publish—put the book online—or have one's book published by an on-demand publisher. Whichever method a writer chooses, she should be aware that there are legal issues that must be resolved as to copyright and other property ownership rights, and how she will be paid for her work.

DISCUSSION QUESTIONS

1. Discuss why the government, under antitrust laws, should not be able to tell a privately held business what it can or cannot do.

2. Why should a cable company have to comply with "must carry" requirements when the stations carried may or may not bring in any revenue to the company?

3. Should the federal government have given satellite television companies so much favorable legislation? Why or why not?

4. Should satellite radio be subject to FCC regulation? Why or why not?

5. Should a movie be allowed to have a final permanent form, regardless as to whether it is in monochrome or color? Argue both sides of the controversy.

6. Argue for and against the RIAA suing individuals for music file sharing.

7. Does the advantage of having a publishing contract outweigh the loss of the copyright to the publisher? Discuss.

CASE FOR REVIEW

On October 10, 2002, the FCC declined to approve the transfer of licenses from EchoStar Communications Corporation and Hughes Electronics Corporation, a subsidiary of General Motors Corporation, to a new entity. EchoStar and Hughes both provide direct broadcast satellite (DBS) service via Dish Network and DirecTV.

FCC commissioners felt that this merger would not be of benefit to consumers. Yet, Consumers' Union stated that this merger could have allowed satellite TV to pose a serious threat to cable monopolies under the proper conditions. Look up this FCC decision under http://www.fcc.gov/, and argue for and against the merger.

KEY TERMS

Aggregate Tuning Hours	Incorporated	Communications Act of 1934
ASCAP—The American Society of	Cable Communications Act	Copyright Royalty Board
Composers, Authors, and	Cable Television Consumer	Digital Performance Right in Sound
Publishers	Protection and Competition Act	Recordings Act
blanket license	Celler-Kefauver Act	Equal Time Rule
BMI—Broadcast Music	Clayton Act	exclusivity agreement

Family Entertainment and Copyright Act

Federal Communications Commission (FCC)

Federal Trade Commission (FTC)

Hart-Scoss-Rodino Antitrust Improvement Act

In-Band On-Channel (IBOC)

international standard book number

must carry

National Association of Broadcasters (NAB)

Notice of Inquiry

Notice of Proposed Rule Making

Recording Artist's Coalition (RAC)

Recording Industry Association of America (RIAA)

retransmission consent

Satellite Home Viewer Improvement Act (SHVIA)

Screen Actors Guild (SAG)

SESAC—Society of European Stage Authors and Composers

Sherman Antitrust Act

time is of the essence

■ ENDNOTES

[1] About the Federal Communications Commission.

[2] http://www.fcc.gov.

[3] 1996 Telecommunications Act.

[4] *CBS v. FCC*, 453 U.S. 367 (1981). The Court held that the First Amendment rights of candidates and the public outweighed the First Amendment rights of broadcasters with regard to federal candidates' political statements.

[5] *Wilson v. A.H. Belo Corp.* , 87 F.3d 393 (9th Cir. 1996). The Court of Appeals holding they have exclusive jurisdiction over rulemaking by the FCC, and this may not be evaded by seeking relief in the district court.

[6] 47 USC 521 Section 601.

[7] *Turner Broadcasting System v. FCC*, 512 U.S. 622 (1994) and 520 U.S. 180 (1997).

[8] Title 17 U.S.C. Sections 111 and 119.

[9] http://www.fcc.gov.

[10] Ibid.

[11] Ibid.

[12] *Mathew v. The Walt Disney Company*, case number cv06-4303 (C.D. Cal. W.D. 2006).

[13] *Lamothe v. Atlantic Recording Corp.*, 847 F.2d 1403 (9th Cir. 1988).

[14] *ESA v. Granholm*, 404 F. Supp. 978 (ED Mich. 2005); *VSDA v. Schwarzenegger*, 401 F. Supp. 2d. 1034 (ND Cal. 2005); *ESA v. Blagojevich*, 404 F. Supp. 2d 1051 (ND Ill. 2005); *VSDA v. Maleng*, 325 F.Supp.2d 1180 (W.D. Wash. 2004); *IDSA v. St. Louis County*, 329 F.3d 954, 957 (8th Cir. 2003); *American Amusement Machine Association v. Kendrick*, 244 F.3d 572 (7th Cir. 2001).

[15] http://www.copyright.gov.

[16] *Courtney Love v. Geffen Records, Inc., UMG Recordings, Inc.*, Case No. BC 223364 (Los Angeles Superior Court, February 28, 2001).

Online Companion™
For additional resources, please go to
http://www.paralegal.delmar.cengage.com

Student CD-ROM
For additional materials, please go to the
CD in this book.

9

Advertising and the Media

CHAPTER OUTLINE

OBJECTIVES

After completing this chapter, you will be able to:

- Know how the Federal Trade Commission affects advertising with regard to deceptive ads.

- Know how the Lanham Act affects advertising with regard to deceptive ads.

- Know how the First Amendment affects advertising—when and how advertisements may be presented.

- Know how the Food and Drug Administration affects advertising.

- Understand the dynamics between the Internet and advertising.

FORCES CONTROLLING ADVERTISING

There are four main forces that control advertising, or what is called commercial speech—the First Amendment to the Constitution, the Federal Trade Commission (FTC), the Lanham Act, and the Food and Drug Administration (FDA).

The FTC became involved in advertising in 1938 with the passage of the **Wheeler-Lea Amendment**. This amendment included a broad prohibition against "unfair and deceptive acts or practices." In 1975, Congress passed the **Magnuson-Moss Warranty Act**; this act gave the FTC the authority to adopt regulations that define unfair or deceptive acts based on the industry involved. The controlling body in the FTC with regard to ads is the *Bureau of Consumer Protection's Division of Advertising Practices*. This division is the U.S. enforcer of federal truth in advertising laws. Their law enforcement activities include:

- Claims for foods, drugs, dietary supplements, and other products promising health benefits.
- Health fraud on the Internet.
- Weight-loss advertising.
- Advertising and marketing directed to children.
- Performance claims for computers, ISPs, and other high-tech products and services.
- Tobacco and alcohol advertising, including monitoring for unfair practices or deceptive claims and reporting to Congress on cigarette and smokeless tobacco labeling, advertising, and promotion.
- Protecting children's privacy online.
- Claims about product performance made in national or regional newspapers and magazines; in radio and TV commercials, including infomercials; through direct mail to consumers; or on the Internet.[1]

If the FTC deems that there have been unfair or deceptive ads, the Division of Enforcement at the FTC can issue cease and desist orders, federal injunctions, and civil penalties. If the court's injunctive order is not followed, there can be criminal sanctions against the offender.

The FTC and Deceptive Ads

In an attempt to help advertisers comply with FTC guidelines, and not put forth unsubstantiated claims with their ads, the Commission has authored several education pieces.[2] This not only helps regulation of potentially deceptive ads but also helps legitimate business, because consumers are less likely to lose faith in advertising.

■ **WHEELER-LEA AMENDMENT**

Under the Wheeler-Lea Amendment to the Federal Trade Commission Act, unfair or deceptive acts or practices (which include advertising) are prohibited.

■ **MAGNUSON-MOSS WARRANTY ACT**

The Magnuson-Moss Warranty Act prohibits "unfair or deceptive acts or practices in or affecting commerce." It is a violation of the FTC Act to advertise a warranty deceptively.

Working in conjunction with the FTC in the monitoring of advertising is the self-regulatory group called the **National Advertising Division (NAD)**. NAD is part of the **National Advertising Review Council (NARC)**. NARC was established to set standards and provide guidance as to the truth and accuracy of national advertising. NARC and NAD are part of the **Better Business Bureau (BBB)**. The mission of the National Advertising Division (NAD), part of the Better Business Bureau (BBB), is to review national advertising for truthfulness and accuracy. It was established to foster public confidence in the credibility of advertising. Policy and procedures for NAD are established by the National Advertising Review Council (NARC). NARC establishes the policies and procedures for the advertising industry's system of self-regulation, which includes the Better Business Bureau's National Advertising Division (NAD). The BBB is a leader in public services related to ethical business practices and dispute resolution—to promote honesty and integrity in the market-place. (The BBB assists businesses and consumers solve marketplace problems via voluntary self-regulation by business and consumer education.) NARC and NAD investigate complaints stemming from consumers and other advertisers, and seek to have an advertiser substantiate their claims. Both NARC and NAD mainly use peer pressure to control the content of advertising, and thus are self-contained, self-regulatory entities.

The FTC realizes one of the areas of advertising receiving the greatest number of complaints, concerns weight-loss products, and it relies on the NAD to encourage the weight-loss industry to regulate them. The FTC also has put the onus on the media to assist in the regulation of these advertisements. The FTC has stated that "...we would have an easier task if these blatantly false ads were never disseminated in the first place."[3]

Most broadcasters and publishers do screen their ads for taste and appropriateness. The FTC has only asked the media to screen out blatantly false ads.[4] The Chairman of the FTC conceded that although the media must contend with First Amendment issues with regard to advertising, there is no constitutional right to run false advertisements. (See the *Central Hudson* case later in this chapter.)

In response to the FTC plea for assistance in the screening of weight-loss advertising, the **Newspaper Association of America (NAA)** appeared at a FTC workshop in 2002.[5] (The NAA is a nonprofit organization that represents over 2,000 papers in the United States and Canada. The NAA members account for nearly 90 percent of the entire daily and nondaily papers in the United States.)

The NAA supports the FTC in its attempt to regulate false weight-loss ads, and pledges to explore all possible ideas with the FTC on how best to address the problem. Yet, the NAA believes advertisers are ultimately responsible for the content of their ads, and the FTC and other governmental authorities are responsible for enforcing advertising laws.

The NAA contends that for a newspaper to have to investigate each ad for potential falsity would have a chilling effect on freedom of the press, and the public's interest in a free flow of information. A newspaper does not have the expertise to evaluate whether or not an ad for a weight-loss product is legitimate, although public

---

■ NATIONAL ADVERTISING DIVISION (NAD)

The mission of the National Advertising Division (NAD), part of the Better Business Bureau (BBB), is to review national advertising for truthfulness and accuracy. It was established to foster public confidence in the credibility of advertising.

■ NATIONAL ADVERTISING REVIEW COUNCIL (NARC)

NARC establishes the policies and procedures for the advertising industry's system of self-regulation, which includes the Better Business Bureau's National Advertising Division (NAD).

■ BETTER BUSINESS BUREAU (BBB)

The BBB is a leader in public services related to ethical business practices and dispute resolution—to promote honesty and integrity in the marketplace.

■ **NEWSPAPER ASSOCIATION OF AMERICA (NAA)**

The NAA is a nonprofit organization representing the newspaper industry. NAA members account for nearly 90 percent of the daily circulation in the United States and a wide range of nondaily U.S. newspapers. The NAA also has Canadian and International members.

■ **AFFIRMATIVE DISCLOSURE**

Affirmative disclosure requires an advertiser to provide customers with any information that could materially affect their purchase decision.

■ **CORRECTIVE AD**

A corrective ad is when the Federal Trade Commission orders a company to run an ad, for the purpose of correcting a consumer's mistaken impression, created by the company's prior advertising.

health professionals and government agencies, such as the FTC, do have such expertise, and under current law, newspapers may not be constrained from printing ads based on the mere possibility that there may be adverse consequences.[6] Furthermore, immunizing newspapers from liability for publishing potentially false advertisements serves the public interest by safeguarding the free flow of information that allows people to make informed decisions.[7]

Affirmative Disclosure and Corrective Ads

If the FTC has determined that a deceptive ad has run, an advertiser may be required to make an **affirmative disclosure**, or run a **corrective ad**. When the FTC asks an advertiser for affirmative disclosure, they require them to disclose all the potential negatives of the product.

In *J.B Williams Co. v. FTC*, 68 F.T.C. 481, 546, 1965, aff'd 381 F.2d 884 (6th Cir. 1967), the FTC made the makers of a product called Geritol put in their ads that it did not help to cure people of certain forms of anemia. Geritol was an iron supplement product, and it was advertised to cure "tired blood." The Commission found that

> "... [Geritol] was effective in only the small minority of cases where tiredness symptoms are due to an iron deficiency, and that it was of no benefit in all other cases ... [the Commission stated] The nature, appearance, or intended use of a product may create the impression on the mind of the consumer . . . and if the impression is false, and if the seller does not take adequate steps to correct it, he is responsible for an unlawful deception."

(Cigarette Rule Statement of Basis and Purpose, 29 FR 8324, 8352 [July 2, 1964]).[8]

Even more oppressive is when the FTC requires an advertiser to run corrective ads to educate the consumer as to what the product does not do, despite prior protestations as to a product's efficacy. In *Warner-Lambert Co. v. FTC*, 562 F.2d 749, 762 (DCC 1977), cert. denied, 435 U.S. 950 (1978), the FTC ordered the manufacturers of Listerine to spend $10 million on ads that stated that Listerine would not cure sore throats or colds. For almost 100 years, Listerine had advertised it would cure these maladies—although medical science never proved this claim.

"The statement 'Kills Germs By Millions On Contact' immediately precedes the assertion 'For General Oral Hygiene Bad Breath, Colds and Resultant Sore Throats.' ... By placing these two statements in close proximity, respondent [Warner-Lambert] has conveyed the message that since Listerine can kill millions of germs, it can cure, prevent and ameliorate colds and sore throats ..."[9]

In 1996, the FTC issued a complaint against Exxon Corporation for deceptive advertising as to its claims, "Exxon gasoline keeps your engine cleaner. . . . So it can help drive down maintenance costs"; and "Exxon 93 *Supreme* [emphasis added] . . .

with the power to drive down maintenance costs. Gas that can save you money. For more reliable performance."[10] The FTC required Exxon to produce, and air, 15-second corrective ads. Exxon also had to produce an informational brochure, informing consumers most cars will run correctly on Exxon's *regular octane gas.*

In 2000, the FTC required the makers of Bayer Aspirin to spend $1 million on consumer education to rectify the company's claim—Bayer Aspirin prevented heart attacks and strokes. "The FTC alleged that since some adults are less likely to benefit from a daily aspirin regime, and some may suffer adverse health effects from taking aspirin on a daily basis, the ad claims were unsubstantiated." Bayer was required to advertise in major magazines that brochures ("Aspirin Regimen Therapy—Is It Right For You?") were available for free by calling a toll-free phone number. The FTC also required Bayer to disclose that "Aspirin is not appropriate for everyone, so be sure to talk to your doctor before you begin an aspirin regimen."[11]

THE LANHAM ACT AND DECEPTIVE ADS

Under the Lanham Act (also discussed in Chapter 7), 15 U.S.C.A. Section 1125 (a) and Section 43 (a), the definition of a deceptive advertising is,

> "... (a)(1) Any person who, on or in connection with any goods or services ... uses in commerce any ... false or misleading description of fact, or false or misleading representation of fact, which ... (B) in commercial advertising or promotion, misrepresents the nature, characteristics, [or] qualities ... of his or her or another person's goods, services or commercial activities, shall be liable in a civil action by any person who believes that he or she is or is likely to be damaged by such act ... 1) that the defendant has made false or misleading statements as to his own product [or another's]; 2) that there is actual deception or at least a tendency to deceive a substantial portion of the intended audience; 3) that the deception is material in that it is likely to influence purchasing decisions; 4) that the advertised goods traveled in interstate commerce; and 5) that there is a likelihood of injury to the plaintiff in terms of declining sales, loss of good will, etc."

False advertising can result from total misstatement to partial misstatements that are potentially misleading to the consumer; a decision as to which advertising is misleading is ultimately made by the courts.

In 1987, a New York court held that a disclosure of information by drug manufacturer Johnson & Johnson that Anacin was a superior pain reliever to its competitor was insufficient. The information failed to disclose all of the side effects of Anacin, whereas Johnson & Johnson exposed all of the side effects found in the competing drug made by American Home Products Corp. Although the Lanham Act does not require full disclosure, there must be sufficient information not to mislead consumers. In this case, when Johnson & Johnson did not make full disclosure, the ad was misleading with regard to the potential health risks of its product.[12]

THE CONSTITUTION AND ADVERTISING

In 1942, the U.S. Supreme Court created the "first commercial speech doctrine." In the *Valentine v. Chrestensen*, 316 U.S. 52 case the Court said that the First Amendment does not apply to commercial speech—the Constitution "imposes no restraint on government as respects commercial advertising." In this case, Mr. Chrestensen had acquired a surplus World War I submarine. He sailed it from port to port and exhibited it for profit. In 1940, he sailed it to New York City and moored it in the East River. To advertise his business, he attempted to distribute handbills on city streets. He was informed that this activity violated a sanitation code that forbids the distribution, in the streets, of *commercial* advertising. He was told, however, that he could distribute handbills that were only informational or for public protest. He then prepared a two-sided handbill; on one side was a revision of the original handbill without a price of admission to the submarine, and on the other side was a protest against the City Dock Department.

The Police Department advised him that the distribution of a bill containing only the protest would not violate the sanitation code, and would not be restrained, but distribution of the two-sided bill was prohibited. Mr. Chrestensen still continued to distribute the two-sided bill. Chrestensen sued in federal court, and obtained an injunction. The U.S. Supreme Court reversed, stating,

> "This court has unequivocally held that the streets are proper places for the exercise of the freedom of communicating information and disseminating opinion and that, although the states and municipalities may appropriately regulate the privilege in the public interest, they may not unduly burden or proscribe its employment in these public thoroughfares. We are equally clear that the Constitution imposes no such restraint on government as [to] ... *purely commercial advertising*" [emphasis added].

It took until the 1970s for the Court to overturn the *Valentine* decision. In *Pittsburgh Press Co. v. Pittsburgh Commission on Human Relations*, 413 U.S. 376 (1973), the Human Relations Commission ordered the *Pittsburgh Press* to stop classifying its help wanted ads into Help Wanted Male and Help Wanted Female—it was discrimination. The U.S. Supreme Court stated in this case, "We hold only that the Commission's modified order, narrowly drawn to prohibit placement in sex-designated columns of advertisements for nonexempt job opportunities, does not infringe the First Amendment rights of *Pittsburgh Press*." Thus, the *Pittsburgh Press* would have to comply with the Commission's order.

In 1975, in *Bigelow v. Virginia*, 421 U.S. 809, the Court struck down a Virginia statute that prohibited abortion ads. In this case, in 1971, Jeffrey Bigelow had published an ad in *The Virginia Weekly* for abortions in New York (this ad appeared before the *Roe v. Wade* decision, and at that time abortions were legal in New York but not in Virginia).

Bigelow was prosecuted for running this ad, and the Supreme Court used his case to rewrite commercial speech law. The Court stated, "... speech is not stripped of First Amendment protection ..." merely because it is in the form of an advertisement. "The advertisement conveyed information of potential interest and value to a diverse audience consisting of not only readers possibly in need of the services offered, but also those concerned with the subject matter or the law of another State, and readers seeking reform in Virginia; and thus appellant's [Bigelow's] First Amendment interests coincided with the constitutional interests of the general public."

The Supreme Court ruled that in the future, with regard to limitations on commercial speech, there would have to be a *compelling state interest* to justify limitations on legal commercial speech. "Virginia's asserted interest in regulating what Virginians may hear or read about the New York services or in shielding its citizens from information about activities outside Virginia's borders (which Virginia's police powers do not reach) is entitled to little, if any, weight under the circumstances."

In another Supreme Court case—*Virginia State Board of Pharmacy v. Virginia Citizens Consumer Council*, 425 U.S. 748 (1976)—the Court held that the state of Virginia's statute to outlaw price advertising by pharmacists was an attempt to regulate commercial speech. Justice Blackmun stated that this was "highly paternalistic" and that the public had the right to receive such information; thus, the speech had First Amendment protections. The Court did make clear that this ruling did not mean that governments could not control false or misleading ads.

The Court continued to recognize the First Amendment aspects of commercial speech. In 1977, in *Carey, Governor of New York v. Population Services International*, 431 U.S. 678, the Supreme Court struck down a New York ban on the advertising of nonprescription contraceptives. These devices were legal in New York, but New York law forbids any displays depicting the contraceptives. The Court held that such a law was in violation of the First Amendment and there was no compelling state interest demonstrated in such a ban. "The prohibition of any advertisement or display of contraceptives that seeks to suppress completely any information about the availability and price of contraceptives cannot be justified on the ground that advertisements of contraceptive products would offend and embarrass those exposed to them and that permitting them would legitimize sexual activity of young people. These are classically not justifications validating suppression of expression protected by the First Amendment, and here the advertisements in question merely state the availability of products that are not only entirely legal but constitutionally protected."

Also decided in 1977, the Court ruled in *Linmark Associates, Inc. v. Township of Willingboro*, 431 U.S. 85 that homeowners do have a constitutional right to put "for sale" and "sold" signs in front of their homes. This residential advertising restriction was put in place by the town of Willingboro, New Jersey, to prevent "white flight." The Supreme Court said that the town could not deprive its citizens of the information that the "for sale" signs denoted. "If dissemination of this information can be restricted, then every locality in the country can suppress any facts that reflect poorly on the locality ..."

The landmark case that solidified the commercial speech doctrine was *Central Hudson Gas & Electric Corp. v. Public Service Commission of New York*. The balancing test handed down by the Court, in this case, remains valid today with regard to the determination of governmental restrictions on commercial speech.

CASE STUDY **Central Hudson Gas & Electric Corp. v. Public Service Commission of New York**

447 U.S. 557 (1980)

Historical background to this case:	In the 1970s, as a result of an oil embargo from the Middle East, and an overdemand for electricity in New York (especially New York City), the Public Service Commission for electric utility companies feared massive electrical shortages.
Facts:	In December 1973, the Public Service Commission for electric utility companies in New York issued an order to stop all ads that promoted the use of electricity. The Commission had found that there were insufficient fuel stocks or electrical production capacity for the winter of 1973–1974. The Commission did allow "informational" advertising, "... designed to encourage 'shifts of consumption' from peak demand times to periods of low electricity demand." The Commission felt that this informational advertising would not create an increase in electrical demand but would "level" demand throughout the day.
	Central Hudson challenged the advertising ban on First and Fourteenth Amendment grounds. The trial court and the New York Court of Appeals upheld the Commission's order. The New York Court of Appeals held the ban on advertising, and thus encouraging conservation outweighed the free speech issue. The U.S. Supreme Court reversed.
Issue:	Does this advertising ban violate Central Hudson's right to free speech?
Decision:	Yes.
Reason:	Justice Powell delivered the opinion of the Court, and found that the ban on advertising would only have a "highly speculative" effect on energy consumption. The First Amendment and commercial speech is based on the informational aspect of advertising, and the Court advanced a four-pronged test as to when commercial speech can be restricted:

(continues)

CASE STUDY **Central Hudson Gas & Electric Corp. v. Public Service Commission of New York** *(continued)*

1. There is no constitutional objection to suppression of advertising that is potentially misleading, or if the advertisement relates to an illegal activity. "If the communication is neither misleading nor related to unlawful activity, the Government's power is more circumscribed.

2. The State must assert a substantial interest to be achieved by restrictions on commercial speech.

3. Moreover, the regulatory technique must be in proportion to that interest." Does the governmental interest justify the restriction on speech? "... the restriction must directly advance the state interest involved; the regulation may not be sustained if it provides only ineffective or remote support for the Government's purpose [and]

4. ... if the governmental interest could be served as well by a more limited restriction on commercial speech, the excessive restrictions cannot survive."

In this case, the Court did not find the ads misleading or unlawful, nor was there any substantial interest shown in proscribing these ads, as their potential energy conservation benefit seemed negligible. The Court also held that the Commission had not shown that its interest in conservation could not be protected in a more limited regulation of commercial speech.

After the *Central Hudson* case, the Court had problems in accepting a commercial speech doctrine; there were a series of conflicting Court decisions. The Court overturned a San Diego ordinance that allowed some billboard advertising but not others. The stated purpose of the ordinance was "... to eliminate hazards to pedestrians and motorists brought about by distracting sign displays" and "... to preserve and improve the appearance of the City." Metromedia, an outdoors advertising firm, sued to enjoin enforcement of the ordinance. The U.S. Supreme Court held the ordinance is unconstitutional on its face "Because the San Diego ordinance reaches too far into the realm of protected speech."[13]

In 1984, the Court ruled in *Members of the Los Angeles City Council v. Taxpayers for Vincent*, 466 U.S. 789, the city of Los Angeles *could* ban political posters on *public* property because this ordinance directly advanced a substantial governmental interest—aesthetics. "The problem addressed by this ordinance—the visual assault on the citizens of Los Angeles presented by an accumulation of signs posted on public property—constitutes a significant substantive evil within the City's power to prohibit." The Court distinguished this decision from *Metromedia* because *Metormedia* was too broad in scope, and the *Vincent* case only banned posters on *public* property.

The "notorious" Tupperware party came under the scrutiny of the Court in *State University of New York v. Fox*, 492 U.S. 469 (1989). The Court upheld SUNY's rules with regard to the restriction of commercial activities on campus. In this case, American Future Systems, Inc. (AFS) was demonstrating and selling its housewares at a party hosted in a student dormitory. The housewares salesperson was arrested when she refused to leave. The Court held that governments have more leeway in regulating commercial speech than applying the "least restrictive means" test. In commercial speech, all that the government is required to show is that there is a "reasonable fit" between the government's purpose in restricting commercial speech and the means chosen to accomplish that purpose.

Justices Blackmun dissented, joined by Justices Brennan and Marshall, stating the majority opinion is rewriting the law in this area, stating, "I would have preferred to leave the least-restrictive-means question to another day, and dispose of the case on the alternative—and, in this case, narrower—ground of overbreadth."

In *Cincinnati v. Discovery Network*, 507 U.S. 410 (1993), the Court held that an ordinance that prohibited all newsracks, yet allowed thousands of newspaper stands, did not meet the "reasonable fit" between the government's purpose and the method of restriction on commercial speech.

The Discovery Network, Inc., is engaged in the business of providing adult educational, recreational, and social programs to individuals in the Cincinnati area. Its means of advertising these programs is via a free magazine, published nine times per year. In 1989, Discovery was granted a permit to distribute these publications in various newsracks, but, in 1990, Cincinnati's Director of Public Works notified Discovery that its permit for the newsracks was revoked, and they had 30 days to remove them. Discovery was told in the notice that their publication was a "commercial handbill" and thus Cincinnati code prohibited distribution on public property.

The Federal District Court held that "... the regulatory scheme advanced by the City of Cincinnati completely prohibiting the distribution of commercial handbills on the public right of way violates the First Amendment." The court held that these publications were commercial speech and thus entitled to First Amendment protection because they promoted lawful activity and were not misleading. The District Court recognized that the city "... may regulate publication dispensing devices pursuant to its substantial interest in promoting safety and esthetics on or about the public right of way," but based on the *SUNY* case the city had the burden to show a "reasonable fit" between the ordinance and the ends sought. The court held that the "fit" in this case was unreasonable because the number of newsracks was small—62, compared with the 1,500–2000 newsstands, and the newsracks only affected public safety in a minimal way. The city could have adequately addressed the aesthetic and safety issues, "... by regulating the size, shape, number or placement of such devices." The Court of Appeals affirmed the District Court's holding.

The U.S. Supreme Court agreed. Justice Stevens, writing for the Court, stated,

"The city's selective and categorical ban on the distribution, via newsrack, of 'commercial handbills' is not consistent with the dictates of the First Amendment. ... In the absence of some basis for distinguishing between 'newspapers' and 'commercial handbills' that is relevant to an interest asserted by the city, we are unwilling to recognize Cincinnati's bare assertion that the 'low value' of commercial speech is a sufficient justification for its selective and categorical ban on newsracks dispensing 'commercial handbills.' Our holding, however, is narrow. As should be clear from the above discussion, we do not reach the question whether, given certain facts and under certain circumstances, a community might be able to justify differential treatment of commercial and noncommercial newsracks. We simply hold that on this record Cincinnati has failed to make such a showing."

There were two dissenters to this decision—Chief Justice Rehnquist and Justice White. Chief Justice Rehnquist, writing the dissent, stated,

"Cincinnati has burdened less speech than necessary to fully accomplish its objective of alleviating the problems caused by the proliferation of newsracks on its street corners. Because I believe the city has established a 'reasonable fit' between its substantial safety and esthetic interests and its prohibition against respondents' newsracks, I would hold that the city's actions are permissible under *Central Hudson*."

In May 2006, the 9th Circuit Court of Appeals upheld the ban on aerial ads in Honolulu, Hawaii. The court rejected an antiabortion rights group argument that they had First Amendment rights to fly banners depicting aborted fetuses over Honolulu's Waikiki Beach.

The court held that the ban did not violate the First Amendment—it was a "... reasonable and viewpoint neutral restriction on speech in a nonpublic forum." The group had other reasonable alternative means of communication. "Preservation of the visual beauty of Honolulu's coastal and scenic areas is of paramount importance."

The antiabortion group's appeal to the U.S. Supreme Court was denied on December 4, 2006, and left standing the Ninth Circuit Court of Appeals' decision that the City's ban on aerial tow-banner advertising was constitutional.[14]

Noncommercial Corporate Speech

Do corporations have constitutional rights to engage in noncommercial speech—speech that is not promoting their product, but in which the corporation is advocating or expressing its views on a subject? According to the U.S. Supreme Court, they do.

In 1980, the Court decided the *Consolidated Edison v. Public Service Commission of New York*, 447 U.S. 530, and held that the Public Service Commission could not prevent Consolidated Edison (Con Ed) from sending inserts with their customers' bills that discussed "issues of public policy." The New York regulation held that no inserts that discuss issues of controversial public policy could be inserted into customer's bills.

New York's appellate court held that the regulation against the insertion of materials that discussed controversial issues was a reasonable regulation. The U.S. Supreme Court reversed, stating that this was not a reasonable restriction on corporate speech.

The facts of this case were that in 1976, Consolidated Edison placed inserts into their bills promoting the need for nuclear energy to diminish the country's dependence on foreign oil. The Natural Resources Defense Council requested Consolidated Edison to enclose a rebuttal in the next billing statement. Con Ed refused. In 1977, the Public Commission put into affect the prohibition with regard to billing inserts. Thus, the issue was did Con Ed have the constitutional right to freedom of speech with regard to its billing inserts?

The Court held that Consolidated Edison was entitled to freedom of speech, the worth of speech as to its informational value does not depend on the speaker, whether it is a corporation, association, union, or individual. The criteria as to governmental regulation of noncommercial corporate speech include the restriction must be of significant governmental interest; it must leave ample alternative channels for communication and such regulations; it "... may not be based upon either the content or subject matter of speech"; the regulation must be a valid restriction on the time, place, or manner of communication; and the state regulation must be "narrowly drawn" and serve a compelling state interest.

In 1986, the U.S. Supreme Court reaffirmed the *Consolidated Edison* case in *Pacific Gas & Electric (PG&E) v. Public Utilities Commission (PUC) of California*, 475 U.S. 1. In the *PG&E* case, the Court held the requirement by the PUC that PG&E place an informational insert, representing a view PG&E did not agree with, in their customer's bills four times a year, violated their First Amendment rights. The Court stated that forcing PG&E to insert another group's insert in place of PG&E's was unconstitutional.

An interesting twist and turn of the U.S. Supreme Court occurred when it first granted certiorari to hear the case of *Nike, Inc. v. Kasky*, 539 U.S. 654 (2003). The Court heard arguments in the case in April 2003, but then announced in June 2003 that they should have not agreed to take the case.

In the trial court case, Nike filed a demurrer, contending that Kasky's suit was absolutely barred by the First Amendment. The trial court dismissed the case, and the California Court of Appeal affirmed this dismissal.

Nike had argued that they had a First Amendment right to defend themselves in the media against charges of unfair labor practices. Marc Kasky, an antiglobalization activist, argued that Nike had participated in unfair and deceptive practices in its defensive labor practices ads, a violation of California's Unfair Competition Law. Kasky alleged Nike made, "... *false statements and/or material omissions of fact* [emphasis added]" concerning the working conditions under which its products are manufactured, thus, Kasky alleged that First Amendment protection should not apply. The California Supreme Court reversed the lower court's ruling, finding that Nike's messages were commercial speech because the speech was designed to increase the company's profitability, but that the suit was at such a preliminary stage that the issue as to whether any false representations had been made had yet to be resolved.[15]

When the U.S. Supreme Court decided that it should not have taken this case, it left the legal door open for Kasky to proceed with his lawsuit. The Supreme Court held that the case should go to trial to resolve the false representations issue before the U.S. Supreme Court should get involved.

There were dissents to this decision not to resolve the case from Justices Breyer and O'Connor, both arguing that by postponing this decision there would be a "chilling" effect on constitutional rights of corporations. Ultimately, Nike settled with Kasky. Nike agreed to fund a labor rights group to oversee working conditions at overseas factories.

Although noncommercial speech does not enjoy the full protection of the First Amendment, it is clear that the Court, at this time, has blurred the line between speech that advances a corporation's profitability and speech that is merely an expression of corporate policy.

Vice and Commercial Speech

In 1986, the U.S. Supreme Court upheld Puerto Rico's 1948 Games of Chance Act. This act prohibited the advertising of casino gambling to Puerto Rican residents, yet it was permissible for casinos to advertise to prospective visitors. Under this law, the Puerto Rican government had decided that they knew what was best for its citizens.

Posadas de Puerto Rico Associates v. Tourism Company of Puerto Rico, 478 U.S. 328 (1986), addressed this Puerto Rican Act. The act stated, "... [n]o gambling room shall be permitted to advertise or otherwise offer their facilities to the public of Puerto Rico." Posadas, a Texas-based operation, and owner of the Condado Holiday Inn Hotel and the Sands Casino, challenged the Act after being fined twice by the Tourism Company for violating the law. The local advertising by Posadas included matchbook covers and elevator signs, both using the word "casino" on them. The Puerto Rican Act specifically forbids the use of the word casino on

"... matchbooks, lighters, envelopes, inter-office and/or external correspondence, invoices, napkins, brochures, menus, elevators, glasses, plates, lobbies, banners, flyers, paper holders, pencils, telephone books, directories, bulletin boards or in any hotel dependency or object which may be accessible to the public in Puerto Rico."

The Puerto Rico Superior Court held that, based on the construction of the act, it was facially constitutional. The Puerto Rico Supreme Court dismissed the appeal on the grounds that the appeal did not address a "substantial constitutional question." The U.S. Supreme Court decided it had jurisdiction over this case because the statute in question may be repugnant to the U.S. Constitution. The Supreme Court, in a 5–4 vote, affirmed the Superior Court ruling, stating the act does pass muster under the four-pronged test of *Central Hudson*. The commercial speech concerns a lawful activity and is not misleading; Puerto Rico has an interest in protecting the health, safety, and welfare of its citizens—a substantial governmental interest. The restrictions on this commercial speech directly advance the government's interest, "... and are not underinclusive simply because other kinds of gambling may be advertised to Puerto Rico residents." Finally, the restrictions are no more broad than necessary to serve the Government's interest, because the restriction only applies to residents, not tourists. The Court also held that it must abide by the narrow construction of the Puerto Rico Superior Court and approved sub silentio by the Puerto Rico Supreme Court. "This would be the rule in a case originating in one of the 50 States, and Puerto Rico's status as a Commonwealth dictates application of the same rule."

There were vehement dissents by four Justices. Brennan, Marshall, and Blackmun joined in one dissent, stating that Puerto Rican law "...seeks to suppress commercial speech in order to deprive consumers of accurate information concerning lawful activity."

Justice Stevens's dissent, with which Justices Marshall and Blackman joined, stated that the law was discriminatory and violated the First Amendment: "Puerto Rico blatantly discriminates in its punishment of speech depending on the publication, audience, and words employed. Moreover, the prohibitions, as now construed by the Puerto Rico courts, establish a regime of prior restraint and articulate a standard that is hopelessly vague and unpredictable." Justice Stevens wrote the Puerto Rican Superior Court's construction discriminates against local media and favors media from outside Puerto Rico.

"With respect to the audience, the newly construed regulations plainly discriminate in terms of the intended listener or reader. Casino advertising must be 'addressed to tourists.' ... It must not 'invite the residents of Puerto Rico to visit the casino.' ... The regulation thus poses what might be viewed as a reverse privileges and immunities problem: Puerto Rico's residents are singled out for disfavored treatment in comparison to all other Americans. ... The First Amendment surely does not permit Puerto Rico's frank discrimination among publications, audiences, and words. Nor, should sanctions for speech be as unpredictable and haphazardous [*sic*] as the roll of dice in a casino."

In 1996, the U.S. Supreme Court rejected much of the *Posadas* decision in *44 Liquormart, Inc. v. Rhode Island*, 517 U.S. 484. 44 Liquormart, a licensed Rhode Island liquor retailer and a licensed Massachusetts liquor retailer, patronized by Rhode Island residents, filed an action for a declaratory judgment as to Rhode Island laws that banned the advertising of retail liquor prices, except at the point-of-sale location. 44 Liquormart alleged that this was a violation of the First Amendment. The Federal District Court concluded the ban was unconstitutional, because it did not directly advance the state's interest in promotion of temperance, and the ban was more extensive than necessary to serve that interest. The Court of Appeals reversed, finding "inherent merit" in the state's contention competitive price advertising would ultimately increase sales, and the Twenty-First Amendment (the amendment that relegalized alcohol after prohibition and gave several states the power to regulate the sale of liquor within their boundaries) gave the ad prohibition a "presumption of validity."

The state of Rhode Island relied on the *Posadas* decision, arguing the ad restrictions are valid because alcoholic beverages are "vice" items. Justice Stevens delivered the opinion of the U.S. Supreme Court, and rejected this "vice" argument:

> "... [O]n reflection, we are now persuaded that Posadas erroneously performed the First Amendment analysis. The casino advertising ban was designed to keep truthful, nonmisleading speech from members of the public for fear that they would be more likely to gamble if they received it. As a result, the advertising ban served to shield the State's antigambling policy from the public scrutiny that more direct, nonspeech regulation would draw. ... Given our longstanding hostility to commercial speech regulation of this type, *Posadas* clearly erred in concluding that it was 'up to the legislature' to choose suppression over a less speech-restrictive policy."

Justice Stevens stated that almost any product that could cause a threat to public health or morals could be considered a "vice."

The Supreme Court also dismissed the contention by Rhode Island that the greater power to ban an activity includes the lesser power to ban its advertisement. "Contrary to the assumption made in *Posadas*, we think it quite clear that banning speech may sometimes prove far more intrusive than banning conduct. As a venerable proverb teaches, it may prove more injurious to prevent people from teaching others how to fish than to prevent fish from being sold."

In *Greater New Orleans Broadcasting Association, Inc. v. United States*, 527 U.S. 173 (1999), the constitutionality of a federal law—Title 18 U.S.C. §1304, and a Federal Communications Commission (FCC) regulation that prohibited radio and television stations from accepting ads from privately operated gambling casinos, regardless of where the station or the casino was located, was at issue.

In the *New Orleans* case, the Broadcasting Association wished to run ads for private commercial casinos that were lawful and regulated in Louisiana and Mississippi. They filed suit for a declaration that section 1304 and the FCC's regulation violate the First Amendment as applied to them. The District Court, in applying the *Central Hudson* four-pronged test with regard to commercial speech, granted the government's cross-motion for summary judgment, the Court of Appeals affirmed.

The U.S. Supreme Court reversed, and held that section 1304 may not be applied if the advertisements are for lawful private casino gambling, and the broadcast by a radio or television station is located where such gambling is legal, such as Louisiana. Section 1304 cannot satisfy the third and fourth parts of the *Central Hudson* test—regulatory regulation must be in proportion to the government's interest and if the governmental interest could be served by a more limited means. As to the government's first assertion the statute is to alleviate casino gambling's social cost by limiting demand: "... the operation of §1304 and its regulatory regime is so pierced by exemptions and inconsistencies that the government cannot hope to exonerate it." Federal law prohibits a broadcaster from carrying ads as to *privately* operated commercial casino gambling, regardless of the casino or broadcaster's location, yet exempts advertising about state-run casinos, tribal casino gambling, and certain occasional commercial casino gambling, even if the broadcaster is located in a jurisdiction of strict antigambling. Along with the FCC's interpretation of the statute, it appears the government wants to prohibit, "... certain accurate product information, not commercial enticements of all kinds, and then only for certain brands of casino gambling." The government cannot abridge non-Indians' freedom of speech more severely than their tribal competitors. It gives no sound reason for these distinctions in freedom of speech.

The government's second asserted interest—"assisting" states with policies that disfavor private casinos is no more convincing to uphold the statute then the first assertion. Section 1304, "... sacrifices an intolerable amount of truthful speech about lawful conduct when compared to the diverse policies at stake and the social ills that one could reasonably hope such a ban to eliminate."

Under the *Greater New Orleans* case, the Court made the *Central Hudson* test, the test whether there should be any limitations on commercial speech or advertising, but what about a legal activity that has been deemed harmful and addictive—tobacco smoking?

Tobacco Ads

In 1997, the Federal Trade Commission (FTC) filed a complaint against the makers of Camel cigarettes—R.J. Reynolds. The complaint alleged that "... the purpose of the Joe Camel campaign was to reposition the Camel brand to make it attractive to young smokers ..." (It has been reported the cigarette industry has purposely marketed its product to children as young as 14.) The FTC dismissed this complaint after the 1998 **Master Settlement Agreement (MSA)** came into effect. The MSA calls for the ban of all cartoon characters in any tobacco advertising, promotion, or packaging.

MASTER SETTLEMENT AGREEMENT (MSA)

The Master Settlement Agreement resolved lawsuits filed by state and U.S. territory attorneys general against the tobacco industry. It provided funds to the states to compensate them for taxpayer money that was spent on patients and family members with tobacco-related diseases. The agreement required that tobacco billboard advertising be taken down, that tobacco companies stop using cartoon characters to sell cigarettes, and that tobacco companies make many of their internal documents available to the public. The tobacco companies also agreed not to target youth in the advertising, marketing and promotion of their products. The Master Settlement Agreement also called for the creation of a foundation—the American Legacy Foundation to counter the use of tobacco.

The MSA also prohibits the tobacco industry from sponsoring any events that may attract a young audience. The tobacco brand name cannot be used in any stadiums or arenas; there cannot be payments to promote tobacco products in movies, television, theater productions, live performance, videos, and video games. Nor can the tobacco brand name or logo be used on specialty (promotional) items.[16]

Despite the MSA, some states decided that agreement did not go far enough, and began to impose more regulation on the promotion of tobacco products. In 1999, the Attorney General of Massachusetts announced new regulations on tobacco products, especially with regard to new ad restrictions. These restrictions were to "close the holes" in the MSA, and to stop tobacco companies, "... from recruiting new customers among the children of Massachusetts."

The Massachusetts regulations called for no outdoor advertising of tobacco products that is visible within a 1,000-foot radius of any public playground, playground area in a public park, elementary school, or secondary school. Another provision called for the prohibition of placing tobacco ads lower than five feet off the floor of any retail establishment (point-of-sale), and tobacco products could not be displayed so customers could have access to them without the assistance of a salesperson.[17]

The tobacco companies filed three separate suits in federal court over these ad restrictions. The tobacco companies alleged these restrictions were preempted by the Federal Cigarette Labeling and Advertising Act, 15 U.S.C. Section 1334 (b). This act prohibits a state from imposing any "... requirement or prohibition based on smoking and health ... with respect to the advertising or promotion of ... cigarettes ..." The smokeless tobacco and cigar industry also argued violation of their First Amendment free speech rights. [18] The U.S. District Court upheld the majority of advertising restrictions, calling tobacco ads "functional pornography." The court did strike down the point-of-sale provision.[19]

The 1st U.S. Circuit Court of Appeals held that federal law does not preempt the Massachusetts Attorney General's regulations; they do not violate the commercial speech protections under the First Amendment, and do not violate the Commerce Clause, except for warning requirements for cigar packages and advertisements. The 1st Circuit reasoned that the federal law only applies to the content of cigarette labels, and in no way prohibits a state from regulating tobacco ads.[20] The tobacco industry appealed.

In 2001, the U.S. Supreme Court reversed the 1st Circuit on both the First Amendment and preemption issues. The Court held that the federal cigarette labeling law did preempt the states from restricting the promotion and advertising of cigarettes, and many of the Massachusetts regulations did violate the First Amendment (*Lorillard Tobacco Co. v. Reilly,* 533 U.S. 525 [2001]).

Writing a 5–4 decision, Justice O'Connor stated,

> "... a distinction between state regulation of the location as opposed to the content of cigarette advertising has no foundation in the text of the pre-emption provision. ... Congress pre-empted state cigarette advertising regulations like the Attorney General's because they would upset federal legislative choices to require specific warnings and to impose the ban on cigarette advertising in electronic media in order to address concerns about smoking and health."

Although the federal statute's preemption provision does

> "... not restrict States' and localities' ability to enact generally applicable zoning restrictions on the location and size of advertisements that apply to cigarettes on equal terms with other products, see, *e.g.*, *Metromedia, Inc.* v. *San Diego* ... or to regulate conduct as it relates to the sale or use of cigarettes, as by prohibiting cigarette sales to minors."

The Court examined the ad restriction on the smokeless tobacco and cigar industry, and held that although the Massachusetts Attorney General had a substantial interest in protecting minors from tobacco products, the 1,000-foot restriction was too broad and violated *Central Hudson's* fourth prong in its commercial speech test. The broad sweep of the ad prohibitions shows that the Attorney General did not carefully calculate

> "... the costs and benefits associated with the burden on speech imposed. ... The record indicates that the regulations prohibit advertising in a substantial portion of Massachusetts' major metropolitan areas; in some areas, they would constitute nearly a complete ban on the communication of truthful information."

The regulations also curtail the information adults could receive. Adult consumers have a First Amendment right to receive information about a *legal* product.

As to the "point-of-sale" restriction, the Court held that

> "... regulations prohibiting indoor, point-of-sale advertising of smokeless tobacco and cigars lower than 5 feet from the floor of a retail establishment located within 1,000 feet of a school or playground fail both the third and fourth steps of the *Central Hudson* analysis. The 5-foot rule does not seem to advance the goals of preventing minors from using tobacco products and curbing demand for that activity by limiting youth exposure to advertising. Not all children are less than 5 feet tall, and those who are can look up and take in their surroundings."

Also, the restriction is not a "reasonable fit" with the goal of preventing under age tobacco use. Although the First Circuit held the restriction's burden on speech was limited, "... there is no *de minimis* exception for a speech restriction that lacks sufficient tailoring or justification."

As to the display of tobacco products, the Court agreed with Massachusetts that prohibiting direct access to tobacco products was permissible and does withstand First Amendment scrutiny. Massachusetts did demonstrate a substantial interest in preventing access to tobacco products by minors, and, by requiring a salesperson to gain access to these products, the state has crafted an appropriate narrow means of advancing this interest.

"Because unattended displays of such products present an opportunity for access without the proper age verification required by law, the State prohibits self-service and other displays that would allow an individual to obtain tobacco without direct contact with a salesperson. It is clear that the regulations leave open ample communication channels. They do not significantly impede adult access to tobacco products, and retailers have other means of exercising any cognizable speech interest in the presentation of their products."

Justice Thomas concurred with the majority decision, writing that commercial speech, including tobacco ads, should receive First Amendment protection: "... when the Government seeks to restrict truthful speech in order to suppress the ideas it conveys, strict scrutiny is appropriate, whether or not the speech in question may be characterized as 'commercial' I would subject all of the advertising restrictions to strict scrutiny and would hold that they violate the First Amendment."

Justice Stevens dissented, stating, "On the First Amendment questions, I agree with the Court both that the outdoor advertising restrictions imposed by Massachusetts serve legitimate and important state interests and that the record does not indicate that the measures were properly tailored to serve those interests." Justice Stevens wanted to remand the case back to the lower courts for the further development of evidence with regard to the breadth of the outdoor advertising regulation.

Lorillard gave the federal government the right to regulate tobacco ads, and the decision overturned hundreds of state and local laws regulating the advertising of tobacco.

Since the *Lorillard* decision, Congress has considered other ways to regulate the advertisement of tobacco products. In 2002, Representative James Hansen (R-Utah) introduced a bill calling for **Stronger Tobacco Warning Labels to Save Lives Act**, HR 3907. This was an attempt to give more detail as to the health hazards of smoking. It allowed showing, on the warning label, a color picture of one of the following—a diseased lung, heart, or mouth; an individual suffering from addiction; children watching an adult smoke a cigarette; and an individual adversely affected by secondhand smoke from a cigarette, including pregnant women or infants.

Also in 2002, Senator Edward Kennedy (D-Mass.) introduced the **Youth Smoking Prevention and Public Health Act**, S. 2626. This measure gave the Food and Drug Administration the power to regulate tobacco products. The sponsors of the Bill stated that tobacco companies had not lived up to the agreement made under the Master Settlement Agreement of 1998, with regard to stopping marketing tobacco products to children.

In February 2006, the U.S. Supreme Court refused to hear an appeal by two North Carolina–based tobacco companies that claimed that California's antismoking ads hurt their reputations. Reynolds American Inc. and Lorillard Tobacco Co. asked the Court to overturn the decision of the 9th Circuit Court of Appeals, which held

■ STRONGER TOBACCO WARNING LABELS TO SAVE LIVES ACT

The Stronger Tobacco Warning Labels to Save Lives Act would require that cigarette packages include health warnings, disclosure of tar and nicotine levels, listings of physical addictions, and health messages, including the hazards of secondhand smoke. In addition, graphic pictures of health effects would have to occupy at least 50% of each side of cigarette packs and cartons.

■ YOUTH SMOKING PREVENTION AND PUBLIC HEALTH ACT

The Youth Smoking Prevention and Public Health Act was introduced to protect public health by providing the Food and Drug Administration with certain authority to regulate tobacco products.

that the companies' First Amendment rights were not violated by California's ad campaign. California uses $.25 of an $.87 tax on each pack of cigarettes sold to educate Californian's about health, and this includes funding for antismoking ads.

The tobacco companies objected to an ad that portrayed them as being only money hungry in their attempt to "hook" 500,000 children per year on smoking, just so they could stay in business. The companies said that California was using tax money, raised on cigarettes, to vilify the tobacco industry.[21]

Compelled Ads—Fruit, Mushrooms, and "Beef, It's What's for Dinner"

Throughout this chapter, the discussion has concerned itself with the First Amendment rights of advertisers and what and how they can convey their commercial messages. What happens when the government steps in and compels an advertiser to speak? The U.S. Supreme Court has addressed this issue three times since 1997.

The U.S. Supreme Court upheld a federal program forcing fruit producers to pay for generic fruit promotional ads in *Glickman v. Wileman Brothers & Elliot*, 521 U.S. 457 (1997).

■ **AGRICULTURAL MARKETING AGREEMENT ACT (AMAA)**

The AMAA is intended "to establish and maintain ... orderly marketing conditions for agricultural commodities in interstate commerce."

In 1937, Congress passed the **Agricultural Marketing Agreement Act (AMAA)**, to promote fair pricing and uniform marketing in agriculture. The administrative cost of the AMAA was covered by assessments made on product advertising and promotion. A group of California tree-fruit growers filed suit for violation of their free speech rights in regard to this mandatory assessment. The U.S. District and U.S. Circuit Court of Appeals ruled against the growers; they appealed to the U.S. Supreme Court.

On appeal, in an opinion written by Justice Stevens, the Court held "The fact that an economic regulation may indirectly lead to a reduction in a handler's individual advertising budget does not itself amount to a restriction on speech." By participating in these ads, the producers were promoting their own welfare by encouraging the sale of their products. Thus, this promotional program raises economic issues not constitutional questions.

Justice Stevens did state that for such marketing requirements to pass constitutional muster, they must not impose any restraint on a producer to communicate their message to any audience; they cannot compel any producer to engage in any specific speech; or they may not compel a producer to endorse or finance any political view.

Justice Souter did dissent, writing that the Court should have applied the *Central Hudson* commercial-speech test.

Although it would appear from the *Glickman* case, compelled promotional ads would withstand Court scrutiny, a 2001 mushroom case would find the Court agreeing with the mushroom producers, and against compelled advertising. In *U.S. v. United Foods*, 533 U.S. 405, the U.S. Supreme Court held that the assessment against the mushroom growers violated the First Amendment.

The **Mushroom Promotion, Research, and Consumer Information Act** mandated that fresh mushroom handlers pay assessments to fund ads promoting mushroom sales. United Foods refused to pay the assessment, alleging that it violated their First Amendment rights. It filed a case in federal district court. The court granted the government a summary judgment because it found the *Glickman* decision applicable, and thus the First Amendment rights of United Foods was not violated. The Sixth Circuit Court of Appeals reversed, holding that *Glickman* did not control, because the mushroom assessment was not part of a statutory agricultural marketing program.

The U.S. Supreme Court agreed with the Court of Appeals and affirmed their decision. Justice Kennedy, writing for the majority, stated that United Foods wished to convey the message that their brand of mushrooms was superior to those grown by other producers. They objected to being charged for conveying a contrary message. "First Amendment values are at serious risk if the Government can compel a citizen or group of citizens to subsidize speech on the side that it favors."

Justice Thomas, in a concurring opinion, wrote, "Any regulation that compels the funding of advertising must be subjected to the most stringent First Amendment scrutiny."

Thus, the Court's ruling in this case is based on compelled speech guidelines, not on the *Central Hudson* guidelines for commercial speech. Future litigants in such cases will challenge such required speech on both compelled and commercial speech issues.

In 2005, the U.S. Supreme Court again dealt with compelled speech in the advertising for beef products, as seen in *Veneman (later becoming Johanns) v. Livestock Marketing Association and Nebraska Cattleman Inc. v. Livestock Marketing Association*, 125 S.Ct. 2055 (2005); *Veneman v. Livestock Mktg. Ass'n*, 124 S. Ct. 2389 (2005). The issue in these cases was whether the First Amendment rights of beef producers were violated when they were required to pay $1 per head of cattle, under the **Beef Promotion and Research Act**, to fund generic beef ads designed to persuade people to eat more red meat.

The Livestock Association argued that the *United Foods* case controlled the legal issues; the Court did not agree. The Court held that the case should be decided on the government-speech doctrine—the government has its own First Amendment rights to advance its own messages. Writing for the Court, Justice Scalia stated that the beef producers did not enjoy the right not to fund government speech. However, Justice Scalia did state that if the "individual beef advertisements were attributed" to certain beef producers they could be unconstitutional when applied to specific advertising situations.

This decision lends constitutional support to as many as 15 other generic advertising programs, including campaigns such as "Got Milk," and "The Other White Meat," a slogan that promotes pork.

How the Court will decide such cases in the future, no one can tell, but for the present time, be legally assured: "Beef, It's What's for Dinner."

■ **MUSHROOM PROMOTION, RESEARCH, AND CONSUMER INFORMATION ACT**

The Mushroom Promotion, Research, and Consumer Information Act calls for the cooperative development, financing, and implementation of a coordinated program of mushroom promotion, research, and consumer information necessary to maintain and expand existing markets for mushrooms.

■ **BEEF PROMOTION AND RESEARCH ACT**

The Beef Promotion and Research Act, 7 U.S.C. 2901 et seq., gives the authority for the collection and expenditures of $1.00 per head of cattle to fund generic beef ads.

THE FDA'S ROLE IN ADVERTISING

Since its inception in 1906, the FDA has had the authority to regulate advertising dealing with pharmaceuticals. The FDA's job is to make sure ads for these products accurately inform a consumer as to the pharmaceuticals' health and safety; yet, at the same time, the FDA must take into consideration the First Amendment rights of the advertiser.

In 2002, the U.S. Supreme Court agreed to hear a case that concerned itself with the advertising of compounded drugs—drugs that a pharmacist mixes to create a medicine that fits that particular patient's needs.

In 1997, the **Food and Drug Modernization Act** allowed compounded drugs to be exempted from the usual FDA approval process. The act did state that providers of such drugs could not advertise particular compound drugs, yet they could advertise the fact they do make compound pharmaceuticals.[22]

Eight pharmacies sued in federal court, alleging that this act violated their First Amendment rights. The FDA countered, alleging that pharmacists only compounded to avoid the lengthy FDA approval process for pharmaceuticals. The U.S. Supreme Court agreed with the pharmacists.

In *Thompson v. Western States Medical Center*, 535 U.S. 357 (2002), the Court applied the *Central Hudson* test with regard to restrictions on commercial speech, and concluded that the act's prohibitions on soliciting prescriptions for and advertising compounded drugs amounted to unconstitutional restrictions on commercial speech.

The Court held that the government's interest in preserving the new drug approval process of the act is important, as is the practice of compounding so that patients with a particular pharmaceutical need may obtain such medications. Because pharmacists compound in small quantities, they do not make enough money from this process to seek FDA approval of the medication. Thus, the government must be able to draw the line between small-scale compounding and large-scale drug manufacturers. Although the government argued that the Modernization Act accomplishes this by not allowing pharmacists to advertise a particular compounded drug, it does allow a pharmacist to advertise that they do compound. The Court stated that the government had not shown the speech restrictions with regard to advertising the compounded drug were "... not more extensive than is necessary to serve [those] interest[s]. *Central Hudson.* ... If the Government can achieve its interests in a manner that does not restrict commercial speech, or that restricts less speech, the Government must do so."

On Nov 6, 2007 H.R. 4083, the **Non-Prescription Drug Modernization Act of 2007** was introduced by Representative Henry Waxman D-CA. This act is to amend the Federal Food, Drug, and Cosmetic Act, and to expand the Food and Drug Administration's authority to regulate drug advertising. It is to regulate false or misleading ads as to drugs other than a prescription drugs.

■ FOOD AND DRUG MODERNIZATION ACT

The Food and Drug Modernization Act creates a special exemption to ensure continued availability of compounded drug products prepared by pharmacists to provide patients with individualized therapies not available commercially. The law, however, seeks to prevent manufacturing under the guise of compounding by establishing parameters within which the practice is appropriate and lawful.

■ NON-PRESCRIPTION DRUG MODERNIZATION ACT OF 2007

The Non-Prescription Drug Modernization Act is to regulate false or misleading ads as to drugs other than a prescription drugs.

THE INTERNET AND ADVERTISING

The FTC and the BBB have both been concerned with deceptive advertising on the Internet. The FTC especially has targeted health claims and weight-loss claims, as discussed earlier in this chapter. After September 11, the FTC began a crackdown on sites that were exploiting fears of communicable diseases such as anthrax and smallpox. The FTC told sites that were potentially deceiving consumers into buying various products such as gas masks, protective suits, or items to sterilize mail to cease and desist.

The FTC also has published Internet advertising guidelines, which an online advertiser should not ignore, although they are not legally binding. "Dot com Disclosures"[23] recognizes the growth of Internet advertising and consumers shopping online. The FTC understands that fraud and deception may lessen consumer confidence. To ensure that products and services are truthfully advertised online, and consumers receive what they order, the FTC is committed to continue to enforce their consumer protection laws. Although general advertising principles apply online, Internet advertising presents some unique challenges, and the FTC will craft new advertising criteria as needed. The FTC advises online businesses to stay current on online advertising law, and comply with these regulations as they are promulgated.

The BBB also has adopted a code of ethics for online advertisers. The code covers everything from truthful and accurate ads, customer satisfaction, protecting children, and advertising disclosure. The code is strictly voluntary, although the BBB suggests the guidelines be adhered to by advertisers.

An area of concern for Internet consumers is "spam"—unsolicited e-mail. In response to the public's concern, Congress implemented the **CAN SPAM Act of 2003 (Controlling the Assault of Non-Solicited Pornography and Marketing Act)**. This act went into effect in January 2004. It banned unsolicited commercial e-mail, and it *preempted state laws* as to spam. The CAN SPAM Act prohibits the sending of spam after a recipient has requested the "spammer" to stop. It requires the spammer to have a valid physical address, opt-out information (how to stop this particular spammer), and a means of reply to the e-mail. If a recipient opts out, the spammer must remove the recipient from its list within 10 business days or face criminal and civil sanctions. The act also forbids a spammer from using another's e-mail address to send out spam.

The FTC is authorized to enforce the CAN SPAM Act, and the Department of Justice has the authority to enforce it with criminal sanctions. Other federal and state agencies can enforce the law against organizations under their jurisdiction, and companies that provide Internet access (Internet Service Providers [ISPs] and other access servers) may sue violators as well.[24]

There is another issue as to the CAN SPAM Act—will it will survive constitutional scrutiny? A Fifth Circuit Court of Appeals decision in 2005 held that CAN SPAM did *not* violate the Constitution.

■ **CAN SPAM ACT OF 2003 (CONTROLLING THE ASSAULT OF NON-SOLICITED PORNOGRAPHY AND MARKETING ACT)**

The CAN SPAM Act of 2003 establishes requirements for those who send commercial email, spells out penalties for spammers and companies whose products are advertised in spam, if they violate the law, and gives consumers the right to ask emailers to stop spamming them.

In February 2003, White Buffalo Ventures filed a Public Information Act request with the University of Texas for a list of all its e-mail addresses. By April 2003, White Buffalo was flooding these addresses with spam for its LonghornSingles.com dating service. When the university asked White Buffalo to cease and desist, White Buffalo refused. When the university began to block the e-mails, White Buffalo sued, claiming violation of their First Amendment rights and a violation of the CAN SPAM Act.

White Buffalo should have read the act, because Section 8(c) provides: "Nothing in this act shall be construed to have any effect on the lawfulness or unlawfulness, under any other provision of law, of the adoption, implementation, or enforcement by a provider of Internet access service of a policy of declining to transmit, route, relay, handle, or store certain types of electronic mail messages." In federal district court, the university's motion for summary judgment was granted based on the findings that the university's spam policy was not preempted by the CAN SPAM Act, nor did it violate the First Amendment. The Fifth Circuit Court of Appeals affirmed.

The Court of Appeals held the University was only filtering "received" e-mails, and CAN SPAM only applied to "sending" spam. Furthermore, "... UT's ITS policy is not a 'statute, regulation, or rule of a State or political subdivision of a state' and is therefore not pre-empted ..."

As to the issue of the First Amendment rights of White Buffalo being violated, the court applied the four-pronged test of *Central Hudson* (cited earlier): (1) whether the speech is unlawful or misleading; (2) whether the government's expressed interest is substantial; (3) whether the state action directly promotes that interest; and (4) whether the state action is more extensive than necessary to promote that interest.

The court found the speech by White Buffalo was legal and contained factual information. Under the substantiality of the government's interest in blocking the spam the court found, "UT advances two primary interests: (1) safeguarding the time and interests of those with UT email accounts (*'user* efficiency') and (2) protecting the efficiency of its networks and servers (*'server* efficiency')." UT's antispam policy, which blocks specific incoming commercial spam, after account holders have complained about it, directly advances a state interest.

With regard to the last prong of the *Central Hudson* test, the university has made policy that is narrowly drawn to protect its system and users from e-mails that have become a problem as adjudged by user complaints. Thus, UT's antispam policy is constitutionally permissible under *Central Hudson*.[25]

In May 2004, the FTC added further regulations to the CAN SPAM Act that require

> "... any person who initiates, to a protected computer, the transmission of a commercial email that includes sexually oriented material must: 1) exclude sexually oriented materials from the subject heading and include in the subject heading of that email the mark 'SEXUALLY-EXPLICIT'; and 2) provide that the matter in the email message that is initially viewable when the message is opened include only certain specified information, not including any sexually oriented materials."[26]

The purpose of this section is an attempt to rectify one of the major complaints as to Internet spam—unsolicited ads for sexually oriented materials and protection of children from such materials.

How well will the CAN SPAM Act work in the alleviation of unwanted e-mails? Only time will tell. However, the FTC has realized that for every spammer they close down there are dozens of others still in business.

Chapter 10 will delve further into the interaction of the Internet and the laws surrounding it.

SUMMARY

There are four main forces that control advertising, or what is called commercial speech—the First Amendment to the Constitution, the Federal Trade Commission (FTC), the Lanham Act, and the Food and Drug Administration (FDA).

The landmark case that solidified the commercial speech doctrine was *Central Hudson Gas & Electric Corp. v. Public Service Commission of New York* in which a four-prong test was devised by the Court to determine when commercial speech can be restricted.

The Master Settlement Agreement bans the use of cartoon characters in the promotion or packaging of tobacco products.

The Internet has spawned concern over deceptive advertising because it is such a ubiquitous and persuasive medium. The FTC has targeted such advertising to protect consumers.

The CAN SPAM Act was implemented to help prevent the proliferation of spam, and to protect children from sexually explicit e-mails. The FTC enforces this act.

▥ DISCUSSION QUESTIONS_____

1. Argue why there should be no controls on advertising. Should it be "buyer beware"?

2. Can the media be a watchdog for deceptive weight-loss ads? Argue why or why not.

3. Argue why the tobacco industry should not be restricted on how it markets its product.

4. Should an industry be compelled to contribute to an advertising campaign to promote its product? Argue for and against this.

5. Should the CAN SPAM Act have preempted state laws on spam?

▥ CASE FOR REVIEW_____

In *United States* v. *Edge Broadcasting Co.*, 509 U.S. 418 (1993), it was held that Title 18 U.S.C. Section 1304 was constitutional as to the preventing of advertising of the Virginia lottery by a broadcaster in North Carolina where no such lottery was authorized. Ninety percent of the station's audience lived in Virginia, but ten percent lived in North Carolina. The Court reasoned that Section 1304 furthered the intent of Congress to support North Carolina's antigambling laws. Compare and contrast this case to the *Greater New Orleans Broadcasting* case.

■ KEY TERMS

affirmative disclosure

Agricultural Marketing Agreement
   Act (AMAA)

Beef Promotion and Research Act

Better Business Bureau (BBB)

CAN SPAM Act of 2003
   (Controlling the Assault of Non-
   Solicited Pornography and
   Marketing Act)

corrective ad

Food and Drug Modernization Act

Magnuson-Moss Warranty Act

Master Settlement Agreement
   (MSA)

Mushroom Promotion, Research,
   and Consumer Information Act

National Advertising Division
   (NAD)

National Advertising Review
   Council (NARC)

Newspaper Association of America
   (NAA)

Non-Prescription Drug
   Modernization Act of 2007

Stronger Tobacco Warning Labels
   to Save Lives Act

Wheeler-Lea Amendment

Youth Smoking Prevention and
   Public Health Act

■ ENDNOTES

1 Guide to the Federal Trade Commission.

2 http://www.ftc.gov.

3 Ibid.

4 Ibid.

5 Ibid.

6 *Near v. Minnesota*, 283 U.S. 697, 720 (1931). The fact that the liberty of the press may be abused does not make the immunity of the press from prior restraint less necessary.

7 *Pittman v. Dow Jones & Co.*, 662 F. Supp. 921, 922 (E.D. La. 1987); *Goldstein v. Garlick*, 318 N.Y.S.2d 370, 374-376 (N.Y. Sup. Ct. 1971).

8 FTC Policy Statement on Deception Appended to Cliffdale Associates, Inc., 103 F.T.C. 110, 174 (1984).

9 Ibid.

10 http://www.ftc.gov.

11 (FTC File No. D. 8919)(Civil Action No. CV 00-132 (NHP))(Bayer).

12 *American Home Products Corp. v. Johnson & Johnson*, 654 F. Supp. 568 (S.D.N.Y. 1987).

13 *Metromedia, Inc. v. San Diego*, 453 U.S. 490 (1981).

14 *Center for Bio-Ethical Reform, Inc. v. City and County of Honolulu*, 455 F.3d 910, 918 (9th Cir. 2006) cert. denied (U.S. Dec. 4, 2006)(No. 06-479).

15 *Kasky v. Nike, Inc.*, 45 P.3d 243 (Cal. 2002).

16 The Surgeon General's Report on Reducing Tobacco Use.

17 Section2(a) of the Massachusetts General Laws.

[18] *Consolidated Cigar Corp. v. Reilly*, 218 F.3d 30 (1st Cir. 2000), petitions for cert. granted sub nom. *Lorillard Tobacco Co. v. Reilly*, 121 S. Ct. 755 (2001).

[19] *Lorillard Tobacco Co. v. Reilly*, 76 F.Supp. 2d 24 (D. Mass. 1999); *Lorillard Tobacco Co. v. Reilly*, 84 F. Supp. 2d 180 (D. Mass. 2000) (Lorillard II).

[20] *Consolidated Cigar Corp. v. Reilly*, 218 F.3d 30 (1st Cir. 2000).

[21] *R.J. Reynolds Tobacco v. Shewry*, 384 F.3d 1126 (9th Cir. 2004).

[22] 21 USC 353a. SEC. 503A. Pharmacy Compounding.

[23] http://www.ftc.gov.

[24] Ibid.

[25] *White Buffalo Ventures, LLC v. University of Texas at Austin*, 420 F.3d 366 (5th Cir. 2005), cert. denied, 126 S.Ct. 1039 (Jan. 9, 2006).

[26] Section 7704(d) CAN SPAM Act.

Online Companion™
For additional resources, please go to
http://www.paralegal.delmar.cengage.com.

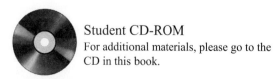

Student CD-ROM
For additional materials, please go to the
CD in this book.

The Media and Cyberspace

■ CHAPTER OUTLINE_____

■ OBJECTIVES_____

After completing this chapter, you will be able to:

- Define what constitutes jurisdiction in cyberspace.

- Understand the issue of libel on the Internet, and who is liable for the posting of defamatory information.

- Understand how international libel jurisdiction issues are resolved.

- Understand how to protect one's work, as to re-publishing it online.

- Understand domain names and the issues surrounding them.

- Understand what cybersquatting is and the laws pertaining to it.

- Understand what the implications are of Net Neutrality.

JURISDICTION IN CYBERSPACE

Before the invention of the World Wide Web and the Internet, a decision as to where a case should be heard—that is, the **jurisdiction** over the matter—was quite easy. **Personal jurisdiction** was achieved by discerning where the person resided or was domiciled; if a business, in what states the entity did business; or, in the case of a corporation, where the corporation was registered to do business. For jurisdiction over a controversy, it requires the defendant do a purposeful act, "... some act by which the defendant purposefully avails itself of the privilege of conducting activities within the forum State, thus invoking the benefits and protections of its laws."[1] With the growth of the Internet, the question is, what allows a court to have jurisdiction when the entire world possibly is affected by the information on a site?

There are two main bases for a court to obtain personal jurisdiction over a defendant, either under **common law**—where a state can assert jurisdiction over anything that is physically present in the state[2]— or under what are called "**long arm statutes**"—these statutes allowing jurisdiction over entities and things outside of the state.

The **Uniform Interstate and International Procedure Act (UIIPA)**, a model long arm statute that several states have enacted, outlines the following as to jurisdiction:

"§ 1.02. [Personal Jurisdiction Based upon Enduring Relationship].

A court may exercise personal jurisdiction over a person domiciled in, organized under the laws of, or maintaining his or its principal place of business in, this state as to any [cause of action] [claim for relief].

§ 1.03. [Personal Jurisdiction Based on Conduct].

(a) A court may exercise personal jurisdiction over a person, who acts directly or by an agent, as to a [cause of action] [claim for relief] arising from the person's

(1) Transacting any business in this state;

(2) Contracting to supply services or things in this state;

(3) Causing tortious injury by an act or omission in this state;

(4) Causing tortious injury in this state by an act or omission outside this state if he regularly does or solicits business, or engages in any other persistent course of conduct, or derives substantial revenue from goods used or consumed or services rendered, in this state. ...

(b) When jurisdiction over a person is based solely upon this section, only a [cause of action] arising from acts enumerated in this section may be asserted against him."[3]

Of course, **due process** must not be violated in the exercise of a long arm statute. To satisfy the Due Process Clause of the Fourteenth Amendment, a plaintiff must show that the defendant has "**minimum contacts**" with the forum state "such that the maintenance of the suit does not offend 'traditional notions of **fair play and substantial justice**.'"[4]

To establish fair play and substantial justice, the court will look to the burden of defending the suit in the state; whether the state claiming jurisdiction has an interest in the dispute; the plaintiff's and the interstate judicial system's interest in the efficient resolution of the controversy; and if the interest of the several states asserting jurisdiction will further substantive social policies. Basically, would the defendant reasonably anticipate being brought into court there?[5]

With these jurisdictional considerations in mind, how does a plaintiff establish jurisdiction with regard to a Web site? To begin the analysis, it is best to look at how the courts have viewed jurisdiction with regard to a medium that spans several jurisdictions—the print media. As we discussed in a previous chapter, in *Keeton v. Hustler Magazine, Inc.* the U.S. Supreme Court held that a state can exercise personal jurisdiction over a publisher accused of publishing libelous material about a resident of that state, when the publisher targets its economic activity at that state. Even though *Hustler Magazine* was an Ohio publication, the circulation of the magazine in New Hampshire created *minimum contacts* in that state, and jurisdiction was appropriate.

In *Calder v. Jones* (cited earlier), the Supreme Court held that a California court could exercise personal jurisdiction against an author and the editor of the *National Enquirer*. Although both were residents of Florida, they had libeled a California resident, and the Supreme Court determined that the defendants had purposefully targeted their libelous activity at California, by publishing their article in a magazine they knew was sold and circulated in that state, and "... must reasonably anticipate being haled [*sic*] into court ..." in California.

There have been *contra* decisions as to extension of personal jurisdiction. In *IDS Life Insurance Company v. Sun America Inc.*, 958 F. Supp. 1258 (N.D. Ill. 1997), the defendant merely advertised in newspapers, magazines, television, and maintained a Web site. The District Court for the Northern District of Illinois held that "... mere advertising did not result in continuous contact with Illinois, and thus the court did not have personal jurisdiction ... it cannot plausibly be argued that any defendant who advertises nationally could expect to be haled [sic] into court in any state, for a cause of action that does not relate to the advertisements." Ads alone are not sufficient to create minimum contacts.

For the courts to establish jurisdiction over Internet activities they have begun to develop a "**sliding scale**" to decide if the minimum contacts requirement has been satisfied. They have established a criterion whether personal jurisdiction can be constitutionally exercised. The criterion is to what extent is the contact "... directly proportionate to the nature and quality of commercial activity that an entity conducts over the Internet." This sliding scale is consistent with well-developed personal jurisdiction principles. At one end of the spectrum are situations in which a

UNIFORM INTERSTATE AND INTERNATIONAL PROCEDURE ACT (UIIPA)

UIIPA is a model long arm statute that several states have enacted.

DUE PROCESS

Due process establishes a course for judicial or governmental proceedings to follow that is designed to safeguard the legal rights of the individual.

MINIMUM CONTACTS

The concept of minimum contacts determines when it is appropriate for a court in one state to assert personal jurisdiction over a defendant from another state.

■ FAIR PLAY AND SUBSTANTIAL JUSTICE

Fair play and substantial justice is a standard of fairness that a court's assertion of personal jurisdiction over a nonresident defendant must meet in order to avoid a violation of the defendant's right to due process.

■ SLIDING SCALE

A sliding scale is a flexible method of determining if personal jurisdiction can be exercised over a defendant.

defendant clearly does business over the Internet. If the defendant enters into contracts with residents of a foreign jurisdiction, which involve the knowing and repeated transmitting of computer files over the Internet, personal jurisdiction is proper, for example, *CompuServe, Inc. v. Patterson*, 89 F.3d 1257 (6th Cir.1996). At the opposite end are situations in which a defendant has simply posted information on an Internet Web site that is accessible to users in foreign jurisdictions. A passive Web site that does little more than make information available to those who are interested in it is not grounds for the exercise [of] personal jurisdiction, for example, *Bensusan Restaurant Corp., v. King*, 937 F.Supp. 295 (S.D.N.Y.1996). The middle ground is occupied by interactive Web sites at which a user can exchange information with the host computer. In these cases, the exercise of jurisdiction is determined by examining the level of interactivity and commercial nature of the exchange of information that occurs on the Web site, for example, *Maritz, Inc. v. Cybergold, Inc.*, 947 F.Supp. 1328 (E.D.Mo.1996).[6]

An example of a passive Web site was discussed in *Hearst Corp. v. Goldberger*, 1997 WL 97097, 1997 US Dis. Lexis 2065 (SDNY Feb. 26, 1997), the federal court decided the New York long arm statute did *not* permit a federal court to exercise personal jurisdiction over an out-of-state defendant, solely because the defendant's Web site is accessible to, and has been electronically "visited" by, computer users in New York.

In this case, the plaintiff—Hearst Corporation, the owner and publisher of *Esquire Magazine*—brought a trademark infringement suit against the defendant, Goldberger. Goldberger had established an Internet domain name and Web site, "ESQWIRE.COM," although he did not have any services to sell at the time that he established the Web site. This site was to provide law information and law office infrastructure networking services. Goldberger lived in New Jersey and worked in Pennsylvania. The court held that his Web site was "... most analogous to an advertisement in a national magazine ... [and] ... New York law is clear ... that advertisements in national publications are not sufficient to provide personal jurisdiction ... and jurisdiction does not exist in New York based merely on his placing the offer on the Internet outside New York." Nor could the court exercise jurisdiction over Goldberger, because he did not regularly transact business or derive substantial revenue in the state; or expect his acts to have consequences in the state. Thus, there were no minimum contacts.

On the other end of the "sliding scale" of Internet personal jurisdiction is *Playboy Enterprises, Inc. v. Chuckleberry Publishing, Inc.* 939 F. Supp. 1032 (S.D.N.Y. 1996). The facts of this case were that the plaintiff, Playboy Enterprises, Inc. (PEI), published *Playboy Magazine*. The defendant, Tattilo Editrice, S.p.A. ("Tattilo"), published a magazine in Italy under the name *Playmen* from 1967. In 1979, after Tattilo announced plans to publish an English language version of *Playmen* in the United States, PEI brought suit to enjoin Tattilo's use of the *Playmen* name in connection with a magazine and related products. PEI alleged that this was a violation of its *Playboy* trademark. PEI was granted an injunction, permanently enjoining Tattilo from using the name *Playmen* in the United States.

The court found that Tattilo had violated this injunction when he had "... actively solicited United States customers to its Internet site, and in doing so ... distributed its product within the United States." One of the defendants' Web sites was a "pay" site —the Internet customer had to subscribe to the service and pay the defendant for a password that would allow access to sexually explicit photos. Thus, the defendant knew that people in the United States were accessing his site in violation of the injunction against such actions. Tattilo was given the choice of shutting down his entire Web site, or denying access to the pay *Playmen* site in the United States. However, the court did state that it did not have the power to "... restrict Tattilo from providing its PLAYMEN Internet service outside the United States. There are many English-speaking countries throughout the world. This Court has no jurisdiction to control Tattilo's activities in those countries." Tattilo was required to honor the injunction against him with regard to using the *Playmen* name in the United States. The court held that there was sufficient commercial activity on the part of Tattilo to constitute minimum contacts.

THE INTERNET AND LIBEL

Cyberspace creates an entirely new venue for potential libel suits. When defamatory information is posted on a Web site, clearly all viewers of the World Wide Web can see this publication. When you add to this the identification, fault, and damages aspect of the tort, a potential lawsuit is born. The issue with regard to the Net is who is actually liable for the posting of a libelous statement.

In a New York case, it originally was ruled that an online service provider— Prodigy—*could* be sued for a libelous statement posted by a subscriber. The decision found that Prodigy was the *publisher* of the words of its subscribers, because it had the capability to delete their messages. The judge ruled that Prodigy could have used filtering software to scan for offensive words or phrases posted online.[7] This decision left service providers with difficult choices—should they use prior restraints on the speech of their customers, or should they accept liability for statements they did not make?

The *Prodigy* case was the impetus behind a provision of **Title V of the Telecommunications Act of 1996-Section 230(c) of the Communications Decency Act (CDA)** that ruled, "No provider or user of an interactive computer service shall be treated as the publisher or speaker of any information provided by another information content provider." Under this act, it was stated by Congress that "It is the policy of the United States—(1) to promote the continued development of the Internet and other interactive computer services and other interactive media. ..."[8] Under Section 230, Internet access providers and Web site operators can post information without liability for the accuracy of the material. Courts have dismissed libel, invasion of privacy, and a host of other civil liability claims against Web site owners, all in the interest of not curtailing the freedom of expression on the Net.

■ **TITLE V OF THE TELECOMMUN- ICATIONS ACT OF 1996-SECTION 230(C) OF THE COMMUNICATIONS DECENCY ACT (CDA)**

The Communications Decency Act held no provider or user of an interactive computer service shall be treated as the publisher or speaker of any information provided by another information content provider.

Does this mean that Section 230(c) gives the Internet a broader freedom of speech than even the First Amendment? In a 2003 case, the 9th Circuit Court of Appeals said yes! In *Batzel v. Smith*, 333 F.3d 1018, the court held that the CDA immunizes Web site operators that post defamatory e-mails authored by a third party. This protection had never been given to the other media.

In the *Batzel* case, attorney Ellen Batzel had hired a handyman—Robert Smith—and, according to Smith, Batzel had told him that she was the granddaughter of Nazi leader Heinrich Himmler. After hearing this, Smith started to wonder about his employer's European art collection. Smith suspected that some of her pieces were stolen during World War II.

Smith e-mailed his suspicions to a Web site for museum security officials and others interested in stolen art—Museum Security Network. Tom Cremers, the owner of the Network, edited Smith's e-mail and posted it in the site's newsletter. Batzel learned of this e-mail and complained to Cremers, stating that she was not related to any Nazi official, and that her artwork was not stolen. Cremers contacted Smith, Smith stated that his e-mail was true, but he had not thought it would be posted. Batzel sued the Museum Security Network and other defendants.

When the case went to court, Cremers sought to have the case dismissed, stating that Section 230(c) of the CDA protected him from liability; the trial court refused, stating that the Network was not an ISP. The 9th Circuit Court of Appeals reversed, stating Section 230(c) was intended to protect *anyone* that republishes information, as long as the republisher of the information reasonably believes that the person presenting the information intended it to be put on the Net. The court held that "Making interactive computer services and their users liable for the speech of third parties would severely restrict the information available on the Internet. Section 230 therefore sought to prevent lawsuits from shutting down Web sites and other services on the Internet." The court also held that the Network was an online service provider as described under Section 230:

> "There is no dispute that the Network uses interactive computer services to distribute its on-line mailing and to post the listserv on its Web site. Indeed, to make its Web site available and to mail out the listserv, the Network *must* access the Internet through some form of 'interactive computer service.' Thus, both the Network Web site, and the listserv are potentially immune under §230."

(The 9th Circuit did remand the case to the trial court for a determination if Cremers reasonably believed that Smith intended the e-mail to be published on Cremers site.)

Judge Gould dissented, stating, "Nothing in the text, legislative history, or human experience would lead me to accept the notion that Congress in § 230 intended to immunize users or providers of interactive computer services who, by their discretionary decisions to spread particular communications, cause trickles of defamation to swell into rivers of harm." Gould instead sought an interpretation of Section 230(c) that would only immunize a Web site operator "... when the defendant took no active role in selecting the questionable information for publication. If the defendant took an active role in selecting information for publication, the information is no longer 'information provided by another' within the meaning of § 230."

It is interesting that the majority of the 9th Circuit Court in *Batzel* held that "There is no dispute that the Network uses interactive computer services to distribute its on-line mailing and to post the listserv on its Web site. Indeed, to make its Web site available and to mail out the listserv, the Network *must* access the Internet through some form of 'interactive computer service.'" Could it be concluded that any Web site that uses some form of "interactive computer service" is an ISP under Section 230(c)?

In 2004 and 2006, two California decisions in *Barrett v. Rosenthal* revisited the issue of defamation republishing liability.

In April 2004, a unanimous California Supreme Court agreed to review the *Barrett* case; the Court heard this case on September 5, 2006, and a decision was rendered on November 20, 2006.[9] The California Supreme Court reversed the California Appeals

---

CASE STUDY **Barrett v. Rosenthal**

First Appellate District, Division Two [Appellate No. A096451] (January 2004)

Facts:
Stephen Barrett and Terry Polevoy are the plaintiffs in this case. As alternative health care physicians, they maintain Web sites that expose "health frauds and quackery." Ilena Rosenthal, the defendant, directs the Humantics Foundation for Women.

Barrett and Polevoy asserted libel claims against Rosenthal as a result of several postings she made on various Usernet and Internet newsgroups. The most controversial of these postings, made on August 14, 2000, wherein Rosenthal republished an e-mail received from another defendant in this case —Timothy Bolen. Mr. Bolen had accused Dr. Polevoy of "stalking women." The e-mail claimed that Polevoy had stalked Christine McPhee, a radio commentator, whose program supported alternative medicine, a program that Polevoy did not like. The e-mail in question urged readers to file complaints against Polevoy for unspecified "criminal conduct."

Polevoy and Barrett informed Rosenthal that Bolen's message was defamatory and asked her to withdraw the posting. Rosenthal refused, instead posting more messages referring to Polevoy and Barrett as "quacks."

Issue:
Is Rosenthal immune from Polevoy and Barrett's defamation suit under Section 230(c) of the CDA?

Decision:
In the California Court of Appeals decision, it was held that Rosenthal would be liable for defamation. The California Supreme Court then heard this case in 2006, and it reversed the California Court of Appeals ruling, holding that Rosenthal would be immune from defamation liability.

(continues)

Reason: In the history of this case, the trial court had held Rosenthal was immune from plaintiff's defamation claim. The trial court following the Fourth Circuit case of *Zeran v. America Online*, 129 F.3d 327 (4th Cir. 1997), cert. denied 524 U.S. 937 (1998). Under *Zeran*, the court concluded, Section 230 *did* immunize providers and users of interactive computer services from liability, not only as *primary publishers* but also as *distributors* of defamation of a third party. This protection is available whether or not the provider or user *knowingly* distributed the defamation, even if the provider or user profits from such conduct.

The California Appellate Court did not agree with the trial court—the CDA did *not* grant Rosenthal immunity from her postings as a "distributor" of third-party information. The appellate court held, under common law, an individual that republishes another's libel is treated as a *primary* publisher or distributor, and as such is held to a strict standard of liability, the same liability as the original author. Yet, an individual that is merely a conduit—secondary publishers may only be liable as publishers "... if they know or have reason to know of the defamatory nature of matter they disseminate." The California Appellate Court relied on the principle that if a statute is capable of more than one construction, then the statute's construction must be construed in accord with the common law, and, under common law, Rosenthal is liable.

The California Appeals Court found that because the CDA was ambiguous as to a user acting "... as the publisher or speaker of information ...," this phrase possibly could encompass common-law liability. If Congress had wanted to immunize *distributors* from liability, it would have been more specific by adding the word "distributor." The court stated, "In any case, in law and as it appears in Section 230, the word 'publisher' is at least capable of two reasonable constructions and therefore ambiguous, which is enough to justify application of the interpretative canon favoring retention of common law principles."

Thus, the appellate court ignored *Zeran's* holding that "... it would be impossible for service providers to screen each of their millions of postings for possible [defamation] problems." *Zeran* concluding any other decision would have a chilling effect on online speech.

The appellate court did not take any position on the aspects of a "chilling effect" on Internet speech, the court stated that the parties and the trial court did not address this issue, and the court would need further information as to whether or not it would be prohibitive for a provider or user of an interactive computer service to remove defamatory material.

Court decision, and upheld the protections of Section 230 of the federal Telecommunications Act of 1996 (the CDA). The California Supreme Court concluded, "... Section 230 prohibits 'distributor' liability for Internet publications. ... Section 230(c) (1) immunizes individual 'users' of interactive computer services, and that no practical or principled distinction can be drawn between active and passive use."

The California Supreme Court did interject some interesting dicta: "We acknowledge that recognizing broad immunity for defamatory republications on the Internet has some troubling consequences. Until Congress chooses to revise the settled law in this area, however, plaintiffs who contend they were defamed in an Internet posting may only seek recovery from the original source of the statement."

International Libel Suits and the Internet

A case that the media must take notice of is *Dow Jones & Company Inc. v. Gutnick*, HCA 56 (2002). In *Gutnick*, the High Court of Australia held that Mr. Gutnick could sue in Australia for defamation on the Internet. In October 2000, the online edition of *Barron's Magazine*, published by Dow Jones, had an article in it called "Unholy Gains." This article included critical comments about Melbourne businessman, Joseph Gutnick. One hundred forty people living in Australia downloaded and read the article. Mr. Gutnick contended that part of the article defamed him. A key issue was whether this Internet defamation suit could be brought in Australia.

The Australian High Court ruled, "If people wish to do business in, or indeed travel to, or live in, or utilize the infrastructure of different countries, they can hardly expect to be absolved from compliance with the laws of those countries. The fact that publication might occur everywhere does not mean that it occurs nowhere." The High Court held defamation occurs on the Net when and where a page is downloaded, and that is the appropriate place to sue. Mr. Gutnick lived, worked, and socialized in the State of Victoria in Australia; thus, this is the appropriate legal forum.

Rather than continue this suit, in 2004 Dow Jones settled the case with Mr. Gutnick.

ONLINE EDITIONS AND THE MEDIA

As a journalist, the Internet can be a blessing because the world has access to the information posted, but it also can be a bane because of jurisdictional issues as discussed earlier. The fact is that a freelance journalist's work, appearing in the print media and later posted on the Web, may lead to copyright ownership and compensation disputes. In *New York Times v. Tasini*, the U.S. Supreme Court ruled that a freelance writer, Jonathan Tasini, owned the electronic rights to his work, unless he had assigned his rights to the publishers of his articles.

As a result of the *Tasini* case, in most publication contracts, the rights to electronic editions are included in any fees or royalties given the author. If an author has different wishes in this matter, it will have to be negotiated with her publisher.

THE INTERNET AND DOMAIN NAMES

By the late 1990s, it was clear that there needed to be a system in place whereby anyone who wanted to access information on the Internet could do so in an efficient manner. In answer to that issue, the **Domain Name System (DNS)** was implemented. What the DNS does is allow users to find their way around the Internet.

Every computer that is connected to the World Wide Web has a unique Internet Protocol (IP) address, just as everyone with a cellular telephone has her own phone number. The problem with an IP address is that it is a complicated string of numbers, for example, 123.4.56.78, which is hard to remember each time an Internet user wants to look up information on a Web site. The DNS helps with this situation by changing this series of numbers into a "mnemonic" that is easier to remember, for example, http://www.uspto.gov (the site that is linked to the United States Patent and Trademark Office).

■ **DOMAIN NAME SYSTEM (DNS)**

The Domain Name System (DNS) is the way that Internet domain names are located and translated into Internet Protocol (IP) addresses.

CASE STUDY   New York Times v. Tasini

533 U.S. 483 (2001)

Facts: Justice Ginsberg, delivering the opinion of the Supreme Court, stated that this case revolves around the rights of freelance authors and the rights of their publishers. Six freelance authors sued three print periodicals for copyright infringement. The print periodical publishers, without the freelancers' consent, placed copies of the freelancers' articles into three computer databases. This made these article retrievable by a user in isolation of the original print publication.

The freelance authors' complaint alleged that their copyrights had been infringed on by the inclusion of their articles in the computer databases. The publishers alleged that they had the privilege of reproduction and distribution of these articles under §201(c) of the Copyright Act. The publishers maintained that because they are the copyright owners of the collective works —the original print publication—they merely have exercised "the privilege" §201(c) accords them to "reproduc[e] and distribut[e]" the author's discretely copyrighted contribution.

Issue: Does §201(c) of the Copyright Act give the publishers "the privilege" to reproduce and distribute the freelancers' articles without their consent?

Decision: No.

(continues)

CASE STUDY **New York Times v. Tasini** *(continued)*

Reason: The Court held that the Copyright Act does not give the publishers such a privilege. Databases reproduce articles standing alone, not "as part of that particular collective work" the author contributed to, nor were the articles "part of ... any revision," or were they "part of ... any later collective work in the same series."

Before the Copyright Act of 1976, an author risked losing her rights if she placed an article in a collective work, because copyright only attached when the work was published and the contributor's copyright notice was properly affixed in the publication. This left authors at the mercy of the publisher as to their legal rights.

In the 1976 Copyright Act revision, Congress sought to clarify and improve this situation. Together, §404(a) and §201(c) "... preserve the author's copyright in a contribution even if the contribution does not bear a separate notice in the author's name, and without requiring any unqualified transfer of rights to the owner of the collective work."

A newspaper or magazine publisher is privileged to reproduce or distribute an article contributed by a freelance author, unless there is some other contractual agreement to the contrary, only "... 'as part of' any (or all) of three categories of collective works: (a) 'that collective work' to which the author contributed her work, (b) 'any revision of that collective work,' or (c) 'any later collective work in the same series.'" Thus, a publishing company could reprint a contribution from one issue to a later issue, or reprint an article in a revised edition of the collective work, but the publisher cannot revise the contribution or include it in an entirely new work or venue without violating the author's copyright.

Under §201(c), a freelancer has the right to benefit from the demand for an article standing alone or placed in a new collection. Thus, after the initial publication, the freelancer may sell the article to others that wish to publish it.

Justice Stevens, with whom Justice Breyer joined, dissented, stating, "No one doubts that the *New York Times* has the right to reprint its issues in Braille, in a foreign language, or in microform, even though such revisions might look and feel quite different from the original. Such differences, however, would largely result from the different medium being employed. Similarly, the decision to convert the single collective work newspaper into a collection of individual ASCII [computer] files can be explained as little more than a decision that reflects the different nature of the electronic medium."

UNIVERSAL RESOLVABILITY

Universal resolvability ensures predictable search results from any place on the Internet. Each IP address will have its own distinctive domain name.

ICANN (INTERNET CORPORATION FOR ASSIGNED NAMES AND NUMBERS)

The tasks of ICANN include managing the assignment of domain names and IP addresses.

TOP LEVEL DOMAIN REGISTRY (TLD REGISTRY)

The right-most label in a domain name is referred to as its "top-level domain" (TLD). The responsibility for operating each TLD (including maintaining a registry of the domain names within the TLD) is delegated to a particular organization. These organizations are referred to as "registry operators" or "sponsors," for example ICANN.

The DNS allows any user of the Internet, anywhere in the world, to reach a Web site or e-mail address; it allows what is called "**universal resolvability**"—ensuring a predictable connection to a particular Web site or e-mail address. When the DNS computer communicates with another computer, it asks (in computer language) if that computer is the intended recipient of the information. The computer answering must answer "yes" or "no," and it does so by identifying its DNS.

This is where the organization called **ICANN (Internet Corporation For Assigned Names and Numbers)** steps in. ICANN is responsible for managing and coordinating the DNS to assure universal resolvability. ICANN is a global, nonprofit, private sector body that acts in the public interest as to the DNS. It oversees the processes and systems that assure each domain name goes to the correct IP address.

ICANN governs what is called the **Top Level Domain Registry (TLD registry)**. A TLD is how a computer begins its search for a DNS. There are several TLDs approved by ICANN, some familiar ones are .com, .org, .gov, and .biz. There are also some 244 country specific registries, for example, .cn (China) and .fr (France). These TLDs help one computer begin the search for that one particular e-mail address or Web site. Once the TLD is located, the computer can refine its search to the final IP address.

ICANN has the authority to grant new TLDs. On May 10, 2006, ICANN's Board voted 9 to 5 *against* a proposed new TLD—.xxx—a voluntary TLD for the adult entertainment industry. On June 1, 2006, the .xxx TLD's chief sponsor, ICM Registry Inc., appealed this decision, and ICM began taking reservations for this TLD from adult sites. ICM had already hired a staff and built the system for the .xxx TLD's registration. Currently, ICM is not charging for a site to reserve an .xxx TLD registration, although ICM plans to charge $60 for each registration, if and when the .xxx TLD is implemented.

In March 2007, ICANN again voted 9 to 5 to deny an application from ICM for the .xxx TLD registration. ICANN decided that ICM's proposal raised too many public policy concerns and ultimately could change the role of the nonprofit organization. ICANN stated if it had approved this new .xxx TLD, the new .xxx TLD would have placed ICANN in a position of having to deal with each country's pornography laws.

Cybersquatting

Cybersquatting started in the early days of the Internet at a time when many businesses were not really sure of the economic impact that this new medium would have on their enterprises. As a form of an electronic "gold rush," there were those who took advantage of this opportunity and began to register trademarked business names 'in the hope that sooner or later a business would have to come to them and buy their trademarked name from the cybersquatter. Hertz, Avon, and Panavision were all victimized by cybersquatters.

When Panavision went to register its trademarked name "Panavision," it discovered that a Mr. Toeppen had already registered that domain name. Panavision's counsel sent a letter to Toeppen informing him, "Panavision held a trademark in the name Panavision ... telling him to stop using that trademark and the domain name Panavision.com. Toeppen responded by mail to Panavision ... stating he had the right to use the name Panavision.com on the Internet as his domain name. Toeppen stated: If your attorney has advised you otherwise, he is trying to screw you. He wants to blaze new trails in the legal frontier at your expense. Why do you want to fund your attorney's purchase of a new boat (or whatever) when you can facilitate the acquisition of 'PanaVision.com' cheaply and simply instead?" Toeppen asked for $13,000 for the release of PanaVision.com.

When this case went to the Federal District Court and the Federal Court of Appeals, it was found that Toeppen was guilty of registering another's trademark, including a violation of the **Federal Trademark Dilution Act** 15 U.S.C. § 1125(c). The Federal Court of Appeals concluded, "Toeppen engaged in a scheme to register Panavision's trademarks as his domain names on the Internet and then to extort money from Panavision by trading on the value of those names."[11]

In response to these domain name issues, in 1999, Congress passed the **Anticybersquatting Consumer Protection Act (ACPA)**. This law criminalizes the act of cybersquatting and allows a court to cancel domain names that were registered in bad faith. The ACPA applies to presently and previously registered names. It also allows for civil fines up to $100,000 for cybersquatting, and if the court finds the registration or use of the registered trademark as an identifier was *willful*, fines can be imposed up to $300,000, per trademark, per identifier, as the court considers just, and full costs and reasonable attorney's fees can be awarded.[12] ICANN also offers the possibility of arbitration to recover a wrongfully registered domain name.

■ **CYBERSQUATTING**

Cybersquatting is using a domain name with bad-faith intent to profit from the goodwill of a trademark belonging to someone else.

■ **FEDERAL TRADEMARK DILUTION ACT**

The Federal Trademark Dilution Act protects famous marks (trademarks and service marks) from uses that dilute their distinctiveness.

■ **ANTICYBER-SQUATTING CONSUMER PROTECTION ACT (ACPA)**

The ACPA is intended to protect the public from acts of Internet "cybersquatting," a term used to describe the bad faith, abusive registration of Internet domain names.

To stop a cybersquatter under the ACPA, the trademark owner will have to prove:

- The domain name was registered by the squatter in bad faith, with intent to profit from the use of the trademark.

- The trademark was distinctive at the time of the domain name registration.

- The domain name registered is confusing or identical with the trademark held.

- The domain name was registered with the intention of diverting consumers from the domain or other online location of the person or entity who is the owner of a trademark to the squatter's domain or other online location.

- The trademark qualifies for protection under federal trademark laws—it is distinctive and the owner was the first to use it in commerce.[13]

In 1999, ICANN adopted and began implementing the **Uniform Domain Name Dispute Resolution Policy (UDNDRP)**. This is an international policy for resolution of domain name disputes. To prevail under the UDNDRP, the complainant must show:

- A domain name is confusingly similar or identical to the mark to which the complainant has legal rights.

- The domain name owner (squatter) has no rights in the registered domain name.

- The domain name was registered and is being used in bad faith.

If the complainant wins in arbitration under UDNDRP, the domain name registered by the squatter will be canceled, or the name will be transferred to the rightful owner. Under arbitration, under the UDNDRP there are no financial recoveries.

NET NEUTRALITY

Unbeknown to many, the growth of the Internet since its humble beginnings in the 1970s has been closely regulated by the **Federal Communications Commission (FCC)**. The FCC requires phone companies that carry Internet information over their lines to stay out of this free flow of information. Under FCC regulation, the telecommunications companies that carry such information are not allowed to interfere with the downloading of information. They cannot tell people

---

■ UNIFORM DOMAIN NAME DISPUTE RESOLUTION POLICY (UDNDRP)

The Uniform Domain Name Dispute Resolution Policy has been adopted by ICANN, and sets forth the terms and conditions in connection with a dispute as to the registration and use of an Internet domain name.

■ FEDERAL COMMUNICATIONS COMMISSION (FCC)

The Federal Communications Commission (FCC) is an independent United States government agency, directly responsible to Congress. The FCC was established by the Communications Act of 1934 and is charged with regulating interstate and international communications.

what applications to run, or what devices they can attach to the network; neither can they discriminate as to whom they carry on their lines, or can they grant the right to use their network services based on how much someone pays.

In 2002, there was an attempt by the U.S. government to change this. The FCC issued a declaratory ruling, defining "... **broadband** cable modem service as an 'information service' but not a 'telecommunications service' ... so that it is not subject to mandatory Title II [FCC] common-carrier regulation."[14] The U.S. Supreme Court affirmed this declaratory ruling in *National Cable Telecommunications Association v. Brand X Internet Service*, 545 U.S. 967 (2005).

The Court opined that a federal court must defer to an agency's (FCCs) construction of a statute (**The Communications Act of 1934**, as amended by the **Telecommunications Act of 1996**) even if the ruling "... differs from what the court believes to be the best interpretation [of that statute, as long as the statute] ... is within the agency's jurisdiction to administer, the statute is ambiguous on the point at issue, and the agency's construction is reasonable." Thus, the FCC has the statutory authority to execute and enforce the Communications Act §151, "... and to 'prescribe such rules and regulations as may be necessary ... to carry out the [Act's] provisions.'"

Yet, when there was a lobbying push by the public and the tech industry against this declaratory ruling, the FCC decided not to totally deregulate broadband, and instead put forth, in August 2005, four broadband principles to recognize some consumer Internet rights. These four principles include:

- *"To encourage broadband deployment and preserve and promote the open and interconnected nature of the public Internet*, consumers are entitled to access the lawful Internet content of their choice.

- *To encourage broadband deployment and preserve and promote the open and interconnected nature of the public Internet*, consumers are entitled to run applications and use services of their choice, subject to the needs of law enforcement.

- *To encourage broadband deployment and preserve and promote the open and interconnected nature of the public Internet*, consumers are entitled to connect their choice of legal devices that do not harm the network.

- *To encourage broadband deployment and preserve and promote the open and interconnected nature of the public Internet*, consumers are entitled to competition among network providers, application and service providers, and content providers."[15]

Thus, what actually occurred was that the FCC did assert some powers over the broadband companies, under the four principles, but these rules are not very clear as to what the broadband providers can or cannot do. These principles also leave Internet consumers at a loss as to how to gain enforcement of these rules, or how to file a complaint against the broadband companies, if necessary.

In March 2006, Congress introduced "**The Communications Opportunity, Promotion and Enhancement Act of 2006**" HR 5252 (COPE). COPE put the FCC's four principles into law, but then took away any rulemaking authority of the FCC.

■ **BROADBAND**

Broadband is also called high-speed Internet, because it usually has a high rate of data transmission.

■ **THE COMMUNICATIONS ACT OF 1934**

The Communications Act of 1934 replaced the Federal Radio Commission with the Federal Communications Commission.

■ **TELECOMMUN-ICATIONS ACT OF 1996**

The Telecommunications Act of 1996 is the first major overhaul of telecommunications law since The Communications Act of 1934. The goal of this law is to let anyone enter any communications business—to let any communications business compete in any market against any other.

■ THE COMMUNICATIONS OPPORTUNITY, PROMOTION AND ENHANCEMENT ACT OF 2006 HR 5252 (COPE)

The Communications Opportunity, Promotion, and Enhancement (COPE) Act of 2006 was a large telecom bill designed to update US laws to address changes in voice, video and data services.

Under COPE the FCC would have had to look at each incidence of potential Internet discrimination on a case-by-case basis. This potentially would put a great burden on any Internet startup business, because it would have to take each discrimination complaint to the FCC.

COPE did encourage the expansion of broadband networks to consumer homes and encouraged the creation of municipal broadband networks, such as the free Google WiFi project in San Francisco. COPE actually prohibited states from banning networks done exclusively by municipalities. But COPE did nothing to preserve the network neutrality the United States had enjoyed since the inception of the Internet. Instead, COPE gave cable and phone companies the authority they wanted to create potentially discriminatory networks.

COPE allowed the cable and telecommunications companies to charge third parties for "premium access" to broadband (faster Internet service, thus, faster downloads of Web sites). This potentially could create an Internet where only rich and powerful corporations could successfully participate, because they would have the money to buy the premium broadband service from the empowered cable and phone companies. COPE had been labeled "Big Business v. Consumer Rights" or "Big Government v. Free-Market Competition." Network neutrality advocates advanced the concept that by allowing the telecommunications industry control over the Internet, there could be violations of the First Amendment right—freedom of speech—because if the Internet was not neutral, then the telecommunications companies could filter out information they did not want on their networks.

The telecommunications industry argued that they need legislation such as COPE, because they are the ones investing billions of dollars in infrastructure for the Internet, and, thus, should be able to determine how their networks operate. They said they are seeing higher traffic in their business but not necessarily higher profits.

On June 8, 2006, the House of Representatives overwhelmingly voted for COPE, and on September 29, 2006, COPE was placed on the Senate Legislative Calendar. This bill died with the ending of the 109th Congress.

There were other bills in Congress dealing with Internet neutrality—for example, S.2360, sponsored by Senator Wyden (D). This bill called for no two-tier Internet, "To ensure and promote a free and open Internet for all Americans." This bill died with the ending of the 109th Congress.

S.2917, sponsored by Senator Snowe (R), Senator Dorgan (D), Senator Clinton (D), and Senator Obama (D), also called for no two-tier Internet and protection of Internet neutrality. This bill was introduced in May 2006. This bill never became law.

HR5417, sponsored by Congressmen Sensenbrenner (R) and Conyers (D), called for Antitrust extended to Internet neutrality: "The lack of competition in the broadband marketplace presents a clear incentive for providers to leverage dominant market power over the broadband bottleneck to pre-select, favor, or prioritize Internet content over their networks," said Judiciary Chairman James Sensenbrenner of Wisconsin. This bill died with the ending of the 109th Congress.

HR5273 was sponsored by Congressman Markey (D), and it called for no two-tier Internet. This bill died with the ending of the 109th Congress.

Another Internet bill that had been introduced in the Senate was **The Communications, Consumer Choice, and Broadband Deployment Act of 2006, S2686**. Senate Commerce Chairman Ted Stevens (R) and ranking member Daniel Inouye (D) were cosponsors of the bill (although Senator Inouye has expressed reservations as to the wording of the bill). This act was another attempt to transform the telecommunications industry.

Unlike the COPE bill, the Stevens bill only encouraged municipal broadband if the municipality partners with a private firm to install the municipal broadband. Governments that try to put broadband in under the auspices of the governmental entity had to subject themselves to a private sector veto, by putting the project out for bid.

As to network neutrality, the Stevens bill stripped the FCC of any power to create network neutrality rules and removed the ability of the FCC to adjudicate any complaints as to the four principles as discussed earlier. Thus, the telecommunications companies could do as they pleased. Under the Stevens bill, the FCC would only be able to write an annual report to Congress on the development of the Internet—traffic, routing, transport, interconnection, and peering; and how these items are impacting the "public" Internet (whatever "public" means). Under the Stevens bill, the FCC could only recommend appropriate "private enforcement mechanisms," again allowing the telecommunication companies more power to do as they wish, even if the FCC finds something wrong. S2686 died with the ending of the 109th Congress.

In January 2007, U.S. Senators Byron Dorgan (D-ND) and Olympia Snowe (R-ME) introduced legislation—the **Internet Freedom Preservation Act S. 215**. According to Senator Dorgan this bill would ensure that broadband service providers do not discriminate against Internet content, applications, or services by offering preferential treatment. The last action on this bill was taken on January 9, 2007, it was read twice and referred to the Senate Committee on Commerce, Science, and Transportation.

In March 2007, at its monthly open meeting in Washington, D.C., the FCC voted to issue a notice of inquiry on "broadband industry practices" that will include a discussion of an open Internet.

At the meeting, FCC Democratic Commissioner Michael J. Copps said,

> "It is time for us [FCC] to go beyond the original four principles and commit (the) industry and the FCC unequivocally to a specific principle of enforceable nondiscrimination, one that allows for reasonable network management but makes clear that broadband network providers will not be allowed to shackle the promise of the Internet in its adolescence."

In response, Republican Commissioner Robert McDowell cautioned, "We [the FCC] must resist the temptation to impose regulation based merely on theory." He pointed out that the commission had not yet received any complaints of abuse.

Yet, consumer groups, supporting Internet neutrality, stated that if the FCC waited to intervene until the phone companies developed discriminatory business models, it could mean waiting until the damage was already done to the Internet.

■ THE COMMUNICATIONS, CONSUMER CHOICE, AND BROADBAND DEPLOYMENT ACT OF 2006, S2686

S2686, consisted of 10 separate titles, aimed to reform existing communications laws.

■ INTERNET FREEDOM PRESERVATION ACT S. 215

A bill to amend the Communications Act of 1934 to ensure net neutrality.

On January 14, 2008, Comcast Corporation received official word that it is being investigated by the Federal Communications Commission in connection with its network management practices. The FCC's Enforcement Bureau, sent a letter to Comcast expressing the FCC's interest in knowing whether Comcast is managing its network in a manner consistent with the agency's August 2005 "policy statement" as to the four "principles" to ensure "that broadband networks are widely deployed, open, affordable, and accessible to all consumers." FCC Chairman Kevin Martin signaled the launch of the investigation in comments made January 8 at the Consumer Electronics Show in Las Vegas.

As was stated at the beginning of this section, the Internet has flourished under the watchful eye and rulemaking of the FCC. If COPE had become law it would have taken away the rulemaking of the FCC, and the proposed Stevens bill would have gone one step further and taken away enforcement of the four principles. It will be of interest to all that use the Internet to see what the future of the Internet will be, with or without Internet neutrality. Hopefully, the Internet will remain the great information system and business equalizer that it has been from its inception.

SUMMARY

Personal jurisdiction in cyberspace is mainly accomplished via "long arm" statutes. These statutes allow jurisdiction over entities and things outside of the state. Long arm statutes cannot violate the Constitution's due process clause. To avoid violating this clause, the defendant must have minimum contacts with the forum state. Minimum contacts on the Internet are based on a sliding scale of contact between the plaintiff and defendant.

Cyberspace creates an entirely new venue for potential libel suits. When defamatory information is posted on a Web site, there is clearly publication to all the potential viewers of the World Wide Web. When the identification, fault, and damages aspect of the tort is added, a potential lawsuit is born. Who is actually liable for the posting of a libelous statement? Where can the defendant be sued for posting libel on the Net?

Under the *Tasini* case, a freelance writer holds the copyright to that article with respect to republishing it on the Internet—placing it in a computer database—and thus should receive additional compensation if so posted. Most publishers now will have an author sign a contract stating that the publisher holds the rights to all online publication of the work, and thus no further compensation will be paid.

The Domain Name System (DNS) changes Internet Protocol numbers into a more Net user-friendly format. ICANN manages and coordinates the DNS. Top Level Domain Registry (TLD) is how a computer begins to search for a domain name, for example, .org, .biz, and .com. Cybersquatting is the process of registering a previously trademarked name as a domain name, in the hopes that the owner of the trademark will have to buy that domain name from the domain name registrant.

The Anticybersquatting Consumer Protection Act (ACPA) criminalizes the act of cybersquatting. Uniform Domain Name Dispute Resolution Policy (UDNDRP) is an international policy for resolution of domain name disputes.

Internet neutrality means that all Internet sites must be treated equally by the telecommunications industry.

■ DISCUSSION QUESTIONS

1. Should the individual who reposts libelous material from another on the Internet be held liable for defamation? Why or why not?

2. If an Internet article defames someone in Zimbabwe, should the defendant in this case have to appear in a Zimbabwe court? Why or why not?

3. Should a journalist be paid twice for an article merely because a print publisher places it in a computer database?

4. Discuss the pros and cons of ICANN refusing to grant the TLD .xxx.

5. Should anyone be entitled to register a domain name, even if they are not the holders of the mark assigned?

6. Should Internet neutrality be made part of federal law? Why or why not?

7. Could the repeal of Internet neutrality lead to violations of the First Amendment?

■ CASE FOR REVIEW

Research the issue of Internet neutrality and argue for and against it.

■ KEY TERMS

Anticybersquatting Consumer Protection Act (ACPA)	Federal Communications Commission (FCC)	long arm statutes
broadband	Federal Trademark Dilution Act	minimum contacts
common law	ICANN (Internet Corporation For	personal jurisdiction
cybersquatting	Assigned Names and Numbers)	sliding scale
Domain Name System (DNS)	Internet Freedom Preservation Act	Telecommunications Act of 1996
due process	S. 215	The Communications Act of 1934
fair play and substantial justice	jurisdiction	

The Communications Opportunity, Promotion and Enhancement Act of 2006 HR 5252 (COPE)

The Communications, Consumer Choice, and Broadband Deployment Act of 2006, S2686

Title V of the Telecommunications Act of 1996-Section 230(c) of the Communications Decency Act (CDA)

Top Level Domain Registry (TLD registry)

Uniform Domain Name Dispute Resolution Policy (UDNDRP)

Uniform Interstate and International Procedure Act (UIIPA)

universal resolvability

■ ENDNOTES

[1] *Hanson v. Denckla*, 357 U.S. 235, 253, 78 S.Ct. 1228, 1240, 2 L.Ed.2d 1283 (1958). *Asahi Metal Indus. Co v. Superior Court*, 480 U.S. 102, 107 S.Ct. 1026, 94 L.Ed.2d 92 (1987).

[2] *Burnham v. Superior Court*, 495 U.S. at 609-620, 110 S.Ct. at 2110-2115; id. at 628-29, 110 S. Ct at 2120 (1990). In *Burnham*, the Supreme Court held that the Due Process Clause does not prohibit a state court from exercising personal jurisdiction over a nonresident who is temporarily in that state and is served personally with process even though the suit is unrelated to her activities in the state.

[3] Uniform Interstate and International Procedure Act, 13 U.L.A. 355 (1986 ed.).

[4] *International Shoe Co. v. Washington*, 326 U.S. 310, 316, 66 S.Ct. 154, 158, 90 L.Ed. 95 (1945).

[5] *World-Wide Volkswagen Corp. v. Woodson*, 444 U.S. 286, 100 S.Ct. 559, 62 L.Ed.2d 490 (1980), *Burger King Corp. v. Rudzewicz*, 471 U.S. 462, 105 S.Ct. 2174, 85 L.Ed.2d 528 (1985).

[6] *Zippo Mfr. Co. v. Zippo Dot Com, Inc.* 952 F. Supp. 1119 (W.D. Pa. 1997).

[7] *Stratton Oakmont Inc. v. Prodigy Services Co.,* 1995 WL 323710 (N.Y. Sup. Ct. 1995).

[8] U.S. Code: Title 47: Section 230(c) Communications Decency Act.

[9] *Barrett v. Rosenthal*, 40 Cal.4th 33, 146 P.3d 510, 51 Cal.Rptr.3d 55 (Cal. Sup. Ct., Nov. 20, 2006).

[10] Footnote 13 in *New York Times v. Tasini*, 533 U.S. 483 (2001).

[11] *Panavision International v. Toeppen*, 141 F.3d 1316 (9th Cir.1998).

[12] 15 USC section 1125(d).

[13] Ibid.

[14] http://www.fcc.gov.

[15] FCC-05-151A1.

Online Companion™
For additional resources, please go to
http://www.paralegal.delmar.cengage.com.

Student CD-ROM
For additional materials, please go to the
CD in this book.

11

Media and Entertainment Ethics

■ OBJECTIVES_____

After completing this chapter, you will be able to:

- Know what the difference is between what is legal and what is ethical?

- Have a better understanding of what is ethical to report on and what is not ethical to report on—for example, is the report an invasion of privacy? Does the story provide balance?

- Realize that ethics is a relative term. What may be acceptable by one group of people may not be ethical to others. What is ethical in the United States may be reprehensible in another country.

WHAT IS ETHICS?

In this book, we have been studying the legal aspects of the media and entertainment industries. Interestingly, the public often views these professions—the law, the media, and entertainment—as being less than ethical. Yet, if asked, most individuals could not give an adequate definition of ethics. Most consider ethics to be the equivalent to law, which it is not. If something is legal, it is the bare minimum of an ethical standard. To be legal means that the individual is merely intent on not "breaking" the law so as to stay out of jail. Ethics is much more than an issue of legality. Ethics encompasses not only the legality of an issue but also the "moral" aspects of an issue—a code of conduct that is put forth by a group, which under specific conditions should be followed.

In the media and entertainment industries, the form of ethics usually followed is that of **moral relativism**—one not reflective of any absolute truths or falsities. Instead, it reflects a code that refers to social and cultural preferences. The public, many times uncomfortable with this ambiguous view of ethics, actually views this as being unethical. If it is not deemed "right" or "wrong" on its face, this makes some individuals quite uncomfortable. In the media and entertainment industries, most ethical issues faced are not so clear-cut; it is more a matter of dealing with subtleties.

▨ MORAL RELATIVISM

Moral relativism is a concept that espouses the fact morality varies between individuals and cultures and so there is no objective right and wrong.

Media Ethics

In the media, a journalist must counterbalance the legality in reporting a story with the rights of privacy of the individual being reported on, the right of the public to know, and how the public will react to how the story is covered. It is this last premise—the perception of the story, and the ethical consideration in reporting that —that we now examine. We turn to a world of "should or should not" reporting.

Should the media report stories that reflect their own biases or promote their own agendas? It is a tempting thought, to have one's own forum to expound on the world as one sees it. The problem with this is that if the media does this overtly, the media consumer that picks up on this, and feels offended by it, will take his news business elsewhere. Because the media is based on a market economy, it cannot ignore the need for subscribers, watchers, and advertisers. Financial ruin could result if any of these segments were alienated. Thus, a media owner and editor keep these concepts in mind when structuring news content. As has been discussed earlier, it is important for a news organization to have policies in place as to what "should or should not be covered." The journalist should feel confident that an editor would back them in whatever story they decide to cover.

For example, a cub reporter is assigned a story to cover conditions in a local barrio. As a new and idealistic journalist, the reporter's story discusses the economic and political problems of the area—how the residents are disenfranchised from the rest of the community. The story runs, and the next day the reporter is called into the community's police chief's office. At the time, the reporter is anticipating being praised by the police chief for a well-reported story. Instead, the chief seriously chastises the story. The exact quote from the chief is, "What are you trying to do, start a riot?" That was not the intention; the intention was to report a truthful and informative story. Although there were job concerns, the reporter stood his ground, and fortunately his editor backed him about how he handled the story.

Should the reporter have been so forthright in reporting on the conditions in the area? Was it ethical to potentially create a disturbance? In retrospect, should the reporter have been more sensitive to the conditions in the barrio?

Another area that affects the reporting of a story is the balance a media owner or editor must find between investigative reporting and the potential of being sued for that media coverage. Case in point: the ABC News Magazine *Prime Time Live* broadcast of a story accusing Food Lion grocery stores of selling old food and spoiled meat washed in bleach.

Two producers of ABC reported the story. They lied on their résumés to get a job at Food Lion. When hired, they went undercover wearing wigs with hidden cameras and concealed microphones. "Food Lion did not sue for defamation, but focused on how ABC gathered its information through claims for fraud, breach of duty of loyalty, trespass, and unfair trade practices. Food Lion won at trial, and judgment for compensatory damages of $1,402 was entered on the various claims." Although Food Lion was originally awarded $5.5 million in punitive damages, this was reduced to $315,000, and, ultimately, to nominal damages of $2. The court held that ABC's producers did breach their duty of loyalty and committed a trespass. The court also held, on First Amendment grounds, that Food Lion could not prove publication damages.[1] Yet, it was estimated that the *Prime Time* story cost Food Lion over $1 billion in stock value in the week following the story, and immeasurable public relations losses later.

Was it ethical for ABC to have its producers lie to get the story? Or could this just be considered journalistic "muck-raking?" Should the media have the power to cause such a large amount of damage to a business?

News stories cannot only cost businesses money, and a police chief's sleepless nights; they can actually cost lives. In 2005, *Newsweek* published an article that reported American soldiers had supposedly flushed a copy of the Qur'an down the toilet. The report stated that the soldiers were attempting to gain information from a detainee at the Guantánamo, Cuba, holding area. This story incited widespread discontent in the Muslim world, and nine people died as a result. Shortly after the story came out in print, *Newsweek* confessed that the report was not true.

What is the ethical duty of *Newsweek* in the reporting of such a volatile story? Should there have been a more extensive investigation of the facts before publication?

Ethics and Invasion of Privacy

Invasion of privacy is a major area in which the media must weigh the public's right to know with the ethics of reporting a story. In *Diaz v. Oakland Tribune*, 139 C.A.3d 118 (1983), the *Tribune* reported on a sex change operation performed on Toni Ann Diaz. Ms. Diaz, originally a man, enrolled in a community college and ultimately was elected student body president. No one on campus knew of the operation before the news article.

Ms. Diaz sued for invasion of privacy, and won a judgment of $775,000 in the California Superior Court. The appellate court overturned the verdict and ordered a new trial, holding the Superior Court (trial court) judge had erred in not requiring Ms. Diaz to prove the story was *not* newsworthy. Ms. Diaz declined to go through a second trial.

Although it could be argued that a community college student body president's history was newsworthy, and thus of interest to the public, was it ethical to report on such a private matter? Would it have been more ethical to do such a report if Ms. Diaz had already revealed she had the sex change operation?

An Ethics Checklist

Taking these scenarios into consideration, how can a journalist determine what is or what is not ethical to report? A series of questions that address the issue can help.

How important is it to report the story?

Has the editor given direct instructions to cover the event? If the story has been assigned, there is little room to decide whether or not it will be covered, but the manner in which the story is handled can make a big difference.

What words or pictures are being used to cover the story?

If a journalist works for a news organization that seeks the sensational, then that is how the story will have to be run. But if the organization is more mainstream, how a story is worded can make a big difference. Are subtle derogations being used against women? Do pictures in the story accurately represent the scene, or are they skewed to depict a specific stereotype? In a report on business, are all white males depicted as decision makers? Are women pictured as wives of victims, or victims of crimes? Be careful of racial stereotyping. Are all reports on blacks or Hispanics about gangs, crimes, or drugs?

How are unnamed sources handled?

As was discussed in a previous chapter with regard to confidential sources, most journalistic codes of ethics require a journalist to maintain a source's confidentiality if so asked. Yet, the public has a right to know if this source of information is reliable. In these situations, a journalist must maintain the secrecy of the source, but still give the public sufficient information to decide if the information reported on is credible.

How should a journalist conduct investigative reporting?

This form of journalism involves issues not normally found in routine reporting. It is important to involve one's editor in the decision to run the story. Always be careful of sources and how the story is phrased. Be careful that the story is scrupulously accurate and fair. As discussed earlier in the *Food Lion* case, always evaluate the legal and ethical ramifications of reporting the story. If the story is detailed in nature, it is best to have an expert review it before publication to ensure that all information is accurate.

How should a news organization handle errors in a story?

Any errors found in a story must be corrected in a timely manner, and must be reported in a prominent position in the publication or broadcast. It is best not to repeat the error in the correction, yet there must be sufficient information so that the reader can understand what is being corrected. If it is an error of context or tone, not one of fact, there may need to be an editor's column or editor's note to correct the inference made by the reader.

Who is missing from the story?

If the demographics of the reporting area are 50 percent white, 30 percent black, and 20 percent Hispanic, do the stories covered adequately represent this ethnic diversity? This may not seem important because the journalist could respond that he is only covering the day's events, yet an observer of the news could find this racially biased.

Is the report balanced?

If a lead story was about the presence of previously convicted sexual predators in various neighborhoods, a description in the same news report on how an individual could find out where such individuals live would give balance to a story.

A story about the political strife in the world would be well balanced with interviews from individuals that had connection with that part of the world. Or a story about a raid on a marijuana growing facility could be ethically balanced with coverage on antidrug programs at local schools.

It is important that the media consider where news coverage appears to be distorted or not representative of the covered area. The media has a role in the community to be its eyes and ears, and to report the news as such. Anything less than that would not be ethical.

International Media Ethics Codes

Although many in the United States wish to impose Western forms of ethics on the world, this may or may not suffice, because each area has its own distinct media needs and concerns. Yet most journalists, wherever they are in the world, have codified their own version of what is or is not ethical reporting. Ironically, despite some minor differences, journalists strive for similar goals.

The **Code of Ethics in East Africa** emphasizes that journalists shall report fair, accurate, and unbiased stories. There should not be any prejudicial language used that would stigmatize an individual. A journalist should not plagiarize, because that is considered to be unethical. Nor should a journalist or his employer accept bribes to influence the running of a news story.

Under Article Three of the **Latin American Federation of Journalists**, journalists are asked to defend freedom of expression and the right to information, to fight for new information that relates to the people's interest and does not deform reality, and to reject propaganda as to the inevitability of war or use of force in international conflicts.

The **Islamic Mass Media Charter** states in its Article Three that the Islamic media should censor all material that may be harmful to Islamic character and values; offensive words should not be used, nor should obscene material be published; anything that goes against public morality should not be published nor anything that incites crime, violence, or anything that arouses terror.

Commercial advertisements that go against morality should be strictly barred from publication.[2]

ENTERTAINMENT ETHICS

Should the entertainment industry be held to an even higher standard of ethics than the media? Some would argue yes. Why? Popular entertainment molds the cultural climate of the world—or does it?

The entertainment industry has been sharply criticized for its derogation of women, its promotion of tobacco use, the antics of its "stars," and its use of graphic violence. Yet, it could be argued, these depictions are legal based on First Amendment grounds, but are these depictions ethical?

■ **CODE OF ETHICS IN EAST AFRICA**

The Code of Ethics in East Africa is that a journalist will be fair and allow a right of reply; the journalist will not accept favors or bribes for running a story; a journalist shall not show discrimination towards race, religion, national origin, or gender; he should show respect for human dignity, and not plagiarize another's work.

Graphic Violence

In 1968, Dr. Martin Luther King Jr. and Senator Robert Kennedy were assassinated. In response, then President Lyndon Johnson appointed the **NCCPV (the National Commission on the Causes and Prevention of Violence)** to review whether the viewing of violence encouraged the commission of violent acts. The Commission concluded "A constant diet of violent behavior has an adverse effect on human behavior." Yet the viewing public is continuously bombarded with violence in the movies, television, and video games.

The entertainment industry would argue that their depiction of violence is only a reflection of what occurs in society, and, more important, that this is what "sells." The dilemma is which came first: the violent society, or the watching of violence in an entertainment format? If it can be shown the watching of graphic violence begets violent behavior, how much violence depicted is ethical? Is "gratuitous" violence in a script even ethical?

Tobacco Use

In the movie *Thank You For Smoking*, it was emphasized how important it was to the tobacco industry for its products be made "sexy" or "the cool thing to do," but of course the potentially serious downside of tobacco's use should not be discussed.

Screenwriter Joe Eszterhaus, writer of movies such as *Flashdance, Sliver,* and *Basic Instinct*, which feature tobacco-using characters, had regrets for his advocacy of smoking when he was diagnosed with cancer of the throat in 2002. Although he felt that smoking was an integral portion of many of his movies, and he was an avid smoker, he has expressed remorse for intentionally promoting cigarettes to a young audience in his movies.

In an ethical response to movies and their subliminal promotion of tobacco use, there is discussion in changing the rating of a movie solely on the basis that someone smokes in the film. The new mandatory rating if smoking were shown in the movie would be "R." What this would do is limit the introduction of smoking to a younger audience. This would be an ethical and economic "wake-up call" to Hollywood because "R" rated movies historically do not do as well at the box office as "PG" movies.

Celebrity Slips of the Tongue

In the third season of the television show *Grey's Anatomy*, Isaiah Washington became embroiled in a backstage controversy. In October 2006, it was reported that Washington had used a derogatory epithet toward his costar T. R. Knight with reference to his sexual orientation. Shortly after this encounter, Mr. Knight disclosed that he was gay.

■ **LATIN AMERICAN FEDERATION OF JOURNALISTS**

The ethical guidelines of the Latin American Federation of Journalists states: journalism should contribute to the strengthening of peace, co-existence, self-determination of the people, disarmament, international cooperation, and mutual understanding among all the peoples of the world; and journalists should fight for equality among human beings. Journalists will adopt the principles of truth and objectivity in their work, and will commit ethical faults when they silence, falsify, or manipulate facts. A journalist is responsible for his information and opinions, will accept the existence of reprinting rights, and will respect the professional secrecy of his sources.

ABC Studios rebuked Mr. Washington for his comments, and he apologized; he even made public service announcements, denouncing individuals that use hateful words against others. These public service announcements were played during the showing of *Grey's Anatomy*. Washington admitted he had "... issues he obviously needs to examine within his own soul," and he sought outside help.

Despite everything that Mr. Washington had done to try to rectify the incident, on June 7, 2007, ABC announced they would not renew his *Grey's Anatomy* contract, and he would be dropped from the show. Was it ethical for Mr. Washington to have commented on Mr. Knight's lifestyle? Was it ethical for ABC to fire him? Do celebrities need to be held to a higher ethical standard?

Also in 2007, radio talk show host Don Imus was fired by CBS for his comments about the Rutgers women's basketball team. Imus found himself in the center of a brewing storm of controversy when he referred to the team as "nappy-headed hos." Protests poured into CBS, and sponsors of Imus' show left one by one, and potential guests to his show began to dwindle in number. Mr. Imus acknowledged his comment was "really stupid." Although he stated that he had apologized enough, "I said it. ... I wouldn't be here if I didn't say it." True, Don Imus has made a career of shocking his audiences, yet CBS could not sanction the ethical, and ultimately the economic, ramifications of his comments.

On December 3, 2007, Don Imus returned to radio courtesy of the Citadel Broadcasting Corporation. Las Vegas-based Citadel, which bought WABC and other ABC radio stations from Walt Disney Company last year, now owns more than 240 radio stations around the country.

Did the firing of Mr. Washington and Mr. Imus mean that the code of ethics of the entertainment industry has changed? Or are the tables turning, and now the entertainment industry is being forced, by public opinion, to adapt to a new cultural climate? Only time will tell.

SUMMARY

In the media and entertainment industries, the form of ethics usually followed is that of moral relativism—one not reflective of any absolute truths or falsities. Instead, it reflects a code that refers to social and cultural preferences.

A journalist must counterbalance the legality in reporting a story with the rights of privacy of the individual being reported on, the right of the public to know, and how the public will react to how the story is covered. Invasion of privacy is a major area in which the media must weigh the public's right to know with the ethics of reporting a story.

When doing international stories, or reporting in a foreign country, a journalist must take into consideration the culture and laws of the countries where the information for the article is gathered. The reporter and broadcaster or publisher also must take into consideration the customs and culture of the county where the article will be viewed or read.

The entertainment industry has been sharply criticized for its derogatory depiction of women, its promotion of tobacco use, the antics of its "stars," and its use of graphic violence. In response to these ethical issues, celebrities and leaders in the entertainment industry have been faced with ethical and economic decisions and setbacks.

▉ DISCUSSION QUESTIONS_____

1. Argue why merely following the law should be ethically sufficient.
2. Discuss why a journalist should or should not worry about how the readers of a story react to its content.
3. Discuss why or why not a journalist should get a story, no matter the cost on the people reported on.
4. Argue why customs or cultures of other countries should conform to those of the United States.
5. Discuss why celebrities should be held to a higher standard of conduct than noncelebrities.

▉ CASE FOR REVIEW_____

In June 2007, Paris Hilton was sentenced to 45 days in jail for violating the terms of her probation for an alcohol-related reckless driving conviction.

In January 2007, she had pled no contest to a reckless driving charge, stemming from a September 2006 arrest for failing a field sobriety test. She was sentenced to 36 months' probation, alcohol education, and $1,500 in fines. After this first sentence, Ms. Hilton was involved in two other traffic stops—one for driving on a suspended license, and the second for speeding and not having any headlights on. Furthermore, she failed to enroll in the mandated alcohol education program as per the terms of her probation. These incidents are what led to her jail sentence.

Although the city attorney in the case, Rocky Delgadillo, said that Ms. Hilton was being treated the same as anyone else, discuss why or why not Ms. Hilton, as a celebrity, should be held to a higher ethical standard in her public conduct.

▉ KEY TERMS_____

Code of Ethics in East Africa	Journalists	on the Causes and Prevention of
Islamic Mass Media Charter	moral relativism	Violence)
Latin American Federation of	NCCPV (the National Commission	

ENDNOTES

[1] *Food Lion, Inc. v. ABC, Inc.*, 194 F.3d 505 (4th Cir. 1999).

[2] http://usinfo.state.gov.

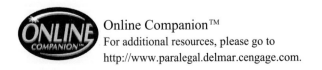

Online Companion™
For additional resources, please go to
http://www.paralegal.delmar.cengage.com.

Student CD-ROM
For additional materials, please go to the
CD in this book.

Helpful Web Sites

FINDLAW

http://www.findlaw.com

Findlaw is the most often visited legal Web site. This site provides legal resources for legal professionals, businesses, students, and individuals, and includes statutes, cases, legal news, and much more.

DOUGLAS LINDER

http://www.law.umkc.edu

Accounts, maps, photos, transcript excerpts, and other materials relating to famous American trials, assembled by Professor Douglas Linder, UMKC School of Law.

WESTLAW

http://westlaw.com

This site provides legal resources for legal professionals, businesses, students, and individuals, and includes statutes, cases, legal news, and much more.

DEPARTMENT OF JUSTICE

http://www.lifeand
liberty.gov

This site is maintained by the U.S. Department of Justice and is dedicated to issues concerning the USA Patriot Act.

The Constitutional Provision Respecting Copyright

The Congress shall have Power ... To promote the Progress of Science and useful Arts, by securing for limited Times to Authors and Inventors the exclusive Right to their respective Writings and Discoveries

(United States Constitution, Article I, Section 8)

PREFACE

This volume contains the text of title 17 of the *United States Code*, including all amendments enacted through the end of the second session of the 109th Congress, in 2006. It includes the Copyright Act of 1976 and all subsequent amendments to copyright law; the Semiconductor Chip Protection Act of 1984, as amended; and the Vessel Hull Design Protection Act, as amended. The Copyright Office is responsible for registering claims under all three.

The United States copyright law is contained in chapters 1 through 8 and 10 through 12 of title 17 of the *United States Code*. The Copyright Act of 1976, which provides the basic framework for the current copyright law, was enacted on October 19, 1976, as Pub. L. No. 94-553, 90 Stat. 2541. Listed below in chronological order of their enactment are subsequent amendments to copyright law.

Chapters 9 and 13 of title 17 contain statutory design protection that is independent of copyright protection. Chapter 9 of title 17 is the Semiconductor Chip Protection Act of 1984 (SCPA), as amended. On November 8, 1984, the SCPA was enacted as title III of Pub. L. No. 98-620,

98 Stat. 3335, 3347. Chapter 13 of title 17 is the Vessel Hull Design Protection Act (VHDPA). It was enacted on October 28, 1998 as title V of the Digital Millennium Copyright Act (DMCA), Pub. L. No. 105-304, 112 Stat. 2860, 2905. Subsequent amendments to the SCPA and the VHDPA are also included in the list below, in chronological order of their enactment.

Significant copyright legislation enacted since the last edition of this circular in June 2003 includes the Copyright Royalty and Distribution Reform Act of 2004, the Satellite Home Viewer Extension and Reauthorization Act of 2004, and the Family Entertainment and Copyright Act of 2005 (including the Artists' Rights and Theft Prevention Act of 2005, the Family Movie Act of 2005, and the Preservation of Orphan Works Act). For more details, these statutes appear at the end of the chronological list below of statutory enactments contained in title 17 of the *United States Code*.

For transitional and supplementary copyright provisions that do not amend title 17, see the appendices.

Statutory Enactments Contained in Title 17 of the United States Code

- [Copyright Act of 1976], Pub. L. No. 94-553, 90 Stat. 2541 (for the general revision of copyright law, title 17 of the *United States Code,* and for other purposes), October 19, 1976.

- Legislative Branch Appropriation Act, 1978, Pub. L. No. 95-94, 91 Stat. 653, 682 (amending §203 and §708, title 17, *United States Code,* regarding the deposit of moneys by the Register of Copyrights in the Treasury of the United States), enacted August 5, 1977.

- [Copyright Amendments], Pub. L. No. 95-598, 92 Stat. 2549, 2676 (amending §201(e), title 17, *United States Code,* to permit involuntary transfer under the Bankruptcy Law), enacted November 6, 1978.

- [Copyright Amendments], Pub. L. No. 96-517, 94 Stat. 3015, 3028 (amending §101 and §117, title 17, *United States Code,* regarding computer programs), enacted December 12, 1980.

- Piracy and Counterfeiting Amendments Act of 1982, Pub. L. No. 97-180, 96 Stat. 91, 93 (amending §506(a), title 17, *United States Code* and title 18 of the *United States Code*), enacted May 24, 1982.

- [Copyright Amendments], Pub. L. No. 97-215, 96 Stat. 178 (amending the manufacturing clause in chapter 6, title 17, *United States Code*), enacted July 13, 1982.

- [Copyright Amendments], Pub. L. No. 97-366, 96 Stat. 1759 (amending §110 and §708, title 17, *United States Code,* regarding the redesignation of registration fees as filing fees, and the exemption from copyright liability of certain performances of nondramatic literary or musical works), enacted October 25, 1982.

- Record Rental Amendment of 1984, Pub. L. No. 98-450, 98 Stat. 1727 (amending §109 and §115, title 17, *United States Code,* with respect to rental, lease or lending of sound recordings), enacted October 4, 1984.

- Semiconductor Chip Protection Act of 1984, title III of Pub. L. No. 98-620, 98 Stat. 3335, 3347 (adding chapter 9, title 17, *United States Code,* to provide design protection for semiconductor chips), November 8, 1984.

- [Copyright Amendments], Pub. L. No. 99-397, 100 Stat. 848 (amending §111 and §801, title 17, *United States Code,* to clarify the definition of the local service area of a primary transmitter in the case of a low power television station), enacted on August 27, 1986.

- [Amendments to the Semiconductor Chip Protection Act of 1984], Pub. L. No. 100-159, 101 Stat. 899 (amending chapter 9, title 17, *United States Code,* regarding protection extended to semiconductor chip products of foreign entities), enacted November 9, 1987.

- Berne Convention Implementation Act of 1988, Pub. L. No. 100-568, 102 Stat. 2853, enacted October 31, 1988. (See the Appendix for certain provisions of this Act that do not amend title 17 of the *United States Code.*)

- [Copyright Amendments], Pub. L. No. 100-617, 102 Stat. 3194 (extending for an additional eight-year period certain provisions of title 17, *United States Code,* relating to the rental of sound recordings and for other purposes), enacted November 5, 1988.

- Satellite Home Viewer Act of 1988, title II of Pub. L. No. 100-667, 102 Stat. 3935, 3949, enacted November 16, 1988.

- Judicial Improvements and Access to Justice Act, Pub. L. No. 100-702, 102 Stat. 4642, 4672 (amending §912, title 17, *United States Code*), enacted November 19, 1988.

- Copyright Fees and Technical Amendments Act of 1989, Pub. L. No. 101-318, 104 Stat. 287, enacted on July 3, 1990.

- Copyright Royalty Tribunal Reform and Miscellaneous Pay Act of 1989, Pub. L. No. 101-319, 104 Stat. 290, enacted July 3, 1990.

- Copyright Remedy Clarification Act, Pub. L. No. 101-553, 104 Stat. 2749, enacted November 15, 1990.

- Visual Artists Rights Act of 1990, title VI of the Judicial Improvements Act of 1990, Pub. L. No. 101-650, 104 Stat. 5089, 5128, enacted December 1, 1990.

- Architectural Works Copyright Protection Act, title VII of the Judicial Improvements Act of 1990, Pub. L. No. 101-650, 104 Stat. 5089, 5133, enacted December 1, 1990.

- Computer Software Rental Amendments Act of 1990, title VIII of the Judicial Improvements Act of 1990, Pub. L. No. 101-650, 104 Stat 5089, 5134, enacted December 1, 1990.

- Semiconductor International Protection Extension Act of 1991, Pub. L. No. 102-64, 105 Stat. 320 (amending chapter 9, title 17, *United States Code,* regarding protection extended to semiconductor chip products of foreign entities), enacted June 28, 1991.

- Copyright Amendments Act of 1992, Pub. L. No. 102-307, 106 Stat. 264, 272 (amending chapter 3, title 17, *United States Code,* as described immediately below and by deleting subsection 108(i)), enacted June 26, 1992. (Also, through an independent provision that does not amend title 17 of the *United States Code,* the Act established the National Film Registry under title II, which is the National Film Preservation Act of 1992.)

- Copyright Renewal Act of 1992, title I of the Copyright Amendments Act of 1992, Pub. L. No. 102-307, 106 Stat. 264 (amending chapter 3, title 17 of the *United States Code*, by providing for automatic renewal of copyright for works copyrighted between January 1, 1964, and December 31, 1977), enacted June 26, 1992.

- [Copyright Amendments], Pub. L. No. 102-492, 106 Stat. 3145 (amending §107, title 17, *United States Code*, regarding unpublished works), enacted October 24, 1992.

- [Copyright Amendments], Pub. L. No. 102-561, 106 Stat. 4233 (amending §2319, title 18, *United States Code*, regarding criminal penalties for copyright infringement), enacted October 28, 1992.

- Audio Home Recording Act of 1992, Pub. L. No. 102-563, 106 Stat. 4237 (amending title 17 of the *United States Code* by adding a new chapter 10), enacted October 28, 1992.

- North American Free Trade Agreement Implementation Act, Pub. L. No. 103-182, 107 Stat. 2057, 2114 and 2115 (amending §109, title 17, *United States Code*, and adding a new §104A), enacted December 8, 1993.

- Copyright Royalty Tribunal Reform Act of 1993, Pub. L. No. 103-198, 107 Stat. 2304 (amending, *inter alia*, chapter 8, title 17, *United States Code*), enacted December 17, 1993.

- Satellite Home Viewer Act of 1994, Pub. L. No. 103-369, 108 Stat. 3477 (amending, *inter alia*, §111 and §119, title 17, *United States Code*, relating to the definition of a local service area of a primary transmitter), enacted October 18, 1994.

- Uruguay Round Agreements Act, Pub. L. No. 103-465, 108 Stat. 4809, 4973 (amending, *inter alia*, §104, title 17, *United States Code*, and adding a new chapter 11), enacted December 8, 1994. (See the Appendix J for the text of certain provisions of this Act that do not amend title 17 of the *United States Code*.)

- Digital Performance Right in Sound Recordings Act of 1995, Pub. L. No. 104-39, 109 Stat. 336 (amending, *inter alia*, §114 and §115, title 17, *United States Code*), enacted November 1, 1995.

- Anticounterfeiting Consumer Protection Act of 1996, Pub. L. No. 104-153, 110 Stat. 1386, 1388 (amending §603(c), title 17, *United States Code* and §2318, title 18, *United States Code*), enacted July 2, 1996.

- Legislative Branch Appropriations Act, 1997, Pub. L. No. 104-197, 110 Stat. 2394, 2416 (amending, *inter alia*, title 17 of the *United States Code*, by adding a new §121 concerning the limitation on exclusive copyrights for literary works in specialized format for the blind and disabled), enacted September 16, 1996.

- [Copyright Amendments and Amendments to the Semiconductor Chip Protection Act of 1984], Pub. L. No. 105-80, 111 Stat. 1529 (making technical amendments to certain provisions of title 17, *United States Code*), enacted November 13, 1997.

- No Electronic Theft (NET) Act, Pub. L. No. 105-147, 111 Stat. 2678, enacted December 16, 1997.

- Sonny Bono Copyright Term Extension Act, title I of Pub. L. No. 105-298, 112 Stat. 2827 (amending chapter 3, title 17, *United States Code*, to extend the term of copyright protection for most works to life plus 70 years), enacted October 27, 1998.

- Fairness in Music Licensing Act of 1998, title II of Pub. L. No. 105-298, 112 Stat. 2827, 2830 (amending, *inter alia,* §110, title 17, *United States Code,* and adding §513 to provide a music licensing exemption for food service and drinking establishments), enacted October 27, 1998.

- Digital Millennium Copyright Act, Pub. L. No. 105-304, 112 Stat. 2860, 2887 (title IV amending §108, §112, §114, chapter 7 and chapter 8, title 17, *United States Code*), enacted October 28, 1998. (This Act also contains four separate acts within titles I, II, III and V that amended title 17 of the *United States Code.* These four acts are each separately listed below. See the Appendix B for additional provisions of this Act that do not amend title 17 of the *United States Code.*)

- WIPO Copyright and Performances and Phonograms Treaties Implementation Act of 1998, title I of the Digital Millennium Copyright Act, Pub. L. No. 105-304, 112 Stat. 2860, 2861 (amending title 17 of the *United States Code, inter alia,* to add a new chapter 12 which prohibits circumvention of copyright protection systems and provides protection for copyright management information), enacted October 28, 1998.

- Online Copyright Infringement Liability Limitation Act, title II of the Digital Millennium Copyright Act, Pub. L. No. 105-304, 112 Stat. 2860, 2877 (amending title 17 of the *United States Code,* to add a new §512), enacted October 28, 1998.

- Computer Maintenance Competition Assurance Act, title III of the Digital Millennium Copyright Act, Pub. L. No. 105-304, 112 Stat. 2860, 2886 (amending §117, title 17, *United States Code*), enacted October 28, 1998.

- Vessel Hull Design Protection Act, title V of the Digital Millennium Copyright Act, Pub. L. No. 105-304, 112 Stat. 2860, 2905 (adding chapter 13, title 17, *United States Code,* to provide design protection for vessel hulls), enacted October 28, 1998.

- [Copyright Amendments and Amendments to the Vessel Hull Design Protection Act], Pub. L. No. 106-44, 113 Stat. 221 (making technical corrections to title 17 of the *United States Code*), enacted August 5, 1999.

- Satellite Home Viewer Improvement Act of 1999, title I of the Intellectual Property and Communications Omnibus Reform Act of 1999, Pub. L. No. 106-113, 113 Stat. 1501, app. I (amending chapters 1 and 5 of title 17 of the *United States Code* to replace the Satellite Home Viewer Act of 1994 and amending chapters 12 and 13 of title 17), enacted November 29, 1999.

- Digital Theft Deterrence and Copyright Damages Improvement Act of 1999, Pub. L. No. 106-160, 113 Stat 1774, (amending chapter 5 of title 17 of the *United States Code* to increase statutory damages for copyright infringement), enacted December 9, 1999.

- Work Made for Hire and Copyright Corrections Act of 2000, Pub. L. No. 106-379, 114 Stat. 1444 (amending the definition of work made for hire in title 17 of the *United States Code,* amending chapter 7 of title 17, including changing the language regarding Copyright Office fees, and making other technical and conforming amendments to title 17), enacted October 27, 2000.

- Intellectual Property and High Technology Technical Amendments Act of 2002, Division C, Title III, Subtitle B of the 21st Century Department of Justice Appropriations Authorization Act, Pub. L. No. 107-273, 116 Stat. 1758, 1901 (making technical corrections both to title 17, *United States*

Code, and, as described in footnotes where appropriate, to title I of the Intellectual Property and Communications Omnibus Reform Act of 1999, entitled the Satellite Home Viewer Improvement Act of 1999, Pub. L. No. 106-113, 113 Stat. 1501, app. I), enacted November 2, 2002.

- Technology, Education, and Copyright Harmonization Act of 2002, Division C, Title III, Subtitle C of the 21st Century Department of Justice Appropriations Authorization Act, Pub. L. No. 107-273, 116 Stat. 1758, 1910 (amending chapter 1, title 17, *United States Code*, to incorporate provisions relating to use of copyrighted works for distance education), enacted November 2, 2002.

- Small Webcaster Settlement Act of 2002, Pub. L. No. 107-321, 116 Stat. 2780 (amending chapter 1, title 17, *United States Code*, to incorporate new language into section 114), enacted December 4, 2002.

- Copyright Royalty and Distribution Reform Act of 2004, Pub. L. No. 108-419, 118 Stat. 2341 (revising chapter 8, title 17, *United States Code*, in its entirety), enacted November 30, 2004.

- Individuals with Disabilities Education Improvement Act of 2004, Title III, Pub. L. No. 108-446, 118 Stat. 2647, 2807 (amending section 121, title 17, *United States Code*, to further expand authorized reproduction of copyrighted works for the blind or people with other disabilities), enacted December 3, 2004.

- Satellite Home Viewer Extension and Reauthorization Act of 2004, Title IX, Division J of the Consolidated Appropriations Act, 2005, Pub. L. No. 108-447, 118 Stat. 2809, 3393 (amending section 119, title 17, *United States Code*, throughout and by extending for an additional five years the statutory license for satellite carriers retransmitting over-the-air television broadcast stations to their subscribers), enacted December 8, 2004.

- Anti-counterfeiting Amendments Act of 2004, Title I of the Intellectual Property Protection and Courts Amendments Act of 2004, Pub. L. No. 108-482, 118 Stat. 3912 (amending section 2318, title 18, of the *United States Code* concerning trafficking in counterfeit or illicit labels in connection with stolen copyrighted works), enacted December 23, 2004.

- Fraudulent Online Identity Sanctions Act, Title II of the Intellectual Property Protection and Courts Amendments Act of 2004, Pub. L. No. 108-482, 118 Stat. 3912, 3916 (amending section 504(c), title 17, *United States Code*, to add language making it a criminal violation to knowingly provide false contact information for a domain name that is used in connection with copyright infringement when registering the domain name with authorities), enacted December 23, 2004.

- Artists' Rights and Theft Prevention Act of 2005 (also known as the "ART Act"), Title I of the Family Entertainment and Copyright Act of 2005, Pub. L. No. 109-9, 119 Stat. 218 (amending chapter 113, title 18, *United States Code*, to add a new section 2319B authorizing criminal penalties for unauthorized recording of motion pictures; amends section 506(a), title 17, United States Code, in its entirety; amending section 2319, title 18, *United States Code*, by adding criminal penalties for section 506(a); amending section 408, title 17, *United States Code*, by adding new language authorizing preregistration of works being prepared for commercial distribution; and directing the United States Sentencing Commission to establish policies and guidelines for intellectual property crimes), enacted April 27, 2005.

- Family Movie Act of 2005, Title II of the Family Entertainment and Copyright Act of 2005, Pub. L. No. 109-9, 119 Stat. 218, 223 (amending section 110, title 17, *United States Code*, to add a new exemption from infringement for imperceptible skipping of audio and video content in motion pictures), enacted April 27, 2005.

- Preservation of Orphan Works Act, Title IV of the Family Entertainment and Copyright Act of 2005, Pub. L. No. 109-9, 119 Stat. 218, 226 (amending section 108(i), title 17, *United States Code*, to add orphan works to the list of works that are exempt from certain limitations on uses by libraries and archives), enacted April 27, 2005.

- Copyright Royalty Judges Program Technical Corrections Act, Pub. L. No. 109-303, 120 Stat. 1478 (to make clarifying and technical corrections to chapter 8, *United States Code*, and related conforming amendments), enacted October 6, 2006.

This 2007 edition would not have been possible without the efforts of Renée Coe, Senior Attorney in the Office of the General Counsel, who was responsible for updating statutory provisions and drafting text, as well as the Information and Records Division's writer-editor Judith Nierman, who was responsible for proofreading and editorial review, and graphic designer Charles Gibbons, who was responsible for the document's design and production.

Marybeth Peters
Register of Copyrights

CHAPTER 1

SUBJECT MATTER AND SCOPE OF COPYRIGHT

- 101. Definitions
- 102. Subject matter of copyright: In general
- 103. Subject matter of copyright: Compilations and derivative works
- 104. Subject matter of copyright: National origin
- 104A. Copyright in restored works
- 105. Subject matter of copyright: United States Government works
- 106. Exclusive rights in copyrighted works
- 106A. Rights of certain authors to attribution and integrity
- 107. Limitations on exclusive rights: Fair use
- 108. Limitations on exclusive rights: Reproduction by libraries and archives
- 109. Limitations on exclusive rights: Effect of transfer of particular copy or phonorecord
- 110. Limitations on exclusive rights: Exemption of certain performances and displays
- 111. Limitations on exclusive rights: Secondary transmissions

- 112. Limitations on exclusive rights: Ephemeral recordings
- 113. Scope of exclusive rights in pictorial, graphic, and sculptural works
- 114. Scope of exclusive rights in sound recordings
- 115. Scope of exclusive rights in nondramatic musical works: Compulsory license for making and distributing phonorecords
- 116. Negotiated licenses for public performances by means of coin-operated phonorecord players
- 117. Limitations on exclusive rights: Computer programs[1]
- 118. Scope of exclusive rights: Use of certain works in connection with noncommercial broadcasting
- 119. Limitations on exclusive rights: Secondary transmissions of superstations and network stations for private home viewing
- 120. Scope of exclusive rights in architectural works
- 121. Limitations on exclusive rights: reproduction for blind or other people with disabilities
- 122. Limitations on exclusive rights; secondary transmissions by satellite carriers within local market

§ 101. Definitions[2]

Except as otherwise provided in this title, as used in this title, the following terms and their variant forms mean the following:

An "anonymous work" is a work on the copies or phonorecords of which no natural person is identified as author.

An "architectural work" is the design of a building as embodied in any tangible medium of expression, including a building, architectural plans, or drawings. The work includes the overall form as well as the arrangement and composition of spaces and elements in the design, but does not include individual standard features.[3]

"Audiovisual works" are works that consist of a series of related images which are intrinsically intended to be shown by the use of machines or devices such as projectors, viewers, or electronic equipment, together with accompanying sounds, if any, regardless of the nature of the material objects, such as films or tapes, in which the works are embodied.

The "Berne Convention" is the Convention for the Protection of Literary and Artistic Works, signed at Berne, Switzerland, on September 9, 1886, and all acts, protocols, and revisions thereto.[4]

The "best edition" of a work is the edition, published in the United States at any time before the date of deposit, that the Library of Congress determines to be most suitable for its purposes.

A person's "children" are that person's immediate offspring, whether legitimate or not, and any children legally adopted by that person.

A "collective work" is a work, such as a periodical issue, anthology, or encyclopedia, in which a number of contributions, constituting separate and independent works in themselves, are assembled into a collective whole.

A "compilation" is a work formed by the collection and assembling of preexisting materials or of data that are selected, coordinated, or arranged in such a way that the resulting work as a whole constitutes an original work of authorship. The term "compilation" includes collective works.

A "computer program" is a set of statements or instructions to be used directly or indirectly in a computer in order to bring about a certain result.[5]

"Copies" are material objects, other than phonorecords, in which a work is fixed by any method now known or later developed, and from which the work can be perceived, reproduced, or otherwise communicated, either directly or with the aid of a machine or device. The term "copies" includes the material object, other than a phonorecord, in which the work is first fixed.

A "Copyright Royalty Judge" is a Copyright Royalty Judge appointed under section 802 of this title, and includes any individual serving as an interim Copyright Royalty Judge under such section.[6]

"Copyright owner", with respect to any one of the exclusive rights comprised in a copyright, refers to the owner of that particular right.

A work is "created" when it is fixed in a copy or phonorecord for the first time; where a work is prepared over a period of time, the portion of it that has been fixed at any particular time constitutes the work as of that time, and where the work has been prepared in different versions, each version constitutes a separate work.

A "derivative work" is a work based upon one or more preexisting works, such as a translation, musical arrangement, dramatization, fictionalization, motion picture version, sound recording, art reproduction, abridgment, condensation, or any other form in which a work may be recast, transformed, or adapted. A work consisting of editorial revisions, annotations, elaborations, or other modifications, which, as a whole, represent an original work of authorship, is a "derivative work".

A "device", "machine", or "process" is one now known or later developed.

A "digital transmission" is a transmission in whole or in part in a digital or other nonanalog format.[7]

To "display" a work means to show a copy of it, either directly or by means of a film, slide, television image, or any other device or process or, in the case of a motion picture or other audiovisual work, to show individual images nonsequentially.

An "establishment" is a store, shop, or any similar place of business open to the general public for the primary purpose of selling goods or services in which the majority of the gross square feet of space that is nonresidential is used for that purpose, and in which nondramatic musical works are performed publicly.[8]

A "food service or drinking establishment" is a restaurant, inn, bar, tavern, or any other similar place of business in which the public or patrons assemble for the primary purpose of being served food or drink, in which the majority of the gross square feet of space that is nonresidential is used for that purpose, and in which nondramatic musical works are performed publicly.[9]

The term "financial gain" includes receipt, or expectation of receipt, of anything of value, including the receipt of other copyrighted works.[10]

A work is "fixed" in a tangible medium of expression when its embodiment in a copy or phonorecord, by or under the authority of the author, is sufficiently permanent or stable to permit it to be perceived, reproduced, or otherwise communicated for a period of more than transitory duration. A work consisting of sounds, images, or both, that are being transmitted, is "fixed" for purposes of this title if a fixation of the work is being made simultaneously with its transmission.

The "Geneva Phonograms Convention" is the Convention for the Protection of Producers of Phonograms Against Unauthorized Duplication of Their Phonograms, concluded at Geneva, Switzerland, on October 29, 1971.[11]

The "gross square feet of space" of an establishment means the entire interior space of that establishment, and any adjoining outdoor space used to serve patrons, whether on a seasonal basis or otherwise.[12]

The terms "including" and "such as" are illustrative and not limitative.

An "international agreement" is   —

(1) the Universal Copyright Convention;

(2) the Geneva Phonograms Convention;

(3) the Berne Convention;

(4) the WTO Agreement;

(5) the WIPO Copyright Treaty;[13]

(6) the WIPO Performances and Phonograms Treaty;[14] and

(7) any other copyright treaty to which the United States is a party.[15]

A "joint work" is a work prepared by two or more authors with the intention that their contributions be merged into inseparable or interdependent parts of a unitary whole.

"Literary works" are works, other than audiovisual works, expressed in words, numbers, or other verbal or numerical symbols or indicia, regardless of the nature of the material objects, such as books, periodicals, manuscripts, phonorecords, film, tapes, disks, or cards, in which they are embodied.

"Motion pictures" are audiovisual works consisting of a series of related images which, when shown in succession, impart an impression of motion, together with accompanying sounds, if any.

The term "motion picture exhibition facility" means a movie theater, screening room, or other venue that is being used primarily for the exhibition of a copyrighted motion picture, if such exhibition is open to the public or is made to an assembled group of viewers outside of a normal circle of a family and its social acquaintances.[16]

To "perform" a work means to recite, render, play, dance, or act it, either directly or by means of any device or process or, in the case of a motion picture or other audiovisual work, to show its images in any sequence or to make the sounds accompanying it audible.

A "performing rights society" is an association, corporation, or other entity that licenses the public performance of nondramatic musical works on behalf of copyright owners of such works, such as the American Society of Composers, Authors and Publishers (ASCAP), Broadcast Music, Inc. (BMI), and SESAC, Inc.[17]

"Phonorecords" are material objects in which sounds, other than those accompanying a motion picture or other audiovisual work, are fixed by any method now known or later developed, and from which the sounds can be perceived, reproduced, or otherwise communicated, either directly or with the aid of a machine or device. The term "phonorecords" includes the material object in which the sounds are first fixed.

"Pictorial, graphic, and sculptural works" include two-dimensional and three-dimensional works of fine, graphic, and applied art, photographs, prints and art reproductions, maps, globes, charts, diagrams, models, and technical drawings, including architectural plans. Such works shall include works of artistic craftsmanship insofar as their form but not their mechanical or utilitarian aspects are concerned; the design of a useful article, as defined in this section, shall be considered a pictorial, graphic, or sculptural work only if, and only to the extent that, such design incorporates pictorial, graphic, or sculptural features that can be identified separately from, and are capable of existing independently of, the utilitarian aspects of the article.[18]

For purposes of section 513, a "proprietor" is an individual, corporation, partnership, or other entity, as the case may be, that owns an establishment or a food service or drinking establishment, except that no owner or operator of a radio or television station licensed by the Federal Communications Commission, cable system or satellite carrier, cable or satellite carrier service or programmer, provider of online services or network access or the operator of facilities therefor, telecommunications company, or any other such audio or audiovisual service or programmer now known or as may be developed in the future, commercial subscription music service, or owner or operator of any other transmission service, shall under any circumstances be deemed to be a proprietor.[19]

A "pseudonymous work" is a work on the copies or phonorecords of which the author is identified under a fictitious name.

"Publication" is the distribution of copies or phonorecords of a work to the public by sale or other transfer of ownership, or by rental, lease, or lending. The offering to distribute copies or phonorecords to a group of persons for purposes of further distribution, public performance, or public display, constitutes publication. A public performance or display of a work does not of itself constitute publication.

To perform or display a work "publicly" means —

(1) to perform or display it at a place open to the public or at any place where a substantial number of persons outside of a normal circle of a family and its social acquaintances is gathered; or

(2) to transmit or otherwise communicate a performance or display of the work to a place specified by clause (1) or to the public, by means of any device or process, whether the members of the public capable of receiving the performance or display receive it in the same place or in separate places and at the same time or at different times.

"Registration", for purposes of sections 205(c)(2), 405, 406, 410(d), 411, 412, and 506(e), means a registration of a claim in the original or the renewed and extended term of copyright.[20]

"Sound recordings" are works that result from the fixation of a series of musical, spoken, or other sounds, but not including the sounds accompanying a motion picture or other audiovisual work, regardless of the nature of the material objects, such as disks, tapes, or other phonorecords, in which they are embodied.

"State" includes the District of Columbia and the Commonwealth of Puerto Rico, and any territories to which this title is made applicable by an Act of Congress.

A "transfer of copyright ownership" is an assignment, mortgage, exclusive license, or any other conveyance, alienation, or hypothecation of a copyright or of any of the exclusive rights comprised in a copyright, whether or not it is limited in time or place of effect, but not including a nonexclusive license.

A "transmission program" is a body of material that, as an aggregate, has been produced for the sole purpose of transmission to the public in sequence and as a unit.

To "transmit" a performance or display is to communicate it by any device or process whereby images or sounds are received beyond the place from which they are sent.

A "treaty party" is a country or intergovernmental organization other than the United States that is a party to an international agreement.[21]

The "United States", when used in a geographical sense, comprises the several States, the District of Columbia and the Commonwealth of Puerto Rico, and the organized territories under the jurisdiction of the United States Government.

For purposes of section 411, a work is a "United States work" only if —

(1) in the case of a published work, the work is first published —

(A) in the United States;

(B) simultaneously in the United States and another treaty party or parties, whose law grants a term of copyright protection that is the same as or longer than the term provided in the United States;

(C) simultaneously in the United States and a foreign nation that is not a treaty party; or

(D) in a foreign nation that is not a treaty party, and all of the authors of the work are nationals, domiciliaries, or habitual residents of, or in the case of an audiovisual work legal entities with headquarters in, the United States;

(2) in the case of an unpublished work, all the authors of the work are nationals, domiciliaries, or habitual residents of the United States, or, in the case of an unpublished audiovisual work, all the authors are legal entities with headquarters in the United States; or

(3) in the case of a pictorial, graphic, or sculptural work incorporated in a building or structure, the building or structure is located in the United States.[22]

A "useful article" is an article having an intrinsic utilitarian function that is not merely to portray the appearance of the article or to convey information. An article that is normally a part of a useful article is considered a "useful article".

The author's "widow" or "widower" is the author's surviving spouse under the law of the author's domicile at the time of his or her death, whether or not the spouse has later remarried.

The "WIPO Copyright Treaty" is the WIPO Copyright Treaty concluded at Geneva, Switzerland, on December 20, 1996.[23]

The "WIPO Performances and Phonograms Treaty" is the WIPO Performances and Phonograms Treaty concluded at Geneva, Switzerland, on December 20, 1996.[24]

A "work of visual art" is —

(1) a painting, drawing, print or sculpture, existing in a single copy, in a limited edition of 200 copies or fewer that are signed and consecutively numbered by the author, or, in the case of a sculpture, in multiple cast, carved, or fabricated sculptures of 200 or fewer that are consecutively numbered by the author and bear the signature or other identifying mark of the author; or

(2) a still photographic image produced for exhibition purposes only, existing in a single copy that is signed by the author, or in a limited edition of 200 copies or fewer that are signed and consecutively numbered by the author.

A work of visual art does not include —

(A)(i) any poster, map, globe, chart, technical drawing, diagram, model, applied art, motion picture or other audiovisual work, book, magazine, newspaper, periodical, data base, electronic information service, electronic publication, or similar publication;

(ii) any merchandising item or advertising, promotional, descriptive, covering, or packaging material or container;

(iii) any portion or part of any item described in clause (i) or (ii);

(B) any work made for hire; or

(C) any work not subject to copyright protection under this title.[25]

A "work of the United States Government" is a work prepared by an officer or employee of the United States Government as part of that person's official duties.

A "work made for hire" is —

(1) a work prepared by an employee within the scope of his or her employment; or

(2) a work specially ordered or commissioned for use as a contribution to a collective work, as a part of a motion picture or other audiovisual work, as a translation, as a supplementary work, as a compilation, as an instructional text, as a test, as answer material for a test, or as an atlas, if the parties expressly agree in a written instrument signed by them that the work shall be considered a work made for hire. For the purpose of the foregoing sentence, a "supplementary work" is a work prepared for publication as a secondary adjunct to a work by another author for the purpose of introducing, concluding, illustrating, explaining, revising, commenting upon, or assisting in the use of the other work, such as forewords, afterwords, pictorial illustrations, maps, charts, tables, editorial notes, musical arrangements, answer material for tests, bibliographies, appendixes, and indexes, and an "instructional text" is a literary, pictorial, or graphic work prepared for publication and with the purpose of use in systematic instructional activities.

In determining whether any work is eligible to be considered a work made for hire under paragraph (2), neither the amendment contained in section 1011(d) of the Intellectual Property and Communications Omnibus Reform Act of 1999, as enacted by section 1000(a)(9) of Public Law 106-113, nor the deletion of the words added by that amendment —

(A) shall be considered or otherwise given any legal significance, or

(B) shall be interpreted to indicate congressional approval or disapproval of, or acquiescence in, any judicial determination,

by the courts or the Copyright Office. Paragraph (2) shall be interpreted as if both section 2(a)(1) of the Work Made For Hire and Copyright Corrections Act of 2000 and section 1011(d) of the Intellectual Property and Communications Omnibus Reform Act of 1999, as enacted by section 1000(a)(9) of Public Law 106-113, were never enacted, and without regard to any inaction or awareness by the Congress at any time of any judicial determinations.[26]

The terms "WTO Agreement" and "WTO member country" have the meanings given those terms in paragraphs (9) and (10), respectively, of section 2 of the Uruguay Round Agreements Act.[27]

§ 102. Subject matter of copyright: In general[28]

(a) Copyright protection subsists, in accordance with this title, in original works of authorship fixed in any tangible medium of expression, now known or later developed, from which they can be perceived, reproduced, or otherwise communicated, either directly or with the aid of a machine or device. Works of authorship include the following categories:

(1) literary works;

(2) musical works, including any accompanying words;

(3) dramatic works, including any accompanying music;

(4) pantomimes and choreographic works;

(5) pictorial, graphic, and sculptural works;

(6) motion pictures and other audiovisual works;

(7) sound recordings; and

(8) architectural works.

(b) In no case does copyright protection for an original work of authorship extend to any idea, procedure, process, system, method of operation, concept, principle, or discovery, regardless of the form in which it is described, explained, illustrated, or embodied in such work.

§ 103. Subject matter of copyright: Compilations and derivative works

(a) The subject matter of copyright as specified by section 102 includes compilations and derivative works, but protection for a work employing preexisting material in which copyright subsists does not extend to any part of the work in which such material has been used unlawfully.

(b) The copyright in a compilation or derivative work extends only to the material contributed by the author of such work, as distinguished from the preexisting material employed in the work, and does not imply any exclusive right in the preexisting material. The copyright in such work is independent of, and does not affect or enlarge the scope, duration, ownership, or subsistence of, any copyright protection in the preexisting material.

§ 104. Subject matter of copyright: National origin[29]

(a) Unpublished Works. — The works specified by sections 102 and 103, while unpublished, are subject to protection under this title without regard to the nationality or domicile of the author.

(b) Published Works. — The works specified by sections 102 and 103, when published, are subject to protection under this title if —

(1) on the date of first publication, one or more of the authors is a national or domiciliary of the United States, or is a national, domiciliary, or sovereign authority of a treaty party, or is a stateless person, wherever that person may be domiciled; or

(2) the work is first published in the United States or in a foreign nation that, on the date of first publication, is a treaty party; or

(3) the work is a sound recording that was first fixed in a treaty party; or

(4) the work is a pictorial, graphic, or sculptural work that is incorporated in a building or other structure, or an architectural work that is embodied in a building and the building or structure is located in the United States or a treaty party; or

(5) the work is first published by the United Nations or any of its specialized agencies, or by the Organization of American States; or

(6) the work comes within the scope of a Presidential proclamation. Whenever the President finds that a particular foreign nation extends, to works by authors who are nationals or domiciliaries of the United States or to works that are first published in the United States, copyright protection on substantially the same basis as that on which the foreign nation extends protection to works of its own nationals and domiciliaries and works first published in that nation, the President may by proclamation extend protection under this title to works of which one or more of the authors is, on the date of first publication, a national, domiciliary, or sovereign authority of that nation, or which was first published in that nation. The President may revise, suspend, or revoke any such proclamation or impose any conditions or limitations on protection under a proclamation.

For purposes of paragraph (2), a work that is published in the United States or a treaty party within 30 days after publication in a foreign nation that is not a treaty party shall be considered to be first published in the United States or such treaty party, as the case may be.

(c) Effect of Berne Convention. — No right or interest in a work eligible for protection under this title may be claimed by virtue of, or in reliance upon, the provisions of the Berne Convention, or the adherence of the United States thereto. Any rights in a work eligible for protection under this title that derive from this title, other Federal or State statutes, or the common law, shall not be expanded or reduced by virtue of, or in reliance upon, the provisions of the Berne Convention, or the adherence of the United States thereto.

(d) Effect of Phonograms Treaties. — Notwithstanding the provisions of subsection (b), no works other than sound recordings shall be eligible for protection under this title solely by virtue of the adherence of the United States to the Geneva Phonograms Convention or the WIPO Performances and Phonograms Treaty.[30]

§ 104A. Copyright in restored works[31]

(a) Automatic Protection and Term. —

    (1) Term. —

        (A) Copyright subsists, in accordance with this section, in restored works, and vests automatically on the date of restoration.

        (B) Any work in which copyright is restored under this section shall subsist for the remainder of the term of copyright that the work would have otherwise been granted in the United States if the work never entered the public domain in the United States.

(2) Exception. — Any work in which the copyright was ever owned or administered by the Alien Property Custodian and in which the restored copyright would be owned by a government or instrumentality thereof, is not a restored work.

(b) Ownership of Restored Copyright. — A restored work vests initially in the author or initial rightholder of the work as determined by the law of the source country of the work.

(c) Filing of Notice of Intent to Enforce Restored Copyright Against Reliance Parties. — On or after the date of restoration, any person who owns a copyright in a restored work or an exclusive right therein may file with the Copyright Office a notice of intent to enforce that person's copyright or exclusive right or may serve such a notice directly on a reliance party. Acceptance of a notice by the Copyright Office is effective as to any reliance parties but shall not create a presumption of the validity of any of the facts stated therein. Service on a reliance party is effective as to that reliance party and any other reliance parties with actual knowledge of such service and of the contents of that notice.

(d) Remedies for Infringement of Restored Copyrights. —

(1) Enforcement of copyright in restored works in the absence of a reliance party. — As against any party who is not a reliance party, the remedies provided in chapter 5 of this title shall be available on or after the date of restoration of a restored copyright with respect to an act of infringement of the restored copyright that is commenced on or after the date of restoration.

(2) Enforcement of copyright in restored works as against reliance parties. — As against a reliance party, except to the extent provided in paragraphs (3) and (4), the remedies provided in chapter 5 of this title shall be available, with respect to an act of infringement of a restored copyright, on or after the date of restoration of the restored copyright if the requirements of either of the following subparagraphs are met:

(A)(i) The owner of the restored copyright (or such owner's agent) or the owner of an exclusive right therein (or such owner's agent) files with the Copyright Office, during the 24-month period beginning on the date of restoration, a notice of intent to enforce the restored copyright; and

(ii)(I) the act of infringement commenced after the end of the 12-month period beginning on the date of publication of the notice in the Federal Register;

(II) the act of infringement commenced before the end of the 12-month period described in subclause (I) and continued after the end of that 12-month period, in which case remedies shall be available only for infringement occurring after the end of that 12-month period; or

(III) copies or phonorecords of a work in which copyright has been restored under this section are made after publication of the notice of intent in the Federal Register.

(B)(i) The owner of the restored copyright (or such owner's agent) or the owner of an exclusive right therein (or such owner's agent) serves upon a reliance party a notice of intent to enforce a restored copyright; and (ii)(I) the act of infringement commenced after the end of the 12-month period beginning on the date the notice of intent is received;

(II) the act of infringement commenced before the end of the 12-month period described in subclause (I) and continued after the end of that 12-month period, in which case remedies shall be available only for the infringement occurring after the end of that 12-month period; or

(III) copies or phonorecords of a work in which copyright has been restored under this section are made after receipt of the notice of intent.

In the event that notice is provided under both subparagraphs (A) and (B), the 12-month period referred to in such subparagraphs shall run from the earlier of publication or service of notice.

(3) Existing derivative works. —

(A) In the case of a derivative work that is based upon a restored work and is created —

(i) before the date of the enactment of the Uruguay Round Agreements Act, if the source country of the restored work is an eligible country on such date, or

(ii) before the date on which the source country of the restored work becomes an eligible country, if that country is not an eligible country on such date of enactment,

a reliance party may continue to exploit that derivative work for the duration of the restored copyright if the reliance party pays to the owner of the restored copyright reasonable compensation for conduct which would be subject to a remedy for infringement but for the provisions of this paragraph.

(B) In the absence of an agreement between the parties, the amount of such compensation shall be determined by an action in United States district court, and shall reflect any harm to the actual or potential market for or value of the restored work from the reliance party's continued exploitation of the work, as well as compensation for the relative contributions of expression of the author of the restored work and the reliance party to the derivative work.

(4) Commencement of infringement for reliance parties. — For purposes of section 412, in the case of reliance parties, infringement shall be deemed to have commenced before registration when acts which would have constituted infringement had the restored work been subject to copyright were commenced before the date of restoration.

(e) Notices of Intent to Enforce a Restored Copyright. —

(1) Notices of intent filed with the copyright office. —

(A)(i) A notice of intent filed with the Copyright Office to enforce a restored copyright shall be signed by the owner of the restored copyright or the owner of an exclusive right therein, who files the notice under subsection (d)(2)(A)(i) (hereafter in this paragraph referred to as the "owner"), or by the owner's agent, shall identify the title of the restored work, and shall include an English translation of the title and any other alternative titles known to the owner by which the restored work may be identified, and an address and telephone number at which the owner may be contacted. If the notice is signed by an agent, the agency relationship must have been constituted in a writing signed by the owner before the filing of the notice. The Copyright Office may specifically require in regulations other information to be included in the notice, but failure to provide such other information shall not invalidate the notice or be a basis for refusal to list the restored work in the Federal Register.

(ii) If a work in which copyright is restored has no formal title, it shall be described in the notice of intent in detail sufficient to identify it.

(iii) Minor errors or omissions may be corrected by further notice at any time after the notice of intent is filed. Notices of corrections for such minor errors or omissions shall be accepted after the period established in subsection (d)(2)(A)(i). Notices shall be published in the Federal Register pursuant to subparagraph (B).

(B)(i) The Register of Copyrights shall publish in the Federal Register, commencing not later than 4 months after the date of restoration for a particular nation and every 4 months thereafter for a period of 2 years, lists identifying restored works and the ownership thereof if a notice of intent to enforce a restored copyright has been filed.

(ii) Not less than 1 list containing all notices of intent to enforce shall be maintained in the Public Information Office of the Copyright Office and shall be available for public inspection and copying during regular business hours pursuant to sections 705 and 708.

(C) The Register of Copyrights is authorized to fix reasonable fees based on the costs of receipt, processing, recording, and publication of notices of intent to enforce a restored copyright and corrections thereto.

(D)(i) Not later than 90 days before the date the Agreement on Trade-Related Aspects of Intellectual Property referred to in section 101(d)(15) of the Uruguay Round Agreements Act enters into force with respect to the United States, the Copyright Office shall issue and publish in the Federal Register regulations governing the filing under this subsection of notices of intent to enforce a restored copyright.

(ii) Such regulations shall permit owners of restored copyrights to file simultaneously for registration of the restored copyright.

(2) Notices of intent served on a reliance party. —

(A) Notices of intent to enforce a restored copyright may be served on a reliance party at any time after the date of restoration of the restored copyright.

(B) Notices of intent to enforce a restored copyright served on a reliance party shall be signed by the owner or the owner's agent, shall identify the restored work and the work in which the restored work is used, if any, in detail sufficient to identify them, and shall include an English translation of the title, any other alternative titles known to the owner by which the work may be identified, the use or uses to which the owner objects, and an address and telephone number at which the reliance party may contact the owner. If the notice is signed by an agent, the agency relationship must have been constituted in writing and signed by the owner before service of the notice.

(3) Effect of material false statements. — Any material false statement knowingly made with respect to any restored copyright identified in any notice of intent shall make void all claims and assertions made with respect to such restored copyright.

(f) Immunity from Warranty and Related Liability. —

(1) In general. — Any person who warrants, promises, or guarantees that a work does not violate an exclusive right granted in section 106 shall not be liable for legal, equitable, arbitral, or administrative relief if the warranty, promise, or guarantee is breached by virtue of the restoration of copyright under this section, if such warranty, promise, or guarantee is made before January 1, 1995.

(2) Performances. — No person shall be required to perform any act if such performance is made infringing by virtue of the restoration of copyright under the provisions of this section, if the obligation to perform was undertaken before January 1, 1995.

(g) Proclamation of Copyright Restoration. — Whenever the President finds that a particular foreign nation extends, to works by authors who are nationals or domiciliaries of the United States, restored copyright protection on substantially the same basis as provided under this section, the President may by proclamation extend restored protection provided under this section to any work —

(1) of which one or more of the authors is, on the date of first publication, a national, domiciliary, or sovereign authority of that nation; or

(2) which was first published in that nation.

The President may revise, suspend, or revoke any such proclamation or impose any conditions or limitations on protection under such a proclamation.

(h) Definitions. — For purposes of this section and section 109(a):

(1) The term "date of adherence or proclamation" means the earlier of the date on which a foreign nation which, as of the date the WTO Agreement enters into force with respect to the United States, is not a nation adhering to the Berne Convention or a WTO member country, becomes —

(A) a nation adhering to the Berne Convention;

(B) a WTO member country;

(C) a nation adhering to the WIPO Copyright Treaty;[32]

(D) a nation adhering to the WIPO Performances and Phonograms Treaty;[33] or

(E) subject to a Presidential proclamation under subsection (g).

(2) The "date of restoration" of a restored copyright is —

(A) January 1, 1996, if the source country of the restored work is a nation adhering to the Berne Convention or a WTO member country on such date, or

(B) the date of adherence or proclamation, in the case of any other source country of the restored work.

(3) The term "eligible country" means a nation, other than the United States, that —

(A) becomes a WTO member country after the date of the enactment of the Uruguay Round Agreements Act;

(B) on such date of enactment is, or after such date of enactment becomes, a nation adhering to the Berne Convention;

(C) adheres to the WIPO Copyright Treaty;[34]

(D) adheres to the WIPO Performances and Phonograms Treaty;[35] or

(E) after such date of enactment becomes subject to a proclamation under subsection (g).

(4) The term "reliance party" means any person who —

(A) with respect to a particular work, engages in acts, before the source country of that work becomes an eligible country, which would have violated section 106 if the restored work had been subject to copyright protection, and who, after the source country becomes an eligible country, continues to engage in such acts;

(B) before the source country of a particular work becomes an eligible country, makes or acquires 1 or more copies or phonorecords of that work; or

(C) as the result of the sale or other disposition of a derivative work covered under subsection (d)(3), or significant assets of a person described in subparagraph (A) or (B), is a successor, assignee, or licensee of that person.

(5) The term "restored copyright" means copyright in a restored work under this section.

(6) The term "restored work" means an original work of authorship that —

(A) is protected under subsection (a);

(B) is not in the public domain in its source country through expiration of term of protection;

(C) is in the public domain in the United States due to —

(i) noncompliance with formalities imposed at any time by United States copyright law, including failure of renewal, lack of proper notice, or failure to comply with any manufacturing requirements;

(ii) lack of subject matter protection in the case of sound recordings fixed before February 15, 1972; or

(iii) lack of national eligibility;

(D) has at least one author or rightholder who was, at the time the work was created, a national or domiciliary of an eligible country, and if published, was first published in an eligible country and not published in the United States during the 30-day period following publication in such eligible country; and

(E) if the source country for the work is an eligible country solely by virtue of its adherence to the WIPO Performances and Phonograms Treaty, is a sound recording.[36]

(7) The term "rightholder" means the person —

(A) who, with respect to a sound recording, first fixes a sound recording with authorization, or

(B) who has acquired rights from the person described in subparagraph (A) by means of any conveyance or by operation of law.

(8) The "source country" of a restored work is —

(A) a nation other than the United States;

(B) in the case of an unpublished work —

(i) the eligible country in which the author or rightholder is a national or domiciliary, or, if a restored work has more than 1 author or rightholder, of which the majority of foreign authors or rightholders are nationals or domiciliaries; or

(ii) if the majority of authors or rightholders are not foreign, the nation other than the United States which has the most significant contacts with the work; and

(C) in the case of a published work —

(i) the eligible country in which the work is first published, or

(ii) if the restored work is published on the same day in 2 or more eligible countries, the eligible country which has the most significant contacts with the work.

§ 105. Subject matter of copyright: United States Government works[37]

Copyright protection under this title is not available for any work of the United States Government, but the United States Government is not precluded from receiving and holding copyrights transferred to it by assignment, bequest, or otherwise.

§ 106. Exclusive rights in copyrighted works[38]

Subject to sections 107 through 122, the owner of copyright under this title has the exclusive rights to do and to authorize any of the following:

(1) to reproduce the copyrighted work in copies or phonorecords;

(2) to prepare derivative works based upon the copyrighted work;

(3) to distribute copies or phonorecords of the copyrighted work to the public by sale or other transfer of ownership, or by rental, lease, or lending;

(4) in the case of literary, musical, dramatic, and choreographic works, pantomimes, and motion pictures and other audiovisual works, to perform the copyrighted work publicly;

(5) in the case of literary, musical, dramatic, and choreographic works, pantomimes, and pictorial, graphic, or sculptural works, including the individual images of a motion picture or other audiovisual work, to display the copyrighted work publicly; and

(6) in the case of sound recordings, to perform the copyrighted work publicly by means of a digital audio transmission.

§ 106A. Rights of certain authors to attribution and integrity[39]

(a) Rights of Attribution and Integrity. — Subject to section 107 and independent of the exclusive rights provided in section 106, the author of a work of visual art —

(1) shall have the right —

(A) to claim authorship of that work, and

(B) to prevent the use of his or her name as the author of any work of visual art which he or she did not create;

(2) shall have the right to prevent the use of his or her name as the author of the work of visual art in the event of a distortion, mutilation, or other modification of the work which would be prejudicial to his or her honor or reputation; and

(3) subject to the limitations set forth in section 113(d), shall have the right —

(A) to prevent any intentional distortion, mutilation, or other modification of that work which would be prejudicial to his or her honor or reputation, and any intentional distortion, mutilation, or modification of that work is a violation of that right, and

(B) to prevent any destruction of a work of recognized stature, and any intentional or grossly negligent destruction of that work is a violation of that right.

(b) Scope and Exercise of Rights. — Only the author of a work of visual art has the rights conferred by subsection (a) in that work, whether or not the author is the copyright owner. The authors of a joint work of visual art are coowners of the rights conferred by subsection (a) in that work.

(c) Exceptions. — (1) The modification of a work of visual art which is the result of the passage of time or the inherent nature of the materials is not a distortion, mutilation, or other modification described in subsection (a)(3)(A).

(2) The modification of a work of visual art which is the result of conservation, or of the public presentation, including lighting and placement, of the work is not a destruction, distortion, mutilation, or other modification described in subsection (a)(3) unless the modification is caused by gross negligence.

(3) The rights described in paragraphs (1) and (2) of subsection (a) shall not apply to any reproduction, depiction, portrayal, or other use of a work in, upon, or in any connection with any item described in subparagraph (A) or (B) of the definition of "work of visual art" in section 101, and any such reproduction, depiction, portrayal, or other use of a work is not a destruction, distortion, mutilation, or other modification described in paragraph (3) of subsection (a).

(d) Duration of Rights. — (1) With respect to works of visual art created on or after the effective date set forth in section 610(a) of the Visual Artists Rights Act of 1990, the rights conferred by subsection (a) shall endure for a term consisting of the life of the author.

(2) With respect to works of visual art created before the effective date set forth in section 610(a) of the Visual Artists Rights Act of 1990, but title to which has not, as of such effective date, been transferred from the author, the rights conferred by subsection (a) shall be coextensive with, and shall expire at the same time as, the rights conferred by section 106.

(3) In the case of a joint work prepared by two or more authors, the rights conferred by subsection (a) shall endure for a term consisting of the life of the last surviving author.

(4) All terms of the rights conferred by subsection (a) run to the end of the calendar year in which they would otherwise expire.

(e) Transfer and Waiver. — (1) The rights conferred by subsection (a) may not be transferred, but those rights may be waived if the author expressly agrees to such waiver in a written instrument signed by the author. Such instrument shall specifically identify the work, and uses of that work, to which the waiver applies, and the waiver shall apply only to the work and uses so identified. In the case of a joint work prepared by two or more authors, a waiver of rights under this paragraph made by one such author waives such rights for all such authors.

(2) Ownership of the rights conferred by subsection (a) with respect to a work of visual art is distinct from ownership of any copy of that work, or of a copyright or any exclusive right under a copyright in that work. Transfer of ownership of any copy of a work of visual art, or of a copyright or any exclusive right under a copyright, shall not constitute a waiver of the rights conferred by subsection (a). Except as may otherwise be agreed by the author in a written instrument signed by the author, a waiver of the rights conferred by subsection (a) with respect to a work of visual art shall not constitute a transfer of ownership of any copy of that work, or of ownership of a copyright or of any exclusive right under a copyright in that work.

§ 107. Limitations on exclusive rights: Fair use[40]

Notwithstanding the provisions of sections 106 and 106A, the fair use of a copyrighted work, including such use by reproduction in copies or phonorecords or by any other means specified by that section, for purposes such as criticism, comment, news reporting, teaching (including multiple copies for classroom use), scholarship, or research, is not an infringement of copyright. In determining whether the use made of a work in any particular case is a fair use the factors to be considered shall include —

(1) the purpose and character of the use, including whether such use is of a commercial nature or is for nonprofit educational purposes;

(2) the nature of the copyrighted work;

(3) the amount and substantiality of the portion used in relation to the copyrighted work as a whole; and

(4) the effect of the use upon the potential market for or value of the copyrighted work.

The fact that a work is unpublished shall not itself bar a finding of fair use if such finding is made upon consideration of all the above factors.

§ 108. *Limitations on exclusive rights: Reproduction by libraries and archives*[41]

(a) Except as otherwise provided in this title and notwithstanding the provisions of section 106, it is not an infringement of copyright for a library or archives, or any of its employees acting within the scope of their employment, to reproduce no more than one copy or phonorecord of a work, except as provided in subsections (b) and (c), or to distribute such copy or phonorecord, under the conditions specified by this section, if —

(1) the reproduction or distribution is made without any purpose of direct or indirect commercial advantage;

(2) the collections of the library or archives are (i) open to the public, or (ii) available not only to researchers affiliated with the library or archives or with the institution of which it is a part, but also to other persons doing research in a specialized field; and

(3) the reproduction or distribution of the work includes a notice of copyright that appears on the copy or phonorecord that is reproduced under the provisions of this section, or includes a legend stating that the work may be protected by copyright if no such notice can be found on the copy or phonorecord that is reproduced under the provisions of this section.

(b) The rights of reproduction and distribution under this section apply to three copies or phonorecords of an unpublished work duplicated solely for purposes of preservation and security or for deposit for research use in another library or archives of the type described by clause (2) of subsection (a), if —

(1) the copy or phonorecord reproduced is currently in the collections of the library or archives; and

(2) any such copy or phonorecord that is reproduced in digital format is not otherwise distributed in that format and is not made available to the public in that format outside the premises of the library or archives.

(c) The right of reproduction under this section applies to three copies or phonorecords of a published work duplicated solely for the purpose of replacement of a copy or phonorecord that is damaged, deteriorating, lost, or stolen, or if the existing format in which the work is stored has become obsolete, if —

(1) the library or archives has, after a reasonable effort, determined that an unused replacement cannot be obtained at a fair price; and

(2) any such copy or phonorecord that is reproduced in digital format is not made available to the public in that format outside the premises of the library or archives in lawful possession of such copy.

For purposes of this subsection, a format shall be considered obsolete if the machine or device necessary to render perceptible a work stored in that format is no longer manufactured or is no longer reasonably available in the commercial marketplace.

(d) The rights of reproduction and distribution under this section apply to a copy, made from the collection of a library or archives where the user makes his or her request or from that of another library or archives, of no more than one article or other contribution to a copyrighted collection or periodical issue, or to a copy or phonorecord of a small part of any other copyrighted work, if —

(1) the copy or phonorecord becomes the property of the user, and the library or archives has had no notice that the copy or phonorecord would be used for any purpose other than private study, scholarship, or research; and

(2) the library or archives displays prominently, at the place where orders are accepted, and includes on its order form, a warning of copyright in accordance with requirements that the Register of Copyrights shall prescribe by regulation.

(e) The rights of reproduction and distribution under this section apply to the entire work, or to a substantial part of it, made from the collection of a library or archives where the user makes his or her request or from that of another library or archives, if the library or archives has first determined, on the basis of a reasonable investigation, that a copy or phonorecord of the copyrighted work cannot be obtained at a fair price, if —

(1) the copy or phonorecord becomes the property of the user, and the library or archives has had no notice that the copy or phonorecord would be used for any purpose other than private study, scholarship, or research; and

(2) the library or archives displays prominently, at the place where orders are accepted, and includes on its order form, a warning of copyright in accordance with requirements that the Register of Copyrights shall prescribe by regulation.

(f) Nothing in this section —

(1) shall be construed to impose liability for copyright infringement upon a library or archives or its employees for the unsupervised use of reproducing equipment located on its premises: *Provided,* That such equipment displays a notice that the making of a copy may be subject to the copyright law;

(2) excuses a person who uses such reproducing equipment or who requests a copy or phonorecord under subsection (d) from liability for copyright infringement for any such act, or for any later use of such copy or phonorecord, if it exceeds fair use as provided by section 107;

(3) shall be construed to limit the reproduction and distribution by lending of a limited number of copies and excerpts by a library or archives of an audiovisual news program, subject to clauses (1), (2), and (3) of subsection (a); or

(4) in any way affects the right of fair use as provided by section 107, or any contractual obligations assumed at any time by the library or archives when it obtained a copy or phonorecord of a work in its collections.

(g) The rights of reproduction and distribution under this section extend to the isolated and unrelated reproduction or distribution of a single copy or phonorecord of the same material on separate occasions, but do not extend to cases where the library or archives, or its employee —

(1) is aware or has substantial reason to believe that it is engaging in the related or concerted reproduction or distribution of multiple copies or phonorecords of the same material, whether made on one occasion or over a period of time, and whether intended for aggregate use by one or more individuals or for separate use by the individual members of a group; or

(2) engages in the systematic reproduction or distribution of single or multiple copies or phonorecords of material described in subsection (d): *Provided,* That nothing in this clause prevents a library or archives from participating in interlibrary arrangements that do not have, as their purpose or effect, that the library or archives receiving such copies or phonorecords for distribution does so in such aggregate quantities as to substitute for a subscription to or purchase of such work.

(h)(1) For purposes of this section, during the last 20 years of any term of copyright of a published work, a library or archives, including a nonprofit educational institution that functions as such, may reproduce, distribute, display, or perform in facsimile or digital form a copy or phonorecord of such work, or portions thereof, for purposes of preservation, scholarship, or research, if such library or archives has first determined, on the basis of a reasonable investigation, that none of the conditions set forth in subparagraphs (A), (B), and (C) of paragraph (2) apply.

(2) No reproduction, distribution, display, or performance is authorized under this subsection if —

(A) the work is subject to normal commercial exploitation;

(B) a copy or phonorecord of the work can be obtained at a reasonable price; or

(C) the copyright owner or its agent provides notice pursuant to regulations promulgated by the Register of Copyrights that either of the conditions set forth in subparagraphs (A) and (B) applies.

(3) The exemption provided in this subsection does not apply to any subsequent uses by users other than such library or archives.

(i) The rights of reproduction and distribution under this section do not apply to a musical work, a pictorial, graphic or sculptural work, or a motion picture or other audiovisual work other than an audiovisual work dealing with news, except that no such limitation shall apply with respect to rights granted by subsections (b), (c), and (h), or with respect to pictorial or graphic works published as illustrations, diagrams, or similar adjuncts to works of which copies are reproduced or distributed in accordance with subsections (d) and (e).

§ 109. *Limitations on exclusive rights: Effect of transfer of particular copy or phonorecord*[42]

(a) Notwithstanding the provisions of section 106(3), the owner of a particular copy or phonorecord lawfully made under this title, or any person authorized by such owner, is entitled, without the authority of the copyright owner, to sell or otherwise dispose of the possession of that copy or phonorecord. Notwithstanding the preceding sentence, copies or phonorecords of works subject to restored copyright under section 104A that are manufactured before the date of restoration of copyright or, with respect to reliance parties, before publication or service of notice under section 104A(e), may be sold or otherwise disposed of without the authorization of the owner of the restored copyright for purposes of direct or indirect commercial advantage only during the 12-month period beginning on —

(1) the date of the publication in the Federal Register of the notice of intent filed with the Copyright Office under section 104A(d)(2)(A), or

(2) the date of the receipt of actual notice served under section 104A(d)(2)(B), whichever occurs first.

(b)(1)(A) Notwithstanding the provisions of subsection (a), unless authorized by the owners of copyright in the sound recording or the owner of copyright in a computer program (including any tape, disk, or other medium embodying such program), and in the case of a sound recording in the musical works embodied therein, neither the owner of a particular phonorecord nor any person in possession of a particular copy of a computer program (including any tape, disk, or other medium embodying such program), may, for the purposes of direct or indirect commercial advantage, dispose of, or authorize the disposal of, the possession of that phonorecord or computer program (including any tape, disk, or other medium embodying such program) by rental, lease, or lending, or by any other act or practice in the nature of rental, lease, or lending. Nothing in the preceding sentence shall apply to the rental, lease, or lending of a phonorecord for nonprofit purposes by a nonprofit library or nonprofit educational institution. The transfer of possession of a lawfully made copy of a computer program by a nonprofit educational institution to another nonprofit educational institution or to faculty, staff, and students does not constitute rental, lease, or lending for direct or indirect commercial purposes under this subsection.

(B) This subsection does not apply to —

(i) a computer program which is embodied in a machine or product and which cannot be copied during the ordinary operation or use of the machine or product; or

(ii) a computer program embodied in or used in conjunction with a limited purpose computer that is designed for playing video games and may be designed for other purposes.

(C) Nothing in this subsection affects any provision of chapter 9 of this title.

(2)(A) Nothing in this subsection shall apply to the lending of a computer program for nonprofit purposes by a nonprofit library, if each copy of a computer program which is lent by such library has affixed to the packaging containing the program a warning of copyright in accordance with requirements that the Register of Copyrights shall prescribe by regulation.

(B) Not later than three years after the date of the enactment of the Computer Software Rental Amendments Act of 1990, and at such times thereafter as the Register of Copyrights considers appropriate, the Register of Copyrights, after consultation with representatives of copyright owners and librarians, shall submit to the Congress a report stating whether this paragraph has achieved its intended purpose of maintaining the integrity of the copyright system while providing nonprofit libraries the capability to fulfill their function. Such report shall advise the Congress as to any information or recommendations that the Register of Copyrights considers necessary to carry out the purposes of this subsection.

(3) Nothing in this subsection shall affect any provision of the antitrust laws. For purposes of the preceding sentence, "antitrust laws" has the meaning given that term in the first section of the Clayton Act and includes section 5 of the Federal Trade Commission Act to the extent that section relates to unfair methods of competition.

(4) Any person who distributes a phonorecord or a copy of a computer program (including any tape, disk, or other medium embodying such program) in violation of paragraph (1) is an infringer of copyright under section 501 of this title and is subject to the remedies set forth in sections 502, 503, 504, 505, and 509. Such violation shall not be a criminal offense under section 506 or cause such person to be subject to the criminal penalties set forth in section 2319 of title 18.

(c) Notwithstanding the provisions of section 106(5), the owner of a particular copy lawfully made under this title, or any person authorized by such owner, is entitled, without the authority of the copyright owner, to display that copy publicly, either directly or by the projection of no more than one image at a time, to viewers present at the place where the copy is located.

(d) The privileges prescribed by subsections (a) and (c) do not, unless authorized by the copyright owner, extend to any person who has acquired possession of the copy or phonorecord from the copyright owner, by rental, lease, loan, or otherwise, without acquiring ownership of it.

(e) Notwithstanding the provisions of sections 106(4) and 106(5), in the case of an electronic audiovisual game intended for use in coin-operated equipment, the owner of a particular copy of such a game lawfully made under this title, is entitled, without the authority of the copyright owner of the game, to publicly perform or display that game in coin-operated equipment, except that this subsection shall not apply to any work of authorship embodied in the audiovisual game if the copyright owner of the electronic audiovisual game is not also the copyright owner of the work of authorship.

§ 110. Limitations on exclusive rights: Exemption of certain performances and displays[43]

Notwithstanding the provisions of section 106, the following are not infringements of copyright:

(1) performance or display of a work by instructors or pupils in the course of face-to-face teaching activities of a nonprofit educational institution, in a classroom or similar place devoted to instruction, unless, in the case of a motion picture or other audiovisual work, the performance, or the display of individual images, is given by means of a copy that was not lawfully made under this title, and that the person responsible for the performance knew or had reason to believe was not lawfully made;

(2) except with respect to a work produced or marketed primarily for performance or display as part of mediated instructional activities transmitted via digital networks, or a performance or display that is given by means of a copy or phonorecord that is not lawfully made and acquired under this title, and the transmitting government body or accredited nonprofit educational institution knew or had reason to believe was not lawfully made and acquired, the performance of a nondramatic literary or musical work or reasonable and limited portions of any other work, or display of a work in an amount comparable to that which is typically displayed in the course of a live classroom session, by or in the course of a transmission, if —

(A) the performance or display is made by, at the direction of, or under the actual supervision of an instructor as an integral part of a class session offered as a regular part of the systematic mediated instructional activities of a governmental body or an accredited nonprofit educational institution;

(B) the performance or display is directly related and of material assistance to the teaching content of the transmission;

(C) the transmission is made solely for, and, to the extent technologically feasible, the reception of such transmission is limited to —

(i) students officially enrolled in the course for which the transmission is made; or

(ii) officers or employees of governmental bodies as a part of their official duties or employment; and

(D) the transmitting body or institution —

(i) institutes policies regarding copyright, provides informational materials to faculty, students, and relevant staff members that accurately describe, and promote compliance with, the laws of the United States relating to copyright, and provides notice to students that materials used in connection with the course may be subject to copyright protection; and

(ii) in the case of digital transmissions —

(I) applies technological measures that reasonably prevent —
(aa) retention of the work in accessible form by recipients of the transmission from the transmitting body or institution for longer than the class session; and

(bb) unauthorized further dissemination of the work in accessible form by such recipients to others; and

(II) does not engage in conduct that could reasonably be expected to interfere with technological measures used by copyright owners to prevent such retention or unauthorized further dissemination;

(3) performance of a nondramatic literary or musical work or of a dramatico-musical work of a religious nature, or display of a work, in the course of services at a place of worship or other religious assembly;

(4) performance of a nondramatic literary or musical work otherwise than in a transmission to the public, without any purpose of direct or indirect commercial advantage and without payment of any fee or other compensation for the performance to any of its performers, promoters, or organizers, if —

(A) there is no direct or indirect admission charge; or

(B) the proceeds, after deducting the reasonable costs of producing the performance, are used exclusively for educational, religious, or charitable purposes and not for private financial gain, except where the copyright owner has served notice of objection to the performance under the following conditions:

(i) the notice shall be in writing and signed by the copyright owner or such owner's duly authorized agent; and

(ii) the notice shall be served on the person responsible for the performance at least seven days before the date of the performance, and shall state the reasons for the objection; and

(iii) the notice shall comply, in form, content, and manner of service, with requirements that the Register of Copyrights shall prescribe by regulation;

(5)(A) except as provided in subparagraph (B), communication of a transmission embodying a performance or display of a work by the public reception of the transmission on a single receiving apparatus of a kind commonly used in private homes, unless —

(i) a direct charge is made to see or hear the transmission; or

(ii) the transmission thus received is further transmitted to the public;

(B) communication by an establishment of a transmission or retransmission embodying a performance or display of a nondramatic musical work intended to be received by the general public, originated by a radio or television broadcast station licensed as such by the Federal Communications Commission, or, if an audiovisual transmission, by a cable system or satellite carrier, if —

(i) in the case of an establishment other than a food service or drinking establishment, either the establishment in which the communication occurs has less than 2,000 gross square feet of space (excluding space used for customer parking and for no other purpose), or the establishment in which the communication occurs has 2,000 or more gross square feet of space (excluding space used for customer parking and for no other purpose) and —

(I) if the performance is by audio means only, the performance is communicated by means of a total of not more than 6 loudspeakers, of which not more than 4 loudspeakers are located in any 1 room or adjoining outdoor space; or

(II) if the performance or display is by audiovisual means, any visual portion of the performance or display is communicated by means of a total of not more than 4 audiovisual devices, of which not more than 1 audiovisual device is located in any 1 room, and no such audiovisual device has a diagonal screen size greater than 55 inches, and any audio portion of the performance or display is communicated by means of a total of not more than 6 loudspeakers, of which not more than 4 loudspeakers are located in any 1 room or adjoining outdoor space;

(ii) in the case of a food service or drinking establishment, either the establishment in which the communication occurs has less than 3,750 gross square feet of space (excluding space used for customer parking and for no other purpose), or the establishment in which the communication occurs has 3,750 gross square feet of space or more (excluding space used for customer parking and for no other purpose) and —

(I) if the performance is by audio means only, the performance is communicated by means of a total of not more than 6 loudspeakers, of which not more than 4 loudspeakers are located in any 1 room or adjoining outdoor space; or

(II) if the performance or display is by audiovisual means, any visual portion of the performance or display is communicated by means of a total of not more than 4 audiovisual devices, of which not more than 1 audiovisual device is located in any 1 room, and no such audiovisual device has a diagonal screen size greater than 55 inches, and any audio portion of the performance or display is communicated by means of a total of not more than 6 loudspeakers, of which not more than 4 loudspeakers are located in any 1 room or adjoining outdoor space;

(iii) no direct charge is made to see or hear the transmission or retransmission;

(iv) the transmission or retransmission is not further transmitted beyond the establishment where it is received; and

(v) the transmission or retransmission is licensed by the copyright owner of the work so publicly performed or displayed;

(6) performance of a nondramatic musical work by a governmental body or a nonprofit agricultural or horticultural organization, in the course of an annual agricultural or horticultural fair or exhibition conducted by such body or organization; the exemption provided by this clause shall extend to any liability for copyright infringement that would otherwise be imposed on such body or organization, under doctrines of vicarious liability or related infringement, for a performance by a concessionnaire, business establishment, or other person at such fair or exhibition, but shall not excuse any such person from liability for the performance;

(7) performance of a nondramatic musical work by a vending establishment open to the public at large without any direct or indirect admission charge, where the sole purpose of the performance is to promote the retail sale of copies or phonorecords of the work, or of the audiovisual or other devices utilized in such performance, and the performance is not transmitted beyond the place where the establishment is located and is within the immediate area where the sale is occurring;

(8) performance of a nondramatic literary work, by or in the course of a transmission specifically designed for and primarily directed to blind or other handicapped persons who are unable to read normal printed material as a result of their handicap, or deaf or other handicapped persons who are unable to hear the aural signals accompanying a transmission of visual signals, if the performance is made without any purpose of direct or indirect commercial advantage and its transmission is made through the facilities of: (i) a governmental body; or (ii) a noncommercial educational broadcast station (as defined in section 397 of title 47); or (iii) a radio subcarrier authorization (as defined in 47 CFR 73.293-73.295 and 73.593-73.595); or (iv) a cable system (as defined in section 111 (f));

(9) performance on a single occasion of a dramatic literary work published at least ten years before the date of the performance, by or in the course of a transmission specifically designed for and primarily directed to blind or other handicapped persons who are unable to read normal printed material as a result of their handicap, if the performance is made without any purpose of direct or indirect commercial advantage and its transmission is made through the facilities of a radio subcarrier authorization referred to in clause (8) (iii), *Provided,* That the provisions of this clause shall not be applicable to more than one performance of the same work by the same performers or under the auspices of the same organization;

(10) notwithstanding paragraph (4), the following is not an infringement of copyright: performance of a nondramatic literary or musical work in the course of a social function which is organized and promoted by a nonprofit veterans' organization or a nonprofit fraternal organization to which the general public is not invited, but not including the invitees of the organizations, if the proceeds from the performance, after deducting the reasonable costs of producing the performance, are used exclusively for charitable purposes and not for financial gain. For purposes of this section the social functions of any college or university fraternity or sorority shall not be included unless the social function is held solely to raise funds for a specific charitable purpose; and

(11) the making imperceptible, by or at the direction of a member of a private household, of limited portions of audio or video content of a motion picture, during a performance in or transmitted to that household for private home viewing, from an authorized copy of the motion picture, or the creation or provision of a computer program or other technology that enables such making imperceptible and that is designed and marketed to be used, at the direction of a member of a private household, for such making imperceptible, if no fixed copy of the altered version of the motion picture is created by such computer program or other technology.

The exemptions provided under paragraph (5) shall not be taken into account in any administrative, judicial, or other governmental proceeding to set or adjust the royalties payable to copyright owners for the public performance or display of their works. Royalties payable to copyright owners for any public performance or display of their works other than such performances or displays as are exempted under paragraph (5) shall not be diminished in any respect as a result of such exemption.

In paragraph (2), the term "mediated instructional activities" with respect to the performance or display of a work by digital transmission under this section refers to activities that use such work as an integral part of the class experience, controlled by or under the actual supervision of the instructor and analogous to the type of performance or display that would take place in a live classroom setting. The term does not refer to activities that use, in 1 or more class sessions of a single course, such works as textbooks, course packs, or other material in any media, copies or phonorecords of which are typically purchased or acquired by the students in higher education for their independent use and retention or are typically purchased or acquired for elementary and secondary students for their possession and independent use.

For purposes of paragraph (2), accreditation —

(A) with respect to an institution providing post-secondary education, shall be as determined by a regional or national accrediting agency recognized by the Council on Higher Education Accreditation or the United States Department of Education; and

(B) with respect to an institution providing elementary or secondary education, shall be as recognized by the applicable state certification or licensing procedures.

For purposes of paragraph (2), no governmental body or accredited nonprofit educational institution shall be liable for infringement by reason of the transient or temporary storage of material carried out through the automatic technical process of a digital transmission of the performance or display of that material as authorized under paragraph (2). No such material stored on the system or network controlled or operated by the transmitting body or institution under this paragraph shall be maintained on such system or network in a manner ordinarily accessible to anyone other than anticipated recipients. No such copy shall be maintained on the system or network in a manner ordinarily accessible to such anticipated recipients for a longer period than is reasonably necessary to facilitate the transmissions for which it was made.

For purposes of paragraph (11), the term "making imperceptible" does not include the addition of audio or video content that is performed or displayed over or in place of existing content in a motion picture.

Nothing in paragraph (11) shall be construed to imply further rights under section 106 of this title, or to have any effect on defenses or limitations on rights granted under any other section of this title or under any other paragraph of this section.

§ 111. Limitations on exclusive rights: Secondary transmissions[44]

(a) Certain Secondary Transmissions Exempted. — The secondary transmission of a performance or display of a work embodied in a primary transmission is not an infringement of copyright if —

(1) the secondary transmission is not made by a cable system, and consists entirely of the relaying, by the management of a hotel, apartment house, or similar establishment, of signals transmitted by a broadcast station licensed by the Federal Communications Commission, within the local service area of such station, to the private lodgings of guests or residents of such establishment, and no direct charge is made to see or hear the secondary transmission; or

(2) the secondary transmission is made solely for the purpose and under the conditions specified by clause (2) of section 110; or

(3) the secondary transmission is made by any carrier who has no direct or indirect control over the content or selection of the primary transmission or over the particular recipients of the secondary transmission, and whose activities with respect to the secondary transmission consist solely of providing wires, cables, or other communications channels for the use of others: *Provided,* That the provisions of this clause extend only to the activities of said carrier with respect to secondary transmissions and do not exempt from liability the activities of others with respect to their own primary or secondary transmissions;

(4) the secondary transmission is made by a satellite carrier pursuant to a statutory license under section 119; or

(5) the secondary transmission is not made by a cable system but is made by a governmental body, or other nonprofit organization, without any purpose of direct or indirect commercial advantage, and without charge to the recipients of the secondary transmission other than assessments necessary to defray the actual and reasonable costs of maintaining and operating the secondary transmission service.

(b) Secondary Transmission of Primary Transmission to Controlled Group. — Notwithstanding the provisions of subsections (a) and (c), the secondary transmission to the public of a performance or display of a work embodied in a primary transmission is actionable as an act of infringement under section 501, and is fully subject to the remedies provided by sections 502 through 506 and 509, if the primary transmission is not made for reception by the public at large but is controlled and limited to reception by particular members of the public: *Provided,* however, That such secondary transmission is not actionable as an act of infringement if —

(1) the primary transmission is made by a broadcast station licensed by the Federal Communications Commission; and

(2) the carriage of the signals comprising the secondary transmission is required under the rules, regulations, or authorizations of the Federal Communications Commission; and

(3) the signal of the primary transmitter is not altered or changed in any way by the secondary transmitter.

(c) Secondary Transmissions by Cable Systems. —

(1) Subject to the provisions of clauses (2), (3), and (4) of this subsection and section 114(d), secondary transmissions to the public by a cable system of a performance or display of a work embodied in a primary transmission made by a broadcast station licensed by the Federal

Communications Commission or by an appropriate governmental authority of Canada or Mexico shall be subject to statutory licensing upon compliance with the requirements of subsection (d) where the carriage of the signals comprising the secondary transmission is permissible under the rules, regulations, or authorizations of the Federal Communications Commission.

(2) Notwithstanding the provisions of clause (1) of this subsection, the willful or repeated secondary transmission to the public by a cable system of a primary transmission made by a broadcast station licensed by the Federal Communications Commission or by an appropriate governmental authority of Canada or Mexico and embodying a performance or display of a work is actionable as an act of infringement under section 501, and is fully subject to the remedies provided by sections 502 through 506 and 509, in the following cases:

(A) where the carriage of the signals comprising the secondary transmission is not permissible under the rules, regulations, or authorizations of the Federal Communications Commission; or

(B) where the cable system has not deposited the statement of account and royalty fee required by subsection (d).

(3) Notwithstanding the provisions of clause (1) of this subsection and subject to the provisions of subsection (e) of this section, the secondary transmission to the public by a cable system of a performance or display of a work embodied in a primary transmission made by a broadcast station licensed by the Federal Communications Commission or by an appropriate governmental authority of Canada or Mexico is actionable as an act of infringement under section 501, and is fully subject to the remedies provided by sections 502 through 506 and sections 509 and 510, if the content of the particular program in which the performance or display is embodied, or any commercial advertising or station announcements transmitted by the primary transmitter during, or immediately before or after, the transmission of such program, is in any way willfully altered by the cable system through changes, deletions, or additions, except for the alteration, deletion, or substitution of commercial advertisements performed by those engaged in television commercial advertising market research: *Provided,* That the research company has obtained the prior consent of the advertiser who has purchased the original commercial advertisement, the television station broadcasting that commercial advertisement, and the cable system performing the secondary transmission: *And provided further,* That such commercial alteration, deletion, or substitution is not performed for the purpose of deriving income from the sale of that commercial time.

(4) Notwithstanding the provisions of clause (1) of this subsection, the secondary transmission to the public by a cable system of a performance or display of a work embodied in a primary transmission made by a broadcast station licensed by an appropriate governmental authority of Canada or Mexico is actionable as an act of infringement under section 501, and is fully subject to the remedies provided by sections 502 through 506 and section 509, if (A) with respect to Canadian signals, the community of the cable system is located more than 150 miles from the United States-Canadian border and is also located south of the forty-second parallel of latitude, or (B) with respect to Mexican signals, the secondary transmission is made by a cable system which received the primary transmission by means other than direct interception of a free space radio wave

emitted by such broadcast television station, unless prior to April 15, 1976, such cable system was actually carrying, or was specifically authorized to carry, the signal of such foreign station on the system pursuant to the rules, regulations, or authorizations of the Federal Communications Commission.

(d) Statutory License for Secondary Transmissions by Cable Systems.[45] —

(1) A cable system whose secondary transmissions have been subject to statutory licensing under subsection (c) shall, on a semiannual basis, deposit with the Register of Copyrights, in accordance with requirements that the Register shall prescribe by regulation —

(A) a statement of account, covering the six months next preceding, specifying the number of channels on which the cable system made secondary transmissions to its subscribers, the names and locations of all primary transmitters whose transmissions were further transmitted by the cable system, the total number of subscribers, the gross amounts paid to the cable system for the basic service of providing secondary transmissions of primary broadcast transmitters, and such other data as the Register of Copyrights may from time to time prescribe by regulation. In determining the total number of subscribers and the gross amounts paid to the cable system for the basic service of providing secondary transmissions of primary broadcast transmitters, the cable system shall not include subscribers and amounts collected from subscribers receiving secondary transmissions pursuant to section 119. Such statement shall also include a special statement of account covering any nonnetwork television programming that was carried by the cable system in whole or in part beyond the local service area of the primary transmitter, under rules, regulations, or authorizations of the Federal Communications Commission permitting the substitution or addition of signals under certain circumstances, together with logs showing the times, dates, stations, and programs involved in such substituted or added carriage; and

(B) except in the case of a cable system whose royalty is specified in subclause (C) or (D), a total royalty fee for the period covered by the statement, computed on the basis of specified percentages of the gross receipts from subscribers to the cable service during said period for the basic service of providing secondary transmissions of primary broadcast transmitters, as follows:

(i) 0.675 of 1 per centum of such gross receipts for the privilege of further transmitting any nonnetwork programming of a primary transmitter in whole or in part beyond the local service area of such primary transmitter, such amount to be applied against the fee, if any, payable pursuant to paragraphs (ii) through (iv);

(ii) 0.675 of 1 per centum of such gross receipts for the first distant signal equivalent;

(iii) 0.425 of 1 per centum of such gross receipts for each of the second, third, and fourth distant signal equivalents;

(iv) 0.2 of 1 per centum of such gross receipts for the fifth distant signal equivalent and each additional distant signal equivalent thereafter; and in computing the amounts payable under paragraph (ii) through (iv), above, any fraction of a distant signal equivalent shall be computed at its fractional value and, in the case of any cable system located partly within and partly without the local service area of a primary transmitter, gross receipts shall be limited to those gross receipts derived from subscribers located without the local service area of such primary transmitter; and

(C) if the actual gross receipts paid by subscribers to a cable system for the period covered by the statement for the basic service of providing secondary transmissions of primary broadcast transmitters total $80,000 or less, gross receipts of the cable system for the purpose of this subclause shall be computed by subtracting from such actual gross receipts the amount by which $80,000 exceeds such actual gross receipts, except that in no case shall a cable system's gross receipts be reduced to less than $3,000. The royalty fee payable under this subclause shall be 0.5 of 1 per centum, regardless of the number of distant signal equivalents, if any; and

(D) if the actual gross receipts paid by subscribers to a cable system for the period covered by the statement, for the basic service of providing secondary transmissions of primary broadcast transmitters, are more than $80,000 but less than $160,000, the royalty fee payable under this subclause shall be

(i) 0.5 of 1 per centum of any gross receipts up to $80,000; and

(ii) 1 per centum of any gross receipts in excess of $80,000 but less than $160,000, regardless of the number of distant signal equivalents, if any.

(2) The Register of Copyrights shall receive all fees deposited under this section and, after deducting the reasonable costs incurred by the Copyright Office under this section, shall deposit the balance in the Treasury of the United States, in such manner as the Secretary of the Treasury directs. All funds held by the Secretary of the Treasury shall be invested in interest-bearing United States securities for later distribution with interest by the Librarian of Congress upon authorization by the Copyright Royalty Judges.

(3) The royalty fees thus deposited shall, in accordance with the procedures provided by clause (4), be distributed to those among the following copyright owners who claim that their works were the subject of secondary transmissions by cable systems during the relevant semiannual period:

(A) any such owner whose work was included in a secondary transmission made by a cable system of a nonnetwork television program in whole or in part beyond the local service area of the primary transmitter; and

(B) any such owner whose work was included in a secondary transmission identified in a special statement of account deposited under clause (1) (A); and

(C) any such owner whose work was included in nonnetwork programming consisting exclusively of aural signals carried by a cable system in whole or in part beyond the local service area of the primary transmitter of such programs.

(4) The royalty fees thus deposited shall be distributed in accordance with the following procedures:

(A) During the month of July in each year, every person claiming to be entitled to statutory license fees for secondary transmissions shall file a claim with the Copyright Royalty Judges, in accordance with requirements that the Copyright Royalty Judges shall prescribe by regulation. Notwithstanding any provisions of the antitrust laws, for purposes of this clause any claimants may agree among themselves as to the proportionate division of statutory licensing fees among them, may lump their claims together and file them jointly or as a single claim, or may designate a common agent to receive payment on their behalf.

(B) After the first day of August of each year, the Copyright Royalty Judges shall determine whether there exists a controversy concerning the distribution of royalty fees. If the Copyright Royalty Judges determine that no such controversy exists, the Copyright Royalty Judges shall authorize the Librarian of Congress to proceed to distribute such fees to the copyright owners entitled to receive them, or to their designated agents, subject to the deduction of reasonable administrative costs under this section. If the Copyright Royalty Judges find the existence of a controversy, the Copyright Royalty Judges shall, pursuant to chapter 8 of this title, conduct a proceeding to determine the distribution of royalty fees.

(C) During the pendency of any proceeding under this subsection, the Copyright Royalty Judges shall have the discretion to authorize the Librarian of Congress to proceed to distribute any amounts that are not in controversy.

(e) Nonsimultaneous Secondary Transmissions by Cable Systems. —

(1) Notwithstanding those provisions of the second paragraph of subsection (f) relating to nonsimultaneous secondary transmissions by a cable system, any such transmissions are actionable as an act of infringement under section 501, and are fully subject to the remedies provided by sections 502 through 506 and sections 509 and 510, unless —

(A) the program on the videotape is transmitted no more than one time to the cable system's subscribers; and

(B) the copyrighted program, episode, or motion picture videotape, including the commercials contained within such program, episode, or picture, is transmitted without deletion or editing; and

(C) an owner or officer of the cable system

(i) prevents the duplication of the videotape while in the possession of the system,

(ii) prevents unauthorized duplication while in the possession of the facility making the videotape for the system if the system owns or controls the facility, or takes reasonable precautions to prevent such duplication if it does not own or control the facility,

(iii) takes adequate precautions to prevent duplication while the tape is being transported, and

(iv) subject to clause (2), erases or destroys, or causes the erasure or destruction of, the videotape; and

(D) within forty-five days after the end of each calendar quarter, an owner or officer of the cable system executes an affidavit attesting

(i) to the steps and precautions taken to prevent duplication of the videotape, and

(ii) subject to clause (2), to the erasure or destruction of all videotapes made or used during such quarter; and

(E) such owner or officer places or causes each such affidavit, and affidavits received pursuant to clause (2)(C), to be placed in a file, open to public inspection, at such system's main office in the community where the transmission is made or in the nearest community where such system maintains an office; and

(F) the nonsimultaneous transmission is one that the cable system would be authorized to transmit under the rules, regulations, and authorizations of the Federal Communications Commission in effect at the time of the nonsimultaneous transmission if the transmission had been made simultaneously, except that this subclause shall not apply to inadvertent or accidental transmissions.

(2) If a cable system transfers to any person a videotape of a program nonsimultaneously transmitted by it, such transfer is actionable as an act of infringement under section 501, and is fully subject to the remedies provided by sections 502 through 506 and 509, except that, pursuant to a written, nonprofit contract providing for the equitable sharing of the costs of such videotape and its transfer, a videotape nonsimultaneously transmitted by it, in accordance with clause (1), may be transferred by one cable system in Alaska to another system in Alaska, by one cable system in Hawaii permitted to make such nonsimultaneous transmissions to another such cable system in Hawaii, or by one cable system in Guam, the Northern Mariana Islands, or the Trust Territory of the Pacific Islands, to another cable system in any of those three territories, if —

(A) each such contract is available for public inspection in the offices of the cable systems involved, and a copy of such contract is filed, within thirty days after such contract is entered into, with the Copyright Office (which Office shall make each such contract available for public inspection); and

(B) the cable system to which the videotape is transferred complies with clause (1) (A), (B), (C) (i), (iii), and (iv), and (D) through (F); and

(C) such system provides a copy of the affidavit required to be made in accordance with clause (1) (D) to each cable system making a previous nonsimultaneous transmission of the same videotape.

(3) This subsection shall not be construed to supersede the exclusivity protection provisions of any existing agreement, or any such agreement hereafter entered into, between a cable system and a television broadcast station in the area in which the cable system is located, or a network with which such station is affiliated.

(4) As used in this subsection, the term "videotape", and each of its variant forms, means the reproduction of the images and sounds of a program or programs broadcast by a television

broadcast station licensed by the Federal Communications Commission, regardless of the nature of the material objects, such as tapes or films, in which the reproduction is embodied.

(f) Definitions. — As used in this section, the following terms and their variant forms mean the following:

A "primary transmission" is a transmission made to the public by the transmitting facility whose signals are being received and further transmitted by the secondary transmission service, regardless of where or when the performance or display was first transmitted.

A "secondary transmission" is the further transmitting of a primary transmission simultaneously with the primary transmission, or nonsimultaneously with the primary transmission if by a "cable system" not located in whole or in part within the boundary of the forty-eight contiguous States, Hawaii, or Puerto Rico: *Provided, however,* That a nonsimultaneous further transmission by a cable system located in Hawaii of a primary transmission shall be deemed to be a secondary transmission if the carriage of the television broadcast signal comprising such further transmission is permissible under the rules, regulations, or authorizations of the Federal Communications Commission.

A "cable system" is a facility, located in any State, Territory, Trust Territory, or Possession, that in whole or in part receives signals transmitted or programs broadcast by one or more television broadcast stations licensed by the Federal Communications Commission, and makes secondary transmissions of such signals or programs by wires, cables, microwave, or other communications channels to subscribing members of the public who pay for such service. For purposes of determining the royalty fee under subsection (d)(1), two or more cable systems in contiguous communities under common ownership or control or operating from one headend shall be considered as one system.

The "local service area of a primary transmitter", in the case of a television broadcast station, comprises the area in which such station is entitled to insist upon its signal being retransmitted by a cable system pursuant to the rules, regulations, and authorizations of the Federal Communications Commission in effect on April 15, 1976, or such station's television market as defined in section 76.55(e) of title 47, Code of Federal Regulations (as in effect on September 18, 1993), or any modifications to such television market made, on or after September 18, 1993, pursuant to section 76.55(e) or 76.59 of title 47 of the Code of Federal Regulations, or in the case of a television broadcast station licensed by an appropriate governmental authority of Canada or Mexico, the area in which it would be entitled to insist upon its signal being retransmitted if it were a television broadcast station subject to such rules, regulations, and authorizations. In the case of a low power television station, as defined by the rules and regulations of the Federal Communications Commission, the "local service area of a primary transmitter" comprises the area within 35 miles of the transmitter site, except that in the case of such a station located in a standard metropolitan statistical area which has one of the 50 largest populations of all standard metropolitan statistical areas (based on the 1980 decennial census of population taken by the Secretary of Commerce), the number of miles shall be 20 miles. The "local service area of a primary transmitter", in the case of a radio broadcast station, comprises the primary service area of such station, pursuant to the rules and regulations of the Federal Communications Commission.

A "distant signal equivalent" is the value assigned to the secondary transmission of any nonnetwork television programming carried by a cable system in whole or in part beyond the local service area of the primary transmitter of such programming. It is computed by assigning a value of one to each independent station and a value of one-quarter to each network station and noncommercial educational station for the nonnetwork programming so carried pursuant to the rules, regulations, and authorizations of the Federal Communications Commission. The foregoing values for independent, network, and noncommercial educational stations are subject, however, to the following exceptions and limitations. Where the rules and regulations of the Federal Communications Commission require a cable system to omit the further transmission of a particular program and such rules and regulations also permit the substitution of another program embodying a performance or display of a work in place of the omitted transmission, or where such rules and regulations in effect on the date of enactment of this Act permit a cable system, at its election, to effect such deletion and substitution of a nonlive program or to carry additional programs not transmitted by primary transmitters within whose local service area the cable system is located, no value shall be assigned for the substituted or additional program; where the rules, regulations, or authorizations of the Federal Communications Commission in effect on the date of enactment of this Act permit a cable system, at its election, to omit the further transmission of a particular program and such rules, regulations, or authorizations also permit the substitution of another program embodying a performance or display of a work in place of the omitted transmission, the value assigned for the substituted or additional program shall be, in the case of a live program, the value of one full distant signal equivalent multiplied by a fraction that has as its numerator the number of days in the year in which such substitution occurs and as its denominator the number of days in the year. In the case of a station carried pursuant to the late-night or specialty programming rules of the Federal Communications Commission, or a station carried on a part-time basis where full-time carriage is not possible because the cable system lacks the activated channel capacity to retransmit on a full-time basis all signals which it is authorized to carry, the values for independent, network, and noncommercial educational stations set forth above, as the case may be, shall be multiplied by a fraction which is equal to the ratio of the broadcast hours of such station carried by the cable system to the total broadcast hours of the station.

A "network station" is a television broadcast station that is owned or operated by, or affiliated with, one or more of the television networks in the United States providing nationwide transmissions, and that transmits a substantial part of the programming supplied by such networks for a substantial part of that station's typical broadcast day.

An "independent station" is a commercial television broadcast station other than a network station.

A "noncommercial educational station" is a television station that is a noncommercial educational broadcast station as defined in section 397 of title 47.

§ 112. Limitations on exclusive rights: Ephemeral recordings[46]

(a)(1) Notwithstanding the provisions of section 106, and except in the case of a motion picture or other audiovisual work, it is not an infringement of copyright for a transmitting organization entitled to transmit to the public a performance or display of a work, under a license, including a statutory license under section 114(f), or transfer of the copyright or under the limitations on exclusive rights in sound recordings specified by section 114 (a) or for a transmitting organization that is a broadcast radio or television station licensed as such by the Federal Communications Commission and that makes a broadcast transmission of a performance of a sound recording in a digital format on a non-subscription basis, to make no more than one copy or phonorecord of a particular transmission program embodying the performance or display, if —

(A) the copy or phonorecord is retained and used solely by the transmitting organization that made it, and no further copies or phonorecords are reproduced from it; and

(B) the copy or phonorecord is used solely for the transmitting organization's own transmissions within its local service area, or for purposes of archival preservation or security; and

(C) unless preserved exclusively for archival purposes, the copy or phonorecord is destroyed within six months from the date the transmission program was first transmitted to the public.

(2) In a case in which a transmitting organization entitled to make a copy or phonorecord under paragraph (1) in connection with the transmission to the public of a performance or display of a work is prevented from making such copy or phonorecord by reason of the application by the copyright owner of technical measures that prevent the reproduction of the work, the copyright owner shall make available to the transmitting organization the necessary means for permitting the making of such copy or phonorecord as permitted under that paragraph, if it is technologically feasible and economically reasonable for the copyright owner to do so. If the copyright owner fails to do so in a timely manner in light of the transmitting organization's reasonable business requirements, the transmitting organization shall not be liable for a violation of section 1201(a)(1) of this title for engaging in such activities as are necessary to make such copies or phonorecords as permitted under paragraph (1) of this subsection.

(b) Notwithstanding the provisions of section 106, it is not an infringement of copyright for a governmental body or other nonprofit organization entitled to transmit a performance or display of a work, under section 110(2) or under the limitations on exclusive rights in sound recordings specified by section 114(a), to make no more than thirty copies or phonorecords of a particular transmission program embodying the performance or display,
if —

(1) no further copies or phonorecords are reproduced from the copies or phonorecords made under this clause; and

(2) except for one copy or phonorecord that may be preserved exclusively for archival purposes, the copies or phonorecords are destroyed within seven years from the date the transmission program was first transmitted to the public.

(c) Notwithstanding the provisions of section 106, it is not an infringement of copyright for a governmental body or other nonprofit organization to make for distribution no more than one copy or phonorecord, for each transmitting organization specified in clause (2) of this subsection, of a particular transmission program embodying a performance of a nondramatic musical work of a religious nature, or of a sound recording of such a musical work, if —

(1) there is no direct or indirect charge for making or distributing any such copies or phonorecords; and

(2) none of such copies or phonorecords is used for any performance other than a single transmission to the public by a transmitting organization entitled to transmit to the public a performance of the work under a license or transfer of the copyright; and

(3) except for one copy or phonorecord that may be preserved exclusively for archival purposes, the copies or phonorecords are all destroyed within one year from the date the transmission program was first transmitted to the public.

(d) Notwithstanding the provisions of section 106, it is not an infringement of copyright for a governmental body or other nonprofit organization entitled to transmit a performance of a work under section 110(8) to make no more than ten copies or phonorecords embodying the performance, or to permit the use of any such copy or phonorecord by any governmental body or nonprofit organization entitled to transmit a performance of a work under section 110(8), if —

(1) any such copy or phonorecord is retained and used solely by the organization that made it, or by a governmental body or nonprofit organization entitled to transmit a performance of a work under section 110(8), and no further copies or phonorecords are reproduced from it; and

(2) any such copy or phonorecord is used solely for transmissions authorized under section 110(8), or for purposes of archival preservation or security; and

(3) the governmental body or nonprofit organization permitting any use of any such copy or phonorecord by any governmental body or nonprofit organization under this subsection does not make any charge for such use.

(e) Statutory License. — (1) A transmitting organization entitled to transmit to the public a performance of a sound recording under the limitation on exclusive rights specified by section 114(d)(1)(C)(iv) or under a statutory license in accordance with section 114(f) is entitled to a statutory license, under the conditions specified by this subsection, to make no more than 1 phonorecord of the sound recording (unless the terms and conditions of the statutory license allow for more), if the following conditions are satisfied:

(A) The phonorecord is retained and used solely by the transmitting organization that made it, and no further phonorecords are reproduced from it.

(B) The phonorecord is used solely for the transmitting organization's own transmissions originating in the United States under a statutory license in accordance with section 114(f) or the limitation on exclusive rights specified by section 114(d)(1)(C)(iv).

(C) Unless preserved exclusively for purposes of archival preservation, the phonorecord is destroyed within 6 months from the date the sound recording was first transmitted to the public using the phonorecord.

(D) Phonorecords of the sound recording have been distributed to the public under the authority of the copyright owner or the copyright owner authorizes the transmitting entity to transmit the sound recording, and the transmitting entity makes the phonorecord under this subsection from a phonorecord lawfully made and acquired under the authority of the copyright owner.

(2) Notwithstanding any provision of the antitrust laws, any copyright owners of sound recordings and any transmitting organizations entitled to a statutory license under this subsection may negotiate and agree upon royalty rates and license terms and conditions for making phonorecords of such sound recordings under this section and the proportionate division of fees paid among copyright owners, and may designate common agents to negotiate, agree to, pay, or receive such royalty payments.

(3) Proceedings under chapter 8 shall determine reasonable rates and terms of royalty payments for the activities specified by paragraph (1) during the 5-year period beginning on January 1 of the second year following the year in which the proceedings are to be commenced, or such other period as the parties may agree. Such rates shall include a minimum fee for each type of service offered by transmitting organizations. Any copyright owners of sound recordings or any transmitting organizations entitled to a statutory license under this subsection may submit to the Copyright Royalty Judges licenses covering such activities with respect to such sound recordings. The parties to each proceeding shall bear their own costs.

(4) The schedule of reasonable rates and terms determined by the Copyright Royalty Judges shall, subject to paragraph (5), be binding on all copyright owners of sound recordings and transmitting organizations entitled to a statutory license under this subsection during the 5-year period specified in paragraph (3), or such other period as the parties may agree. Such rates shall include a minimum fee for each type of service offered by transmitting organizations. The Copyright Royalty Judges shall establish rates that most clearly represent the fees that would have been negotiated in the marketplace between a willing buyer and a willing seller. In determining such rates and terms, the Copyright Royalty Judges shall base their decision on economic, competitive, and programming information presented by the parties, including —

(A) whether use of the service may substitute for or may promote the sales of phonorecords or otherwise interferes with or enhances the copyright owner's traditional streams of revenue; and

(B) the relative roles of the copyright owner and the transmitting organization in the copyrighted work and the service made available to the public with respect to relative creative contribution, technological contribution, capital investment, cost, and risk.

In establishing such rates and terms, the Copyright Royalty Judges may consider the rates and terms under voluntary license agreements described in paragraphs (2) and (3). The Copyright Royalty Judges shall also establish requirements by which copyright owners may receive reasonable notice of the use of their sound recordings under this section, and under which records of such use shall be kept and made available by transmitting organizations entitled to obtain a statutory license under this subsection.

(5) License agreements voluntarily negotiated at any time between 1 or more copyright owners of sound recordings and 1 or more transmitting organizations entitled to obtain a statutory license under this subsection shall be given effect in lieu of any decision by the Librarian of Congress or determination by the Copyright Royalty Judges.

(6)(A) Any person who wishes to make a phonorecord of a sound recording under a statutory license in accordance with this subsection may do so without infringing the exclusive right of the copyright owner of the sound recording under section 106(1)—

(i) by complying with such notice requirements as the Copyright Royalty Judges shall prescribe by regulation and by paying royalty fees in accordance with this subsection; or

(ii) if such royalty fees have not been set, by agreeing to pay such royalty fees as shall be determined in accordance with this subsection.

(B) Any royalty payments in arrears shall be made on or before the 20th day of the month next succeeding the month in which the royalty fees are set.

(7) If a transmitting organization entitled to make a phonorecord under this subsection is prevented from making such phonorecord by reason of the application by the copyright owner of technical measures that prevent the reproduction of the sound recording, the copyright owner shall make available to the transmitting organization the necessary means for permitting the making of such phonorecord as permitted under this subsection, if it is technologically feasible and economically reasonable for the copyright owner to do so. If the copyright owner fails to do so in a timely manner in light of the transmitting organization's reasonable business requirements, the transmitting organization shall not be liable for a violation of section 1201(a)(1) of this title for engaging in such activities as are necessary to make such phonorecords as permitted under this subsection.

(8) Nothing in this subsection annuls, limits, impairs, or otherwise affects in any way the existence or value of any of the exclusive rights of the copyright owners in a sound recording, except as otherwise provided in this subsection, or in a musical work, including the exclusive rights to reproduce and distribute a sound recording or musical work, including by means of a digital phonorecord delivery, under section 106(1), 106(3), and 115, and the right to perform publicly a sound recording or musical work, including by means of a digital audio transmission, under sections 106(4) and 106(6).

(f)(1) Notwithstanding the provisions of section 106, and without limiting the application of subsection (b), it is not an infringement of copyright for a governmental body or other nonprofit educational institution entitled under section 110(2) to transmit a performance or display to make copies or phonorecords of a work that is in digital form and, solely to the extent permitted in paragraph (2), of a work that is in analog form, embodying the performance or display to be used for making transmissions authorized under section 110(2), if —

(A) such copies or phonorecords are retained and used solely by the body or institution that made them, and no further copies or phonorecords are reproduced from them, except as authorized under section 110(2); and

(B) such copies or phonorecords are used solely for transmissions authorized under section 110(2).

(2) This subsection does not authorize the conversion of print or other analog versions of works into digital formats, except that such conversion is permitted hereunder, only with respect to the amount of such works authorized to be performed or displayed under section 110(2), if —

(A) no digital version of the work is available to the institution; or

(B) the digital version of the work that is available to the institution is subject to technological protection measures that prevent its use for section 110(2).

(g) The transmission program embodied in a copy or phonorecord made under this section is not subject to protection as a derivative work under this title except with the express consent of the owners of copyright in the preexisting works employed in the program.

§ 113. Scope of exclusive rights in pictorial, graphic, and sculptural works[47]

(a) Subject to the provisions of subsections (b) and (c) of this section, the exclusive right to reproduce a copyrighted pictorial, graphic, or sculptural work in copies under section 106, includes the right to reproduce the work in or on any kind of article, whether useful or otherwise.

(b) This title does not afford, to the owner of copyright in a work that portrays a useful article as such, any greater or lesser rights with respect to the making, distribution, or display of the useful article so portrayed than those afforded to such works under the law, whether title 17 or the common law or statutes of a State, in effect on December 31, 1977, as held applicable and construed by a court in an action brought under this title.

(c) In the case of a work lawfully reproduced in useful articles that have been offered for sale or other distribution to the public, copyright does not include any right to prevent the making, distribution, or display of pictures or photographs of such articles in connection with advertisements or commentaries related to the distribution or display of such articles, or in connection with news reports.

(d)(1) In a case in which —

(A) a work of visual art has been incorporated in or made part of a building in such a way that removing the work from the building will cause the destruction, distortion, mutilation, or other modification of the work as described in section 106A(a)(3), and

(B) the author consented to the installation of the work in the building either before the effective date set forth in section 610(a) of the Visual Artists Rights Act of 1990, or in a written instrument executed on or after such effective date that is signed by the owner of the building and the author and that specifies that installation of the work may subject the work to destruction, distortion, mutilation, or other modification, by reason of its removal, then the rights conferred by paragraphs (2) and (3) of section 106A(a) shall not apply.

(2) If the owner of a building wishes to remove a work of visual art which is a part of such building and which can be removed from the building without the destruction, distortion, mutilation, or other modification of the work as described in section 106A(a)(3), the author's rights under paragraphs (2) and (3) of section 106A(a) shall apply unless —

(A) the owner has made a diligent, good faith attempt without success to notify the author of the owner's intended action affecting the work of visual art, or

(B) the owner did provide such notice in writing and the person so notified failed, within 90 days after receiving such notice, either to remove the work or to pay for its removal.

For purposes of subparagraph (A), an owner shall be presumed to have made a diligent, good faith attempt to send notice if the owner sent such notice by registered mail to the author at the most recent address of the author that was recorded with the Register of Copyrights pursuant to paragraph (3). If the work is removed at the expense of the author, title to that copy of the work shall be deemed to be in the author.

(3) The Register of Copyrights shall establish a system of records whereby any author of a work of visual art that has been incorporated in or made part of a building, may record his or her identity and address with the Copyright Office. The Register shall also establish procedures under which any such author may update the information so recorded, and procedures under which owners of buildings may record with the Copyright Office evidence of their efforts to comply with this subsection.

§ 114. Scope of exclusive rights in sound recordings[48]

(a) The exclusive rights of the owner of copyright in a sound recording are limited to the rights specified by clauses (1), (2), (3) and (6) of section 106, and do not include any right of performance under section 106(4).

(b) The exclusive right of the owner of copyright in a sound recording under clause (1) of section 106 is limited to the right to duplicate the sound recording in the form of phonorecords or copies that directly or indirectly recapture the actual sounds fixed in the recording. The exclusive right of the owner of copyright in a sound recording under clause (2) of section 106 is limited to the right to prepare a derivative work in which the actual sounds fixed in the sound recording are rearranged, remixed, or otherwise altered in sequence or quality. The exclusive rights of the owner of copyright in a sound recording under clauses (1) and (2) of section 106 do not extend to the making or duplication of another sound recording that consists entirely of an independent fixation of other sounds, even though such sounds imitate or simulate those in the copyrighted sound recording. The exclusive rights of the owner of copyright in a sound recording under clauses (1), (2), and (3) of section 106 do not apply to sound recordings included in educational television and radio programs (as defined in section 397 of title 47) distributed or transmitted by or through public broadcasting entities (as defined by section 118(g)): *Provided,* That copies or phonorecords of said programs are not commercially distributed by or through public broadcasting entities to the general public.

(c) This section does not limit or impair the exclusive right to perform publicly, by means of a phonorecord, any of the works specified by section 106(4).

(d) Limitations on Exclusive Right. — Notwithstanding the provisions of section 106(6) —

(1) Exempt transmissions and retransmissions. — The performance of a sound recording publicly by means of a digital audio transmission, other than as a part of an interactive service, is not an infringement of section 106(6) if the performance is part of —

(A) a nonsubscription broadcast transmission;

(B) a retransmission of a nonsubscription broadcast transmission: *Provided,* That, in the case of a retransmission of a radio station's broadcast transmission —

(i) the radio station's broadcast transmission is not willfully or repeatedly retransmitted more than a radius of 150 miles from the site of the radio broadcast transmitter, however —

(I) the 150 mile limitation under this clause shall not apply when a nonsubscription broadcast transmission by a radio station licensed by the Federal Communications Commission is retransmitted on a nonsubscription basis by a terrestrial broadcast station, terrestrial translator, or terrestrial repeater licensed by the Federal Communications Commission; and

(II) in the case of a subscription retransmission of a nonsubscription broadcast retransmission covered by subclause (I), the 150 mile radius shall be measured from the transmitter site of such broadcast retransmitter;

(ii) the retransmission is of radio station broadcast transmissions that are —

(I) obtained by the retransmitter over the air;

(II) not electronically processed by the retransmitter to deliver separate and discrete signals; and

(III) retransmitted only within the local communities served by the retransmitter;

(iii) the radio station's broadcast transmission was being retransmitted to cable systems (as defined in section 111(f)) by a satellite carrier on January 1, 1995, and that retransmission was being retransmitted by cable systems as a separate and discrete signal, and the satellite carrier obtains the radio station's broadcast transmission in an analog format: *Provided,* That the broadcast transmission being retransmitted may embody the programming of no more than one radio station; or

(iv) the radio station's broadcast transmission is made by a noncommercial educational broadcast station funded on or after January 1, 1995, under section 396(k) of the Communications Act of 1934 (47 U.S.C. 396(k)), consists solely of noncommercial educational and cultural radio programs, and the retransmission, whether or not simultaneous, is a nonsubscription terrestrial broadcast retransmission; or

(C) a transmission that comes within any of the following categories —

(i) a prior or simultaneous transmission incidental to an exempt transmission, such as a feed received by and then retransmitted by an exempt transmitter: *Provided,* That such incidental transmissions do not include any subscription transmission directly for reception by members of the public;

(ii) a transmission within a business establishment, confined to its premises or the immediately surrounding vicinity;

(iii) a retransmission by any retransmitter, including a multichannel video programming distributor as defined in section 602(12) of the Communications Act of 1934 (47 U.S.C. 522 (12)), of a transmission by a transmitter licensed to publicly perform the sound recording as a part of that transmission, if the retransmission is simultaneous with the licensed transmission and authorized by the transmitter; or

(iv) a transmission to a business establishment for use in the ordinary course of its business: *Provided,* That the business recipient does not retransmit the transmission outside of its premises or the immediately surrounding vicinity, and that the transmission does not exceed the sound recording performance complement. Nothing in this clause shall limit the scope of the exemption in clause (ii).

(2) Statutory licensing of certain transmissions. —

The performance of a sound recording publicly by means of a subscription digital audio transmission not exempt under paragraph (1), an eligible nonsubscription transmission, or a transmission not exempt under paragraph (1) that is made by a preexisting satellite digital audio radio service shall be subject to statutory licensing, in accordance with subsection (f) if —

(A)(i) the transmission is not part of an interactive service;

(ii) except in the case of a transmission to a business establishment, the transmitting entity does not automatically and intentionally cause any device receiving the transmission to switch from one program channel to another; and

(iii) except as provided in section 1002(e), the transmission of the sound recording is accompanied, if technically feasible, by the information encoded in that sound recording, if any, by or under the authority of the copyright owner of that sound recording, that identifies the title of the sound recording, the featured recording artist who performs on the sound recording, and related information, including information concerning the underlying musical work and its writer;

(B) in the case of a subscription transmission not exempt under paragraph (1) that is made by a preexisting subscription service in the same transmission medium used by such service on July 31, 1998, or in the case of a transmission not exempt under paragraph (1) that is made by a preexisting satellite digital audio radio service —

(i) the transmission does not exceed the sound recording performance complement; and

(ii) the transmitting entity does not cause to be published by means of an advance program schedule or prior announcement the titles of the specific sound recordings or phonorecords embodying such sound recordings to be transmitted; and

(C) in the case of an eligible nonsubscription transmission or a subscription transmission not exempt under paragraph (1) that is made by a new subscription service or by a preexisting subscription service other than in the same transmission medium used by such service on July 31, 1998 —

(i) the transmission does not exceed the sound recording performance complement, except that this requirement shall not apply in the case of a retransmission of a broadcast transmission if the retransmission is made by a transmitting entity that does not have the right or ability to control the programming of the broadcast station making the broadcast transmission, unless —

(I) the broadcast station makes broadcast transmissions —
(aa) in digital format that regularly exceed the sound recording performance complement; or
(bb) in analog format, a substantial portion of which, on a weekly basis, exceed the sound recording performance complement; and

(II) the sound recording copyright owner or its representative has notified the transmitting entity in writing that broadcast transmissions of the copyright owner's sound recordings exceed the sound recording performance complement as provided in this clause;

(ii) the transmitting entity does not cause to be published, or induce or facilitate the publication, by means of an advance program schedule or prior announcement, the titles of the specific sound recordings to be transmitted, the phonorecords embodying such sound recordings, or, other than for illustrative purposes, the names of the featured recording artists, except that this clause does not disqualify a transmitting entity that makes a prior announcement that a particular artist will be featured within an unspecified future time period, and in the case of a retransmission of a broadcast transmission by a transmitting entity that does not have the right or ability to control the programming of the broadcast transmission, the requirement of this clause shall not apply to a prior oral announcement by the broadcast station, or to an advance program schedule published, induced, or facilitated by the broadcast station, if the transmitting entity does not have actual knowledge and has not received written notice from the copyright owner or its representative that the broadcast station publishes or induces or facilitates the publication of such advance program schedule, or if such advance program schedule is a schedule of classical music programming published by the broadcast station in the same manner as published by that broadcast station on or before September 30, 1998;

(iii) the transmission —

(I) is not part of an archived program of less than 5 hours duration;

(II) is not part of an archived program of 5 hours or greater in duration that is made available for a period exceeding 2 weeks;

(III) is not part of a continuous program which is of less than 3 hours duration; or

(IV) is not part of an identifiable program in which performances of sound recordings are rendered in a predetermined order, other than an archived or continuous program, that is transmitted at —

(aa) more than 3 times in any 2-week period that have been publicly announced in advance, in the case of a program of less than 1 hour in duration, or

(bb) more than 4 times in any 2-week period that have been publicly announced in advance, in the case of a program of 1 hour or more in duration, except that the requirement of this subclause shall not apply in the case of a retransmission of a broadcast transmission by a transmitting entity that does not have the right or ability to control the programming of the broadcast transmission, unless the transmitting entity is given notice in writing by the copyright owner of the sound recording that the broadcast station makes broadcast transmissions that regularly violate such requirement;

(iv) the transmitting entity does not knowingly perform the sound recording, as part of a service that offers transmissions of visual images contemporaneously with transmissions of sound recordings, in a manner that is likely to cause confusion, to cause mistake, or to deceive, as to the affiliation, connection, or association of the copyright owner or featured recording artist with the transmitting entity or a particular product or service advertised by the transmitting entity, or as to the origin, sponsorship, or approval by the copyright owner or featured recording artist of the activities of the transmitting entity other than the performance of the sound recording itself;

(v) the transmitting entity cooperates to prevent, to the extent feasible without imposing substantial costs or burdens, a transmission recipient or any other person or entity from automatically scanning the transmitting entity's transmissions alone or together with transmissions by other transmitting entities in order to select a particular sound recording to be transmitted to the transmission recipient, except that the requirement of this clause shall not apply to a satellite digital audio service that is in operation, or that is licensed by the Federal Communications Commission, on or before July 31, 1998;

(vi) the transmitting entity takes no affirmative steps to cause or induce the making of a phonorecord by the transmission recipient, and if the technology used by the transmitting entity enables the transmitting entity to limit the making by the transmission recipient of phonorecords of the transmission directly in a digital format, the transmitting entity sets such technology to limit such making of phonorecords to the extent permitted by such technology;

(vii) phonorecords of the sound recording have been distributed to the public under the authority of the copyright owner or the copyright owner authorizes the transmitting entity to transmit the sound recording, and the transmitting entity makes the transmission from a phonorecord lawfully made under the authority of the copyright owner, except that the requirement of this clause shall not apply to a retransmission of a broadcast transmission by a transmitting entity that does not have the right or ability to control the programming of the broadcast transmission, unless the transmitting entity is given notice in writing by the copyright owner of the sound recording that the broadcast station makes broadcast transmissions that regularly violate such requirement;

(viii) the transmitting entity accommodates and does not interfere with the transmission of technical measures that are widely used by sound recording copyright owners to identify or protect copyrighted works, and that are technically feasible of being transmitted by the transmitting entity without imposing substantial costs on the transmitting entity or resulting in perceptible aural or visual degradation of the digital signal, except that the requirement of this clause shall not apply to a satellite digital audio service that is in operation, or that is licensed under the authority of the Federal Communications Commission, on or before July 31, 1998, to the extent that such service has designed, developed, or made commitments to procure equipment or technology that is not compatible with such technical measures before such technical measures are widely adopted by sound recording copyright owners; and

(ix) the transmitting entity identifies in textual data the sound recording during, but not before, the time it is performed, including the title of the sound recording, the title of the phonorecord embodying such sound recording, if any, and the featured recording artist, in a manner to permit it to be displayed to the transmission recipient by the device or technology intended for receiving the service provided by the transmitting entity, except that the obligation in this clause shall not take effect until 1 year after the date of the enactment of the Digital Millennium Copyright Act and shall not apply in the case of a retransmission of a broadcast transmission by a transmitting entity that does not have the right or ability to control the programming of the broadcast transmission, or in the case in which devices or technology intended for receiving the service provided by the transmitting entity that have the capability to display such textual data are not common in the marketplace.

(3) Licenses for transmissions by interactive services. —

(A) No interactive service shall be granted an exclusive license under section 106(6) for the performance of a sound recording publicly by means of digital audio transmission for a period in excess of 12 months, except that with respect to an exclusive license granted to an interactive service by a licensor that holds the copyright to 1,000 or fewer sound recordings, the period of such license shall not exceed 24 months: *Provided, however,* That the grantee of such exclusive license shall be ineligible to receive another exclusive license for the performance of that sound recording for a period of 13 months from the expiration of the prior exclusive license.

(B) The limitation set forth in subparagraph (A) of this paragraph shall not apply if —

(i) the licensor has granted and there remain in effect licenses under section 106(6) for the public performance of sound recordings by means of digital audio transmission by at least

5 different interactive services; *Provided, however,* That each such license must be for a minimum of 10 percent of the copyrighted sound recordings owned by the licensor that have been licensed to interactive services, but in no event less than 50 sound recordings; or

(ii) the exclusive license is granted to perform publicly up to 45 seconds of a sound recording and the sole purpose of the performance is to promote the distribution or performance of that sound recording.

(C) Notwithstanding the grant of an exclusive or nonexclusive license of the right of public performance under section 106(6), an interactive service may not publicly perform a sound recording unless a license has been granted for the public performance of any copyrighted musical work contained in the sound recording: *Provided,* That such license to publicly perform the copyrighted musical work may be granted either by a performing rights society representing the copyright owner or by the copyright owner.

(D) The performance of a sound recording by means of a retransmission of a digital audio transmission is not an infringement of section 106(6) if —

(i) the retransmission is of a transmission by an interactive service licensed to publicly perform the sound recording to a particular member of the public as part of that transmission; and

(ii) the retransmission is simultaneous with the licensed transmission, authorized by the transmitter, and limited to that particular member of the public intended by the interactive service to be the recipient of the transmission.

(E) For the purposes of this paragraph —

(i) a "licensor" shall include the licensing entity and any other entity under any material degree of common ownership, management, or control that owns copyrights in sound recordings; and

(ii) a "performing rights society" is an association or corporation that licenses the public performance of nondramatic musical works on behalf of the copyright owner, such as the American Society of Composers, Authors and Publishers, Broadcast Music, Inc., and SESAC, Inc.

(4) Rights not otherwise limited. —

(A) Except as expressly provided in this section, this section does not limit or impair the exclusive right to perform a sound recording publicly by means of a digital audio transmission under section 106(6).

(B) Nothing in this section annuls or limits in any way —

(i) the exclusive right to publicly perform a musical work, including by means of a digital audio transmission, under section 106(4);

(ii) the exclusive rights in a sound recording or the musical work embodied therein under sections 106(1), 106(2) and 106(3); or

(iii) any other rights under any other clause of section 106, or remedies available under this title as such rights or remedies exist either before or after the date of enactment of the Digital Performance Right in Sound Recordings Act of 1995.

(C) Any limitations in this section on the exclusive right under section 106(6) apply only to the exclusive right under section 106(6) and not to any other exclusive rights under section 106. Nothing in this section shall be construed to annul, limit, impair or otherwise affect in any way the ability of the owner of a copyright in a sound recording to exercise the rights under sections 106(1), 106(2) and 106(3), or to obtain the remedies available under this title pursuant to such rights, as such rights and remedies exist either before or after the date of enactment of the Digital Performance Right in Sound Recordings Act of 1995.

(e) Authority for Negotiations. —

(1) Notwithstanding any provision of the antitrust laws, in negotiating statutory licenses in accordance with subsection (f), any copyright owners of sound recordings and any entities performing sound recordings affected by this section may negotiate and agree upon the royalty rates and license terms and conditions for the performance of such sound recordings and the proportionate division of fees paid among copyright owners, and may designate common agents on a nonexclusive basis to negotiate, agree to, pay, or receive payments.

(2) For licenses granted under section 106(6), other than statutory licenses, such as for performances by interactive services or performances that exceed the sound recording performance complement —

(A) copyright owners of sound recordings affected by this section may designate common agents to act on their behalf to grant licenses and receive and remit royalty payments: *Provided,* That each copyright owner shall establish the royalty rates and material license terms and conditions unilaterally, that is, not in agreement, combination, or concert with other copyright owners of sound recordings; and

(B) entities performing sound recordings affected by this section may designate common agents to act on their behalf to obtain licenses and collect and pay royalty fees: *Provided,* That each entity performing sound recordings shall determine the royalty rates and material license terms and conditions unilaterally, that is, not in agreement, combination, or concert with other entities performing sound recordings.

(f) Licenses for Certain Nonexempt Transmissions.

(1)(A) Proceedings under chapter 8 shall determine reasonable rates and terms of royalty payments for subscription transmissions by preexisting subscription services and transmissions by preexisting satellite digital audio radio services specified by subsection (d)(2) during the 5-year period beginning on January 1 of the second year following the year in which the proceedings are to be commenced, except in the case of a different transitional period provided under section 6(b)(3) of the Copyright Royalty and Distribution Reform Act of 2004, or such other period as the parties may agree. Such terms and rates shall distinguish among the different types of digital audio transmission services then in operation. Any copyright owners of sound recordings, preexisting subscription services, or preexisting satellite digital audio radio services may submit to the Copyright Royalty Judges licenses covering such subscription transmissions with respect to such sound recordings. The parties to each proceeding shall bear their own costs.

(B) The schedule of reasonable rates and terms determined by the Copyright Royalty Judges shall, subject to paragraph (3), be binding on all copyright owners of sound recordings and entities performing sound recordings affected by this paragraph during the 5-year period specified in subparagraph (A), a transitional period provided under section 6(b)(3) of the Copyright Royalty and Distribution Reform Act of 2004, or such other period as the parties may agree. In establishing rates and terms for preexisting subscription services and preexisting satellite digital audio radio services, in addition to the objectives set forth in section 801(b)(1), the Copyright Royalty Judges may consider the rates and terms for comparable types of subscription digital audio transmission services and comparable circumstances under voluntary license agreements described in subparagraph (A).

(C) The procedures under subparagraphs (A) and (B) also shall be initiated pursuant to a petition filed by any copyright owners of sound recordings, any preexisting subscription services, or any preexisting satellite digital audio radio services indicating that a new type of subscription digital audio transmission service on which sound recordings are performed is or is about to become operational, for the purpose of determining reasonable terms and rates of royalty payments with respect to such new type of transmission service for the period beginning with the inception of such new type of service and ending on the date on which the royalty rates and terms for subscription digital audio transmission services most recently determined under subparagraph (A) or (B) and chapter 8 expire, or such other period as the parties may agree.

(2)(A) Proceedings under chapter 8 shall determine reasonable rates and terms of royalty payments for public performances of sound recordings by means of eligible nonsubscription transmission services and new subscription services specified by subsection (d)(2) during the 5-year period beginning on January 1 of the second year following the year in which the proceedings are to be commenced, except in the case of a different transitional period provided under section 6(b)(3) of the Copyright Royalty and Distribution Reform Act of 2004, or such other period as the parties may agree. Such rates and terms shall distinguish among the different types of eligible nonsubscription transmission services and new subscription services then in operation and shall include a minimum fee for each such type of service. Any copyright owners of sound recordings or any entities performing sound recordings affected by this paragraph may submit to the Copyright Royalty Judges licenses covering such eligible nonsubscription transmissions and new subscription services with respect to such sound recordings. The parties to each proceeding shall bear their own costs.

(B) The schedule of reasonable rates and terms determined by the Copyright Royalty Judges shall, subject to paragraph (3), be binding on all copyright owners of sound recordings and entities performing sound recordings affected by this paragraph during the 5-year period specified in subparagraph (A), a transitional period provided under section 6(b)(3) of the Copyright Royalty and Distribution Act of 2004, or such other period as the parties may agree. Such rates and terms shall distinguish among the different types of eligible nonsubscription transmission services then in operation and shall include a minimum fee for each such type of service, such differences to be based on criteria including, but not limited to, the quantity and nature of the use of sound recordings and the degree to which use of the service may substitute for or may promote the purchase of phonorecords by consumers. In establishing rates and terms for transmissions by eligible nonsubscription services and new subscription services, the Copyright Royalty Judges shall establish rates and terms that most clearly represent the rates and terms that would have been negotiated in the marketplace between a willing buyer and a willing seller. In determining such rates and terms, the Copyright Royalty Judges shall base [its][49] decision on economic, competitive and programming information presented by the parties, including —

(i) whether use of the service may substitute for or may promote the sales of phonorecords or otherwise may interfere with or may enhance the sound recording copyright owner's other streams of revenue from its sound recordings; and

(ii)the relative roles of the copyright owner and the transmitting entity in the copyrighted work and the service made available to the public with respect to relative creative contribution, technological contribution, capital investment, cost, and risk.

In establishing such rates and terms, the Copyright Royalty Judges may consider the rates and terms for comparable types of digital audio transmission services and comparable circumstances under voluntary license agreements described in subparagraph (A).

(C) The procedures under subparagraphs (A) and (B) shall also be initiated pursuant to a petition filed by any copyright owners of sound recordings or any eligible nonsubscription service or new subscription service indicating that a new type of eligible nonsubscription service or new subscription service on which sound recordings are performed is or is about to become operational, for the purpose of determining reasonable terms and rates of royalty payments with respect to such new type of service for the period beginning with the inception of such new type of service and ending on the date on which the royalty rates and terms for preexisting subscription digital audio transmission services or preexisting satellite digital radio audio services, as the case may be, most recently determined under subparagraph (A) or (B) and chapter 8 expire, or such other period as the parties may agree.

(3) License agreements voluntarily negotiated at any time between 1 or more copyright owners of sound recordings and 1 or more entities performing sound recordings shall be given effect in lieu of any decision by the Librarian of Congress or determination by the Copyright Royalty Judges.

(4)(A) The Copyright Royalty Judges shall also establish requirements by which copyright owners may receive reasonable notice of the use of their sound recordings under this section, and under which records of such use shall be kept and made available by entities performing sound recordings. The notice and recordkeeping rules in effect on the day before the effective date of the Copyright Royalty and Distribution Reform Act of 2004 shall remain in effect unless and until new regulations are promulgated by the Copyright Royalty Judges. If new regulations are promulgated under this subparagraph, the Copyright Royalty Judges shall take into account the substance and effect of the rules in effect on the day before the effective date of the Copyright Royalty and Distribution Reform Act of 2004 and shall, to the extent practicable, avoid significant disruption of the functions of any designated agent authorized to collect and distribute royalty fees.

(B) Any person who wishes to perform a sound recording publicly by means of a transmission eligible for statutory licensing under this subsection may do so without infringing the exclusive right of the copyright owner of the sound recording —

(i) by complying with such notice requirements as the Copyright Royalty Judges shall prescribe by regulation and by paying royalty fees in accordance with this subsection; or

(ii) if such royalty fees have not been set, by agreeing to pay such royalty fees as shall be determined in accordance with this subsection.

(C) Any royalty payments in arrears shall be made on or before the twentieth day of the month next succeeding the month in which the royalty fees are set.

(5)(A) Notwithstanding section 112(e) and the other provisions of this subsection, the receiving agent may enter into agreements for the reproduction and performance of sound recordings under section 112(e) and this section by any 1 or more small commercial webcasters or noncommercial webcasters during the period beginning on October 28, 1998, and ending on December 31, 2004, that, once published in the Federal Register pursuant to subparagraph (B), shall be binding on all copyright owners of sound recordings and other persons entitled to payment under this section, in lieu of any determination by a copyright arbitration royalty panel or decision by the Librarian of Congress. Any such agreement for small commercial webcasters shall include provisions for payment of royalties on the basis of a percentage of revenue or expenses, or both, and include a minimum fee. Any such agreement may include other terms and conditions, including requirements by which copyright owners may receive notice of the use of their sound recordings and under which records of such use shall be kept and made available by small commercial webcasters or noncommercial webcasters. The receiving agent shall be under no obligation to negotiate any such agreement. The receiving agent shall have no obligation to any copyright owner of sound recordings or any other person entitled to payment under this section in negotiating any such agreement, and no liability to any copyright owner of sound recordings or any other person entitled to payment under this section for having entered into such agreement.

(B) The Copyright Office shall cause to be published in the Federal Register any agreement entered into pursuant to subparagraph (A). Such publication shall include a statement containing the substance of subparagraph (C). Such agreements shall not be included in the Code of Federal Regulations. Thereafter, the terms of such agreement shall be available, as an option, to any small commercial webcaster or noncommercial webcaster meeting the eligibility conditions of such agreement.

(C) Neither subparagraph (A) nor any provisions of any agreement entered into pursuant to subparagraph (A), including any rate structure, fees, terms, conditions, or notice and record-keeping requirements set forth therein, shall be admissible as evidence or otherwise taken into account in any administrative, judicial, or other government proceeding involving the setting or adjustment of the royalties payable for the public performance or reproduction in ephemeral phonorecords or copies of sound recordings, the determination of terms or conditions related thereto, or the establishment of notice or recordkeeping requirements by the Librarian of Congress under paragraph (4) or section 112(e)(4). It is the intent of Congress that any royalty rates, rate structure, definitions, terms, conditions, or notice and recordkeeping requirements, included in such agreements shall be considered as a compromise motivated by the unique business, economic and political circumstances of small webcasters, copyright owners, and performers rather than as matters that would have been negotiated in the marketplace between a willing buyer and a willing seller, or otherwise meet the objectives set forth in section 801(b).

(D) Nothing in the Small Webcaster Settlement Act of 2002 or any agreement entered into pursuant to subparagraph (A) shall be taken into account by the United States Court of Appeals for the District of Columbia Circuit in its review of the determination by the Librarian of Congress of July 8, 2002, of rates and terms for the digital performance of sound recordings and ephemeral recordings, pursuant to sections 112 and 114.

(E) As used in this paragraph —

  (i) the term "noncommercial webcaster" means a webcaster that —

    (I) is exempt from taxation under section 501 of the Internal Revenue Code of 1986 (26 U.S.C. 501);

    (II) has applied in good faith to the Internal Revenue Service for exemption from taxation under section 501 of the Internal Revenue Code and has a commercially reasonable expectation that such exemption shall be granted; or

    (III) is operated by a State or possession or any governmental entity or subordinate thereof, or by the United States or District of Columbia, for exclusively public purposes;

  (ii) the term "receiving agent" shall have the meaning given that term in section 261.2 of title 37, Code of Federal Regulations, as published in the Federal Register on July 8, 2002; and

  (iii) the term "webcaster" means a person or entity that has obtained a compulsory license under section 112 or 114 and the implementing regulations therefor to make eligible nonsubscription transmissions and ephemeral recordings.

(F) The authority to make settlements pursuant to subparagraph (A) shall expire December 15, 2002, except with respect to noncommercial webcasters for whom the authority shall expire May 31, 2003.

(g) Proceeds from Licensing of Transmissions. —

  (1) Except in the case of a transmission licensed under a statutory license in accordance with subsection (f) of this section —

  (A) a featured recording artist who performs on a sound recording that has been licensed for a transmission shall be entitled to receive payments from the copyright owner of the sound recording in accordance with the terms of the artist's contract; and

(B) a nonfeatured recording artist who performs on a sound recording that has been licensed for a transmission shall be entitled to receive payments from the copyright owner of the sound recording in accordance with the terms of the nonfeatured recording artist's applicable contract or other applicable agreement.

(2) An agent designated to distribute receipts from the licensing of transmissions in accordance with subsection (f) shall distribute such receipts as follows:

(A) 50 percent of the receipts shall be paid to the copyright owner of the exclusive right under section 106(6) of this title to publicly perform a sound recording by means of a digital audio transmission.

(B) 2½ percent of the receipts shall be deposited in an escrow account managed by an independent administrator jointly appointed by copyright owners of sound recordings and the American Federation of Musicians (or any successor entity) to be distributed to nonfeatured musicians (whether or not members of the American Federation of Musicians) who have performed on sound recordings.

(C) 2½ percent of the receipts shall be deposited in an escrow account managed by an independent administrator jointly appointed by copyright owners of sound recordings and the American Federation of Television and Radio Artists (or any successor entity) to be distributed to nonfeatured vocalists (whether or not members of the American Federation of Television and Radio Artists) who have performed on sound recordings.

(D) 45 percent of the receipts shall be paid, on a per sound recording basis, to the recording artist or artists featured on such sound recording (or the persons conveying rights in the artists' performance in the sound recordings).

(3) A nonprofit agent designated to distribute receipts from the licensing of transmissions in accordance with subsection (f) may deduct from any of its receipts, prior to the distribution of such receipts to any person or entity entitled thereto other than copyright owners and performers who have elected to receive royalties from another designated agent and have notified such nonprofit agent in writing of such election, the reasonable costs of such agent incurred after November 1, 1995, in —

(A) the administration of the collection, distribution, and calculation of the royalties;

(B) the settlement of disputes relating to the collection and calculation of the royalties; and

(C) the licensing and enforcement of rights with respect to the making of ephemeral recordings and performances subject to licensing under section 112 and this section, including those incurred in participating in negotiations or arbitration proceedings under section 112 and this section, except that all costs incurred relating to the section 112 ephemeral recordings right may only be deducted from the royalties received pursuant to section 112.

(4) Notwithstanding paragraph (3), any designated agent designated to distribute receipts from the licensing of transmissions in accordance with subsection (f) may deduct from any of its receipts, prior to the distribution of such receipts, the reasonable costs identified in paragraph (3) of such

agent incurred after November 1, 1995, with respect to such copyright owners and performers who have entered with such agent a contractual relationship that specifies that such costs may be deducted from such royalty receipts.

(h) Licensing to Affiliates. —

(1) If the copyright owner of a sound recording licenses an affiliated entity the right to publicly perform a sound recording by means of a digital audio transmission under section 106(6), the copyright owner shall make the licensed sound recording available under section 106(6) on no less favorable terms and conditions to all bona fide entities that offer similar services, except that, if there are material differences in the scope of the requested license with respect to the type of service, the particular sound recordings licensed, the frequency of use, the number of subscribers served, or the duration, then the copyright owner may establish different terms and conditions for such other services.

(2) The limitation set forth in paragraph (1) of this subsection shall not apply in the case where the copyright owner of a sound recording licenses —

(A) an interactive service; or

(B) an entity to perform publicly up to 45 seconds of the sound recording and the sole purpose of the performance is to promote the distribution or performance of that sound recording.

(i) No Effect on Royalties for Underlying Works. — License fees payable for the public performance of sound recordings under section 106(6) shall not be taken into account in any administrative, judicial, or other governmental proceeding to set or adjust the royalties payable to copyright owners of musical works for the public performance of their works. It is the intent of Congress that royalties payable to copyright owners of musical works for the public performance of their works shall not be diminished in any respect as a result of the rights granted by section 106(6).

(j) Definitions. — As used in this section, the following terms have the following meanings:

(1) An "affiliated entity" is an entity engaging in digital audio transmissions covered by section 106(6), other than an interactive service, in which the licensor has any direct or indirect partnership or any ownership interest amounting to 5 percent or more of the outstanding voting or non-voting stock.

(2) An "archived program" is a predetermined program that is available repeatedly on the demand of the transmission recipient and that is performed in the same order from the beginning, except that an archived program shall not include a recorded event or broadcast transmission that makes no more than an incidental use of sound recordings, as long as such recorded event or broadcast transmission does not contain an entire sound recording or feature a particular sound recording.

(3) A "broadcast" transmission is a transmission made by a terrestrial broadcast station licensed as such by the Federal Communications Commission.

(4) A "continuous program" is a predetermined program that is continuously performed in the same order and that is accessed at a point in the program that is beyond the control of the transmission recipient.

(5) A "digital audio transmission" is a digital transmission as defined in section 101, that embodies the transmission of a sound recording. This term does not include the transmission of any audiovisual work.

(6) An "eligible nonsubscription transmission" is a noninteractive nonsubscription digital audio transmission not exempt under subsection (d)(1) that is made as part of a service that provides audio programming consisting, in whole or in part, of performances of sound recordings, including retransmissions of broadcast transmissions, if the primary purpose of the service is to provide to the public such audio or other entertainment programming, and the primary purpose of the service is not to sell, advertise, or promote particular products or services other than sound recordings, live concerts, or other music-related events.

(7) An "interactive service" is one that enables a member of the public to receive a transmission of a program specially created for the recipient, or on request, a transmission of a particular sound recording, whether or not as part of a program, which is selected by or on behalf of the recipient. The ability of individuals to request that particular sound recordings be performed for reception by the public at large, or in the case of a subscription service, by all subscribers of the service, does not make a service interactive, if the programming on each channel of the service does not substantially consist of sound recordings that are performed within 1 hour of the request or at a time designated by either the transmitting entity or the individual making such request. If an entity offers both interactive and noninteractive services (either concurrently or at different times), the noninteractive component shall not be treated as part of an interactive service.

(8) A "new subscription service" is a service that performs sound recordings by means of noninteractive subscription digital audio transmissions and that is not a preexisting subscription service or a preexisting satellite digital audio radio service.

(9) A "nonsubscription" transmission is any transmission that is not a subscription transmission.

(10) A "preexisting satellite digital audio radio service" is a subscription satellite digital audio radio service provided pursuant to a satellite digital audio radio service license issued by the Federal Communications Commission on or before July 31, 1998, and any renewal of such license to the extent of the scope of the original license, and may include a limited number of sample channels representative of the subscription service that are made available on a nonsubscription basis in order to promote the subscription service.

(11) A "preexisting subscription service" is a service that performs sound recordings by means of noninteractive audio-only subscription digital audio transmissions, which was in existence and was making such transmissions to the public for a fee on or before July 31, 1998, and may include a limited number of sample channels representative of the subscription service that are made available on a nonsubscription basis in order to promote the subscription service.

(12) A "retransmission" is a further transmission of an initial transmission, and includes any further retransmission of the same transmission. Except as provided in this section, a transmission qualifies as a "retransmission" only if it is simultaneous with the initial transmission. Nothing in this

definition shall be construed to exempt a transmission that fails to satisfy a separate element required to qualify for an exemption under section 114(d)(1).

(13) The "sound recording performance complement" is the transmission during any 3-hour period, on a particular channel used by a transmitting entity, of no more than —

(A) 3 different selections of sound recordings from any one phonorecord lawfully distributed for public performance or sale in the United States, if no more than 2 such selections are transmitted consecutively; or

(B) 4 different selections of sound recordings —

(i) by the same featured recording artist; or

(ii) from any set or compilation of phonorecords lawfully distributed together as a unit for public performance or sale in the United States,

if no more than three such selections are transmitted consecutively:

Provided, That the transmission of selections in excess of the numerical limits provided for in clauses (A) and (B) from multiple phonorecords shall nonetheless qualify as a sound recording performance complement if the programming of the multiple phonorecords was not willfully intended to avoid the numerical limitations prescribed in such clauses.

(14) A "subscription" transmission is a transmission that is controlled and limited to particular recipients, and for which consideration is required to be paid or otherwise given by or on behalf of the recipient to receive the transmission or a package of transmissions including the transmission.

(15) A "transmission" is either an initial transmission or a retransmission.

§ 115. Scope of exclusive rights in nondramatic musical works: Compulsory license for making and distributing phonorecords[50]

In the case of nondramatic musical works, the exclusive rights provided by clauses (1) and (3) of section 106, to make and to distribute phonorecords of such works, are subject to compulsory licensing under the conditions specified by this section.

(a) Availability and Scope of Compulsory License. —

(1) When phonorecords of a nondramatic musical work have been distributed to the public in the United States under the authority of the copyright owner, any other person, including those who make phonorecords or digital phonorecord deliveries, may, by complying with the provisions of this section, obtain a compulsory license to make and distribute phonorecords of the work. A person may obtain a compulsory license only if his or her primary purpose in making phonorecords is to distribute them to the public for private use, including by means of a digital phonorecord delivery. A person may not obtain a compulsory license for use of the work in the making of phonorecords duplicating a sound recording fixed by another, unless:

(i) such sound recording was fixed lawfully; and

(ii) the making of the phonorecords was authorized by the owner of copyright in the sound recording or, if the sound recording was fixed before February 15, 1972, by any person who fixed the sound recording pursuant to an express license from the owner of the copyright in the musical work or pursuant to a valid compulsory license for use of such work in a sound recording.

(2) A compulsory license includes the privilege of making a musical arrangement of the work to the extent necessary to conform it to the style or manner of interpretation of the performance involved, but the arrangement shall not change the basic melody or fundamental character of the work, and shall not be subject to protection as a derivative work under this title, except with the express consent of the copyright owner.

(b) Notice of Intention to Obtain Compulsory License. —

(1) Any person who wishes to obtain a compulsory license under this section shall, before or within thirty days after making, and before distributing any phonorecords of the work, serve notice of intention to do so on the copyright owner. If the registration or other public records of the Copyright Office do not identify the copyright owner and include an address at which notice can be served, it shall be sufficient to file the notice of intention in the Copyright Office. The notice shall comply, in form, content, and manner of service, with requirements that the Register of Copyrights shall prescribe by regulation.

(2) Failure to serve or file the notice required by clause (1) forecloses the possibility of a compulsory license and, in the absence of a negotiated license, renders the making and distribution of phonorecords actionable as acts of infringement under section 501 and fully subject to the remedies provided by sections 502 through 506 and 509.

(c) Royalty Payable under Compulsory License.[51] —

(1) To be entitled to receive royalties under a compulsory license, the copyright owner must be identified in the registration or other public records of the Copyright Office. The owner is entitled to royalties for phonorecords made and distributed after being so identified, but is not entitled to recover for any phonorecords previously made and distributed.

(2) Except as provided by clause (1), the royalty under a compulsory license shall be payable for every phonorecord made and distributed in accordance with the license. For this purpose, and other than as provided in paragraph (3), a phonorecord is considered "distributed" if the person exercising the compulsory license has voluntarily and permanently parted with its possession. With respect to each work embodied in the phonorecord, the royalty shall be either two and three-fourths cents, or one-half of one cent per minute of playing time or fraction thereof, whichever amount is larger.

(3)(A) A compulsory license under this section includes the right of the compulsory licensee to distribute or authorize the distribution of a phonorecord of a nondramatic musical work by means of a digital transmission which constitutes a digital phonorecord delivery, regardless of whether the digital transmission is also a public performance of the sound recording under section 106(6) of this title or of any nondramatic musical work embodied therein under section 106(4) of this title. For every digital phonorecord delivery by or under the authority of the compulsory licensee —

(i) on or before December 31, 1997, the royalty payable by the compulsory licensee shall be the royalty prescribed under paragraph (2) and chapter 8 of this title; and

(ii) on or after January 1, 1998, the royalty payable by the compulsory licensee shall be the royalty prescribed under subparagraphs (B) through (E) and chapter 8 of this title.

(B) Notwithstanding any provision of the antitrust laws, any copyright owners of nondramatic musical works and any persons entitled to obtain a compulsory license under subsection (a)(1) may negotiate and agree upon the terms and rates of royalty payments this section and the proportionate division of fees paid among copyright owners, and may designate common agents to negotiate, agree to, pay or receive such royalty payments. Such authority to negotiate the terms and rates of royalty payments includes, but is not limited to, the authority to negotiate the year during which the royalty rates prescribed under this subparagraph and subparagraphs (C) through (E) and chapter 8 of this title shall next be determined.

(C) Proceedings under chapter 8 shall determine reasonable rates and terms of royalty payments for the activities specified by this section during the period beginning with the effective date of such rates and terms, but not earlier than January 1 of the second year following the year in which the petition requesting the proceeding is filed, and ending on the effective date of successor rates and terms, or such other period as the parties may agree. Such terms and rates shall distinguish between (i) digital phonorecord deliveries where the reproduction or distribution of a phonorecord is incidental to the transmission which constitutes the digital phonorecord delivery, and (ii) digital phonorecord deliveries in general. Any copyright owners of nondramatic musical works and any persons entitled to obtain a compulsory license under subsection (a)(1) may submit to the Copyright Royalty Judges licenses covering such activities. The parties to each proceeding shall bear their own costs.

(D) The schedule of reasonable rates and terms determined by the Copyright Royalty Judges shall, subject to subparagraph (E), be binding on all copyright owners of nondramatic musical works and persons entitled to obtain a compulsory license under subsection (a)(1) during the period specified in subparagraph (C), such other period as may be determined pursuant to subparagraphs (B) and (C), or such other period as the parties may agree. Such terms and rates shall distinguish between (i) digital phonorecord deliveries where the reproduction or distribution of a phonorecord is incidental to the transmission which constitutes the digital phonorecord delivery, and (ii) digital phonorecord deliveries in general. In addition to the objectives set forth in section 801(b)(1), in establishing such rates and terms, the Copyright Royalty Judges may consider rates and terms under voluntary license agreements described in subparagraphs (B) and (C). The royalty rates payable for a compulsory license for a digital phonorecord delivery under this section shall be established de novo and no precedential effect shall be given to the amount of the royalty payable by a compulsory licensee for digital phonorecord deliveries on or before December 31, 1997. The Copyright Royalty Judges shall also establish requirements by which copyright owners may receive reasonable notice of the use of their works under this section, and under which records of such use shall be kept and made available by persons making digital phonorecord deliveries.

(E)(i) License agreements voluntarily negotiated at any time between one or more copyright owners of nondramatic musical works and one or more persons entitled to obtain a compulsory license under subsection (a)(1) shall be given effect in lieu of any determination by the Librarian of Congress and Copyright Royalty Judges. Subject to clause (ii), the royalty rates determined pursuant to subparagraph (C) and (D) shall be given effect as to digital phonorecord deliveries in lieu of any contrary royalty rates specified in a contract pursuant to which a recording artist who is the author of a nondramatic musical work grants a license under that person's exclusive rights in the musical work under paragraphs (1) and (3) of section 106 or commits another person to grant a license in that musical work under paragraphs (1) and (3) of section 106, to a person desiring to fix in a tangible medium of expression a sound recording embodying the musical work.

(ii) The second sentence of clause (i) shall not apply to —

(I) a contract entered into on or before June 22, 1995 and not modified thereafter for the purpose of reducing the royalty rates determined pursuant to subparagraph (C) and (D) or of increasing the number of musical works within the scope of the contract covered by the reduced rates, except if a contract entered into on or before June 22, 1995, is modified thereafter for the purpose of increasing the number of musical works within the scope of the contract, any contrary royalty rates specified in the contract shall be given effect in lieu of royalty rates determined pursuant to subparagraph (C) and (D) for the number of musical works within the scope of the contract as of June 22, 1995; and

(II) a contract entered into after the date that the sound recording is fixed in a tangible medium of expression substantially in a form intended for commercial release, if at the time the contract is entered into, the recording artist retains the right to grant licenses as to the musical work under paragraphs (1) and (3) of section 106.

(F) Except as provided in section 1002(e) of this title, a digital phonorecord delivery licensed under this paragraph shall be accompanied by the information encoded in the sound recording, if any, by or under the authority of the copyright owner of that sound recording, that identifies the title of the sound recording, the featured recording artist who performs on the sound recording, and related information, including information concerning the underlying musical work and its writer.

(G)(i) A digital phonorecord delivery of a sound recording is actionable as an act of infringement under section 501, and is fully subject to the remedies provided by sections 502 through 506 and section 509, unless —

(I) the digital phonorecord delivery has been authorized by the copyright owner of the sound recording; and

(II) the owner of the copyright in the sound recording or the entity making the digital phonorecord delivery has obtained a compulsory license under this section or has otherwise been authorized by the copyright owner of the musical work to distribute or authorize the distribution, by means of a digital phonorecord delivery, of each musical work embodied in the sound recording.

(ii) Any cause of action under this subparagraph shall be in addition to those available to the owner of the copyright in the nondramatic musical work under subsection (c)(6) and section 106(4) and the owner of the copyright in the sound recording under section 106(6).

(H) The liability of the copyright owner of a sound recording for infringement of the copyright in a nondramatic musical work embodied in the sound recording shall be determined in accordance with applicable law, except that the owner of a copyright in a sound recording shall not be liable for a digital phonorecord delivery by a third party if the owner of the copyright in the sound recording does not license the distribution of a phonorecord of the nondramatic musical work.

(I) Nothing in section 1008 shall be construed to prevent the exercise of the rights and remedies allowed by this paragraph, paragraph (6), and chapter 5 in the event of a digital phonorecord delivery, except that no action alleging infringement of copyright may be brought under this title against a manufacturer, importer or distributor of a digital audio recording device, a digital audio recording medium, an analog recording device, or an analog recording medium, or against a consumer, based on the actions described in such section.

(J) Nothing in this section annuls or limits

(i) the exclusive right to publicly perform a sound recording or the musical work embodied therein, including by means of a digital transmission, under sections 106(4) and 106(6), (ii) except for compulsory licensing under the conditions specified by this section, the exclusive rights to reproduce and distribute the sound recording and the musical work embodied therein under sections 106(1) and 106(3), including by means of a digital phonorecord delivery, or (iii) any other rights under any other provision of section 106, or remedies available under this title, as such rights or remedies exist either before or after the date of enactment of the Digital Performance Right in Sound Recordings Act of 1995.

(K) The provisions of this section concerning digital phonorecord deliveries shall not apply to any exempt transmissions or retransmissions under section 114(d)(1). The exemptions created in section 114(d)(1) do not expand or reduce the rights of copyright owners under section 106(1) through (5) with respect to such transmissions and retransmissions.

(4) A compulsory license under this section includes the right of the maker of a phonorecord of a nondramatic musical work under subsection (a)(1) to distribute or authorize distribution of such phonorecord by rental, lease, or lending (or by acts or practices in the nature of rental, lease, or lending). In addition to any royalty payable under clause (2) and chapter 8 of this title, a royalty shall be payable by the compulsory licensee for every act of distribution of a phonorecord by or in the nature of rental, lease, or lending, by or under the authority of the compulsory licensee. With respect to each nondramatic musical work embodied in the phonorecord, the royalty shall be a proportion of the revenue received by the compulsory licensee from every such act of distribution

of the phonorecord under this clause equal to the proportion of the revenue received by the compulsory licensee from distribution of the phonorecord under clause (2) that is payable by a compulsory licensee under that clause and under chapter 8. The Register of Copyrights shall issue regulations to carry out the purpose of this clause.

(5) Royalty payments shall be made on or before the twentieth day of each month and shall include all royalties for the month next preceding. Each monthly payment shall be made under oath and shall comply with requirements that the Register of Copyrights shall prescribe by regulation. The Register shall also prescribe regulations under which detailed cumulative annual statements of account, certified by a certified public accountant, shall be filed for every compulsory license under this section. The regulations covering both the monthly and the annual statements of account shall prescribe the form, content, and manner of certification with respect to the number of records made and the number of records distributed.

(6) If the copyright owner does not receive the monthly payment and the monthly and annual statements of account when due, the owner may give written notice to the licensee that, unless the default is remedied within thirty days from the date of the notice, the compulsory license will be automatically terminated. Such termination renders either the making or the distribution, or both, of all phonorecords for which the royalty has not been paid, actionable as acts of infringement under section 501 and fully subject to the remedies provided by sections 502 through 506 and 509.

(d) Definition. — As used in this section, the following term has the following meaning: A "digital phonorecord delivery" is each individual delivery of a phonorecord by digital transmission of a sound recording which results in a specifically identifiable reproduction by or for any transmission recipient of a phonorecord of that sound recording, regardless of whether the digital transmission is also a public performance of the sound recording or any nondramatic musical work embodied therein. A digital phonorecord delivery does not result from a real-time, non-interactive subscription transmission of a sound recording where no reproduction of the sound recording or the musical work embodied therein is made from the inception of the transmission through to its receipt by the transmission recipient in order to make the sound recording audible.

§ 116. Negotiated licenses for public performances by means of coin-operated phonorecord players[52]

(a) Applicability of Section. — This section applies to any nondramatic musical work embodied in a phonorecord.

(b) Negotiated Licenses. —

(1) Authority for negotiations. — Any owners of copyright in works to which this section applies and any operators of coin-operated phonorecord players may negotiate and agree upon the terms and rates of royalty payments for the performance of such works and the proportionate division of fees paid among copyright owners, and may designate common agents to negotiate, agree to, pay, or receive such royalty payments.

(2) Chapter 8 proceeding. — Parties not subject to such a negotiation may have the terms and rates and the division of fees described in paragraph (1) determined in a proceeding in accordance with the provisions of chapter 8.

(c) License Agreements Superior to Determinations by Copyright Royalty Judges. — License agreements between one or more copyright owners and one or more operators of coin-operated phonorecord players, which are negotiated in accordance with subsection (b), shall be given effect in lieu of any otherwise applicable determination by the Copyright Royalty Judges.

(d) Definitions. — As used in this section, the following terms mean the following:

(1) A "coin-operated phonorecord player" is a machine or device that —

(A) is employed solely for the performance of nondramatic musical works by means of phonorecords upon being activated by the insertion of coins, currency, tokens, or other monetary units or their equivalent;

(B) is located in an establishment making no direct or indirect charge for admission;

(C) is accompanied by a list which is comprised of the titles of all the musical works available for performance on it, and is affixed to the phonorecord player or posted in the establishment in a prominent position where it can be readily examined by the public; and

(D) affords a choice of works available for performance and permits the choice to be made by the patrons of the establishment in which it is located.

(2) An "operator" is any person who, alone or jointly with others —

(A) owns a coin-operated phonorecord player;

(B) has the power to make a coin-operated phonorecord player available for placement in an establishment for purposes of public performance; or

(C) has the power to exercise primary control over the selection of the musical works made available for public performance on a coin-operated phonorecord player.

§ 117. Limitations on exclusive rights: Computer programs[53]

(a) Making of Additional Copy or Adaptation by Owner of Copy. — Notwithstanding the provisions of section 106, it is not an infringement for the owner of a copy of a computer program to make or authorize the making of another copy or adaptation of that computer program provided:

(1) that such a new copy or adaptation is created as an essential step in the utilization of the computer program in conjunction with a machine and that it is used in no other manner, or

(2) that such new copy or adaptation is for archival purposes only and that all archival copies are destroyed in the event that continued possession of the computer program should cease to be rightful.

(b) Lease, Sale, or Other Transfer of Additional Copy or Adaptation. — Any exact copies prepared in accordance with the provisions of this section may be leased, sold, or otherwise transferred, along with the copy from which such copies were prepared, only as part of the lease, sale, or other transfer of all rights in the program. Adaptations so prepared may be transferred only with the authorization of the copyright owner.

(c) Machine Maintenance or Repair. — Notwithstanding the provisions of section 106, it is not an infringement for the owner or lessee of a machine to make or authorize the making of a copy of a computer program if such copy is made solely by virtue of the activation of a machine that lawfully contains an authorized copy of the computer program, for purposes only of maintenance or repair of that machine, if —

(1) such new copy is used in no other manner and is destroyed immediately after the maintenance or repair is completed; and

(2) with respect to any computer program or part thereof that is not necessary for that machine to be activated, such program or part thereof is not accessed or used other than to make such new copy by virtue of the activation of the machine.

(d) Definitions. — For purposes of this section —

(1) the "maintenance" of a machine is the servicing of the machine in order to make it work in accordance with its original specifications and any changes to those specifications authorized for that machine; and

(2) the "repair" of a machine is the restoring of the machine to the state of working in accordance with its original specifications and any changes to those specifications authorized for that machine.

§ 118. Scope of exclusive rights: Use of certain works in connection with noncommercial broadcasting[54]

(a) The exclusive rights provided by section 106 shall, with respect to the works specified by subsection (b) and the activities specified by subsection (d), be subject to the conditions and limitations prescribed by this section.

(b) Notwithstanding any provision of the antitrust laws, any owners of copyright in published nondramatic musical works and published pictorial, graphic, and sculptural works and any public broadcasting entities, respectively, may negotiate and agree upon the terms and rates of royalty payments and the proportionate division of fees paid among various copyright owners, and may designate common agents to negotiate, agree to, pay, or receive payments.

(1) Any owner of copyright in a work specified in this subsection or any public broadcasting entity may submit to the Copyright Royalty Judges proposed licenses covering such activities with respect to such works.

(2) License agreements voluntarily negotiated at any time between one or more copyright owners and one or more public broadcasting entities shall be given effect in lieu of any determination by the Librarian of Congress or the Copyright Royalty Judges, if copies of such agreements are filed with the Copyright Royalty Judges within 30 days of execution in accordance with regulations that the Copyright Royalty Judges shall issue.

(3) Voluntary negotiation proceedings initiated pursuant to a petition filed under section 804(a) for the purpose of determining a schedule of terms and rates of royalty payments by public broadcasting entities to owners of copyright in works specified by this subsection and the proportionate division of fees paid among various copyright owners shall cover the 5-year period beginning on January 1 of the second year following the year in which the petition is filed. The parties to each negotiation proceeding shall bear their own costs.

(4) In the absence of license agreements negotiated under paragraph (2) or (3), the Copyright Royalty Judges shall, pursuant to chapter 8, conduct a proceeding to determine and publish in the Federal Register a schedule of rates and terms which, subject to paragraph (2), shall be binding on all owners of copyright in works specified by this subsection and public broadcasting entities, regardless of whether such copyright owners have submitted proposals to the Copyright Royalty Judges. In establishing such rates and terms the Copyright Royalty Judges may consider the rates for comparable circumstances under voluntary license agreements negotiated as provided in paragraph (2) or (3). The Copyright Royalty Judges shall also establish requirements by which copyright owners may receive reasonable notice of the use of their works under this section, and under which records of such use shall be kept by public broadcasting entities.

(c) Subject to the terms of any voluntary license agreements that have been negotiated as provided by subsection (b) (2) or (3), a public broadcasting entity may, upon compliance with the provisions of this section, including the rates and terms established by the Copyright Royalty Judges under subsection (b)(4), engage in the following activities with respect to published nondramatic musical works and published pictorial, graphic, and sculptural works:

(1) performance or display of a work by or in the course of a transmission made by a noncommercial educational broadcast station referred to in subsection (f); and

(2) production of a transmission program, reproduction of copies or phonorecords of such a transmission program, and distribution of such copies or phonorecords, where such production, reproduction, or distribution is made by a nonprofit institution or organization solely for the purpose of transmissions specified in paragraph (1); and

(3) the making of reproductions by a governmental body or a nonprofit institution of a transmission program simultaneously with its transmission as specified in paragraph (1), and the performance or display of the contents of such program under the conditions specified by paragraph (1) of section 110, but only if the reproductions are used for performances or displays for a period of no more than seven days from the date of the transmission specified in paragraph (1), and are destroyed before or at the end of such period. No person supplying, in accordance with paragraph (2), a reproduction of a transmission program to governmental bodies or nonprofit institutions

under this paragraph shall have any liability as a result of failure of such body or institution to destroy such reproduction: *Provided,* That it shall have notified such body or institution of the requirement for such destruction pursuant to this paragraph: *And provided further,* That if such body or institution itself fails to destroy such reproduction it shall be deemed to have infringed.

(d) Except as expressly provided in this subsection, this section shall have no applicability to works other than those specified in subsection (b). Owners of copyright in nondramatic literary works and public broadcasting entities may, during the course of voluntary negotiations, agree among themselves, respectively, as to the terms and rates of royalty payments without liability under the antitrust laws. Any such terms and rates of royalty payments shall be effective upon filing with the Copyright Royalty Judges, in accordance with regulations that the Copyright Royalty Judges shall prescribe as provided in section 803(b)(6).

(e) Nothing in this section shall be construed to permit, beyond the limits of fair use as provided by section 107, the unauthorized dramatization of a nondramatic musical work, the production of a transmission program drawn to any substantial extent from a published compilation of pictorial, graphic, or sculptural works, or the unauthorized use of any portion of an audiovisual work.

(f) As used in this section, the term "public broadcasting entity" means a noncommercial educational broadcast station as defined in section 397 of title 47 and any nonprofit institution or organization engaged in the activities described in paragraph (2) of subsection (c).

§ 119. *Limitations on exclusive rights: Secondary transmissions of superstations and network stations for private home viewing*[55]

(a) Secondary Transmissions by Satellite Carriers. —

(1) Superstations. — Subject to the provisions of paragraphs (5), (6), and (8) of this subsection and section 114(d), secondary transmissions of a performance or display of a work embodied in a primary transmission made by a superstation shall be subject to statutory licensing under this section if the secondary transmission is made by a satellite carrier to the public for private home viewing or for viewing in a commercial establishment, with regard to secondary transmissions the satellite carrier is in compliance with the rules, regulations, or authorizations of the Federal Communications Commission governing the carriage of television broadcast station signals, and the carrier makes a direct or indirect charge for each retransmission service to each subscriber receiving the secondary transmission or to a distributor that has contracted with the carrier for direct or indirect delivery of the secondary transmission to the public for private home viewing or for viewing in a commercial establishment.[56]

(2) Network stations. —

(A) In general. — Subject to the provisions of subparagraphs (B) and (C) of this paragraph and paragraphs (5), (6), (7), and (8) of this subsection and section 114(d), secondary transmissions of a performance or display of a work embodied in a primary transmission made by a network station shall be subject to statutory licensing under this section if the secondary transmission is made by a satellite carrier to the public for private home viewing, with regard to secondary transmissions the satellite carrier is in compliance with the rules, regulations, or authorizations of the Federal Communications Commission governing the carriage of television broadcast station signals, and the carrier makes a direct or indirect charge for such retransmission service to each subscriber receiving the secondary transmission.

(B) Secondary transmissions to unserved households. —

(i) In general. — The statutory license provided for in subparagraph (A) shall be limited to secondary transmissions of the signals of no more than two network stations in a single day for each television network to persons who reside in unserved households. The limitation in this clause shall not apply to secondary transmissions under paragraph (3).

(ii) Accurate determinations of eligibility. —

(I) Accurate predictive model. — In determining presumptively whether a person resides in an unserved household under subsection (d)(10)(A), a court shall rely on the Individual Location Longley-Rice model set forth by the Federal Communications Commission in Docket No. 98-201, as that model may be amended by the Commission over time under section 339(c)(3) of the Communications Act of 1934 to increase the accuracy of that model.

(II) Accurate measurements. — For purposes of site measurements to determine whether a person resides in an unserved household under subsection (d)(10)(A), a court shall rely on section 339(c)(4) of the Communications Act of 1934.

(iii) C-band exemption to unserved households. —

(I) In general. — The limitations of clause (i) shall not apply to any secondary transmissions by C-band services of network stations that a subscriber to C-band service received before any termination of such secondary transmissions before October 31, 1999.

(II) Definition. — In this clause the term "C-band service" means a service that is licensed by the Federal Communications Commission and operates in the Fixed Satellite Service under part 25 of title 47 of the Code of Federal Regulations.

(C) Exceptions. —

(i) States with single full-power network station. — In a State in which there is licensed by the Federal Communications Commission a single full-power station that was a network station on January 1, 1995, the statutory license provided for in subparagraph (A) shall apply to the secondary transmission by a satellite carrier of the primary transmission of that station to any subscriber in a community that is located within that State and that is not within the first 50 television markets as listed in the regulations of the Commission as in effect on such date (47 CFR 76.51).

(ii) States with all network stations and superstations in same local market. — In a State in which all network stations and superstations licensed by the Federal Communications

Commission within that State as of January 1, 1995, are assigned to the same local market and that local market does not encompass all counties of that State, the statutory license provided under subparagraph (A) shall apply to the secondary transmission by a satellite carrier of the primary transmissions of such station to all subscribers in the State who reside in a local market that is within the first 50 major television markets as listed in the regulations of the Commission as in effect on such date (section 76.51 of title 47 of the Code of Federal Regulations).

(iii) Additional stations. — In the case of that State in which are located 4 counties that —

(I) on January 1, 2004, were in local markets principally comprised of counties in another State, and

(II) had a combined total of 41,340 television households, according to the U.S. Television Household Estimates by Nielsen Media Research for 2004,

the statutory license provided under subparagraph (A) shall apply to secondary transmissions by a satellite carrier to subscribers in any such county of the primary transmissions of any network station located in that State, if the satellite carrier was making such secondary transmissions to any subscribers in that county on January 1, 2004.

(iv) Certain additional stations. — If 2 adjacent counties in a single State are in a local market comprised principally of counties located in another State, the statutory license provided for in subparagraph (A) shall apply to the secondary transmission by a satellite carrier to subscribers in those 2 counties of the primary transmissions of any network station located in the capital of the State in which such 2 counties are located, if —

(I) the 2 counties are located in a local market that is in the top 100 markets for the year 2003 according to Nielsen Media Research; and

(II) the total number of television households in the 2 counties combined did not exceed 10,000 for the year 2003 according to Nielsen Media Research.

(v) Applicability of royalty rates. — The royalty rates under subsection (b)(1)(B) apply to the secondary transmissions to which the statutory license under subparagraph (A) applies under clauses (i), (ii), (iii), and (iv).

(D) Submission of subscriber lists to networks. —

(i) Initial lists. — A satellite carrier that makes secondary transmissions of a primary transmission made by a network station pursuant to subparagraph (A) shall, 90 days after commencing such secondary transmissions, submit to the network that owns or is affiliated with the network station —

(I) a list identifying (by name and address, including street or rural route number, city, State, and zip code) all subscribers to which the satellite carrier makes secondary transmissions of that primary transmission to subscribers in unserved households; and

(II) a separate list, aggregated by designated market area (as defined in section 122(j)) (by name and address, including street or rural route number, city, State, and zip code), which shall indicate those subscribers being served pursuant to paragraph (3), relating to significantly viewed stations.

(ii) Monthly lists. — After the submission of the initial lists under clause (i), on the 15th of each month, the satellite carrier shall submit to the network —

(I) a list identifying (by name and address, including street or rural route number, city, State, and zip code) any persons who have been added or dropped as subscribers under clause (i)(I) since the last submission under clause (i); and

(II) a separate list, aggregated by designated market area (by name and street address, including street or rural route number, city, State, and zip code), identifying those subscribers whose service pursuant to paragraph (3), relating to significantly viewed stations, has been added or dropped.

(iii) Use of subscriber information. — Subscriber information submitted by a satellite carrier under this subparagraph may be used only for purposes of monitoring compliance by the satellite carrier with this subsection.

(iv) Applicability. — The submission requirements of this subparagraph shall apply to a satellite carrier only if the network to which the submissions are to be made places on file with the Register of Copyrights a document identifying the name and address of the person to whom such submissions are to be made. The Register shall maintain for public inspection a file of all such documents.

(3) Secondary transmissions of significantly viewed signals. —

(A) In general. — Notwithstanding the provisions of paragraph (2)(B), and subject to subparagraph (B) of this paragraph, the statutory license provided for in paragraphs (1) and (2) shall apply to the secondary transmission of the primary transmission of a network station or a superstation to a subscriber who resides outside the station's local market (as defined in section 122(j)) but within a community in which the signal has been determined by the Federal Communications Commission, to be significantly viewed in such community, pursuant to the rules, regulations, and authorizations of the Federal Communications Commission in effect on April 15, 1976, applicable to determining with respect to a cable system whether signals are significantly viewed in a community.

(B) Limitation. — Subparagraph (A) shall apply only to secondary transmissions of the primary transmissions of network stations and superstations to subscribers who receive secondary transmissions from a satellite carrier pursuant to the statutory license under section 122.

(C) Waiver. —

(i) In general. — A subscriber who is denied the secondary transmission of the primary transmission of a network station under subparagraph (B) may request a waiver from such denial by submitting a request, through the subscriber's satellite carrier, to the network station in the local market affiliated with the same network where the subscriber is located. The network station shall accept or reject the subscriber's request for a waiver within 30 days after receipt of the request. If the network station fails to accept or reject the subscriber's request for a waiver within that 30-day period, that network station shall be deemed to agree to the waiver request. Unless specifically stated by the network station, a waiver that was granted before the date of the enactment of the Satellite Home Viewer Extension and Reauthorization Act of 2004 under section 339(c)(2) of the Communications Act of 1934 shall not constitute a waiver for purposes of this subparagraph.

(ii) Sunset. — The authority under clause (i) to grant waivers shall terminate on December 31, 2008, and any such waiver in effect shall terminate on that date.

(4) Statutory license where retransmissions into local market available. —

(A) Rules for subscribers to analog signals under sub-section (e). —

(i) For those receiving distant analog signals. — In the case of a subscriber of a satellite carrier who is eligible to receive the secondary transmission of the primary analog transmission of a network station solely by reason of subsection (e) (in this subparagraph referred to as a "distant analog signal"), and who, as of October 1, 2004, is receiving the distant analog signal of that network station, the following shall apply:

(I) In a case in which the satellite carrier makes available to the subscriber the secondary transmission of the primary analog transmission of a local network station affiliated with the same television network pursuant to the statutory license under section 122, the statutory license under paragraph (2) shall apply only to secondary transmissions by that satellite carrier to that subscriber of the distant analog signal of a station affiliated with the same television network —
(aa) if, within 60 days after receiving the notice of the satellite carrier under section 338(h)(1) of the Communications Act of 1934, the subscriber elects to retain the distant analog signal; but
(bb) only until such time as the subscriber elects to receive such local analog signal.

(II) Notwithstanding subclause (I), the statutory license under paragraph (2) shall not apply with respect to any subscriber who is eligible to receive the distant analog signal of a television network station solely by reason of subsection (e), unless the satellite carrier, within 60 days after the date of the enactment of the Satellite Home Viewer Extension and Reauthorization Act of 2004, submits to that television network a list, aggregated by designated market area (as defined in section 122(j)(2)(C)), that —
(aa) identifies that subscriber by name and address (street or rural route number, city, State, and zip code) and specifies the distant analog signals received by the subscriber; and
(bb) states, to the best of the satellite carrier's knowledge and belief, after having made diligent and good faith inquiries, that the subscriber is eligible under subsection (e) to receive the distant analog signals.

(ii) For those not receiving distant analog signals. — In the case of any subscriber of a satellite carrier who is eligible to receive the distant analog signal of a network station solely by reason of subsection (e) and who did not receive a distant analog signal of a station affiliated with the same network on October 1, 2004, the statutory license under paragraph (2) shall not apply to secondary transmissions by that satellite carrier to that subscriber of the distant analog signal of a station affiliated with the same network.

(B) Rules for other subscribers. — In the case of a subscriber of a satellite carrier who is eligible to receive the secondary transmission of the primary analog transmission of a network station under the statutory license under paragraph (2) (in this subparagraph referred to as a "distant analog signal"), other than subscribers to whom subparagraph (A) applies, the following shall apply:

(i) In a case in which the satellite carrier makes available to that subscriber, on January 1, 2005, the secondary transmission of the primary analog transmission of a local network station affiliated with the same television network pursuant to the statutory license under section 122, the statutory license under paragraph (2) shall apply only to secondary transmissions by that satellite carrier to that subscriber of the distant analog signal of a station affiliated with the same television network if the subscriber's satellite carrier, not later than March 1, 2005, submits to that television network a list, aggregated by designated market area (as defined in section 122(j)(2)(C)), that identifies that subscriber by name and address (street or rural route number, city, State, and zip code) and specifies the distant analog signals received by the subscriber.

(ii) In a case in which the satellite carrier does not make available to that subscriber, on January 1, 2005, the secondary transmission of the primary analog transmission of a local network station affiliated with the same television network pursuant to the statutory license under section 122, the statutory license under paragraph (2) shall apply only to secondary transmissions by that satellite carrier of the distant analog signal of a station affiliated with the same network to that subscriber if —

(I) that subscriber seeks to subscribe to such distant analog signal before the date on which such carrier commences to provide pursuant to the statutory license under section 122 the secondary transmissions of the primary analog transmission of stations from the local market of such local network station; and

(II) the satellite carrier, within 60 days after such date, submits to each television network a list that identifies each subscriber in that local market provided such an analog signal by name and address (street or rural route number, city, State, and zip code) and specifies the distant analog signals received by the subscriber.

(C) Future applicability.—The statutory license under paragraph (2) shall not apply to the secondary transmission by a satellite carrier of a primary analog transmission of a network station to a person who—

(i) is not a subscriber lawfully receiving such secondary transmission as of the date of the enactment of the Satellite Home Viewer Extension and Reauthorization Act of 2004; and

(ii) at the time such person seeks to subscribe to receive such secondary transmission, resides in a local market where the satellite carrier makes available to that person the secondary transmission of the primary analog transmission of a local network station affiliated with the same television network pursuant to the statutory license under section 122, and such secondary transmission of such primary transmission can reach such person.

(D) Special rules for distant digital signals.—The statutory license under paragraph (2) shall apply to secondary transmissions by a satellite carrier to a subscriber of primary digital transmissions of network stations if such secondary transmissions to such subscriber are permitted under section 339(a)(2)(D) of the Communications Act of 1934, as in effect on the day after the date of the enactment of the Satellite Home Viewer Extension and Reauthorization Act of 2004, except that the reference to section 73.683(a) of title 47, Code of Federal Regulations, referred to in section 339(a)(2)(D)(i)(I) shall refer to such section as in effect on the date of the enactment of the Satellite Home Viewer Extension and Reauthorization Act of 2004.

(E) Other provisions not affected.—This paragraph shall not affect the applicability of the statutory license to secondary transmissions under paragraph (3) or to unserved households included under paragraph (12).

(F) Waiver.—A subscriber who is denied the secondary transmission of a network station under subparagraph (C) or (D) may request a waiver from such denial by submitting a request, through the subscriber's satellite carrier, to the network station in the local market affiliated with the same network where the subscriber is located. The network station shall accept or reject the subscriber's request for a waiver within 30 days after receipt of the request. If the network station fails to accept or reject the subscriber's request for a waiver within that 30-day period, that network station shall be deemed to agree to the waiver request. Unless specifically stated by the network station, a waiver that was granted before the date of the enactment of the Satellite Home Viewer Extension and Reauthorization Act of 2004 under section 339(c)(2) of the Communications Act of 1934 shall not constitute a waiver for purposes of this subparagraph.

(G) Available defined.—For purposes of this paragraph, a satellite carrier makes available a secondary transmission of the primary transmission of a local station to a subscriber or person if the satellite carrier offers that secondary transmission to other subscribers who reside in the same zip code as that subscriber or person.

(5) Noncompliance with reporting and payment requirements. — Notwithstanding the provisions of paragraphs (1) and (2), the willful or repeated secondary transmission to the public by a satellite carrier of a primary transmission made by a superstation or a network station and embodying a performance or display of a work is actionable as an act of infringement under section 501, and is fully subject to the remedies provided by sections 502 through 506 and 509, where the satellite carrier has not deposited the statement of account and royalty fee required by subsection (b), or has failed to make the submissions to networks required by paragraph (2)(C).

(6) Willful alterations. — Notwithstanding the provisions of paragraphs (1) and (2), the secondary transmission to the public by a satellite carrier of a performance or display of a work embodied in a primary transmission made by a superstation or a network station is actionable as an act of infringement under section 501, and is fully subject to the remedies provided by sections 502 through 506 and sections 509 and 510, if the content of the particular program in which the performance or display is embodied, or any commercial advertising or station announcement transmitted by the primary transmitter during, or immediately before or after, the transmission of such program, is in any way willfully altered by the satellite carrier through changes, deletions, or additions, or is combined with programming from any other broadcast signal.

(7) Violation of territorial restrictions on statutory license for network stations. —

(A) Individual violations. — The willful or repeated secondary transmission by a satellite carrier of a primary transmission made by a network station and embodying a performance or display of a work to a subscriber who is not eligible to receive the transmission under this section is actionable as an act of infringement under section 501 and is fully subject to the remedies provided by sections 502 through 506 and 509, except that —

(i) no damages shall be awarded for such act of infringement if the satellite carrier took corrective action by promptly withdrawing service from the ineligible subscriber, and

(ii) any statutory damages shall not exceed $5 for such subscriber for each month during which the violation occurred.

(B) Pattern of violations. — If a satellite carrier engages in a willful or repeated pattern or practice of delivering a primary transmission made by a network station and embodying a performance or display of a work to subscribers who are not eligible to receive the transmission under this section, then in addition to the remedies set forth in subparagraph (A) —

(i) if the pattern or practice has been carried out on a substantially nationwide basis, the court shall order a permanent injunction barring the secondary transmission by the satellite carrier, for private home viewing, of the primary transmissions of any primary network station affiliated with the same network, and the court may order statutory damages of not to exceed $250,000 for each 6-month period during which the pattern or practice was carried out; and

(ii) if the pattern or practice has been carried out on a local or regional basis, the court shall order a permanent injunction barring the secondary transmission, for private home viewing in that locality or region, by the satellite carrier of the primary transmissions of any primary network station affiliated with the same network, and the court may order statutory damages of not to exceed $250,000 for each 6-month period during which the pattern or practice was carried out.

(C) Previous subscribers excluded. — Subparagraphs (A) and (B) do not apply to secondary transmissions by a satellite carrier to persons who subscribed to receive such secondary transmissions from the satellite carrier or a distributor before November 16, 1988.

(D) Burden of proof.[57] — In any action brought under this paragraph, the satellite carrier shall have the burden of proving that its secondary transmission of a primary transmission by a network station is to a subscriber who is eligible to receive the secondary transmission under this section.

(E) Exception. — The secondary transmission by a satellite carrier of a performance or display of a work embodied in a primary transmission made by a network station to subscribers who do not reside in unserved households shall not be an act of infringement if —

> (i) the station on May 1, 1991, was retransmitted by a satellite carrier and was not on that date owned or operated by or affiliated with a television network that offered interconnected program service on a regular basis for 15 or more hours per week to at least 25 affiliated television licensees in 10 or more States;

> (ii) as of July 1, 1998, such station was retransmitted by a satellite carrier under the statutory license of this section; and

> (iii) the station is not owned or operated by or affiliated with a television network that, as of January 1, 1995, offered interconnected program service on a regular basis for 15 or more hours per week to at least 25 affiliated television licensees in 10 or more States.

(8) Discrimination by a satellite carrier. — Notwithstanding the provisions of paragraph (1), the willful or repeated secondary transmission to the public by a satellite carrier of a performance or display of a work embodied in a primary transmission made by a superstation or a network station is actionable as an act of infringement under section 501, and is fully subject to the remedies provided by sections 502 through 506 and 509, if the satellite carrier unlawfully discriminates against a distributor.[58]

(9) Geographic limitation on secondary transmissions. — The statutory license created by this section shall apply only to secondary transmissions to households located in the United States.

(10) Loser pays for signal intensity measurement; recovery of measurement costs in a civil action. — In any civil action filed relating to the eligibility of subscribing households as unserved households —

> (A) a network station challenging such eligibility shall, within 60 days after receipt of the measurement results and a statement of such costs, reimburse the satellite carrier for any signal intensity measurement that is conducted by that carrier in response to a challenge by the network station and that establishes the household is an unserved household; and

> (B) a satellite carrier shall, within 60 days after receipt of the measurement results and a statement of such costs, reimburse the network station challenging such eligibility for any signal intensity measurement that is conducted by that station and that establishes the household is not an unserved household.

(11) Inability to conduct measurement. — If a network station makes a reasonable attempt to conduct a site measurement of its signal at a subscriber's household and is denied access for the purpose of conducting the measurement, and is otherwise unable to conduct a measurement,

the satellite carrier shall within 60 days notice thereof, terminate service of the station's network to that household.

(12) Service to recreational vehicles and commercial trucks. —

  (A) Exemption. —

   (i) In general. — For purposes of this subsection, and subject to clauses (ii) and (iii), the term "unserved household" shall include —

    (I) recreational vehicles as defined in regulations of the Secretary of Housing and Urban Development under section 3282.8 of title 24 of the Code of Federal Regulations; and

    (II) commercial trucks that qualify as commercial motor vehicles under regulations of the Secretary of Transportation under section 383.5 of title 49 of the Code of Federal Regulations.

   (ii) Limitation. — Clause (i) shall apply only to a recreational vehicle or commercial truck if any satellite carrier that proposes to make a secondary transmission of a network station to the operator of such a recreational vehicle or commercial truck complies with the documentation requirements under subparagraphs (B) and (C).

   (iii) Exclusion. — For purposes of this subparagraph, the terms "recreational vehicle" and "commercial truck" shall not include any fixed dwelling, whether a mobile home or otherwise.

  (B) Documentation requirements. — A recreational vehicle or commercial truck shall be deemed to be an unserved household beginning 10 days after the relevant satellite carrier provides to the network that owns or is affiliated with the network station that will be secondarily transmitted to the recreational vehicle or commercial truck the following documents:

   (i) Declaration. — A signed declaration by the operator of the recreational vehicle or commercial truck that the satellite dish is permanently attached to the recreational vehicle or commercial truck, and will not be used to receive satellite programming at any fixed dwelling.

   (ii) Registration. — In the case of a recreational vehicle, a copy of the current State vehicle registration for the recreational vehicle.

   (iii) Registration and license. — In the case of a commercial truck, a copy of —

    (I) the current State vehicle registration for the truck; and

    (II) a copy of a valid, current commercial driver's license, as defined in regulations of the Secretary of Transportation under section 383 of title 49 of the Code of Federal Regulations, issued to the operator.

  (C) Updated documentation requirements. — If a satellite carrier wishes to continue to make secondary transmissions to a recreational vehicle or commercial truck for more than a 2-year period, that carrier shall provide each network, upon request, with updated documentation in the form described under subparagraph (B) during the 90 days before expiration of that 2-year period.

(13) Statutory license contingent on compliance with FCC rules and remedial steps. — Notwithstanding any other provision of this section, the willful or repeated secondary transmission to the public by a satellite carrier of a primary transmission embodying a performance or display of a work made by a broadcast station licensed by the Federal Communications Commission is actionable as an act of infringement under section 501, and is fully subject to the remedies provided by sections 502 through 506 and 509, if, at the time of such transmission, the satellite carrier is not in compliance with the rules, regulations, and authorizations of the Federal Communications Commission concerning the carriage of television broadcast station signals.[59]

(14) Waivers. — A subscriber who is denied the secondary transmission of a signal of a network station under subsection (a)(2)(B) may request a waiver from such denial by submitting a request, through the subscriber's satellite carrier, to the network station asserting that the secondary transmission is prohibited. The network station shall accept or reject a subscriber's request for a waiver within 30 days after receipt of the request. If a television network station fails to accept or reject a subscriber's request for a waiver within the 30-day period after receipt of the request, that station shall be deemed to agree to the waiver request and have filed such written waiver. Unless specifically stated by the network station, a waiver that was granted before the date of the enactment of the Satellite Home Viewer Extension and Reauthorization Act of 2004 under section 339(c)(2) of the Communications Act of 1934, and that was in effect on such date of enactment, shall constitute a waiver for purposes of this paragraph.

(15) Carriage of low power television stations. —

(A) In general. — Notwithstanding paragraph (2)(B), and subject to subparagraphs (B) through (F) of this paragraph, the statutory license provided for in paragraphs (1) and (2) shall apply to the secondary transmission of the primary transmission of a network station or a superstation that is licensed as a low power television station, to a subscriber who resides within the same local market.

(B) Geographic limitation. —

(i) Network stations. — With respect to network stations, secondary transmissions provided for in subparagraph (A) shall be limited to secondary transmissions to subscribers who —

(I) reside in the same local market as the station originating the signal; and

(II) reside within 35 miles of the transmitter site of such station, except that in the case of such a station located in a standard metropolitan statistical area which has 1 of the 50 largest populations of all standard metropolitan statistical areas (based on the 1980 decennial census of population taken by the Secretary of Commerce), the number of miles shall be 20.

(ii) Superstations. — With respect to superstations, secondary transmissions provided for in subparagraph (A) shall be limited to secondary transmissions to subscribers who reside in the same local market as the station originating the signal.

(C) No applicability to repeaters and translators. — Secondary transmissions provided for in subparagraph (A) shall not apply to any low power television station that retransmits the programs and signals of another television station for more than 2 hours each day.

(D) Royalty fees. — Notwithstanding subsection (b)(1)(B), a satellite carrier whose secondary transmissions of the primary transmissions of a low power television station are subject to statutory licensing under this section shall have no royalty obligation for secondary transmissions to a subscriber who resides within 35 miles of the transmitter site of such station, except that in the case of such a station located in a standard metropolitan statistical area which has 1 of the 50 largest populations of all standard metropolitan statistical areas (based on the 1980 decennial census of population taken by the Secretary of Commerce), the number of miles shall be 20. Carriage of a superstation that is a low power television station within the station's local market, but outside of the 35-mile or 20-mile radius described in the preceding sentence, shall be subject to royalty payments under subsection (b)(1)(B).

(E) Limitation to subscribers taking local-into-local service. — Secondary transmissions provided for in subparagraph (A) may be made only to subscribers who receive secondary transmissions of primary transmissions from that satellite carrier pursuant to the statutory license under section 122, and only in conformity with the requirements under 340(b) of the Communications Act of 1934, as in effect on the date of the enactment of the Satellite Home Viewer Extension and Reauthorization Act of 2004.[60]

(16) Restricted transmission of out-of-state distant network signals into certain markets. —

(A) Out-of-state network affiliates. — Notwithstanding any other provision of this title, the statutory license in this subsection and subsection (b) shall not apply to any secondary transmission of the primary transmission of a network station located outside of the State of Alaska to any subscriber in that State to whom the secondary transmission of the primary transmission of a television station located in that State is made available by the satellite carrier pursuant to section 122.

(B) Exception. — The limitation in subparagraph (A) shall not apply to the secondary transmission of the primary transmission of a digital signal of a network station located outside of the State of Alaska if at the time that the secondary transmission is made, no television station licensed to a community in the State and affiliated with the same network makes primary transmissions of a digital signal.

(b) Statutory License for Secondary Transmissions. —

(1) Deposits with the Register of Copyrights. — A satellite carrier whose secondary transmissions are subject to statutory licensing under subsection (a) shall, on a semiannual basis, deposit with the Register of Copyrights, in accordance with requirements that the Register shall prescribe by regulation —

(A) a statement of account, covering the preceding 6-month period, specifying the names and locations of all superstations and network stations whose signals were retransmitted, at any time during that period, to subscribers as described in subsections (a)(1) and (a)(2), the total number of subscribers that received such retransmissions, and such other data as the Register of Copyrights may from time to time prescribe by regulation; and

(B) a royalty fee for that 6-month period, computed by multiplying the total number of subscribers receiving each secondary transmission of each superstation or network station during each calendar month by the appropriate rate in effect under this section.

Notwithstanding the provisions of subparagraph (B), a satellite carrier whose secondary transmissions are subject to statutory licensing under paragraph (1) or (2) of subsection (a) shall have no royalty obligation for secondary transmissions to a subscriber under paragraph (3) of such subsection.

(2) Investment of fees. — The Register of Copyrights shall receive all fees deposited under this section and, after deducting the reasonable costs incurred by the Copyright Office under this section (other than the costs deducted under paragraph (4)), shall deposit the balance in the Treasury of the United States, in such manner as the Secretary of the Treasury directs. All funds held by the Secretary of the Treasury shall be invested in interest-bearing securities of the United States for later distribution with interest by the Librarian of Congress as provided by this title.

(3) Persons to whom fees are distributed. — The royalty fees deposited under paragraph (2) shall, in accordance with the procedures provided by paragraph (4), be distributed to those copyright owners whose works were included in a secondary transmission made by a satellite carrier during the applicable 6-month accounting period and who file a claim with the Copyright Royalty Judges under paragraph (4).

(4) Procedures for distribution. — The royalty fees deposited under paragraph (2) shall be distributed in accordance with the following procedures:

(A) Filing of claims for fees. — During the month of July in each year, each person claiming to be entitled to statutory license fees for secondary transmissions shall file a claim with the Copyright Royalty Judges, in accordance with requirements that the Copyright Royalty Judges shall prescribe by regulation. For purposes of this paragraph, any claimants may agree among themselves as to the proportionate division of statutory license fees among them, may lump their claims together and file them jointly or as a single claim, or may designate a common agent to receive payment on their behalf.

(B) Determination of controversy; distributions. — After the first day of August of each year, the Copyright Royalty Judges shall determine whether there exists a controversy concerning the distribution of royalty fees. If the Copyright Royalty Judges determine that no such controversy exists, the Copyright Royalty Judges shall authorize the Librarian of Congress to proceed to distribute such fees to the copyright owners entitled to receive them, or to their designated agents, subject to the deduction of reasonable administrative costs under this section. If the Copyright Royalty Judges find the existence of a controversy, the Copyright Royalty Judges shall, pursuant to chapter 8 of this title, conduct a proceeding to determine the distribution of royalty fees.

(C) Withholding of fees during controversy. — During the pendency of any proceeding under this subsection, the Copyright Royalty Judges shall have the discretion to authorize the Librarian of Congress to proceed to distribute any amounts that are not in controversy.

(c) Adjustment of Royalty Fees. —

  (1) Applicability and determination of royalty fees for analog signals. —

    (A) Initial fee. — The appropriate fee for purposes of determining the royalty fee under subsection (b)(1)(B) for the secondary transmission of the primary analog transmissions of network stations and superstations shall be the appropriate fee set forth in part 258 of title 37, Code of Federal Regulations, as in effect on July 1, 2004, as modified under this paragraph.

    (B) Fee set by voluntary negotiation. — On or before January 2, 2005, the Librarian of Congress shall cause to be published in the Federal Register of the initiation of voluntary negotiation proceedings for the purpose of determining the royalty fee to be paid by satellite carriers for the secondary transmission of the primary analog transmission of network stations and superstations under subsection (b)(1)(B).

    (C) Negotiations. — Satellite carriers, distributors, and copyright owners entitled to royalty fees under this section shall negotiate in good faith in an effort to reach a voluntary agreement or agreements for the payment of royalty fees. Any such satellite carriers, distributors and copyright owners may at any time negotiate and agree to the royalty fee, and may designate common agents to negotiate, agree to, or pay such fees. If the parties fail to identify common agents, the Librarian of Congress shall do so, after requesting recommendations from the parties to the negotiation proceeding. The parties to each negotiation proceeding shall bear the cost thereof.

    (D) Agreements binding on parties; filing of agreements; public notice. — (i) Voluntary agreements negotiated at any time in accordance with this paragraph shall be binding upon all satellite carriers, distributors, and copyright owners that a parties thereto. Copies of such agreements shall be filed with the Copyright Office within 30 days after execution in accordance with regulations that the Register of Copyrights shall prescribe.

      (ii)(I) Within 10 days after publication in the Federal Register of a notice of the initiation of voluntary negotiation proceedings, parties who have reached a voluntary agreement may request that the royalty fees in that agreement be applied to all satellite carriers, distributors, and copyright owners without convening an arbitration proceeding pursuant to subparagraph (E).

      (II) Upon receiving a request under subclause (I), the Librarian of Congress shall immediately provide public notice of the royalty fees from the voluntary agreement and afford parties an opportunity to state that they object to those fees.

      (III) The Librarian shall adopt the royalty fees from the voluntary agreement for all satellite carriers, distributors, and copyright owners without convening an arbitration proceeding unless a party with an intent to participate in the arbitration proceeding and a significant interest in the outcome of that proceeding objects under subclause (II).

    (E) Period agreement is in effect. — The obligation to pay the royalty fees established under a voluntary agreement which has been filed with the Copyright Office in accordance with this paragraph shall become effective on the date specified in the agreement, and shall remain in effect until December 31, 2009, or in accordance with the terms of the agreement, whichever is later.

(F) Fee set by compulsory arbitration. —

(i) Notice of initiation of proceedings. — On or before May 1, 2005, the Librarian of Congress shall cause notice to be published in the Federal Register of the initiation of arbitration proceedings for the purpose of determining the royalty fee to be paid for the secondary transmission of primary analog transmission of network stations and superstations under subsection (b)(1)(B) by satellite carriers and distributors

(I) in the absence of a voluntary agreement filed in accordance with subparagraph (D) that establishes royalty fees to be paid by all satellite carriers and distributors; or

(II) if an objection to the fees from a voluntary agreement submitted for adoption by the Librarian of Congress to apply to all satellite carriers, distributors, and copyright owners is received under subparagraph (D) from a party with an intent to participate in the arbitration proceeding and a significant interest in the outcome of that proceeding.

Such arbitration proceeding shall be conducted under chapter 8 as in effect on the day before the date of the enactment of the Copyright Royalty and Distribution Act of 2004.

(ii) Establishment of royalty fees. — In determining royalty fees under this subparagraph, the copyright arbitration royalty panel appointed under chapter 8, as in effect on the day before the date of the enactment of the Copyright Royalty and Distribution Act of 2004 shall establish fees for the secondary transmissions of the primary analog transmission of network stations and superstations that most clearly represent the fair market value of secondary transmissions, except that the Librarian of Congress and any copyright arbitration royalty panel shall adjust those fees to account for the obligations of the parties under any applicable voluntary agreement filed with the Copyright Office pursuant to subparagraph (D). In determining the fair market value, the panel shall base its decision on economic, competitive, and programming information presented by the parties, including —

(I) the competitive environment in which such programming is distributed, the cost of similar signals in similar private and compulsory license marketplaces, and any special features and conditions of the retransmission marketplace;

(II) the economic impact of such fees on copyright owners and satellite carriers; and

(III) the impact on the continued availability of secondary transmissions to the public.

(iii) Period during which decision of arbitration panel or order of librarian effective. — The obligation to pay the royalty fee established under a determination which —

(I) is made by a copyright arbitration royalty panel in an arbitration proceeding under this paragraph and is adopted by the Librarian of Congress under section 802(f), as in effect on the day before the date of the enactment of the Copyright Royalty and Distribution Act of 2004; or

(II) is established by the Librarian under section 802(f) as in effect on the day before such date of enactment shall be effective as of January 1, 2005.

(iv) Persons subject to royalty fee. — The royalty fee referred to in (iii) shall be binding on all satellite carriers, distributors and copyright owners, who are not party to a voluntary agreement filed with the Copyright Office under subparagraph (D).

(2) Applicability and determination of royalty fees for digital signals. — The process and requirements for establishing the royalty fee payable under subsection (b)(1)(B) for the secondary transmission of the primary digital transmissions of network stations and superstations shall be the same as that set forth in paragraph (1) for the secondary transmission of the primary analog transmission of network stations and superstations, except that —

(A) the initial fee under paragraph (1)(A) shall be the rates set forth in section 298.3(b)(1) and (2) of title 37, Code of Federal Regulations, as in effect on the date of the enactment of the Satellite Home Viewer Extension and Reauthorization Act of 2004, reduced by 22.5 percent;

(B) the notice of initiation of arbitration proceedings required in paragraph (1)(F)(i) shall be published on or before December 31, 2005; and

(C) the royalty fees that are established for the secondary transmission of the primary digital transmission of network stations and superstations in accordance with to the procedures set forth in paragraph (1)(F)(iii) and are payable under subsection (b)(1)(B) —

(i) shall be reduced by 22.5 percent; and

(ii) shall be adjusted by the Librarian of Congress on January 1, 2007, and on January 1 of each year thereafter, to reflect any changes occurring during the preceding 12 months in the cost of living as determined by the most recent Consumer Price Index (for all consumers and items) published by the Secretary of Labor.

(d) Definitions. — As used in this section —

(1) Distributor. — The term "distributor" means an entity which contracts to distribute secondary transmissions from a satellite carrier and, either as a single channel or in a package with other programming, provides the secondary transmission either directly to individual subscribers or indirectly through other program distribution entities in accordance with the provisions of this section.

(2) Network station. — The term "network station" means —

(A) a television station licensed by the Federal Communications Commission, including any translator station or terrestrial satellite station that rebroadcasts all or substantially all of the programming broadcast by a network station, that is owned or operated by, or affiliated with, one or more of the television networks in the United States which offer an interconnected program service on a regular basis for 15 or more hours per week to at least 25 of its affiliated television licensees in 10 or more States; or

(B) a noncommercial educational broadcast station (as defined in section 397 of the Communications Act of 1934).

(3) Primary network station. — The term "primary network station" means a network station that broadcasts or rebroadcasts the basic programming service of a particular national network.

(4) Primary transmission. — The term "primary transmission" has the meaning given that term in section 111(f) of this title.

(5) Private home viewing. — The term "private home viewing" means the viewing, for private use in a household by means of satellite reception equipment which is operated by an individual in that household and which serves only such household, of a secondary transmission delivered by a satellite carrier of a primary transmission of a television station licensed by the Federal Communications Commission.

(6) Satellite carrier. — The term "satellite carrier" means an entity that uses the facilities of a satellite or satellite service licensed by the Federal Communications Commission and operates in the Fixed-Satellite Service under part 25 of title 47 of the Code of Federal Regulations or the Direct Broadcast Satellite Service under part 100 of title 47 of the Code of Federal Regulations to establish and operate a channel of communications for point-to-multipoint distribution of television station signals, and that owns or leases a capacity or service on a satellite in order to provide such point-to-multipoint distribution, except to the extent that such entity provides such distribution pursuant to tariff under the Communications Act of 1934, other than for private home viewing pursuant to this section.

(7) Secondary transmission. — The term "secondary transmission" has the meaning given that term in section 111(f) of this title.

(8) Subscriber. — The term "subscriber" means an individual or entity that receives a secondary transmission service by means of a secondary transmission from a satellite carrier and pays a fee for the service, directly or indirectly, to the satellite carrier or to a distributor in accordance with the provisions of this section.

(9) Superstation. — The term "superstation" means a television station, other than a network station, licensed by the Federal Communications Commission, that is secondarily transmitted by a satellite carrier.

(10) Unserved household. — The term "unserved household", with respect to a particular television network, means a household that —

    (A) cannot receive, through the use of a conventional, stationary, outdoor rooftop receiving antenna, an over-the-air signal of a primary network station affiliated with that network of Grade B intensity as defined by the Federal Communications Commission under section 73.683(a) of title 47 of the Code of Federal Regulations, as in effect on January 1, 1999;

    (B) is subject to a waiver that meets the standards of subsection (a)(14) whether or not the waiver was granted before the date of the enactment of the Satellite Home Viewer Extension and Reauthorization Act of 2004;[61]

    (C) is a subscriber to whom subsection (e) applies;

(D) is a subscriber to whom subsection (a)(12) applies; or

(E) is a subscriber to whom the exemption under subsection (a)(2)(B)(iii) applies.

(11) Local market. — The term "local market" has the meaning given such term under section 122(j), except that with respect to a low power television station, the term "local market" means the designated market area in which the station is located.

(12) Low power television station. — The term "low power television station" means a low power television as defined under section 74.701(f) of title 47, Code of Federal Regulations, as in effect on June 1, 2004. For purposes of this paragraph, the term "low power television station" includes a low power television station that has been accorded primary status as a Class A television licensee under section 73.6001(a) of title 47, Code of Federal Regulations.

(13) Commercial establishment. — The term "commercial establishment" —

(A) means an establishment used for commercial purposes, such as a bar, restaurant, private office, fitness club, oil rig, retail store, bank or other financial institution, supermarket, automobile or boat dealership, or any other establishment with a common business area; and

(B) does not include a multi-unit permanent or temporary dwelling where private home viewing occurs, such as a hotel, dormitory, hospital, apartment, condominium, or prison.

(e) Moratorium on Copyright Liability. — Until December 31, 2009, a subscriber who does not receive a signal of Grade A intensity (as defined in the regulations of the Federal Communications Commission under section 73.683(a) of title 47 of the Code of Federal Regulations, as in effect on January 1, 1999, or predicted by the Federal Communications Commission using the Individual Location Longley-Rice methodology described by the Federal Communications Commission in Docket No. 98-201) of a local network television broadcast station shall remain eligible to receive signals of network stations affiliated with the same network, if that subscriber had satellite service of such network signal terminated after July 11, 1998, and before October 31, 1999, as required by this section, or received such service on October 31, 1999.

(f) Expedited Consideration by Justice Department of Voluntary Agreements to Provide Satellite Secondary Transmissions to Local Markets. —

(1) In general. — In a case in which no satellite carrier makes available, to subscribers located in a local market, as defined in section 122(j)(2), the secondary transmission into that market of a primary transmission of one or more television broadcast stations licensed by the Federal Communications Commission, and two or more satellite carriers request a business review letter in accordance with section 50.6 of title 28, Code of Federal Regulations (as in effect on July 7, 2004), in order to assess the legality under the antitrust laws of proposed business conduct to make or carry out an agreement to provide such secondary transmission into such local market, the appropriate official of the Department of Justice shall respond to the request no later than 90 days after the date on which the request is received.

(2) Definition. — For purposes of this subsection, the term "antitrust laws" —

(A) has the meaning given that term in subsection (a) of the first section of the Clayton Act (15 U.S.C. 12(a)), except that such term includes section 5 of the Federal Trade Commission Act (15 U.S.C. 45) to the extent such section 5 applies to unfair methods of competition; and

(B) includes any State law similar to the laws referred to in paragraph (1).

§ 120. Scope of exclusive rights in architectural works[62]

(a) Pictorial Representations Permitted. — The copyright in an architectural work that has been constructed does not include the right to prevent the making, distributing, or public display of pictures, paintings, photographs, or other pictorial representations of the work, if the building in which the work is embodied is located in or ordinarily visible from a public place.

(b) Alterations to and Destruction of Buildings. — Notwithstanding the provisions of section 106(2), the owners of a building embodying an architectural work may, without the consent of the author or copyright owner of the architectural work, make or authorize the making of alterations to such building, and destroy or authorize the destruction of such building.

§ 121. Limitations on exclusive rights: reproduction for blind or other people with disabilities[63]

(a) Notwithstanding the provisions of section 106, it is not an infringement of copyright for an authorized entity to reproduce or to distribute copies or phonorecords of a previously published, nondramatic literary work if such copies or phonorecords are reproduced or distributed in specialized formats exclusively for use by blind or other persons with disabilities.

(b)(1) Copies or phonorecords to which this section applies shall —

(A) not be reproduced or distributed in a format other than a specialized format exclusively for use by blind or other persons with disabilities;

(B) bear a notice that any further reproduction or distribution in a format other than a specialized format is an infringement; and

(C) include a copyright notice identifying the copyright owner and the date of the original publication.

(2) The provisions of this subsection shall not apply to standardized, secure, or norm-referenced tests and related testing material, or to computer programs, except the portions thereof that are in conventional human language (including descriptions of pictorial works) and displayed to users in the ordinary course of using the computer programs.

(c) Notwithstanding the provisions of section 106, it is not an infringement of copyright for a publisher of print instructional materials for use in elementary or secondary schools to create and distribute to the National Instructional Materials Access Center copies of the electronic files described in sections 612(a)(23)(C), 613(a)(6), and section 674(e) of the Individuals with Disabilities Education Act that contain the contents of print instructional materials using the National Instructional Material Accessibility Standard (as defined in section 674(e)(3) of that Act), if —

(1) the inclusion of the contents of such print instructional materials is required by any State educational agency or local educational agency;

(2) the publisher had the right to publish such print instructional materials in print formats; and

(3) such copies are used solely for reproduction or distribution of the contents of such print instructional materials in specialized formats.

(d) For purposes of this section, the term —

(1) "authorized entity" means a nonprofit organization or a governmental agency that has a primary mission to provide specialized services relating to training, education, or adaptive reading or information access needs of blind or other persons with disabilities;

(2) "blind or other persons with disabilities" means individuals who are eligible or who may qualify in accordance with the Act entitled "An Act to provide books for the adult blind", approved March 3, 1931 (2 U.S.C. 135a; 46 Stat. 1487) to receive books and other publications produced in specialized formats; and

(3) "print instructional materials" has the meaning given under section 674(e)(3)(C) of the Individuals with Disabilities Education Act; and

(4) "specialized formats" means —

(A) braille, audio, or digital text which is exclusively for use by blind or other persons with disabilities; and

(B) with respect to print instructional materials, includes large print formats when such materials are distributed exclusively for use by blind or other persons with disabilities.

§ 122. *Limitations on exclusive rights; secondary transmissions by satellite carriers within local markets*[64]

(a) Secondary Transmissions of Television Broadcast Stations by Satellite Carriers. — A secondary transmission of a performance or display of a work embodied in a primary transmission of a television broadcast station into the station's local market shall be subject to statutory licensing under this section if —

(1) the secondary transmission is made by a satellite carrier to the public;

(2) with regard to secondary transmissions, the satellite carrier is in compliance with the rules, regulations, or authorizations of the Federal Communications Commission governing the carriage of television broadcast station signals; and

(3) the satellite carrier makes a direct or indirect charge for the secondary transmission to —

(A) each subscriber receiving the secondary transmission; or

(B) a distributor that has contracted with the satellite carrier for direct or indirect delivery of the secondary transmission to the public.

(b) Reporting Requirements. —

(1) Initial lists. — A satellite carrier that makes secondary transmissions of a primary transmission made by a network station under subsection (a) shall, within 90 days after commencing such secondary transmissions, submit to the network that owns or is affiliated with the network station a list identifying (by name in alphabetical order and street address, including county and zip code) all subscribers to which the satellite carrier makes secondary transmissions of that primary transmission under subsection (a).

(2) Subsequent lists. — After the list is submitted under paragraph (1), the satellite carrier shall, on the 15th of each month, submit to the network a list identifying (by name in alphabetical order and street address, including county and zip code) any subscribers who have been added or dropped as subscribers since the last submission under this subsection.

(3) Use of subscriber information. — Subscriber information submitted by a satellite carrier under this subsection may be used only for the purposes of monitoring compliance by the satellite carrier with this section.

(4) Requirements of networks. — The submission requirements of this subsection shall apply to a satellite carrier only if the network to which the submissions are to be made places on file with the Register of Copyrights a document identifying the name and address of the person to whom such submissions are to be made. The Register of Copyrights shall maintain for public inspection a file of all such documents.

(c) No Royalty Fee Required. — A satellite carrier whose secondary transmissions are subject to statutory licensing under subsection (a) shall have no royalty obligation for such secondary transmissions.

(d) Noncompliance with Reporting and Regulatory Requirements. — Notwithstanding subsection (a), the willful or repeated secondary transmission to the public by a satellite carrier into the local market of a television broadcast station of a primary transmission embodying a performance or display of a work made by that television broadcast station is actionable as an act of infringement under section 501, and is fully subject to the remedies provided under sections 502 through 506 and 509, if the satellite carrier has not complied with the reporting requirements of subsection (b) or with the rules, regulations, and authorizations of the Federal Communications Commission concerning the carriage of television broadcast signals.

(e) Willful Alterations. — Notwithstanding subsection (a), the secondary transmission to the public by a satellite carrier into the local market of a television broadcast station of a performance or display of a work embodied in a primary transmission made by that television broadcast station is actionable as an act of infringement under section 501, and is fully subject to the remedies provided by sections 502 through 506 and sections 509 and 510, if the content of the particular program in which the performance or display is embodied, or any commercial advertising or station announcement transmitted by the primary transmitter during, or immediately before or after, the transmission of such program, is in any way willfully altered by the satellite carrier through changes, deletions, or additions, or is combined with programming from any other broadcast signal.

(f) Violation of Territorial Restrictions on Statutory License for Television Broadcast Stations. —

(1) Individual violations. — The willful or repeated secondary transmission to the public by a satellite carrier of a primary transmission embodying a performance or display of a work made by a television broadcast station to a subscriber who does not reside in that station's local market, and is not subject to statutory licensing under section 119 or a private licensing agreement, is actionable as an act of infringement under section 501 and is fully subject to the remedies provided by sections 502 through 506 and 509, except that —

(A) no damages shall be awarded for such act of infringement if the satellite carrier took corrective action by promptly withdrawing service from the ineligible subscriber; and

(B) any statutory damages shall not exceed $5 for such subscriber for each month during which the violation occurred.

(2) Pattern of violations. — If a satellite carrier engages in a willful or repeated pattern or practice of secondarily transmitting to the public a primary transmission embodying a performance or display of a work made by a television broadcast station to subscribers who do not reside in that station's local market, and are not subject to statutory licensing under section 119 or a private licensing agreement, then in addition to the remedies under paragraph (1) —

(A) if the pattern or practice has been carried out on a substantially nationwide basis, the court —

(i) shall order a permanent injunction barring the secondary transmission by the satellite carrier of the primary transmissions of that television broadcast station (and if such television broadcast station is a network station, all other television broadcast stations affiliated with such network); and

(ii) may order statutory damages not exceeding $250,000 for each 6-month period during which the pattern or practice was carried out; and

(B) if the pattern or practice has been carried out on a local or regional basis with respect to more than one television broadcast station, the court —

(i) shall order a permanent injunction barring the secondary transmission in that locality or region by the satellite carrier of the primary transmissions of any television broadcast station; and

(ii) may order statutory damages not exceeding $250,000 for each 6-month period during which the pattern or practice was carried out.

(g) Burden of Proof. — In any action brought under subsection (f), the satellite carrier shall have the burden of proving that its secondary transmission of a primary transmission by a television broadcast station is made only to subscribers located within that station's local market or subscribers being served in compliance with section 119 or a private licensing agreement.

(h) Geographic Limitations on Secondary Transmissions. — The statutory license created by this section shall apply to secondary transmissions to locations in the United States.

(i) Exclusivity with Respect to Secondary Transmissions of Broadcast Stations by Satellite to Members of the Public. — No provision of section 111 or any other law (other than this section and section 119) shall be construed to contain any authorization, exemption, or license through which secondary transmissions by satellite carriers of programming contained in a primary transmission made by a television broadcast station may be made without obtaining the consent of the copyright owner.

(j) Definitions. — In this section —

(1) Distributor. — The term "distributor" means an entity which contracts to distribute secondary transmissions from a satellite carrier and, either as a single channel or in a package with other programming, provides the secondary transmission either directly to individual subscribers or indirectly through other program distribution entities.

(2) Local market. —

(A) In general. — The term "local market", in the case of both commercial and noncommercial television broadcast stations, means the designated market area in which a station is located, and —

(i) in the case of a commercial television broadcast station, all commercial television broadcast stations licensed to a community within the same designated market area are within the same local market; and

(ii) in the case of a noncommercial educational television broadcast station, the market includes any station that is licensed to a community within the same designated market area as the noncommercial educational television broadcast station.

(B) County of license. — In addition to the area described in subparagraph (A), a station's local market includes the county in which the station's community of license is located.

(C) Designated market area. — For purposes of subparagraph (A), the term "designated market area" means a designated market area, as determined by Nielsen Media Research and published in the 1999-2000 Nielsen Station Index Directory and Nielsen Station Index United States Television Household Estimates or any successor publication.

(D) Certain areas outside of any designated market area. — Any census area, borough, or other area in the State of Alaska that is outside of a designated market area, as determined by Nielsen Media Research, shall be deemed to be part of one of the local markets in the State of Alaska.

A satellite carrier may determine which local market in the State of Alaska will be deemed to be the relevant local market in connection with each subscriber in such census area, borough, or other area.

(3) Network station; satellite carrier; secondary transmission. — The terms "network station", "satellite carrier", and "secondary transmission" have the meanings given such terms under section 119(d).

(4) Subscriber. — The term "subscriber" means a person who receives a secondary transmission service from a satellite carrier and pays a fee for the service, directly or indirectly, to the satellite carrier or to a distributor.

(5) Television broadcast station. — The term "television broadcast station" —

(A) means an over-the-air, commercial or noncommercial television broadcast station licensed by the Federal Communications Commission under subpart E of part 73 of title 47, Code of Federal Regulations, except that such term does not include a low-power or translator television station; and

(B) includes a television broadcast station licensed by an appropriate governmental authority of Canada or Mexico if the station broadcasts primarily in the English language and is a network station as defined in section 119(d)(2)(A).

Chapter 1 Endnotes

[1] In 1980, section 117 was amended in its entirety and given a new title. However, the table of sections was not changed to reflect the new title. Pub. L. No. 96-517, 94 Stat. 3015, 3028. In 1997, a technical amendment made that change. Pub. L. No. 105-80, 111 Stat. 1529, 1534.

[2] The Audio Home Recording Act of 1992 amended section 101 by inserting "Except as otherwise provided in this title," at the beginning of the first sentence. Pub. L. No. 102-563, 106 Stat. 4237, 4248.

The Berne Convention Implementation Act of 1988 amended section 101 by adding a definition for "Berne Convention work." Pub. L. No. 100-568, 102 Stat. 2853, 2854. In 1990, the Architectural Works Copyright Protection Act amended the definition of "Berne Convention work" by adding paragraph (5). Pub. L. No. 101-650, 104 Stat. 5089, 5133. The WIPO Copyright and Performances and Phonograms Treaties Implementation Act of 1998 deleted the definition of "Berne Convention work" from section 101. Pub. L. No. 105-304, 112 Stat. 2860, 2861. The definition of "Berne Convention work," as deleted, as deleted, is contained in Appendix L.

[3] In 1990, the Architectural Works Copyright Protection Act amended section 101 by adding the definition for "architectural work." Pub. L. No. 101-650, 104 Stat. 5089, 5133. That Act states that the definition is applicable to "any architectural work that, on the date of the enactment of this Act, is unconstructed and embodied in unpublished plans or drawings, except that protection for such architectural work under title 17, United States Code, by virtue of the amendments made by this title, shall terminate on December 31, 2002, unless the work is constructed by that date."

[4] The Berne Convention Implementation Act of 1988 amended section 101 by adding the definition of "Berne Convention." Pub. L. No. 100-568, 102 Stat. 2853, 2854.

[5] In 1980, the definition of "computer program" was added to section 101 and placed at the end. Pub. L. No. 96-517, 94 Stat. 3015, 3028. The Intellectual Property and High Technology Technical Amendments Act of 2002 amended section 101 by moving the definition for computer program from the end of section 101 to be in alphabetical order, after "compilation." Pub. L. No. 107-273, 116 Stat. 1758, 1909.

[6] The Copyright Royalty and Distribution Reform Act of 2004 amended section 101 by adding the definition for "Copyright Royalty Judge." It inserted the definition in the wrong alphabetical order, placing it after "copies," instead of "copyright owner." Pub. L. No. 108-419, 118 Stat. 2341, 2361.

[7] The Digital Performance Right in Sound Recordings Act of 1995 amended section 101 by adding the definition of "digital transmission." Pub. L. No.104-39, 109 Stat. 336, 348.

[8] The Fairness in Music Licensing Act of 1998 amended section 101 by adding the definition of "establishment." Pub. L. No. 105-298, 112 Stat. 2827, 2833.

[9] The Fairness in Music Licensing Act of 1998 amended section 101 by adding the definition of "food service or drinking establishment." Pub. L. No. 105-298, 112 Stat. 2827, 2833.

[10] In 1997, the No Electronic Theft (NET) Act amended section 101 by adding the definition for "financial gain." Pub. L. No. 105-147, 111 Stat. 2678.

[11] The WIPO Copyright and Performances and Phonograms Treaties Implementation Act of 1998 amended section 101 by adding the definition of "Geneva Phonograms Convention." Pub. L. No. 105-304, 112 Stat. 2860, 2861.

[12] The Fairness in Music Licensing Act of 1998 amended section 101 by adding the definition of "gross square feet of space." Pub. L. No. 105-298, 112 Stat. 2827, 2833.

[13] The WIPO Copyright and Performances and Phonograms Treaties Implementation Act of 1998 requires that paragraph (5) of the definition of "international agreement" take effect upon entry into force of the WIPO Copyright Treaty with respect to the United States, which occurred March 6, 2002. Pub. L. No. 105-304, 112 Stat. 2860, 2877.

[14] The WIPO Copyright and Performances and Phonograms Treaties Implementation Act of 1998 requires that paragraph (5) of the definition of "international agreement" take effect upon entry into force of the WIPO Copyright Treaty with respect to the United States, which occurred May 20, 2002. Pub. L. No. 105-304, 112 Stat. 2860, 2877.

[15] The WIPO Copyright and Performances and Phonograms Treaties Implementation Act of 1998 amended section 101 by adding the definition of "international agreement." Pub. L. No. 105-304, 112 Stat. 2860, 2861.

[16] The Artists' Rights and Theft Prevention Act of 2005 amended section 101 by adding the definition for "motion picture exhibition facility." It inserted the definition in the wrong alphabetical order, placing it after "motion pictures," instead of before. Pub. L. No. 109-9, 119 Stat. 218, 220.

[17] The Fairness in Music Licensing Act of 1998 amended section 101 by adding the definition of "performing rights society." Pub. L. No. 105-298, 112 Stat. 2827, 2833.

[18] The Berne Convention Implementation Act of 1988 amended the definition of "Pictorial, graphic, and sculptural works" by inserting "diagrams, models, and technical drawings, including architectural plans" in the first sentence, in lieu of "technical drawings, diagrams, and models." Pub. L. No. 100-568, 102 Stat. 2853, 2854.

[19] The Fairness in Music Licensing Act of 1998 amended section 101 by adding the definition of "proprietor." Pub. L. No. 105-298, 112 Stat. 2827, 2833. In 1999, a technical amendment added the phrase "For purposes of section 513,", to the beginning of the definition of "proprietor." Pub. L. No. 106-44, 113 Stat. 221, 222.

[20] The Copyright Renewal Act of 1992 amended section 101 by adding the definition of "registration." Pub. L. No. 102-307, 106 Stat. 264, 266.

[21] The WIPO Copyright and Performances and Phonograms Treaties Implementation Act of 1998 amended section 101 by adding the definition of "treaty party." Pub. L. No. 105-304, 112 Stat. 2860, 2861.

[22] The Berne Convention Implementation Act of 1988 amended section 101 by adding the definition of "country of origin" of a Berne Convention work, for purposes of section 411. Pub. L. No. 100-568, 102 Stat. 2853, 2854. The WIPO Copyright and Performances and Phonograms Treaties Implementation Act of 1998 amended that definition by changing it to a definition for "United States work," for purposes of section 411. Pub. L. No. 105-304, 112 Stat. 2860, 2861. In 1999, a technical amendment moved the definition of "United States work" to place it in alphabetical order, after the definition for "United States." Pub. L. No. 106-44, 113 Stat. 221, 222.

[23]The WIPO Copyright and Performances and Phonograms Treaties Implementation Act of 1998 amended section 101 by adding the definition of "WIPO Copyright Treaty." Pub. L. No. 105-304, 112 Stat. 2860, 2861. That definition is required to take effect upon entry into force of the WIPO Copyright Treaty with respect to the United States, which occurred March 6, 2002. Pub. L. No. 105-304, 112 Stat. 2860, 2877.

[24]The WIPO Copyright and Performances and Phonograms Treaties Implementation Act of 1998 amended section 101 by adding the definition of "WIPO Performances and Phonograms Treaty." Pub. L. No. 105-304, 112 Stat. 2860, 2862. That definition is required to take effect upon entry into force of the WIPO Performances and Phonograms Treaty with respect to the United States, which occurred May 20, 2002. Pub. L. No. 105-304, 112 Stat. 2860, 2877.

[25]The Visual Artists Rights Act of 1990 amended section 101 by adding the definition of "work of visual art." Pub. L. No. 101-650, 104 Stat. 5089, 5128.

[26]The Satellite Home Viewer Improvement Act of 1999 amended the definition of "a work made for hire" by inserting "as a sound recording" after "audiovisual work." Pub. L. No. 106-113, 113 Stat. 1501, app. I at 1501A-544. The Work Made for Hire and Copyright Corrections Act of 2000 amended the definition of "work made for hire" by deleting "as a sound recording" after "audiovisual work." Pub. L. No. 106-379, 114 Stat. 1444. The Act also added a second paragraph to part (2) of that definition. *Id.* These changes are effective retroactively, as of November 29, 1999.

[27]The WIPO Copyright and Performances and Phonograms Treaties Implementation Act of 1998 amended section 101 by adding the definitions of "WTO Agreement" and "WTO member country," thereby transferring those definitions to section 101 from section 104A. Pub. L. No. 105-304, 112 Stat. 2860, 2862. See also endnote 31, *infra*.

[28]In 1990, the Architectural Works Copyright Protection Act amended subsection 102(a) by adding at the end thereof paragraph (8). Pub. L. No. 101-650, 104 Stat. 5089, 5133.

[29]The Berne Convention Implementation Act of 1988 amended section 104(b) by redesignating paragraph (4) as paragraph (5), by inserting after paragraph (3) a new paragraph (4), and by adding subsection (c) at the end. Pub. L. No. 100-568, 102 Stat. 2853, 2855. The WIPO Copyright and Performances and Phonograms Treaties Implementation Act of 1998 amended section 104 as follows: 1) by amending subsection (b) to redesignate paragraphs (3) and (5) as (5) and (6), respectively, and by adding a new paragraph (3); 2) by amending section 104(b), throughout; and 3) by adding section 104(d). Pub. L. No. 105-304, 112 Stat. 2860, 2862.

[30]The WIPO Copyright and Performances and Phonograms Treaties Implementation Act of 1998 requires that subsection (d), regarding the effect of phonograms treaties, take effect upon entry into force of the WIPO Performances and Phonograms Treaty with respect to the United States, which occurred May 20, 2002. Pub. L. No. 105-304, 112 Stat. 2860, 2877.

[31]In 1993, the North American Free Trade Agreement Implementation Act added section 104A. Pub. L. No. 103-182, 107 Stat. 2057, 2115. In 1994, the Uruguay Round Agreements Act amended section 104A in its entirety with an amendment in the nature of a substitute. Pub. L. No. 103-465, 108 Stat. 4809, 4976. On November 13, 1997, section 104A was amended by replacing subsection (d)(3)(A), by striking the last sentence of subsection (e)(1)(B)(ii), and by rewriting paragraphs (2) and (3) of subsection (h). Pub. L. No. 105-80, 111 Stat. 1529, 1530. The WIPO Copyright and Performances and Phonograms Treaties Implementation Act of 1998 amended section 104A by rewriting paragraphs (1) and (3) of subsection (h); by adding subparagraph (E) to subsection (h)(6); and by amending subsection (h)(8)(B)(i). Pub. L. No. 105-304, 112 Stat. 2860, 2862. That Act also deleted paragraph (9), thereby transferring the definitions for "WTO Agreement" and "WTO member country" from section 104A to section 101. Pub. L. No. 105-304, 112 Stat. 2860, 2863. See also endnote 27, *supra*.

[32]The WIPO Copyright and Performances and Phonograms Treaties Implementation Act of 1998 requires that subparagraph (C) of the definition of "date of adherence or proclamation" take effect upon entry into force of the WIPO Copyright Treaty with respect to the United States, which occurred March 6, 2002. Pub. L. No. 105-304, 112 Stat. 2860, 2877.

[33]The WIPO Copyright and Performances and Phonograms Treaties Implementation Act of 1998 requires that subparagraph (D) of the definition of "date of adherence or proclamation" take effect upon entry into force of the WIPO Performances and Phonograms Treaty with respect to the United States, which occurred May 20, 2002. Pub. L. No. 105-304, 112 Stat. 2860, 2877.

[34]The WIPO Copyright and Performances and Phonograms Treaties Implementation Act of 1998 requires that subparagraph (C) of the definition of "eligible country" take effect upon entry into force of the WIPO Copyright Treaty with respect to the United States, which occurred March 6, 2002. Pub. L. No. 105-304, 112 Stat. 2860, 2877.

[35]The WIPO Copyright and Performances and Phonograms Treaties Implementation Act of 1998 requires that subparagraph (D) of the definition of "eligible country" take effect upon entry into force of the WIPO Performance and Phonograms Treaty with respect to the United States, which occurred May 20, 2002. Pub. L. No. 105-304, 112 Stat. 2860, 2877.

[36]The WIPO Copyright and Performances and Phonograms Treaties Implementation Act of 1998 requires that subparagraph (E) of the definition of "restored work" take effect upon entry into force of the WIPO Performances and Phonograms Treaty with respect to the United States, which occurred May 20, 2002. Pub. L. No. 105-304, 112 Stat. 2860, 2877.

[37]In 1968, the Standard Reference Data Act provided an exception to section 105, Pub. L. No. 90-396, 82 Stat. 339. Section 6 of that act amended title 15 of the *United States Code* by authorizing the Secretary of Commerce, at 15 U.S.C. 290e, to secure copyright and renewal thereof on behalf of the United States as author or proprietor "in all or any part of any standard reference data which he prepares or makes available under this chapter," and to "authorize the reproduction and publication thereof by others." See also section 105(f) of the Transitional and Supplementary Provisions of the Copyright Act of 1976, in Appendix A. Pub. L. No. 94-553, 90 Stat. 2541.

Concerning the liability of the United States Government for copyright infringement, also see 28 U.S.C. 1498. Title 28 of the *United States Code* is entitled "Judiciary and Judicial Procedure," included in the appendices to this volume.

[38]The Digital Performance Right in Sound Recordings Act of 1995 amended section 106 by adding paragraph (6). Pub. L. No. 104-39, 109 Stat. 336. In 1999, a technical amendment substituted "121" for "120." Pub. L. No. 106-44, 113 Stat. 221, 222. The Intellectual Property and High Technology Technical Amendments Act of 2002 amended section 106 by substituting sections "107 through 122" for "107 through 121." Pub. L. No. 107-273, 116 Stat. 1758, 1909.

[39]The Visual Artists Rights Act of 1990 added section 106A. Pub. L. No. 101-650, 104 Stat. 5089, 5128. The Act states that, generally, section 106A is to take effect 6 months after its date of enactment, December 1, 1990, and that the rights created by section 106A shall apply to (1) works created before such effective date but title to which has not, as of such effective date, been transferred from the author and (2) works created on or after such effective date, but shall not apply to any destruction, distortion, mutilation, or other modification (as described in section 106A(a)(3)) of any work which occurred before such effective date. See also, endnote 3, chapter 3.

[40]The Visual Artists Rights Act of 1990 amended section 107 by adding the reference to section 106A. Pub. L. No. 101-650, 104 Stat. 5089, 5132. In 1992, section 107 was also amended to add the last sentence. Pub. L. No. 102-492, 106 Stat. 3145.

[41]The Copyright Amendments Act of 1992 amended section 108 by repealing subsection (i) in its entirety. Pub. L. No. 102-307, 106 Stat. 264, 272. In 1998, the Sonny Bono Copyright Term Extension Act amended section 108 by redesignating subsection (h) as (i) and adding a new subsection (h). Pub. L. No. 105-298, 112 Stat. 2827, 2829. Also in 1998, the Digital Millennium Copyright Act amended section 108 by making changes in subsections (a), (b), and (c). Pub. L. No. 105-304, 112 Stat. 2860, 2889.

In 2005, the Preservation of Orphan Works Act amended subsection 108(i) by adding a reference to subsection (h). It substituted "(b), (c), and (h)" for "(b) and (c)." Pub. L. No. 109-9, 119 Stat. 218, 226, 227.

[42]The Record Rental Amendment of 1984 amended section 109 by redesignating subsections (b) and (c) as subsections (c) and (d), respectively, and by inserting a new subsection (b) after subsection (a). Pub. L. No. 98-450, 98 Stat. 1727. Section 4(b) of the Act states that the provisions of section 109(b), as added by section 2 of the Act, "shall not affect the right of an owner of a particular phonorecord of a sound recording, who acquired such ownership before [October 4, 1984], to dispose of the possession of that particular phonorecord on or after such date of enactment in any manner permitted by section 109 of title 17, United States Code, as in effect on the day before the date of the enactment of this Act." Pub. L. No. 98-450, 98 Stat. 1727, 1728. Section 4(c) of the Act also states that the amendments "shall not apply to rentals, leasings, lendings (or acts or practices in the nature of rentals, leasings, or lendings) occurring after the date which is 13 years after

[October 4, 1984]" In 1988, the Record Rental Amendment Act of 1984 was amended to extend the time period in section 4(c) from 5 years to 13 years. Pub. L. No. 100-617, 102 Stat. 3194. In 1993, the North American Free Trade Agreement Implementation Act repealed section 4(c) of the Record Rental Amendment of 1984. Pub. L. No. 103-182, 107 Stat. 2057, 2114. Also in 1988, technical amendments to section 109(d) inserted "(c)" in lieu of "(b)" and substituted "copyright" in lieu of "coyright" Pub. L. No. 100-617, 102 Stat. 3194.

The Computer Software Rental Amendments Act of 1990 amended section 109(b) as follows: 1) paragraphs (2) and (3) were redesignated as paragraphs (3) and (4), respectively; 2) paragraph (1) was struck out and new paragraphs (1) and (2) were inserted in lieu thereof; and 3) paragraph (4), as redesignated, was amended in its entirety with a new paragraph (4) inserted in lieu thereof. Pub. L. No. 101-650, 104 Stat. 5089, 5134. The Act states that section 109(b), as amended, "shall not affect the right of a person in possession of a particular copy of a computer program, who acquired such copy before the date of the enactment of this Act, to dispose of the possession of that copy on or after such date of enactment in any manner permitted by section 109 of title 17, United States Code, as in effect on the day before such date of enactment." The Act also states that the amendments made to section 109(b) "shall not apply to rentals, leasings, or lendings (or acts or practices in the nature of rentals, leasings, or lendings) occurring on or after October 1, 1997." However, this limitation, which is set forth in the first sentence of section 804 (c) of the Computer Software Rental Amendments Act of 1990, at 104 Stat. 5136, was subsequently deleted in 1994 by the Uruguay Round Agreements Act. Pub. L. No. 103-465, 108 Stat. 4809, 4974.

The Computer Software Rental Amendments Act of 1990 also amended section 109 by adding at the end thereof subsection (e). Pub. L. No. 101-650, 104 Stat. 5089, 5135. That Act states that the provisions contained in the new subsection (e) shall take effect 1 year after its date of enactment. It was enacted on December 1, 1990. The Act also states that such amendments so made "shall not apply to public performances or displays that occur on or after October 1, 1995."

In 1994, the Uruguay Round Agreements Act amended section 109(a) by adding the second sentence, which begins with "Notwithstanding the preceding sentence." Pub. L. No. 103-465, 108 Stat. 4809, 4981.

[43]In 1988, the Extension of Record Rental Amendment amended section 110 by adding paragraph (10). Pub. L. No. 97-366, 96 Stat. 1759. In 1997, the Technical Corrections to the Satellite Home Viewer Act amended section 110 by inserting a semicolon in lieu of the period at the end of paragraph (8); by inserting "; and" in lieu of the period at the end of paragraph (9); and by inserting "(4)" in lieu of "4 above" in paragraph (10). Pub. L. No. 105-80, 111 Stat. 1529, 1534. The Fairness in Music Licensing Act of 1998 amended section 110, in paragraph 5, by adding subparagraph (B) and by making conforming amendments to subparagraph (A); by adding the phrase "or of the audiovisual or other devices utilized in such performance" to paragraph 7; and by adding the last paragraph to section 110 that begins "The exemptions provided under paragraph (5)." Pub. L. No. 105-298, 112 Stat. 2827, 2830. In 1999, a technical amendment made corrections to conform paragraph designations that were affected by amendments previously made by the Fairness in Music Licensing Act of 1998. Pub. L. No. 106-44, 113 Stat. 221. The Technology, Education, and Copyright Harmonization Act of 2002 amended section 110 by substituting new language for paragraph 110(2) and by adding all the language at the end of section 110 that concerns paragraph 110(2). Pub. L. No. 107-273, 116 Stat. 1758, 1910.

The Family Movie Act of 2005 amended section 110 by adding paragraph (11) and by adding a new paragraph at the end of that section. Pub. L. No. 109-9, 119 Stat. 218, 223.

[44]In 1986, section 111(d) was amended by striking out paragraph (1) and by redesignating paragraphs (2), (3), (4), and (5) as paragraphs (1), (2), (3), and (4), respectively. Pub. L. 99-397, 100 Stat. 848. Also, in 1986, section 111(f) was amended by substituting "subsection (d)(1)" for "subsection (d)(2)" in the last sentence of the definition of "secondary transmission" and by adding a new sentence after the first sentence in the definition of "local service area of a primary transmitter." Pub. L. No. 99-397, 100 Stat. 848.

The Satellite Home Viewer Act of 1988 amended subsection 111(a) by striking "or" at the end of paragraph (3), by redesignating paragraph (4) as paragraph (5), and by inserting a new paragraph (4). Pub. L. No. 100-667, 102 Stat. 3935, 3949. That Act also amended section (d)(1)(A) by adding the second sentence, which begins with "In determining the total number." *Id.*

The Copyright Royalty Tribunal Reform Act of 1993 amended section 111(d) by substituting "Librarian of Congress" for "Copyright Royalty Tribunal" where appropriate, by inserting a new sentence in lieu of the second and third sentences of paragraph (2), and, in paragraph (4), by amending subparagraph (B) in its entirety. Pub. L. No. 103-198, 107 Stat. 2304, 2311.

The Satellite Home Viewer Act of 1994 amended section 111(f) by inserting "microwave" after "wires, cables," in the paragraph relating to the definition of "cable system" and by inserting new matter after "April 15, 1976," in the paragraph relating to the definition of "local service area of a primary transmitter." Pub. L. No. 103-369, 108 Stat. 3477, 3480. That Act provides that the amendment "relating to the definition of the local service area of a primary transmitter, shall take effect on July 1, 1994." *Id.*

In 1995, the Digital Performance in Sound Recordings Act amended section 111(c)(1) by inserting "and section 114(d)" in the first sentence, after "of this subsection." Pub. L. No. 104-39, 109 Stat. 336, 348.

The Satellite Home Viewer Improvement Act of 1999 amended section 111 by substituting "statutory" for "compulsory" and "programming" for "programing," wherever they appeared. Pub. L. No. 106-113, 113 Stat. 1501, app. I at 1501A-543. The Act also amended sections 111(a) and (b) by inserting "performance or display of a work embodied in a primary transmission" in lieu of "primary transmission embodying a performance or display of a work." It amended paragraph (1) of section 111(c) by inserting "a performance or display of a work embodied in" after "by a cable system of" and by striking "and embodying a performance or display of a work." It amended subparagraphs (3) and (4) of section 111(a) by inserting "a performance or display of a work embodied in a primary transmission" in lieu of "a primary transmission" and by striking "and embodying a performance or display of a work." *Id.*

The Copyright Royalty and Distribution Reform Act of 2004 made amendments to subsection 111(d) to conform it to revised chapter 8, substituting "Copyright Royalty Judges" for "Librarian of Congress" where appropriate, along with making other conforming amendments. Pub. L. No. 108-419, 118 Stat. 2341, 2361. The Satellite Home Viewer Extension and Reauthorization Act of 2004 amended section 111 by deleting "for private home viewing" in subsections (a)(4) and (d)(1)(A). Pub. L. No. 108-447, 118 Stat. 2809, 3393, 3406.

In 2006, the Copyright Royalty Judges Program Technical Corrections Act amended section 111(d)(2) by substituting "upon authorization by the Copyright Royalty Judges for everything in the second sentence after "Librarian of Congress"; by substituting new text for the second sentence of (4)(B); by making a technical correction in the last sentence of (4)(B) to change "finds" to "find"; and by revising (4)(C) in its entirety. Pub. L. No. 109-303, 120 Stat. 1478, 1481.

[45]Royalty rates specified by the compulsory licensing provisions of this section are subject to adjustment by copyright royalty judges appointed by the Librarian of Congress in accordance with the provisions of chapter 8 of title 17 of the *United States Code*, as amended by the Copyright Royalty and Distribution Reform Act of 2004, Pub. L. No. 108-419, 118 Stat. 2341. See, *infra*. Regulations for adjusting royalty rates may be found in subchapter B of chapter 11, title 37, *Code of Federal Regulations*.

[46]In 1998, the Digital Millennium Copyright Act amended section 112 by redesignating subsection (a) as subsection (a)(1); by redesignating former sections (a)(1), (a)(2), and (a)(3) as subsections (a)(1)(A), (a)(1)(B), and (a)(1)(C), respectively; by adding subsection (a)(2); and by amending the language in new subsection (a)(1). Pub. L. No. 105-304, 112 Stat. 2860, 2888. The Digital Millennium Copyright Act also amended section 112 by redesignating subsection (e) as subsection (f) and adding a new subsection (e). Pub. L. No. 105-304, 112 Stat. 2860, 2899. In 1999, a technical amendment to section 112(e) redesignated paragraphs (3) through (10) as (2) through (9) and corrected the paragraph references throughout that section to conform to those redesignations. Pub. L. No. 106-44, 113 Stat. 221. The Technology, Education, and Copyright Harmonization Act of 2002 amended section 112 by redesignating subsection 112(f) as 112(g) and adding a new paragraph (f). Pub. L. No. 107-273, 116 Stat. 1758, 1912.

The Copyright Royalty and Distribution Reform Act of 2004 amended subsection 112(e) to conform it to revised chapter 8, by substituting new language for the first sentences of paragraphs (3) and (4); by deleting paragraph (6) and renumbering paragraphs (7) through (9) as (6) through (8); by changing references to the "Librarian of Congress" to "Copyright Royalty Judges," with corresponding grammatical changes, throughout; and by striking references to negotiations in paragraphs (3) and (4) along with making other conforming amendments. Pub. L. No. 108-419, 118 Stat. 2341, 2361.

[47]The Visual Artists Rights Act of 1990 amended section 113 by adding subsection (d) at the end thereof. Pub. L. No. 101-650, 104 Stat. 5089, 5130.

[48]The Digital Performance Right in Sound Recordings Act of 1995 amended section 114 as follows: 1) in subsection (a), by striking "and (3)" and inserting in lieu thereof "(3) and (6)"; 2) in subsection (b) in the first sentence, by striking "phonorecords, or of copies of motion pictures and other audiovisual works," and inserting "phonorecords or copies"; and 3) by striking subsection (d) and inserting in lieu thereof new subsections (d), (e), (f), (g), (h), (i), and (j). Pub. L. No. 104-39, 109 Stat. 336. In 1997, subsection 114(f) was amended by inserting all the text that appears after "December 31, 2000" and by striking "and publish in the Federal Register." Pub. L. No. 105-80, 111 Stat. 1529, 1531.

In 1998, the Digital Millennium Copyright Act amended section 114(d) by replacing paragraphs (1)(A) and (2) with amendments in the nature of substitutes. Pub. L. No. 105-304, 112 Stat. 2860, 2890. That Act also amended section 114(f) by revising the title; by redesignating paragraph (1) as paragraph (1)(A); by adding paragraph (1)(B) in lieu of paragraphs (2), (3), (4), and (5); and by amending the language in newly designated paragraph (1)(A), including revising the effective date from December 31, 2000, to December 31, 2001. Pub. L. No. 105-304, 112 Stat. 2860, 2894. The Digital Millennium Copyright Act also amended subsection 114(g) by substituting "transmission" in lieu of "subscription transmission," wherever it appears and, in the first sentence in paragraph (g)(1), by substituting "transmission licensed under a statutory license" in lieu of "subscription transmission licensed." Pub. L. No. 105-304, 112 Stat. 2860, 2897. That Act also amended subsection 114(j) by redesignating paragraphs (2), (3), (5), (6), (7), and (8) as (3), (5), (9), (12), (13), and (14), respectively; by amending paragraphs (4) and (9) in their entirety and redesignating them as paragraphs (7) and (15), respectively; and by adding new definitions, including, paragraph (2) defining "archived program," paragraph (4) defining "continuous program," paragraph (6) defining "eligible nonsubscription transmission," paragraph (8) defining "new subscription service," paragraph (10) defining "preexisting satellite digital audio radio service," and paragraph (11) defining "preexisting subscription service." Pub. L. No. 105-304, 112 Stat. 2860, 2897.

The Small Webcaster Settlement Act of 2002 amended section 114 by adding paragraph (5) to subsection 114(f), by amending paragraph 114(g)(2), and by adding paragraph 114(g)(3). Pub. L. No. 107-321, 116 Stat. 2780, 2781 and 2784.

The Copyright Royalty and Distribution Reform Act of 2004 amended subsection 114(f) to conform it to revised chapter 8, by substituting new language for the first sentences of subparagraphs (1)(A), (1)(B), (2)(A), and (2)(B); by substituting new language for subparagraphs (1)(C) and (2)(C); by changing references to the "Librarian of Congress" in paragraphs (1), (2), (3), and (4) to "Copyright Royalty Judges," and making corresponding grammatical changes; by striking references to negotiations in paragraphs (1), (2), (3), and (4) and replacing with corresponding grammatical changes and conforming language; and by adding new language at the end of subparagraph (4)(A). Pub. L. No. 108-419, 118 Stat. 2341, 2362-2364.

In 2006, the Copyright Royalty Judges Program Technical Corrections Act amended section 114 by substituting new text after "proceedings are to be commenced" in the first sentence in (f)(1)(A); by amending (2)(A) in its entirety; and by inserting "described in" in the last sentence of (2)(B) which repeats an amendment already made by the Copyright Royalty and Distribution Reform Act of 2004, Pub. L. No. 108 419, 118 Stat. 2341, 2364. Pub. L. No. 109-303, 120 Stat. 1478, 1481-82.

[49]The Copyright Royalty and Distribution Reform Act of 2004 did not conform the pronoun "its" to "their" when it substituted "Copyright Royalty Judges" for "copyright arbitration royalty panel." Pub. L. No. 108-419, 118 Stat. 2341, 2362.

[50]The Record Rental Amendment of 1984 amended section 115 by redesignating paragraphs (3) and (4) of subsection (c) as paragraphs (4) and (5), respectively, and by adding a new paragraph (3). Pub. L. No. 98-450, 98 Stat. 1727.

The Digital Performance Right in Sound Recordings Act of 1995 amended section 115 as follows: 1) in the first sentence of subsection (a)(1), by striking "any other person" and inserting in lieu thereof "any other person, including those who make phonorecords or digital phonorecord deliveries,"; 2) in the second sentence of the same subsection, by inserting before the period "including by means of a digital phonorecord delivery"; 3) in the second sentence of subsection (c)(2), by inserting "and other than as provided in paragraph (3)," after "For this purpose,"; 4) by redesignating paragraphs (3), (4), and (5) of subsection (c) as paragraphs (4), (5), and (6), respectively, and by inserting after paragraph (2) a new paragraph (3); and (5) by adding after subsection (c) a new subsection (d). Pub. L. No. 104-39, 109 Stat. 336, 344.

In 1997, section 115 was amended by striking "and publish in the Federal Register" in subparagraph 115(c)(3)(D). Pub. L. No. 105-80, 111 Stat. 1529, 1531. The same legislation also amended section 115(c)(3)(E) by replacing the phrases "sections 106(1) and (3)" and "sections 106(1) and 106(3)" with "paragraphs (1) and (3) of section 106." Pub. L. No. 105-80, 111 Stat. 1529, 1534.

The Copyright Royalty and Distribution Reform Act of 2004 amended paragraph 115(c)(3) to conform it to revised chapter 8, by substituting new language for the first sentences of subparagraphs (3)(C) and (3)(D); by changing references to the "Librarian of Congress" in subparagraphs (3)(C), (3)(D), and (3)(E) to "Copyright Royalty Judges," with corresponding grammatical changes; by striking references to negotiations in subparagraphs (3)(C) and (D) and making corresponding grammatical changes and conforming language; by deleting subparagraph (F); and by redesignating paragraphs (G) through (L) as paragraphs (F) through (K) with corresponding technical changes in subparagraphs (A), (B), and (E) to conform references to the subparagraphs subject to that redesignation. Pub. L. No. 108-419, 118 Stat. 2341, 2364-2365. The Copyright Royalty and Distribution Act of 2004 also amended the first sentence of subparagraph 115(c)(3)(B) by substituting "section" for "paragraph" and by inserting "on a nonexclusive basis" after "common agents." *Id.* at 2364. It also amended subparagraph 115(c)(3)(E) by inserting "as to digital phonorecord deliveries" after "shall be given effect." *Id.* at 2365.

In 2006, the Copyright Royalty Judges Program Technical Corrections Act amended 115(c)(3)(B) by inserting "this subparagraph and subparagraphs (C) through (E)" in lieu of "subparagraphs (B) through (F)." The Act also amended the third sentence of 115(c)(3)(D) by inserting "in subparagraphs (B) and (C)" after "described"; and 115(c)(3)(E)(i) and (ii)(I) by substituting "(C) and (D)" for "(C) or (D)" wherever it appears. Pub. L. No. 109-303, 120 Stat. 1478, 1482.

[51]See endnote 45, *supra*.

[52]The Berne Convention Implementation Act of 1988 added section 116A. Pub. L. No. 100-568, 102 Stat. 2853, 2855. The Copyright Royalty Tribunal Reform Act of 1993 redesignated section 116A as section 116; repealed the preexisting section 116; in the redesignated section 116, struck subsections (b), (e), (f), and (g), and redesignated subsections (c) and (d) as subsections (b) and (c), respectively; and substituted, where appropriate, "Librarian of Congress" or "copyright arbitration royalty panel" for "Copyright Royalty Tribunal." Pub. L. No. 103-198, 107 Stat. 2304, 2309. In 1997, section 116 was amended by rewriting subsection (b)(2) and by adding a new subsection (d). Pub. L. No. 105-80, 111 Stat. 1529, 1531.

The Copyright Royalty and Distribution Reform Act of 2004 amended section 116 to conform it to revised chapter 8, by substituting new language for subsection (b)(2); by changing the title of subsection (c) to "License Agreements Superior to Determinations by Copyright Royalty Judges" from "License Agreements Superior to Copyright Arbitration Royalty Panel Determinations"; and, in subsection (c), by striking "copyright arbitration royalty panel" and replacing it with "Copyright Royalty Judges." Pub. L. No. 108-419, 118 Stat. 2341, 2365.

[53]In 1980, section 117 was amended in its entirety. Pub. L. No. 96-517, 94 Stat. 3015, 3028. In 1998, the Computer Maintenance Competition Assurance Act amended section 117 by inserting headings for subsections (a) and (b) and by adding subsections (c) and (d). Pub. L. No. 105-304, 112 Stat. 2860, 2887.

[54]The Copyright Royalty Tribunal Reform Act of 1993 amended section 118 by striking the first two sentences of subsection (b), by substituting a new first sentence in paragraph (3), and by making general conforming amendments throughout. Pub. L. No. 103-198, 107 Stat. 2304, 2309. In 1999, a technical amendment deleted paragraph (2) from section 118(e). Pub. L. No. 106-44, 113 Stat. 221, 222. The Intellectual Property and High Technology Technical Amendments Act of 2002 amended section 118 by deleting "to it" in the second sentence in subsection (b)(1). Pub. L. No. 107-273, 116 Stat. 1758, 1909.

The Copyright Royalty and Distribution Reform Act of 2004 amended section 118 to conform it to revised chapter 8, by deleting the last sentence in paragraph (b)(1); by revising paragraph (b)(2) by rewriting the end of sentence after "determination by the"; by substituting new language for the first sentence of paragraph (3), thereby, creating new paragraphs (3) and (4); by deleting subsection (c) and redesignating sections (d) through (g) as (c) through (f) with a corresponding technical change in section (f) to refer to "subsection (c)" instead of "subsection (d)"; and by changing references to the "Librarian of Congress" in subsections (b) and (d), as redesignated, to "Copyright Royalty Judges," with corresponding grammatical or procedural changes. Pub. L. No. 108-419, 118 Stat. 2341, 2365-2366. The Copyright Royalty and Distribution Act of 2004 also amended section 116 in text that became the second sentence of new subparagraph (4), see *supra*, by inserting "or (3)" after "paragraph 2". *Id*. at 2366. It further amended section 116(c) by inserting "or (3)" after "provided by subsection (b)(2)" and by inserting "to the extent that they were accepted by the Librarian of Congress" after "under subsection (b)(3)" and before the comma. *Id*.

In 2006, the Copyright Royalty Judges Program Technical Corrections Act amended subsection 118(b)(3) by inserting "owners of copyright in works" in lieu of "copyright owners in works"; by amending the first sentence of (c); and by substituting "(f)" for "(g)" in (c)(1). Pub. L. No. 109-303, 120 Stat. 1478, 1482.

[55]The Satellite Home Viewer Act of 1988 added section 119. Pub. L. No. 100-667, 102 Stat. 3935, 3949. The Copyright Royalty Tribunal Reform Act of 1993 amended subsections (b) and (c) of section 119 by substituting "Librarian of Congress" in lieu of "Copyright Royalty Tribunal" wherever it appeared and by making related conforming amendments. Pub. L. No. 103-198, 107 Stat. 2304, 2310. The Copyright Royalty Tribunal Reform Act of 1993 also amended paragraph (c)(3) by deleting subparagraphs (B), (C), (E), and (F) and by redesignating subparagraph (D) as (B), (G) as (C), and (H) as (D). The redesignated subparagraph (C) was amended in its entirety and paragraph (c)(4) was deleted. *Id*.

The Satellite Home Viewer Act of 1994 further amended section 119. Pub. L. No. 103-369, 108 Stat. 3477. In 1997, technical corrections and clarifications were made to the Satellite Home Viewer Act of 1994. Pub. L. No. 105-80, 111 Stat. 1529. Those two acts amended section 119 as follows: 1) by deleting or replacing obsolete effective dates; 2) in subsection (a)(5), by adding subparagraph (D); 3) in subsection (a), by adding paragraphs (8), (9), and (10); 4) in subsection (b)(1)(B), by adjusting the royalty rate for retransmitted superstations; 5) in subsection (c)(3), by replacing subparagraph (B) with an amendment in the nature of a substitute; 6) in subsections (d)(2) and (d)(6), by modifying the definition of "network station" and "satellite carrier"; and 7) in subsection (d), by adding paragraph 11 to define "local market."

Pursuant to section 4 of the Satellite Home Viewer Act of 1994, the changes made by that Act to section 119 of the *United States Code* ceased to be effective on December 31, 1999. Pub. L. No. 103-369, 108 Stat. 3477, 3481. However, section 1003 of the Satellite Home Viewer Improvement Act of 1999 extended that date to December 31, 2004. Pub. L. No. 106-113, 113 Stat. 1501, app. I at 1501A-527.

The Digital Performance Right in Sound Recordings Act of 1995 amended section 119 in the first sentence of subsections (a)(1) and (a)(2)(A), respectively, by inserting the words "and section 114(d)" after "of this subsection." Pub. L. No. 104-39, 109 Stat. 336, 348. In 1999, a technical amendment substituted "network station's" for "network's stations" in section 119(a)(8)(C)(ii). Pub. L. No. 106-44, 113 Stat. 221, 222.

The Satellite Home Viewer Improvement Act of 1999 amended section 119(a)(1) as follows: 1) by inserting "and PBS satellite feed" after "Superstations" in the paragraph heading; 2) by inserting "performance or display of a work embodied in a primary transmission made by a superstation or by the Public Broadcasting Service satellite feed" in lieu of "primary transmission made by a superstation and embodying a performance or display of a work," (see this endnote, *infra*) and 3) by adding the last sentence, which begins "In the case of the Public Broadcasting Service." Pub. L. No. 106-113, 113 Stat. 1501, app. I at 1501A-530 and 543. The Act states that these amendments shall be effective as of July 1, 1999, except for a portion of the second item, starting with "performance or display" through "superstation." Pub. L. No. 106-113, 113 Stat. 1501, app. I at 1501A-544. The Act also amended section 119(a) by inserting the phrase "with regard to secondary transmissions the satellite carrier is in compliance with the rules, regulations, or authorization of the Federal Communications Commission governing the carriage of television broadcast stations signals" in paragraphs (1) and (2) and by inserting into paragraph (2), "a performance or display of a work embodied in a primary transmission made by a network station" in lieu of "programming contained in a primary transmission made by a network station and embodying a performance or display of a work." *Id*. at 1501A-531 and 544. The Act amended section 119(a)(2) by substituting new language for paragraph (B) and, in paragraph (C), by deleting "currently" after "the satellite carrier" near the end of the first sentence. *Id*. at 1501A-528 and 544. It also amended section 119(a)(4) by inserting "a performance or display of a work embodied in" after "by a satellite carrier of" and by deleting "and embodying a performance or display of a work." *Id*. at

1501A-544. The Satellite Home Viewer Improvement Act of 1999 further amended section 119(a) by adding subparagraph (E) to paragraph (5). *Id.* at 1501A-528. It amended section 119(a)(6) by inserting "performance or display of a work embodied in" after "by a satellite carrier of" and by deleting "and embodying a performance or display of a work." *Id.* The Act also amended section 119(a) by adding paragraphs (11) and (12). *Id.* at 1501A-529 and 531.

The Satellite Home Viewer Improvement Act of 1999 amended section 119(b)(1) by inserting "or the Public Broadcasting Service satellite feed" into subparagraph (B). (See endnote 59, *infra.*) *Id.* at 1501A-530. The Act amended section 119(c) by adding a new paragraph (4). *Id.* at 1501A-527. The Act amended section 119(d) by substituting new language for paragraphs (9) through (11) and by adding paragraph (12). *Id.* at 1501A-527, 530, and 531. The Act substituted new language for section 119(e). *Id.* at 1501A-529.

The Intellectual Property and High Technology Technical Amendments Act of 2002 amended section 119(a)(6) by substituting "of a performance" for "of performance." Pub. L. No. 107-273, 116 Stat. 1758, 1909. The Act also amended section 119(b)(1)(A) by substituting "retransmitted" and "retransmissions" for "transmitted" and "transmitted," respectively, in paragraph (1)(A). *Id.*

The Copyright Royalty and Distribution Reform Act of 2004 amended section 119 to conform it to revised chapter 8 by changing references to the "Librarian of Congress" in subsections (b) and (c) to "Copyright Royalty Judges," with corresponding grammatical adjustments and procedural references; by substituting new language for subparagraphs (b)(4)(B) and (C); by deleting the term "arbitration" wherever it appears with "proceedings," along with corresponding grammatical adjustments; by amending the title of subparagraph 119(c)(3)(C) to insert "Determination under Chapter 8" in lieu of "Decision of Arbitration Panel or Order of Librarian"; and, also, in subparagraph (c)(3)(C), by substituting new language for clauses (i) and (ii). Pub. L. No. 108-419, 118 Stat. 2341, 2364-2365.

The Satellite Home Viewer Extension and Reauthorization Act of 2004 amended paragraph 119(a)(1) by deleting "and PBS satellite feed" from the title; by deleting "or by the Public Broadcasting Service satellite feed" from the first sentence; by deleting the last sentence, which concerned Public Broadcasting Service satellite feed; by inserting "or for viewing in a commercial establishment" after "for private home viewing"; and by substituting "subscriber" for "household." Pub. L. No. 108-447, 118 Stat. 2809, 3393, 3394 and 3406. It amended subparagraph 119(a)(2)(B) by inserting at the end of clause (i) "The limitation in this clause shall not apply to secondary transmissions under paragraph (3)." *Id.* at 3397. It amended subsection (C) in its entirety by substituting new language. *Id.* at 3394. It amended paragraph 119(a)(5), which is now renumbered as 119(a)(7), in the first sentence of subparagraph (A), by inserting "who is not eligible to receive the transmission under this section" in lieu of "who does not reside in an unserved household" and, in the first sentence of subparagraph (B), by making the same change but using "are" instead of "is"; and, in subparagraph (D), by substituting "is to a subscriber who is eligible to receive the secondary transmission under this section" in lieu of "is for private home viewing to an unserved household." *Id.* at 3404. The Act further amended subsection 119(a) by adding new paragraphs, redesignated as paragraphs (3) and (4); by deleting paragraph eight; by renumbering the paragraphs affected by those changes; and by revising the references to old paragraph numbers, accordingly, in paragraphs (1) and (2), to be the new numbers as redesignated. *Id.* at 3394, 3396, and 3397. The Act further amended subsection 119(a) by adding at the end three new paragraphs, designated as new paragraphs (14), (15) and (16). *Id.* at 3400, 3404 and 3408.

The Satellite Home Viewer Extension and Reauthorization Act of 2004 amended the title of subsection 119(b) by deleting "for Private Home Viewing." *Id.* at 3406. It also amended subparagraph 119(b)(A) and paragraph 119(b)(3) by deleting "for private home viewing." *Id.* The Act amended subparagraph (119)(b)(1)(B) in its entirety by substituting new language. *Id.* at 3400. It added a new paragraph at the end of paragraph 119(b)(1). *Id.* at 3401.

The Satellite Home Viewer Extension and Reauthorization Act of 2004 amended subsection 119(c) in its entirety. *Id.* The Satellite Home Viewer Extension and Reauthorization Act of 2004 amended paragraph 119(d)(1) by deleting "for private home viewing" after "individual subscribers" and by adding at the end "in accordance with the provisions of this section." *Id.* at 3406. It amended paragraph 119(d)(2)(A) by substituting, at the beginning of the first sentence, "a television station licensed by the Federal Communications Commission" in lieu of "a television broadcast station." *Id.* The Act amended paragraph 119(d)(8) by substituting "or entity that" in lieu of "who"; by deleting "for private home viewing"; and by inserting at the end "in accordance with the provisions of this section." *Id.* It amended subparagraph 119(d)(10)(D) by changing "(a)(11)" to "(a)(12)". *Id.* at 3405. It amended in their entireties paragraph 119(d)(9), subparagraph (119)(d)(10)(B) and paragraphs 119(d)(11) and (12). *Id.* at 3405 and 3406.

The Satellite Home Viewer Extension and Reauthorization Act of 2004 amended subsection 119(e) by changing the date at the beginning of the sentence from "December 31, 2004" to "December 31, 2009". *Id.* at 3394. The Satellite Home Viewer Extension and Reauthorization Act of 2004 amended section 119 by adding a new subsection (f). *Id.* at 3394.

In 2006, the Copyright Royalty Judges Program Technical Corrections Act amended section 119 by revising the second sentence of (b)(4)(B); by amending (b)(4)(C) in its entirety; and by making a technical correction to substitute "arbitration" for "arbitrary" in (c)(1)(F)(i). Pub. L. No. 109-303, 120 Stat. 1478, 1482-83.

[56]The Satellite Home Viewer Improvement Act of 1999 amended section 119(a)(1) by deleting "primary transmission made by a superstation and embodying a performance or display of a work" and inserting in its place "performance or display of a work embodied in a primary transmission made by a superstation." Pub. L. No. 106-113, 113 Stat. 1501, app. I at 1501A-543. This amendatory language did not take into account a prior amendment that had inserted "or by the Public Broadcasting Service satellite feed" after "superstation" into the phrase quoted above that was deleted. Pub. L. No. 106-113, 113 Stat. 1501, app. I at 1501A-530. There was no mention of the phrase "or by the Public Broadcasting Service satellite feed" in that second amendment. that second amendment. The Intellectual Property and High Technology Technical Amendments Act of 2002 clarified these provisions. Pub. L. No. 107-273, 116 Stat. 1758, 1908. The Act deleted the first change and amended the second to clarify that the amended language should read, "performance or display of a work embodied in a primary transmission made by a superstation or by the Public Broadcasting Service satellite feed." *Id.*

[57]The Satellite Home Viewer Act of 1994 states that "The provisions of section 119(a)(5)(D) . . . relating to the burden of proof of satellite carriers, shall take effect on January 1, 1997, with respect to civil actions relating to the eligibility of subscribers who subscribed to service as an unserved household before the date of the enactment of this Act [, October 18, 1994]." Pub. L. No. 103-369, 108 Stat. 3477, 3481.

[58]The Intellectual Property and High Technology Technical Amendments Act of 2002 made a technical correction to insert the word "a" before "performance." Pub. L. No. 107-273, 116 Stat. 1758, 1909.

[59]The Satellite Home Viewer Improvement Act of 1999 stated that section 119(a), "as amended by section 1005(e)" of the same Act, was amended to add a new paragraph at the end of that subsection. Pub. L. No. 106-113, 113 Stat. 1501, app. I at 1501A-531. The Intellectual Property and High Technology Technical Amendments Act of 2002 made a technical correction to clarify that the amendment was to section 119(a) as amended by "section 1005(d)" of the Satellite Home Viewer Improvement Act of 1999 rather than "section 1005(e)." Pub. L. No. 107-273, 116 Stat. 1758, 1908.

[60]The Satellite Home Viewer Extension and Reauthorization Act of 2004 was enacted on December 8, 2004.

[61]See endnote 60, *supra*.

[62] In 1990, the Architectural Works Copyright Protection Act added section 120. Pub. L. No. 101-650, 104 Stat. 5089, 5133. The effective date provision of the Act states that its amendments apply to any work created on or after the date it was enacted, which was December 1, 1990. It also states that the amendments apply to "any architectural work that, on [December 1, 1990], is unconstructed and embodied in unpublished plans or drawings, except that protection for such architectural work under title 17, United States Code, by virtue of the amendments made by [the Act], shall terminate on December 31, 2002, unless the work is constructed by that date." *Id.*, 104 Stat. 5089, 5134.

[63]The Legislative Branch Appropriations Act, 1997, added section 121. Pub. L. No. 104-197, 110 Stat. 2394, 2416. The Work Made for Hire and Copyright Corrections Act of 2000 amended section 121 by substituting "section 106" for "sections 106 and 710." Pub. L. No. 106-379, 114 Stat. 1444, 1445.

The Individuals with Disabilities Education Improvement Act of 2004 amended section 121 by amending paragraph (c)(3) in its entirety; by adding a new paragraph (c)(4); by redesignating subsection (c) as (d); and by adding a new subsection (c). Pub. L. No. 108-446, 118 Stat. 2647, 2807.

[64]The Satellite Home Viewer Improvement Act of 1999 added section 122. Pub. L. No. 106-113, 113 Stat. 1501, app. I at 1501A-523. The Act states that section 122 shall be effective as of November 29, 1999. Pub. L. No. 106-113, 113 Stat. 1501, app. I at 1501A-544.

The Satellite Home Viewer Extension and Reauthorization Act of 2004 amended section 122 by adding a subparagraph (D) to paragraph (j)(2). Pub. L. No. 108-447, 118 Stat. 2809, 3393, 3409.

CHAPTER 2

COPYRIGHT OWNERSHIP AND TRANSFER

- 201. Ownership of copyright
- 202. Ownership of copyright as distinct from ownership of material object
- 203. Termination of transfers and licenses granted by the author
- 204. Execution of transfers of copyright ownership
- 205. Recordation of transfers and other documents

§ 201. Ownership of copyright[1]

(a) Initial Ownership. — Copyright in a work protected under this title vests initially in the author or authors of the work. The authors of a joint work are coowners of copyright in the work.

(b) Works Made for Hire. — In the case of a work made for hire, the employer or other person for whom the work was prepared is considered the author for purposes of this title, and, unless the parties have expressly agreed otherwise in a written instrument signed by them, owns all of the rights comprised in the copyright.

(c) Contributions to Collective Works. — Copyright in each separate contribution to a collective work is distinct from copyright in the collective work as a whole, and vests initially in the author of the contribution. In the absence of an express transfer of the copyright or of any rights under it, the owner of copyright in the collective work is presumed to have acquired only the privilege of reproducing and distributing the contribution as part of that particular collective work, any revision of that collective work, and any later collective work in the same series.

(d) Transfer of Ownership. —

(1) The ownership of a copyright may be transferred in whole or in part by any means of conveyance or by operation of law, and may be bequeathed by will or pass as personal property by the applicable laws of intestate succession.

(2) Any of the exclusive rights comprised in a copyright, including any subdivision of any of the rights specified by section 106, may be transferred as provided by clause (1) and owned separately. The owner of any particular exclusive right is entitled, to the extent of that right, to all of the protection and remedies accorded to the copyright owner by this title.

(e) Involuntary Transfer. — When an individual author's ownership of a copyright, or of any of the exclusive rights under a copyright, has not previously been transferred voluntarily by that individual author, no action by any governmental body or other official or organization purporting to seize, expropriate, transfer, or exercise rights of ownership with respect to the copyright, or any of the exclusive rights under a copyright, shall be given effect under this title, except as provided under title 11.[2]

§ 202. *Ownership of copyright as distinct from ownership of material object*

Ownership of a copyright, or of any of the exclusive rights under a copyright, is distinct from ownership of any material object in which the work is embodied. Transfer of ownership of any material object, including the copy or phonorecord in which the work is first fixed, does not of itself convey any rights in the copyrighted work embodied in the object; nor, in the absence of an agreement, does transfer of ownership of a copyright or of any exclusive rights under a copyright convey property rights in any material object.

§ 203. *Termination of transfers and licenses granted by the author*[3]

(a) Conditions for Termination. — In the case of any work other than a work made for hire, the exclusive or nonexclusive grant of a transfer or license of copyright or of any right under a copyright, executed by the author on or after January 1, 1978, otherwise than by will, is subject to termination under the following conditions:

(1) In the case of a grant executed by one author, termination of the grant may be effected by that author or, if the author is dead, by the person or persons who, under clause (2) of this subsection, own and are entitled to exercise a total of more than one-half of that author's termination interest. In the case of a grant executed by two or more authors of a joint work, termination of the grant may be effected by a majority of the authors who executed it; if any of such authors is dead, the termination interest of any such author may be exercised as a unit by the person or persons who, under clause (2) of this subsection, own and are entitled to exercise a total of more than one-half of that author's interest.

(2) Where an author is dead, his or her termination interest is owned, and may be exercised, as follows:

(A) The widow or widower owns the author's entire termination interest unless there are any surviving children or grandchildren of the author, in which case the widow or widower owns one-half of the author's interest.

(B) The author's surviving children, and the surviving children of any dead child of the author, own the author's entire termination interest unless there is a widow or widower, in which case the ownership of one-half of the author's interest is divided among them.

(C) The rights of the author's children and grandchildren are in all cases divided among them and exercised on a per stirpes basis according to the number of such author's children represented; the share of the children of a dead child in a termination interest can be exercised only by the action of a majority of them.

(D) In the event that the author's widow or widower, children, and grandchildren are not living, the author's executor, administrator, personal representative, or trustee shall own the author's entire termination interest.

(3) Termination of the grant may be effected at any time during a period of five years beginning at the end of thirty-five years from the date of execution of the grant; or, if the grant covers the right of publication of the work, the period begins at the end of thirty-five years from the date of publication of the work under the grant or at the end of forty years from the date of execution of the grant, whichever term ends earlier.

(4) The termination shall be effected by serving an advance notice in writing, signed by the number and proportion of owners of termination interests required under clauses (1) and (2) of this subsection, or by their duly authorized agents, upon the grantee or the grantee's successor in title.

(A) The notice shall state the effective date of the termination, which shall fall within the five-year period specified by clause (3) of this subsection, and the notice shall be served not less than two or more than ten years before that date. A copy of the notice shall be recorded in the Copyright Office before the effective date of termination, as a condition to its taking effect.

(B) The notice shall comply, in form, content, and manner of service, with requirements that the Register of Copyrights shall prescribe by regulation.

(5) Termination of the grant may be effected notwithstanding any agreement to the contrary, including an agreement to make a will or to make any future grant.

(b) Effect of Termination. — Upon the effective date of termination, all rights under this title that were covered by the terminated grants revert to the author, authors, and other persons owning termination interests under clauses (1) and (2) of subsection (a), including those owners who did not join in signing the notice of termination under clause (4) of subsection (a), but with the following limitations:

(1) A derivative work prepared under authority of the grant before its termination may continue to be utilized under the terms of the grant after its termination, but this privilege does not extend to the preparation after the termination of other derivative works based upon the copyrighted work covered by the terminated grant.

(2) The future rights that will revert upon termination of the grant become vested on the date the notice of termination has been served as provided by clause (4) of subsection (a). The rights vest in the author, authors, and other persons named in, and in the proportionate shares provided by, clauses (1) and (2) of subsection (a).

(3) Subject to the provisions of clause (4) of this subsection, a further grant, or agreement to make a further grant, of any right covered by a terminated grant is valid only if it is signed by the same number and proportion of the owners, in whom the right has vested under clause (2) of this subsection, as are required to terminate the grant under clauses (1) and (2) of subsection (a). Such further grant or agreement is effective with respect to all of the persons in whom the right it covers has vested under clause (2) of this subsection, including those who did not join in signing it. If any person dies after rights under a terminated grant have vested in him or her, that person's legal representatives, legatees, or heirs at law represent him or her for purposes of this clause.

(4) A further grant, or agreement to make a further grant, of any right covered by a terminated grant is valid only if it is made after the effective date of the termination. As an exception, however, an agreement for such a further grant may be made between the persons provided by clause (3) of this subsection and the original grantee or such grantee's successor in title, after the notice of termination has been served as provided by clause (4) of subsection (a).

(5) Termination of a grant under this section affects only those rights covered by the grants that arise under this title, and in no way affects rights arising under any other Federal, State, or foreign laws.

(6) Unless and until termination is effected under this section, the grant, if it does not provide otherwise, continues in effect for the term of copyright provided by this title.

§ 204. Execution of transfers of copyright ownership

(a) A transfer of copyright ownership, other than by operation of law, is not valid unless an instrument of conveyance, or a note or memorandum of the transfer, is in writing and signed by the owner of the rights conveyed or such owner's duly authorized agent.

(b) A certificate of acknowledgment is not required for the validity of a transfer, but is prima facie evidence of the execution of the transfer if —

(1) in the case of a transfer executed in the United States, the certificate is issued by a person authorized to administer oaths within the United States; or

(2) in the case of a transfer executed in a foreign country, the certificate is issued by a diplomatic or consular officer of the United States, or by a person authorized to administer oaths whose authority is proved by a certificate of such an officer.

§ 205. Recordation of transfers and other documents[4]

(a) Conditions for Recordation. — Any transfer of copyright ownership or other document pertaining to a copyright may be recorded in the Copyright Office if the document filed for recordation bears the actual signature of the person who executed it, or if it is accompanied by a sworn or official certification that it is a true copy of the original, signed document.

(b) Certificate of Recordation. — The Register of Copyrights shall, upon receipt of a document as provided by subsection (a) and of the fee provided by section 708, record the document and return it with a certificate of recordation.

(c) Recordation as Constructive Notice. — Recordation of a document in the Copyright Office gives all persons constructive notice of the facts stated in the recorded document, but only if —

(1) the document, or material attached to it, specifically identifies the work to which it pertains so that, after the document is indexed by the Register of Copyrights, it would be revealed by a reasonable search under the title or registration number of the work; and

(2) registration has been made for the work.

(d) Priority between Conflicting Transfers. — As between two conflicting transfers, the one executed first prevails if it is recorded, in the manner required to give constructive notice under subsection (c), within one month after its execution in the United States or within two months after its execution outside the United States, or at any time before recordation in such manner of the later transfer. Otherwise the later transfer prevails if recorded first in such manner, and if taken in good faith, for valuable consideration or on the basis of a binding promise to pay royalties, and without notice of the earlier transfer.

(e) Priority between Conflicting Transfer of Ownership and Nonexclusive License. — A nonexclusive license, whether recorded or not, prevails over a conflicting transfer of copyright ownership if the license is evidenced by a written instrument signed by the owner of the rights licensed or such owner's duly authorized agent, and if

(1) the license was taken before execution of the transfer; or

(2) the license was taken in good faith before recordation of the transfer and without notice of it.

Chapter 2 Endnotes

[1] In 1978, section 201(e) was amended by deleting the period at the end and adding ", except as provided under title 11."

[2] Title 11 of the *United States Code* is entitled "Bankruptcy."

[3] In 1998, the Sonny Bono Copyright Term Extension Act amended section 203 by deleting "by his widow or her widower and his or her grandchildren" from the first sentence in paragraph (2) of subsection (a) and by adding subparagraph (D) to paragraph (2). Pub. L. No. 105-298, 112 Stat. 2827, 2829.

[4] The Berne Convention Implementation Act of 1988 amended section 205 by deleting subsection (d) and redesignating subsections (e) and (f) as subsections (d) and (e), respectively. Pub. L. No. 100-568, 102 Stat. 2853, 2857.

CHAPTER 3[1]

DURATION OF COPYRIGHT

- 301. Preemption with respect to other laws
- 302. Duration of copyright: Works created on or after January 1, 1978
- 303. Duration of copyright: Works created but not published or copyrighted before January 1, 1978
- 304. Duration of copyright: Subsisting copyrights
- 305. Duration of copyright: Terminal date

§ 301. Preemption with respect to other laws[2]

(a) On and after January 1, 1978, all legal or equitable rights that are equivalent to any of the exclusive rights within the general scope of copyright as specified by section 106 in works of authorship that are fixed in a tangible medium of expression and come within the subject matter of copyright as specified by sections 102 and 103, whether created before or after that date and whether published or unpublished, are governed exclusively by this title. Thereafter, no person is entitled to any such right or equivalent right in any such work under the common law or statutes of any State.

(b) Nothing in this title annuls or limits any rights or remedies under the common law or statutes of any State with respect to —

(1) subject matter that does not come within the subject matter of copyright as specified by sections 102 and 103, including works of authorship not fixed in any tangible medium of expression; or

(2) any cause of action arising from undertakings commenced before January 1, 1978;

(3) activities violating legal or equitable rights that are not equivalent to any of the exclusive rights within the general scope of copyright as specified by section 106; or

(4) State and local landmarks, historic preservation, zoning, or building codes, relating to architectural works protected under section 102(a)(8).

(c) With respect to sound recordings fixed before February 15, 1972, any rights or remedies under the common law or statutes of any State shall not be annulled or limited by this title until February 15, 2067. The preemptive provisions of subsection (a) shall apply to any such rights and remedies pertaining to any cause of action arising from undertakings commenced on and after February 15, 2067. Notwithstanding the provisions of section 303, no sound recording fixed before February 15, 1972, shall be subject to copyright under this title before, on, or after February 15, 2067.

(d) Nothing in this title annuls or limits any rights or remedies under any other Federal statute.

(e) The scope of Federal preemption under this section is not affected by the adherence of the United States to the Berne Convention or the satisfaction of obligations of the United States thereunder.

(f)(1) On or after the effective date set forth in section 610(a) of the Visual Artists Rights Act of 1990, all legal or equitable rights that are equivalent to any of the rights conferred by section 106A with respect to works of visual art to which the rights conferred by section 106A apply are governed exclusively by section 106A and section 113(d) and the provisions of this title relating to such sections. Thereafter, no person is entitled to any such right or equivalent right in any work of visual art under the common law or statutes of any State.[3]

(2) Nothing in paragraph (1) annuls or limits any rights or remedies under the common law or statutes of any State with respect to —

(A) any cause of action from undertakings commenced before the effective date set forth in section 610(a) of the Visual Artists Rights Act of 1990;

(B) activities violating legal or equitable rights that are not equivalent to any of the rights conferred by section 106A with respect to works of visual art; or

(C) activities violating legal or equitable rights which extend beyond the life of the author.

§ 302. *Duration of copyright: Works created on or after January 1, 1978*[4]

(a) In General. — Copyright in a work created on or after January 1, 1978, subsists from its creation and, except as provided by the following subsections, endures for a term consisting of the life of the author and 70 years after the author's death.

(b) Joint Works. — In the case of a joint work prepared by two or more authors who did not work for hire, the copyright endures for a term consisting of the life of the last surviving author and 70 years after such last surviving author's death.

(c) Anonymous Works, Pseudonymous Works, and Works Made for Hire. — In the case of an anonymous work, a pseudonymous work, or a work made for hire, the copyright endures for a term of 95 years from the year of its first publication, or a term of 120 years from the year of its creation, whichever expires first. If, before the end of such term, the identity of one or more of the authors of an anonymous or pseudonymous work is revealed in the records of a registration made for that work under subsections (a) or (d) of section 408, or in the records provided by this subsection, the copyright in the work endures for the term specified by subsection (a) or (b), based on the life of the author or authors whose identity has been revealed. Any person having an interest in the copyright in an anonymous or pseudonymous work may at any time record, in records to be maintained by the Copyright Office for that purpose, a statement identifying one or more authors of the work; the statement shall also identify the person filing it, the nature of that person's interest, the source of the information recorded, and the particular work affected, and shall comply in form and content with requirements that the Register of Copyrights shall prescribe by regulation.

(d) Records Relating to Death of Authors. — Any person having an interest in a copyright may at any time record in the Copyright Office a statement of the date of death of the author of the copyrighted work, or a statement that the author is still living on a particular date. The statement shall identify the person filing it, the nature of that person's interest, and the source of the information recorded, and shall comply in form and content with requirements that the Register of Copyrights shall prescribe by regulation. The Register shall maintain current records of information relating to the death of authors of copyrighted works, based on such recorded statements and, to the extent the Register considers practicable, on data contained in any of the records of the Copyright Office or in other reference sources.

(e) Presumption as to Author's Death. — After a period of 95 years from the year of first publication of a work, or a period of 120 years from the year of its creation, whichever expires first, any person who obtains from the Copyright Office a certified report that the records provided by subsection (d) disclose nothing to indicate that the author of the work is living, or died less than 70 years before, is entitled to the benefit of a presumption that the author has been dead for at least 70 years. Reliance in good faith upon this presumption shall be a complete defense to any action for infringement under this title.

§ 303. Duration of copyright: Works created but not published or copyrighted before January 1, 1978[5]

(a) Copyright in a work created before January 1, 1978, but not theretofore in the public domain or copyrighted, subsists from January 1, 1978, and endures for the term provided by section 302. In no case, however, shall the term of copyright in such a work expire before December 31, 2002; and, if the work is published on or before December 31, 2002, the term of copyright shall not expire before December 31, 2047.

(b) The distribution before January 1, 1978, of a phonorecord shall not for any purpose constitute a publication of the musical work embodied therein.

§ 304. Duration of copyright: Subsisting copyrights[6]

(a) Copyrights in Their First Term on January 1, 1978. —

(1)(A) Any copyright, in the first term of which is subsisting on January 1, 1978, shall endure for 28 years from the date it was originally secured.

(B) In the case of —

(i) any posthumous work or of any periodical, cyclopedic, or other composite work upon which the copyright was originally secured by the proprietor thereof, or

(ii) any work copyrighted by a corporate body (otherwise than as assignee or licensee of the individual author) or by an employer for whom such work is made for hire,

the proprietor of such copyright shall be entitled to a renewal and extension of the copyright in such work for the further term of 67 years.

(C) In the case of any other copyrighted work, including a contribution by an individual author to a periodical or to a cyclopedic or other composite work —

(i) the author of such work, if the author is still living,

(ii) the widow, widower, or children of the author, if the author is not living,

(iii) the author's executors, if such author, widow, widower, or children are not living, or

(iv) the author's next of kin, in the absence of a will of the author, shall be entitled to a renewal and extension of the copyright in such work for a further term of 67 years.

(2)(A) At the expiration of the original term of copyright in a work specified in paragraph (1)(B) of this subsection, the copyright shall endure for a renewed and extended further term of 67 years, which —

(i) if an application to register a claim to such further term has been made to the Copyright Office within 1 year before the expiration of the original term of copyright, and the claim is registered, shall vest, upon the beginning of such further term, in the proprietor of the copyright who is entitled to claim the renewal of copyright at the time the application is made; or

(ii) if no such application is made or the claim pursuant to such application is not registered, shall vest, upon the beginning of such further term, in the person or entity that was the proprietor of the copyright as of the last day of the original term of copyright.

(B) At the expiration of the original term of copyright in a work specified in paragraph (1)(C) of this subsection, the copyright shall endure for a renewed and extended further term of 67 years, which —

(i) if an application to register a claim to such further term has been made to the Copyright Office within 1 year before the expiration of the original term of copyright, and the claim is registered, shall vest, upon the beginning of such further term, in any person who is entitled under paragraph (1)(C) to the renewal and extension of the copyright at the time the application is made; or

(ii) if no such application is made or the claim pursuant to such application is not registered, shall vest, upon the beginning of such further term, in any person entitled under paragraph (1)(C), as of the last day of the original term of copyright, to the renewal and extension of the copyright.

(3)(A) An application to register a claim to the renewed and extended term of copyright in a work may be made to the Copyright Office —

(i) within 1 year before the expiration of the original term of copyright by any person entitled under paragraph (1)(B) or (C) to such further term of 67 years; and

(ii) at any time during the renewed and extended term by any person in whom such further term vested, under paragraph (2)(A) or (B), or by any successor or assign of such person, if the application is made in the name of such person.

(B) Such an application is not a condition of the renewal and extension of the copyright in a work for a further term of 67 years.

(4)(A) If an application to register a claim to the renewed and extended term of copyright in a work is not made within 1 year before the expiration of the original term of copyright in a work, or if the claim pursuant to such application is not registered, then a derivative work prepared under authority of a grant of a transfer or license of the copyright that is made before the expiration of the original term of copyright may continue to be used under the terms of the grant during the renewed and extended term of copyright without infringing the copyright, except that such use does not extend to the preparation during such renewed and extended term of other derivative works based upon the copyrighted work covered by such grant.

(B) If an application to register a claim to the renewed and extended term of copyright in a work is made within 1 year before its expiration, and the claim is registered, the certificate of such registration shall constitute prima facie evidence as to the validity of the copyright during its renewed and extended term and of the facts stated in the certificate. The evidentiary weight to be accorded the certificates of a registration of a renewed and extended term of copyright made after the end of that 1-year period shall be within the discretion of the court.

(b) Copyrights in Their Renewal Term at the Time of the Effective Date of the Sonny Bono Copyright Term Extension Act.[7] — Any copyright still in its renewal term at the time that the Sonny Bono Copyright Term Extension Act becomes effective shall have a copyright term of 95 years from the date copyright was originally secured.[8]

(c) Termination of Transfers and Licenses Covering Extended Renewal Term. — In the case of any copyright subsisting in either its first or renewal term on January 1, 1978, other than a copyright in a work made for hire, the exclusive or nonexclusive grant of a transfer or license of the renewal copyright or any right under it, executed before January 1, 1978, by any of the persons designated by subsection (a)(1)(C) of this section, otherwise than by will, is subject to termination under the following conditions:

(1) In the case of a grant executed by a person or persons other than the author, termination of the grant may be effected by the surviving person or persons who executed it. In the case of a grant executed by one or more of the authors of the work, termination of the grant may be effected, to the extent of a particular author's share in the ownership of the renewal copyright, by the author who executed it or, if such author is dead, by the person or persons who, under clause (2) of this subsection, own and are entitled to exercise a total of more than one-half of that author's termination interest.

(2) Where an author is dead, his or her termination interest is owned, and may be exercised, as follows:

(A) The widow or widower owns the author's entire termination interest unless there are any surviving children or grandchildren of the author, in which case the widow or widower owns one-half of the author's interest.

(B) The author's surviving children, and the surviving children of any dead child of the author, own the author's entire termination interest unless there is a widow or widower, in which case the ownership of one-half of the author's interest is divided among them.

(C) The rights of the author's children and grandchildren are in all cases divided among them and exercised on a per stirpes basis according to the number of such author's children represented; the share of the children of a dead child in a termination interest can be exercised only by the action of a majority of them.

(D) In the event that the author's widow or widower, children, and grandchildren are not living, the author's executor, administrator, personal representative, or trustee shall own the author's entire termination interest.

(3) Termination of the grant may be effected at any time during a period of five years beginning at the end of fifty-six years from the date copyright was originally secured, or beginning on January 1, 1978, whichever is later.

(4) The termination shall be effected by serving an advance notice in writing upon the grantee or the grantee's successor in title. In the case of a grant executed by a person or persons other than the author, the notice shall be signed by all of those entitled to terminate the grant under clause (1) of this subsection, or by their duly authorized agents. In the case of a grant executed by one or more of the authors of the work, the notice as to any one author's share shall be signed by that author or his or her duly authorized agent or, if that author is dead, by the number and proportion of the owners of his or her termination interest required under clauses (1) and (2) of this subsection, or by their duly authorized agents.

(A) The notice shall state the effective date of the termination, which shall fall within the five-year period specified by clause (3) of this subsection, or, in the case of a termination under subsection (d), within the five-year period specified by subsection (d)(2), and the notice shall be served not less than two or more than ten years before that date. A copy of the notice shall be recorded in the Copyright Office before the effective date of termination, as a condition to its taking effect.

(B) The notice shall comply, in form, content, and manner of service, with requirements that the Register of Copyrights shall prescribe by regulation.

(5) Termination of the grant may be effected notwithstanding any agreement to the contrary, including an agreement to make a will or to make any future grant.

(6) In the case of a grant executed by a person or persons other than the author, all rights under this title that were covered by the terminated grant revert, upon the effective date of termination, to all of those entitled to terminate the grant under clause (1) of this subsection. In the case of a grant executed by one or more of the authors of the work, all of a particular author's rights under this title that were covered by the terminated grant revert, upon the effective date of termination, to that author or, if that author is dead, to the persons owning his or her termination interest under clause (2) of this subsection, including those owners who did not join in signing the notice of termination under clause (4) of this subsection. In all cases the reversion of rights is subject to the following limitations:

(A) A derivative work prepared under authority of the grant before its termination may continue to be utilized under the terms of the grant after its termination, but this privilege does not extend to the preparation after the termination of other derivative works based upon the copyrighted work covered by the terminated grant.

(B) The future rights that will revert upon termination of the grant become vested on the date the notice of termination has been served as provided by clause (4) of this subsection.

(C) Where the author's rights revert to two or more persons under clause (2) of this subsection, they shall vest in those persons in the proportionate shares provided by that clause. In such a case, and subject to the provisions of subclause (D) of this clause, a further grant, or agreement to make a further grant, of a particular author's share with respect to any right covered by a terminated grant is valid only if it is signed by the same number and proportion of the owners, in whom the right has vested under this clause, as are required to terminate the grant under clause (2) of this subsection. Such further grant or agreement is effective with respect to all of the persons in whom the right it covers has vested under this subclause, including those who did not join in signing it. If any person dies after rights under a terminated grant have vested in him or her, that person's legal representatives, legatees, or heirs at law represent him or her for purposes of this subclause.

(D) A further grant, or agreement to make a further grant, of any right covered by a terminated grant is valid only if it is made after the effective date of the termination. As an exception, however, an agreement for such a further grant may be made between the author or any of the persons provided by the first sentence of clause (6) of this subsection, or between the persons provided by subclause (C) of this clause, and the original grantee or such grantee's successor in title, after the notice of termination has been served as provided by clause (4) of this subsection.

(E) Termination of a grant under this subsection affects only those rights covered by the grant that arise under this title, and in no way affects rights arising under any other Federal, State, or foreign laws.

(F) Unless and until termination is effected under this subsection, the grant, if it does not provide otherwise, continues in effect for the remainder of the extended renewal term.

(d) Termination Rights Provided in Subsection (c) Which Have Expired on or before the Effective Date of the Sonny Bono Copyright Term Extension Act. — In the case of any copyright other than a work made for hire, subsisting in its renewal term on the effective date of the Sonny Bono Copyright Term Extension Act[9] for which the termination right provided in subsection (c) has expired by such date, where the author or owner of the termination right has not previously exercised such termination right, the exclusive or nonexclusive grant of a transfer or license of the renewal copyright or any right under it, executed before January 1, 1978, by any of the persons designated in subsection (a)(1)(C) of this section, other than by will, is subject to termination under the following conditions:

(1) The conditions specified in subsections (c) (1), (2), (4), (5), and (6) of this section apply to terminations of the last 20 years of copyright term as provided by the amendments made by the Sonny Bono Copyright Term Extension Act.

(2) Termination of the grant may be effected at any time during a period of 5 years beginning at the end of 75 years from the date copyright was originally secured.

§ 305. *Duration of copyright: Terminal date*

All terms of copyright provided by sections 302 through 304 run to the end of the calendar year in which they would otherwise expire.

Chapter 3 Endnotes

[1] Private Law 92-60, 85 Stat. 857, effective December 15, 1971, states that:

[A]ny provision of law to the contrary notwithstanding, copyright is hereby granted to the trustees under the will of Mary Baker Eddy, their successors, and assigns, in the work "Science and Health with Key to the Scriptures" (entitled also in some editions "Science and Health" or "Science and Health; with a Key to the Scriptures"), by Mary Baker Eddy, including all editions thereof in English and translation heretofore published, or hereafter published by or on behalf of said trustees, their successors or assigns, for a term of seventy-five years from the effective date of this Act or from the date of first publication, whichever is later.

But *cf. United Christian Scientists* v. *Christian Science Board of Directors, First Church of Christ, Scientist*, 829 F.2d 1152, 4 USPQ2d 1177 (D.C. Cir. 1987) (holding Priv. L. 92-60, 85 Stat. 857, to be unconstitutional because it violates the Establishment Clause).

[2] The Berne Convention Implementation Act of 1988 amended section 301 by adding at the end thereof subsection (e). Pub. L. No. 100-568, 102 Stat. 2853, 2857. In 1990, the Architectural Works Copyright Protection Act amended section 301(b) by adding at the end thereof paragraph (4). Pub. L. No. 101-650, 104 Stat. 5133, 5134. The Visual Artists Rights Act of 1990 amended section 301 by adding at the end thereof subsection (f). Pub. L. No. 101-650, 104 Stat. 5089, 5131. In 1998, the Sonny Bono Copyright Term Extension Act amended section 301 by changing "February 15, 2047" to "February 15, 2067" each place it appeared in subsection (c). Pub. L. No. 105-298, 112 Stat. 2827.

[3] The Visual Artists Rights Act of 1990, which added subsection (f), states, "Subject to subsection (b) and except as provided in subsection (c), this title and the amendments made by this title take effect 6 months after the date of the enactment of this Act," that is, six months after December 1, 1990. Pub. L. No. 101-650, 104 Stat. 5089, 5132. See also endnote 39, chapter 1.

[4] In 1998, the Sonny Bono Copyright Term Extension Act amended section 302 by substituting "70" for "fifty," "95" for "seventy-five," and "120" for "one hundred" each place they appeared. Pub. L. No. 105-298, 112 Stat. 2827. This change was effective October 27, 1998. *Id.*

[5] In 1997, section 303 was amended by adding subsection (b). Pub. L. No. 105-80, 111 Stat. 1529, 1534. In 1998, the Sonny Bono Copyright Term Extension Act amended section 303 by substituting "December 31, 2047" for "December 31, 2027." Pub. L. No. 105-298, 112 Stat. 2827.

[6] The Copyright Renewal Act of 1992 amended section 304 by substituting a new subsection (a) and by making a conforming amendment in the matter preceding paragraph (1) of subsection (c). Pub. L. No. 102-307, 106 Stat. 264. The Act, as amended by the Sonny Bono Copyright Term Extension Act, states that the renewal and extension of a copyright for a further term of 67 years "shall have the same effect with respect to any grant, before the effective date of the Sonny Bono Copyright Term Extension Act [October 27, 1998], of a transfer or license of the further term as did the renewal of a copyright before the effective date of the Sonny Bono Copyright Term Extension Act [October 27, 1998] under the law in effect at the time of such grant." The Act also states that the 1992 amendments "shall apply only to those copyrights secured between January 1, 1964, and December 31, 1977. Copyrights secured before January 1, 1964, shall be governed by the provisions of section 304(a) of title 17, United States Code, as in effect on the day before . . .[enactment on June 26, 1992], except each reference to forty-seven years in such provisions shall be deemed to be 67 years." Pub. L. No. 102-307, 106 Stat. 264, 266, as amended by the Sonny Bono Copyright Term Extension Act, Pub. L. No. 105-298, 112 Stat. 2827, 2828.

In 1998, the Sonny Bono Copyright Term Extension Act amended section 304 by substituting "67" for "47" wherever it appeared in subsection (a), by substituting a new subsection (b), and by adding subsection (d) at the end thereof. Pub. L. No. 105-298, 112 Stat. 2827. That Act also amended subsection 304(c) by deleting "by his widow or her widower and his or her children or grandchildren" from the first sentence of paragraph (2), by adding subparagraph (D) at the end of paragraph (2), and by inserting "or, in the case of a termination under subsection (d), within the five-year period specified by subsection (d)(2)," into the first sentence of subparagraph (4)(A). *Id.*

[7] In 1998, the Sonny Bono Copyright Term Extension Act amendment to subsection 304(b) completely deleted the previous language that was originally part of the 1976 Copyright Act. Pub. L. No. 105-298, 112 Stat. 2827. That earlier statutory language continues to be relevant for calculating the term of protection for copyrights commencing between September 19, 1906, and December 31, 1949. The 1976 Copyright Act extended the terms for those copyrights by 20 years, provided they were in their renewal term between December 31, 1976, and December 31, 1977. The deleted language states:

The duration of any copyright, the renewal term of which is subsisting at any time between December 31, 1976, and December 31, 1977, inclusive, or for which renewal registration is made between December 31, 1976, and December 31, 1977, inclusive, is extended to endure for a term of seventy-five years from the date copyright was originally secured.

The effective date of this provision was October 19, 1976. That effective date provision is contained in Appendix A, herein, as section 102 of the Transitional and Supplementary Provisions of the Copyright Act of 1976. Copyright Act of 1976, Pub. L. No. 94-553, 90 Stat. 2541, 2598.

In addition, prior to the 1976 Copyright Act, Congress enacted a series of nine interim extensions for works whose copyright protection began between September 19, 1906, and December 31, 1918, if they were in their renewal terms. Without these interim extensions, copyrights commencing during that time period would have otherwise expired after 56 years, at the end of their renewal terms, between September 19, 1962, and December 31, 1976. The nine Acts authorizing the interim extensions are as follows, in chronological order:

Pub. L. No. 87-668, 76 Stat. 555 (extending copyrights from September 19, 1962, to December 31, 1965)

Pub. L. No. 89-142, 79 Stat. 581 (extending copyrights to December 31, 1967)

Pub. L. No. 90-141, 81 Stat. 464 (extending copyrights to December 31, 1968)

Pub. L. No. 90-416, 82 Stat. 397 (extending copyrights to December 31, 1969)

Pub. L. No. 91-147, 83 Stat. 360 (extending copyrights to December 31, 1970)

Pub. L. No. 91-555, 84 Stat. 1441 (extending copyrights to December 31, 1971)

Pub. L. No. 92-170, 85 Stat. 490 (extending copyrights to December 31, 1972)

Pub. L. No. 92-566, 86 Stat. 1181 (extending copyrights to December 31, 1974)

Pub. L. No. 93-573, 88 Stat. 1873 (extending copyrights to December 31, 1976)

[8] The effective date of the Sonny Bono Copyright Term Extension Act is October 27, 1998.

[9] See endnote 8, *supra.*

CHAPTER 4

COPYRIGHT NOTICE, DEPOSIT, AND REGISTRATION

- 401. Notice of copyright: Visually perceptible copies
- 402. Notice of copyright: Phonorecords of sound recordings
- 403. Notice of copyright: Publications incorporating United States Government works
- 404. Notice of copyright: Contributions to collective works
- 405. Notice of copyright: Omission of notice on certain copies and phonorecords
- 406. Notice of copyright: Error in name or date on certain copies and phonorecords
- 407. Deposit of copies or phonorecords for Library of Congress

§ 401. Notice of copyright: Visually perceptible copies[1]

(a) General Provisions. — Whenever a work protected under this title is published in the United States or elsewhere by authority of the copyright owner, a notice of copyright as provided by this section may be placed on publicly distributed copies from which the work can be visually perceived, either directly or with the aid of a machine or device.

(b) Form of Notice. — If a notice appears on the copies, it shall consist of the following three elements:

(1) the symbol (c) (the letter C in a circle), or the word "Copyright", or the abbreviation "Copr."; and

(2) the year of first publication of the work; in the case of compilations or derivative works incorporating previously published material, the year date of first publication of the compilation or derivative work is sufficient. The year date may be omitted where a pictorial, graphic, or sculptural work, with accompanying text matter, if any, is reproduced in or on greeting cards, postcards, stationery, jewelry, dolls, toys, or any useful articles; and

(3) the name of the owner of copyright in the work, or an abbreviation by which the name can be recognized, or a generally known alternative designation of the owner.

(c) Position of Notice. — The notice shall be affixed to the copies in such manner and location as to give reasonable notice of the claim of copyright. The Register of Copyrights shall prescribe by regulation, as examples, specific methods of affixation and positions of the notice on various types of works that will satisfy this requirement, but these specifications shall not be considered exhaustive.

(d) Evidentiary Weight of Notice. — If a notice of copyright in the form and position specified by this section appears on the published copy or copies to which a defendant in a copyright infringement suit had access, then no weight shall be given to such a defendant's interposition of a defense based on innocent infringement in mitigation of actual or statutory damages, except as provided in the last sentence of section 504(c)(2).

§ 402. Notice of copyright: Phonorecords of sound recordings[2]

(a) General Provisions. — Whenever a sound recording protected under this title is published in the United States or elsewhere by authority of the copyright owner, a notice of copyright as provided by this section may be placed on publicly distributed phonorecords of the sound recording.

(b) Form of Notice. — If a notice appears on the phonorecords, it shall consist of the following three elements:

(1) the symbol (the letter P in a circle); and

(2) the year of first publication of the sound recording; and

(3) the name of the owner of copyright in the sound recording, or an abbreviation by which the name can be recognized, or a generally known alternative designation of the owner; if the producer of the sound recording is named on the phonorecord labels or containers, and if no other name appears in conjunction with the notice, the producer's name shall be considered a part of the notice.

(c) Position of Notice. — The notice shall be placed on the surface of the phonorecord, or on the phonorecord label or container, in such manner and location as to give reasonable notice of the claim of copyright.

(d) Evidentiary Weight of Notice. — If a notice of copyright in the form and position specified by this section appears on the published phonorecord or phonorecords to which a defendant in a copyright infringement suit had access, then no weight shall be given to such a defendant's interposition of a defense based on innocent infringement in mitigation of actual or statutory damages, except as provided in the last sentence of section 504(c)(2).

§ 403. Notice of copyright: Publications incorporating United States Government works[3]

Sections 401(d) and 402(d) shall not apply to a work published in copies or phonorecords consisting predominantly of one or more works of the United States Government unless the notice of copyright appearing on the published copies or phonorecords to which a defendant in the copyright infringement suit had access includes a statement identifying, either affirmatively or negatively, those portions of the copies or phonorecords embodying any work or works protected under this title.

§ 404. Notice of copyright: Contributions to collective works[4]

(a) A separate contribution to a collective work may bear its own notice of copyright, as provided by sections 401 through 403. However, a single notice applicable to the collective work as a whole is sufficient to invoke the provisions of section 401(d) or 402(d), as applicable with respect to the separate contributions it contains (not including advertisements inserted on behalf of persons other than the owner of copyright in the collective work), regardless of the ownership of copyright in the contributions and whether or not they have been previously published.

(b) With respect to copies and phonorecords publicly distributed by authority of the copyright owner before the effective date of the Berne Convention Implementation Act of 1988, where the person named in a single notice applicable to a collective work as a whole is not the owner of copyright in a separate contribution that does not bear its own notice, the case is governed by the provisions of section 406(a).

§ 405. Notice of copyright: Omission of notice on certain copies and phonorecords[5]

(a) Effect of Omission on Copyright. — With respect to copies and phonorecords publicly distributed by authority of the copyright owner before the effective date of the Berne Convention Implementation Act of 1988, the omission of the copyright notice described in sections 401 through 403 from copies or phonorecords publicly distributed by authority of the copyright owner does not invalidate the copyright in a work if —

(1) the notice has been omitted from no more than a relatively small number of copies or phonorecords distributed to the public; or

(2) registration for the work has been made before or is made within five years after the publication without notice, and a reasonable effort is made to add notice to all copies or phonorecords that are distributed to the public in the United States after the omission has been discovered; or

(3) the notice has been omitted in violation of an express requirement in writing that, as a condition of the copyright owner's authorization of the public distribution of copies or phonorecords, they bear the prescribed notice.

(b) Effect of Omission on Innocent Infringers. — Any person who innocently infringes a copyright, in reliance upon an authorized copy or phonorecord from which the copyright notice has been omitted and which was publicly distributed by authority of the copyright owner before the effective date of the Berne Convention Implementation Act of 1988, incurs no liability for actual or statutory damages under section 504 for any infringing acts committed before receiving actual notice that registration for the work has been made under section 408, if such person proves that he or she was misled by the omission of notice. In a suit for infringement in such a case the court may allow or disallow recovery of any of the infringer's profits attributable to the infringement, and may enjoin the continuation of the infringing undertaking or may require, as a condition for permitting the continuation of the infringing undertaking, that the infringer pay the copyright owner a reasonable license fee in an amount and on terms fixed by the court.

(c) Removal of Notice. — Protection under this title is not affected by the removal, destruction, or obliteration of the notice, without the authorization of the copyright owner, from any publicly distributed copies or phonorecords.

§ 406. *Notice of copyright: Error in name or date on certain copies and phonorecords*[6]

(a) Error in Name. — With respect to copies and phonorecords publicly distributed by authority of the copyright owner before the effective date of the Berne Convention Implementation Act of 1988, where the person named in the copyright notice on copies or phonorecords publicly distributed by authority of the copyright owner is not the owner of copyright, the validity and ownership of the copyright are not affected. In such a case, however, any person who innocently begins an undertaking that infringes the copyright has a complete defense to any action for such infringement if such person proves that he or she was misled by the notice and began the undertaking in good faith under a purported transfer or license from the person named therein, unless before the undertaking was begun-

(1) registration for the work had been made in the name of the owner of copyright; or

(2) a document executed by the person named in the notice and showing the ownership of the copyright had been recorded.

The person named in the notice is liable to account to the copyright owner for all receipts from transfers or licenses purportedly made under the copyright by the person named in the notice.

(b) Error in Date. — When the year date in the notice on copies or phonorecords distributed before the effective date of the Berne Convention Implementation Act of 1988 by authority of the copyright owner is earlier than the year in which publication first occurred, any period computed from the year of first publication under section 302 is to be computed from the year in the notice. Where the year date is more than one year later than the year in which publication first occurred, the work is considered to have been published without any notice and is governed by the provisions of section 405.

(c) Omission of Name or Date. — Where copies or phonorecords publicly distributed before the effective date of the Berne Convention Implementation Act of 1988 by authority of the copyright owner contain no name or no date that could reasonably be considered a part of the notice, the work is considered to have been published without any notice and is governed by the provisions of section 405 as in effect on the day before the effective date of the Berne Convention Implementation Act of 1988.

§ 407. *Deposit of copies or phonorecords for Library of Congress*[7]

(a) Except as provided by subsection (c), and subject to the provisions of subsection (e), the owner of copyright or of the exclusive right of publication in a work published in the United States shall deposit, within three months after the date of such publication —

(1) two complete copies of the best edition; or

(2) if the work is a sound recording, two complete phonorecords of the best edition, together with any printed or other visually perceptible material published with such phonorecords.

Neither the deposit requirements of this subsection nor the acquisition provisions of subsection (e) are conditions of copyright protection.

(b) The required copies or phonorecords shall be deposited in the Copyright Office for the use or disposition of the Library of Congress. The Register of Copyrights shall, when requested by the depositor and upon payment of the fee prescribed by section 708, issue a receipt for the deposit.

(c) The Register of Copyrights may by regulation exempt any categories of material from the deposit requirements of this section, or require deposit of only one copy or phonorecord with respect to any categories. Such regulations shall provide either for complete exemption from the deposit requirements of this section, or for alternative forms of deposit aimed at providing a satisfactory archival record of a work without imposing practical or financial hardships on the depositor, where the individual author is the owner of copyright in a pictorial, graphic, or sculptural work and (i) less than five copies of the work have been published, or (ii) the work has been published in a limited edition consisting of numbered copies, the monetary value of which would make the mandatory deposit of two copies of the best edition of the work burdensome, unfair, or unreasonable.

(d) At any time after publication of a work as provided by subsection(a), the Register of Copyrights may make written demand for the required deposit on any of the persons obligated to make the deposit under subsection (a). Unless deposit is made within three months after the demand is received, the person or persons on whom the demand was made are liable —

(1) to a fine of not more than $250 for each work; and

(2) to pay into a specially designated fund in the Library of Congress the total retail price of the copies or phonorecords demanded, or, if no retail price has been fixed, the reasonable cost to the Library of Congress of acquiring them; and

(3) to pay a fine of $2,500, in addition to any fine or liability imposed under clauses (1) and (2), if such person willfully or repeatedly fails or refuses to comply with such a demand.

(e) With respect to transmission programs that have been fixed and transmitted to the public in the United States but have not been published, the Register of Copyrights shall, after consulting with the Librarian of Congress and other interested organizations and officials, establish regulations governing the acquisition, through deposit or otherwise, of copies or phonorecords of such programs for the collections of the Library of Congress.

(1) The Librarian of Congress shall be permitted, under the standards and conditions set forth in such regulations, to make a fixation of a transmission program directly from a transmission to the public, and to reproduce one copy or phonorecord from such fixation for archival purposes.

(2) Such regulations shall also provide standards and procedures by which the Register of Copyrights may make written demand, upon the owner of the right of transmission in the United States, for the deposit of a copy or phonorecord of a specific transmission program. Such deposit may, at the option of the owner of the right of transmission in the United States, be accomplished by gift, by loan for purposes of reproduction, or by sale at a price not to exceed the cost of reproducing and supplying the copy or phonorecord. The regulations established under this clause shall

provide reasonable periods of not less than three months for compliance with a demand, and shall allow for extensions of such periods and adjustments in the scope of the demand or the methods for fulfilling it, as reasonably warranted by the circumstances. Willful failure or refusal to comply with the conditions prescribed by such regulations shall subject the owner of the right of transmission in the United States to liability for an amount, not to exceed the cost of reproducing and supplying the copy or phonorecord in question, to be paid into a specially designated fund in the Library of Congress.

(3) Nothing in this subsection shall be construed to require the making or retention, for purposes of deposit, of any copy or phonorecord of an unpublished transmission program, the transmission of which occurs before the receipt of a specific written demand as provided by clause (2).

(4) No activity undertaken in compliance with regulations prescribed under clauses (1) and (2) of this subsection shall result in liability if intended solely to assist in the acquisition of copies or phonorecords under this subsection.

§ 408. Copyright registration in general[8]

(a) Registration Permissive. — At any time during the subsistence of the first term of copyright in any published or unpublished work in which the copyright was secured before January 1, 1978, and during the subsistence of any copyright secured on or after that date, the owner of copyright or of any exclusive right in the work may obtain registration of the copyright claim by delivering to the Copyright Office the deposit specified by this section, together with the application and fee specified by sections 409 and 708. Such registration is not a condition of copyright protection.

(b) Deposit for Copyright Registration. — Except as provided by subsection (c), the material deposited for registration shall include —

   (1) in the case of an unpublished work, one complete copy or phonorecord;

   (2) in the case of a published work, two complete copies or phonorecords of the best edition;

   (3) in the case of a work first published outside the United States, one complete copy or phonorecord as so published;

   (4) in the case of a contribution to a collective work, one complete copy or phonorecord of the best edition of the collective work.

Copies or phonorecords deposited for the Library of Congress under section 407 may be used to satisfy the deposit provisions of this section, if they are accompanied by the prescribed application and fee, and by any additional identifying material that the Register may, by regulation, require. The Register shall also prescribe regulations establishing requirements under which copies or phonorecords acquired for the Library of Congress under subsection (e) of section 407, otherwise than by deposit, may be used to satisfy the deposit provisions of this section.

(c) Administrative Classification and Optional Deposit. —

(1) The Register of Copyrights is authorized to specify by regulation the administrative classes into which works are to be placed for purposes of deposit and registration, and the nature of the copies or phonorecords to be deposited in the various classes specified. The regulations may require or permit, for particular classes, the deposit of identifying material instead of copies or phonorecords, the deposit of only one copy or phonorecord where two would normally be required, or a single registration for a group of related works. This administrative classification of works has no significance with respect to the subject matter of copyright or the exclusive rights provided by this title.

(2) Without prejudice to the general authority provided under clause (1), the Register of Copyrights shall establish regulations specifically permitting a single registration for a group of works by the same individual author, all first published as contributions to periodicals, including newspapers, within a twelve-month period, on the basis of a single deposit, application, and registration fee, under the following conditions —

(A) if the deposit consists of one copy of the entire issue of the periodical, or of the entire section in the case of a newspaper, in which each contribution was first published; and

(B) if the application identifies each work separately, including the periodical containing it and its date of first publication.

(3) As an alternative to separate renewal registrations under subsection (a) of section 304, a single renewal registration may be made for a group of works by the same individual author, all first published as contributions to periodicals, including newspapers, upon the filing of a single application and fee, under all of the following conditions:

(A) the renewal claimant or claimants, and the basis of claim or claims under section 304(a), is the same for each of the works; and

(B) the works were all copyrighted upon their first publication, either through separate copyright notice and registration or by virtue of a general copyright notice in the periodical issue as a whole; and

(C) the renewal application and fee are received not more than twenty-eight or less than twenty-seven years after the thirty-first day of December of the calendar year in which all of the works were first published; and

(D) the renewal application identifies each work separately, including the periodical containing it and its date of first publication.

(d) Corrections and Amplifications. — The Register may also establish, by regulation, formal procedures for the filing of an application for supplementary registration, to correct an error in a copyright registration or to amplify the information given in a registration. Such application shall be accompanied by the fee provided by section 708, and shall clearly identify the registration to be corrected or amplified. The information contained in a supplementary registration augments but does not supersede that contained in the earlier registration.

(e) Published Edition of Previously Registered Work. — Registration for the first published edition of a work previously registered in unpublished form may be made even though the work as published is substantially the same as the unpublished version.

(f) Preregistration of Works Being Prepared for Commercial Distribution. —

(1) Rulemaking. — Not later than 180 days after the date of enactment of this subsection, the Register of Copyrights shall issue regulations to establish procedures for preregistration of a work that is being prepared for commercial distribution and has not been published.

(2) Class of works. — The regulations established under paragraph (1) shall permit preregistration for any work that is in a class of works that the Register determines has had a history of infringement prior to authorized commercial distribution.

(3) Application for registration. — Not later than 3 months after the first publication of a work preregistered under this subsection, the applicant shall submit to the Copyright Office-

(A) an application for registration of the work;

(B) a deposit; and

(C) the applicable fee.

(4) Effect of untimely application. — An action under this chapter for infringement of a work preregistered under this subsection, in a case in which the infringement commenced no later than 2 months after the first publication of the work, shall be dismissed if the items described in paragraph (3) are not submitted to the Copyright Office in proper form within the earlier of —

(A) 3 months after the first publication of the work; or

(B) 1 month after the copyright owner has learned of the infringement.

§ 409. Application for copyright registration[9]

The application for copyright registration shall be made on a form prescribed by the Register of Copyrights and shall include —

(1) the name and address of the copyright claimant;

(2) in the case of a work other than an anonymous or pseudonymous work, the name and nationality or domicile of the author or authors, and, if one or more of the authors is dead, the dates of their deaths;

(3) if the work is anonymous or pseudonymous, the nationality or domicile of the author or authors;

(4) in the case of a work made for hire, a statement to this effect;

(5) if the copyright claimant is not the author, a brief statement of how the claimant obtained ownership of the copyright;

(6) the title of the work, together with any previous or alternative titles under which the work can be identified;

(7) the year in which creation of the work was completed;

(8) if the work has been published, the date and nation of its first publication;

(9) in the case of a compilation or derivative work, an identification of any preexisting work or works that it is based on or incorporates, and a brief, general statement of the additional material covered by the copyright claim being registered;

(10) in the case of a published work containing material of which copies are required by section 601 to be manufactured in the United States, the names of the persons or organizations who performed the processes specified by subsection (c) of section 601 with respect to that material, and the places where those processes were performed; and

(11) any other information regarded by the Register of Copyrights as bearing upon the preparation or identification of the work or the existence, ownership, or duration of the copyright.

If an application is submitted for the renewed and extended term provided for in section 304(a)(3)(A) and an original term registration has not been made, the Register may request information with respect to the existence, ownership, or duration of the copyright for the original term.

§ 410. Registration of claim and issuance of certificate

(a) When, after examination, the Register of Copyrights determines that, in accordance with the provisions of this title, the material deposited constitutes copyrightable subject matter and that the other legal and formal requirements of this title have been met, the Register shall register the claim and issue to the applicant a certificate of registration under the seal of the Copyright Office. The certificate shall contain the information given in the application, together with the number and effective date of the registration.

(b) In any case in which the Register of Copyrights determines that, in accordance with the provisions of this title, the material deposited does not constitute copyrightable subject matter or that the claim is invalid for any other reason, the Register shall refuse registration and shall notify the applicant in writing of the reasons for such refusal.

(c) In any judicial proceedings the certificate of a registration made before or within five years after first publication of the work shall constitute *prima facie* evidence of the validity of the copyright and of the facts stated in the certificate. The evidentiary weight to be accorded the certificate of a registration made thereafter shall be within the discretion of the court.

(d) The effective date of a copyright registration is the day on which an application, deposit, and fee, which are later determined by the Register of Copyrights or by a court of competent jurisdiction to be acceptable for registration, have all been received in the Copyright Office.

§ 411. Registration and infringement actions[10]

(a) Except for an action brought for a violation of the rights of the author under section 106A(a), and subject to the provisions of subsection (b), no action for infringement of the copyright in any United States work shall be instituted until preregistration or registration of the copyright claim has been made in accordance with this title. In any case, however, where the deposit, application, and fee required for registration have been delivered to the Copyright Office in proper form and registration has been refused, the applicant is entitled to institute an action for infringement if notice thereof, with a copy of the complaint, is served on the Register of Copyrights. The Register may, at his or her option, become a party to the action with respect to the issue of registrability of the copyright claim by entering an appearance within sixty days after such service, but the Register's failure to become a party shall not deprive the court of jurisdiction to determine that issue.

(b) In the case of a work consisting of sounds, images, or both, the first fixation of which is made simultaneously with its transmission, the copyright owner may, either before or after such fixation takes place, institute an action for infringement under section 501, fully subject to the remedies provided by sections 502 through 506 and sections 509 and 510, if, in accordance with requirements that the Register of Copyrights shall prescribe by regulation, the copyright owner —

(1) serves notice upon the infringer, not less than 48 hours before such fixation, identifying the work and the specific time and source of its first transmission, and declaring an intention to secure copyright in the work; and

(2) makes registration for the work, if required by subsection (a), within three months after its first transmission.

§ 412. Registration as prerequisite to certain remedies for infringement[11]

In any action under this title, other than an action brought for a violation of the rights of the author under section 106A(a), an action for infringement of the copyright of a work that has been preregistered under section 408(f) before the commencement of the infringement and that has an effective date of registration not later than the earlier of 3 months after the first publication of the work or 1 month after the copyright owner has learned of the infringement, or an action instituted under section 411(b), no award of statutory damages or of attorney's fees, as provided by sections 504 and 505, shall be made for —

(1) any infringement of copyright in an unpublished work commenced before the effective date of its registration; or

(2) any infringement of copyright commenced after first publication of the work and before the effective date of its registration, unless such registration is made within three months after the first publication of the work.

Chapter 4 Endnotes

[1]The Berne Convention Implementation Act of 1988 amended section 401 as follows: 1) in subsection (a), by changing the heading to "General Provisions" and by inserting "may be placed on" in lieu of "shall be placed on all"; 2) in subsection (b), by inserting "If a notice appears on the copies, it" in lieu of "The notice appearing on the copies"; and 3) by adding subsection (d). Pub. L. No. 100-568, 102 Stat. 2853, 2857.

[2]The Berne Convention Implementation Act of 1988 amended section 402 as follows: 1) in subsection (a), by changing the heading to "General Provisions" and by inserting "may be placed on" in lieu of "shall be placed on all"; 2) in subsection (b), by inserting "If a notice appears on the phonorecords, it" in lieu of "The notice appearing on the phonorecords"; and 3) by adding subsection (d). Pub. L. No. 100-568, 102 Stat. 2853, 2857.

[3]The Berne Convention Implementation Act of 1988 amended section 403 in its entirety. Pub. L. No. 100-568, 102 Stat. 2853, 2858.

[4]The Berne Convention Implementation Act of 1988 amended section 404 as follows: 1) in the second sentence of subsection (a), by inserting "to invoke the provisions of section 401(d) or 402(d), as applicable" in lieu of "to satisfy the requirements of sections 401 through 403" and 2) in subsection (b), by inserting "With respect to copies and phonorecords publicly distributed by authority of the copyright owner before the effective date of the Berne Convention Implementation Act of 1988," at the beginning of the sentence. Pub. L. No. 100-568, 102 Stat. 2853, 2858.

[5]The Berne Convention Implementation Act of 1988 amended section 405 as follows: 1) in subsection (a), by inserting "With respect to copies and phonorecords publicly distributed by authority of the copyright owner before the effective date of the Berne Convention Implementation Act of 1988, the omission of the copyright notice described in" at the beginning of the first sentence, in lieu of "The omission of the copyright notice prescribed by"; 2) in subsection (b), by inserting after "omitted," in the first sentence, "and which was publicly distributed by authority of the copyright owner before the effective date of the Berne Convention Implementation Act of 1988"; and 3) by amending the section heading to add "on certain copies and phonorecords" at the end thereof. Pub. L. No. 100-568, 102 Stat. 2853, 2858.

[6]The Berne Convention Implementation Act of 1988 amended section 406 as follows: 1) in subsection (a), by inserting "With respect to copies and phonorecords publicly distributed by authority of the copyright owner before the effective date of the Berne Convention Implementation Act of 1988," at the beginning of the first sentence; 2) in subsection (b), by inserting "before the effective date of the Berne Convention Implementation Act of 1988" after "distributed"; 3) in subsection (c), by inserting "before the effective date of the Berne Convention Implementation Act of 1988" after "publicly distributed" and by inserting "as in effect on the day before the effective date of the Berne Convention Implementation Act of 1988" after "405"; and 4) by amending the section heading to add "on certain copies and phonorecords" at the end thereof. Pub. L. No. 100-568, 102 Stat. 2853, 2858.

[7]The Berne Convention Implementation Act of 1988 amended section 407 by striking out the words "with notice of copyright" in subsection (a). Pub. L. No. 100-568, 102 Stat. 2853, 2859.

[8]The Berne Convention Implementation Act of 1988 amended section 408 by deleting "Subject to the provisions of section 405(a)," at the beginning of the second sentence of subsection (a). Pub. L. No. 100-568, 102 Stat. 2853, 2859. That Act also amended section 408(c)(2) by inserting "the following conditions:" in lieu of "all of the following conditions" and by striking subparagraph (A) and by redesignating subparagraphs (B) and (C) as subparagraphs (A) and (B), respectively. *Id.* The Copyright Renewal Act of 1992 amended section 408 by revising the first sentence of subsection (a), preceding the words "the owner of copyright or of any exclusive right." Pub. L. No. 102-307, 106 Stat. 264, 266.

The Artists' Rights and Theft Prevention Act of 2005 amended section 408 by adding a new subsection (f). Pub. L. No. 109-9, 119 Stat. 218, 221.

[9]The Copyright Renewal Act of 1992 amended section 409 by adding the last sentence. Pub. L. No. 102-307, 106 Stat. 264, 266.

[10]The Berne Convention Implementation Act of 1988 amended section 411 as follows: 1) in subsection (a), by inserting "Except for actions for infringement of copyright in Berne Convention works whose country of origin is not the United States, and" before "subject"; 2) in paragraph (b)(2), by inserting ", if required by subsection (a)," after "work"; and 3) by

inserting "and infringement actions" in the heading, in lieu of "as prerequisite to infringement suit." Pub. L. No. 100-568, 102 Stat. 2853, 2859.

The Visual Artists Rights Act of 1990 amended section 411(a) by inserting "and an action brought for a violation of the rights of the author under section 106A(a)" after "United States." Pub. L. No. 101-650, 104 Stat. 5089, 5131. In 1997, section 411(b)(1) was amended in its entirety. Pub. L. No. 105-80, 111 Stat. 1529, 1532.

The WIPO Copyright and Performances and Phonograms Treaties Implementation Act of 1998 amended the first sentence in section 411(a) by deleting "actions for infringement of copyright in Berne Convention works whose country of origin is not the United and" and by inserting "United States" after "no action for infringement of the copyright in any." Pub. L. No. 105-304, 112 Stat. 2860, 2863.

The Artists' Rights and Theft Prevention Act of 2005 amended subsection 411(a) by inserting "preregistration" in the first sentence, after "shall be instituted until" in the first sentence. Pub. L. No. 109-9, 119 Stat. 218, 222.

[11]The Visual Artists Rights Act of 1990 amended section 412 by inserting "an action brought for a violation of the rights of the author under section 106A(a) or" after "other than." Pub. L. No. 101-650, 104 Stat. 5089, 5131.

The Artists' Rights and Theft Prevention Act of 2005 amended subsection 412 by inserting the clause that follows "section 106A(a)," in the text preceding subparagraph (1). Pub. L. No. 109-9, 119 Stat. 218, 222.

CHAPTER 5

COPYRIGHT INFRINGEMENT AND REMEDIES

- 501. Infringement of copyright
- 502. Remedies for infringement: Injunctions
- 503. Remedies for infringement: Impounding and disposition of infringing articles
- 504. Remedies for infringement: Damages and profits
- 505. Remedies for infringement: Costs and attorney's fees
- 506. Criminal offenses
- 507. Limitations on actions
- 508. Notification of filing and determination of actions
- 509. Seizure and forfeiture
- 510. Remedies for alteration of programming by cable systems
- 511. Liability of States, instrumentalities of States, and State officials for infringement of copyright
- 512. Limitations on liability relating to material online
- 513. Determination of reasonable license fees for individual proprietors[1]

§ 501. Infringement of copyright[2]

(a) Anyone who violates any of the exclusive rights of the copyright owner as provided by sections 106 through 122 or of the author as provided in section 106A(a), or who imports copies or phonorecords into the United States in violation of section 602, is an infringer of the copyright or right of the author, as the case may be. For purposes of this chapter (other than section 506), any reference to copyright shall be deemed to include the rights conferred by section 106A(a). As used in this subsection, the term "anyone" includes any State, any instrumentality of a State, and any officer or employee of a State or instrumentality of a State acting in his or her official capacity. Any State, and any such instrumentality, officer, or employee, shall be subject to the provisions of this title in the same manner and to the same extent as any nongovernmental entity.

(b) The legal or beneficial owner of an exclusive right under a copyright is entitled, subject to the requirements of section 411, to institute an action for any infringement of that particular right committed while he or she is the owner of it. The court may require such owner to serve written notice of the action with a copy of the complaint upon any person shown, by the records of the Copyright Office or otherwise, to have or claim an interest in the copyright, and shall require that such notice be served upon any person whose interest is likely to be affected by a decision in the case. The court may require the joinder, and shall permit the intervention, of any person having or claiming an interest in the copyright.

(c) For any secondary transmission by a cable system that embodies a performance or a display of a work which is actionable as an act of infringement under subsection (c) of section 111, a television broadcast station holding a copyright or other license to transmit or perform the same version of that work shall, for purposes of subsection (b) of this section, be treated as a legal or beneficial owner if such secondary transmission occurs within the local service area of that television station.

(d) For any secondary transmission by a cable system that is actionable as an act of infringement pursuant to section 111(c)(3), the following shall also have standing to sue: (i) the primary transmitter whose transmission has been altered by the cable system; and (ii) any broadcast station within whose local service area the secondary transmission occurs.

(e) With respect to any secondary transmission that is made by a satellite carrier of a performance or display of a work embodied in a primary transmission and is actionable as an act of infringement under section 119(a)(5), a network station holding a copyright or other license to transmit or perform the same version of that work shall, for purposes of subsection (b) of this section, be treated as a legal or beneficial owner if such secondary transmission occurs within the local service area of that station.

(f)(1) With respect to any secondary transmission that is made by a satellite carrier of a performance or display of a work embodied in a primary transmission and is actionable as an act of infringement under section 122, a television broadcast station holding a copyright or other license to transmit or perform the same version of that work shall, for purposes of subsection (b) of this section, be treated as a legal or beneficial owner if such secondary transmission occurs within the local market of that station.

(2) A television broadcast station may file a civil action against any satellite carrier that has refused to carry television broadcast signals, as required under section 122(a)(2), to enforce that television broadcast station's rights under section 338(a) of the Communications Act of 1934.

§ 502. Remedies for infringement: Injunctions

(a) Any court having jurisdiction of a civil action arising under this title may, subject to the provisions of section 1498 of title 28, grant temporary and final injunctions on such terms as it may deem reasonable to prevent or restrain infringement of a copyright.

(b) Any such injunction may be served anywhere in the United States on the person enjoined; it shall be operative throughout the United States and shall be enforceable, by proceedings in contempt or otherwise, by any United States court having jurisdiction of that person. The clerk of the court granting the injunction shall, when requested by any other court in which enforcement of the injunction is sought, transmit promptly to the other court a certified copy of all the papers in the case on file in such clerk's office.

§ 503. Remedies for infringement: Impounding and disposition of infringing articles

(a) At any time while an action under this title is pending, the court may order the impounding, on such terms as it may deem reasonable, of all copies or phonorecords claimed to have been made or used in violation of the copyright owner's exclusive rights, and of all plates, molds, matrices, masters, tapes, film negatives, or other articles by means of which such copies or phonorecords may be reproduced.

(b) As part of a final judgment or decree, the court may order the destruction or other reasonable disposition of all copies or phonorecords found to have been made or used in violation of the copyright owner's exclusive rights, and of all plates, molds, matrices, masters, tapes, film negatives, or other articles by means of which such copies or phonorecords may be reproduced.

§ 504. Remedies for infringement: Damages and profits[3]

(a) In General. — Except as otherwise provided by this title, an infringer of copyright is liable for either —

(1) the copyright owner's actual damages and any additional profits of the infringer, as provided by subsection (b); or

(2) statutory damages, as provided by subsection (c).

(b) Actual Damages and Profits. — The copyright owner is entitled to recover the actual damages suffered by him or her as a result of the infringement, and any profits of the infringer that are attributable to the infringement and are not taken into account in computing the actual damages. In establishing the infringer's profits, the copyright owner is required to present proof only of the infringer's gross revenue, and the infringer is required to prove his or her deductible expenses and the elements of profit attributable to factors other than the copyrighted work.

(c) Statutory Damages. —

(1) Except as provided by clause (2) of this subsection, the copyright owner may elect, at any time before final judgment is rendered, to recover, instead of actual damages and profits, an award of statutory damages for all infringements involved in the action, with respect to any one work, for which any one infringer is liable individually, or for which any two or more infringers are liable jointly and severally, in a sum of not less than $750 or more than $30,000 as the court considers just. For the purposes of this subsection, all the parts of a compilation or derivative work constitute one work.

(2) In a case where the copyright owner sustains the burden of proving, and the court finds, that infringement was committed willfully, the court in its discretion may increase the award of statutory damages to a sum of not more than $150,000. In a case where the infringer sustains the burden of proving, and the court finds, that such infringer was not aware and had no reason to believe that his or her acts constituted an infringement of copyright, the court in its discretion may reduce the award of statutory damages to a sum of not less than $200. The court shall remit statutory damages in any case where an infringer believed and had reasonable grounds for believing that his or her use of the copyrighted work was a fair use under section 107, if the infringer was: (i) an employee or agent of a nonprofit educational institution, library, or archives acting within the scope of his or her employment who, or such institution, library, or archives itself, which infringed by reproducing the work in copies or phonorecords; or (ii) a public broadcasting entity which or a person who, as a regular part of the nonprofit activities of a public broadcasting entity (as defined in subsection (g) of section 118) infringed by performing a published nondramatic literary work or by reproducing a transmission program embodying a performance of such a work.

(3) (A) In a case of infringement, it shall be a rebuttable presumption that the infringement was committed willfully for purposes of determining relief if the violator, or a person acting in concert with the violator, knowingly provided or knowingly caused to be provided materially false contact information to a domain name registrar, domain name registry, or other domain name registration authority in registering, maintaining, or renewing a domain name used in connection with the infringement.

(B) Nothing in this paragraph limits what may be considered willful infringement under this subsection.

(C) For purposes of this paragraph, the term "domain name" has the meaning given that term in section 45 of the Act entitled "An Act to provide for the registration and protection of trademarks used in commerce, to carry out the provisions of certain international conventions, and for other purposes" approved July 5, 1946 (commonly referred to as the "Trademark Act of 1946"; 15 U.S.C. 1127).

(d) Additional Damages in Certain Cases. — In any case in which the court finds that a defendant proprietor of an establishment who claims as a defense that its activities were exempt under section 110(5) did not have reasonable grounds to believe that its use of a copyrighted work was exempt under such section, the plaintiff shall be entitled to, in addition to any award of damages under this section, an additional award of two times the amount of the license fee that the proprietor of the establishment concerned should have paid the plaintiff for such use during the preceding period of up to 3 years.

§ 505. Remedies for infringement: Costs and attorney's fees

In any civil action under this title, the court in its discretion may allow the recovery of full costs by or against any party other than the United States or an officer thereof. Except as otherwise provided by this title, the court may also award a reasonable attorney's fee to the prevailing party as part of the costs.

§ 506. Criminal offenses[4]

(a) Criminal Infringement. —

(1) In general. — Any person who willfully infringes a copyright shall be punished as provided under section 2319 of title 18, if the infringement was committed —

(A) for purposes of commercial advantage or private financial gain;

(B) by the reproduction or distribution, including by electronic means, during any 180-day period, of 1 or more copies or phonorecords of 1 or more copyrighted works, which have a total retail value of more than $1,000; or

(C) by the distribution of a work being prepared for commercial distribution, by making it available on a computer network accessible to members of the public, if such person knew or should have known that the work was intended for commercial distribution.

(2) Evidence. — For purposes of this subsection, evidence of reproduction or distribution of a copyrighted work, by itself, shall not be sufficient to establish willful infringement of a copyright.

(3) Definition. — In this subsection, the term "work being prepared for commercial distribution" means —

(A) a computer program, a musical work, a motion picture or other audiovisual work, or a sound recording, if, at the time of unauthorized distribution —

(i) the copyright owner has a reasonable expectation of commercial distribution; and

(ii) the copies or phonorecords of the work have not been commercially distributed; or

(B) a motion picture, if, at the time of unauthorized distribution, the motion picture —

(i) has been made available for viewing in a motion picture exhibition facility; and

(ii) has not been made available in copies for sale to the general public in the United States in a format intended to permit viewing outside a motion picture exhibition facility.

(b) Forfeiture and Destruction. — When any person is convicted of any violation of subsection (a), the court in its judgment of conviction shall, in addition to the penalty therein prescribed, order the forfeiture and destruction or other disposition of all infringing copies or phonorecords and all implements, devices, or equipment used in the manufacture of such infringing copies or phonorecords.

(c) Fraudulent Copyright Notice. — Any person who, with fraudulent intent, places on any article a notice of copyright or words of the same purport that such person knows to be false, or who, with fraudulent intent, publicly distributes or imports for public distribution any article bearing such notice or words that such person knows to be false, shall be fined not more than $2,500.

(d) Fraudulent Removal of Copyright Notice. — Any person who, with fraudulent intent, removes or alters any notice of copyright appearing on a copy of a copyrighted work shall be fined not more than $2,500.

(e) False Representation. — Any person who knowingly makes a false representation of a material fact in the application for copyright registration provided for by section 409, or in any written statement filed in connection with the application, shall be fined not more than $2,500.

(f) Rights of Attribution and Integrity. — Nothing in this section applies to infringement of the rights conferred by section 106A(a).

§ 507. Limitations on actions[5]

(a) Criminal Proceedings. — Except as expressly provided otherwise in this title, no criminal proceeding shall be maintained under the provisions of this title unless it is commenced within 5 years after the cause of action arose.

(b) Civil Actions. — No civil action shall be maintained under the provisions of this title unless it is commenced within three years after the claim accrued.

§ 508. Notification of filing and determination of actions

(a) Within one month after the filing of any action under this title, the clerks of the courts of the United States shall send written notification to the Register of Copyrights setting forth, as far as is shown by the papers filed in the court, the names and addresses of the parties and the title, author, and registration number of each work involved in the action. If any other copyrighted work is later included in the action by amendment, answer, or other pleading, the clerk shall also send a notification concerning it to the Register within one month after the pleading is filed.

(b) Within one month after any final order or judgment is issued in the case, the clerk of the court shall notify the Register of it, sending with the notification a copy of the order or judgment together with the written opinion, if any, of the court.

(c) Upon receiving the notifications specified in this section, the Register shall make them a part of the public records of the Copyright Office.

§ 509. *Seizure and forfeiture*

(a) All copies or phonorecords manufactured, reproduced, distributed, sold, or otherwise used, intended for use, or possessed with intent to use in violation of section 506 (a), and all plates, molds, matrices, masters, tapes, film negatives, or other articles by means of which such copies or phonorecords may be reproduced, and all electronic, mechanical, or other devices for manufacturing, reproducing, or assembling such copies or phonorecords may be seized and forfeited to the United States.

(b) The applicable procedures relating to

(i) the seizure, summary and judicial forfeiture, and condemnation of vessels, vehicles, merchandise, and baggage for violations of the customs laws contained in title 19,

(ii) the disposition of such vessels, vehicles, merchandise, and baggage or the proceeds from the sale thereof,

(iii) the remission or mitigation of such forfeiture,

(iv) the compromise of claims, and

(v) the award of compensation to informers in respect of such forfeitures, shall apply to seizures and forfeitures incurred, or alleged to have been incurred, under the provisions of this section, insofar as applicable and not inconsistent with the provisions of this section; except that such duties as are imposed upon any officer or employee of the Treasury Department or any other person with respect to the seizure and forfeiture of vessels, vehicles, merchandise, and baggage under the provisions of the customs laws contained in title 19 shall be performed with respect to seizure and forfeiture of all articles described in subsection (a) by such officers, agents, or other persons as may be authorized or designated for that purpose by the Attorney General.

§ 510. *Remedies for alteration of programming by cable systems*[6]

(a) In any action filed pursuant to section 111(c)(3), the following remedies shall be available:

(1) Where an action is brought by a party identified in subsections (b) or (c) of section 501, the remedies provided by sections 502 through 505, and the remedy provided by subsection (b) of this section; and

(2) When an action is brought by a party identified in subsection (d) of section 501, the remedies provided by sections 502 and 505, together with any actual damages suffered by such party as a result of the infringement, and the remedy provided by subsection (b) of this section.

(b) In any action filed pursuant to section 111(c)(3), the court may decree that, for a period not to exceed thirty days, the cable system shall be deprived of the benefit of a statutory license for one or more distant signals carried by such cable system.

§ 511. Liability of States, instrumentalities of States, and State officials for infringement of copyright[7]

(a) In General. — Any State, any instrumentality of a State, and any officer or employee of a State or instrumentality of a State acting in his or her official capacity, shall not be immune, under the Eleventh Amendment of the Constitution of the United States or under any other doctrine of sovereign immunity, from suit in Federal Court by any person, including any governmental or nongovernmental entity, for a violation of any of the exclusive rights of a copyright owner provided by sections 106 through 122, for importing copies of phonorecords in violation of section 602, or for any other violation under this title.

(b) Remedies. — In a suit described in subsection (a) for a violation described in that subsection, remedies (including remedies both at law and in equity) are available for the violation to the same extent as such remedies are available for such a violation in a suit against any public or private entity other than a State, instrumentality of a State, or officer or employee of a State acting in his or her official capacity. Such remedies include impounding and disposition of infringing articles under section 503, actual damages and profits and statutory damages under section 504, costs and attorney's fees under section 505, and the remedies provided in section 510.

§ 512. Limitations on liability relating to material online[8]

(a) Transitory Digital Network Communications. — A service provider shall not be liable for monetary relief, or, except as provided in subsection (j), for injunctive or other equitable relief, for infringement of copyright by reason of the provider's transmitting, routing, or providing connections for, material through a system or network controlled or operated by or for the service provider, or by reason of the intermediate and transient storage of that material in the course of such transmitting, routing, or providing connections, if —

(1) the transmission of the material was initiated by or at the direction of a person other than the service provider;

(2) the transmission, routing, provision of connections, or storage is carried out through an automatic technical process without selection of the material by the service provider;

(3) the service provider does not select the recipients of the material except as an automatic response to the request of another person;

(4) no copy of the material made by the service provider in the course of such intermediate or transient storage is maintained on the system or network in a manner ordinarily accessible to

anyone other than anticipated recipients, and no such copy is maintained on the system or network in a manner ordinarily accessible to such anticipated recipients for a longer period than is reasonably necessary for the transmission, routing, or provision of connections; and

(5) the material is transmitted through the system or network without modification of its content.

(b) System Caching.—

(1) Limitation on liability. — A service provider shall not be liable for monetary relief, or, except as provided in subsection (j), for injunctive or other equitable relief, for infringement of copyright by reason of the intermediate and temporary storage of material on a system or network controlled or operated by or for the service provider in a case in which —

(A) the material is made available online by a person other than the service provider;

(B) the material is transmitted from the person described in subparagraph (A) through the system or network to a person other than the person described in subparagraph (A) at the direction of that other person; and

(C) the storage is carried out through an automatic technical process for the purpose of making the material available to users of the system or network who, after the material is transmitted as described in subparagraph (B), request access to the material from the person described in subparagraph (A), if the conditions set forth in paragraph (2) are met.

(2) Conditions. — The conditions referred to in paragraph (1) are that —

(A) the material described in paragraph (1) is transmitted to the subsequent users described in paragraph (1)(C) without modification to its content from the manner in which the material was transmitted from the person described in paragraph (1)(A);

(B) the service provider described in paragraph (1) complies with rules concerning the refreshing, reloading, or other updating of the material when specified by the person making the material available online in accordance with a generally accepted industry standard data communications protocol for the system or network through which that person makes the material available, except that this subparagraph applies only if those rules are not used by the person described in paragraph (1)(A) to prevent or unreasonably impair the intermediate storage to which this subsection applies;

(C) the service provider does not interfere with the ability of technology associated with the material to return to the person described in paragraph (1)(A) the information that would have been available to that person if the material had been obtained by the subsequent users described in paragraph (1)(C) directly from that person, except that this subparagraph applies only if that technology —

(i) does not significantly interfere with the performance of the provider's system or network or with the intermediate storage of the material;

(ii) is consistent with generally accepted industry standard communications protocols; and

(iii) does not extract information from the provider's system or network other than the information that would have been available to the person described in paragraph (1)(A) if the subsequent users had gained access to the material directly from that person;

(D) if the person described in paragraph (1)(A) has in effect a condition that a person must meet prior to having access to the material, such as a condition based on payment of a fee or provision of a password or other information, the service provider permits access to the stored material in significant part only to users of its system or network that have met those conditions and only in accordance with those conditions; and

(E) if the person described in paragraph (1)(A) makes that material available online without the authorization of the copyright owner of the material, the service provider responds expeditiously to remove, or disable access to, the material that is claimed to be infringing upon notification of claimed infringement as described in subsection (c)(3), except that this subparagraph applies only if —

(i) the material has previously been removed from the originating site or access to it has been disabled, or a court has ordered that the material be removed from the originating site or that access to the material on the originating site be disabled; and

(ii) the party giving the notification includes in the notification a statement confirming that the material has been removed from the originating site or access to it has been disabled or that a court has ordered that the material be removed from the originating site or that access to the material on the originating site be disabled.

(c) Information Residing on Systems or Networks at Direction of Users.—

(1) In general. — A service provider shall not be liable for monetary relief, or, except as provided in subsection (j), for injunctive or other equitable relief, for infringement of copyright by reason of the storage at the direction of a user of material that resides on a system or network controlled or operated by or for the service provider, if the service provider —

(A)(i) does not have actual knowledge that the material or an activity using the material on the system or network is infringing;

(ii) in the absence of such actual knowledge, is not aware of facts or circumstances from which infringing activity is apparent; or

(iii) upon obtaining such knowledge or awareness, acts expeditiously to remove, or disable access to, the material;

(B) does not receive a financial benefit directly attributable to the infringing activity, in a case in which the service provider has the right and ability to control such activity; and

(C) upon notification of claimed infringement as described in paragraph (3), responds expeditiously to remove, or disable access to, the material that is claimed to be infringing or to be the subject of infringing activity.

(2) Designated agent. — The limitations on liability established in this subsection apply to a service provider only if the service provider has designated an agent to receive notifications of claimed

infringement described in paragraph (3), by making available through its service, including on its website in a location accessible to the public, and by providing to the Copyright Office, substantially the following information:

(A) the name, address, phone number, and electronic mail address of the agent.

(B) other contact information which the Register of Copyrights may deem appropriate. The Register of Copyrights shall maintain a current directory of agents available to the public for inspection, including through the Internet, in both electronic and hard copy formats, and may require payment of a fee by service providers to cover the costs of maintaining the directory.

(3) Elements of notification. —

(A) To be effective under this subsection, a notification of claimed infringement must be a written communication provided to the designated agent of a service provider that includes substantially the following:

(i) A physical or electronic signature of a person authorized to act on behalf of the owner of an exclusive right that is allegedly infringed.

(ii) Identification of the copyrighted work claimed to have been infringed, or, if multiple copyrighted works at a single online site are covered by a single notification, a representative list of such works at that site.

(iii) Identification of the material that is claimed to be infringing or to be the subject of infringing activity and that is to be removed or access to which is to be disabled, and information reasonably sufficient to permit the service provider to locate the material.

(iv) Information reasonably sufficient to permit the service provider to contact the complaining party, such as an address, telephone number, and, if available, an electronic mail address at which the complaining party may be contacted.

(v) A statement that the complaining party has a good faith belief that use of the material in the manner complained of is not authorized by the copyright owner, its agent, or the law.

(vi) A statement that the information in the notification is accurate, and under penalty of perjury, that the complaining party is authorized to act on behalf of the owner of an exclusive right that is allegedly infringed.

(B)(i) Subject to clause (ii), a notification from a copyright owner or from a person authorized to act on behalf of the copyright owner that fails to comply substantially with the provisions of subparagraph (A) shall not be considered under paragraph (1)(A) in determining whether a service provider has actual knowledge or is aware of facts or circumstances from which infringing activity is apparent.

(ii) In a case in which the notification that is provided to the service provider's designated agent fails to comply substantially with all the provisions of subparagraph (A) but substantially complies with clauses (ii), (iii), and (iv) of subparagraph (A), clause (i) of this subparagraph applies only if the service provider promptly attempts to contact the person making the notification or takes other reasonable steps to assist in the receipt of notification that substantially complies with all the provisions of subparagraph (A).

(d) Information Location Tools. — A service provider shall not be liable for monetary relief, or, except as provided in subsection (j), for injunctive or other equitable relief, for infringement of copyright by reason of the provider referring or linking users to an online location containing infringing material or infringing activity, by using information location tools, including a directory, index, reference, pointer, or hypertext link, if the service provider —

(1)(A) does not have actual knowledge that the material or activity is infringing;

(B) in the absence of such actual knowledge, is not aware of facts or circumstances from which infringing activity is apparent; or

(C) upon obtaining such knowledge or awareness, acts expeditiously to remove, or disable access to, the material;

(2) does not receive a financial benefit directly attributable to the infringing activity, in a case in which the service provider has the right and ability to control such activity; and

(3) upon notification of claimed infringement as described in subsection (c)(3), responds expeditiously to remove, or disable access to, the material that is claimed to be infringing or to be the subject of infringing activity, except that, for purposes of this paragraph, the information described in subsection (c)(3)(A)(iii) shall be identification of the reference or link, to material or activity claimed to be infringing, that is to be removed or access to which is to be disabled, and information reasonably sufficient to permit the service provider to locate that reference or link.

(e) Limitation on Liability of Nonprofit Educational Institutions. — (1) When a public or other nonprofit institution of higher education is a service provider, and when a faculty member or graduate student who is an employee of such institution is performing a teaching or research function, for the purposes of subsections (a) and (b) such faculty member or graduate student shall be considered to be a person other than the institution, and for the purposes of subsections (c) and (d) such faculty member's or graduate student's knowledge or awareness of his or her infringing activities shall not be attributed to the institution, if —

(A) such faculty member's or graduate student's infringing activities do not involve the provision of online access to instructional materials that are or were required or recommended, within the preceding 3-year period, for a course taught at the institution by such faculty member or graduate student;

(B) the institution has not, within the preceding 3-year period, received more than 2 notifications described in subsection (c)(3) of claimed infringement by such faculty member or graduate student, and such notifications of claimed infringement were not actionable under subsection (f); and

(C) the institution provides to all users of its system or network informational materials that accurately describe, and promote compliance with, the laws of the United States relating to copyright.

(2) For the purposes of this subsection, the limitations on injunctive relief contained in subsections (j)(2) and (j)(3), but not those in (j)(1), shall apply.

(f) Misrepresentations. - Any person who knowingly materially misrepresents under this section —

(1) that material or activity is infringing, or

(2) that material or activity was removed or disabled by mistake or misidentification, shall be liable for any damages, including costs and attorneys' fees, incurred by the alleged infringer, by any copyright owner or copyright owner's authorized licensee, or by a service provider, who is injured by such misrepresentation, as the result of the service provider relying upon such misrepresentation in removing or disabling access to the material or activity claimed to be infringing, or in replacing the removed material or ceasing to disable access to it.

(g) Replacement of Removed or Disabled Material and Limitation on Other Liability.—

(1) No liability for taking down generally. — Subject to paragraph (2), a service provider shall not be liable to any person for any claim based on the service provider's good faith disabling of access to, or removal of, material or activity claimed to be infringing or based on facts or circumstances from which infringing activity is apparent, regardless of whether the material or activity is ultimately determined to be infringing.

(2) Exception. — Paragraph (1) shall not apply with respect to material residing at the direction of a subscriber of the service provider on a system or network controlled or operated by or for the service provider that is removed, or to which access is disabled by the service provider, pursuant to a notice provided under subsection (c)(1)(C), unless the service provider —

(A) takes reasonable steps promptly to notify the subscriber that it has removed or disabled access to the material;

(B) upon receipt of a counter notification described in paragraph (3), promptly provides the person who provided the notification under subsection (c)(1)(C) with a copy of the counter notification, and informs that person that it will replace the removed material or cease disabling access to it in 10 business days; and

(C) replaces the removed material and ceases disabling access to it not less than 10, nor more than 14, business days following receipt of the counter notice, unless its designated agent first receives notice from the person who submitted the notification under subsection (c)(1)(C) that such person has filed an action seeking a court order to restrain the subscriber from engaging in infringing activity relating to the material on the service provider's system or network.

(3) Contents of counter notification. — To be effective under this subsection, a counter notification must be a written communication provided to the service provider's designated agent that includes substantially the following:

(A) A physical or electronic signature of the subscriber.

(B) Identification of the material that has been removed or to which access has been disabled and the location at which the material appeared before it was removed or access to it was disabled.

(C) A statement under penalty of perjury that the subscriber has a good faith belief that the material was removed or disabled as a result of mistake or misidentification of the material to be removed or disabled.

(D) The subscriber's name, address, and telephone number, and a statement that the subscriber consents to the jurisdiction of Federal District Court for the judicial district in which the address is located, or if the subscriber's address is outside of the United States, for any judicial district in which the service provider may be found, and that the subscriber will accept service of process from the person who provided notification under subsection (c)(1)(C) or an agent of such person.

(4) Limitation on other liability. — A service provider's compliance with paragraph (2) shall not subject the service provider to liability for copyright infringement with respect to the material identified in the notice provided under subsection (c)(1)(C).

(h) Subpoena to Identify Infringer.—

(1) Request. — A copyright owner or a person authorized to act on the owner's behalf may request the clerk of any United States district court to issue a subpoena to a service provider for identification of an alleged infringer in accordance with this subsection.

(2) Contents of request — The request may be made by filing with the clerk —

(A) a copy of a notification described in subsection (c)(3)(A);

(B) a proposed subpoena; and

(C) a sworn declaration to the effect that the purpose for which the subpoena is sought is to obtain the identity of an alleged infringer and that such information will only be used for the purpose of protecting rights under this title.

(3) Contents of subpoena. — The subpoena shall authorize and order the service provider receiving the notification and the subpoena to expeditiously disclose to the copyright owner or person authorized by the copyright owner information sufficient to identify the alleged infringer of the material described in the notification to the extent such information is available to the service provider.

(4) Basis for granting subpoena. — If the notification filed satisfies the provisions of subsection (c)(3)(A), the proposed subpoena is in proper form, and the accompanying declaration is properly executed, the clerk shall expeditiously issue and sign the proposed subpoena and return it to the requester for delivery to the service provider.

(5) Actions of service provider receiving subpoena. — Upon receipt of the issued subpoena, either accompanying or subsequent to the receipt of a notification described in subsection (c)(3)(A), the service provider shall expeditiously disclose to the copyright owner or person authorized by the copyright owner the information required by the subpoena, notwithstanding any other provision of law and regardless of whether the service provider responds to the notification.

(6) Rules applicable to subpoena. — Unless otherwise provided by this section or by applicable rules of the court, the procedure for issuance and delivery of the subpoena, and the remedies for

noncompliance with the subpoena, shall be governed to the greatest extent practicable by those provisions of the Federal Rules of Civil Procedure governing the issuance, service, and enforcement of a subpoena duces tecum.

(i) Conditions for Eligibility.—

(1) Accommodation of technology. — The limitations on liability established by this section shall apply to a service provider only if the service provider —

(A) has adopted and reasonably implemented, and informs subscribers and account holders of the service provider's system or network of, a policy that provides for the termination in appropriate circumstances of subscribers and account holders of the service provider's system or network who are repeat infringers; and

(B) accommodates and does not interfere with standard technical measures.

(2) Definition. — As used in this subsection, the term "standard technical measures" means technical measures that are used by copyright owners to identify or protect copyrighted works and —

(A) have been developed pursuant to a broad consensus of copyright owners and service providers in an open, fair, voluntary, multi-industry standards process;

(B) are available to any person on reasonable and nondiscriminatory terms; and

(C) do not impose substantial costs on service providers or substantial burdens on their systems or networks.

(j) Injunctions. — The following rules shall apply in the case of any application for an injunction under section 502 against a service provider that is not subject to monetary remedies under this section:

(1) Scope of relief. — (A) With respect to conduct other than that which qualifies for the limitation on remedies set forth in subsection (a), the court may grant injunctive relief with respect to a service provider only in one or more of the following forms:

(i) An order restraining the service provider from providing access to infringing material or activity residing at a particular online site on the provider's system or network.

(ii) An order restraining the service provider from providing access to a subscriber or account holder of the service provider's system or network who is engaging in infringing activity and is identified in the order, by terminating the accounts of the subscriber or account holder that are specified in the order.

(iii) Such other injunctive relief as the court may consider necessary to prevent or restrain infringement of copyrighted material specified in the order of the court at a particular online location, if such relief is the least burdensome to the service provider among the forms of relief comparably effective for that purpose.

(B) If the service provider qualifies for the limitation on remedies described in subsection (a), the court may only grant injunctive relief in one or both of the following forms:

(i) An order restraining the service provider from providing access to a subscriber or account holder of the service provider's system or network who is using the provider's service to engage in infringing activity and is identified in the order, by terminating the accounts of the subscriber or account holder that are specified in the order.

(ii) An order restraining the service provider from providing access, by taking reasonable steps specified in the order to block access, to a specific, identified, online location outside the United States.

(2) Considerations. — The court, in considering the relevant criteria for injunctive relief under applicable law, shall consider —

(A) whether such an injunction, either alone or in combination with other such injunctions issued against the same service provider under this subsection, would significantly burden either the provider or the operation of the provider's system or network;

(B) the magnitude of the harm likely to be suffered by the copyright owner in the digital network environment if steps are not taken to prevent or restrain the infringement;

(C) whether implementation of such an injunction would be technically feasible and effective, and would not interfere with access to noninfringing material at other online locations; and

(D) whether other less burdensome and comparably effective means of preventing or restraining access to the infringing material are available.

(3) Notice and ex parte orders. — Injunctive relief under this subsection shall be available only after notice to the service provider and an opportunity for the service provider to appear are provided, except for orders ensuring the preservation of evidence or other orders having no material adverse effect on the operation of the service provider's communications network.

(k) Definitions.—

(1) Service provider. — (A) As used in subsection (a), the term "service provider" means an entity offering the transmission, routing, or providing of connections for digital online communications, between or among points specified by a user, of material of the user's choosing, without modification to the content of the material as sent or received.

(B) As used in this section, other than subsection (a), the term "service provider" means a provider of online services or network access, or the operator of facilities therefor, and includes an entity described in subparagraph (A).

(2) Monetary relief. — As used in this section, the term "monetary relief" means damages, costs, attorneys' fees, and any other form of monetary payment.

(l) Other Defenses Not Affected. — The failure of a service provider's conduct to qualify for limitation of liability under this section shall not bear adversely upon the consideration of a defense by the service provider that the service provider's conduct is not infringing under this title or any other defense.

(m) Protection of Privacy. — Nothing in this section shall be construed to condition the applicability of subsections (a) through (d) on —

(1) a service provider monitoring its service or affirmatively seeking facts indicating infringing activity, except to the extent consistent with a standard technical measure complying with the provisions of subsection (i); or

(2) a service provider gaining access to, removing, or disabling access to material in cases in which such conduct is prohibited by law.

(n) Construction. — Subsections (a), (b), (c), and (d) describe separate and distinct functions for purposes of applying this section. Whether a service provider qualifies for the limitation on liability in any one of those subsections shall be based solely on the criteria in that subsection, and shall not affect a determination of whether that service provider qualifies for the limitations on liability under any other such subsection.

§ 513. Determination of reasonable license fees for individual proprietors[9]

In the case of any performing rights society subject to a consent decree which provides for the determination of reasonable license rates or fees to be charged by the performing rights society, notwithstanding the provisions of that consent decree, an individual proprietor who owns or operates fewer than 7 non-publicly traded establishments in which nondramatic musical works are performed publicly and who claims that any license agreement offered by that performing rights society is unreasonable in its license rate or fee as to that individual proprietor, shall be entitled to determination of a reasonable license rate or fee as follows:

(1) The individual proprietor may commence such proceeding for determination of a reasonable license rate or fee by filing an application in the applicable district court under paragraph (2) that a rate disagreement exists and by serving a copy of the application on the performing rights society. Such proceeding shall commence in the applicable district court within 90 days after the service of such copy, except that such 90-day requirement shall be subject to the administrative requirements of the court.

(2) The proceeding under paragraph (1) shall be held, at the individual proprietor's election, in the judicial district of the district court with jurisdiction over the applicable consent decree or in that place of holding court of a district court that is the seat of the Federal circuit (other than the Court of Appeals for the Federal Circuit) in which the proprietor's establishment is located.

(3) Such proceeding shall be held before the judge of the court with jurisdiction over the consent decree governing the performing rights society. At the discretion of the court, the proceeding shall be held before a special master or magistrate judge appointed by such judge. Should that consent decree provide for the appointment of an advisor or advisors to the court for any purpose, any such advisor shall be the special master so named by the court.

(4) In any such proceeding, the industry rate shall be presumed to have been reasonable at the time it was agreed to or determined by the court. Such presumption shall in no way affect a determination of whether the rate is being correctly applied to the individual proprietor.

(5) Pending the completion of such proceeding, the individual proprietor shall have the right to perform publicly the copyrighted musical compositions in the repertoire of the performing rights society by paying an interim license rate or fee into an interest bearing escrow account with the clerk of the court, subject to retroactive adjustment when a final rate or fee has been determined, in an amount equal to the industry rate, or, in the absence of an industry rate, the amount of the most recent license rate or fee agreed to by the parties.

(6) Any decision rendered in such proceeding by a special master or magistrate judge named under paragraph (3) shall be reviewed by the judge of the court with jurisdiction over the consent decree governing the performing rights society. Such proceeding, including such review, shall be concluded within 6 months after its commencement.

(7) Any such final determination shall be binding only as to the individual proprietor commencing the proceeding, and shall not be applicable to any other proprietor or any other performing rights society, and the performing rights society shall be relieved of any obligation of nondiscrimination among similarly situated music users that may be imposed by the consent decree governing its operations.

(8) An individual proprietor may not bring more than one proceeding provided for in this section for the determination of a reasonable license rate or fee under any license agreement with respect to any one performing rights society.

(9) For purposes of this section, the term "industry rate" means the license fee a performing rights society has agreed to with, or which has been determined by the court for, a significant segment of the music user industry to which the individual proprietor belongs.

Chapter 5 Endnotes

[1]In 1998, two sections 512 were enacted into law. On October 17, 1998, the Fairness in Music Licensing Act of 1998 was enacted. This Act amended chapter 5 to add section 512 entitled "Determination of reasonable license fees for individual proprietors." Pub. L. No. 105-298, 112 Stat. 2827, 2831. On October 28, 1998, the Online Copyright Infringement Liability Limitation Act was enacted. This Act amended chapter 5 to add section 512 entitled "Limitations on liability relating to material online." Pub. L. No. 105-304, 112 Stat. 2860, 2877. In 1999, a technical correction was enacted to redesignate the section 512 that was entitled "Determination of reasonable license fees for individual proprietors" as section 513. Also, the table of sections was amended to reflect that change. Pub. L. No. 106-44, 113 Stat. 221. See also endnote 9, *infra.*

[2]The Berne Convention Implementation Act of 1988 amended section 501(b) by striking out "sections 205(d) and 411" and inserting in lieu thereof "section 411." Pub. L. No. 100-568, 102 Stat. 2853, 2860. The Satellite Home Viewer Act of 1988 amended section 501 by adding subsection (e). Pub. L. No. 100-667, 102 Stat. 3935, 3957.

In 1990, the Copyright Remedy Clarification Act amended section 501(a) by adding the last two sentences. Pub. L. No. 101-553, 104 Stat. 2749. The Visual Artists Rights Act of 1990 also amended section 501(a) as follows: 1) by inserting "or of the author as provided in section 106A(a)" after "118" and 2) by striking out "copyright." and inserting in lieu thereof "copyright or right of the author, as the case may be. For purposes of this chapter (other than section 506), any reference to copyright shall be deemed to include the rights conferred by section 106A(a)." Pub. L. No. 101-650, 104 Stat. 5089, 5131.

In 1999, a technical correction amended the first sentence in subsection 501(a) by inserting "121" in lieu of "118." Pub. L. No. 106-44, 113 Stat. 221, 222. The Satellite Home Viewer Improvement Act of 1999 amended section 501 by adding a subsection (f) and, in subsection (e), by inserting "performance or display of a work embodied in a primary transmission" in lieu of "primary transmission embodying the performance or display of a work." Pub. L. No. 106-113, 113 Stat. 1501, app. I at 1501A-527 and 544. The Satellite Home Viewer Improvement Act of 1999 states that section 501(f) shall be effective as of July 1, 1999. Pub. L. No. 106-113, 113 Stat. 1501, app. I at 1501A-544.

The Intellectual Property and High Technology Technical Amendments Act of 2002 amended section 501(a) by substituting sections "106 through 122" for "106 through 121." Pub. L. No. 107-273, 116 Stat. 1758, 1909.

[3]The Berne Convention Implementation Act of 1988 amended section 504(c) as follows: 1) in paragraph (1), by inserting "$500" in lieu of "$250" and by inserting "$20,000" in lieu of "$10,000" and 2) in paragraph (2), by inserting "$100,000" in lieu of "$50,000" and by inserting "$200" in lieu of "$100." Pub. L. No. 100-568, 102 Stat. 2853, 2860. The Digital Theft Deterrence and Copyright Damages Improvement Act of 1999 amended section 504(c), in paragraph (1), by substituting "$750" for "$500" and "$30,000" for "$20,000" and, in paragraph (2), by substituting "$150,000" for "$100,000." Pub. L. No. 106-160, 113 Stat. 1774.

The Fraudulent Online Identity Sanctions Act amended section 504(c) by adding a new subparagraph (3). Pub. L. No. 108-482, 118 Stat. 3912, 3916.

[4]The Piracy and Counterfeiting Amendments Act of 1982 amended section 506 by substituting a new subsection(a). Pub. L. No. 97-180, 96 Stat. 91, 93. The Visual Artists Rights Act of 1990 amended section 506 by adding subsection (f). Pub. L. No.101-650, 104 Stat. 5089, 5131. In 1997, the No Electronic Theft (NET) Act again amended section 506 by amending subsection (a) in its entirety. Pub. L. No. 105-147, 111 Stat. 2678. That Act also directed the United States Sentencing Commission to "ensure that the applicable guideline range for a defendant convicted of a crime against intellectual property . . . is sufficiently stringent to deter such a crime" and to "ensure that the guidelines provide for consideration of the retail value and quantity of the items with respect to which the crime against intellectual property was committed." Pub. L. No. 105-147, 111 Stat. 2678, 2680. See also endnote 2 in Appendix F.

The Artists' Rights and Theft Prevention Act of 2005 amended subsection 506(a) in its entirety. Pub. L. No. 109-9, 119 Stat. 218, 220.

[5]In 1997, the No Electronic Theft (NET) Act amended section 507(a) by inserting "5" in lieu of "three." Pub. L. No. 105-147, 111 Stat. 2678.

[6]The Satellite Home Viewer Improvement Act of 1999 amended the heading for section 510 by substituting "programming" for "programing" and, in subsection (b), by substituting "statutory" for "compulsory." Pub. L. No. 106-113, 113 Stat. 1501, app. I at 1501A-543.

[7]In 1990, the Copyright Remedy Clarification Act added section 511. Pub. L. No. 101-553, 104 Stat. 2749. In 1999, a technical correction amended subsection 511(a) by inserting "121" in lieu of "119." Pub. L. No. 106-44, 113 Stat. 221, 222. The Intellectual Property and High Technology Technical Amendments Act of 2002 amended section 511(a) by substituting sections "106 through 122" for "106 through 121." Pub. L. No. 107-273, 116 Stat. 1758, 1909.

[8]In 1998, the Online Copyright Infringement Liability Limitation Act added section 512. Pub. L. No. 105-304, 112 Stat. 2860, 2877. In 1999, a technical correction deleted the heading for paragraph (2) of section 512(e), which was "Injunctions." Pub. L. No. 106-44, 113 Stat. 221, 222.

[9]The Fairness in Music Licensing Act of 1998 added section 513. Pub. L. No. 105-298, 112 Stat. 2827, 2831. This section was originally designated as section 512. However, because two sections 512 had been enacted into law in 1998, a technical amendment redesignated this as section 513. Pub. L. No. 106-44, 113 Stat. 221. See also endnote 1, *supra*.

CHAPTER 6

MANUFACTURING REQUIREMENTS AND IMPORTATION

- 601. Manufacture, importation, and public distribution of certain copies
- 602. Infringing importation of copies or phonorecords
- 603. Importation prohibitions: Enforcement and disposition of excluded articles

§ 601. *Manufacture, importation, and public distribution of certain copies*[1]

(a) Prior to July 1, 1986, and except as provided by subsection (b), the importation into or public distribution in the United States of copies of a work consisting preponderantly of nondramatic literary material that is in the English language and is protected under this title is prohibited unless the portions consisting of such material have been manufactured in the United States or Canada.

(b) The provisions of subsection (a) do not apply —

(1) where, on the date when importation is sought or public distribution in the United States is made, the author of any substantial part of such material is neither a national nor a domiciliary of the United States or, if such author is a national of the United States, he or she has been domiciled outside the United States for a continuous period of at least one year immediately preceding that date; in the case of a work made for hire, the exemption provided by this clause does not apply unless a substantial part of the work was prepared for an employer or other person who is not a national or domiciliary of the United States or a domestic corporation or enterprise;

(2) where the United States Customs Service is presented with an import statement issued under the seal of the Copyright Office, in which case a total of no more than two thousand copies of any one such work shall be allowed entry; the import statement shall be issued upon request to the copyright owner or to a person designated by such owner at the time of registration for the work under section 408 or at any time thereafter;

(3) where importation is sought under the authority or for the use, other than in schools, of the Government of the United States or of any State or political subdivision of a State;

(4) where importation, for use and not for sale, is sought —

(A) by any person with respect to no more than one copy of any work at any one time;

(B) by any person arriving from outside the United States, with respect to copies forming part of such person's personal baggage; or

(C) by an organization operated for scholarly, educational, or religious purposes and not for private gain, with respect to copies intended to form a part of its library;

(5) where the copies are reproduced in raised characters for the use of the blind; or

(6) where, in addition to copies imported under clauses (3) and (4) of this subsection, no more than two thousand copies of any one such work, which have not been manufactured in the United States or Canada, are publicly distributed in the United States; or

(7) where, on the date when importation is sought or public distribution in the United States is made —

   (A) the author of any substantial part of such material is an individual and receives compensation for the transfer or license of the right to distribute the work in the United States; and

   (B) the first publication of the work has previously taken place outside the United States under a transfer or license granted by such author to a transferee or licensee who was not a national or domiciliary of the United States or a domestic corporation or enterprise; and

   (C) there has been no publication of an authorized edition of the work of which the copies were manufactured in the United States; and

   (D) the copies were reproduced under a transfer or license granted by such author or by the transferee or licensee of the right of first publication as mentioned in subclause (B), and the transferee or the licensee of the right of reproduction was not a national or domiciliary of the United States or a domestic corporation or enterprise.

(c) The requirement of this section that copies be manufactured in the United States or Canada is satisfied if —

   (1) in the case where the copies are printed directly from type that has been set, or directly from plates made from such type, the setting of the type and the making of the plates have been performed in the United States or Canada; or

   (2) in the case where the making of plates by a lithographic or photoengraving process is a final or intermediate step preceding the printing of the copies, the making of the plates has been performed in the United States or Canada; and

   (3) in any case, the printing or other final process of producing multiple copies and any binding of the copies have been performed in the United States or Canada.

(d) Importation or public distribution of copies in violation of this section does not invalidate protection for a work under this title. However, in any civil action or criminal proceeding for infringement of the exclusive rights to reproduce and distribute copies of the work, the infringer has a complete defense with respect to all of the nondramatic literary material comprised in the work and any other parts of the work in which the exclusive rights to reproduce and distribute copies are owned by the same person who owns such exclusive rights in the nondramatic literary material, if the infringer proves —

   (1) that copies of the work have been imported into or publicly distributed in the United States in violation of this section by or with the authority of the owner of such exclusive rights; and

   (2) that the infringing copies were manufactured in the United States or Canada in accordance with the provisions of subsection (c); and

(3) that the infringement was commenced before the effective date of registration for an authorized edition of the work, the copies of which have been manufactured in the United States or Canada in accordance with the provisions of subsection (c).

(e) In any action for infringement of the exclusive rights to reproduce and distribute copies of a work containing material required by this section to be manufactured in the United States or Canada, the copyright owner shall set forth in the complaint the names of the persons or organizations who performed the processes specified by subsection (c) with respect to that material, and the places where those processes were performed.

§ 602. *Infringing importation of copies or phonorecords*

(a) Importation into the United States, without the authority of the owner of copyright under this title, of copies or phonorecords of a work that have been acquired outside the United States is an infringement of the exclusive right to distribute copies or phonorecords under section 106, actionable under section 501. This subsection does not apply to —

(1) importation of copies or phonorecords under the authority or for the use of the Government of the United States or of any State or political subdivision of a State, but not including copies or phonorecords for use in schools, or copies of any audiovisual work imported for purposes other than archival use;

(2) importation, for the private use of the importer and not for distribution, by any person with respect to no more than one copy or phonorecord of any one work at any one time, or by any person arriving from outside the United States with respect to copies or phonorecords forming part of such person's personal baggage; or

(3) importation by or for an organization operated for scholarly, educational, or religious purposes and not for private gain, with respect to no more than one copy of an audiovisual work solely for its archival purposes, and no more than five copies or phonorecords of any other work for its library lending or archival purposes, unless the importation of such copies or phonorecords is part of an activity consisting of systematic reproduction or distribution, engaged in by such organization in violation of the provisions of section 108(g)(2).

(b) In a case where the making of the copies or phonorecords would have constituted an infringement of copyright if this title had been applicable, their importation is prohibited. In a case where the copies or phonorecords were lawfully made, the United States Customs Service has no authority to prevent their importation unless the provisions of section 601 are applicable. In either case, the Secretary of the Treasury is authorized to prescribe, by regulation, a procedure under which any person claiming an interest in the copyright in a particular work may, upon payment of a specified fee, be entitled to notification by the Customs Service of the importation of articles that appear to be copies or phonorecords of the work.

§ 603. Importation prohibitions: Enforcement and disposition of excluded articles[2]

(a) The Secretary of the Treasury and the United States Postal Service shall separately or jointly make regulations for the enforcement of the provisions of this title prohibiting importation.

(b) These regulations may require, as a condition for the exclusion of articles under section 602 —

(1) that the person seeking exclusion obtain a court order enjoining importation of the articles; or

(2) that the person seeking exclusion furnish proof, of a specified nature and in accordance with prescribed procedures, that the copyright in which such person claims an interest is valid and that the importation would violate the prohibition in section 602; the person seeking exclusion may also be required to post a surety bond for any injury that may result if the detention or exclusion of the articles proves to be unjustified.

(c) Articles imported in violation of the importation prohibitions of this title are subject to seizure and forfeiture in the same manner as property imported in violation of the customs revenue laws. Forfeited articles shall be destroyed as directed by the Secretary of the Treasury or the court, as the case may be.

Chapter 6 Endnotes

[1] In 1982, section 601(a) was amended in the first sentence by substituting "1986" for "1982." Pub. L. No. 97-215, 96 Stat. 178.
[2] The Anticounterfeiting Consumer Protection Act of 1996 amended the last sentence of section 603(c) by deleting the semicolon and all text immediately following the words "as the case may be." Pub. L. No. 104-153, 110 Stat. 1386, 1388.

CHAPTER 7[1]

COPYRIGHT OFFICE

- 701. The Copyright Office: General responsibilities and organization
- 702. Copyright Office regulations
- 703. Effective date of actions in Copyright Office
- 704. Retention and disposition of articles deposited in Copyright Office
- 705. Copyright Office records: Preparation, maintenance, public inspection, and searching
- 706. Copies of Copyright Office records
- 707. Copyright Office forms and publications
- 708. Copyright Office fees
- 709. Delay in delivery caused by disruption of postal or other services

§ 701. The Copyright Office: General responsibilities and organization[2]

(a) All administrative functions and duties under this title, except as otherwise specified, are the responsibility of the Register of Copyrights as director of the Copyright Office of the Library of Congress. The Register of Copyrights, together with the subordinate officers and employees of the Copyright Office, shall be appointed by the Librarian of Congress, and shall act under the Librarian's general direction and supervision.

(b) In addition to the functions and duties set out elsewhere in this chapter, the Register of Copyrights shall perform the following functions:

(1) Advise Congress on national and international issues relating to copyright, other matters arising under this title, and related matters.

(2) Provide information and assistance to Federal departments and agencies and the Judiciary on national and international issues relating to copyright, other matters arising under this title, and related matters.

(3) Participate in meetings of international intergovernmental organizations and meetings with foreign government officials relating to copyright, other matters arising under this title, and related matters, including as a member of United States delegations as authorized by the appropriate Executive branch authority.

(4) Conduct studies and programs regarding copyright, other matters arising under this title, and related matters, the administration of the Copyright Office, or any function vested in the Copyright Office by law, including educational programs conducted cooperatively with foreign intellectual property offices and international intergovernmental organizations.

(5) Perform such other functions as Congress may direct, or as may be appropriate in furtherance of the functions and duties specifically set forth in this title.

(c) The Register of Copyrights shall adopt a seal to be used on and after January 1, 1978, to authenticate all certified documents issued by the Copyright Office.

(d) The Register of Copyrights shall make an annual report to the Librarian of Congress of the work and accomplishments of the Copyright Office during the previous fiscal year. The annual report of the Register of Copyrights shall be published separately and as a part of the annual report of the Librarian of Congress.

(e) Except as provided by section 706(b) and the regulations issued thereunder, all actions taken by the Register of Copyrights under this title are subject to the provisions of the Administrative Procedure Act of June 11, 1946, as amended (c. 324, 60 Stat. 237, title 5, United States Code, Chapter 5, Subchapter II and Chapter 7).

(f) The Register of Copyrights shall be compensated at the rate of pay in effect for level III of the Executive Schedule under section 5314 of title 5.[3] The Librarian of Congress shall establish not more than four positions for Associate Registers of Copyrights, in accordance with the recommendations of the Register of Copyrights. The Librarian shall make appointments to such positions after consultation with the Register of Copyrights. Each Associate Register of Copyrights shall be paid at a rate not to exceed the maximum annual rate of basic pay payable for GS-18 of the General Schedule under section 5332 of title 5.

§ 702. Copyright Office regulations[4]

The Register of Copyrights is authorized to establish regulations not inconsistent with law for the administration of the functions and duties made the responsibility of the Register under this title. All regulations established by the Register under this title are subject to the approval of the Librarian of Congress.

§ 703. Effective date of actions in Copyright Office

In any case in which time limits are prescribed under this title for the performance of an action in the Copyright Office, and in which the last day of the prescribed period falls on a Saturday, Sunday, holiday, or other nonbusiness day within the District of Columbia or the Federal Government, the action may be taken on the next succeeding business day, and is effective as of the date when the period expired.

§ 704. Retention and disposition of articles deposited in Copyright Office

(a) Upon their deposit in the Copyright Office under sections 407 and 408, all copies, phonorecords, and identifying material, including those deposited in connection with claims that have been refused registration, are the property of the United States Government.

(b) In the case of published works, all copies, phonorecords, and identifying material deposited are available to the Library of Congress for its collections, or for exchange or transfer to any other library. In the case of unpublished works, the Library is entitled, under regulations that the Register of Copyrights shall prescribe, to select any deposits for its collections or for transfer to the National Archives of the United States or to a Federal records center, as defined in section 2901 of title 44.

(c) The Register of Copyrights is authorized, for specific or general categories of works, to make a facsimile reproduction of all or any part of the material deposited under section 408, and to make such reproduction a part of the Copyright Office records of the registration, before transferring such material to the Library of Congress as provided by subsection (b), or before destroying or otherwise disposing of such material as provided by subsection (d).

(d) Deposits not selected by the Library under subsection (b), or identifying portions or reproductions of them, shall be retained under the control of the Copyright Office, including retention in Government storage facilities, for the longest period considered practicable and desirable by the Register of Copyrights and the Librarian of Congress. After that period it is within the joint discretion of the Register and the Librarian to order their destruction or other disposition; but, in the case of unpublished works, no deposit shall be knowingly or intentionally destroyed or otherwise disposed of during its term of copyright unless a facsimile reproduction of the entire deposit has been made a part of the Copyright Office records as provided by subsection (c).

(e) The depositor of copies, phonorecords, or identifying material under section 408, or the copyright owner of record, may request retention, under the control of the Copyright Office, of one or more of such articles for the full term of copyright in the work. The Register of Copyrights shall prescribe, by regulation, the conditions under which such requests are to be made and granted, and shall fix the fee to be charged under section 708(a)(10) if the request is granted.

§ 705. Copyright Office records: Preparation, maintenance, public inspection, and searching[5]

(a) The Register of Copyrights shall ensure that records of deposits, registrations, recordations, and other actions taken under this title are maintained, and that indexes of such records are prepared.

(b) Such records and indexes, as well as the articles deposited in connection with completed copyright registrations and retained under the control of the Copyright Office, shall be open to public inspection.

(c) Upon request and payment of the fee specified by section 708, the Copyright Office shall make a search of its public records, indexes, and deposits, and shall furnish a report of the information they disclose with respect to any particular deposits, registrations, or recorded documents.

§ 706. Copies of Copyright Office records

(a) Copies may be made of any public records or indexes of the Copyright Office; additional certificates of copyright registration and copies of any public records or indexes may be furnished upon request and payment of the fees specified by section 708.

(b) Copies or reproductions of deposited articles retained under the control of the Copyright Office shall be authorized or furnished only under the conditions specified by the Copyright Office regulations.

§ 707. Copyright Office forms and publications

(a) Catalog of Copyright Entries. — The Register of Copyrights shall compile and publish at periodic intervals catalogs of all copyright registrations. These catalogs shall be divided into parts in accordance with the various classes of works, and the Register has discretion to determine, on the basis of practicability and usefulness, the form and frequency of publication of each particular part.

(b) Other Publications. — The Register shall furnish, free of charge upon request, application forms for copyright registration and general informational material in connection with the functions of the Copyright Office. The Register also has the authority to publish compilations of information, bibliographies, and other material he or she considers to be of value to the public.

(c) Distribution of Publications. — All publications of the Copyright Office shall be furnished to depository libraries as specified under section 1905 of title 44, and, aside from those furnished free of charge, shall be offered for sale to the public at prices based on the cost of reproduction and distribution.

§ 708. Copyright Office fees[6]

(a) Fees. — Fees shall be paid to the Register of Copyrights —

(1) on filing each application under section 408 for registration of a copyright claim or for a supplementary registration, including the issuance of a certificate of registration if registration is made;

(2) on filing each application for registration of a claim for renewal of a subsisting copyright under section 304(a), including the issuance of a certificate of registration if registration is made;

(3) for the issuance of a receipt for a deposit under section 407;

(4) for the recordation, as provided by section 205, of a transfer of copyright ownership or other document;

(5) for the filing, under section 115(b), of a notice of intention to obtain a compulsory license;

(6) for the recordation, under section 302(c), of a statement revealing the identity of an author of an anonymous or pseudonymous work, or for the recordation, under section 302(d), of a statement relating to the death of an author;

(7) for the issuance, under section 706, of an additional certificate of registration;

(8) for the issuance of any other certification; and

(9) for the making and reporting of a search as provided by section 705, and for any related services.
   The Register of Copyrights is authorized to fix fees for other services, including the cost of preparing copies of Copyright Office records, whether or not such copies are certified, based on the cost of providing the service.

(b) Adjustment of Fees. — The Register of Copyrights may, by regulation, adjust the fees for the services specified in paragraphs (1) through (9) of subsection (a) in the following manner:[7]

(1) The Register shall conduct a study of the costs incurred by the Copyright Office for the registration of claims, the recordation of documents, and the provision of services. The study shall also consider the timing of any adjustment in fees and the authority to use such fees consistent with the budget.

(2) The Register may, on the basis of the study under paragraph (1), and subject to paragraph (5), adjust fees to not more than that necessary to cover the reasonable costs incurred by the

Copyright Office for the services described in paragraph (1), plus a reasonable inflation adjustment to account for any estimated increase in costs.

(3) Any fee established under paragraph (2) shall be rounded off to the nearest dollar, or for a fee less than $12, rounded off to the nearest 50 cents.

(4) Fees established under this subsection shall be fair and equitable and give due consideration to the objectives of the copyright system.

(5) If the Register determines under paragraph (2) that fees should be adjusted, the Register shall prepare a proposed fee schedule and submit the schedule with the accompanying economic analysis to the Congress. The fees proposed by the Register may be instituted after the end of 120 days after the schedule is submitted to the Congress unless, within that 120-day period, a law is enacted stating in substance that the Congress does not approve the schedule.

(c) The fees prescribed by or under this section are applicable to the United States Government and any of its agencies, employees, or officers, but the Register of Copyrights has discretion to waive the requirement of this subsection in occasional or isolated cases involving relatively small amounts.

(d) (1) Except as provided in paragraph (2), all fees received under this section shall be deposited by the Register of Copyrights in the Treasury of the United States and shall be credited to the appropriations for necessary expenses of the Copyright Office. Such fees that are collected shall remain available until expended. The Register may, in accordance with regulations that he or she shall prescribe, refund any sum paid by mistake or in excess of the fee required by this section.

(2) In the case of fees deposited against future services, the Register of Copyrights shall request the Secretary of the Treasury to invest in interest-bearing securities in the United States Treasury any portion of the fees that, as determined by the Register, is not required to meet current deposit account demands. Funds from such portion of fees shall be invested in securities that permit funds to be available to the Copyright Office at all times if they are determined to be necessary to meet current deposit account demands. Such investments shall be in public debt securities with maturities suitable to the needs of the Copyright Office, as determined by the Register of Copyrights, and bearing interest at rates determined by the Secretary of the Treasury, taking into consideration current market yields on outstanding marketable obligations of the United States of comparable maturities.

(3) The income on such investments shall be deposited in the Treasury of the United States and shall be credited to the appropriations for necessary expenses of the Copyright Office.

§ 709. *Delay in delivery caused by disruption of postal or other services*

In any case in which the Register of Copyrights determines, on the basis of such evidence as the Register may by regulation require, that a deposit, application, fee, or any other material to be delivered to the Copyright Office by a particular date, would have been received in the Copyright Office in due time except for a general disruption or suspension of postal or other transportation or communications services, the actual receipt of such material in the Copyright Office within one month after the date on which the Register determines that the disruption or suspension of such services has terminated, shall be considered timely.

Chapter 7 Endnotes

[1] The Work Made for Hire and Copyright Corrections Act of 2000 amended the table of sections for chapter 7 by deleting section 710, entitled, "Reproduction for use of the blind and physically handicapped: Voluntary licensing forms and procedures." Pub. L. No. 106-379, 114 Stat. 1444, 1445.

[2] The Copyright Fees and Technical Amendments Act of 1989 amended section 701 by adding subsection (e). Pub. L. No. 101-319, 104 Stat. 290. In 1998, the Digital Millennium Copyright Act amended section 701 by adding a new subsection (b), redesignating former subsections (b) through (e) as (c) through (f) respectively, and, in the new subsection (f), by substituting "III" for "IV" and "5314" for "5315." Pub. L. No. 105-304, 112 Stat. 2860, 2887.

[3] Title 5 of the *United States Code* is entitled "Government Organization and Employees."

[4] Copyright Office regulations are published in the *Federal Register* and in title 37, chapter II, of the *Code of Federal Regulations.*

[5] The Work Made for Hire and Copyright Corrections Act of 2000 amended section 705 by rewriting paragraph (a). Pub. L. No. 106-379, 114 Stat. 1444, 1445.

[6] The Copyright Fees and Technical Amendments Act of 1989 amended section 708 . by substituting a new subsection (a), by redesignating subsections (b) and (c) as subsections (c) and (d), respectively, and by adding a new subsection (b). Pub. L. No. 101-318, 104 Stat. 287. The Act states that these amendments "shall take effect 6 months after the date of the enactment of this Act" and shall apply to:

(A) claims to original, supplementary, and renewal copyright received for registration, and to items received for recordation in the Copyright Office, on or after such effective date, and

(B) other requests for services received on or after such effective date, or received before such effective date for services not yet rendered as of such date.

With respect to prior claims, the Act states that claims to original, supplementary, and renewal copyright received for registration and items received for recordation in acceptable form in the Copyright Office before the above mentioned effective date, and requests for services which are rendered before such effective date "shall be governed by section 708 of title 17, United States Code, as in effect before such effective date." Pub. L. No. 101-318, 104 Stat. 287, 288.

The Copyright Renewal Act of 1992 amended paragraph (2) of section 708(a) by striking the words "in its first term" and by substituting "$20" in lieu of "$12." Pub. L. No. 102-307, 106 Stat. 264, 266.

In 1997, section 708 was amended by rewriting subsections (b) and (d) in their entirety. Pub. L. No. 105-80, 111 Stat. 1529, 1532.

The Work Made for Hire and Copyright Corrections Act of 2000 amended section 708 by rewriting subsection (a), by substituting new language for the first sentence in subsection (b) and by substituting "adjustment" for "increase" in paragraph (b)(1), the word "adjust" for "increase" in paragraph (b)(2) and the word "adjusted" for "increased" in paragraph (b)(5). Pub. L. No. 106-379, 114 Stat. 1444, 1445. The Act also stated that "The fees under section 708(a) of title 17, United States Code, on the date of the enactment of this Act shall be the fees in effect under section 708(a) of such title on the day before such date of enactment."

[7] The current fees may be found in the *Code of Federal Regulations*, at 37 CFR §201.3, as as authorized by Pub. L. No. 105-80, 111 Stat. 1529, 1532. In Pub. L. No. 105-80, Congress amended section 708(b) to require that the Register of Copyrights establish fees by regulation rather than by codifying them in title 17, *United States Code*, as was previously done.

CHAPTER 8[1]

PROCEEDINGS BY COPYRIGHT ROYALTY JUDGES

§ 801. Copyright Royalty Judges; appointment and functions[2]

(a) Appointment. — The Librarian of Congress shall appoint 3 full-time Copyright Royalty Judges, and shall appoint 1 of the 3 as the Chief Copyright Royalty Judge. The Librarian shall make appointments to such positions after consultation with the Register of Copyrights.

(b) Functions. — Subject to the provisions of this chapter, the functions of the Copyright Royalty Judges shall be as follows:

(1) To make determinations and adjustments of reasonable terms and rates of royalty payments as provided in sections 112(e), 114, 115, 116, 118, 119, and 1004. The rates applicable under sections 114(f)(1)(B), 115, and 116 shall be calculated to achieve the following objectives:

(A) To maximize the availability of creative works to the public.

(B) To afford the copyright owner a fair return for his or her creative work and the copyright user a fair income under existing economic conditions.

(C) To reflect the relative roles of the copyright owner and the copyright user in the product made available to the public with respect to relative creative contribution, technological contribution, capital investment, cost, risk, and contribution to the opening of new markets for creative expression and media for their communication.

(D) To minimize any disruptive impact on the structure of the industries involved and on generally prevailing industry practices.

(2) To make determinations concerning the adjustment of the copyright royalty rates under section 111 solely in accordance with the following provisions:

(A) The rates established by section 111(d)(1)(B) may be adjusted to reflect —

(i) national monetary inflation or deflation; or

(ii) changes in the average rates charged cable subscribers for the basic service of providing secondary transmissions to maintain the real constant dollar level of the royalty fee per subscriber which existed as of the date of October 19, 1976, except that —

(I) if the average rates charged cable system subscribers for the basic service of providing secondary transmissions are changed so that the average rates exceed national monetary inflation, no change in the rates established by section 111(d)(1)(B) shall be permitted; and

(II) no increase in the royalty fee shall be permitted based on any reduction in the average number of distant signal equivalents per subscriber.

The Copyright Royalty Judges may consider all factors relating to the maintenance of such level of payments, including, as an extenuating factor, whether the industry has been restrained by subscriber rate regulating authorities from increasing the rates for the basic service of providing secondary transmissions.

(B) In the event that the rules and regulations of the Federal Communications Commission are amended at any time after April 15, 1976, to permit the carriage by cable systems of additional television broadcast signals beyond the local service area of the primary transmitters of such signals, the royalty rates established by section 111(d)(1)(B) may be adjusted to ensure that the rates for the additional distant signal equivalents resulting from such carriage are reasonable in the light of the changes effected by the amendment to such rules and regulations. In determining the reasonableness of rates proposed following an amendment of Federal Communications Commission rules and regulations, the Copyright Royalty Judges shall consider, among other factors, the economic impact on copyright owners and users; except that no adjustment in royalty rates shall be made under this subparagraph with respect to any distant signal equivalent or fraction thereof represented by —

(i) carriage of any signal permitted under the rules and regulations of the Federal Communications Commission in effect on April 15, 1976, or the carriage of a signal of the same type (that is, independent, network, or noncommercial educational) substituted for such permitted signal; or

(ii) a television broadcast signal first carried after April 15, 1976, pursuant to an individual waiver of the rules and regulations of the Federal Communications Commission, as such rules and regulations were in effect on April 15, 1976.

(C) In the event of any change in the rules and regulations of the Federal Communications Commission with respect to syndicated and sports program exclusivity after April 15, 1976, the rates established by section 111(d)(1)(B) may be adjusted to assure that such rates are reasonable in light of the changes to such rules and regulations, but any such adjustment shall apply only to the affected television broadcast signals carried on those systems affected by the change.

(D) The gross receipts limitations established by section 111(d)(1) (C) and (D) shall be adjusted to reflect national monetary inflation or deflation or changes in the average rates charged cable system subscribers for the basic service of providing secondary transmissions to maintain the real constant dollar value of the exemption provided by such section, and the royalty rate specified therein shall not be subject to adjustment.

(3)(A) To authorize the distribution, under sections 111, 119, and 1007, of those royalty fees collected under sections 111, 119, and 1005, as the case may be, to the extent that the Copyright Royalty Judges have found that the distribution of such fees is not subject to controversy.

(B) In cases where the Copyright Royalty Judges determine that controversy exists, the Copyright Royalty Judges shall determine the distribution of such fees, including partial distributions, in accordance with section 111, 119, or 1007, as the case may be.

(C) Notwithstanding section 804(b)(8), the Copyright Royalty Judges, at any time after the filing of claims under section 111, 119, or 1007, may, upon motion of one or more of the claimants and after publication in the Federal Register of a request for responses to the motion from interested claimants, make a partial distribution of such fees, if, based upon all responses received during the 30-day period beginning on the date of such publication, the Copyright Royalty Judges conclude that no claimant entitled to receive such fees has stated a reasonable objection to the partial distribution, and all such claimants —

(i) agree to the partial distribution;

(ii) sign an agreement obligating them to return any excess amounts to the extent necessary to comply with the final determination on the distribution of the fees made under subparagraph (B);

(iii) file the agreement with the Copyright Royalty Judges; and

(iv) agree that such funds are available for distribution.

(D) The Copyright Royalty Judges and any other officer or employee acting in good faith in distributing funds under subparagraph (C) shall not be held liable for the payment of any excess fees under subparagraph (C). The Copyright Royalty Judges shall, at the time the final determination is made, calculate any such excess amounts.

(4) To accept or reject royalty claims filed under sections 111, 119, and 1007, on the basis of timeliness or the failure to establish the basis for a claim.

(5) To accept or reject rate adjustment petitions as provided in section 804 and petitions to participate as provided in section 803(b) (1) and (2).

(6) To determine the status of a digital audio recording device or a digital audio interface device under sections 1002 and 1003, as provided in section 1010.

(7)(A) To adopt as a basis for statutory terms and rates or as a basis for the distribution of statutory royalty payments, an agreement concerning such matters reached among some or all of the participants in a proceeding at any time during the proceeding, except that —

(i) the Copyright Royalty Judges shall provide to those that would be bound by the terms, rates, or other determination set by any agreement in a proceeding to determine royalty rates an opportunity to comment on the agreement and shall provide to participants in the proceeding under section 803(b)(2) that would be bound by the terms, rates, or other determination set by the agreement an opportunity to comment on the agreement and object to its adoption as a basis for statutory terms and rates; and

(ii) the Copyright Royalty Judges may decline to adopt the agreement as a basis for statutory terms and rates for participants that are not parties to the agreement, if any participant described in clause (i) objects to the agreement and the Copyright Royalty Judges conclude, based on the record before them if one exists, that the agreement does not provide a reasonable basis for setting statutory terms or rates.

(B) License agreements voluntarily negotiated pursuant to section 112(e)(5), 114(f)(3), 115(c)(3)(E)(i), 116(c), or 118(b)(2) that do not result in statutory terms and rates shall not be subject to clauses (i) and (ii) of subparagraph (A).

(C) Interested parties may negotiate and agree to, and the Copyright Royalty Judges may adopt, an agreement that specifies as terms notice and recordkeeping requirements that apply in lieu of those that would otherwise apply under regulations.

(8) To perform other duties, as assigned by the Register of Copyrights within the Library of Congress, except as provided in section 802(g), at times when Copyright Royalty Judges are not engaged in performing the other duties set forth in this section.

(c) Rulings. — The Copyright Royalty Judges may make any necessary procedural or evidentiary rulings in any proceeding under this chapter and may, before commencing a proceeding under this chapter, make any such rulings that would apply to the proceedings conducted by the Copyright Royalty Judges.

(d) Administrative Support. — The Librarian of Congress shall provide the Copyright Royalty Judges with the necessary administrative services related to proceedings under this chapter.

(e) Location in Library of Congress. — The offices of the Copyright Royalty Judges and staff shall be in the Library of Congress.

(f) Effective Date of Actions. — On and after the date of the enactment of the Copyright Royalty and Distribution Reform Act of 2004, in any case in which time limits are prescribed under this title for performance of an action with or by the Copyright Royalty Judges, and in which the last day of the prescribed period falls on a Saturday, Sunday, holiday, or other nonbusiness day within the District of Columbia or the Federal Government, the action may be taken on the next succeeding business day, and is effective as of the date when the period expired.

§ 802. Copyright Royalty Judgeships; staff[3]

(a) Qualifications of Copyright Royalty Judges. —

(1) In general. — Each Copyright Royalty Judge shall be an attorney who has at least 7 years of legal experience. The Chief Copyright Royalty Judge shall have at least 5 years of experience in adjudications, arbitrations, or court trials. Of the other 2 Copyright Royalty Judges, 1 shall have significant knowledge of copyright law, and the other shall have significant knowledge of economics. An individual may serve as a Copyright Royalty Judge only if the individual is free of any financial conflict of interest under subsection (h).

(2) Definition. — In this subsection, the term "adjudication" has the meaning given that term in section 551 of title 5, but does not include mediation.

(b) Staff. — The Chief Copyright Royalty Judge shall hire 3 full-time staff members to assist the Copyright Royalty Judges in performing their functions.

(c) Terms. — The individual first appointed as the Chief Copyright Royalty Judge shall be appointed to a term of 6 years, and of the remaining individuals first appointed as Copyright Royalty Judges, 1 shall be appointed to a term of 4 years, and the other shall be appointed to a term of 2 years. Thereafter, the terms of succeeding Copyright Royalty Judges shall each be 6 years. An individual serving as a Copyright Royalty Judge may be reappointed to subsequent terms. The term of a Copyright Royalty Judge shall begin when the term of the predecessor of that Copyright Royalty Judge ends. When the term of office of a Copyright Royalty Judge ends, the individual serving that term may continue to serve until a successor is selected.

(d) Vacancies or Incapacity. —

(1) Vacancies. — If a vacancy should occur in the position of Copyright Royalty Judge, the Librarian of Congress shall act expeditiously to fill the vacancy, and may appoint an interim Copyright Royalty Judge to serve until another Copyright Royalty Judge is appointed under this section. An individual appointed to fill the vacancy occurring before the expiration of the term for which the predecessor of that individual was appointed shall be appointed for the remainder of that term.

(2) Incapacity. — In the case in which a Copyright Royalty Judge is temporarily unable to perform his or her duties, the Librarian of Congress may appoint an interim Copyright Royalty Judge to perform such duties during the period of such incapacity.

(e) Compensation. —

(1) Judges. — The Chief Copyright Royalty Judge shall receive compensation at the rate of basic pay payable for level AL-1 for administrative law judges pursuant to section 5372(b) of title 5, and each of the other two Copyright Royalty Judges shall receive compensation at the rate of basic pay payable for level AL-2 for administrative law judges pursuant to such section. The compensation of the Copyright Royalty Judges shall not be subject to any regulations adopted by the Office of Personnel Management pursuant to its authority under section 5376(b)(1) of title 5.

(2) Staff members. — Of the staff members appointed under subsection (b) —

(A) the rate of pay of 1 staff member shall be not more than the basic rate of pay payable for level 10 of GS-15 of the General Schedule;

(B) the rate of pay of 1 staff member shall be not less than the basic rate of pay payable for GS-13 of the General Schedule and not more than the basic rate of pay payable for level 10 of GS-14 of such Schedule; and

(C) the rate of pay for the third staff member shall be not less than the basic rate of pay payable for GS-8 of the General Schedule and not more than the basic rate of pay payable for level 10 of GS-11 of such Schedule.

(3) Locality pay. — All rates of pay referred to under this subsection shall include locality pay.

(f) Independence of Copyright Royalty Judge. —

(1) In making determinations. —

(A) In general. — (i) Subject to subparagraph (B) and clause (ii) of this subparagraph, the Copyright Royalty Judges shall have full independence in making determinations concerning adjustments and determinations of copyright royalty rates and terms, the distribution of copyright royalties, the acceptance or rejection of royalty claims, rate adjustment petitions, and petitions to participate, and in issuing other rulings under this title, except that the Copyright Royalty Judges may consult with the Register of Copyrights on any matter other than a question of fact.

(ii) One or more Copyright Royalty Judges may, or by motion to the Copyright Royalty Judges, any participant in a proceeding may, request from the Register of Copyrights an interpretation of any material questions of substantive law that relate to the construction of provisions of this title and arise in the course of the proceeding. Any request for a written interpretation shall be in writing and on the record, and reasonable provision shall be made to permit participants in the proceeding to comment on the material questions of substantive law in a manner that minimizes duplication and delay. Except as provided in subparagraph (B), the Register of Copyrights shall deliver to the Copyright Royalty Judges a written response within 14 days after the receipt of all briefs and comments from the participants. The Copyright Royalty Judges shall apply the legal interpretation embodied in the response of the Register of Copyrights if it is timely delivered, and the response shall be included in the record that accompanies the final determination. The authority under this clause shall not be construed to authorize the Register of Copyrights to provide an interpretation of questions of procedure before the Copyright Royalty Judges, the ultimate adjustments and determinations of copyright royalty rates and terms, the ultimate distribution of copyright royalties, or the acceptance or rejection of royalty claims, rate adjustment petitions, or petitions to participate in a proceeding.

(B) Novel questions. — (i) In any case in which a novel material question of substantive law concerning an interpretation of those provisions of this title that are the subject of the proceeding is presented, the Copyright Royalty Judges shall request a decision of the Register of Copyrights, in writing, to resolve such novel question. Reasonable provision shall be made for comment on such request by the participants in the proceeding, in such a way as to minimize duplication and delay. The Register of Copyrights shall transmit his or her decision to the Copyright Royalty Judges within 30 days after the Register of Copyrights receives all of the briefs or comments of the participants. Such decision shall be in writing and included by the Copyright Royalty Judges in the record that accompanies their final determination. If such a decision is timely delivered to the Copyright Royalty Judges, the Copyright Royalty Judges shall apply the legal determinations embodied in the decision of the Register of Copyrights in resolving material questions of substantive law.

(ii) In clause (i), a "novel question of law" is a question of law that has not been determined in prior decisions, determinations, and rulings described in section 803(a).

(C) Consultation. — Notwithstanding the provisions of subparagraph (A), the Copyright Royalty Judges shall consult with the Register of Copyrights with respect to any determination or ruling that would require that any act be performed by the Copyright Office, and any such determination or ruling shall not be binding upon the Register of Copyrights.

(D) Review of legal conclusions by the register of copyrights. — The Register of Copyrights may review for legal error the resolution by the Copyright Royalty Judges of a material question of substantive law under this title that underlies or is contained in a final determination of the Copyright Royalty Judges. If the Register of Copyrights concludes, after taking into consideration the views of the participants in the proceeding, that any resolution reached by the Copyright Royalty Judges was in material error, the Register of Copyrights shall issue a written decision correcting such legal error, which shall be made part of the record of the proceeding. The Register of Copyrights shall issue such written decision not later than 60 days after the date on which the final determination by the Copyright Royalty Judges is issued. Additionally, the Register of Copyrights shall cause to be published in the Federal Register such written decision, together with a specific identification of the legal conclusion of the Copyright Royalty Judges that is determined to be erroneous. As to conclusions of substantive law involving an interpretation of the statutory provisions of this title, the decision of the Register of Copyrights shall be binding as precedent upon the Copyright Royalty Judges in subsequent proceedings under this chapter. When a decision has been rendered pursuant to this subparagraph, the Register of Copyrights may, on the basis of and in accordance with such decision, intervene as of right in any appeal of a final determination of the Copyright Royalty Judges pursuant to section 803(d) in the United States Court of Appeals for the District of Columbia Circuit. If, prior to intervening in such an appeal, the Register of Copyrights gives notification to, and undertakes to consult with, the Attorney General with respect to such intervention, and the Attorney General fails, within a reasonable period after receiving such notification, to intervene in such appeal, the Register of Copyrights may intervene in such appeal in his or her own name by any attorney designated by the Register of Copyrights for such purpose. Intervention by the Register of Copyrights in his or her own name shall not preclude the Attorney General from intervening on behalf of the United States in such an appeal as may be otherwise provided or required by law.

(E) Effect on judicial review. — Nothing in this section shall be interpreted to alter the standard applied by a court in reviewing legal determinations involving an interpretation or construction of the provisions of this title or to affect the extent to which any construction or interpretation of the provisions of this title shall be accorded deference by a reviewing court.

(2) Performance appraisals. —

(A) In general. — Notwithstanding any other provision of law or any regulation of the Library of Congress, and subject to subparagraph (B), the Copyright Royalty Judges shall not receive performance appraisals.

(B) Relating to sanction or removal. — To the extent that the Librarian of Congress adopts regulations under subsection (h) relating to the sanction or removal of a Copyright Royalty Judge and such regulations require documentation to establish the cause of such sanction or removal, the Copyright Royalty Judge may receive an appraisal related specifically to the cause of the sanction or removal.

(g) Inconsistent Duties Barred. — No Copyright Royalty Judge may undertake duties that conflict with his or her duties and responsibilities as a Copyright Royalty Judge.

(h) Standards of Conduct. — The Librarian of Congress shall adopt regulations regarding the standards of conduct, including financial conflict of interest and restrictions against ex parte communications, which shall govern the Copyright Royalty Judges and the proceedings under this chapter.

(i) Removal or Sanction. — The Librarian of Congress may sanction or remove a Copyright Royalty Judge for violation of the standards of conduct adopted under subsection (h), misconduct, neglect of duty, or any disqualifying physical or mental disability. Any sanction or removal may be made only after notice and opportunity for a hearing, but the Librarian of Congress may suspend the Copyright Royalty Judge during the pendency of such hearing. The Librarian shall appoint an interim Copyright Royalty Judge during the period of any such suspension.

§ 803. Institution and conclusion of proceedings[4]

(a) Proceedings. —

(1) In general. — The Copyright Royalty Judges shall act in accordance with this title, and to the extent not inconsistent with this title, in accordance with subchapter II of chapter 5 of title 5, in carrying out the purposes set forth in section 801. The Copyright Royalty Judges shall act in accordance with regulations issued by the Copyright Royalty Judges and the Librarian of Congress, and on the basis of a written record, prior determinations and interpretations of the Copyright Royalty Tribunal, Librarian of Congress, the Register of Copyrights, copyright arbitration royalty panels (to the extent those determinations are not inconsistent with a decision of the Librarian of Congress or the Register of Copyrights), and the Copyright Royalty Judges (to the extent those determinations are not inconsistent with a decision of the Register of Copyrights that was timely delivered to the Copyright Royalty Judges pursuant to section 802(f)(1) (A) or (B), or with a decision of the Register of Copyrights pursuant to section 802(f)(1)(D)), under this chapter, and decisions of the court of appeals under this chapter before, on, or after the effective date of the Copyright Royalty and Distribution Reform Act of 2004.

(2) Judges acting as panel and individually. — The Copyright Royalty Judges shall preside over hearings in proceedings under this chapter en banc. The Chief Copyright Royalty Judge may designate a Copyright Royalty Judge to preside individually over such collateral and administrative proceedings, and over such proceedings under paragraphs (1) through (5) of subsection (b), as the Chief Judge considers appropriate.

(3) Determinations. — Final determinations of the Copyright Royalty Judges in proceedings under this chapter shall be made by majority vote. A Copyright Royalty Judge dissenting from the majority on any determination under this chapter may issue his or her dissenting opinion, which shall be included with the determination.

(b) Procedures. —

(1) Initiation. —

(A) Call for petitions to participate. — (i) The Copyright Royalty Judges shall cause to be published in the Federal Register notice of commencement of proceedings under this chapter, calling for the filing of petitions to participate in a proceeding under this chapter for the purpose of making the relevant determination under section 111, 112, 114, 115, 116, 118, 119, 1004, or 1007, as the case may be —

(I) promptly upon a determination made under section 804(a);

(II) by no later than January 5 of a year specified in paragraph (2) of section 804(b) for the commencement of proceedings;

(III) by no later than January 5 of a year specified in subparagraph (A) or (B) of paragraph (3) of section 804(b) for the commencement of proceedings, or as otherwise provided in subparagraph (A) or (C) of such paragraph for the commencement of proceedings;

(IV) as provided under section 804(b)(8); or

(V) by no later than January 5 of a year specified in any other provision of section 804(b) for the filing of petitions for the commencement of proceedings, if a petition has not been filed by that date, except that the publication of notice requirement shall not apply in the case of proceedings under section 111 that are scheduled to commence in 2005.

(ii) Petitions to participate shall be filed by no later than 30 days after publication of notice of commencement of a proceeding under clause (i), except that the Copyright Royalty Judges may, for substantial good cause shown and if there is no prejudice to the participants that have already filed petitions, accept late petitions to participate at any time up to the date that is 90 days before the date on which participants in the proceeding are to file their written direct statements. Notwithstanding the preceding sentence, petitioners whose petitions are filed more than 30 days after publication of notice of commencement of a proceeding are not eligible to object to a settlement reached during the voluntary negotiation period under paragraph (3), and any objection filed by such a petitioner shall not be taken into account by the Copyright Royalty Judges.

(B) Petitions to participate. — Each petition to participate in a proceeding shall describe the petitioner's interest in the subject matter of the proceeding. Parties with similar interests may file a single petition to participate.

(2) Participation in general. — Subject to paragraph (4), a person may participate in a proceeding under this chapter, including through the submission of briefs or other information, only if —

(A) that person has filed a petition to participate in accordance with paragraph (1) (either individually or as a group under paragraph (1)(B));

(B) the Copyright Royalty Judges have not determined that the petition to participate is facially invalid;

(C) the Copyright Royalty Judges have not determined, sua sponte or on the motion of another participant in the proceeding, that the person lacks a significant interest in the proceeding; and

(D) the petition to participate is accompanied by either —

(i) in a proceeding to determine royalty rates, a filing fee of $150; or

(ii) in a proceeding to determine distribution of royalty fees —

(I) a filing fee of $150; or

(II) a statement that the petitioner (individually or as a group) will not seek a distribution of more than $1000, in which case the amount distributed to the petitioner shall not exceed $1000.

(3) Voluntary negotiation period. —

(A) Commencement of proceedings. —

(i) Rate adjustment proceeding. — Promptly after the date for filing of petitions to participate in a proceeding, the Copyright Royalty Judges shall make available to all participants in the proceeding a list of such participants and shall initiate a voluntary negotiation period among the participants.

(ii) Distribution proceeding. — Promptly after the date for filing of petitions to participate in a proceeding to determine the distribution of royalties, the Copyright Royalty Judges shall make available to all participants in the proceeding a list of such participants. The initiation of a voluntary negotiation period among the participants shall be set at a time determined by the Copyright Royalty Judges.

(B) Length of proceedings. — The voluntary negotiation period initiated under subparagraph (A) shall be 3 months.

(C) Determination of subsequent proceedings. — At the close of the voluntary negotiation proceedings, the Copyright Royalty Judges shall, if further proceedings under this chapter are necessary, determine whether and to what extent paragraphs (4) and (5) will apply to the parties.

(4) Small claims procedure in distribution proceedings. —

(A) In general. — If, in a proceeding under this chapter to determine the distribution of royalties, the contested amount of a claim is $10,000 or less, the Copyright Royalty Judges shall decide the controversy on the basis of the filing of the written direct statement by the participant, the response by any opposing participant, and 1 additional response by each such party.

(B) Bad faith inflation of claim. — If the Copyright Royalty Judges determine that a participant asserts in bad faith an amount in controversy in excess of $10,000 for the purpose of avoiding a determination under the procedure set forth in subparagraph (A), the Copyright Royalty Judges shall impose a fine on that participant in an amount not to exceed the difference between the actual amount distributed and the amount asserted by the participant.

(5) Paper proceedings. — The Copyright Royalty Judges in proceedings under this chapter may decide, sua sponte or upon motion of a participant, to determine issues on the basis of the filing of the written direct statement by the participant, the response by any opposing participant, and one additional response by each such participant. Prior to making such decision to proceed on such a paper record only, the Copyright Royalty Judges shall offer to all parties to the proceeding the opportunity to comment on the decision. The procedure under this paragraph —

(A) shall be applied in cases in which there is no genuine issue of material fact, there is no need for evidentiary hearings, and all participants in the proceeding agree in writing to the procedure; and

(B) may be applied under such other circumstances as the Copyright Royalty Judges consider appropriate.

(6) Regulations. —

(A) In general. — The Copyright Royalty Judges may issue regulations to carry out their functions under this title. All regulations issued by the Copyright Royalty Judges are subject to the approval of the Librarian of Congress. Not later than 120 days after Copyright Royalty Judges or interim Copyright Royalty Judges, as the case may be, are first appointed after the enactment of the Copyright Royalty and Distribution Reform Act of 2004, such judges shall issue regulations to govern proceedings under this chapter.

(B) Interim regulations. — Until regulations are adopted under subparagraph (A), the Copyright Royalty Judges shall apply the regulations in effect under this chapter on the day before the effective date of the Copyright Royalty and Distribution Reform Act of 2004, to the extent such regulations are not inconsistent with this chapter, except that functions carried out under such regulations by the Librarian of Congress, the Register of Copyrights, or copyright arbitration royalty panels that, as of such date of enactment, are to be carried out by the Copyright Royalty Judges under this chapter, shall be carried out by the Copyright Royalty Judges under such regulations.

(C) Requirements. — Regulations issued under subparagraph (A) shall include the following:

(i) The written direct statements and written rebuttal statements of all participants in a proceeding under paragraph (2) shall be filed by a date specified by the Copyright Royalty Judges, which, in the case of written direct statements, may be not earlier than 4 months, and not later than 5 months, after the end of the voluntary negotiation period under paragraph (3). Notwithstanding the preceding sentence, the Copyright Royalty Judges may allow a participant in a proceeding to file an amended written direct statement based on new information received during the discovery process, within 15 days after the end of the discovery period specified in clause (iv).

(ii)(I) Following the submission to the Copyright Royalty Judges of written direct statements and written rebuttal statements by the participants in a proceeding under paragraph (2), the Copyright Royalty Judges, after taking into consideration the views of the participants in the proceeding, shall determine a schedule for conducting and completing discovery.

   (II) In this chapter, the term "written direct statements" means witness statements, testimony, and exhibits to be presented in the proceedings, and such other information that is necessary to establish terms and rates, or the distribution of royalty payments, as the case may be, as set forth in regulations issued by the Copyright Royalty Judges.

(iii) Hearsay may be admitted in proceedings under this chapter to the extent deemed appropriate by the Copyright Royalty Judges.

(iv) Discovery in connection with written direct statements shall be permitted for a period of 60 days, except for discovery ordered by the Copyright Royalty Judges in connection with the resolution of motions, orders, and disputes pending at the end of such period. The Copyright Royalty Judges may order a discovery schedule in connection with written rebuttal statements.

(v) Any participant under paragraph (2) in a proceeding under this chapter to determine royalty rates may request of an opposing participant nonprivileged documents directly related to the written direct statement or written rebuttal statement of that participant. Any objection to such a request shall be resolved by a motion or request to compel production made to the Copyright Royalty Judges in accordance with regulations adopted by the Copyright Royalty Judges. Each motion or request to compel discovery shall be determined by the Copyright Royalty Judges, or by a Copyright Royalty Judge when permitted under subsection (a)(2). Upon such motion, the Copyright Royalty Judges may order discovery pursuant to regulations established under this paragraph.

(vi)(I) Any participant under paragraph (2) in a proceeding under this chapter to determine royalty rates may, by means of written motion or on the record, request of an opposing participant or witness other relevant information and materials if, absent the discovery sought, the Copyright Royalty Judges' resolution of the proceeding would be substantially impaired. In determining whether discovery will be granted under this clause, the Copyright Royalty Judges may consider —
   (aa) whether the burden or expense of producing the requested information or materials outweighs the likely benefit, taking into account the needs and resources of the participants, the importance of the issues at stake, and the probative value of the requested information or materials in resolving such issues;
   (bb) whether the requested information or materials would be unreasonably cumulative or duplicative, or are obtainable from another source that is more convenient, less burdensome, or less expensive; and
   (cc) whether the participant seeking discovery has had ample opportunity by discovery in the proceeding or by other means to obtain the information sought.

(II) This clause shall not apply to any proceeding scheduled to commence after December 31, 2010.

(vii) In a proceeding under this chapter to determine royalty rates, the participants entitled to receive royalties shall collectively be permitted to take no more than 10 depositions and secure responses to no more than 25 interrogatories, and the participants obligated to pay royalties shall collectively be permitted to take no more than 10 depositions and secure responses to no more than 25 interrogatories. The Copyright Royalty Judges shall resolve any disputes among similarly aligned participants to allocate the number of depositions or interrogatories permitted under this clause.

(viii) The rules and practices in effect on the day before the effective date of the Copyright Royalty and Distribution Reform Act of 2004, relating to discovery in proceedings under this chapter to determine the distribution of royalty fees, shall continue to apply to such proceedings on and after such effective date.

(ix) In proceedings to determine royalty rates, the Copyright Royalty Judges may issue a subpoena commanding a participant or witness to appear and give testimony, or to produce and permit inspection of documents or tangible things, if the Copyright Royalty Judges' resolution of the proceeding would be substantially impaired by the absence of such testimony or production of documents or tangible things. Such subpoena shall specify with reasonable particularity the materials to be produced or the scope and nature of the required testimony. Nothing in this clause shall preclude the Copyright Royalty Judges from requesting the production by a nonparticipant of information or materials relevant to the resolution by the Copyright Royalty Judges of a material issue of fact.

(x) The Copyright Royalty Judges shall order a settlement conference among the participants in the proceeding to facilitate the presentation of offers of settlement among the participants. The settlement conference shall be held during a 21-day period following the 60-day discovery period specified in clause (iv) and shall take place outside the presence of the Copyright Royalty Judges.

(xi) No evidence, including exhibits, may be submitted in the written direct statement or written rebuttal statement of a participant without a sponsoring witness, except where the Copyright Royalty Judges have taken official notice, or in the case of incorporation by reference of past records, or for good cause shown.

(c) Determination of Copyright Royalty Judges. —

(1) Timing. — The Copyright Royalty Judges shall issue their determination in a proceeding not later than 11 months after the conclusion of the 21-day settlement conference period under subsection (b)(6)(C)(x), but, in the case of a proceeding to determine successors to rates or terms that expire on a specified date, in no event later than 15 days before the expiration of the then current statutory rates and terms.

(2) Rehearings. —

(A) In general. — The Copyright Royalty Judges may, in exceptional cases, upon motion of a participant in a proceeding under subsection (b)(2), order a rehearing, after the determination in the proceeding is issued under paragraph (1), on such matters as the Copyright Royalty Judges determine to be appropriate.

(B) Timing for filing motion. — Any motion for a rehearing under subparagraph (A) may only be filed within 15 days after the date on which the Copyright Royalty Judges deliver to the participants in the proceeding their initial determination.

(C) Participation by opposing party not required. — In any case in which a rehearing is ordered, any opposing party shall not be required to participate in the rehearing, except that nonparticipation may give rise to the limitations with respect to judicial review provided for in subsection (d)(1).

(D) No negative inference. — No negative inference shall be drawn from lack of participation in a rehearing.

(E) Continuity of rates and terms. — (i) If the decision of the Copyright Royalty Judges on any motion for a rehearing is not rendered before the expiration of the statutory rates and terms that were previously in effect, in the case of a proceeding to determine successors to rates and terms that expire on a specified date, then —

(I) the initial determination of the Copyright Royalty Judges that is the subject of the rehearing motion shall be effective as of the day following the date on which the rates and terms that were previously in effect expire; and

(II) in the case of a proceeding under section 114(f)(1)(C) or 114(f)(2)(C), royalty rates and terms shall, for purposes of section 114(f)(4)(B), be deemed to have been set at those rates and terms contained in the initial determination of the Copyright Royalty Judges that is the subject of the rehearing motion, as of the date of that determination.

(ii) The pendency of a motion for a rehearing under this paragraph shall not relieve persons obligated to make royalty payments who would be affected by the determination on that motion from providing the statements of account and any reports of use, to the extent required, and paying the royalties required under the relevant determination or regulations.

(iii) Notwithstanding clause (ii), whenever royalties described in clause (ii) are paid to a person other than the Copyright Office, the entity designated by the Copyright Royalty Judges to which such royalties are paid by the copyright user (and any successor thereto) shall, within 60 days after the motion for rehearing is resolved or, if the motion is granted, within 60 days after the rehearing is concluded, return any excess amounts previously paid to the extent necessary to comply with the final determination of royalty rates by the Copyright Royalty Judges. Any underpayment of royalties resulting from a rehearing shall be paid within the same period.

(3) Contents of determination. — A determination of the Copyright Royalty Judges shall be supported by the written record and shall set forth the findings of fact relied on by the Copyright Royalty Judges. Among other terms adopted in a determination, the Copyright Royalty Judges may specify notice and recordkeeping requirements of users of the copyrights at issue that apply in lieu of those that would otherwise apply under regulations.

(4) Continuing jurisdiction. — The Copyright Royalty Judges may issue an amendment to a written determination to correct any technical or clerical errors in the determination or to modify the terms, but not the rates, of royalty payments in response to unforeseen circumstances that would frustrate the proper implementation of such determination. Such amendment shall be set forth in a written addendum to the determination that shall be distributed to the participants of the proceeding and shall be published in the Federal Register.

(5) Protective order. — The Copyright Royalty Judges may issue such orders as may be appropriate to protect confidential information, including orders excluding confidential information from the record of the determination that is published or made available to the public, except that any terms or rates of royalty payments or distributions may not be excluded.

(6) Publication of determination. — By no later than the end of the 60-day period provided in section 802(f)(1)(D), the Librarian of Congress shall cause the determination, and any corrections thereto, to be published in the Federal Register. The Librarian of Congress shall also publicize the determination and corrections in such other manner as the Librarian considers appropriate, including, but not limited to, publication on the Internet. The Librarian of Congress shall also make the determination, corrections, and the accompanying record available for public inspection and copying.

(7) Late payment. — A determination of the Copyright Royalty Judges may include terms with respect to late payment, but in no way shall such terms prevent the copyright holder from asserting other rights or remedies provided under this title.

(d) Judicial Review. —

(1) Appeal. — Any determination of the Copyright Royalty Judges under subsection (c) may, within 30 days after the publication of the determination in the Federal Register, be appealed, to the United States Court of Appeals for the District of Columbia Circuit, by any aggrieved participant in the proceeding under subsection (b)(2) who fully participated in the proceeding and who would be bound by the determination. Any participant that did not participate in a rehearing may not raise any issue that was the subject of that rehearing at any stage of judicial review of the hearing determination. If no appeal is brought within that 30-day period, the determination of the Copyright Royalty Judges shall be final, and the royalty fee or determination with respect to the distribution of fees, as the case may be, shall take effect as set forth in paragraph (2).

(2) Effect of rates. —

(A) Expiration on specified date. — When this title provides that the royalty rates and terms that were previously in effect are to expire on a specified date, any adjustment or determination by the Copyright Royalty Judges of successor rates and terms for an ensuing statutory license period shall be effective as of the day following the date of expiration of the rates and terms that were previously in effect, even if the determination of the Copyright Royalty Judges is rendered on a later date. A licensee shall be obligated to continue making payments under the rates and terms previously in effect until such time as rates and terms for the successor period are established. Whenever royalties pursuant to this section are paid to a person other than the Copyright Office, the entity designated by the Copyright Royalty Judges to which such royalties are paid by the copyright user (and any successor thereto) shall, within 60 days after the final determination of the Copyright Royalty Judges establishing rates and terms for a successor period or the exhaustion of all rehearings or appeals of such determination, if any, return any excess amounts previously paid to the extent necessary to comply with the final determination of royalty rates. Any underpayment of royalties by a copyright user shall be paid to the entity designated by the Copyright Royalty Judges within the same period.

(B) Other cases. — In cases where rates and terms have not, prior to the inception of an activity, been established for that particular activity under the relevant license, such rates and terms shall be retroactive to the inception of activity under the relevant license covered by such rates and terms. In other cases where rates and terms do not expire on a specified date, successor rates and terms shall take effect on the first day of the second month that begins after the publication of the determination of the Copyright Royalty Judges in the Federal Register, except as otherwise provided in this title, or by the Copyright Royalty Judges, or as agreed by the participants in a proceeding that would be bound by the rates and terms. Except as otherwise provided in this title, the rates and terms, to the extent applicable, shall remain in effect until such successor rates and terms become effective.

(C) Obligation to make payments. —

(i) The pendency of an appeal under this subsection shall not relieve persons obligated to make royalty payments under section 111, 112, 114, 115, 116, 118, 119, or 1003, who would be affected by the determination on appeal, from —

(I) providing the applicable statements of account and report of use; and

(II) paying the royalties required under the relevant determination or regulations.

(ii) Notwithstanding clause (i), whenever royalties described in clause (i) are paid to a person other than the Copyright Office, the entity designated by the Copyright Royalty Judges to which such royalties are paid by the copyright user (and any successor thereto) shall, within 60 days after the final resolution of the appeal, return any excess amounts previously paid (and interest thereon, if ordered pursuant to paragraph (3)) to the extent necessary to comply with the final determination of royalty rates on appeal. Any underpayment of royalties resulting from an appeal (and interest thereon, if ordered pursuant to paragraph (3)) shall be paid within the same period.

(3) Jurisdiction of court. — Section 706 of title 5 shall apply with respect to review by the court of appeals under this subsection. If the court modifies or vacates a determination of the Copyright Royalty Judges, the court may enter its own determination with respect to the amount or

distribution of royalty fees and costs, and order the repayment of any excess fees, the payment of any underpaid fees, and the payment of interest pertaining respectively thereto, in accordance with its final judgment. The court may also vacate the determination of the Copyright Royalty Judges and remand the case to the Copyright Royalty Judges for further proceedings in accordance with subsection (a).

(e) Administrative Matters. —

(1) Deduction of costs of Library of Congress and Copyright Office from filing fees. —

(A) Deduction from filing fees. — The Librarian of Congress may, to the extent not otherwise provided under this title, deduct from the filing fees collected under subsection (b) for a particular proceeding under this chapter the reasonable costs incurred by the Librarian of Congress, the Copyright Office, and the Copyright Royalty Judges in conducting that proceeding, other than the salaries of the Copyright Royalty Judges and the 3 staff members appointed under section 802(b).

(B) Authorization of appropriations. — There are authorized to be appropriated such sums as may be necessary to pay the costs incurred under this chapter not covered by the filing fees collected under subsection (b). All funds made available pursuant to this subparagraph shall remain available until expended.

(2) Positions required for administration of compulsory licensing. — Section 307 of the Legislative Branch Appropriations Act, 1994, shall not apply to employee positions in the Library of Congress that are required to be filled in order to carry out section 111, 112, 114, 115, 116, 118, or 119 or chapter 10.

§ 804. Institution of proceedings[5]

(a) Filing of Petition. — With respect to proceedings referred to in paragraphs (1) and (2) of section 801(b) concerning the determination or adjustment of royalty rates as provided in sections 111, 112, 114, 115, 116, 118, 119, and 1004, during the calendar years specified in the schedule set forth in subsection (b), any owner or user of a copyrighted work whose royalty rates are specified by this title, or are established under this chapter before or after the enactment of the Copyright Royalty and Distribution Reform Act of 2004, may file a petition with the Copyright Royalty Judges declaring that the petitioner requests a determination or adjustment of the rate. The Copyright Royalty Judges shall make a determination as to whether the petitioner has such a significant interest in the royalty rate in which a determination or adjustment is requested. If the Copyright Royalty Judges determine that the petitioner has such a significant interest, the Copyright Royalty Judges shall cause notice of this determination, with the reasons for such determination, to be published in the Federal Register, together with the notice of commencement of proceedings under this chapter. With respect to proceedings under paragraph (1) of section 801(b) concerning the determination or adjustment of royalty rates as provided in sections 112 and 114, during the calendar years specified in the schedule set forth in subsection (b), the Copyright Royalty Judges shall cause notice of commencement of proceedings under this chapter to be published in the Federal Register as provided in section 803(b)(1)(A).

(b) Timing of Proceedings. —

(1) Section 111 proceedings. — (A) A petition described in subsection (a) to initiate proceedings under section 801(b)(2) concerning the adjustment of royalty rates under section 111 to which subparagraph (A) or (D) of section 801(b)(2) applies may be filed during the year 2005 and in each subsequent fifth calendar year.

(B) In order to initiate proceedings under section 801(b)(2) concerning the adjustment of royalty rates under section 111 to which subparagraph (B) or (C) of section 801(b)(2) applies, within 12 months after an event described in either of those subsections, any owner or user of a copyrighted work whose royalty rates are specified by section 111, or by a rate established under this chapter before or after the enactment of the Copyright Royalty and Distribution Reform Act of 2004, may file a petition with the Copyright Royalty Judges declaring that the petitioner requests an adjustment of the rate. The Copyright Royalty Judges shall then proceed as set forth in subsection (a) of this section. Any change in royalty rates made under this chapter pursuant to this subparagraph may be reconsidered in the year 2005, and each fifth calendar year thereafter, in accordance with the provisions in section 801(b)(2) (B) or (C), as the case may be. A petition for adjustment of rates established by section 111(d)(1)(B) as a result of a change in the rules and regulations of the Federal Communications Commission shall set forth the change on which the petition is based.

(C) Any adjustment of royalty rates under section 111 shall take effect as of the first accounting period commencing after the publication of the determination of the Copyright Royalty Judges in the Federal Register, or on such other date as is specified in that determination.

(2) Certain section 112 proceedings. — Proceedings under this chapter shall be commenced in the year 2007 to determine reasonable terms and rates of royalty payments for the activities described in section 112(e)(1) relating to the limitation on exclusive rights specified by section 114(d)(1)(C)(iv), to become effective on January 1, 2009. Such proceedings shall be repeated in each subsequent fifth calendar year.

(3) Section 114 and corresponding 112 proceedings. —

(A) For eligible nonsubscription services and new subscription services. — Proceedings under this chapter shall be commenced as soon as practicable after the date of enactment of the Copyright Royalty and Distribution Reform Act of 2004 to determine reasonable terms and rates of royalty payments under sections 114 and 112 for the activities of eligible nonsubscription transmission services and new subscription services, to be effective for the period beginning on January 1, 2006, and ending on December 31, 2010. Such proceedings shall next be commenced in January 2009 to determine reasonable terms and rates of royalty payments, to become effective on January 1, 2011. Thereafter, such proceedings shall be repeated in each subsequent fifth calendar year.

(B) For preexisting subscription and satellite digital audio radio services. — Proceedings under this chapter shall be commenced in January 2006 to determine reasonable terms and rates of royalty payments under sections 114 and 112 for the activities of preexisting subscription services, to be effective during the period beginning on January 1, 2008, and ending on December 31, 2012, and preexisting satellite digital audio radio services, to be effective during the period beginning on January 1, 2007, and ending on December 31, 2012. Such proceedings shall next be commenced in 2011 to determine reasonable terms and rates of royalty payments, to become effective on January 1, 2013. Thereafter, such proceedings shall be repeated in each subsequent fifth calendar year.

(C)(i) Notwithstanding any other provision of this chapter, this subparagraph shall govern proceedings commenced pursuant to section 114(f)(1)(C) and 114(f)(2)(C) concerning new types of services.

(ii) Not later than 30 days after a petition to determine rates and terms for a new type of service is filed by any copyright owner of sound recordings, or such new type of service, indicating that such new type of service is or is about to become operational, the Copyright Royalty Judges shall issue a notice for a proceeding to determine rates and terms for such service.

(iii) The proceeding shall follow the schedule set forth in subsections (b), (c), and (d) of section 803, except that —

(I) the determination shall be issued by not later than 24 months after the publication of the notice under clause (ii); and

(II) the decision shall take effect as provided in subsections (c)(2) and (d)(2) of section 803 and section 114(f)(4)(B)(ii) and (C).

(iv) The rates and terms shall remain in effect for the period set forth in section 114(f)(1)(C) or 114(f)(2)(C), as the case may be.

(4) Section 115 proceedings. — A petition described in subsection (a) to initiate proceedings under section 801(b)(1) concerning the adjustment or determination of royalty rates as provided in section 115 may be filed in the year 2006 and in each subsequent fifth calendar year, or at such other times as the parties have agreed under section 115(c)(3) (B) and (C).

(5) Section 116 proceedings. — (A) A petition described in subsection (a) to initiate proceedings under section 801(b) concerning the determination of royalty rates and terms as provided in section 116 may be filed at any time within 1 year after negotiated licenses authorized by section 116 are terminated or expire and are not replaced by subsequent agreements.

(B) If a negotiated license authorized by section 116 is terminated or expires and is not replaced by another such license agreement which provides permission to use a quantity of musical works not substantially smaller than the quantity of such works performed on coin-operated phonorecord players during the 1-year period ending March 1, 1989, the Copyright Royalty Judges shall, upon petition filed under paragraph (1) within 1 year after such termination or expiration, commence a proceeding to promptly establish an interim royalty rate or rates for the public performance by means of a coin-operated phonorecord player of nondramatic musical works embodied in phonorecords which had been subject to the terminated or expired negotiated license agreement. Such rate or rates shall be the same as the last such rate or rates and shall remain in force until the conclusion of proceedings by the Copyright Royalty Judges, in accordance with section 803, to adjust the royalty rates applicable to such works, or until superseded by a new negotiated license agreement, as provided in section 116(b).

(6) Section 118 proceedings. — A petition described in subsection (a) to initiate proceedings under section 801(b)(1) concerning the determination of reasonable terms and rates of royalty payments as provided in section 118 may be filed in the year 2006 and in each subsequent fifth calendar year.

(7) Section 1004 proceedings. — A petition described in subsection (a) to initiate proceedings under section 801(b)(1) concerning the adjustment of reasonable royalty rates under section 1004 may be filed as provided in section 1004(a)(3).

(8) Proceedings concerning distribution of royalty fees. — With respect to proceedings under section 801(b)(3) concerning the distribution of royalty fees in certain circumstances under section 111, 119, or 1007, the Copyright Royalty Judges shall, upon a determination that a controversy exists concerning such distribution, cause to be published in the Federal Register notice of commencement of proceedings under this chapter.

§ 805. General rule for voluntarily negotiated agreements

Any rates or terms under this title that —

(1) are agreed to by participants to a proceeding under section 803(b)(3),

(2) are adopted by the Copyright Royalty Judges as part of a determination under this chapter, and

(3) are in effect for a period shorter than would otherwise apply under a determination pursuant to this chapter,

shall remain in effect for such period of time as would otherwise apply under such determination, except that the Copyright Royalty Judges shall adjust the rates pursuant to the voluntary negotiations to reflect national monetary inflation during the additional period the rates remain in effect.

Chapter 8 Endnotes

[1]The Copyright Royalty and Distribution Reform Act of 2004 amended chapter 8 in its entirety. Pub. L. No. 108-419, 118 Stat. 2341.

In 2006, the Copyright Royalty Judges Program Technical Corrections Act amended chapter 8 throughout. Pub. L. No. 109-303, 120 Stat. 1478. Section 6 of that Act states, "Except as provided under subsection (b), this Act and the amendments made by this Act shall be effective as if included in the Copyright Royalty and Distribution Reform Act of 2004." *Id.* at 1483.

[2]In 2006, the Copyright Royalty Judges Program Technical Corrections Act amended section 801 by inserting a comma after "119" in the first sentence of subsection (b)(1) and by adding a new subsection (f) at the end. Pub. L. No. 109-303, 120 Stat. 1478. It also amended the language in 803(b)(3)(C) that preceded (i) and substituted "the" for "such" in (i). *Id.* at 1483.

[3]In 2006, the Copyright Royalty Judges Program Technical Corrections Act amended 802(f)(1)(A)(i) by substituting "subparagraph (B) and clause (ii) of this subparagraph" for "clause (ii) of this subparagraph and subparagraph (B),"; by amending (f)(1)(A)(ii) in its entirety; and by inserting a comma after "undertakes to consult with" in the seventh sentence of (f)(1)(D). Pub. L. No. 109-303, 120 Stat. 1478-79.

[4]The Satellite Home Viewer Extension and Reauthorization Act of 2004 amended section 803(b)(1)(A)(i)(V) by inserting at the end, "except that in the case of proceedings under section 111 that are scheduled to commence in 2005, such notice may not be published." Pub. L. No. 108-447, 118 Stat. 2809, 3393, 3409.

In 2006, the Copyright Royalty Judges Program Technical Corrections Act amended paragraph 803(a)(1) by inserting a new sentence at the beginning and by amending the second sentence. Pub. L. No. 109-303, 120 Stat. 1478, 1479. It amended (b)(1)(A)(i)(V) by inserting "the publication of notice requirement shall not apply" prior to "in the case of" and deleting from the end of the sentence "such notice may not be published." *Id.* It amended (b)(2)(A) by deleting from the end "together with a filing fee of $150" and by adding a new clause (D). *Id.* at 1479-80. It amended (b)(3)(A) by changing the heading and adding the text for (ii). *Id.* at 1480. It amended (b)(4)(A) by deleting the last sentence. Id. It amended the first sentence of (b)(6)(C)(i) by inserting "and written rebuttal statements" after "direct statements" and inserting "in the case of written direct statements" after "Copyright Royalty Judge." Id. It entirely amended (b)(6)(C)(ii)(I), iv, and x. *Id.* It amended (c)(2)(B) by deleting "concerning rates and terms" at the end of the sentence; (c)(4) by deleting "with the approval of the Register of Copyrights" in the first sentence after "Copyright Royalty Judges;" and (c)(7) by making a technical correction to add "the" before "Copyright Royalty Judges." Id. It amended (d)(2)C)(i)(I) by inserting "applicable" before "statements of account" and deleting "any" before "reports of use." Id. at 1481. It amended (d)(3) by inserting a new sentence at the beginning and by deleting "pursuant to section 706 of title 5" at the beginning of what was previously the first sentence, now the second sentence. *Id.*

[5]In 2006, the Copyright Royalty Judges Program Technical Corrections Act amended paragraph 804(b)(1)(B) by substituting "801(b)(2)(B) or (C)" for "801(b)(3)(B) or (C)" in the third sentence. Pub. L. No. 109-303, 120 Stat. 1478, 1481. It amended (b)(3)(A) by substituting "date of enactment" for "effective date" and (b)(3)(C)(i) and (ii) by making technical corrections to correct grammatical errors. *Id.*

CHAPTER 9[1]

PROTECTION OF SEMICONDUCTOR CHIP PRODUCTS

- 901. Definitions
- 902. Subject matter of protection
- 903. Ownership, transfer, licensing, and recordation[2]
- 904. Duration of protection
- 905. Exclusive rights in mask works
- 906. Limitation on exclusive rights: reverse engineering; first sale
- 907. Limitation on exclusive rights: innocent infringement
- 908. Registration of claims of protection
- 909. Mask work notice

§ 901. Definitions

(a) As used in this chapter —

(1) a "semiconductor chip product" is the final or intermediate form of any product —

(A) having two or more layers of metallic, insulating, or semiconductor material, deposited or otherwise placed on, or etched away or otherwise removed from, a piece of semiconductor material in accordance with a predetermined pattern; and

(B) intended to perform electronic circuitry functions;

(2) a "mask work" is a series of related images, however fixed or encoded —

(A) having or representing the predetermined, three-dimensional pattern of metallic, insulating, or semiconductor material present or removed from the layers of a semiconductor chip product; and

(B) in which series the relation of the images to one another is that each image has the pattern of the surface of one form of the semiconductor chip product;

(3) a mask work is "fixed" in a semiconductor chip product when its embodiment in the product is sufficiently permanent or stable to permit the mask work to be perceived or reproduced from the product for a period of more than transitory duration;

(4) to "distribute" means to sell, or to lease, bail, or otherwise transfer, or to offer to sell, lease, bail, or otherwise transfer;

(5) to "commercially exploit" a mask work is to distribute to the public for commercial purposes a semiconductor chip product embodying the mask work; except that such term includes an offer to sell or transfer a semiconductor chip product only when the offer is in writing and occurs after the mask work is fixed in the semiconductor chip product;

(6) the "owner" of a mask work is the person who created the mask work, the legal representative of that person if that person is deceased or under a legal incapacity, or a party to whom all the rights under this chapter of such person or representative are transferred in accordance with section 903(b); except that, in the case of a work made within the scope of a person's employment, the owner is the employer for whom the person created the mask work or a party to whom all the rights under this chapter of the employer are transferred in accordance with section 903(b);

(7) an "innocent purchaser" is a person who purchases a semiconductor chip product in good faith and without having notice of protection with respect to the semiconductor chip product;

(8) having "notice of protection" means having actual knowledge that, or reasonable grounds to believe that, a mask work is protected under this chapter; and

(9) an "infringing semiconductor chip product" is a semiconductor chip product which is made, imported, or distributed in violation of the exclusive rights of the owner of a mask work under this chapter.

(b) For purposes of this chapter, the distribution or importation of a product incorporating a semiconductor chip product as a part thereof is a distribution or importation of that semiconductor chip product.

§ 902. Subject matter of protection[3]

(a)(1) Subject to the provisions of subsection (b), a mask work fixed in a semiconductor chip product, by or under the authority of the owner of the mask work, is eligible for protection under this chapter if —

(A) on the date on which the mask work is registered under section 908, or is first commercially exploited anywhere in the world, whichever occurs first, the owner of the mask work is (i) a national or domiciliary of the United States, (ii) a national, domiciliary, or sovereign authority of a foreign nation that is a party to a treaty affording protection to mask works to which the United States is also a party, or (iii) a stateless person, wherever that person may be domiciled;

(B) the mask work is first commercially exploited in the United States; or

(C) the mask work comes within the scope of a Presidential proclamation issued under paragraph (2).

(2) Whenever the President finds that a foreign nation extends, to mask works of owners who are nationals or domiciliaries of the United States protection (A) on substantially the same basis as that on which the foreign nation extends protection to mask works of its own nationals and domiciliaries and mask works first commercially exploited in that nation, or (B) on substantially the same basis as provided in this chapter, the President may by proclamation extend protection under this chapter to mask works (i) of owners who are, on the date on which the mask works are registered under section 908, or the date on which the mask works are first commercially exploited anywhere in the world, whichever occurs first, nationals, domiciliaries, or sovereign authorities of that nation, or (ii) which are first commercially exploited in that nation. The President may revise, suspend, or revoke any such proclamation or impose any conditions or limitations on protection extended under any such proclamation.

(b) Protection under this chapter shall not be available for a mask work that —

(1) is not original; or

(2) consists of designs that are staple, commonplace, or familiar in the semiconductor industry, or variations of such designs, combined in a way that, considered as a whole, is not original.

(c) In no case does protection under this chapter for a mask work extend to any idea, procedure, process, system, method of operation, concept, principle, or discovery, regardless of the form in which it is described, explained, illustrated, or embodied in such work.

§ 903. Ownership, transfer, licensing, and recordation

(a) The exclusive rights in a mask work subject to protection under this chapter belong to the owner of the mask work.

(b) The owner of the exclusive rights in a mask work may transfer all of those rights, or license all or less than all of those rights, by any written instrument signed by such owner or a duly authorized agent of the owner. Such rights may be transferred or licensed by operation of law, may be bequeathed by will, and may pass as personal property by the applicable laws of intestate succession.

(c)(1) Any document pertaining to a mask work may be recorded in the Copyright Office if the document filed for recordation bears the actual signature of the person who executed it, or if it is accompanied by a sworn or official certification that it is a true copy of the original, signed document. The Register of Copyrights shall, upon receipt of the document and the fee specified pursuant to section 908(d), record the document and return it with a certificate of recordation. The recordation of any transfer or license under this paragraph gives all persons constructive notice of the facts stated in the recorded document concerning the transfer or license.

(2) In any case in which conflicting transfers of the exclusive rights in a mask work are made, the transfer first executed shall be void as against a subsequent transfer which is made for a valuable consideration and without notice of the first transfer, unless the first transfer is recorded in accordance with paragraph (1) within three months after the date on which it is executed, but in no case later than the day before the date of such subsequent transfer.

(d) Mask works prepared by an officer or employee of the United States Government as part of that person's official duties are not protected under this chapter, but the United States Government is not precluded from receiving and holding exclusive rights in mask works transferred to the Government under subsection (b).

§ 904. Duration of protection

(a) The protection provided for a mask work under this chapter shall commence on the date on which the mask work is registered under section 908, or the date on which the mask work is first commercially exploited anywhere in the world, whichever occurs first.

(b) Subject to subsection (c) and the provisions of this chapter, the protection provided under this chapter to a mask work shall end ten years after the date on which such protection commences under subsection (a).

(c) All terms of protection provided in this section shall run to the end of the calendar year in which they would otherwise expire.

§ 905. Exclusive rights in mask works

The owner of a mask work provided protection under this chapter has the exclusive rights to do and to authorize any of the following:

(1) to reproduce the mask work by optical, electronic, or any other means;

(2) to import or distribute a semiconductor chip product in which the mask work is embodied; and

(3) to induce or knowingly to cause another person to do any of the acts described in paragraphs (1) and (2).

§ 906. Limitation on exclusive rights: reverse engineering; first sale

(a) Notwithstanding the provisions of section 905, it is not an infringement of the exclusive rights of the owner of a mask work for —

(1) a person to reproduce the mask work solely for the purpose of teaching, analyzing, or evaluating the concepts or techniques embodied in the mask work or the circuitry, logic flow, or organization of components used in the mask work; or

(2) a person who performs the analysis or evaluation described in paragraph (1) to incorporate the results of such conduct in an original mask work which is made to be distributed.

(b) Notwithstanding the provisions of section 905(2), the owner of a particular semiconductor chip product made by the owner of the mask work, or by any person authorized by the owner of the mask work, may import, distribute, or otherwise dispose of or use, but not reproduce, that particular semiconductor chip product without the authority of the owner of the mask work.

§ 907. Limitation on exclusive rights: innocent infringement

(a) Notwithstanding any other provision of this chapter, an innocent purchaser of an infringing semiconductor chip product —

(1) shall incur no liability under this chapter with respect to the importation or distribution of units of the infringing semiconductor chip product that occurs before the innocent purchaser has notice of protection with respect to the mask work embodied in the semiconductor chip product; and

(2) shall be liable only for a reasonable royalty on each unit of the infringing semiconductor chip product that the innocent purchaser imports or distributes after having notice of protection with respect to the mask work embodied in the semiconductor chip product.

(b) The amount of the royalty referred to in subsection (a)(2) shall be determined by the court in a civil action for infringement unless the parties resolve the issue by voluntary negotiation, mediation, or binding arbitration.

(c) The immunity of an innocent purchaser from liability referred to in subsection (a)(1) and the limitation of remedies with respect to an innocent purchaser referred to in subsection (a)(2) shall extend to any person who directly or indirectly purchases an infringing semiconductor chip product from an innocent purchaser.

(d) The provisions of subsections (a), (b), and (c) apply only with respect to those units of an infringing semiconductor chip product that an innocent purchaser purchased before having notice of protection with respect to the mask work embodied in the semiconductor chip product.

§ 908. Registration of claims of protection

(a) The owner of a mask work may apply to the Register of Copyrights for registration of a claim of protection in a mask work. Protection of a mask work under this chapter shall terminate if application for registration of a claim of protection in the mask work is not made as provided in this chapter within two years after the date on which the mask work is first commercially exploited anywhere in the world.

(b) The Register of Copyrights shall be responsible for all administrative functions and duties under this chapter. Except for section 708, the provisions of chapter 7 of this title relating to the general responsibilities, organization, regulatory authority, actions, records, and publications of the Copyright Office shall apply to this chapter, except that the Register of Copyrights may make such changes as may be necessary in applying those provisions to this chapter.

(c) The application for registration of a mask work shall be made on a form prescribed by the Register of Copyrights. Such form may require any information regarded by the Register as bearing upon the preparation or identification of the mask work, the existence or duration of protection of the mask work under this chapter, or ownership of the mask work. The application shall be accompanied by the fee set pursuant to subsection (d) and the identifying material specified pursuant to such subsection.

(d) The Register of Copyrights shall by regulation set reasonable fees for the filing of applications to register claims of protection in mask works under this chapter, and for other services relating to the administration of this chapter or the rights under this chapter, taking into consideration the cost of providing those services, the benefits of a public record, and statutory fee schedules under this title. The Register shall also specify the identifying material to be deposited in connection with the claim for registration.

(e) If the Register of Copyrights, after examining an application for registration, determines, in accordance with the provisions of this chapter, that the application relates to a mask work which is entitled to protection under this chapter, then the Register shall register the claim of protection and issue to the applicant a certificate of registration of the claim of protection under the seal of the Copyright Office. The effective date of registration of a claim of protection shall be the date on which an application, deposit of identifying material, and fee, which are determined by the Register of Copyrights or by a court of competent jurisdiction to be acceptable for registration of the claim, have all been received in the Copyright Office.

(f) In any action for infringement under this chapter, the certificate of registration of a mask work shall constitute prima facie evidence (1) of the facts stated in the certificate, and (2) that the applicant issued the certificate has met the requirements of this chapter, and the regulations issued under this chapter, with respect to the registration of claims.

(g) Any applicant for registration under this section who is dissatisfied with the refusal of the Register of Copyrights to issue a certificate of registration under this section may seek judicial review of that refusal by bringing an action for such review in an appropriate United States district court not later than sixty days after the refusal. The provisions of chapter 7 of title 5 shall apply to such judicial review. The failure of the Register of Copyrights to issue a certificate of registration within four months after an application for registration is filed shall be deemed to be a refusal to issue a certificate of registration for purposes of this subsection and section 910(b)(2), except that, upon a showing of good cause, the district court may shorten such four-month period.

§ 909. Mask work notice[4]

(a) The owner of a mask work provided protection under this chapter may affix notice to the mask work, and to masks and semiconductor chip products embodying the mask work, in such manner and location as to give reasonable notice of such protection. The Register of Copyrights shall prescribe by regulation, as examples, specific methods of affixation and positions of notice for purposes of this section, but these specifications shall not be considered exhaustive. The affixation of such notice is not a condition of protection under this chapter, but shall constitute prima facie evidence of notice of protection.

(b) The notice referred to in subsection (a) shall consist of —

(1) the words "mask work", the symbol *M*, or the symbol Ⓜ (the letter M in a circle); and

(2) the name of the owner or owners of the mask work or an abbreviation by which the name is recognized or is generally known.

§ 910. *Enforcement of exclusive rights*[5]

(a) Except as otherwise provided in this chapter, any person who violates any of the exclusive rights of the owner of a mask work under this chapter, by conduct in or affecting commerce, shall be liable as an infringer of such rights. As used in this subsection, the term "any person" includes any State, any instrumentality of a State, and any officer or employee of a State or instrumentality of a State acting in his or her official capacity. Any State, and any such instrumentality, officer, or employee, shall be subject to the provisions of this chapter in the same manner and to the same extent as any nongovernmental entity.

(b)(1) The owner of a mask work protected under this chapter, or the exclusive licensee of all rights under this chapter with respect to the mask work, shall, after a certificate of registration of a claim of protection in that mask work has been issued under section 908, be entitled to institute a civil action for any infringement with respect to the mask work which is committed after the commencement of protection of the mask work under section 904(a).

(2) In any case in which an application for registration of a claim of protection in a mask work and the required deposit of identifying material and fee have been received in the Copyright Office in proper form and registration of the mask work has been refused, the applicant is entitled to institute a civil action for infringement under this chapter with respect to the mask work if notice of the action, together with a copy of the complaint, is served on the Register of Copyrights, in accordance with the Federal Rules of Civil Procedure. The Register may, at his or her option, become a party to the action with respect to the issue of whether the claim of protection is eligible for registration by entering an appearance within sixty days after such service, but the failure of the Register to become a party to the action shall not deprive the court of jurisdiction to determine that issue.

(c)(1) The Secretary of the Treasury and the United States Postal Service shall separately or jointly issue regulations for the enforcement of the rights set forth in section 905 with respect to importation. These regulations may require, as a condition for the exclusion of articles from the United States, that the person seeking exclusion take any one or more of the following actions:

(A) Obtain a court order enjoining, or an order of the International Trade Commission under section 337 of the Tariff Act of 1930 excluding, importation of the articles.

(B) Furnish proof that the mask work involved is protected under this chapter and that the importation of the articles would infringe the rights in the mask work under this chapter.

(C) Post a surety bond for any injury that may result if the detention or exclusion of the articles proves to be unjustified.

(2) Articles imported in violation of the rights set forth in section 905 are subject to seizure and forfeiture in the same manner as property imported in violation of the customs laws. Any such forfeited articles shall be destroyed as directed by the Secretary of the Treasury or the court, as the case may be, except that the articles may be returned to the country of export whenever it is

shown to the satisfaction of the Secretary of the Treasury that the importer had no reasonable grounds for believing that his or her acts constituted a violation of the law.

§ 911. Civil actions[6]

(a) Any court having jurisdiction of a civil action arising under this chapter may grant temporary restraining orders, preliminary injunctions, and permanent injunctions on such terms as the court may deem reasonable to prevent or restrain infringement of the exclusive rights in a mask work under this chapter.

(b) Upon finding an infringer liable, to a person entitled under section 910(b)(1) to institute a civil action, for an infringement of any exclusive right under this chapter, the court shall award such person actual damages suffered by the person as a result of the infringement. The court shall also award such person the infringer's profits that are attributable to the infringement and are not taken into account in computing the award of actual damages. In establishing the infringer's profits, such person is required to present proof only of the infringer's gross revenue, and the infringer is required to prove his or her deductible expenses and the elements of profit attributable to factors other than the mask work.

(c) At any time before final judgment is rendered, a person entitled to institute a civil action for infringement may elect, instead of actual damages and profits as provided by subsection (b), an award of statutory damages for all infringements involved in the action, with respect to any one mask work for which any one infringer is liable individually, or for which any two or more infringers are liable jointly and severally, in an amount not more than $250,000 as the court considers just.

(d) An action for infringement under this chapter shall be barred unless the action is commenced within three years after the claim accrues.

(e)(1) At any time while an action for infringement of the exclusive rights in a mask work under this chapter is pending, the court may order the impounding, on such terms as it may deem reasonable, of all semiconductor chip products, and any drawings, tapes, masks, or other products by means of which such products may be reproduced, that are claimed to have been made, imported, or used in violation of those exclusive rights. Insofar as practicable, applications for orders under this paragraph shall be heard and determined in the same manner as an application for a temporary restraining order or preliminary injunction.

(2) As part of a final judgment or decree, the court may order the destruction or other disposition of any infringing semiconductor chip products, and any masks, tapes, or other articles by means of which such products may be reproduced.

(f) In any civil action arising under this chapter, the court in its discretion may allow the recovery of full costs, including reasonable attorneys' fees, to the prevailing party.

(g)(1) Any State, any instrumentality of a State, and any officer or employee of a State or instrumentality of a State acting in his or her official capacity, shall not be immune, under the Eleventh

Amendment of the Constitution of the United States or under any other doctrine of sovereign immunity, from suit in Federal court by any person, including any governmental or nongovernmental entity, for a violation of any of the exclusive rights of the owner of a mask work under this chapter, or for any other violation under this chapter.

(2) In a suit described in paragraph (1) for a violation described in that paragraph, remedies (including remedies both at law and in equity) are available for the violation to the same extent as such remedies are available for such a violation in a suit against any public or private entity other than a State, instrumentality of a State, or officer or employee of a State acting in his or her official capacity. Such remedies include actual damages and profits under subsection (b), statutory damages under subsection (c), impounding and disposition of infringing articles under subsection (e), and costs and attorney's fees under subsection (f).

§ 912. Relation to other laws[7]

(a) Nothing in this chapter shall affect any right or remedy held by any person under chapters 1 through 8 or 10 of this title, or under title 35.

(b) Except as provided in section 908(b) of this title, references to "this title" or "title 17" in chapters 1 through 8 or 10 of this title shall be deemed not to apply to this chapter.

(c) The provisions of this chapter shall preempt the laws of any State to the extent those laws provide any rights or remedies with respect to a mask work which are equivalent to those rights or remedies provided by this chapter, except that such preemption shall be effective only with respect to actions filed on or after January 1, 1986.

(d) Notwithstanding subsection (c), nothing in this chapter shall detract from any rights of a mask work owner, whether under Federal law (exclusive of this chapter) or under the common law or the statutes of a State, heretofore or hereafter declared or enacted, with respect to any mask work first commercially exploited before July 1, 1983.

§ 913. Transitional provisions

(a) No application for registration under section 908 may be filed, and no civil action under section 910 or other enforcement proceeding under this chapter may be instituted, until sixty days after the date of the enactment of this chapter.

(b) No monetary relief under section 911 may be granted with respect to any conduct that occurred before the date of the enactment of this chapter, except as provided in subsection (d).

(c) Subject to subsection (a), the provisions of this chapter apply to all mask works that are first commercially exploited or are registered under this chapter, or both, on or after the date of the enactment of this chapter.

(d)(1) Subject to subsection (a), protection is available under this chapter to any mask work that was first commercially exploited on or after July 1, 1983, and before the date of the enactment of this chapter, if a claim of protection in the mask work is registered in the Copyright Office before July 1, 1985, under section 908.

(2) In the case of any mask work described in paragraph (1) that is provided protection under this chapter, infringing semiconductor chip product units manufactured before the date of the enactment of this chapter may, without liability under sections 910 and 911, be imported into or distributed in the United States, or both, until two years after the date of registration of the mask work under section 908, but only if the importer or distributor, as the case may be, first pays or offers to pay the reasonable royalty referred to in section 907(a)(2) to the mask work owner, on all such units imported or distributed, or both, after the date of the enactment of this chapter.

(3) In the event that a person imports or distributes infringing semiconductor chip product units described in paragraph (2) of this subsection without first paying or offering to pay the reasonable royalty specified in such paragraph, or if the person refuses or fails to make such payment, the mask work owner shall be entitled to the relief provided in sections 910 and 911.

§ 914. International transitional provisions[8]

(a) Notwithstanding the conditions set forth in subparagraphs (A) and (C) of section 902(a)(1) with respect to the availability of protection under this chapter to nationals, domiciliaries, and sovereign authorities of a foreign nation, the Secretary of Commerce may, upon the petition of any person, or upon the Secretary's own motion, issue an order extending protection under this chapter to such foreign nationals, domiciliaries, and sovereign authorities if the Secretary finds —

(1) that the foreign nation is making good faith efforts and reasonable progress toward —

(A) entering into a treaty described in section 902(a)(1)(A); or

(B) enacting or implementing legislation that would be in compliance with subparagraph (A) or (B) of section 902(a)(2); and

(2) that the nationals, domiciliaries, and sovereign authorities of the foreign nation, and persons controlled by them, are not engaged in the misappropriation, or unauthorized distribution or commercial exploitation, of mask works; and

(3) that issuing the order would promote the purposes of this chapter and international comity with respect to the protection of mask works.

(b) While an order under subsection (a) is in effect with respect to a foreign nation, no application for registration of a claim for protection in a mask work under this chapter may be denied solely because the owner of the mask work is a national, domiciliary, or sovereign authority of that foreign nation, or solely because the mask work was first commercially exploited in that foreign nation.

(c) Any order issued by the Secretary of Commerce under subsection (a) shall be effective for such a period as the Secretary designates in the order, except that no such order may be effective after that date on which the authority of the Secretary of Commerce terminates under subsection (e). The effective date of any such order shall also be designated in the order. In the case of an order issued upon the petition of a person, such effective date may be no earlier than the date on which the Secretary receives such petition.

(d)(1) Any order issued under this section shall terminate if —

(A) the Secretary of Commerce finds that any of the conditions set forth in paragraphs (1), (2), and (3) of subsection (a) no longer exist; or

(B) mask works of nationals, domiciliaries, and sovereign authorities of that foreign nation or mask works first commercially exploited in that foreign nation become eligible for protection under subparagraph (A) or (C) of section 902(a)(1).

(2) Upon the termination or expiration of an order issued under this section, registrations of claims of protection in mask works made pursuant to that order shall remain valid for the period specified in section 904.

(e) The authority of the Secretary of Commerce under this section shall commence on the date of the enactment of this chapter, and shall terminate on July 1, 1995.

(f) (1) The Secretary of Commerce shall promptly notify the Register of Copyrights and the Committees on the Judiciary of the Senate and the House of Representatives of the issuance or termination of any order under this section, together with a statement of the reasons for such action. The Secretary shall also publish such notification and statement of reasons in the Federal Register.

(2) Two years after the date of the enactment of this chapter, the Secretary of Commerce, in consultation with the Register of Copyrights, shall transmit to the Committees on the Judiciary of the Senate and the House of Representatives a report on the actions taken under this section and on the current status of international recognition of mask work protection. The report shall include such recommendation for modifications of the protection accorded under this chapter to mask works owned by nationals, domiciliaries, or sovereign authorities of foreign nations as the Secretary, in consultation with the Register of Copyrights, considers would promote the purposes of this chapter and international comity with respect to mask work protection. Not later than July 1, 1994, the Secretary of Commerce, in consultation with the Register of Copyrights, shall transmit to the Committees on the Judiciary of the Senate and the House of Representatives a report updating the matters contained in the report transmitted under the preceding sentence.

Chapter 9 Endnotes

[1] In 1984, the Semiconductor Chip Protection Act amended title 17 of the *United States Code* to add a new chapter 9 entitled "Protection of Semiconductor Chip Products." Pub. L. No. 98-620, 98 Stat. 3347.

[2] In 1997, the heading for section 903 in the table of sections was amended by adding ", transfer, licensure, and recordation" at the end thereof, in lieu of "and transfer." Pub. L. No. 105-80, 111 Stat. 1529, 1535. The Intellectual Property and High

Technology Technical Amendments Act of 2002 amended the heading for section 903 in the table of sections for chapter 9 by substituting "licensing" for "licensure." Pub. L. No. 107-273, 116 Stat. 1758, 1910.

[3]In 1987, section 902 was amended by adding the last sentence in subsection (a)(2). Pub. L. No. 100-159, 101 Stat. 899, 900.

[4]In 1997, section 909 was amended by correcting misspellings in subsection (b)(1). Pub. L. No. 105-80, 111 Stat. 1529, 1535.

[5]In 1990, the Copyright Remedy Clarification Act amended section 910 by adding the last two sentences to subsection (a). Pub. L. No. 101-553, 104 Stat. 2749, 2750. In 1997, a technical correction amended section 910(a) by capitalizing the first word of the second sentence. Pub. L. No. 105-80, 111 Stat. 1529 1535.

[6]In 1990, the Copyright Remedy Clarification Act amended section 911 by adding subsection (g). Pub. L. No. 101-553, 104 Stat. 2749, 2750.

[7]In 1988, the Judicial Improvements and Access to Justice Act amended section 912 by deleting subsection (d) and redesignating subsection (e) as subsection (d). Pub. L. No. 100-702, 102 Stat. 4642, 4672. The Audio Home Recording Act of 1992 amended section 912 by inserting "or 10" after "8" in subsections (a) and (b). Pub. L. No. 102-563, 106 Stat. 4237, 4248.

[8]In 1987, section 914 was amended in subsection (e) by inserting "on July 1, 1991" in lieu of "three years after such date of enactment" and by adding the last sentence to subsection (f)(2). Pub. L. No. 100-159, 101 Stat. 899. The Semiconductor International Protection Extension Act of 1991 amended section 914 by inserting "or implementing" after "enacting" in the first sentence of subsection (a)(1)(B), by changing the date in subsection (e) to "July 1, 1995" and by changing the date in the last sentence of subsection (f)(2) to "July 1, 1994." Pub. L. No. 102-64, 105 Stat. 320.

On July 1, 1995, section 914 expired as required by subsection (e). It was rendered largely unnecessary upon the entry into force on January 1, 1995, of the Agreement on Trade-Related Aspects of Intellectual Property Rights (TRIPs)(Annex 1C to the World Trade Organization (WTO) Agreement). Part II, section 6 of TRIPs protects semiconductor chip products and was the basis for Presidential Proclamation No. 6780, March 23, 1995, under section 902(a)(2) extending protection to all present and future WTO members (146 countries as of April 4, 2003), as of January 1, 1996. See Appendix K.

For a discussion of Congressional findings regarding extending protection to semiconductor chip products of foreign entities, see Pub. L. No. 100-159, 101 Stat. 899, and the Semiconductor International Protection Extension Act of 1991, Pub. L. No. 102-64, 105 Stat. 320.5

CHAPTER 10[1]
DIGITAL AUDIO RECORDING DEVICES AND MEDIA

- Subchapter A — Definitions
  - 1001. Definitions
- Subchapter B — Copying Controls
  - 1002. Incorporation of copying controls
- Subchapter C — Royalty Payments
  - 1003. Obligation to make royalty payments
  - 1004. Royalty payments
  - 1005. Deposit of royalty payments and deduction of expenses
  - 1006. Entitlement to royalty payments
  - 1007. Procedures for distributing royalty payments

Subchapter A — Definitions

§ 1001. Definitions

As used in this chapter, the following terms have the following meanings:

(1) A "digital audio copied recording" is a reproduction in a digital recording format of a digital musical recording, whether that reproduction is made directly from another digital musical recording or indirectly from a transmission.

(2) A "digital audio interface device" is any machine or device that is designed specifically to communicate digital audio information and related interface data to a digital audio recording device through a nonprofessional interface.

(3) A "digital audio recording device" is any machine or device of a type commonly distributed to individuals for use by individuals, whether or not included with or as part of some other machine or device, the digital recording function of which is designed or marketed for the primary purpose of, and that is capable of, making a digital audio copied recording for private use, except for —

(A) professional model products, and

(B) dictation machines, answering machines, and other audio recording equipment that is designed and marketed primarily for the creation of sound recordings resulting from the fixation of nonmusical sounds.

(4)(A) A "digital audio recording medium" is any material object in a form commonly distributed for use by individuals, that is primarily marketed or most commonly used by consumers for the purpose of making digital audio copied recordings by use of a digital audio recording device.

(B) Such term does not include any material object —

(i) that embodies a sound recording at the time it is first distributed by the importer or manufacturer; or

(ii) that is primarily marketed and most commonly used by consumers either for the purpose of making copies of motion pictures or other audiovisual works or for the purpose of making copies of nonmusical literary works, including computer programs or data bases.

(5)(A) A "digital musical recording" is a material object —

(i) in which are fixed, in a digital recording format, only sounds, and material, statements, or instructions incidental to those fixed sounds, if any, and

(ii) from which the sounds and material can be perceived, reproduced, or otherwise communicated, either directly or with the aid of a machine or device.

(B) A "digital musical recording" does not include a material object —

(i) in which the fixed sounds consist entirely of spoken word recordings, or

(ii) in which one or more computer programs are fixed, except that a digital musical recording may contain statements or instructions constituting the fixed sounds and incidental material, and statements or instructions to be used directly or indirectly in order to bring about the perception, reproduction, or communication of the fixed sounds and incidental material.

(C) For purposes of this paragraph —

(i) a "spoken word recording" is a sound recording in which are fixed only a series of spoken words, except that the spoken words may be accompanied by incidental musical or other sounds, and

(ii) the term "incidental" means related to and relatively minor by comparison.

(6) "Distribute" means to sell, lease, or assign a product to consumers in the United States, or to sell, lease, or assign a product in the United States for ultimate transfer to consumers in the United States.

(7) An "interested copyright party" is —

(A) the owner of the exclusive right under section 106(1) of this title to reproduce a sound recording of a musical work that has been embodied in a digital musical recording or analog musical recording lawfully made under this title that has been distributed;

(B) the legal or beneficial owner of, or the person that controls, the right to reproduce in a digital musical recording or analog musical recording a musical work that has been embodied in a digital musical recording or analog musical recording lawfully made under this title that has been distributed;

(C) a featured recording artist who performs on a sound recording that has been distributed; or

(D) any association or other organization —

(i) representing persons specified in subparagraph (A), (B), or (C), or

(ii) engaged in licensing rights in musical works to music users on behalf of writers and publishers.

(8) To "manufacture" means to produce or assemble a product in the United States. A "manufacturer" is a person who manufactures.

(9) A "music publisher" is a person that is authorized to license the reproduction of a particular musical work in a sound recording.

(10) A "professional model product" is an audio recording device that is designed, manufactured, marketed, and intended for use by recording professionals in the ordinary course of a lawful business, in accordance with such requirements as the Secretary of Commerce shall establish by regulation.

(11) The term "serial copying" means the duplication in a digital format of a copyrighted musical work or sound recording from a digital reproduction of a digital musical recording. The term "digital reproduction of a digital musical recording" does not include a digital musical recording as distributed, by authority of the copyright owner, for ultimate sale to consumers.

(12) The "transfer price" of a digital audio recording device or a digital audio recording medium —

(A) is, subject to subparagraph (B) —

(i) in the case of an imported product, the actual entered value at United States Customs (exclusive of any freight, insurance, and applicable duty), and

(ii) in the case of a domestic product, the manufacturer's transfer price (FOB the manufacturer, and exclusive of any direct sales taxes or excise taxes incurred in connection with the sale); and

(B) shall, in a case in which the transferor and transferee are related entities or within a single entity, not be less than a reasonable arms-length price under the principles of the regulations adopted pursuant to section 482 of the Internal Revenue Code of 1986, or any successor provision to such section.

(13) A "writer" is the composer or lyricist of a particular musical work.

Subchapter B — Copying Controls

§ 1002. Incorporation of copying controls

(a) Prohibition on Importation, Manufacture, and Distribution. — No person shall import, manufacture, or distribute any digital audio recording device or digital audio interface device that does not conform to —

(1) the Serial Copy Management System;

(2) a system that has the same functional characteristics as the Serial Copy Management System and requires that copyright and generation status information be accurately sent, received, and acted upon between devices using the system's method of serial copying regulation and devices using the Serial Copy Management System; or

(3) any other system certified by the Secretary of Commerce as prohibiting unauthorized serial copying.

(b) Development of Verification Procedure. — The Secretary of Commerce shall establish a procedure to verify, upon the petition of an interested party, that a system meets the standards set forth in subsection (a)(2).

(c) Prohibition on Circumvention of the System. — No person shall import, manufacture, or distribute any device, or offer or perform any service, the primary purpose or effect of which is to avoid, bypass, remove, deactivate, or otherwise circumvent any program or circuit which implements, in whole or in part, a system described in subsection (a).

(d) Encoding of Information on Digital Musical Recordings.—

(1) Prohibition on encoding inaccurate information. — No person shall encode a digital musical recording of a sound recording with inaccurate information relating to the category code, copyright status, or generation status of the source material for the recording.

(2) Encoding of copyright status not required. — Nothing in this chapter requires any person engaged in the importation or manufacture of digital musical recordings to encode any such digital musical recording with respect to its copyright status.

(e) Information Accompanying Transmission in Digital Format. — Any person who transmits or otherwise communicates to the public any sound recording in digital format is not required under this chapter to transmit or otherwise communicate the information relating to the copyright status of the sound recording. Any such person who does transmit or otherwise communicate such copyright status information shall transmit or communicate such information accurately.

Subchapter C — Royalty Payments

§ 1003. Obligation to make royalty payments

(a) Prohibition on Importation and Manufacture. — No person shall import into and distribute, or manufacture and distribute, any digital audio recording device or digital audio recording medium unless such person records the notice specified by this section and subsequently deposits the statements of account and applicable royalty payments for such device or medium specified in section 1004.

(b) Filing of Notice. — The importer or manufacturer of any digital audio recording device or digital audio recording medium, within a product category or utilizing a technology with respect to which such manufacturer or importer has not previously filed a notice under this subsection, shall file with the Register of Copyrights a notice with respect to such device or medium, in such form and content as the Register shall prescribe by regulation.

(c) Filing of Quarterly and Annual Statements of Account.—

(1) Generally. — Any importer or manufacturer that distributes any digital audio recording device or digital audio recording medium that it manufactured or imported shall file with the Register of Copyrights, in such form and content as the Register shall prescribe by regulation, such quarterly and annual statements of account with respect to such distribution as the Register shall prescribe by regulation.

(2) Certification, verification, and confidentiality. — Each such statement shall be certified as accurate by an authorized officer or principal of the importer or manufacturer. The Register shall issue regulations to provide for the verification and audit of such statements and to protect the confidentiality of the information contained in such statements. Such regulations shall provide for the disclosure, in confidence, of such statements to interested copyright parties.

(3) Royalty payments. — Each such statement shall be accompanied by the royalty payments specified in section 1004.

§ 1004. Royalty payments[2]

(a) Digital Audio Recording Devices. —

(1) Amount of payment. — The royalty payment due under section 1003 for each digital audio recording device imported into and distributed in the United States, or manufactured and distributed in the United States, shall be 2 percent of the transfer price. Only the first person to manufacture and distribute or import and distribute such device shall be required to pay the royalty with respect to such device.

(2) Calculation for devices distributed with other devices. — With respect to a digital audio recording device first distributed in combination with one or more devices, either as a physically integrated unit or as separate components, the royalty payment shall be calculated as follows:

(A) If the digital audio recording device and such other devices are part of a physically integrated unit, the royalty payment shall be based on the transfer price of the unit, but shall be reduced by any royalty payment made on any digital audio recording device included within the unit that was not first distributed in combination with the unit.

(B) If the digital audio recording device is not part of a physically integrated unit and substantially similar devices have been distributed separately at any time during the preceding 4 calendar quarters, the royalty payment shall be based on the average transfer price of such devices during those 4 quarters.

(C) If the digital audio recording device is not part of a physically integrated unit and substantially similar devices have not been distributed separately at any time during the preceding 4 calendar quarters, the royalty payment shall be based on a constructed price reflecting the proportional value of such device to the combination as a whole.

(3) Limits on royalties. —Notwithstanding paragraph (1) or (2), the amount of the royalty payment for each digital audio recording device shall not be less than $1 nor more than the royalty maximum. The royalty maximum shall be $8 per device, except that in the case of a physically integrated unit containing more than 1 digital audio recording device, the royalty maximum for such unit shall be $12. During the 6th year after the effective date of this chapter, and not more than once each year thereafter, any interested copyright party may petition the Copyright Royalty Judges to increase the royalty maximum and, if more than 20 percent of the royalty payments are at the relevant royalty maximum, the Copyright Royalty Judges shall prospectively increase such royalty maximum with the goal of having no more than 10 percent of such payments at the new royalty maximum; however the amount of any such increase as a percentage of the royalty maximum shall in no event exceed the percentage increase in the Consumer Price Index during the period under review.

(b) Digital Audio Recording Media. — The royalty payment due under section 1003 for each digital audio recording medium imported into and distributed in the United States, or manufactured and distributed in the United States, shall be 3 percent of the transfer price. Only the first person to manufacture and distribute or import and distribute such medium shall be required to pay the royalty with respect to such medium.

§ 1005. Deposit of royalty payments and deduction of expenses[3]

The Register of Copyrights shall receive all royalty payments deposited under this chapter and, after deducting the reasonable costs incurred by the Copyright Office under this chapter, shall deposit the balance in the Treasury of the United States as offsetting receipts, in such manner as the Secretary of the Treasury directs. All funds held by the Secretary of the Treasury shall be invested in interest-bearing United States securities for later distribution with interest under section 1007. The Register may, in the Register's discretion, 4 years after the close of any calendar year, close out the royalty payments account for that calendar year, and may treat any funds remaining in such account and any subsequent deposits that would otherwise be attributable to that calendar year as attributable to the succeeding calendar year.

§ 1006. Entitlement to royalty payments[4]

(a) Interested Copyright Parties. — The royalty payments deposited pursuant to section 1005 shall, in accordance with the procedures specified in section 1007, be distributed to any interested copyright party —

(1) whose musical work or sound recording has been —

(A) embodied in a digital musical recording or an analog musical recording lawfully made under this title that has been distributed, and

(B) distributed in the form of digital musical recordings or analog musical recordings or disseminated to the public in transmissions, during the period to which such payments pertain; and

(2) who has filed a claim under section 1007.

(b) Allocation of Royalty Payments to Groups. — The royalty payments shall be divided into 2 funds as follows:

(1) The sound recordings fund. — 66⅔ percent of the royalty payments shall be allocated to the Sound Recordings Fund. 2⅝ percent of the royalty payments allocated to the Sound Recordings Fund shall be placed in an escrow account managed by an independent administrator jointly appointed by the interested copyright parties described in section 1001(7)(A) and the American Federation of Musicians (or any successor entity) to be distributed to nonfeatured musicians (whether or not members of the American Federation of Musicians or any successor entity) who have performed on sound recordings distributed in the United States. 1⅜ percent of the royalty

payments allocated to the Sound Recordings Fund shall be placed in an escrow account managed by an independent administrator jointly appointed by the interested copyright parties described in section 1001(7)(A) and the American Federation of Television and Radio Artists (or any successor entity) to be distributed to nonfeatured vocalists (whether or not members of the American Federation of Television and Radio Artists or any successor entity) who have performed on sound recordings distributed in the United States. 40 percent of the remaining royalty payments in the Sound Recordings Fund shall be distributed to the interested copyright parties described in section 1001(7)(C), and 60 percent of such remaining royalty payments shall be distributed to the interested copyright parties described in section 1001(7)(A).

(2) The Musical Works Fund. —

(A) 33⅓ percent of the royalty payments shall be allocated to the Musical Works Fund for distribution to interested copyright parties described in section 1001(7)(B).

(B)(i) Music publishers shall be entitled to 50 percent of the royalty payments allocated to the Musical Works Fund.

(ii) Writers shall be entitled to the other 50 percent of the royalty payments allocated to the Musical Works Fund.

(c) Allocation of Royalty Payments Within Groups. — If all interested copyright parties within a group specified in subsection (b) do not agree on a voluntary proposal for the distribution of the royalty payments within each group, the Copyright Royalty Judges shall, pursuant to the procedures specified under section 1007(c), allocate royalty payments under this section based on the extent to which, during the relevant period —

(1) for the Sound Recordings Fund, each sound recording was distributed in the form of digital musical recordings or analog musical recordings; and

(2) for the Musical Works Fund, each musical work was distributed in the form of digital musical recordings or analog musical recordings or disseminated to the public in transmissions.

§ 1007. Procedures for distributing royalty payments[5]

(a) Filing of Claims and Negotiations. —

(1) Filing of claims. — During the first 2 months of each calendar year, every interested copyright party seeking to receive royalty payments to which such party is entitled under section 1006 shall file with the Copyright Royalty Judges a claim for payments collected during the preceding year in such form and manner as the Copyright Royalty Judges shall prescribe by regulation.

(2) Negotiations. — Notwithstanding any provision of the antitrust laws, for purposes of this section interested copyright parties within each group specified in section 1006(b) may agree among themselves to the proportionate division of royalty payments, may lump their claims together and file them jointly or as a single claim, or may designate a common agent, including any organization

described in section 1001(7)(D), to negotiate or receive payment on their behalf; except that no agreement under this subsection may modify the allocation of royalties specified in section 1006(b).

(b) Distribution of Payments in the Absence of a Dispute. — After the period established for the filing of claims under subsection (a), in each year, the Copyright Royalty Judges shall determine whether there exists a controversy concerning the distribution of royalty payments under section 1006(c). If the Copyright Royalty Judges determine that no such controversy exists, the Copyright Royalty Judges shall, within 30 days after such determination, authorize the distribution of the royalty payments as set forth in the agreements regarding the distribution of royalty payments entered into pursuant to subsection (a). The Librarian of Congress shall, before such royalty payments are distributed, deduct the reasonable administrative costs incurred under this section.

(c) Resolution of Disputes. — If the Copyright Royalty Judges find the existence of a controversy, the Copyright Royalty Judges shall, pursuant to chapter 8 of this title, conduct a proceeding to determine the distribution of royalty payments. During the pendency of such a proceeding, the Copyright Royalty Judges shall withhold from distribution an amount sufficient to satisfy all claims with respect to which a controversy exists, but shall, to the extent feasible, authorize the distribution of any amounts that are not in controversy. The Librarian of Congress shall, before such royalty payments are distributed, deduct the reasonable administrative costs incurred under this section.

Subchapter D —Prohibition on Certain Infringement Actions, Remedies, and Arbitration

§ 1008. Prohibition on certain infringement actions

No action may be brought under this title alleging infringement of copyright based on the manufacture, importation, or distribution of a digital audio recording device, a digital audio recording medium, an analog recording device, or an analog recording medium, or based on the noncommercial use by a consumer of such a device or medium for making digital musical recordings or analog musical recordings.

§ 1009. Civil remedies

(a) Civil Actions. — Any interested copyright party injured by a violation of section 1002 or 1003 may bring a civil action in an appropriate United States district court against any person for such violation.

(b) Other Civil Actions. — Any person injured by a violation of this chapter may bring a civil action in an appropriate United States district court for actual damages incurred as a result of such violation.

(c) Powers of the Court. — In an action brought under subsection (a), the court —

(1) may grant temporary and permanent injunctions on such terms as it deems reasonable to prevent or restrain such violation;

(2) in the case of a violation of section 1002, or in the case of an injury resulting from a failure to make royalty payments required by section 1003, shall award damages under subsection (d);

(3) in its discretion may allow the recovery of costs by or against any party other than the United States or an officer thereof; and

(4) in its discretion may award a reasonable attorney's fee to the prevailing party.

(d) Award of Damages. —

(1) Damages for section 1002 or 1003 violations. —

(A) Actual damages. —

(i) In an action brought under subsection (a), if the court finds that a violation of section 1002 or 1003 has occurred, the court shall award to the complaining party its actual damages if the complaining party elects such damages at any time before final judgment is entered.

(ii) In the case of section 1003, actual damages shall constitute the royalty payments that should have been paid under section 1004 and deposited under section 1005. In such a case, the court, in its discretion, may award an additional amount of not to exceed 50 percent of the actual damages.

(B) Statutory damages for section 1002 violations. —

(i) Device. — A complaining party may recover an award of statutory damages for each violation of section 1002(a) or (c) in the sum of not more than $2,500 per device involved in such violation or per device on which a service prohibited by section 1002(c) has been performed, as the court considers just.

(ii) Digital musical recording. — A complaining party may recover an award of statutory damages for each violation of section 1002(d) in the sum of not more than $25 per digital musical recording involved in such violation, as the court considers just.

(iii) Transmission. — A complaining party may recover an award of damages for each transmission or communication that violates section 1002(e) in the sum of not more than $10,000, as the court considers just.

(2) Repeated violations. — In any case in which the court finds that a person has violated section 1002 or 1003 within 3 years after a final judgment against that person for another such violation was entered, the court may increase the award of damages to not more than double the amounts that would otherwise be awarded under paragraph (1), as the court considers just.

(3) Innocent violations of section 1002. — The court in its discretion may reduce the total award of damages against a person violating section 1002 to a sum of not less than $250 in any case in which the court finds that the violator was not aware and had no reason to believe that its acts constituted a violation of section 1002.

(e) Payment of Damages. — Any award of damages under subsection (d) shall be deposited with the Register pursuant to section 1005 for distribution to interested copyright parties as though such funds were royalty payments made pursuant to section 1003.

(f) Impounding of Articles. — At any time while an action under subsection (a) is pending, the court may order the impounding, on such terms as it deems reasonable, of any digital audio recording device, digital musical recording, or device specified in section 1002(c) that is in the custody or control of the alleged violator and that the court has reasonable cause to believe does not comply with, or was involved in a violation of, section 1002.

(g) Remedial Modification and Destruction of Articles. — In an action brought under subsection (a), the court may, as part of a final judgment or decree finding a violation of section 1002, order the remedial modification or the destruction of any digital audio recording device, digital musical recording, or device specified in section 1002(c) that —

(1) does not comply with, or was involved in a violation of, section 1002, and

(2) is in the custody or control of the violator or has been impounded under subsection (f).

§ 1010. Determination of certain disputes[6]

(a) Scope of Determination. — Before the date of first distribution in the United States of a digital audio recording device or a digital audio interface device, any party manufacturing, importing, or distributing such device, and any interested copyright party may mutually agree to petition the Copyright Royalty Judges to determine whether such device is subject to section 1002, or the basis on which royalty payments for such device are to be made under section 1003.

(b) Initiation of Proceedings. — The parties under subsection (a) shall file the petition with the Copyright Royalty Judges requesting the commencement of a proceeding. Within 2 weeks after receiving such a petition, the Chief Copyright Royalty Judge shall cause notice to be published in the Federal Register of the initiation of the proceeding.

(c) Stay of Judicial Proceedings. — Any civil action brought under section 1009 against a party to a proceeding under this section shall, on application of one of the parties to the proceeding, be stayed until completion of the proceeding.

(d) Proceeding. — The Copyright Royalty Judges shall conduct a proceeding with respect to the matter concerned, in accordance with such procedures as the Copyright Royalty Judges may adopt. The Copyright Royalty Judges shall act on the basis of a fully documented written record. Any party to the proceeding may submit relevant information and proposals to the Copyright Royalty Judges. The parties to the proceeding shall each bear their respective costs of participation.

(e) Judicial Review. — Any determination of the Copyright Royalty Judges under subsection (d) may be appealed, by a party to the proceeding, in accordance with section 803(d) of this title. The pendency of an appeal under this subsection shall not stay the determination of the Copyright Royalty

Judges. If the court modifies the determination of the Copyright Royalty Judges, the court shall have jurisdiction to enter its own decision in accordance with its final judgment. The court may further vacate the determination of the Copyright Royalty Judges and remand the case for proceedings as provided in this section.

Chapter 10 Endnotes

[1] The Audio Home Recording Act of 1992 added chapter 10, entitled "Digital Audio Recording Devices and Media," to title 17. Pub. L. No. 102-563, 106 Stat. 4237.

[2] The Copyright Royalty Tribunal Reform Act of 1993 amended section 1004(a)(3) by substituting "Librarian of Congress" in lieu of "Copyright Royalty Tribunal," where appropriate. Pub. L. No. 103-198, 107 Stat. 2304, 2312.

The Copyright Royalty and Distribution Reform Act of 2004 amended paragraph 1004(a)(3) by substituting "Copyright Royalty Judges" in lieu of "Librarian of Congress," wherever it appeared. Pub. L. No. 108-419, 118 Stat. 2341, 2368.

[3] The Copyright Royalty Tribunal Reform Act of 1993 amended section 1005 by striking the last sentence which began "The Register shall submit to the Copyright Royalty Tribunal." Pub. L. No. 103-198, 107 Stat. 2304, 2312.

[4] The Copyright Royalty Tribunal Reform Act of 1993 amended section 1006(c) by substituting "Librarian of Congress" in lieu of "Copyright Royalty Tribunal," where appropriate. Pub. L. No. 103-198, 107 Stat. 2304, 2312. In 1997, section 1006(b)(1) was amended to insert "Federation of Television" in lieu of "Federation Television" wherever it appeared. Pub. L. No. 105-80, 111 Stat. 1529, 1535.

The Copyright Royalty and Distribution Reform Act of 2004 amended subsection 1006(c) by substituting "Copyright Royalty Judges" for "Librarian of Congress shall convene a copyright arbitration royalty panel which" in matter preceding paragraph (1). Pub. L. No. 108-419, 118 Stat. 2341, 2368.

[5] The Copyright Royalty Tribunal Reform Act of 1993 amended section 1007 by substituting "Librarian of Congress" in lieu of "Copyright Royalty Tribunal" or "Tribunal," where appropriate, by amending the first sentence in subsection (c) and by inserting "the reasonable administrative costs incurred by the Librarian" in the last sentence of subsection (c), in lieu of "its reasonable administrative costs." Pub. L. No. 103-198, 107 Stat. 2304, 2312.

In 1997, section 1007 was amended, in subsection (a)(1), by inserting "calendar year 1992" in lieu of "the calendar year in which this chapter takes effect" and, in subsection (b), by inserting "1992" in lieu of "the year in which this section takes effect," and also in subsection (b), by inserting "After" in lieu of "Within 30 days after." Pub. L. No. 105-80, 111 Stat. 1529, 1534 and 1535.

The Copyright Royalty and Distribution Reform Act of 2004 amended paragraph 1007(a)(1) and subsections (b) and (c) in their entirety. Pub. L. No. 108-419, 118 Stat. 2341, 2368.

In 2006, the Copyright Royalty Judges Program Technical Corrections Act amended subsections 1007(b) and (c) by making technical and conforming amendments to correct references to the Copyright Royalty Board and deleting "Librarian of Congress," where appropriate. Pub. L. No. 109-303, 120 Stat. 1478, 1483.

[6] The Copyright Royalty Tribunal Reform Act of 1993 amended section 1010 by substituting "Librarian of Congress" in lieu of "Copyright Royalty Tribunal" or "Tribunal," where appropriate, and by inserting "Librarian's" in lieu of "its." Pub. L. No. 103-198, 107 Stat. 2304, 2312. That Act, which established copyright arbitration royalty panels, states that "[a]ll royalty rates and all determinations with respect to the proportionate division of compulsory license fees among copyright claimants, whether made by the Copyright Royalty Tribunal, or by voluntary agreement, before the effective date set forth in subsection (a) [December 17, 1993] shall remain in effect until modified by voluntary agreement or pursuant to the amendments made by this Act." Pub. L. No. 103-198, 107 Stat. 2304, 2313.

The Copyright Royalty and Distribution Reform Act of 2004 amended section 1010 in its entirety. Pub. L. No. 108-419, 118 Stat. 2341, 2368.

CHAPTER 11[1]

SOUND RECORDINGS AND MUSIC VIDEOS

- 1101. Unauthorized fixation and trafficking in sound recordings and music videos

§ 1101. Unauthorized fixation and trafficking in sound recordings and music videos

(a) Unauthorized Acts. — Anyone who, without the consent of the performer or performers involved —

(1) fixes the sounds or sounds and images of a live musical performance in a copy or phonorecord, or reproduces copies or phonorecords of such a performance from an unauthorized fixation,

(2) transmits or otherwise communicates to the public the sounds or sounds and images of a live musical performance, or

(3) distributes or offers to distribute, sells or offers to sell, rents or offers to rent, or traffics in any copy or phonorecord fixed as described in paragraph (1), regardless of whether the fixations occurred in the United States,

shall be subject to the remedies provided in sections 502 through 505, to the same extent as an infringer of copyright.

(b) Definition. — As used in this section, the term "traffic in" means transport, transfer, or otherwise dispose of, to another, as consideration for anything of value, or make or obtain control of with intent to transport, transfer, or dispose of.

(c) Applicability. — This section shall apply to any act or acts that occur on or after the date of the enactment of the Uruguay Round Agreements Act.

(d) State Law Not Preempted. — Nothing in this section may be construed to annul or limit any rights or remedies under the common law or statutes of any State.

Chapter 11 Endnote

[1]In 1994, the Uruguay Round Agreements Act added chapter 11, entitled "Sound Recordings and Music Videos," to title 17. Pub. L. No. 103-465, 108 Stat. 4809, 4974.

CHAPTER 12[1]

COPYRIGHT PROTECTION AND MANAGEMENT SYSTEMS

§ 1201. Circumvention of copyright protection systems[2]

(a) Violations Regarding Circumvention of Technological Measures. — (1)(A) No person shall circumvent a technological measure that effectively controls access to a work protected under this title. The prohibition contained in the preceding sentence shall take effect at the end of the 2-year period beginning on the date of the enactment of this chapter.

(B) The prohibition contained in subparagraph (A) shall not apply to persons who are users of a copyrighted work which is in a particular class of works, if such persons are, or are likely to be in the succeeding 3-year period, adversely affected by virtue of such prohibition in their ability to make noninfringing uses of that particular class of works under this title, as determined under subparagraph (C).

(C) During the 2-year period described in subparagraph (A), and during each succeeding 3-year period, the Librarian of Congress, upon the recommendation of the Register of Copyrights, who shall consult with the Assistant Secretary for Communications and Information of the Department of Commerce and report and comment on his or her views in making such recommendation, shall make the determination in a rulemaking proceeding for purposes of subparagraph (B) of whether persons who are users of a copyrighted work are, or are likely to be in the succeeding 3-year period, adversely affected by the prohibition under subparagraph (A) in their ability to make noninfringing uses under this title of a particular class of copyrighted works. In conducting such rulemaking, the Librarian shall examine —

(i) the availability for use of copyrighted works;

(ii) the availability for use of works for nonprofit archival, preservation, and educational purposes;

(iii) the impact that the prohibition on the circumvention of technological measures applied to copyrighted works has on criticism, comment, news reporting, teaching, scholarship, or research;

(iv) the effect of circumvention of technological measures on the market for or value of copyrighted works; and

(v) such other factors as the Librarian considers appropriate.

(D) The Librarian shall publish any class of copyrighted works for which the Librarian has determined, pursuant to the rulemaking conducted under subparagraph (C), that noninfringing uses by persons who are users of a copyrighted work are, or are likely to be, adversely affected, and the prohibition contained in subparagraph (A) shall not apply to such users with respect to such class of works for the ensuing 3-year period.

(E) Neither the exception under subparagraph (B) from the applicability of the prohibition contained in subparagraph (A), nor any determination made in a rulemaking conducted under subparagraph (C), may be used as a defense in any action to enforce any provision of this title other than this paragraph.

(2) No person shall manufacture, import, offer to the public, provide, or otherwise traffic in any technology, product, service, device, component, or part thereof, that —

(A) is primarily designed or produced for the purpose of circumventing a technological measure that effectively controls access to a work protected under this title;

(B) has only limited commercially significant purpose or use other than to circumvent a technological measure that effectively controls access to a work protected under this title; or

(C) is marketed by that person or another acting in concert with that person with that person's knowledge for use in circumventing a technological measure that effectively controls access to a work protected under this title.

(3) As used in this subsection —

(A) to "circumvent a technological measure" means to descramble a scrambled work, to decrypt an encrypted work, or otherwise to avoid, bypass, remove, deactivate, or impair a technological measure, without the authority of the copyright owner; and

(B) a technological measure "effectively controls access to a work" if the measure, in the ordinary course of its operation, requires the application of information, or a process or a treatment, with the authority of the copyright owner, to gain access to the work.

(b) Additional Violations. — (1) No person shall manufacture, import, offer to the public, provide, or otherwise traffic in any technology, product, service, device, component, or part thereof, that —

(A) is primarily designed or produced for the purpose of circumventing protection afforded by a technological measure that effectively protects a right of a copyright owner under this title in a work or a portion thereof;

(B) has only limited commercially significant purpose or use other than to circumvent protection afforded by a technological measure that effectively protects a right of a copyright owner under this title in a work or a portion thereof; or

(C) is marketed by that person or another acting in concert with that person with that person's knowledge for use in circumventing protection afforded by a technological measure that effectively protects a right of a copyright owner under this title in a work or a portion thereof.

(2) As used in this subsection —

(A) to "circumvent protection afforded by a technological measure" means avoiding, bypassing, removing, deactivating, or otherwise impairing a technological measure; and

(B) a technological measure "effectively protects a right of a copyright owner under this title" if the measure, in the ordinary course of its operation, prevents, restricts, or otherwise limits the exercise of a right of a copyright owner under this title.

(c) Other Rights, Etc., Not Affected. — (1) Nothing in this section shall affect rights, remedies, limitations, or defenses to copyright infringement, including fair use, under this title.

(2) Nothing in this section shall enlarge or diminish vicarious or contributory liability for copyright infringement in connection with any technology, product, service, device, component, or part thereof.

(3) Nothing in this section shall require that the design of, or design and selection of parts and components for, a consumer electronics, telecommunications, or computing product provide for a response to any particular technological measure, so long as such part or component, or the product in which such part or component is integrated, does not otherwise fall within the prohibitions of subsection (a)(2) or (b)(1).

(4) Nothing in this section shall enlarge or diminish any rights of free speech or the press for activities using consumer electronics, telecommunications, or computing products.

(d) Exemption for Nonprofit Libraries, Archives, and Educational Institutions. — (1) A nonprofit library, archives, or educational institution which gains access to a commercially exploited copyrighted work solely in order to make a good faith determination of whether to acquire a copy of that work for the sole purpose of engaging in conduct permitted under this title shall not be in violation of subsection (a)(1)(A). A copy of a work to which access has been gained under this paragraph —

(A) may not be retained longer than necessary to make such good faith determination; and

(B) may not be used for any other purpose.

(2) The exemption made available under paragraph (1) shall only apply with respect to a work when an identical copy of that work is not reasonably available in another form.

(3) A nonprofit library, archives, or educational institution that willfully for the purpose of commercial advantage or financial gain violates paragraph (1) —

(A) shall, for the first offense, be subject to the civil remedies under section 1203; and

(B) shall, for repeated or subsequent offenses, in addition to the civil remedies under section 1203, forfeit the exemption provided under paragraph (1).

(4) This subsection may not be used as a defense to a claim under subsection (a)(2) or (b), nor may this subsection permit a nonprofit library, archives, or educational institution to manufacture, import, offer to the public, provide, or otherwise traffic in any technology, product, service, component, or part thereof, which circumvents a technological measure.

(5) In order for a library or archives to qualify for the exemption under this subsection, the collections of that library or archives shall be —

(A) open to the public; or

(B) available not only to researchers affiliated with the library or archives or with the institution of which it is a part, but also to other persons doing research in a specialized field.

(e) Law Enforcement, Intelligence, and Other Government Activities. — This section does not prohibit any lawfully authorized investigative, protective, information security, or intelligence activity of an officer, agent, or employee of the United States, a State, or a political subdivision of a State, or a person acting pursuant to a contract with the United States, a State, or a political subdivision of a State. For purposes of this subsection, the term "information security" means activities carried out in order to identify and address the vulnerabilities of a government computer, computer system, or computer network.

(f) Reverse Engineering. — (1) Notwithstanding the provisions of subsection (a)(1)(A), a person who has lawfully obtained the right to use a copy of a computer program may circumvent a technological measure that effectively controls access to a particular portion of that program for the sole purpose of identifying and analyzing those elements of the program that are necessary to achieve interoperability of an independently created computer program with other programs, and that have not previously been readily available to the person engaging in the circumvention, to the extent any such acts of identification and analysis do not constitute infringement under this title.

(2) Notwithstanding the provisions of subsections (a)(2) and (b), a person may develop and employ technological means to circumvent a technological measure, or to circumvent protection afforded by a technological measure, in order to enable the identification and analysis under paragraph (1), or for the purpose of enabling interoperability of an independently created computer program with other programs, if such means are necessary to achieve such interoperability, to the extent that doing so does not constitute infringement under this title.

(3) The information acquired through the acts permitted under paragraph (1), and the means permitted under paragraph (2), may be made available to others if the person referred to in paragraph (1) or (2), as the case may be, provides such information or means solely for the purpose of enabling interoperability of an independently created computer program with other programs, and to the extent that doing so does not constitute infringement under this title or violate applicable law other than this section.

(4) For purposes of this subsection, the term "interoperability" means the ability of computer programs to exchange information, and of such programs mutually to use the information which has been exchanged.

(g) Encryption Research. —

(1) Definitions. — For purposes of this subsection —

(A) the term "encryption research" means activities necessary to identify and analyze flaws and vulnerabilities of encryption technologies applied to copyrighted works, if these activities are conducted to advance the state of knowledge in the field of encryption technology or to assist in the development of encryption products; and

(B) the term "encryption technology" means the scrambling and descrambling of information using mathematical formulas or algorithms.

(2) Permissible acts of encryption research. — Notwithstanding the provisions of subsection (a)(1)(A), it is not a violation of that subsection for a person to circumvent a technological measure as applied to a copy, phonorecord, performance, or display of a published work in the course of an act of good faith encryption research if —

(A) the person lawfully obtained the encrypted copy, phonorecord, performance, or display of the published work;

(B) such act is necessary to conduct such encryption research;

(C) the person made a good faith effort to obtain authorization before the circumvention; and

(D) such act does not constitute infringement under this title or a violation of applicable law other than this section, including section 1030 of title 18 and those provisions of title 18 amended by the Computer Fraud and Abuse Act of 1986.

(3) Factors in determining exemption. — In determining whether a person qualifies for the exemption under paragraph (2), the factors to be considered shall include —

(A) whether the information derived from the encryption research was disseminated, and if so, whether it was disseminated in a manner reasonably calculated to advance the state of knowledge or development of encryption technology, versus whether it was disseminated in a manner that facilitates infringement under this title or a violation of applicable law other than this section, including a violation of privacy or breach of security;

(B) whether the person is engaged in a legitimate course of study, is employed, or is appropriately trained or experienced, in the field of encryption technology; and

(C) whether the person provides the copyright owner of the work to which the technological measure is applied with notice of the findings and documentation of the research, and the time when such notice is provided.

(4) Use of technological means for research activities. — Notwithstanding the provisions of subsection (a)(2), it is not a violation of that subsection for a person to —

(A) develop and employ technological means to circumvent a technological measure for the sole purpose of that person performing the acts of good faith encryption research described in paragraph (2); and

(B) provide the technological means to another person with whom he or she is working collaboratively for the purpose of conducting the acts of good faith encryption research described in paragraph (2) or for the purpose of having that other person verify his or her acts of good faith encryption research described in paragraph (2).

(5) Report to Congress. — Not later than 1 year after the date of the enactment of this chapter, the Register of Copyrights and the Assistant Secretary for Communications and Information of the Department of Commerce shall jointly report to the Congress on the effect this subsection has had on —

(A) encryption research and the development of encryption technology;

(B) the adequacy and effectiveness of technological measures designed to protect copyrighted works; and

(C) protection of copyright owners against the unauthorized access to their encrypted copyrighted works.

The report shall include legislative recommendations, if any.

(h) Exceptions Regarding Minors. — In applying subsection (a) to a component or part, the court may consider the necessity for its intended and actual incorporation in a technology, product, service, or device, which —

(1) does not itself violate the provisions of this title; and

(2) has the sole purpose to prevent the access of minors to material on the Internet.

(i) Protection of Personally Identifying Information. —

(1) Circumvention permitted. — Notwithstanding the provisions of subsection (a)(1)(A), it is not a violation of that subsection for a person to circumvent a technological measure that effectively controls access to a work protected under this title, if —

(A) the technological measure, or the work it protects, contains the capability of collecting or disseminating personally identifying information reflecting the online activities of a natural person who seeks to gain access to the work protected;

(B) in the normal course of its operation, the technological measure, or the work it protects, collects or disseminates personally identifying information about the person who seeks to gain access to the work protected, without providing conspicuous notice of such collection or dissemination to such person, and without providing such person with the capability to prevent or restrict such collection or dissemination;

(C) the act of circumvention has the sole effect of identifying and disabling the capability described in subparagraph (A), and has no other effect on the ability of any person to gain access to any work; and

(D) the act of circumvention is carried out solely for the purpose of preventing the collection or dissemination of personally identifying information about a natural person who seeks to gain access to the work protected, and is not in violation of any other law.

(2) Inapplicability to certain technological measures. —

This subsection does not apply to a technological measure, or a work it protects, that does not collect or disseminate personally identifying information and that is disclosed to a user as not having or using such capability.

(j) Security Testing. —

(1) Definition. — For purposes of this subsection, the term "security testing" means accessing a computer, computer system, or computer network, solely for the purpose of good faith testing, investigating, or correcting, a security flaw or vulnerability, with the authorization of the owner or operator of such computer, computer system, or computer network.

(2) Permissible acts of security testing. — Notwithstanding the provisions of subsection (a)(1)(A), it is not a violation of that subsection for a person to engage in an act of security testing, if such act does not constitute infringement under this title or a violation of applicable law other than this section, including section 1030 of title 18 and those provisions of title 18 amended by the Computer Fraud and Abuse Act of 1986.

(3) Factors in determining exemption. — In determining whether a person qualifies for the exemption under paragraph (2), the factors to be considered shall include —

(A) whether the information derived from the security testing was used solely to promote the security of the owner or operator of such computer, computer system or computer network, or shared directly with the developer of such computer, computer system, or computer network; and

(B) whether the information derived from the security testing was used or maintained in a manner that does not facilitate infringement under this title or a violation of applicable law other than this section, including a violation of privacy or breach of security.

(4) Use of technological means for security testing. — Notwithstanding the provisions of subsection (a)(2), it is not a violation of that subsection for a person to develop, produce, distribute or employ technological means for the sole purpose of performing the acts of security testing described in subsection (2), provided such technological means does not otherwise violate section (a)(2).

(k) Certain Analog Devices and Certain Technological Measures. —

(1) Certain analog devices. —

(A) Effective 18 months after the date of the enactment of this chapter, no person shall manufacture, import, offer to the public, provide or otherwise traffic in any —

(i) VHS format analog video cassette recorder unless such recorder conforms to the automatic gain control copy control technology;

(ii) 8mm format analog video cassette camcorder unless such camcorder conforms to the automatic gain control technology;

(iii) Beta format analog video cassette recorder, unless such recorder conforms to the automatic gain control copy control technology, except that this requirement shall not apply until there are 1,000 Beta format analog video cassette recorders sold in the United States in any one calendar year after the date of the enactment of this chapter;

(iv) 8mm format analog video cassette recorder that is not an analog video cassette camcorder, unless such recorder conforms to the automatic gain control copy control technology, except that this requirement shall not apply until there are 20,000 such recorders sold in the United States in any one calendar year after the date of the enactment of this chapter; or

(v) analog video cassette recorder that records using an NTSC format video input and that is not otherwise covered under clauses (i) through (iv), unless such device conforms to the automatic gain control copy control technology.

(B) Effective on the date of the enactment of this chapter, no person shall manufacture, import, offer to the public, provide or otherwise traffic in —

(i) any VHS format analog video cassette recorder or any 8mm format analog video cassette recorder if the design of the model of such recorder has been modified after such date of enactment so that a model of recorder that previously conformed to the automatic gain control copy control technology no longer conforms to such technology; or

(ii) any VHS format analog video cassette recorder, or any 8mm format analog video cassette recorder that is not an 8mm analog video cassette camcorder, if the design of the model of such recorder has been modified after such date of enactment so that a model of recorder that previously conformed to the four-line colorstripe copy control technology no longer conforms to such technology.

Manufacturers that have not previously manufactured or sold a VHS format analog video cassette recorder, or an 8mm format analog cassette recorder, shall be required to conform to the four-line colorstripe copy control technology in the initial model of any such recorder manufactured after the date of the enactment of this chapter, and thereafter to continue conforming to the four-line colorstripe copy control technology. For purposes of this subparagraph, an analog video cassette recorder "conforms to" the four-line colorstripe copy control technology if it records a signal that, when played back by the playback function of that recorder in the normal viewing mode, exhibits, on a reference display device, a display containing distracting visible lines through portions of the viewable picture.

(2) Certain encoding restrictions. — No person shall apply the automatic gain control copy control technology or colorstripe copy control technology to prevent or limit consumer copying except such copying —

(A) of a single transmission, or specified group of transmissions, of live events or of audiovisual works for which a member of the public has exercised choice in selecting the transmissions, including the content of the transmissions or the time of receipt of such transmissions, or both, and as to which such member is charged a separate fee for each such transmission or specified group of transmissions;

(B) from a copy of a transmission of a live event or an audiovisual work if such transmission is provided by a channel or service where payment is made by a member of the public for such channel or service in the form of a subscription fee that entitles the member of the public to receive all of the programming contained in such channel or service;

(C) from a physical medium containing one or more prerecorded audiovisual works; or

(D) from a copy of a transmission described in subparagraph (A) or from a copy made from a physical medium described in subparagraph (C).

In the event that a transmission meets both the conditions set forth in subparagraph (A) and those set forth in subparagraph (B), the transmission shall be treated as a transmission described in subparagraph (A).

(3) Inapplicability. — This subsection shall not —

(A) require any analog video cassette camcorder to conform to the automatic gain control copy control technology with respect to any video signal received through a camera lens;

(B) apply to the manufacture, importation, offer for sale, provision of, or other trafficking in, any professional analog video cassette recorder; or

(C) apply to the offer for sale or provision of, or other trafficking in, any previously owned analog video cassette recorder, if such recorder was legally manufactured and sold when new and not subsequently modified in violation of paragraph (1)(B).

(4) Definitions. — For purposes of this subsection:

(A) An "analog video cassette recorder" means a device that records, or a device that includes a function that records, on electromagnetic tape in an analog format the electronic impulses produced by the video and audio portions of a television program, motion picture, or other form of audiovisual work.

(B) An "analog video cassette camcorder" means an analog video cassette recorder that contains a recording function that operates through a camera lens and through a video input that may be connected with a television or other video playback device.

(C) An analog video cassette recorder "conforms" to the automatic gain control copy control technology if it —

(i) detects one or more of the elements of such technology and does not record the motion picture or transmission protected by such technology; or

(ii) records a signal that, when played back, exhibits a meaningfully distorted or degraded display.

(D) The term "professional analog video cassette recorder" means an analog video cassette recorder that is designed, manufactured, marketed, and intended for use by a person who regularly employs such a device for a lawful business or industrial use, including making, performing, displaying, distributing, or transmitting copies of motion pictures on a commercial scale.

(E) The terms "VHS format," "8mm format," "Beta format," "automatic gain control copy control technology," "colorstripe copy control technology," "four-line version of the colorstripe copy control technology," and "NTSC" have the meanings that are commonly understood in the consumer electronics and motion picture industries as of the date of the enactment of this chapter.

(5) Violations. — Any violation of paragraph (1) of this subsection shall be treated as a violation of subsection (b)(1) of this section. Any violation of paragraph (2) of this subsection shall be deemed an "act of circumvention" for the purposes of section 1203(c)(3)(A) of this chapter.

§ 1202. *Integrity of copyright management information*[3]

(a) False Copyright Management Information. — No person shall knowingly and with the intent to induce, enable, facilitate, or conceal infringement —

(1) provide copyright management information that is false, or

(2) distribute or import for distribution copyright management information that is false.

(b) Removal or Alteration of Copyright Management Information. — No person shall, without the authority of the copyright owner or the law —

(1) intentionally remove or alter any copyright management information,

(2) distribute or import for distribution copyright management information knowing that the copyright management information has been removed or altered without authority of the copyright owner or the law, or

(3) distribute, import for distribution, or publicly perform works, copies of works, or phonorecords, knowing that copyright management information has been removed or altered without authority of the copyright owner or the law,

knowing, or, with respect to civil remedies under section 1203, having reasonable grounds to know, that it will induce, enable, facilitate, or conceal an infringement of any right under this title.

(c) Definition. — As used in this section, the term "copyright management information" means any of the following information conveyed in connection with copies or phonorecords of a work or performances or displays of a work, including in digital form, except that such term does not include any personally identifying information about a user of a work or of a copy, phonorecord, performance, or display of a work:

(1) The title and other information identifying the work, including the information set forth on a notice of copyright.

(2) The name of, and other identifying information about, the author of a work.

(3) The name of, and other identifying information about, the copyright owner of the work, including the information set forth in a notice of copyright.

(4) With the exception of public performances of works by radio and television broadcast stations, the name of, and other identifying information about, a performer whose performance is fixed in a work other than an audiovisual work.

(5) With the exception of public performances of works by radio and television broadcast stations, in the case of an audiovisual work, the name of, and other identifying information about, a writer, performer, or director who is credited in the audiovisual work.

(6) Terms and conditions for use of the work.

(7) Identifying numbers or symbols referring to such information or links to such information.

(8) Such other information as the Register of Copyrights may prescribe by regulation, except that the Register of Copyrights may not require the provision of any information concerning the user of a copyrighted work.

(d) Law Enforcement, Intelligence, and Other Government Activities. — This section does not prohibit any lawfully authorized investigative, protective, information security, or intelligence activity of an officer, agent, or employee of the United States, a State, or a political subdivision of a State, or a person acting pursuant to a contract with the United States, a State, or a political subdivision of a State. For purposes of this subsection, the term "information security" means activities carried out in order to identify and address the vulnerabilities of a government computer, computer system, or computer network.

(e) Limitations on Liability. —

(1) Analog transmissions. — In the case of an analog transmission, a person who is making transmissions in its capacity as a broadcast station, or as a cable system, or someone who provides programming to such station or system, shall not be liable for a violation of subsection (b) if —

(A) avoiding the activity that constitutes such violation is not technically feasible or would create an undue financial hardship on such person; and

(B) such person did not intend, by engaging in such activity, to induce, enable, facilitate, or conceal infringement of a right under this title.

(2) Digital transmissions. —

(A) If a digital transmission standard for the placement of copyright management information for a category of works is set in a voluntary, consensus standard-setting process involving a representative cross-section of broadcast stations or cable systems and copyright owners of a category of works that are intended for public performance by such stations or systems, a person identified in paragraph (1) shall not be liable for a violation of subsection (b) with respect to the particular copyright management information addressed by such standard if —

(i) the placement of such information by someone other than such person is not in accordance with such standard; and

(ii) the activity that constitutes such violation is not intended to induce, enable, facilitate, or conceal infringement of a right under this title.

(B) Until a digital transmission standard has been set pursuant to subparagraph (A) with respect to the placement of copyright management information for a category of works, a person identified in paragraph (1) shall not be liable for a violation of subsection (b) with respect to such copyright management information, if the activity that constitutes such violation is not intended to induce, enable, facilitate, or conceal infringement of a right under this title, and if —

(i) the transmission of such information by such person would result in a perceptible visual or aural degradation of the digital signal; or

(ii) the transmission of such information by such person would conflict with —

(I) an applicable government regulation relating to transmission of information in a digital signal;

(II) an applicable industry-wide standard relating to the transmission of information in a digital signal that was adopted by a voluntary consensus standards body prior to the effective date of this chapter; or

(III) an applicable industry-wide standard relating to the transmission of information in a digital signal that was adopted in a voluntary, consensus standards-setting process open to participation by a representative cross-section of broadcast stations or cable systems and copyright owners of a category of works that are intended for public performance by such stations or systems.

(3) Definitions. — As used in this subsection —

(A) the term "broadcast station" has the meaning given that term in section 3 of the Communications Act of 1934 (47 U.S.C. 153); and

(B) the term "cable system" has the meaning given that term in section 602 of the Communications Act of 1934 (47 U.S.C. 522).

§ 1203. Civil remedies[4]

(a) Civil Actions. — Any person injured by a violation of section 1201 or 1202 may bring a civil action in an appropriate United States district court for such violation.

(b) Powers of the Court. — In an action brought under subsection (a), the court —

(1) may grant temporary and permanent injunctions on such terms as it deems reasonable to prevent or restrain a violation, but in no event shall impose a prior restraint on free speech or the press protected under the 1st amendment to the Constitution;

(2) at any time while an action is pending, may order the impounding, on such terms as it deems reasonable, of any device or product that is in the custody or control of the alleged violator and that the court has reasonable cause to believe was involved in a violation;

(3) may award damages under subsection (c);

(4) in its discretion may allow the recovery of costs by or against any party other than the United States or an officer thereof;

(5) in its discretion may award reasonable attorney's fees to the prevailing party; and

(6) may, as part of a final judgment or decree finding a violation, order the remedial modification or the destruction of any device or product involved in the violation that is in the custody or control of the violator or has been impounded under paragraph (2).

(c) Award of Damages. —

(1) In general. — Except as otherwise provided in this title, a person committing a violation of section 1201 or 1202 is liable for either —

(A) the actual damages and any additional profits of the violator, as provided in paragraph (2), or

(B) statutory damages, as provided in paragraph (3).

(2) Actual damages. — The court shall award to the complaining party the actual damages suffered by the party as a result of the violation, and any profits of the violator that are attributable to the violation and are not taken into account in computing the actual damages, if the complaining party elects such damages at any time before final judgment is entered.

(3) Statutory damages. — (A) At any time before final judgment is entered, a complaining party may elect to recover an award of statutory damages for each violation of section 1201 in the sum of not less than $200 or more than $2,500 per act of circumvention, device, product, component, offer, or performance of service, as the court considers just.

(B) At any time before final judgment is entered, a complaining party may elect to recover an award of statutory damages for each violation of section 1202 in the sum of not less than $2,500 or more than $25,000.

(4) Repeated violations. — In any case in which the injured party sustains the burden of proving, and the court finds, that a person has violated section 1201 or 1202 within three years after a final judgment was entered against the person for another such violation, the court may increase the award of damages up to triple the amount that would otherwise be awarded, as the court considers just.

(5) Innocent violations. —

(A) In general. — The court in its discretion may reduce or remit the total award of damages in any case in which the violator sustains the burden of proving, and the court finds, that the violator was not aware and had no reason to believe that its acts constituted a violation.

(B) Nonprofit library, archives, educational institutions, or public broadcasting entities. —

(i) Definition. — In this subparagraph, the term "public broadcasting entity" has the meaning given such term under section 118(g).

(ii) In general. — In the case of a nonprofit library, archives, educational institution, or public broadcasting entity, the court shall remit damages in any case in which the library, archives, educational institution, or public broadcasting entity sustains the burden of proving, and the court finds, that the library, archives, educational institution, or public broadcasting entity was not aware and had no reason to believe that its acts constituted a violation.

§ 1204. Criminal offenses and penalties[5]

(a) In General. — Any person who violates section 1201 or 1202 willfully and for purposes of commercial advantage or private financial gain —

(1) shall be fined not more than $500,000 or imprisoned for not more than 5 years, or both, for the first offense; and

(2) shall be fined not more than $1,000,000 or imprisoned for not more than 10 years, or both, for any subsequent offense.

(b) Limitation for Nonprofit Library, Archives, Educational Institution, or Public Broadcasting Entity. — Subsection (a) shall not apply to a nonprofit library, archives, educational institution, or public broadcasting entity (as defined under section 118(g)).

(c) Statute of Limitations. — No criminal proceeding shall be brought under this section unless such proceeding is commenced within five years after the cause of action arose.

§ 1205. Savings clause

Nothing in this chapter abrogates, diminishes, or weakens the provisions of, nor provides any defense or element of mitigation in a criminal prosecution or civil action under, any Federal or State law that prevents the violation of the privacy of an individual in connection with the individual's use of the Internet.

Chapter 12 Endnotes

[1]The WIPO Copyright and Performances and Phonograms Treaties Implementation Act of 1998 added chapter 12, entitled "Copyright Protection and Management Systems," to title 17. Pub. L. No. 105-304, 112 Stat. 2860, 2863. The WIPO Copyright and Performances and Phonograms Treaties Implementation Act of 1998 is title I of the Digital Millennium Copyright Act. Pub. L. No. 105-304, 112 Stat. 2860.

[2]The Satellite Home Viewer Improvement Act of 1999 amended section 1201(a)(1)(C) by deleting "on the record." Pub. L. No. 106-113, 113 Stat. 1501, app. I at 1501A-594.

[3]In 1999, section 1202 was amended by inserting "category of works" for "category or works," in subsection (e)(2)(B). Pub. L. No. 106-44, 113 Stat. 221, 222.

[4]The Satellite Home Viewer Improvement Act of 1999 amended section 1203(c)(5)(B) in its entirety. Pub. L. No. 106-113, 113 Stat. 1501, app. I at 1501A-593.

[5]The Satellite Home Viewer Improvement Act of 1999 amended section 1204(b) in its entirety. Pub. L. No. 106-113, 113 Stat. 1501, app. I at 1501A-593.

CHAPTER 13[1]

PROTECTION OF ORIGINAL DESIGNS

- 1301. Designs protected
- 1302. Designs not subject to protection
- 1303. Revisions, adaptations, and rearrangements
- 1304. Commencement of protection
- 1305. Term of protection
- 1306. Design notice
- 1307. Effect of omission of notice
- 1308. Exclusive rights
- 1309. Infringement
- 1310. Application for registration
- 1311. Benefit of earlier filing date in foreign country
- 1312. Oaths and acknowledgments
- 1313. Examination of application and issue or refusal of registration
- 1314. Certification of registration
- 1315. Publication of announcements and indexes
- 1316. Fees
- 1317. Regulations
- 1318. Copies of records
- 1319. Correction of errors in certificates
- 1320. Ownership and transfer
- 1321. Remedy for infringement
- 1322. Injunctions
- 1323. Recovery for infringement
- 1324. Power of court over registration
- 1325. Liability for action on registration fraudulently obtained
- 1326. Penalty for false marking
- 1327. Penalty for false representation
- 1328. Enforcement by Treasury and Postal Service
- 1329. Relation to design patent law unaffected
- 1330. Common law and other rights unaffected

- 1331. Administrator; Office of the Administrator
- 1332. No retroactive effect

§ 1301. Designs protected[2]

(a) Designs protected. —

(1) In general. — The designer or other owner of an original design of a useful article which makes the article attractive or distinctive in appearance to the purchasing or using public may secure the protection provided by this chapter upon complying with and subject to this chapter.

(2) Vessel hulls. — The design of a vessel hull, including a plug or mold, is subject to protection under this chapter, notwithstanding section 1302(4).

(b) Definitions. — For the purpose of this chapter, the following terms have the following meanings:

(1) A design is "original" if it is the result of the designer's creative endeavor that provides a distinguishable variation over prior work pertaining to similar articles which is more than merely trivial and has not been copied from another source.

(2) A "useful article" is a vessel hull, including a plug or mold, which in normal use has an intrinsic utilitarian function that is not merely to portray the appearance of the article or to convey information. An article which normally is part of a useful article shall be deemed to be a useful article.

(3) A "vessel" is a craft —

(A) that is designed and capable of independently steering a course on or through water through its own means of propulsion; and

(B) that is designed and capable of carrying and transporting one or more passengers.

(4) A "hull" is the frame or body of a vessel, including the deck of a vessel, exclusive of masts, sails, yards, and rigging.

(5) A "plug" means a device or model used to make a mold for the purpose of exact duplication, regardless of whether the device or model has an intrinsic utilitarian function that is not only to portray the appearance of the product or to convey information.

(6) A "mold" means a matrix or form in which a substance for material is used, regardless of whether the matrix or form has an intrinsic utilitarian function that is not only to portray the appearance of the product or to convey information.

§ 1302. Designs not subject to protection[3]

Protection under this chapter shall not be available for a design that is —

(1) not original;

(2) staple or commonplace, such as a standard geometric figure, a familiar symbol, an emblem, or a motif, or another shape, pattern, or configuration which has become standard, common, prevalent, or ordinary;

(3) different from a design excluded by paragraph (2) only in insignificant details or in elements which are variants commonly used in the relevant trades;

(4) dictated solely by a utilitarian function of the article that embodies it; or

(5) embodied in a useful article that was made public by the designer or owner in the United States or a foreign country more than 2 years before the date of the application for registration under this chapter.

§ 1303. Revisions, adaptations, and rearrangements

Protection for a design under this chapter shall be available notwithstanding the employment in the design of subject matter excluded from protection under section 1302 if the design is a substantial revision, adaptation, or rearrangement of such subject matter. Such protection shall be independent of any subsisting protection in subject matter employed in the design, and shall not be construed as securing any right to subject matter excluded from protection under this chapter or as extending any subsisting protection under this chapter.

§ 1304. Commencement of protection

The protection provided for a design under this chapter shall commence upon the earlier of the date of publication of the registration under section 1313(a) or the date the design is first made public as defined by section 1310(b).

§ 1305. Term of protection

(a) In General. — Subject to subsection (b), the protection provided under this chapter for a design shall continue for a term of 10 years beginning on the date of the commencement of protection under section 1304.

(b) Expiration. — All terms of protection provided in this section shall run to the end of the calendar year in which they would otherwise expire.

(c) Termination of Rights. — Upon expiration or termination of protection in a particular design under this chapter, all rights under this chapter in the design shall terminate, regardless of the number of different articles in which the design may have been used during the term of its protection.

§ 1306. Design notice

(a) Contents of Design Notice. — (1) Whenever any design for which protection is sought under this chapter is made public under section 1310(b), the owner of the design shall, subject to the provisions of section 1307, mark it or have it marked legibly with a design notice consisting of —

> (A) the words "Protected Design", the abbreviation "Prot'd Des.", or the letter "D" with a circle, Ⓓ, or the symbol "*D*";

> (B) the year of the date on which protection for the design commenced; and

> (C) the name of the owner, an abbreviation by which the name can be recognized, or a generally accepted alternative designation of the owner.

Any distinctive identification of the owner may be used for purposes of subparagraph (C) if it has been recorded by the Administrator before the design marked with such identification is registered.

> (2) After registration, the registration number may be used instead of the elements specified in subparagraphs (B) and (C) of paragraph (1).

(b) Location of Notice. — The design notice shall be so located and applied as to give reasonable notice of design protection while the useful article embodying the design is passing through its normal channels of commerce.

(c) Subsequent Removal of Notice. — When the owner of a design has complied with the provisions of this section, protection under this chapter shall not be affected by the removal, destruction, or obliteration by others of the design notice on an article.

§ 1307. Effect of omission of notice

(a) Actions with Notice. — Except as provided in subsection (b), the omission of the notice prescribed in section 1306 shall not cause loss of the protection under this chapter or prevent recovery for infringement under this chapter against any person who, after receiving written notice of the design protection, begins an undertaking leading to infringement under this chapter.

(b) Actions without Notice. — The omission of the notice prescribed in section 1306 shall prevent any recovery under section 1323 against a person who began an undertaking leading to infringement under this chapter before receiving written notice of the design protection. No injunction shall be issued under this chapter with respect to such undertaking unless the owner of the design reimburses that person for any reasonable expenditure or contractual obligation in connection with such undertaking that was incurred before receiving written notice of the design protection, as the court in its discretion directs. The burden of providing written notice of design protection shall be on the owner of the design.

§ 1308. Exclusive rights

The owner of a design protected under this chapter has the exclusive right to —

(1) make, have made, or import, for sale or for use in trade, any useful article embodying that design; and

(2) sell or distribute for sale or for use in trade any useful article embodying that design.

§ 1309. Infringement

(a) Acts of Infringement. — Except as provided in subsection (b), it shall be infringement of the exclusive rights in a design protected under this chapter for any person, without the consent of the owner of the design, within the United States and during the term of such protection, to —

(1) make, have made, or import, for sale or for use in trade, any infringing article as defined in subsection (e); or

(2) sell or distribute for sale or for use in trade any such infringing article.

(b) Acts of Sellers and Distributors. — A seller or distributor of an infringing article who did not make or import the article shall be deemed to have infringed on a design protected under this chapter only if that person —

(1) induced or acted in collusion with a manufacturer to make, or an importer to import such article, except that merely purchasing or giving an order to purchase such article in the ordinary course of business shall not of itself constitute such inducement or collusion; or

(2) refused or failed, upon the request of the owner of the design, to make a prompt and full disclosure of that person's source of such article, and that person orders or reorders such article after receiving notice by registered or certified mail of the protection subsisting in the design.

(c) Acts without Knowledge. — It shall not be infringement under this section to make, have made, import, sell, or distribute, any article embodying a design which was created without knowledge that a design was protected under this chapter and was copied from such protected design.

(d) Acts in Ordinary Course of Business. — A person who incorporates into that person's product of manufacture an infringing article acquired from others in the ordinary course of business, or who, without knowledge of the protected design embodied in an infringing article, makes or processes the infringing article for the account of another person in the ordinary course of business, shall not be deemed to have infringed the rights in that design under this chapter except under a condition contained in paragraph (1) or (2) of subsection (b). Accepting an order or reorder from the source of the infringing article shall be deemed ordering or reordering within the meaning of subsection (b)(2).

(e) Infringing Article Defined. — As used in this section, an "infringing article" is any article the design of which has been copied from a design protected under this chapter, without the consent of the owner of the protected design. An infringing article is not an illustration or picture of a protected design in an advertisement, book, periodical, newspaper, photograph, broadcast, motion picture, or similar medium. A design shall not be deemed to have been copied from a protected design if it is original and not substantially similar in appearance to a protected design.

(f) Establishing Originality. — The party to any action or proceeding under this chapter who alleges rights under this chapter in a design shall have the burden of establishing the design's originality whenever the opposing party introduces an earlier work which is identical to such design, or so similar as to make prima facie showing that such design was copied from such work.

(g) Reproduction for Teaching or Analysis. — It is not an infringement of the exclusive rights of a design owner for a person to reproduce the design in a useful article or in any other form solely for the purpose of teaching, analyzing, or evaluating the appearance, concepts, or techniques embodied in the design, or the function of the useful article embodying the design.

§ 1310. *Application for registration*

(a) Time Limit for Application for Registration. — Protection under this chapter shall be lost if application for registration of the design is not made within 2 years after the date on which the design is first made public.

(b) When Design Is Made Public. — A design is made public when an existing useful article embodying the design is anywhere publicly exhibited, publicly distributed, or offered for sale or sold to the public by the owner of the design or with the owner's consent.

(c) Application by Owner of Design. — Application for registration may be made by the owner of the design.

(d) Contents of Application. — The application for registration shall be made to the Administrator and shall state —

(1) the name and address of the designer or designers of the design;

(2) the name and address of the owner if different from the designer;

(3) the specific name of the useful article embodying the design;

(4) the date, if any, that the design was first made public, if such date was earlier than the date of the application;

(5) affirmation that the design has been fixed in a useful article; and

(6) such other information as may be required by the Administrator.

The application for registration may include a description setting forth the salient features of the design, but the absence of such a description shall not prevent registration under this chapter.

(e) Sworn Statement. — The application for registration shall be accompanied by a statement under oath by the applicant or the applicant's duly authorized agent or representative, setting forth, to the best of the applicant's knowledge and belief —

(1) that the design is original and was created by the designer or designers named in the application;

(2) that the design has not previously been registered on behalf of the applicant or the applicant's predecessor in title; and

(3) that the applicant is the person entitled to protection and to registration under this chapter.

If the design has been made public with the design notice prescribed in section 1306, the statement shall also describe the exact form and position of the design notice.

(f) Effect of Errors. — (1) Error in any statement or assertion as to the utility of the useful article named in the application under this section, the design of which is sought to be registered, shall not affect the protection secured under this chapter.

(2) Errors in omitting a joint designer or in naming an alleged joint designer shall not affect the validity of the registration, or the actual ownership or the protection of the design, unless it is shown that the error occurred with deceptive intent.

(g) Design Made in Scope of Employment. — In a case in which the design was made within the regular scope of the designer's employment and individual authorship of the design is difficult or impossible to ascribe and the application so states, the name and address of the employer for whom the design was made may be stated instead of that of the individual designer.

(h) Pictorial Representation of Design. — The application for registration shall be accompanied by two copies of a drawing or other pictorial representation of the useful article embodying the design, having one or more views, adequate to show the design, in a form and style suitable for reproduction, which shall be deemed a part of the application.

(i) Design in More than One Useful Article. — If the distinguishing elements of a design are in substantially the same form in different useful articles, the design shall be protected as to all such useful articles when protected as to one of them, but not more than one registration shall be required for the design.

(j) Application for More than One Design. — More than one design may be included in the same application under such conditions as may be prescribed by the Administrator. For each design included in an application the fee prescribed for a single design shall be paid.

§ 1311. Benefit of earlier filing date in foreign country

An application for registration of a design filed in the United States by any person who has, or whose legal representative or predecessor or successor in title has, previously filed an application for registration of the same design in a foreign country which extends to designs of owners who are citizens of the United States, or to applications filed under this chapter, similar protection to that provided under this chapter shall have that same effect as if filed in the United States on the date on which the application was first filed in such foreign country, if the application in the United States is filed within 6 months after the earliest date on which any such foreign application was filed.

§ 1312. Oaths and acknowledgments

(a) In General. — Oaths and acknowledgments required by this chapter —

    (1) may be made —

        (A) before any person in the United States authorized by law to administer oaths; or

        (B) when made in a foreign country, before any diplomatic or consular officer of the United States authorized to administer oaths, or before any official authorized to administer oaths in the foreign country concerned, whose authority shall be proved by a certificate of a diplomatic or consular officer of the United States; and

    (2) shall be valid if they comply with the laws of the State or country where made.

(b) Written Declaration in Lieu of Oath. — (1) The Administrator may by rule prescribe that any document which is to be filed under this chapter in the Office of the Administrator and which is required by any law, rule, or other regulation to be under oath, may be subscribed to by a written declaration in such form as the Administrator may prescribe, and such declaration shall be in lieu of the oath otherwise required.

    (2) Whenever a written declaration under paragraph (1) is used, the document containing the declaration shall state that willful false statements are punishable by fine or imprisonment, or both, pursuant to section 1001 of title 18, and may jeopardize the validity of the application or document or a registration resulting therefrom.

§ 1313. Examination of application and issue or refusal of registration[4]

(a) Determination of Registrability of Design; Registration. — Upon the filing of an application for registration in proper form under section 1310, and upon payment of the fee prescribed under section 1316, the Administrator shall determine whether or not the application relates to a design which on its face appears to be subject to protection under this chapter, and, if so, the Register shall register the design. Registration under this subsection shall be announced by publication. The date of registration shall be the date of publication.

(b) Refusal to Register; Reconsideration. — If, in the judgment of the Administrator, the application for registration relates to a design which on its face is not subject to protection under this chapter, the Administrator shall send to the applicant a notice of refusal to register and the grounds for the refusal. Within 3 months after the date on which the notice of refusal is sent, the applicant may, by written request, seek reconsideration of the application. After consideration of such a request, the Administrator shall either register the design or send to the applicant a notice of final refusal to register.

(c) Application to Cancel Registration. — Any person who believes he or she is or will be damaged by a registration under this chapter may, upon payment of the prescribed fee, apply to the Administrator at any time to cancel the registration on the ground that the design is not subject to protection under this chapter, stating the reasons for the request. Upon receipt of an application for cancellation, the Administrator shall send to the owner of the design, as shown in the records of the Office of the Administrator, a notice of the application, and the owner shall have a period of 3 months after the date on which such notice is mailed in which to present arguments to the Administrator for support of the validity of the registration. The Administrator shall also have the authority to establish, by regulation, conditions under which the opposing parties may appear and be heard in support of their arguments. If, after the periods provided for the presentation of arguments have expired, the Administrator determines that the applicant for cancellation has established that the design is not subject to protection under this chapter, the Administrator shall order the registration stricken from the record. Cancellation under this subsection shall be announced by publication, and notice of the Administrator's final determination with respect to any application for cancellation shall be sent to the applicant and to the owner of record. Costs of the cancellation procedure under this subsection shall be borne by the nonprevailing party or parties, and the Administrator shall have the authority to assess and collect such costs.

§ 1314. Certification of registration

Certificates of registration shall be issued in the name of the United States under the seal of the Office of the Administrator and shall be recorded in the official records of the Office. The certificate shall state the name of the useful article, the date of filing of the application, the date of registration, and the date the design was made public, if earlier than the date of filing of the application, and shall contain a reproduction of the drawing or other pictorial representation of the design. If a description of the salient features of the design appears in the application, the description shall also appear in the certificate. A certificate of registration shall be admitted in any court as prima facie evidence of the facts stated in the certificate.

§ 1315. Publication of announcements and indexes

(a) Publications of the Administrator. — The Administrator shall publish lists and indexes of registered designs and cancellations of designs and may also publish the drawings or other pictorial representations of registered designs for sale or other distribution.

(b) File of Representatives of Registered Designs. — The Administrator shall establish and maintain a file of the drawings or other pictorial representations of registered designs. The file shall be available for use by the public under such conditions as the Administrator may prescribe.

§ 1316. Fees

The Administrator shall by regulation set reasonable fees for the filing of applications to register designs under this chapter and for other services relating to the administration of this chapter, taking into consideration the cost of providing these services and the benefit of a public record.

§ 1317. Regulations

The Administrator may establish regulations for the administration of this chapter.

§ 1318. Copies of records

Upon payment of the prescribed fee, any person may obtain a certified copy of any official record of the Office of the Administrator that relates to this chapter. That copy shall be admissible in evidence with the same effect as the original.

§ 1319. Correction of errors in certificates

The Administrator may, by a certificate of correction under seal, correct any error in a registration incurred through the fault of the Office, or, upon payment of the required fee, any error of a clerical or typographical nature occurring in good faith but not through the fault of the Office. Such registration, together with the certificate, shall thereafter have the same effect as if it had been originally issued in such corrected form.

§ 1320. Ownership and transfer[5]

(a) Property Right in Design. — The property right in a design subject to protection under this chapter shall vest in the designer, the legal representatives of a deceased designer or of one under legal incapacity, the employer for whom the designer created the design in the case of a design made within the regular scope of the designer's employment, or a person to whom the rights of the designer or of such employer have been transferred. The person in whom the property right is vested shall be considered the owner of the design.

(b) Transfer of Property Right. — The property right in a registered design, or a design for which an application for registration has been or may be filed, may be assigned, granted, conveyed, or mortgaged by an instrument in writing, signed by the owner, or may be bequeathed by will.

(c) Oath or Acknowledgment of Transfer. — An oath or acknowledgment under section 1312 shall be prima facie evidence of the execution of an assignment, grant, conveyance, or mortgage under subsection (b).

(d) Recordation of Transfer. — An assignment, grant, conveyance, or mortgage under subsection (b) shall be void as against any subsequent purchaser or mortgagee for a valuable consideration, unless it is recorded in the Office of the Administrator within 3 months after its date of execution or before the date of such subsequent purchase or mortgage.

§ 1321. *Remedy for infringement*

(a) In General. — The owner of a design is entitled, after issuance of a certificate of registration of the design under this chapter, to institute an action for any infringement of the design.

(b) Review of Refusal to Register. — (1) Subject to paragraph (2), the owner of a design may seek judicial review of a final refusal of the Administrator to register the design under this chapter by bringing a civil action, and may in the same action, if the court adjudges the design subject to protection under this chapter, enforce the rights in that design under this chapter.

(2) The owner of a design may seek judicial review under this section if —

(A) the owner has previously duly filed and prosecuted to final refusal an application in proper form for registration of the design;

(B) the owner causes a copy of the complaint in the action to be delivered to the Administrator within 10 days after the commencement of the action; and

(C) the defendant has committed acts in respect to the design which would constitute infringement with respect to a design protected under this chapter.

(c) Administrator as Party to Action. — The Administrator may, at the Administrator's option, become a party to the action with respect to the issue of registrability of the design claim by entering an appearance within 60 days after being served with the complaint, but the failure of the Administrator to become a party shall not deprive the court of jurisdiction to determine that issue.

(d) Use of Arbitration to Resolve Dispute. — The parties to an infringement dispute under this chapter, within such time as may be specified by the Administrator by regulation, may determine the dispute, or any aspect of the dispute, by arbitration. Arbitration shall be governed by title 9. The parties shall give notice of any arbitration award to the Administrator, and such award shall, as between the parties to the arbitration, be dispositive of the issues to which it relates. The arbitration award shall be unenforceable until such notice is given. Nothing in this subsection shall preclude the Administrator from determining whether a design is subject to registration in a cancellation proceeding under section 1313(c).

§ 1322. *Injunctions*

(a) In General. — A court having jurisdiction over actions under this chapter may grant injunctions in accordance with the principles of equity to prevent infringement of a design under this chapter, including, in its discretion, prompt relief by temporary restraining orders and preliminary injunctions.

(b) Damages for Injunctive Relief Wrongfully Obtained. — A seller or distributor who suffers damage by reason of injunctive relief wrongfully obtained under this section has a cause of action against the applicant for such injunctive relief and may recover such relief as may be appropriate, including damages for lost profits, cost of materials, loss of good will, and punitive damages in instances where the injunctive relief was sought in bad faith, and, unless the court finds extenuating circumstances, reasonable attorney's fees.

§ 1323. Recovery for infringement

(a) Damages. — Upon a finding for the claimant in an action for infringement under this chapter, the court shall award the claimant damages adequate to compensate for the infringement. In addition, the court may increase the damages to such amount, not exceeding $50,000 or $1 per copy, whichever is greater, as the court determines to be just. The damages awarded shall constitute compensation and not a penalty. The court may receive expert testimony as an aid to the determination of damages.

(b) Infringer's Profits. — As an alternative to the remedies provided in subsection (a), the court may award the claimant the infringer's profits resulting from the sale of the copies if the court finds that the infringer's sales are reasonably related to the use of the claimant's design. In such a case, the claimant shall be required to prove only the amount of the infringer's sales and the infringer shall be required to prove its expenses against such sales.

(c) Statute of Limitations. — No recovery under subsection (a) or (b) shall be had for any infringement committed more than 3 years before the date on which the complaint is filed.

(d) Attorney's Fees. — In an action for infringement under this chapter, the court may award reasonable attorney's fees to the prevailing party.

(e) Disposition of Infringing and Other Articles. — The court may order that all infringing articles, and any plates, molds, patterns, models, or other means specifically adapted for making the articles, be delivered up for destruction or other disposition as the court may direct.

§ 1324. Power of court over registration

In any action involving the protection of a design under this chapter, the court, when appropriate, may order registration of a design under this chapter or the cancellation of such a registration. Any such order shall be certified by the court to the Administrator, who shall make an appropriate entry upon the record.

§ 1325. Liability for action on registration fraudulently obtained

Any person who brings an action for infringement knowing that registration of the design was obtained by a false or fraudulent representation materially affecting the rights under this chapter, shall be liable in the sum of $10,000, or such part of that amount as the court may determine. That amount shall be to compensate the defendant and shall be charged against the plaintiff and paid to the defendant, in addition to such costs and attorney's fees of the defendant as may be assessed by the court.

§ 1326. Penalty for false marking

(a) In General. — Whoever, for the purpose of deceiving the public, marks upon, applies to, or uses in advertising in connection with an article made, used, distributed, or sold, a design which is not protected under this chapter, a design notice specified in section 1306, or any other words or symbols importing that the design is protected under this chapter, knowing that the design is not so protected, shall pay a civil fine of not more than $500 for each such offense.

(b) Suit by Private Persons. — Any person may sue for the penalty established by subsection (a), in which event one-half of the penalty shall be awarded to the person suing and the remainder shall be awarded to the United States.

§ 1327. Penalty for false representation

Whoever knowingly makes a false representation materially affecting the rights obtainable under this chapter for the purpose of obtaining registration of a design under this chapter shall pay a penalty of not less than $500 and not more than $1,000, and any rights or privileges that individual may have in the design under this chapter shall be forfeited.

§ 1328. Enforcement by Treasury and Postal Service

(a) Regulations. — The Secretary of the Treasury and the United States Postal Service shall separately or jointly issue regulations for the enforcement of the rights set forth in section 1308 with respect to importation. Such regulations may require, as a condition for the exclusion of articles from the United States, that the person seeking exclusion take any one or more of the following actions:

(1) Obtain a court order enjoining, or an order of the International Trade Commission under section 337 of the Tariff Act of 1930 excluding, importation of the articles.

(2) Furnish proof that the design involved is protected under this chapter and that the importation of the articles would infringe the rights in the design under this chapter.

(3) Post a surety bond for any injury that may result if the detention or exclusion of the articles proves to be unjustified.

(b) Seizure and Forfeiture. — Articles imported in violation of the rights set forth in section 1308 are subject to seizure and forfeiture in the same manner as property imported in violation of the customs laws. Any such forfeited articles shall be destroyed as directed by the Secretary of the Treasury or the court, as the case may be, except that the articles may be returned to the country of export whenever it is shown to the satisfaction of the Secretary of the Treasury that the importer had no reasonable grounds for believing that his or her acts constituted a violation of the law.

§ 1329. Relation to design patent law

The issuance of a design patent under title 35, United States Code, for an original design for an article of manufacture shall terminate any protection of the original design under this chapter.

§ 1330. Common law and other rights unaffected

Nothing in this chapter shall annul or limit —

(1) common law or other rights or remedies, if any, available to or held by any person with respect to a design which has not been registered under this chapter; or

(2) any right under the trademark laws or any right protected against unfair competition.

§ 1331. Administrator; Office of the Administrator

In this chapter, the "Administrator" is the Register of Copyrights, and the "Office of the Administrator" and the "Office" refer to the Copyright Office of the Library of Congress.

§ 1332. No retroactive effect

Protection under this chapter shall not be available for any design that has been made public under section 1310(b) before the effective date of this chapter.[6]

Chapter 13 · Endnotes

[1] In 1998, the Vessel Hull Design Protection Act added chapter 13, entitled "Protection of Original Designs," to title 17. Pub. L. No. 105-304, 112 Stat. 2860, 2905. The Vessel Hull Design Protection Act is title V of the Digital Millennium Copyright Act, Pub. L. No. 105-304, 112 Stat. 2860, 2905.

[2] The Satellite Home Viewer Improvement Act of 1999 amended section 1301(b)(3) in its entirety. Pub. L. No. 106-113, 113 Stat. 1501, app. I at 1501A-593.

[3] In 1999, section 1302(5) was amended to substitute "2 years" in lieu of "1 year." Pub. L. No. 106-44, 113 Stat. 221, 222.

[4] The Satellite Home Viewer Improvement Act of 1999 amended section 1313(c) by adding at the end thereof the last sentence, which begins "Costs of the cancellation procedure." Pub. L. No. 106-113, 113 Stat. 1501, app. I at 1501A-594.

[5] In 1999, section 1320 was amended to change the spelling in the heading of subsection (c) from "acknowledgement" to "acknowledgment." Pub. L. No. 106-44, 113 Stat. 221, 222.

[6] The effective date of chapter 13 is October 28, 1998. See section 505 of the Digital Millennium Copyright Act, which appears in Appendix B.

APPENDIX A THE COPYRIGHT ACT OF 1976[1]

Title I — General Revision of Copyright Law
* * * * * * *

Transitional and Supplementary Provisions

Sec. 102. This Act becomes effective on January 1, 1978, except as otherwise expressly provided by this Act, including provisions of the first section of this Act. The provisions of sections 118, 304(b), and chapter 8 of title 17, as amended by the first section of this Act, take effect upon enactment of this Act.[2]

Sec. 103. This Act does not provide copyright protection for any work that goes into the public domain before January 1, 1978. The exclusive rights, as provided by section 106 of title 17 as amended by the first section of this Act, to reproduce a work in phonorecords and to distribute phonorecords of the work, do not extend to any nondramatic musical work copyrighted before July 1, 1909.

Sec. 104. All proclamations issued by the President under section 1(e) or 9(b) of title 17 as it existed on December 31, 1977, or under previous copyright statutes of the United States, shall continue in force until terminated, suspended, or revised by the President.

Sec. 105. (a)(1) Section 505 of title 44 is amended to read as follows:

§ 505. Sale of duplicate plates

"The Public Printer shall sell, under regulations of the Joint Committee on Printing to persons who may apply, additional or duplicate stereotype or electrotype plates from which a Government publication is printed, at a price not to exceed the cost of composition, the metal, and making to the Government, plus 10 per centum, and the full amount of the price shall be paid when the order is filed.".

(2) The item relating to section 505 in the sectional analysis at the beginning of chapter 5 of title 44, is amended to read as follows:

"505. Sale of duplicate plates.".

(b) Section 2113 of title 44 is amended to read as follows:

[To assist the reader, section 2113 of title 44, now designated section 2117, appears in Appendix H, *infra*, as currently amended.]

(c) In section 1498(b) of title 28, the phrase "section 101(b) of title 17" is amended to read "section 504(c) of title 17".

(d) Section 543(a)(4) of the Internal Revenue Code of 1954, as amended, is amended by striking out "(other than by reason of section 2 or 6 thereof)".

(e) Section 3202(a) of title 39 is amended by striking out clause (5). Section 3206 of title 39 is amended by deleting the words "subsections (b) and (c)" and inserting "subsection (b)" in subsection (a), and by deleting subsection (c). Section 3206(d) is renumbered (c).

(f) Subsection (a) of section 6 of the Standard Reference Data Act (15 U.S.C. 290e) is amended by deleting the phrase "section 8" and inserting in lieu thereof the phrase "section 105".[3]

(g) Section 131 of title 2 is amended by deleting the phrase "deposit to secure copyright," and inserting in lieu thereof the phrase "acquisition of material under the copyright law,".

Sec. 106. In any case where, before January 1, 1978, a person has lawfully made parts of instruments serving to reproduce mechanically a copyrighted work under the compulsory license provisions of section 1(e) of title 17 as it existed on December 31, 1977, such person may continue to make and distribute such parts embodying the same mechanical reproduction without obtaining a new compulsory license under the terms of section 115 of title 17 as amended by the first section of this Act. However, such parts made on or after January 1, 1978, constitute phonorecords and are otherwise subject to the provisions of said section 115.

Sec. 107. In the case of any work in which an ad interim copyright is subsisting or is capable of being secured on December 31, 1977, under section 22 of title 17 as it existed on that date, copyright protection is hereby extended to endure for the term or terms provided by section 304 of title 17 as amended by the first section of this Act.

Sec. 108. The notice provisions of sections 401 through 403 of title 17 as amended by the first section of this Act apply to all copies or phonorecords publicly distributed on or after January 1, 1978. However, in the case of a work published before January 1, 1978, compliance with the notice provisions of title 17 either as it existed on December 31, 1977, or as amended by the first section of this Act, is adequate with respect to copies publicly distributed after December 31, 1977.

Sec. 109. The registration of claims to copyright for which the required deposit, application, and fee were received in the Copyright Office before January 1, 1978, and the recordation of assignments of copyright or other instruments received in the Copyright Office before January 1, 1978, shall be made in accordance with title 17 as it existed on December 31, 1977.

Sec. 110. The demand and penalty provisions of section 14 of title 17 as it existed on December 31, 1977, apply to any work in which copyright has been secured by publication with notice of copyright on or before that date, but any deposit and registration made after that date in response to a demand under that section shall be made in accordance with the provisions of title 17 as amended by the first section of this Act.

Sec. 111. Section 2318 of title 18 of the United States Code is amended to read as follows:

[To assist the reader, section 2318 of title 18, as currently amended, along with related criminal provisions, appears in Appendix F, *infra*.]

Sec. 112. All causes of action that arose under title 17 before January 1, 1978, shall be governed by title 17 as it existed when the cause of action arose.

Sec. 113. (a) The Librarian of Congress (hereinafter referred to as the "Librarian") shall establish and maintain in the Library of Congress a library to be known as the American Television and Radio Archives (hereinafter referred to as the "Archives"). The purpose of the Archives shall be to preserve a permanent record of the television and radio programs which are the heritage of the people of the United States and to provide access to such programs to historians and scholars without encouraging or causing copyright infringement.

(1) The Librarian, after consultation with interested organizations and individuals, shall determine and place in the Archives such copies and phonorecords of television and radio programs transmitted to the public in the United States and in other countries which are of present or potential public or cultural interest, historical significance, cognitive value, or otherwise worthy of preservation, including copies and phonorecords of published and unpublished transmission programs —

(A) acquired in accordance with sections 407 and 408 of title 17 as amended by the first section of this Act; and

(B) transferred from the existing collections of the Library of Congress; and

(C) given to or exchanged with the Archives by other libraries, archives, organizations, and individuals; and

(D) purchased from the owner thereof.

(2) The Librarian shall maintain and publish appropriate catalogs and indexes of the collections of the Archives, and shall make such collections available for study and research under the conditions prescribed under this section.

(b) Notwithstanding the provisions of section 106 of title 17 as amended by the first section of this Act, the Librarian is authorized with respect to a transmission program which consists of a regularly scheduled newscast or on-the-spot coverage of news events and, under standards and conditions that the Librarian shall prescribe by regulation —

(1) to reproduce a fixation of such a program, in the same or another tangible form, for the purposes of preservation or security or for distribution under the conditions of clause (3) of this subsection; and

(2) to compile, with out abridgment or any other editing, portions of such fixations according to subject matter, and to reproduce such compilations for the purpose of clause (1) of this subsection; and

(3) to distribute a reproduction made under clause (1) or (2) of this subsection —

(A) by loan to a person engaged in research; and

(B) for deposit in a library or archives which meets the requirements of section 108(a) of title 17 as amended by the first section of this Act,

in either case for use only in research and not for further reproduction or performance.

(c) The Librarian or any employee of the Library who is acting under the authority of this section shall not be liable in any action for copyright infringement committed by any other person unless the

Librarian or such employee knowingly participated in the act of infringement committed by such person. Nothing in this section shall be construed to excuse or limit liability under title 17 as amended by the first section of this Act for any act not authorized by that title or this section, or for any act performed by a person not authorized to act under that title or this section.

(d) This section may be cited as the "American Television and Radio Archives Act".

Sec. 114. There are hereby authorized to be appropriated such funds as may be necessary to carry out the purposes of this Act.

Sec. 115. If any provision of title 17, as amended by the first section of this Act, is declared unconstitutional, the validity of the remainder of this title is not affected.

Appendix A · Endnotes

[1]This appendix contains the Transitional and Supplementary Provisions of the Copyright Act of 1976, Pub. L. No. 94-533, 90 Stat. 2541, that do not amend title 17 of the *United States Code.*

[2]The Copyright Act of 1976 was enacted on October 19, 1976.

[3]The Intellectual Property and High Technology Technical Amendments Act of 2002 amended section 105(f) by substituting "section 6 of the Standard Reference Data Act (15 U.S.C. 290e)" for "section 290(e) of title 15." Pub. L. No. 107-273, 116 Stat. 1758, 1910.

APPENDIX B   THE DIGITAL MILLENNIUM COPYRIGHT ACT OF 1998[1]

Section 1. Short Title.

This Act may be cited as the "Digital Millennium Copyright Act".

Title I — WIPO Treaties Implementation

Sec. 101. Short Title.
This title may be cited as the "WIPO Copyright and Performances and Phonograms Treaties Implementation Act of 1998".

* * * * * * *

Sec. 105. Effective Date.

(a) In General. — Except as otherwise provided in this title, this title and the amendments made by this title shall take effect on the date of the enactment of this Act.

(b) Amendments Relating to Certain International Agreements. — (1) The following shall take effect upon the entry into force of the WIPO Copyright Treaty with respect to the United States:

(A) Paragraph (5) of the definition of "international agreement" contained in section 101 of title 17, United States Code, as amended by section 102(a)(4) of this Act.

(B) The amendment made by section 102(a)(6) of this Act.

(C) Subparagraph (C) of section 104A(h)(1) of title 17, United States Code, as amended by section 102(c)(1) of this Act.

(D) Subparagraph (C) of section 104A(h)(3) of title 17, United States Code, as amended by section 102(c)(2) of this Act.

(2) The following shall take effect upon the entry into force of the WIPO Performances and Phonograms Treaty with respect to the United States:

(A) Paragraph (6) of the definition of "international agreement" contained in section 101 of title 17, United States Code, as amended by section 102(a)(4) of this Act.

(B) The amendment made by section 102(a)(7) of this Act.

(C) The amendment made by section 102(b)(2) of this Act.

(D) Subparagraph (D) of section 104A(h)(1) of title 17, United States Code, as amended by section 102(c)(1) of this Act.

(E) Subparagraph (D) of section 104A(h)(3) of title 17, United States Code, as amended by section 102(c)(2) of this Act.

(F) The amendments made by section 102(c)(3) of this Act.

* * * * * * *

Title II — Online Copyright Infringement Liability Limitation

Sec. 201. Short Title.
This title may be cited as the "Online Copyright Infringement Liability Limitation Act".

* * * * * * *

Sec. 203. Effective Date.
This title and the amendments made by this title shall take effect on the date of the enactment of this Act.

* * * * * * *

Title IV — Miscellaneous Provisions

Sec. 401. Provisions Relating to the Commissioner of Patents and Trademarks and the Register of Copyrights

(a) Compensation. — (1) Section 3(d) of title 35, United States Code, is amended by striking "prescribed by law for Assistant Secretaries of Commerce" and inserting "in effect for level III of the Executive Schedule under section 5314 of title 5, United States Code".

* * * * * * *

(3) Section 5314 of title 5, United States Code, is amended by adding at the end the following:

"Assistant Secretary of Commerce and Commissioner of Patents and Trademarks.

"Register of Copyrights.".

* * * * * * *

Sec. 405. Scope of Exclusive Rights in Sound Recordings; Ephemeral Recordings.

(a) Scope of Exclusive Rights in Sound Recordings.

* * * * * * *

(5) The amendment made by paragraph (2)(B)(i)(III) of this subsection shall be deemed to have been enacted as part of the Digital Performance Right in Sound Recordings Act of 1995, and the publication of notice of proceedings under section 114(f)(1) of title 17, United States Code, as in effect upon the effective date of that Act, for the determination of royalty payments shall be deemed to have been made for the period beginning on the effective date of that Act and ending on December 1, 2001.

(6) The amendments made by this subsection do not annul, limit, or otherwise impair the rights that are preserved by section 114 of title 17, United States Code, including the rights preserved by subsections (c), (d)(4), and (i) of such section.

* * * * * * *

(c) Scope of Section 112(a) of Title 17 Not Affected. —

Nothing in this section or the amendments made by this section shall affect the scope of section 112(a) of title 17, United States Code, or the entitlement of any person to an exemption thereunder.

* * * * * * *

Sec. 406. Assumption of Contractual Obligations Related to Transfers of Rights in Motion Pictures.

(a) In General. — Part VI of title 28, United States Code, is amended by adding at the end the following new chapter:

"Chapter 180 — Assumption of Certain Contractual Obligations

"Sec. 4001. Assumption of contractual obligations related to transfers of rights in motion pictures.

"§4001. Assumption of contractual obligations related to transfers of rights in motion pictures

"(a) Assumption of Obligations. — (1) In the case of a transfer of copyright ownership under United States law in a motion picture (as the terms 'transfer of copyright ownership' and 'motion picture' are defined in section 101 of title 17) that is produced subject to 1 or more collective bargaining agreements negotiated under the laws of the United States, if the transfer is executed on or after the effective date of this chapter and is not limited to public performance rights, the transfer instrument shall be deemed to incorporate the assumption agreements applicable to the copyright ownership being transferred that are required by the applicable collective bargaining agreement, and the transferee shall be subject to the obligations under each such assumption agreement to make residual payments and provide related notices, accruing after the effective date of the transfer and applicable to the exploitation of the rights transferred, and any remedies under each such assumption agreement for breach of those obligations, as those obligations and remedies are set forth in the applicable collective bargaining agreement, if —

"(A) the transferee knows or has reason to know at the time of the transfer that such collective bargaining agreement was or will be applicable to the motion picture; or

"(B) in the event of a court order confirming an arbitration award against the transferor under the collective bargaining agreement, the transferor does not have the financial ability to satisfy the award within 90 days after the order is issued.

"(2) For purposes of paragraph (1)(A), 'knows or has reason to know' means any of the following:

"(A) Actual knowledge that the collective bargaining agreement was or will be applicable to the motion picture.

"(B)(i) Constructive knowledge that the collective bargaining agreement was or will be applicable to the motion picture, arising from recordation of a document pertaining to copyright in the motion picture under section 205 of title 17 or from publication, at a site available to the public on-line that is operated by the relevant union, of information that identifies the motion picture as subject to a collective bargaining agreement with that union, if the site permits commercially reasonable verification of the date on which the information was available for access.

"(ii) Clause (i) applies only if the transfer referred to in subsection (a)(1) occurs —

"(I) after the motion picture is completed, or

"(II) before the motion picture is completed and -
"(aa) within 18 months before the filing of an application for copyright registration for the motion picture under section 408 of title 17, or
"(bb) if no such application is filed, within 18 months before the first publication of the motion picture in the United States.

"(C) Awareness of other facts and circumstances pertaining to a particular transfer from which it is apparent that the collective bargaining agreement was or will be applicable to the motion picture.

"(b) Scope of Exclusion of Transfers of Public Performance Rights. — For purposes of this section, the exclusion under subsection (a) of transfers of copyright ownership in a motion picture that are limited to public performance rights includes transfers to a terrestrial broadcast station, cable system, or programmer to the extent that the station, system, or programmer is functioning as an exhibitor of the motion picture, either by exhibiting the motion picture on its own network, system, service, or station, or by initiating the transmission of an exhibition that is carried on another network, system, service, or station. When a terrestrial broadcast station, cable system, or programmer, or other transferee, is also functioning otherwise as a distributor or as a producer of the motion picture, the public performance exclusion does not affect any obligations imposed on the transferee to the extent that it is engaging in such functions.

"(c) Exclusion for Grants of Security Interests. — Subsection (a) shall not apply to —

"(1) a transfer of copyright ownership consisting solely of a mortgage, hypothecation, or other security interest; or

"(2) a subsequent transfer of the copyright ownership secured by the security interest described in paragraph (1) by or under the authority of the secured party, including a transfer through the exercise of the secured party's rights or remedies as a secured party, or by a subsequent transferee.

The exclusion under this subsection shall not affect any rights or remedies under law or contract.

"(d) Deferral Pending Resolution of Bona Fide Dispute. — A transferee on which obligations are imposed under subsection (a) by virtue of paragraph (1) of that subsection may elect to defer performance of such obligations that are subject to a bona fide dispute between a union and a prior transferor until that dispute is resolved, except that such deferral shall not stay accrual of any union claims due under an applicable collective bargaining agreement.

"(e) Scope of Obligations Determined by Private Agreement. — Nothing in this section shall expand or diminish the rights, obligations, or remedies of any person under the collective bargaining agreements or assumption agreements referred to in this section.

"(f) Failure to Notify. — If the transferor under subsection (a) fails to notify the transferee under subsection (a) of applicable collective bargaining obligations before the execution of the transfer instrument, and subsection (a) is made applicable to the transferee solely by virtue of subsection (a)(1)(B), the transferor shall be liable to the transferee for any damages suffered by the transferee as a result of the failure to notify.

"(g) Determination of Disputes and Claims. — Any dispute concerning the application of subsections (a) through (f) shall be determined by an action in United States district court, and the court in its discretion may allow the recovery of full costs by or against any party and may also award a reasonable attorney's fee to the prevailing party as part of the costs.

"(h) Study. — The Comptroller General, in consultation with the Register of Copyrights, shall conduct a study of the conditions in the motion picture industry that gave rise to this section, and the impact of this section on the motion picture industry. The Comptroller General shall report the findings of the study to the Congress within 2 years after the effective date of this chapter.".

* * * * * * *

SEC. 407. EFFECTIVE Date.

Except as otherwise provided in this title, this title and the amendments made by this title shall take effect on the date of the enactment of this Act.

* * * * * * *

Title V — Protection of Certain Original Designs

Sec. 501. Short Title.
This Act may be referred to as the "Vessel Hull Design Protection Act".

* * * * * * *

Sec. 505. Effective Date.[2]
The amendments made by sections 502 and 503 shall take effect on the date of the enactment of this Act.[3]

Appendix B · Endnotes

[1]This appendix contains contains provisions from the Digital Millennium Copyright Act (DMCA), Pub. L. No. 105-304, 112 Stat. 2860, that do not amend title 17 of the *United States Code.*

[2]The Intellectual Property and Communications Omnibus Reform Act of 1999 amended section 505 by deleting everything at the end of the sentence, after "Act." Pub. L. No. 106-113, 113 Stat. 1501, app. I at 1501A-521, 593.

[3]Section 502 of the DMCA added chapter 13 to title 17 of the *United States Code.* Section 503 made conforming amendments. The date of enactment of this Act is October 28, 1998.

APPENDIX C THE COPYRIGHT ROYALTY AND DISTRIBUTION REFORM ACT OF 2004[1]

Section 1. Short Title.
This Act may be cited as the "Copyright Royalty and Distribution Reform Act of 2004".

Sec. 2. Reference.
Except as otherwise expressly provided, whenever in this Act an amendment or repeal is expressed in terms of an amendment to, or repeal of, a section or other provision, the reference shall be considered to be made to a section or other provision of title 17, United States Code.

* * * * * * *

Sec. 6. Effective Date and Transition Provisions.[2]

(a) Effective Date. — This Act and the amendments made by this Act shall take effect 6 months after the date of enactment of this Act, except that the Librarian of Congress shall appoint 1 or more interim Copyright Royalty Judges under section 802(d) of title 17, United States Code, as amended by this Act, within 90 days after such date of enactment to carry out the functions of the Copyright Royalty Judges under title 17, United States Code, to the extent that Copyright Royalty Judges provided for in section 801(a) of title 17, United States Code, as amended by this Act, have not been appointed before the end of that 90-day period.

(b) Transition Provisions. —

(1) In general. — Subject to paragraphs (2) and (3), the amendments made by this Act shall not affect any proceedings commenced, petitions filed, or voluntary agreements entered into before the effective date provided in subsection (a) under the provisions of title 17, United States Code, as amended by this Act, and pending on such effective date. Such proceedings shall continue, determinations made in such proceedings, and appeals taken therefrom, as if this Act had not been enacted, and shall continue in effect until modified under title 17, United States Code, as amended by this Act. Such petitions filed and voluntary agreements entered into shall remain in effect as if this Act had not been enacted. For purposes of this paragraph, the Librarian of Congress may determine whether a proceeding has commenced. The Librarian of Congress may terminate any proceeding commenced before the effective date provided in subsection (a) pursuant to chapter 8 of title 17, United States Code, and any proceeding so terminated shall become null and void. In such cases, the Copyright Royalty Judges may initiate a new proceeding in accordance with regulations adopted pursuant to section 803(b)(6) of title 17, United States Code.

(2) Certain royalty rate proceedings. — Notwithstanding paragraph (1), the amendments made by this Act shall not affect proceedings to determine royalty rates pursuant to section 119(c) of title 17, United States Code, that are commenced before January 31, 2006.

(3) Pending proceedings. — Notwithstanding paragraph (1), any proceedings to establish or adjust rates and terms for the statutory licenses under section 114(f)(2) or 112(e) of title 17, United States Code, for a statutory period commencing on or after January 1, 2005, shall be terminated upon the date of enactment of this Act and shall be null and void. The rates and terms in effect under section 114(f)(2) or 112(e) of title 17, United States Code, on December 31, 2004, for new subscription services, eligible nonsubscription services, and services exempt under section 114(d)(1)(C)(iv) of such title, and the rates and terms published in the Federal Register under the authority of the Small Webcaster Settlement Act of 2002 (17 U.S.C. 114 note; Public Law 107-321) (including the amendments made by that Act) for the years 2003 through 2004, as well as any notice and recordkeeping provisions adopted pursuant thereto, shall remain in effect until the later of the first applicable effective date for successor terms and rates specified in section 804(b) (2) or (3)(A) of title 17, United States Code, or such later date as the parties may agree or the Copyright Royalty Judges may establish. For the period commencing January 1, 2005, an eligible small webcaster or a noncommercial webcaster, as defined in the regulations published by the Register of Copyrights pursuant to the Small Webcaster Settlement Act of 2002 (17 U.S.C. 114 note; Public Law 107-321) (including the amendments made by that Act), may elect to be subject to the rates and terms published in those regulations by complying with the procedures governing the election process set forth in those regulations not later than the first date on which the webcaster would be obligated to make a royalty payment for such period. Until successor terms and rates have been established for the period commencing January 1, 2006, licensees shall continue to make royalty payments at the rates and on the terms previously in effect, subject to retroactive adjustment when successor rates and terms for such services are established.

(4) Interim proceedings. — Notwithstanding subsection (a), as soon as practicable after the date of enactment of this Act, the Copyright Royalty Judges or interim Copyright Royalty Judges shall

publish the notice described in section 803(b)(1)(A) of title 17, United States Code, as amended by this Act, to initiate a proceeding to establish or adjust rates and terms for the statutory licenses under section 114(f)(2) or 112(e) of title 17, United States Code, for new subscription services and eligible nonsubscription services for the period commencing January 1, 2006. The Copyright Royalty Judges or Interim Copyright Royalty Judges are authorized to cause that proceeding to take place as provided in subsection (b) of section 803 of that title within the time periods set forth in that subsection. Notwithstanding section 803(c)(1) of that title, the Copyright Royalty Judges shall not be required to issue their determination in that proceeding before the expiration of the statutory rates and terms in effect on December 31, 2004.

(c) Existing Appropriations. — Any funds made available in an appropriations Act to carry out chapter 8 of title 17, United States Code, shall be available to the extent necessary to carry out this section.

Appendix C · Endnotes

[1] This appendix contains provisions from the Copyright Royalty and Distribution Reform Act of 2004, Pub. L. No. 108-419, 118 Stat. 2341, that do not amend title 17 of the *United States Code*.

[2] In 2006, the Copyright Royalty Judges Program Technical Corrections Act amended section 6(b)(1) by substituting "effective date provided in subsection (a)" for "date of enactment of this Act" in the third sentence. Pub. L. No. 109-303, 120 Stat. 1478, 1483.

APPENDIX D THE SATELLITE HOME VIEWER EXTENSION AND REAUTHORIZATION ACT OF 2004[1]

* * * * * * *

Title IX — Satellite Home Viewer Extension and Reauthorization Act of 2004

Section 1 · Short Titles; Table of Contents.

(a) Short Titles. — This title may be cited as the "Satellite Home Viewer Extension and Reauthorization Act of 2004" or the "W. J. (Billy) Tauzin Satellite Television Act of 2004".

* * * * * * *

Title I — Statutory License for Satellite Carriers

Sec. 101 · Extension of Authority.

(a) In General. — Section 4(a) of the Satellite Home Viewer Act of 1994 (17 U.S.C. 119 note; Public Law 103-369; 108 Stat. 3481) is amended by striking "'December 31, 2004" and inserting "'December 31, 2009".

(b) Extension for Certain Subscribers. — Section 119(e) of title 17, United States Code, is amended by striking "'December 31, 2004" and inserting "'December 31, 2009".

* * * * * * *

Sec. 106 · Effect on Certain Proceedings.

Nothing in this title shall modify any remedy imposed on a party that is required by the judgment of a court in any action that was brought before May 1, 2004, against that party for a violation of section 119 of title 17, United States Code.

* * * * * * *

Sec. 109 · Study.

No later than June 30, 2008, the Register of Copyrights shall report to the Committee on the Judiciary of the House of Representatives and the Committee on the Judiciary of the Senate the Register's findings and recommendations on the operation and revision of the statutory licenses under sections 111, 119, and 122 of title 17, United States Code. The report shall include, but not be limited to, the following:

(1) A comparison of the royalties paid by licensees under such sections, including historical rates of increases in these royalties, a comparison between the royalties under each such section and the prices paid in the marketplace for comparable programming.

(2) An analysis of the differences in the terms and conditions of the licenses under such sections, an analysis of whether these differences are required or justified by historical, technological, or regulatory differences that affect the satellite and cable industries, and an analysis of whether the cable or satellite industry is placed in a competitive disadvantage due to these terms and conditions.

(3) An analysis of whether the licenses under such sections are still justified by the bases upon which they were originally created.

(4) An analysis of the correlation, if any, between the royalties, or lack thereof, under such sections and the fees charged to cable and satellite subscribers, addressing whether cable and satellite companies have passed to subscribers any savings realized as a result of the royalty structure and amounts under such sections.

(5) An analysis of issues that may arise with respect to the application of the licenses under such sections to the secondary transmissions of the primary transmissions of network stations and superstations that originate as digital signals, including issues that relate to the application of the unserved household limitations under section 119 of title 17, United States Code, and to the determination of royalties of cable systems and satellite carriers.

Appendix D · Endnote

[1]This appendix contains provisions from the Satellite Home Viewer Extension and Reauthorization Act of 2004, Title IX, Division J of the Consolidated Appropriations Act, 2005, Pub. L. No. 108-447, 118 Stat. 2809, 3393, that do not amend title 17 of the *United States Code*.

APPENDIX E THE INTELLECTUAL PROPERTY PROTECTION AND COURTS AMENDMENTS ACT OF 2004[1]

Section 1 · Short Title.

This Act may be cited as the "Intellectual Property Protection and Courts Amendments Act of 2004".

Title I — Anti-counterfeiting Provisions

Sec. 101 · Short Title.

This title may be cited as the "'Anti-counterfeiting Amendments Act of 2004".

* * * * * * *

Sec. 103 · Other Rights Not Affected.

(a) Chapters 5 and 12 of Title 17; Electronic Transmissions. — The amendments made by this title —

(1) shall not enlarge, diminish, or otherwise affect any liability or limitations on liability under sections 512, 1201 or 1202 of title 17, United States Code; and

(2) shall not be construed to apply —

(A) in any case, to the electronic transmission of a genuine certificate, licensing document, registration card, similar labeling component, or documentation or packaging described in paragraph (4) or (5) of section 2318(b) of title 18, United States Code, as amended by this title; and

(B) in the case of a civil action under section 2318(f) of title 18, United States Code, to the electronic transmission of a counterfeit label or counterfeit documentation or packaging defined in paragraph (1) or (6) of section 2318(b) of title 18, United States Code.

(b) Fair Use. — The amendments made by this title shall not affect the fair use, under section 107 of title 17, United States Code, of a genuine certificate, licensing document, registration card, similar labeling component, or documentation or packaging described in paragraph (4) or (5) of section 2318(b) of title 18, United States Code, as amended by this title.

Title II — Fraudulent Online Identity Sanctions

Sec. 201 · Short Title.

This title may be cited as the "'Fraudulent Online Identity Sanctions Act".

* * * * * * *

Sec. 205 · Construction.

(a) Free Speech and Press. — Nothing in this title shall enlarge or diminish any rights of free speech or of the press for activities related to the registration or use of domain names.

(b) Discretion of Courts in Determining Relief. — Nothing in this title shall restrict the discretion of a court in determining damages or other relief to be assessed against a person found liable for the infringement of intellectual property rights.

(c) Discretion of Courts in Determining Terms of Imprisonment. — Nothing in this title shall be construed to limit the discretion of a court to determine the appropriate term of imprisonment for an offense under applicable law.

Appendix E · Endnote

[1]This appendix contains provisions from the Intellectual Property Protection and Courts Amendments Act of 2004, Pub. L. No. 108-482, 118 Stat. 3912, that do not amend title 17 of the *United States Code*.

APPENDIX F TITLE 18 — CRIMES AND CRIMINAL PROCEDURE, U.S. CODE

Part I — Crimes Chapter 113 — Stolen Property

* * * * * * *

§ 2318 · Trafficking in counterfeit labels, illicit labels, or counterfeit documentation or packaging[1]

(a) Whoever, in any of the circumstances described in subsection (c), knowingly traffics in —

(1) a counterfeit label or illicit label affixed to, enclosing, or accompanying, or designed to be affixed to, enclose, or accompany —

(A) a phonorecord;

(B) a copy of a computer program;

(C) a copy of a motion picture or other audiovisual work;

(D) a copy of a literary work;

(E) a copy of a pictorial, graphic, or sculptural work;

(F) a work of visual art; or

(G) documentation or packaging; or

(2) counterfeit documentation or packaging, shall be fined under this title or imprisoned for not more than 5 years, or both.

(b) As used in this section —

(1) the term "counterfeit label" means an identifying label or container that appears to be genuine, but is not;

(2) the term "traffic" means to transport, transfer or otherwise dispose of, to another, as consideration for anything of value or to make or obtain control of with intent to so transport, transfer or dispose of;

(3) the terms "copy", "phonorecord", "motion picture", "computer program", "audiovisual work", "literary work", "pictorial, graphic, or sculptural work", "sound recording", "work of visual art", and "copyright owner" have, respectively, the meanings given those terms in section 101 (relating to definitions) of title 17;

(4) the term "illicit label" means a genuine certificate, licensing document, registration card, or similar labeling component —

(A) that is used by the copyright owner to verify that a phonorecord, a copy of a computer program, a copy of a motion picture or other audiovisual work, a copy of a literary work, a copy of a pictorial, graphic, or sculptural work, a work of visual art, or documentation or packaging is not counterfeit or infringing of any copyright; and

(B) that is, without the authorization of the copyright owner —

(i) distributed or intended for distribution not in connection with the copy, phonorecord, or work of visual art to which such labeling component was intended to be affixed by the respective copyright owner; or

(ii) in connection with a genuine certificate or licensing document, knowingly falsified in order to designate a higher number of licensed users or copies than authorized by the copyright owner, unless that certificate or document is used by the copyright owner solely for the purpose of monitoring or tracking the copyright owner's distribution channel and not for the purpose of verifying that a copy or phonorecord is noninfringing;

(5) the term "documentation or packaging" means documentation or packaging, in physical form, for a phonorecord, copy of a computer program, copy of a motion picture or other audiovisual work, copy of a literary work, copy of a pictorial, graphic, or sculptural work, or work of visual art; and

(6) the term "counterfeit documentation or packaging" means documentation or packaging that appears to be genuine, but is not.

(c) The circumstances referred to in subsection (a) of this section are —

(1) the offense is committed within the special maritime and territorial jurisdiction of the United States; or within the special aircraft jurisdiction of the United States (as defined in section 46501 of title 49);

(2) the mail or a facility of interstate or foreign commerce is used or intended to be used in the commission of the offense;

(3) the counterfeit label or illicit label is affixed to, encloses, or accompanies, or is designed to be affixed to, enclose, or accompany —

(A) a phonorecord of a copyrighted sound recording or copyrighted musical work;

(B) a copy of a copyrighted computer program;

(C) a copy of a copyrighted motion picture or other audiovisual work;

(D) a copy of a literary work;

(E) a copy of a pictorial, graphic, or sculptural work;

(F) a work of visual art; or

(G) copyrighted documentation or packaging; or

(4) the counterfeited documentation or packaging is copyrighted.

(d) When any person is convicted of any violation of subsection (a), the court in its judgment of conviction shall in addition to the penalty therein prescribed, order the forfeiture and destruction or other disposition of all counterfeit labels or illicit labels and all articles to which counterfeit labels or illicit labels have been affixed or which were intended to have had such labels affixed and of any equipment, device, or material used to manufacture, reproduce, or assemble the counterfeit labels or illicit labels.

(e) Except to the extent they are inconsistent with the provisions of this title, all provisions of section 509, title 17, United States Code, are applicable to violations of subsection (a).

(f) Civil Remedies. —

(1) In general. — Any copyright owner who is injured, or is threatened with injury, by a violation of subsection (a) may bring a civil action in an appropriate United States district court.

(2) Discretion of court. —In any action brought under paragraph (1), the court —

(A) may grant 1 or more temporary or permanent injunctions on such terms as the court determines to be reasonable to prevent or restrain a violation of subsection (a);

(B) at any time while the action is pending, may order the impounding, on such terms as the court determines to be reasonable, of any article that is in the custody or control of the alleged violator and that the court has reasonable cause to believe was involved in a violation of subsection (a); and

(C) may award to the injured party —

(i) reasonable attorney fees and costs; and

(ii)(I) actual damages and any additional profits of the violator, as provided in paragraph (3); or

(II) statutory damages, as provided in paragraph (4).

(3) Actual damages and profits. —

(A) In general. — The injured party is entitled to recover —

(i) the actual damages suffered by the injured party as a result of a violation of subsection (a), as provided in subparagraph (B) of this paragraph; and

(ii) any profits of the violator that are attributable to a violation of subsection (a) and are not taken into account in computing the actual damages.

(B) Calculation of damages. —The court shall calculate actual damages by multiplying —

(i) the value of the phonorecords, copies, or works of visual art which are, or are intended to be, affixed with, enclosed in, or accompanied by any counterfeit labels, illicit labels, or counterfeit documentation or packaging, by

(ii) the number of phonorecords, copies, or works of visual art which are, or are intended to be, affixed with, enclosed in, or accompanied by any counterfeit labels, illicit labels, or counterfeit documentation or packaging.

(C) Definition. — For purposes of this paragraph, the "value" of a phonorecord, copy, or work of visual art is —

(i) in the case of a copyrighted sound recording or copyrighted musical work, the retail value of an authorized phonorecord of that sound recording or musical work;

(ii) in the case of a copyrighted computer program, the retail value of an authorized copy of that computer program;

(iii) in the case of a copyrighted motion picture or other audiovisual work, the retail value of an authorized copy of that motion picture or audiovisual work;

(iv) in the case of a copyrighted literary work, the retail value of an authorized copy of that literary work;

(v) in the case of a pictorial, graphic, or sculptural work, the retail value of an authorized copy of that work; and

(vi) in the case of a work of visual art, the retail value of that work.

(4) Statutory damages. — The injured party may elect, at any time before final judgment is rendered, to recover, instead of actual damages and profits, an award of statutory damages for each violation of subsection (a) in a sum of not less than $2,500 or more than $25,000, as the court considers appropriate.

(5) Subsequent violation. — The court may increase an award of damages under this subsection by 3 times the amount that would otherwise be awarded, as the court considers appropriate, if the court finds that a person has subsequently violated subsection (a) within 3 years after a final judgment was entered against that person for a violation of that subsection.

(6) Limitation on actions. — A civil action may not be commenced under section unless it is commenced within 3 years after the date on which the claimant discovers the violation of subsection (a).

§ 2319 · *Criminal infringement of a copyright*[2]

(a) Any person who violates section 506(a) (relating to criminal offenses) of title 17 shall be punished as provided in subsections (b), (c), and (d) and such penalties shall be in addition to any other provisions of title 17 or any other law.

(b) Any person who commits an offense under section 506 (a)(1)(A) of title 17 —

(1) shall be imprisoned not more than 5 years, or fined in the amount set forth in this title, or both, if the offense consists of the reproduction or distribution, including by electronic means, during any 180-day period, of at least 10 copies or phonorecords, of 1 or more copyrighted works, which have a total retail value of more than $2,500;

(2) shall be imprisoned not more than 10 years, or fined in the amount set forth in this title, or both, if the offense is a second or subsequent offense under paragraph (1); and

(3) shall be imprisoned not more than 1 year, or fined in the amount set forth in this title, or both, in any other case.

(c) Any person who commits an offense under section 506(a)(1)(B) of title 17 —

(1) shall be imprisoned not more than 3 years, or fined in the amount set forth in this title, or both, if the offense consists of the reproduction or distribution of 10 or more copies or phonorecords of 1 or more copyrighted works, which have a total retail value of $2,500 or more;

(2) shall be imprisoned not more than 6 years, or fined in the amount set forth in this title, or both, if the offense is a second or subsequent offense under paragraph (1); and

(3) shall be imprisoned not more than 1 year, or fined in the amount set forth in this title, or both, if the offense consists of the reproduction or distribution of 1 or more copies or phonorecords of 1 or more copyrighted works, which have a total retail value of more than $1,000.

(d) Any person who commits an offense under section 506(a)(1)(C) of title 17 —

(1) shall be imprisoned not more than 3 years, fined under this title, or both;

(2) shall be imprisoned not more than 5 years, fined under this title, or both, if the offense was committed for purposes of commercial advantage or private financial gain;

(3) shall be imprisoned not more than 6 years, fined under this title, or both, if the offense is a second or subsequent offense; and

(4) shall be imprisoned not more than 10 years, fined under this title, or both, if the offense is a second or subsequent offense under paragraph (2).

(e) (1) During preparation of the presentence report pursuant to Rule 32(c) of the Federal Rules of Criminal Procedure, victims of the offense shall be permitted to submit, and the probation officer shall receive, a victim impact statement that identifies the victim of the offense and the extent and scope of the injury and loss suffered by the victim, including the estimated economic impact of the offense on that victim.

(2) Persons permitted to submit victim impact statements shall include —

   (A) producers and sellers of legitimate works affected by conduct involved in the offense;

   (B) holders of intellectual property rights in such works; and

   (C) the legal representatives of such producers, sellers, and holders.

(f) As used in this section —

   (1) the terms "phonorecord" and "copies" have, respectively, the meanings set forth in section 101 (relating to definitions) of title 17;

   (2) the terms "reproduction" and "distribution" refer to the exclusive rights of a copyright owner under clauses (1) and (3) respectively of section 106 (relating to exclusive rights in copyrighted works), as limited by sections 107 through 122, of title 17;

   (3) the term "financial gain" has the meaning given the term in section 101 of title 17; and

   (4) the term "work being prepared for commercial distribution" has the meaning given the term in section 506(a) of title 17.

2319A · *Unauthorized fixation of and trafficking in sound recordings and music videos of live musical performances*[3]

(a) Offense. — Whoever, without the consent of the performer or performers involved, knowingly and for purposes of commercial advantage or private financial gain —

   (1) fixes the sounds or sounds and images of a live musical performance in a copy or phonorecord, or reproduces copies or phonorecords of such a performance from an unauthorized fixation;

   (2) transmits or otherwise communicates to the public the sounds or sounds and images of a live musical performance; or

   (3) distributes or offers to distribute, sells or offers to sell, rents or offers to rent, or traffics in any copy or phonorecord fixed as described in paragraph (1), regardless of whether the fixations occurred in the United States;

shall be imprisoned for not more than 5 years or fined in the amount set forth in this title, or both, or if the offense is a second or subsequent offense, shall be imprisoned for not more than 10 years or fined in the amount set forth in this title, or both.

(b) Forfeiture and Destruction. — When a person is convicted of a violation of subsection (a), the court shall order the forfeiture and destruction of any copies or phonorecords created in violation thereof, as well as any plates, molds, matrices, masters, tapes, and film negatives by means of which such copies or phonorecords may be made. The court may also, in its discretion, order the forfeiture and destruction of any other equipment by means of which such copies or phonorecords may be reproduced, taking into account the nature, scope, and proportionality of the use of the equipment in the offense.

(c) Seizure and Forfeiture. — If copies or phonorecords of sounds or sounds and images of a live musical performance are fixed outside of the United States without the consent of the performer or performers involved, such copies or phonorecords are subject to seizure and forfeiture in the United States in the same manner as property imported in violation of the customs laws. The Secretary of the Treasury shall, not later than 60 days after the date of the enactment of the Uruguay Round Agreements Act, issue regulations to carry out this subsection, including regulations by which any performer may, upon payment of a specified fee, be entitled to notification by the United States Customs Service of the importation of copies or phonorecords that appear to consist of unauthorized fixations of the sounds or sounds and images of a live musical performance.

(d) Victim Impact Statement. —

(1) During preparation of the presentence report pursuant to Rule 32(c) of the Federal Rules of Criminal Procedure, victims of the offense shall be permitted to submit, and the probation officer shall receive, a victim impact statement that identifies the victim of the offense and the extent and scope of the injury and loss suffered by the victim, including the estimated economic impact of the offense on that victim.

(2) Persons permitted to submit victim impact statements shall include —

(A) producers and sellers of legitimate works affected by conduct involved in the offense;

(B) holders of intellectual property rights in such works; and

(C) the legal representatives of such producers, sellers, and holders.

(e) Definitions. — As used in this section —

(1) the terms "copy", "fixed", "musical work", "phonorecord", "reproduce", "sound recordings", and "transmit" mean those terms within the meaning of title 17; and

(2) the term "traffic in" means transport, transfer, or otherwise dispose of, to another, as consideration for anything of value, or make or obtain control of with intent to transport, transfer, or dispose of.

(f) Applicability. — This section shall apply to any Act or Acts that occur on or after the date of the enactment of the Uruguay Round Agreements Act.[4]

§ 2319B · *Unauthorized recording of Motion pictures in a Motion picture exhibition facility*[5]

(a) Offense. — Any person who, without the authorization of the copyright owner, knowingly uses or attempts to use an audiovisual recording device to transmit or make a copy of a motion picture or other audiovisual work protected under title 17, or any part thereof, from a performance of such work in a motion picture exhibition facility, shall —

(1) be imprisoned for not more than 3 years, fined under this title, or both; or

(2) if the offense is a second or subsequent offense, be imprisoned for no more than 6 years, fined under this title, or both.

The possession by a person of an audiovisual recording device in a motion picture exhibition facility may be considered as evidence in any proceeding to determine whether that person committed an offense under this subsection, but shall not, by itself, be sufficient to support a conviction of that person for such offense.

(b) Forfeiture and Destruction. — When a person is convicted of a violation of subsection (a), the court in its judgment of conviction shall, in addition to any penalty provided, order the forfeiture and destruction or other disposition of all unauthorized copies of motion pictures or other audiovisual works protected under title 17, or parts thereof, and any audiovisual recording devices or other equipment used in connection with the offense.

(c) Authorized Activities. — This section does not prevent any lawfully authorized investigative, protective, or intelligence activity by an officer, agent, or employee of the United States, a State, or a political subdivision of a State, or by a person acting under a contract with the United States, a State, or a political subdivision of a State.

(d) Immunity for Theaters. — With reasonable cause, the owner or lessee of a motion picture exhibition facility where a motion picture or other audiovisual work is being exhibited, the authorized agent or employee of such owner or lessee, the licensor of the motion picture or other audiovisual work being exhibited, or the agent or employee of such licensor —

   (1) may detain, in a reasonable manner and for a reasonable time, any person suspected of a violation of this section with respect to that motion picture or audiovisual work for the purpose of questioning or summoning a law enforcement officer; and

   (2) shall not be held liable in any civil or criminal action arising out of a detention under paragraph (1).

(e) Victim Impact Statement. —

   (1) In general. — During the preparation of the presentence report under rule 32(c) of the Federal Rules of Criminal Procedure, victims of an offense under this section shall be permitted to submit to the probation officer a victim impact statement that identifies the victim of the offense and the extent and scope of the injury and loss suffered by the victim, including the estimated economic impact of the offense on that victim.

   (2) Contents. — A victim impact statement submitted under this subsection shall include:

      (A) producers and sellers of legitimate works affected by conduct involved in the offense;

      (B) holders of intellectual property rights in the works described in subparagraph (A); and

      (C) the legal representatives of such producers, sellers, and holders.

(f) State Law Not Preempted. — Nothing in this section may be construed to annul or limit any rights or remedies under the laws of any State.

(g) Definitions. — In this section, the following definitions shall apply:

(1) Title 17 definitions. — The terms "audiovisual work", "copy", "copyright owner", "motion picture", "motion picture exhibition facility", and "transmit" have, respectively, the meanings given those terms in section 101 of title 17.

(2) Audiovisual recording device. — The term "audiovisual recording device" means a digital or analog photographic or video camera, or any other technology or device capable of enabling the recording or transmission of a copyrighted motion picture or other audiovisual work, or any part thereof, regardless of whether audiovisual recording is the sole or primary purpose of the device.

Appendix F · Endnotes

[1]In 1962, section 2318, entitled "Transportation, sale, or receipt of phonograph records bearing forged or counterfeit labels," was added to title 18 of the *United States Code*. Pub. L. No. 87-773, 76 Stat. 775. In 1974, section 2318 was amended to change the penalties. Pub. L. No. 93-573, 88 Stat. 1873. The Copyright Act of 1976 revised section 2318 with an amendment in the nature of a substitute. Pub. L. No. 94-553, 90 Stat. 2541, 2600. The Piracy and Counterfeiting Amendments Act of 1982 again revised section 2318 with an amendment in the nature of a substitute that included a new title, "Trafficking in counterfeit labels for phonorecords, and copies of motion pictures or other audiovisual works." Pub. L. No. 97-180, 96 Stat. 91. The Crime Control Act of 1990 made a technical amendment to section 2318 to delete the comma after "phonorecords" in the title. Pub. L. No. 101-647, 104 Stat. 4789, 4928. In 1994, section 2318(c)(1) was amended by inserting "section 46501 of title 49" in lieu of "section 101 of the Federal Aviation Act of 1958. Pub. L. No. 103-272, 108 Stat. 745, 1374. The Violent Crime Control and Law Enforcement Act of 1994 amended section 2318(a) by inserting "under this title" in lieu of "not more than $250,000." Pub. L. No. 103-322, 108 Stat. 1796, 2148. (As provided in 18 USC §3571, the maximum fine for an individual is $250,000, and the maximum fine for an organization is $500,000.)

The Anticounterfeiting Consumer Protection Act of 1996 amended section 2318 by changing the title, by amending subsection (a) to insert "a computer program or documentation" through to "knowingly traffics in counterfeit documentation or packaging for a computer program" in lieu of "a motion picture or other audiovisual work" and by amending subsection (b)(3) to insert "computer program" after "motion picture." Pub. L. No. 104-153, 110 Stat. 1386. The Act also amended section 2318(c) by inserting "a copy of a copyrighted computer program or copyrighted documentation or packaging for a computer program" into paragraph (3) and by adding paragraph (4). *Id*. at 1387.

The Anti-counterfeiting Amendments Act of 2004 amended section 2318 by changing its title, by amending subsection 2318(a) in its entirety; and by amending paragraph 2318(c)(3) in its entirety. Pub. L. No. 108-482, 118 Stat. 3912-3913. It amended paragraph 2318(c)(4) by deleting "for a computer program" after "packaging." *Id*. at 3914. It amended subsection 2318(d) by inserting "or illicit labels" after "counterfeit labels," wherever it appears and by inserting the text at the end of the sentence, after "such labels affixed." *Id*. The Act also added a new subsection (f). *Id*.

[2]The Piracy and Counterfeiting Amendments Act of 1982 added section 2319 to title 18 of the *United States Code*. This section was entitled "Criminal infringement of a copyright." Pub. L. No. 97-180, 96 Stat. 91, 92. In 1992, section 2319 was amended by substituting a new subsection (b), by deleting "sound recording," "motion picture" and "audiovisual work" from subsection (c)(1) and by substituting "120" for "118" in subsection (c)(2). Pub. L. No. 102-561, 106 Stat. 4233. In 1997, a technical amendment corrected the spelling of "last" in subsection (b)(1) to "least." Pub. L. No. 105-80, 111 Stat. 1529, 1536.

In 1997, the No Electronic Theft Act amended section 2319 of title 18 as follows: 1) in subsection (a) by inserting "and (c)" after "subsection (b),"; 2) in subsection (b), in the matter preceding paragraph (1), by inserting "section 506(a)(1) of title 17" in lieu of "subsection (a) of this section,"; 3) in subsection (b)(1) by inserting "including by electronic means" and by inserting "which have a total retail value" in lieu of "with a retail value," 4) by redesignating subsection (c) as subsection (e); and 5) by adding new subsections (c) and (d). Pub. L. No. 105-147, 111 Stat. 2678. The Act also directed the United States Sentencing Commission to "ensure that the applicable guideline range for a defendant convicted of a crime against intellectual property . . . is sufficiently stringent to deter such a crime" and to "ensure that the guidelines provide for consideration of the retail value and quantity of the items with respect to which the crime against intellectual property was committed." *Id*. See also endnote 4, chapter 5, *supra*.

The Intellectual Property and High Technology Technical Amendments Act of 2002 amended paragraph (2) of section 2319(e) by substituting sections "107 through 122" for "107 through 120." Pub. L. No. 107-273, 116 Stat. 1758, 1910.

The Artists' Rights and Theft Prevention Act of 2005 amended the beginning of the first sentence of 5 U.S.C. 2319(a) by substituting "Any person who" in lieu of "Whoever." Pub. L. No. 109-9, 119 Stat. 218, 220-221. It amended subsection 2319(a) by substituting "subsections (b), (c) and (d)" in lieu of "subsections (b) and (c). *Id*. at 221. It amended the first line of subsection 2319(b) by inserting "section 506(a)(1)(A)" in lieu of "section 506(a)(1)." *Id*. The Act amended the first line of subsection 2319(c) by inserting "section 506(a)(1)(B) of title 17" in lieu of "section 506(a)(2) of title 17, United States Code." Id. It also amended subsection (e) by adding a new paragraph (3). Id. Finally, the Act amended section 2319 by adding a new subsection (d) and redesignating the following subsections accordingly, as (e) and (f). *Id*.

[3]In 1994, the Uruguay Round Agreements Act added section 2319A to title 18 of the *United States Code*. This section was entitled "Unauthorized fixation of and trafficking in sound recordings and music videos of live musical performances." Pub. L. No. 103-465, 108 Stat. 4809, 4974. In 1997, the No Electronic Theft Act amended section 2319A by redesignating subsections (d) and (e) as subsections (e) and (f), respectively, and by adding subsection (d). Pub. L. No. 105-147, 111 Stat. 2678. See also endnote 2, *supra*, regarding the United States Sentencing Commission.

[4]The Uruguay Round Agreements Act was enacted on December 8, 1994.

[5]The Artists' Rights and Theft Prevention Act of 2005 added a new section 2319B to title 5 of the *United States Code*. Pub. L. No. 109-9, 119 Stat. 218.6.

APPENDIX G TITLE 28 — JUDICIARY AND JUDICIAL PROCEDURE, U.S. CODE

Part IV — Jurisdiction and Venue Chapter 85 — District Courts; Jurisdiction

* * * * * * *

§ 1338 · Patents, plant variety protection, copyrights, mask works, designs, trademarks, and unfair competition[1]

(a) The district courts shall have original jurisdiction of any civil action arising under any Act of Congress relating to patents, plant variety protection, copyrights and trademarks. Such jurisdiction shall be exclusive of the courts of the states in patent, plant variety protection and copyright cases.

(b) The district courts shall have original jurisdiction of any civil action asserting a claim of unfair competition when joined with a substantial and related claim under the copyright, patent, plant variety protection or trademark laws.

(c) Subsections (a) and (b) apply to exclusive rights in mask works under chapter 9 of title 17, and to exclusive rights in designs under chapter 13 of title 17, to the same extent as such subsections apply to copyrights.

* * * * * * *

Chapter 87 — District Courts; Venue

* * * * * * *

§ 1400 · Patents and copyrights, mask works, and designs[2]

* * * * * * *

(a) Civil actions, suits, or proceedings arising under any Act of Congress relating to copyrights or exclusive rights in mask works or designs may be instituted in the district in which the defendant or his agent resides or may be found.

(b) Any civil action for patent infringement may be brought in the judicial district where the defendant resides, or where the defendant has committed acts of infringement and has a regular and established place of business.

* * * * * * *

Chapter 91 — United States Court of Federal Claims

* * * * * * *

§ 1498 · Patent and copyright cases[3]

* * * * * * *

(b) Hereafter, whenever the copyright in any work protected under the copyright laws of the United States shall be infringed by the United States, by a corporation owned or controlled by the United States, or by a contractor, subcontractor, or any person, firm, or corporation acting for the Government and with the authorization or consent of the Government, the exclusive action which may be brought for such infringement shall be an action by the copyright owner against the United States in the Court of Federal Claims for the recovery of his reasonable and entire compensation as damages for such infringement, including the minimum statutory damages as set forth in section 504(c) of title 17, United States Code: Provided, That a Government employee shall have a right of action against the Government under this subsection except where he was in a position to order, influence, or induce use of the copyrighted work by the Government: Provided, however, That this subsection shall not confer a right of action on any copyright owner or any assignee of such owner with respect to any copyrighted work prepared by a person while in the employment or service of the United States, where the copyrighted work was prepared as a part of the official functions of the employee, or in the preparation of which Government time, material, or facilities were used: And provided further, That before such action against the United States has been instituted the appropriate corporation owned or controlled by the United States or the head of the appropriate department or agency of the Government, as the case may be, is authorized to enter into an agreement with the copyright owner in full settlement and compromise for the damages accruing to him by reason of such infringement and to settle the claim administratively out of available appropriations.

Except as otherwise provided by law, no recovery shall be had for any infringement of a copyright covered by this subsection committed more than three years prior to the filing of the complaint or counterclaim for infringement in the action, except that the period between the date of receipt of a written claim for compensation by the Department or agency of the Government or corporation owned or controlled by the United States, as the case may be, having authority to settle such claim and the date of mailing by the Government of a notice to the claimant that his claim has been denied shall not be counted as a part of the three years, unless suit is brought before the last-mentioned date.

(c) The provisions of this section shall not apply to any claim arising in a foreign country.

* * * * * * *

(e) Subsections (b) and (c) of this section apply to exclusive rights in mask works under chapter 9 of title 17, and to exclusive rights in designs under chapter 13 of title 17, to the same extent as such subsections apply to copyrights.

Appendix G · Endnotes

[1]In 1948, section 1338, entitled "Patents, copyrights, trademarks, and unfair competition," was added to title 28 of the *United States Code*. Pub. L. No. 773, 62 Stat. 869, 931. In 1970, the title of section 1338 and the text of subsection (b) were amended to insert "plant variety protection " after "patent." Pub. L. No. 91-577, 84 Stat. 1542, 1559. In 1988, the Judicial Improvements and Access to Justice Act amended section 1338 by adding "mask works" to the title and by adding subsection (c). Pub. L. No. 100-702, 102 Stat. 4642, 4671. In 1998, the Digital Millennium Copyright Act (DMCA) amended the title by inserting "designs," after "mask works." Pub. L. No. 105-304, 112 Stat. 2860, 2917. The DMCA also amended subsection (c) by inserting ", and to exclusive rights in designs under chapter 13 of title 17," after "chapter 9 of title 17." *Id.* In 1999, the Anticybersquatting Consumer Protection Act amended section 1338 throughout to change "trade-mark" and "trade-marks" to "trademark" and "trademarks," respectively. Pub. L. No. 106-113, 113 Stat. 1501, 1501A-551, app I.

[2]In 1948, section 1400, entitled "Patents and copyrights," was added to title 28 of the *United States Code*. Pub. L. No. 773, 62 Stat. 869, 936. In 1988, the Judicial Improvements and Access to Justice Act amended subsection (a) by inserting "or exclusive rights in mask works" after "copyrights." Pub. L. No. 100-702, 102 Stat. 4642, 4671. In 1998, the Digital Millenium Copyright Act (DMCA) amended subsection (a) to insert "or designs" after "mask works." Pub. L. No. 105-304, 112 Stat. 2860, 2917. The DMCA also amended the section heading to "Patents and copyrights, mask works, and designs." This amendment included a period at the end, after "designs." In 1999, a technical amendment deleted the period. Pub. L. No. 106-44, 113 Stat. 221, 223.

[3]In 1960, section 1498 of the *United States Code* was amended to add subsections (b) and (c). Pub. L. No. 86-726, 74 Stat. 855. The Copyright Act of 1976 amended section 1498(b) to insert "section 504(c) of title 17" in lieu of "section 101(b) of title 17." Pub. L. No. 94-553, 90 Stat. 2541, 2599. The Federal Courts Improvement Act of 1982 amended section 1498(a) to insert "United States Claims Court" in lieu of "Court of Claims" and, in subsections (b) and (d), to insert "Claims Court" in lieu of "Court of Claims," wherever it appeared. Pub. L. No. 97-164, 96 Stat. 25, 40. In 1988, the Judicial Improvements and Access to Justice Act amended section 1498 by adding subsection (e). Pub. L. No. 100-702, 102 Stat. 4642, 4671. The Federal Courts Administration Act of 1992 amended section 1498 by inserting "United States Court of Federal Claims" in lieu of "United States Claims Court," wherever it appeared, and by inserting "Court of Federal Claims" in lieu of "Claims Court," wherever it appeared. Pub. L. No. 102-572, 106 Stat. 4506, 4516. In 1997, the No Electronic Theft (NET) Act amended section 1498(b) to insert "action which may be brought for such infringement shall be an action by the copyright owner" in lieu of "remedy of the owner of such copyright shall be by action." Pub. L.

No. 105-147, 111 Stat. 2678, 2680. In 1998, the Digital Millennium Copyright Act amended subsection (e) by inserting, ", and to exclusive rights in designs under chapter 13 of title 17," after "chapter 9 of title 17." Pub. L. No. 105-304, 112 Stat. 2860, 2917.

APPENDIX H TITLE 44 — PUBLIC PRINTING AND DOCUMENTS, U.S. CODE

Chapter 21 — National Archives and Records Administration

* * * * * * *

§ 2117 · Limitation on liability[1]

When letters and other intellectual productions (exclusive of patented material, published works under copyright protection, and unpublished works for which copyright registration has been made) come into the custody or possession of the Archivist, the United States or its agents are not liable for infringement of copyright or analogous rights arising out of use of the materials for display, inspection, research, reproduction, or other purposes.

Appendix H · Endnote

[1]In 1968, this section, originally designated as section 2113, which is entitled "Limitation on liability," was added to title 44 of the *United States Code*. Pub. L. No. 90-620, 82 Stat. 1238, 1291. The 1976 Copyright Act amended section 2113 in its entirety. Pub. L. No. 94-553, 90 Stat. 2541, 2599. The National Archives and Records Administration Act of 1984 amended section 2113 by redesignating it as section 2117 and by inserting "Archivist" in lieu of "Administrator of General Services." Pub. L. No. 98-497, 98 Stat. 2280 and 2286.

APPENDIX I BERNE CONVENTION IMPLEMENTATION ACT OF 1988[1]

Sec.1 · Short Title and References to Title 17, United States Code.

(a) Short Title. — This Act, may be cited as the "Berne Convention Implementation Act of 1988".

(b) References to Title 17, United States Code. — Whenever in this Act an amendment or repeal is expressed in terms of an amendment to or a repeal of a section or other provision, the reference shall be considered to be made to a section or other provision of title 17, United States Code.

Sec. 2 · Declarations.

The Congress makes the following declarations:

(1) The Convention for the Protection of Literary and Artistic Works, signed at Berne, Switzerland, on September 9, 1886, and all acts, protocols, and revisions thereto (hereafter in this Act referred to as the "Berne Convention") are not self-executing under the Constitution and laws of the United States.

(2) The obligations of the United States under the Berne Convention may be performed only pursuant to appropriate domestic law.

(3) The amendments made by this Act, together with the law as it exists on the date of the enactment of this Act, satisfy the obligations of the United States in adhering to the Berne Convention and no further rights or interests shall be recognized or created for that purpose.

Sec. 3 · Construction of the Berne Convention.

(a) Relationship with Domestic Law. — The provisions of the Berne Convention —

(1) shall be given effect under title 17, as amended by this Act, and any other relevant provision of Federal or State law, including the common law; and

(2) shall not be enforceable in any action brought pursuant to the provisions of the Berne Convention itself.

(b) Certain Rights Not Affected. — The provisions of the Berne Convention, the adherence of the United States thereto, and satisfaction of United States obligations thereunder, do not expand or reduce any right of an author of a work, whether claimed under Federal, State, or the common law —

(1) to claim authorship of the work; or

(2) to object to any distortion, mutilation, or other modification of, or other derogatory action in relation to, the work, that would prejudice the author's honor or reputation.

* * * * * * *

Sec. 12 · Works in the public domain.

Title 17, United States Code, as amended by this Act, does not provide copyright protection for any work that is in the public domain in the United States.

Sec. 13 · Effective date: effect on pending cases.

(a) Effective Date. — This Act and the amendments made by this Act take effect on the date on which the Berne Convention (as defined in section 101 of title 17, United States Code) enters into force with respect to the United States.[2]

(b) Effect on Pending Cases. — Any cause of action arising under title 17, United States Code, before the effective date of this Act shall be governed by the provisions of such title as in effect when the cause of action arose.

Appendix I · Endnotes

[1]This appendix consists of provisions of the Berne Convention Implementation Act of 1988, Pub. L. No. 100-568, 102 Stat. 2853, that do not amend title 17 of the *United States Code*.

[2]The Berne Convention entered into force in the United States on March 1, 1989.

APPENDIX J URUGUAY ROUND AGREEMENTS ACT OF 1994[1]

Sec. 1. Short Title and Table of Contents

(a) Short Title. — This act may be cited as the "Uruguay Round Agreements Act".

* * * * * * *

Sec. 2. Definitions.

For purposes of this Act:

(1) GATT 1947; GATT 1994. —

(A) GATT 1947. — The term "GATT 1947" means the General Agreement on Tariffs and Trade, dated October 30, 1947, annexed to the Final Act Adopted at the Conclusion of the Second Session of the Preparatory Committee of the United Nations Conference on Trade and Employment, as subsequently rectified, amended, or modified by the terms of legal instruments which have entered into force before the date of entry into force of the WTO Agreement.

(B) GATT 1994. — The term "GATT 1994" means the General Agreement on Tariffs and Trade annexed to the WTO Agreement.

(2) HTS. — The term "HTS" means the Harmonized Tariff Schedule of the United States.

(3) International trade commission. — The term "International Trade Commission" means the United States International Trade Commission.

(4) Multilateral trade agreement. — The term "multilateral trade agreement" means an agreement described in section 101(d) of this Act (other than an agreement described in paragraph (17) or (18) of such section).

(5) Schedule XX. - The term "Schedule XX" means Schedule XX — United States of America annexed to the Marrakesh Protocol to the GATT 1994.

(6) Trade representative. — The term "Trade Representative" means the United States Trade Representative.

(7) Uruguay round agreements. — The term "Uruguay Round Agreements" means the agreements approved by the Congress under section 101(a)(1).

(8) World trade organization and WTO. — The terms "World Trade Organization" and "WTO" mean the organization established pursuant to the WTO Agreement.

(9) WTO agreement. — The term "WTO Agreement" means the Agreement Establishing the World Trade Organization entered into on April 15, 1994.

(10) WTO member and WTO member country. — The terms "WTO member" and "WTO member country" mean a state, or separate customs territory (within the meaning of Article XII of the WTO Agreement), with respect to which the United States applies the WTO Agreement.

Title I — Approval of, and General Provisions Relating to, the Uruguay Round Agreements Subtitle A — Approval of Agreements and Related Provisions

Sec. 101 · Approval and entry into force of the Uruguay Round Agreements.

(a) Approval of Agreements and Statement of Administrative Action. — Pursuant to section 1103 of the Omnibus Trade and Competitiveness Act of 1988 (19 U.S.C. 2903) and section 151 of the Trade Act of 1974 (19 U.S.C. 2191), the Congress approves —

(1) the trade agreements described in subsection (d) resulting from the Uruguay Round of multilateral trade negotiations under the auspices of the General Agreement on Tariffs and Trade, entered into on April 15, 1994, and submitted to the Congress on September 27, 1994; and

(2) the statement of administrative action proposed to implement the agreements that was submitted to the Congress on September 27, 1994.

(b) Entry into Force. — At such time as the President determines that a sufficient number of foreign countries are accepting the obligations of the Uruguay Round Agreements, in accordance with article XIV of the WTO Agreement, to ensure the effective operation of, and adequate benefits for the United States under, those Agreements, the President may accept the Uruguay Round Agreements and implement article VIII of the WTO Agreement.

(c) Authorization of Appropriations. — There are authorized to be appropriated annually such sums as may be necessary for the payment by the United States of its share of the expenses of the WTO.

(d) Trade Agreements to Which This Act Applies. — Subsection (a) applies to the WTO Agreement and to the following agreements annexed to that Agreement:

(1) The General Agreement on Tariffs and Trade 1994.

(2) The Agreement on Agriculture.

(3) The Agreement on the Application of Sanitary and Phytosanitary Measures.

(4) The Agreement on Textiles and Clothing.

(5) The Agreement on Technical Barriers to Trade.

(6) The Agreement on Trade-Related Investment Measures.

(7) The Agreement on Implementation of Article VI of the General Agreement on Tariffs and Trade 1994.

(8) The Agreement on Implementation of Article VII of the General Agreement on Tariffs and Trade 1994.

(9) The Agreement on Preshipment Inspection.

(10) The Agreement on Rules of Origin.

(11) The Agreement on Import Licensing Procedures.

(12) The Agreement on Subsidies and Countervailing Measures.

(13) The Agreement on Safeguards.

(14) The General Agreement on Trade in Services.

(15) The Agreement on Trade-Related Aspects of Intellectual Property Rights.

(16) The Understanding on Rules and Procedures Governing the Settlement of Disputes.

(17) The Agreement on Government Procurement.

(18) The International Bovine Meat Agreement.

Sec. 102 · Relationship of the agreements to United States law and state law.

(a) Relationship of Agreements to United States Law. —

(1) United States law to prevail in conflict. — No provision of any of the Uruguay Round Agreements, nor the application of any such provision to any person or circumstance, that is inconsistent with any law of the United States shall have effect.

(2) Construction. — Nothing in this Act shall be construed

(A) to amend or modify any law of the United States, including any law relating to —

(i) the protection of human, animal, or plant life or health,

(ii) the protection of the environment, or

(iii) worker safety, or

(B) to limit any authority conferred under any law of the United States, including section 301 of the Trade Act of 1974,

unless specifically provided for in this Act.

(b) Relationship of Agreements to State Law. —

(1) Federal-State Consultation. —

(A) In General. — Upon the enactment of this Act, the President shall, through the intergovernmental policy advisory committees on trade established under section 306(c)(2)(A) of the Trade and Tariff Act of 1984 (19 U.S.C. 2114c(2)(A)), consult with the States for the purpose of achieving conformity of State laws and practices with the Uruguay Round Agreements.

(B) Federal-State Consultation Process. — The Trade Representative shall establish within the Office of the United States Trade Representative a Federal-State consultation process for addressing issues relating to the Uruguay Round Agreements that directly relate to, or will potentially have a direct effect on, the States. The Federal-State consultation process shall include procedures under which —

(i) the States will be informed on a continuing basis of matters under the Uruguay Round Agreements that directly relate to, or will potentially have a direct impact on, the States;

(ii) the States will be provided an opportunity to submit, on a continuing basis, to the Trade Representative information and advice with respect to matters referred to in clause (i); and

(iii) the Trade Representative will take into account the information and advice received from the States under clause (ii) when formulating United States positions regarding matters referred to in clause (i).

The Federal Advisory Committee Act (5 U.S.C. App.) shall not apply to the Federal-State consultation process established by this paragraph.

(C) Federal-State Cooperation in WTO Dispute Settlement. —

(i) When a WTO member requests consultations with the United States under Article 4 of the Understanding on Rules and Procedures Governing the Settlement of Disputes referred to in section 101(d)(16) (hereafter in this subsection referred to as the "Dispute Settlement Understanding") concerning whether the law of a State is inconsistent with the obligations undertaken by the United States in any of the Uruguay Round Agreements, the Trade Representative shall notify the Governor of the State or the Governor's designee, and the chief legal officer of the jurisdiction whose law is the subject of the consultations, as soon as possible after the request is received, but in no event later than 7 days thereafter.

(ii) Not later than 30 days after receiving such a request for consultations, the Trade Representative shall consult with representatives of the State concerned regarding the matter. If the consultations involve the laws of a large number of States, the Trade Representative may consult with an appropriate group of representatives of the States concerned, as determined by those States.

(iii) The Trade Representative shall make every effort to ensure that the State concerned is involved in the development of the position of the United States at each stage of the consultations and each subsequent stage of dispute settlement proceedings regarding the matter. In particular, the Trade Representative shall —

(I) notify the State concerned not later than 7 days after a WTO member requests the establishment of a dispute settlement panel or gives notice of the WTO member's decision to appeal a report by a dispute settlement panel regarding the matter; and

(II) provide the State concerned with the opportunity to advise and assist the Trade Representative in the preparation of factual information and argumentation for any written or oral presentations by the United States in consultations or in proceedings of a panel or the Appellate Body regarding the matter.

(iv) If a dispute settlement panel or the Appellate Body finds that the law of a State is inconsistent with any of the Uruguay Round Agreements, the Trade Representative shall consult with the State concerned in an effort to develop a mutually agreeable response to the report of the panel or the Appellate Body and shall make every effort to ensure that the State concerned is involved in the development of the United States position regarding the response.

(D) Notice to States Regarding Consultations on Foreign Subcentral Government Laws. —

(i) Subject to clause (ii), the Trade Representative shall, at least 30 days before making a request for consultations under Article 4 of the Dispute Settlement Understanding regarding a subcentral government measure of another WTO member, notify, and solicit the views of, appropriate representatives of each State regarding the matter.

(ii) In exigent circumstances clause (i) shall not apply, in which case the Trade Representative shall notify the appropriate representatives of each State not later than 3 days after making the request for consultations referred to in clause (i).

(2) Legal Challenge. —

(A) In General. — No State law, or the application of such a State law, may be declared invalid as to any person or circumstance on the ground that the provision or application is inconsistent with any of the Uruguay Round Agreements, except in an action brought by the United States for the purpose of declaring such law or application invalid.

(B) Procedures Governing Action. — In any action described in subparagraph (A) that is brought by the United States against a State or any subdivision thereof

(i) a report of a dispute settlement panel or the Appellate Body convened under the Dispute Settlement Understanding regarding the State law, or the law of any political subdivision thereof, shall not be considered as binding or otherwise accorded deference;

(ii) the United States shall have the burden of proving that the law that is the subject of the action, or the application of that law, is inconsistent with the agreement in question;

(iii) any State whose interests may be impaired or impeded in the action shall have the unconditional right to intervene in the action as a party, and the United States shall be entitled to amend its complaint to include a claim or cross-claim concerning the law of a State that so intervenes; and

(iv) any State law that is declared invalid shall not be deemed to have been invalid in its application during any period before the court's judgment becomes final and all timely appeals, including discretionary review, of such judgment are exhausted.

(C) Reports to Congressional Committees. — At least 30 days before the United States brings an action described in subparagraph (A), the Trade Representative shall provide a report to the Committee on Ways and Means of the House of Representatives and the Committee on Finance of the Senate —

(i) describing the proposed action;

(ii) describing efforts by the Trade Representative to resolve the matter with the State concerned by other means; and

(iii) if the State law was the subject of consultations under the Dispute Settlement Understanding, certifying that the Trade Representative has substantially complied with the requirements of paragraph (1)(C) in connection with the matter.

Following the submission of the report, and before the action is brought, the Trade Representative shall consult with the committees referred to in the preceding sentence concerning the matter.

(3) Definition of State Law. — For purposes of this subsection —

(A) the term "State law" includes —

(i) any law of a political subdivision of a State; and

(ii) any State law regulating or taxing the business of insurance; and

(B) the terms "dispute settlement panel" and "Appellate Body" have the meanings given those terms in section 121.

(c) Effect of Agreement with Respect to Private Remedies. —

(1) Limitations. — No person other than the United States —

(A) shall have any cause of action or defense under any of the Uruguay Round Agreements or by virtue of congressional approval of such an agreement, or

(B) may challenge, in any action brought under any provision of law, any action or inaction by any department, agency, or other instrumentality of the United States, any State, or any political subdivision of a State on the ground that such action or inaction is inconsistent with such agreement.

(2) Intent of Congress. — It is the intention of the Congress through paragraph (1) to occupy the field with respect to any cause of action or defense under or in connection with any of the Uruguay Round Agreements, including by precluding any person other than the United States from bringing any action against any State or political subdivision thereof or raising any defense to the application of State law under or in connection with any of the Uruguay Round Agreements —

(A) on the basis of a judgment obtained by the United States in an action brought under any such agreement; or

(B) on any other basis.

(d) Statement of Administrative Action. — The statement of administrative action approved by the Congress under section 101(a) shall be regarded as an authoritative expression by the United States concerning the interpretation and application of the Uruguay Round Agreements and this Act in any judicial proceeding in which a question arises concerning such interpretation or application.

Sec. 103 · *Implementing actions in anticipation of entry into force; regulations.*

(a) Implementing Actions. — After the date of the enactment of this Act —

(1) the President may proclaim such actions, and

(2) other appropriate officers of the United States Government may issue such regulations,

as may be necessary to ensure that any provision of this Act, or amendment made by this Act, that takes effect on the date any of the Uruguay Round Agreements enters into force with respect to the United States is appropriately implemented on such date. Such proclamation or regulation may not have an effective date earlier than the date of entry into force with respect to the United States of the agreement to which the proclamation or regulation relates.

(b) Regulations. — Any interim regulation necessary or appropriate to carry out any action proposed in the statement of administrative action approved under section 101(a) to implement an agreement described in section 101(d) (7), (12), or (13) shall be issued not later than 1 year after the date on which the agreement enters into force with respect to the United States.

Appendix J · Endnote

[1]This appendix consists of provisions of the Uruguay Round Agreements Act, Pub. L. No. 103-465, 108 Stat. 4809, that do not amend title 17 of the *United States Code*.

APPENDIX K GATT/TRADE-RELATED ASPECTS OF INTELLECTUAL PROPERTY RIGHTS (TRIPS) AGREEMENT, PART II[1]

* * * * * * *

Section 6: Layout-Designs (Topographies) of Integrated Circuits

* * * * * * *

Article 35 · Relation to IPIC Treaty

Members agree to provide protection to the layout-designs (topographies) of integrated circuits (hereinafter referred to as "layout-designs") in accordance with Articles 2-7 (other than paragraph 3 of

Article 6), Article 12 and paragraph 3 of Article 16 of the Treaty on Intellectual Property in Respect of Integrated Circuits and, in addition, to comply with the following provisions.

Article 36 · Scope of the Protection

Subject to the provisions of paragraph 1 of Article 37 below, Members shall consider unlawful the following acts if performed without the authorization of the right holder:[2] importing, selling, or otherwise distributing for commercial purposes a protected layout-design, an integrated circuit in which a protected layout-design is incorporated, or an article incorporating such an integrated circuit only insofar as it continues to contain an unlawfully reproduced layout-design.

Article 37 · Acts Not Requiring the Authorization of the Right Holder[3]

1. Notwithstanding Article 36 above, no Member shall consider unlawful the performance of any of the acts referred to in that Article in respect of an integrated circuit incorporating an unlawfully reproduced layout-design or any article incorporating such an integrated circuit where the person performing or ordering such acts did not know and had no reasonable ground to know, when acquiring the integrated circuit or article incorporating such an integrated circuit, that it incorporated an unlawfully reproduced layout-design. Members shall provide that, after the time that such person has received sufficient notice that the layout-design was unlawfully reproduced, he may perform any of the acts with respect to the stock on hand or ordered before such time, but shall be liable to pay to the right holder a sum equivalent to a reasonable royalty such as would be payable under a freely negotiated license in respect of such a layout-design.

2. The conditions set out in sub-paragraphs (a)-(k) of Article 31 above shall apply *mutatis mutandis* in the event of any non-voluntary licensing of a layout-design or of its use by or for the government without the authorization of the right holder.

Article 38· Term of Protection

1. In Members requiring registration as a condition of protection, the term of protection of layout-designs shall not end before the expiration of a period of ten years counted from the date of filing an application for registration or from the first commercial exploitation wherever in the world it occurs.

2. In Members not requiring registration as a condition for protection, layout-designs shall be protected for a term of no less than ten years from the date of the first commercial exploitation wherever in the world it occurs.

3. Notwithstanding paragraphs 1 and 2 above, a Member may provide that protection shall lapse fifteen years after the creation of the layout-design.

Appendix K · Endnotes

[1]For an explanation of the relationship of this section of TRIPs to title 17 of the *United States Code*, see the second paragraph of endnote 8, chapter 9, *supra*.

[2]Article 36 includes footnote 9 that states, "The term 'right holder' in this Section shall be understood as having the same meaning as the term 'holder of the right' in the IPIC Treaty." The IPIC Treaty, which was signed in Washington, D.C., on May 26, 1989, is also known as the Treaty on Intellectual Property in Respect of Integrated Circuits.

[3]See endnote 2, *supra*.

APPENDIX L DEFINITION OF "BERNE CONVENTION WORK"

The WIPO Copyright and Performances and Phonograms Treaties Implementation Act of 1998 deleted the definition of "Berne Convention work" from section 101.[1] Pub. L. No. 105-304, 112 Stat. 2861. The definition of Berne Convention work, as deleted, is as follows:

A work is a "Berne Convention work" if —

(1) in the case of an unpublished work, one or more of the authors is a national of a nation adhering to the Berne Convention, or in the case of a published work, one or more of the authors is a national of a nation adhering to the Berne Convention on the date of first publication;

(2) the work was first published in a nation adhering to the Berne Convention, or was simultaneously first published in a nation adhering to the Berne convention and in a foreign nation that does not adhere to the Berne Convention;

(3) in the case of an audiovisual work —

(A) if one or more of the authors is a legal entity, that author has its headquarters in a nation adhering to the Berne Convention; or

(B) if one or more of the authors is an individual, that author is domiciled, or has his or her habitual residence in, a nation adhering to the Berne Convention; or

(4) in the case of a pictorial, graphic, or sculptural work that is incorporated in a building or other structure, the building or structure is located in a nation adhering to the Berne Convention; or

(5) in the case of an architectural work embodied in a building, such building is erected in a country adhering to the Berne Convention.

For purposes of paragraph (1), an author who is domiciled in or has his or her habitual residence in, a nation adhering to the Berne Convention is considered to be a national of that nation. For purposes of paragraph (2), a work is considered to have been simultaneously published in two or more nations if its dates of publication are within 30 days of one another.

Appendix L · Endnote

[1]For the legislative history of the definition of "Berne Convention work," see endnote 2, chapter 1, *supra*.

Glossary

1998 Sonny Bono Copyright Term Extension Act (CTEA)
The 1998 Sonny Bono Copyright Term Extension Act (CTEA), extended copyright protection to the duration of the author's life plus 70 years, or 95 years for works made for hire.

A

abolitionist literature Literature encouraging the freeing of slaves and ending the importation of slaves.

absolute privilege Absolute privilege is immunity from libel, given to government officials, administrative proceedings, and judicial proceedings.

acquitted The finding of insufficient evidence to prove guilt.

affirmative disclosure Affirmative disclosure requires an advertiser to provide customers with any information that could materially affect their purchase decision.

Aggregate Tuning Hours Aggregate Tuning Hours are the cumulative hours of reception of a broadcast, per listener, for a given timeframe.

Agricultural Marketing Agreement Act (AMAA) The AMAA is intended "to establish and maintain ... orderly marketing conditions for agricultural commodities in interstate commerce."

Alien and Sedition Acts These were laws passed that intended to suppress seditious newspapers, and extended the time required for aliens to live in the United States to gain the right to become naturalized citizens.

all rights All rights refer to the transfer of all of the copyright owner's exclusive rights.

American Civil Liberties Union (ACLU) The ACLU is a national organization advocating individual rights, by litigating, legislating, and educating the public on a broad array of issues affecting individual freedoms.

American Society of Composers, Authors, and Publishers (ASCAP) The American Society of Composers, Authors and Publishers is a membership association of composers, songwriters, lyricists, and music publishers. Its function is to protect the rights of its members by licensing and paying royalties for the public performances of their copyrighted works.

Anticybersquatting Consumer Protection Act (ACPA) The ACPA is intended to protect the public from acts of Internet "cybersquatting," a term used to describe the bad faith, abusive registration of Internet domain names.

Articles of Confederation The first governing document, or constitution, of the United States.

Australian Record Industry Association (ARIA) The Australian Record Industry Association is a trade group representing the Australian recording industry.

Authorization for the use of Military Force The Authorization for use of Military Force, Public Law 107-40, of September 18, 2001, states the President has authority, under the Constitution, to take action to deter and prevent acts of international terrorism against the United States.

average person An average person is one with an average and normal attitude toward, and interest in, sex.

B

Beef Promotion and Research Act The Beef Promotion and Research Act, 7 U.S.C. 2901 et seq., gives the authority for the collection and expenditures of $1.00 per head of cattle to fund generic beef ads.

Berne Convention for the Protection of Literary and Artistic Works The Berne Convention is an international agreement about copyrights, which was first adopted in Berne, Switzerland.

Better Business Bureau (BBB) The BBB is a leader in public services related to ethical business practices and dispute resolution —to promote honesty and integrity in the marketplace.

Bill of Rights These are the first 10 amendments to the Constitution of the United States. Included in them are the freedoms of speech and freedom of the press.

blanket license A blanket license allows the music user to perform a performance rights organization's entire copyrighted song list as much or as little as they like.

broadband Broadband is also called high-speed Internet, because it usually has a high rate of data transmission.

Broadcast Decency Enforcement Act The Broadcast Decency Enforcement Act was passed by Congress, and became Public Law 109-235 on 6/15/2006. This act was passed to increase the penalties for violations by television and radio broadcasters of the prohibitions against transmission of obscene, indecent, and profane material, and for other purposes.

Broadcast Music Incorporated (BMI) Broadcast Music Incorporated is a performance rights organization that collects license fees on behalf of its composers, songwriters, and music publishers and distributes them as royalties to members whose works have been performed.

burden of proof The obligation on a party, to establish the facts at issue in a case, to the required degree of certainty in order to prove its case.

C

Cable Communications Act The purpose of the Cable Communications Act is to establish a national policy concerning cable communications and establish franchise procedures and standards which encourage the growth and development of cable systems and which assure that cable systems are responsive to the needs and interests of the local community.

Cable Television Consumer Protection and Competition Act The Cable Television Consumer Protection and Competition Act was passed to amend the Communication Act of 1934 to provide increased consumer protection and to promote increased competition in the cable television and related markets.

California Anti-Paparazzi Act The California Anti-Paparazzi Act imposed heightened penalties on people who physically invaded another's privacy "with the intent to capture any type of visual image, sound recording, or other physical impression of the plaintiff engaging in personal or familial activity and the physical invasion occurs in a manner that is offensive to a reasonable person."

CAN SPAM Act of 2003 (Controlling the Assault of Non-Solicited Pornography and Marketing Act) The CAN SPAM Act of 2003 establishes requirements for those who send commercial email, spells out penalties for spammers and companies whose products are advertised in spam, if they violate the law, and gives consumers the right to ask emailers to stop spamming them.

Celebrity Rights Act The Celebrity Rights Act grants statutory post-mortem rights which prohibit the unsanctioned use of the "name, voice, signature, photograph or likeness on or in products, merchandise, or goods" of any person for 70 years after a celebrity's death.

Celler-Kefauver Act The Cellar-Kefauver Act reformed and strengthened the Clayton Antitrust Act of 1914. The Cellar-Kefauver Act was passed to close a loophole regarding certain asset acquisitions and acquisitions involving firms that were not direct competitors.

Child Online Protection Act (COPA) A law passed with the declared purpose of protecting minors from harmful sexual material on the Internet.

Child Pornography Prevention Act (CPPA) The Child Pornography Prevention Act extended the existing federal criminal laws against child pornography to the new computer media. As part of the overhaul, the definition of "child pornography" was extended to include "morphed" or computer generated images.

civil contempt Civil contempt occurs when the contemnor willfully disobeys a court order.

Civil War The War Between the States.

Clayton Act The Clayton Antitrust Act of 1914 was passed by the United States Congress as an amendment to clarify and supplement the Sherman Antitrust Act of 1890.

clear and present danger If there is a clear and present danger it requires a governmental limitation on Constitutional First Amendment freedoms of speech to avoid damage to the government.

Code of Civil Procedure section 425.16 The California Code of Civil Procedure section 425.16—anti-SLAPP legislation, states, "A cause of action against a person arising from any act of that person in furtherance of the person's right of petition or free speech under the United States or California Constitution in connection with a public issue shall be subject to a special motion to strike, unless the court determines that the plaintiff has established that there is a probability that the plaintiff will prevail on the claim."

Code of Ethics in East Africa The Code of Ethics in East Africa is that a journalist will be fair and allow a right of reply; the journalist will not accept favors or bribes for running a story; a journalist shall not show discrimination towards race, religion, national origin, or gender; he should show respect for human dignity, and not plagiarize another's work.

Cold War A Cold War is a state of political hostility between two countries, stopping just short of full scale conflict.

commercial appropriation Commercial appropriation is the use of a person's name or picture for another person's gain or commercial advantage.

common law Common law is the traditional law of an area or region; also known as case law. This is the law created by judges when deciding individual disputes or cases.

Communications Act of 1934 The Communications Act of 1934 replaced the Federal Radio Commission with the Federal Communications Commission (FCC). The 1988 amendment to this act, dealt with dial-a-porn. Sections of the act were amended or repealed with the Telecommunications Act of 1996.

Communications Decency Act The 1996 federal legislation which attempted to ban the transmission of obscene or indecent material across the Internet.

Communications Opportunity, Promotion and Enhancement Act of 2006 HR 5252 (COPE) The Communications Opportunity, Promotion, and Enhancement (COPE) Act of 2006 was a large telecom bill designed to update United States laws to address changes in voice, video and data services.

Communications, Consumer Choice, and Broadband Deployment Act of 2006, S2686 S2686, consisted of 10 separate titles, aimed to reform existing communications laws.

Community Trade Mark (CTM) The Community Trade Mark system is one that applies to the members of the European Union.

compelling state interest Compelling state interest is when the speech restriction by the government is justifiable based on a superior governmental interest, and as such, an individual's rights must cede to such interest.

Comstock Act The Comstock Act, a United States federal law, made it illegal to send any "obscene, lewd, and/or lascivious" materials through the mail, including contraceptive devices and information. The act also banned the distribution of information on abortion.

consent Giving consent is giving permission to do something.

contemporary community standards Contemporary community standards are set by what is accepted in the community as a whole—by society at large, or people in general.

contempt of court Any willful disobedience to, or disregard of, a court order or any misconduct in the presence of a court; action that interferes with a judge's ability to administer justice or that insults the dignity of the court. The judge has the power to declare the defiant person (called the contemnor) in contempt of court.

contempt powers Contempt powers allow the highest remedy of a judge to impose sanctions on an individual for acts that excessively disrupt the normal process of a court hearing.

content-based Content based regulation of speech means restrictions are placed on specific speech depending on what it says.

continue To continue a case is to postpone the trial date to a later time.

Copyright Act of 1976 The 1976 Copyright Act preempts the former copyright act of 1909, and all relevant common law and state copyright laws that conflict with this Act.

Copyright Royalty Board The three Copyright Royalty Judges, who make up the Copyright Royalty Board, determine the rates and terms for the copyright statutory licenses and make determinations on distribution of statutory license royalties collected by the copyright office.

Copyrights Copyrights are a group of exclusive rights granted by the federal government, which can be obtained for a variety of intellectual works from movies to literature.

corrective ad A corrective ad is when the Federal Trade Commission orders a company to run an ad, for the purpose of correcting a consumer's mistaken impression, created by the company's prior advertising.

criminal contempt Criminal contempt occurs when the contemnor actually interferes with the ability of the court to function properly.

cybersquatting Cybersquatting is using a domain name with bad-faith intent to profit from the goodwill of a trademark belonging to someone else.

D

defamation The publication of false statements that causes a person to suffer damages.

depositions A deposition is a form of discovery during which a person is questioned while under oath.

Digital Millennium Copyright Act (DMCA) The Digital Millennium Copyright Act (DMCA) makes it a crime to use any measures that circumvent antipiracy measures built into software. The DMCA does offer limited protection to Internet Service Providers in merely distributing information over the Net.

Digital Performance Right in Sound Recordings Act The Digital Performance Right in Sound Recordings Act allows the record companies, who hold the rights in sound recordings, to collect a royalty on digital "performances" of the sound recording.

direct contempt Direct contempt occurs under the court's own eye and within its own hearing.

diversity of citizenship Diversity of citizenship is a case involving questions that must be answered according to state law, but the case may be heard in federal court if the parties on the two sides of the case are from different states.

Domain Name System (DNS) The Domain Name System (DNS) is the way that Internet domain names are located and translated into Internet Protocol (IP) addresses.

due process Due process establishes a course for judicial or governmental proceedings to follow that is designed to safeguard the legal rights of the individual.

E

emotional distress For a plaintiff to recover for emotional distress she must prove that the media acted intentionally or recklessly (some jurisdictions allow recovery for negligent infliction of emotional distress), that the media's conduct was extreme and outrageous, and that the media's conduct was the cause of severe emotional distress.

Equal Time Rule The equal-time rule specifies that radio and television stations must provide equal access to the airwaves to any opposing political candidates who request it.

Espionage Act of 1917 This is a federal law that made it a crime for a person to convey information with intent to interfere with the operation or success of the armed forces of the United States.

exclusivity agreement An exclusivity agreement would prevent an artist from entering a similar recording agreement with another recording company.

F

fair comment Fair comments are statements of opinion made by the media in an honest belief in their truth, even though the statements are not in fact true.

fair play and substantial justice Fair play and substantial justice is a standard of fairness that a court's assertion of personal jurisdiction over a nonresident defendant must meet in order to avoid a violation of the defendant's right to due process.

fair use Fair use is when a person can use material that is copyrighted, by someone else, without paying them royalties, or getting permission to use the work.

false light False light is publicity that invades a person's privacy by disseminating a false statement that would be highly offensive to a reasonable person.

Family Entertainment and Copyright Act The Family Entertainment and Copyright Act provides for the protection of intellectual property rights, and for other purposes.

fault Fault is a neglect of care, an error, or a defect of judgment.

Federal Communications Commission (FCC) The Federal Communications Commission (FCC) is an independent United States government agency, directly responsible to Congress. The FCC was established by the Communications Act of 1934 and is charged with regulating interstate and international communications.

Federal Trade Commission (FTC) Congress created the FTC in 1914 to prevent "unfair methods of competition," and was designed to complement the antitrust laws.

Federal Trademark Dilution Act The Federal Trademark Dilution Act gives a federal right to a mark holder to sue an infringer if they lessen the ability of a mark to identify goods or services, or if the infringer creates confusion in the mind of the consumer.

First North American rights First North American rights mean a periodical acquires the right to be the first publisher of a work in North America.

First serial rights First serial rights refer to the first publication of a work in a magazine.

Food and Drug Modernization Act The Food and Drug Modernization Act creates a special exemption to ensure continued availability of compounded drug products prepared by pharmacists to provide patients with individualized therapies not available commercially. The law, however, seeks to prevent manufacturing under the guise of compounding by establishing parameters within which the practice is appropriate and lawful.

Foreign Intelligence Surveillance Act (FISA) FISA prescribes procedures for requesting judicial authorization for electronic surveillance and physical search of persons engaged in espionage or international terrorism against the United States on behalf of a foreign power.

Fourteenth Amendment's due process clause "No state shall make or enforce any law, which shall abridge the privileges or immunities of citizens of the United States, nor shall any state deprive any person of life, liberty or property without due process of law . . . ."

freedom of expression Allows an individual to speak freely without censorship.

Freedom of Information Act (FOIA) The Freedom of Information Act (FOIA) is a federal law that establishes the public's and the media's right to obtain information from federal government agencies.

freedom of the press The guarantee by a government of free public press.

G

gag order A tool to prevent the media from publishing unwanted information on a particular topic.

general damages General damages are subjective in determination, for example, pain and suffering, mental anguish, loss of reputation (especially in libel suits), and loss of anticipated business.

Government in the Sunshine Act The Government in the Sunshine Act was intended to create greater openness in government. The purpose of the act is to provide the public with information, while protecting the rights of individuals, and the ability of the government to carry out its responsibilities.

grand jury A grand jury reviews the evidence presented by the prosecutor and determines whether there is probable cause to return an indictment against the accused. An indictment is a formal accusation of a criminal offense.

H

Hart-Scoss-Rodino Antitrust Improvement Act The Hart-Scoss-Rodino Antitrust Improvement Act (1976) made it easier for regulators to investigate mergers for antitrust violations.

hearsay Hearsay is secondhand information that occurs if a witness testifies about something that she did not personally see or hear—that is, someone else told her what occurred.

I

ICANN (Internet Corporation For Assigned Names and Numbers) The tasks of ICANN include managing the assignment of domain names and IP addresses.

Immigration and Naturalization Service (INS) The INS, now called the United States Citizenship and Immigration Services, enforces the laws that apply to the entry of non-United States citizens—foreign nationals—into the United States.

impartial jury An impartial jury is one without bias, prejudice, or other preconceptions as to the case before it. The juror should have no opinion about or vested interest in a case at the start of the trial and should base his verdict only on competent legal evidence presented during the trial.

In-Band On-Channel (IBOC) In-Band On-Channel is a method of transmitting digital radio and analog radio broadcast signals simultaneously on the same frequency.

indecent Something that is indecent offends decency.

indirect contempt Contempt is indirect when it occurs out of the presence of the court, thereby requiring the court to rely on the testimony of third parties for proof of the offense.

injunctions Judicial orders restraining or compelling some form of action. To obtain an injunction, one must show that there is potentially irreparable damage if the injunction order is not granted.

Intelligence Identities Protection Act The Intelligence Identities Protection Act is a United States federal law that makes it a federal crime to intentionally reveal the identity of an agent whom one knows to be in or recently in certain covert roles with a United States intelligence agency.

international standard book number The ISBN (International Standard Book Number) is a 13-digit number that uniquely identifies books and book-like products published internationally.

Internet Freedom Preservation Act S. 215 A bill to amend the Communications Act of 1934 to ensure net neutrality.

intrusion Intrusion is the unlawful entry upon or appropriation of the property of another.

Islamic Mass Media Charter The Islamic Mass Media Charter calls for the censorship of all material that may be harmful to Islamic character and values such as offensive words or obscene material. Anything that goes against public morality should not be published nor anything that incites crime, violence, or anything that arouses terror.

J

jurisdiction Jurisdiction is the authority granted to a legal body to make legal decisions in a case.

L

Lanham Act The Lanham Act defines the scope of a trademark, the process by which a federal registration can be obtained from the Patent and Trademark Office for a trademark, and penalties for trademark infringement.

Latin American Federation of Journalists The ethical guidelines of the Latin American Federation of Journalists states: journalism should contribute to the strengthening of peace, co-existence, self-determination of the people, disarmament, international cooperation, and mutual understanding among all the peoples of the world; and journalists should fight for equality among human beings. Journalists will adopt the principles of truth and objectivity in their work, and will commit ethical faults when they silence, falsify, or manipulate facts. A journalist is responsible for his information and opinions, will accept the existence of reprinting rights, and will respect the professional secrecy of his sources.

legal precedent This is a court decision that gives an example or authority, to other courts, on how to decide subsequent cases involving similar or identical facts.

libel insurance Insurance against claims arising from alleged defamation of character.

libel per quod Libel per quod is where more information is needed to determine if a statement is libelous.

libel per se Libel per se is where the words themselves would injure the person's reputation.

libel-proof plaintiffs A person is libel-proof if her character is so bad that anything else bad said about her still would not lead to an action for defamation.

libel The making of defamatory statements in printed form, or via the spoken word if it is disseminated to a large audience.

long arm statutes Long arm statutes give local state courts jurisdiction over an out-of-state company or individual, if its actions caused damage locally or to a local resident.

M

Madrid system for international registration of marks This simplifies the international registration of marks.

Magnuson-Moss Warranty Act The Magnuson-Moss Warranty Act prohibits "unfair or deceptive acts or practices in or affecting commerce." It is a violation of the FTC Act to advertise a warranty deceptively.

Master Settlement Agreement (MSA) The Master Settlement Agreement resolved lawsuits filed by state and United States territory attorneys general against the tobacco industry. It provided funds to the states to compensate them for taxpayer money that was spent on patients and family members with tobacco-related diseases. The agreement required that tobacco billboard advertising be taken down, that tobacco companies stop using cartoon characters to sell cigarettes, and that tobacco companies make many of their internal documents available to the public. The tobacco companies also agreed not to target youth in the advertising, marketing and promotion of their products. The Master Settlement Agreement also called for the creation of a foundation—the American Legacy Foundation to counter the use of tobacco.

minimum contacts Minimum contacts are that degree of contact with a forum state sufficient to maintain a suit there and not offend traditional notions of fair play and substantial justice.

misappropriation or **unfair competition** Misappropriation or unfair competition is a "taking," of a business value of another without consent.

monetary bonds A form of insurance that would protect the government from the publishing of information against it.

moral relativism Moral relativism is a concept that espouses the fact morality varies between individuals and cultures and so there is no objective right and wrong.

moral rights Moral rights, under copyrights, refer to the ability of authors to control the eventual fate of their works.

Motion Picture Association of America (MPAA) The Motion Picture Association of America was formed to advance the business interests of the movie studios.

Mushroom Promotion, Research, and Consumer Information Act The Mushroom Promotion, Research, and Consumer Information Act calls for the cooperative development, financing, and implementation of a coordinated program of mushroom promotion, research, and consumer information necessary to maintain and expand existing markets for mushrooms.

must carry The must carry rule mandates that cable companies carry various local and public television stations within a cable provider's service area.

N

National Advertising Division (NAD) The mission of the National Advertising Division (NAD), part of the Better Business Bureau (BBB), is to review national advertising for truthfulness and accuracy. It was established to foster public confidence in the credibility of advertising.

National Advertising Review Council (NARC) NARC establishes the policies and procedures for the advertising industry's system of self-regulation, which includes the Better Business Bureau's National Advertising Division (NAD).

National Association of Broadcasters (NAB) The National Association of Broadcasters (NAB) is a nonprofit, incorporated association of radio and television broadcast stations. NAB serves and represents the American broadcasting industry.

NCCPV (the National Commission on the Causes and Prevention of Violence) The NCCPV examined the role of the media and entertainment industry as to their influence in the rise of the rate of violence in the United States.

negligence Negligence is a violation of a duty of due care—a reckless disregard for the truth. In media law, negligence may occur from sloppy journalism, not adequately checking a source based on a how a "reasonable person" would check on information in a story.

neutral-reporting privilege The neutral-reporting privilege extends to the media when they function as a "bulletin board," serving merely as a vehicle for the dissemination of newsworthy statements, without espousing or even necessarily believing the contradictory charges and countercharges made by participants in a public debate.

Newspaper Association of America (NAA) The NAA is a nonprofit organization representing the newspaper industry. NAA members account for nearly 90 percent of the daily circulation in the United States and a wide range of nondaily United States newspapers. The NAA also has Canadian and International members.

newsworthy If something is newsworthy is has generated sufficient interest or importance to the public to warrant reporting in the media.

Non-Prescription Drug Modernization Act of 2007 The Non-Prescription Drug Modernization Act regulates false or misleading ads as to drugs other than prescription drugs.

Notice of Inquiry A notice of inquiry is issued by the FCC when it is seeking information or ideas on a given topic.

Notice of Proposed Rule Making A notice of proposed rule making is issued by the FCC when it proposes a new body of regulations or changes to existing regulations. Before any changes to regulations can be made, interested parties are given a time period during which they can comment on the proposed changes.

O

obscene For something to be obscene means it is offensively indecent.

one-time rights One time rights grants a publication the non-exclusive right to use the material once (non-exclusive means the work can be licensed to more than one publication at a time).

orphan works Orphan works are copyrighted works whose owners may be impossible to identify and locate.

over breadth When a law proscribes constitutionally *unprotected* speech, but it also potentially proscribes constitutionally *protected* speech.

P

patently offensive When material so exceeds the generally accepted limits of candor as to be clearly offensive.

personal jurisdiction Personal jurisdiction is a court's power over a particular defendant, also called *in personam* jurisdiction.

petit juror A petit juror is one that sits on a trial jury.

plurality If a court cannot come to a majority opinion, two or more judges will publish concurring opinions. The other judges will then decide which concurring opinion they will join. The concurring opinion with the most number of judges creates a plurality opinion and, thus, a decision for the case.

preliminary hearing A hearing to determine if there is sufficient evidence to charge and try a person for a felony (a serious crime punishable by a term in the state prison).

prior restraint This is the requirement to get prepublication approval. It is censorship that forbids the publishing of objectionable material.

Privacy Protection Act of 1980 The Privacy Protection Act of 1980 protects journalists from being required to turn over to law enforcement any work product and documentary materials, including sources, before it is disseminated to the public.

prurient interest An appeal to "prurient" interest is an appeal to a morbid, degrading, and unhealthy interest in sex, as distinguished from a mere interest in sex.

public domain Works in the public domain are considered to be a part of the public's cultural heritage. They are open for anybody to make use of, for any purpose.

public figures A public figure is someone that is newsworthy and in the public eye.

public interest or newsworthy Public interest refers to the information that affects the well-being of the general public.

public officials A public official is a person in public office.

public trial Proceedings presumptively open to the public.

publication of private facts Publication of private facts is the public disclosure of embarrassing private information.

punitive damages Punitive or exemplary damages are meant to punish or set a public example to others not to commit the tort.

Q

qualified privilege A qualified privilege in defamation suits may be defeated especially by a showing of actual malice on the part of the media.

quash the subpoenas To quash a subpoena means to attempt to nullify or void it.

R

Reardon Report A study that advocated restrictions on the release and publication of information about people accused of crimes.

Recording Artist's Coalition (RAC) The Recording Artist's Coalition is an American music industry organization that represents the recording artist, and attempts to defend her rights and interests.

Recording Industry Association of America (RIAA) The Recording Industry Association of America is a trade group that represents the U.S. recording industry.

remanded To remand is to return a case to a lower court for further proceedings.

retraction Retraction is a formal recanting of the libelous material.

retransmission consent Retransmission consent is an alternative to must carry. Under retransmission a local station can demand compensation from a cable company when the cable company carries their station signal.

right of reply The right of reply is when the media or an individual feels that when she has been misrepresented she should have the right to respond to the allegations.

S

Satellite Home Viewer Improvement Act (SHVIA) The Satellite Home Viewer Improvement Act, for the first time, permitted satellite carriers to transmit local television broadcast signals into local markets, also known as "local-into-local." This act also authorizes satellite carriers to provide distant or national broadcast programming to subscribers.

Screen Actors Guild (SAG) The Screen Actors Guild is an American labor union that represents film and television performers. The Guild seeks to negotiate and enforce collective bargaining agreements that establish equitable levels of compensation, benefits, and working conditions for its performers.

Sedition Act The Sedition Act made it illegal to speak out against the government.

seditious libel laws Sedition is when the government or its officers is criticized. The Sedition Act of 1798 made it a federal crime to publish contemptible writings against the government.

sequestered To sequester a jury is to remove or set it apart from the public.

service mark A service mark is any word, name, symbol, device, or any combination, used, or intended to be used, in commerce, to identify and distinguish the services of one provider from services provided by others, and to indicate the source of the services.

SESAC—Society of European Stage Authors and Composers SESAC is the smallest of the three performance rights organizations in the United States. Based in Nashville, Tennessee, SESAC deals with all aspects of the music business from creation, to licensing, and administration.

Sherman Antitrust Act The Sherman Antitrust Act declared every contract, combination, or conspiracy in restraint of interstate and foreign trade to be illegal, based on Congress' right to control interstate commerce.

shield laws Shield laws vary significantly from state to state, but most provide that privileged information cannot be obtained unless the party seeking the information can allege that the information is highly material and relevant to the case at issue; a compelling need exists for the information, and the information cannot be obtained by other means.

simultaneous rights Simultaneous rights are the right to print material in different publications at approximately the same time.

slander The making of defamatory statements via the spoken word.

sliding scale A sliding scale is a flexible method of determining if personal jurisdiction can be exercised over a defendant.

Smith Act This act made it a criminal offense to advocate the violent overthrow of the federal or state government, or for anyone to organize any association that teaches or encourages such overthrow, or for anyone to belong to or affiliate with such an association that would advocate such overthrow.

special damages Special damages are those that are actually caused by the tort; they are out-of-pocket damages, for example, loss of wages, loss of money due on a contract, and medical bills.

Statute of Anne The Statute of Anne vested authors, rather than printers, with the monopoly on the reproduction of their works.

statute of limitations A statute of limitations limits the amount of time within which legal action may be taken.

Strategic Lawsuits Against Public Participation (SLAPP) suit These are suits usually filed by citizens or companies against journalists or citizen advocates when they speak out against specific projects or corporate policies.

strict liability The imposition of liability regardless of fault.

Stronger Tobacco Warning Labels to Save Lives Act The Stronger Tobacco Warning Labels to Save Lives Act would require that cigarette packages include health warnings, disclosure of tar and nicotine levels, listings of physical addictions, and health messages, including the hazards of secondhand smoke. In addition, graphic pictures of health effects would have to occupy at least 50% of each side of cigarette packs and cartons.

substantial-truth Substantial-truth is where the substance, the gist of the matter, is true.

summary judgment A summary judgment is a decision based on the statements and evidence presented on the record without a trial. Summary judgment is used if there are no disputed facts in the case, and it is decided one party is entitled to judgment in its favor as a matter of law.

T

tangible medium of expression A tangible medium of expression means a work is embodied in a material object of some kind, such as the pages of a book, a canvas, magnetic tape, or a computer's hard disk.

Tax Stamp Act The act required all legal documents, permits, commercial contracts, newspapers, wills, pamphlets, and playing cards in the American Colonies to carry a tax stamp.

Telecommunications Act of 1996 The Telecommunications Act of 1996 is the first major overhaul of telecommunications law since The Communications Act of 1934. The goal of this law is to let anyone enter any communications business—to let any communications business compete in any market against any other.

time is of the essence It is a contract term, and it is meant to specify that the time and dates mentioned in a contract are very important to maintain and should not be ignored by any of the parties under any circumstances.

time, place, and manner restrictions Limits that government can impose on the occasion, location, and type of individual expression in some circumstances.

Title V of the Telecommunications Act of 1996-Section 230 (c) of the Communications Decency Act (CDA) The Communications Decency Act held no provider or user of an interactive computer service shall be treated as the publisher or speaker of any information provided by another information content provider.

Top Level Domain Registry (TLD registry) The right-most label in a domain name is referred to as its "top-level domain" (TLD). The responsibility for operating each TLD (including maintaining a registry of the domain names within the TLD) is delegated to a particular organization. These organizations are referred to as "registry operators" or "sponsors," for example ICANN.

tort The breach of a legal duty that proximately causes injury or harm to another. This is a civil wrong, not a criminal, or a contractual wrong.

trademark A trademark is a form of intellectual property. It is a distinctive indication used by a business, organization, or other legal entity to uniquely identify and distinguish its products from other businesses, organizations, or other legal entities—a brand name.

trespass Trespass is an unauthorized entry upon land.

trier of fact The trier of fact is the authority at a trial, be it jury or judge, who decides what the truth is.

truth Truth is the actual state of things.

U

U.S. Constitution The supreme law of the United States.

U.S. National Security Agency (NSA) The NSA coordinates, directs, and performs highly specialized activities to protect United States government information systems and produce foreign intelligence information.

Uniform Correction or Clarification of Defamation Act (UCCDA) This act is a proposal by the National Conference of Commissioners on Uniform State Laws (NCCUSL) to make the retraction laws more uniform among the states.

Uniform Domain Name Dispute Resolution Policy (UDNDRP) The Uniform Domain Name Dispute Resolution Policy has been adopted by ICANN, and sets forth the terms and conditions in connection with a dispute as to the registration and use of an Internet domain name.

Uniform Interstate and International Procedure Act (UIIPA) UIIPA is a model long arm statute that several states have enacted.

universal resolvability Universal resolvability ensures predictable search results from any place on the Internet. Each IP address will have its own distinctive domain name.

USA Patriot Act The USA Patriot Act was implemented after September 11, 2001, to combat terrorism.

utterly without redeeming social value Material that has not even a modicum of redeeming social value.

V

veggie libel Veggie libel is the false disparagement of a perishable food item.

venue The place of a trial.

video clip businesses Video clip businesses make videotapes or DVDs of segments of a news or public affairs show.

Vietnam War The Vietnam War occurred from 1965 to April 30, 1975. This war was fought between the Democratic Republic of Vietnam—North Vietnam and the Republic of Vietnam—South Vietnam. The United States supported South Vietnam.

voir dire The questioning of prospective jurors by a judge and attorneys in court. It is used to determine if any juror cannot deal with the trial issues fairly.

W

Wheeler-Lea Amendment Under the Wheeler-Lea Amendment to the Federal Trade Commission Act, unfair or deceptive acts or practices (which include advertising) are prohibited.

without prejudice Without prejudice is when a case is dismissed but the plaintiff is allowed to bring a new suit on the same claim.

works made for hire A work made for hire is a work prepared by an employee within the scope of his or her employment. In this case the employer, and not the employee, is considered the author of the work.

World Intellectual Property Organization (WIPO) WIPO administers the Madrid system for international registration of marks.

Y

Youth Smoking Prevention and Public Health Act The Youth Smoking Prevention and Public Health Act was introduced to protect public health by providing the Food and Drug Administration with certain authority to regulate tobacco products.

Index